ROUTLEDGE HANDBOOK OF THE SOCIOLOGY OF SPORT

The sociology of sport is a core discipline within the academic study of sport. It helps us to understand what sport is and why it matters. Sociological knowledge, implicit or explicit, therefore underpins scholarly enquiry into sport in every aspect. The *Routledge Handbook of the Sociology of Sport* is a landmark publication that brings together the most important themes, theories and issues within the sociology of sport, tracing the contours of the discipline and surveying the state of the art.

Part One explores the main theories and analytical approaches that define contemporary sport sociology and introduces the most important methodological issues confronting researchers working in the social scientific study of sport. Part Two examines the connections and divisions between sociology and cognate disciplines within sport studies, including anthropology, economics, geography, history, leisure, philosophy, politics, psychology and tourism studies. Part Three investigates how the most important social divisions within sport, and in wider society, are addressed in sport sociology, including 'race', gender, class, sexuality and disability. Part Four explores a wide range of pressing contemporary issues associated with sport, including sport and the body; social problems associated with sport; sport places and settings; and the global aspects of sport.

Written by a team of leading international sport scholars, including many of the most well-known, respected and innovative thinkers working in the discipline, the *Routledge Handbook of the Sociology of Sport* is an essential reference for any student, researcher or professional with an interest in sport.

Richard Giulianotti is Professor of Sociology at Loughborough University, UK, and also Professor II at Telemark University College, Norway. His main research interests are in the fields of sport, globalization, development and peace, sport mega-events, crime and deviance, cultural identities and qualitative methods. He has headed several projects on these subjects, funded by the UK ESRC, European Commission and Nuffield Foundation. He is author of the books *Football: A Sociology of the Global Game* (1999), *Sport: A Critical Sociology* (2005, revised 2015), *Ethics, Money and Sport* (with A.J. Walsh, 2007), and *Globalization and Football* (with R. Robertson, 2009). He has guest-co-edited special issues of *British Journal of Sociology*, *Global Networks* and *Urban Studies*, edited a further dozen books and published numerous articles in international journals and edited collections. His work has been translated and published in twelve languages.

ROUTLEDGE HANDBOOK OF THE SOCIOLOGY OF SPORT

Edited by Richard Giulianotti

Routledge
Taylor & Francis Group

LONDON AND NEW YORK

First published in paperback 2018

First published 2015
by Routledge
2 Park Square, Milton Park, Abingdon, Oxon OX14 4RN

and by Routledge
711 Third Avenue, New York, NY 10017

Routledge is an imprint of the Taylor & Francis Group, an informa business

British Library Cataloguing in Publication Data
A catalogue record for this book is available from the British Library

Library of Congress Cataloging-in-Publication Data
Routledge handbook of the sociology of sport / edited by Richard Giulianott.
    pages cm
    Includes bibliographical references and index.
    1. Sports—Sociological aspects.   I. Giulianotti, Richard, 1966–
    GV706.5.R68 2015
    306.4'83—dc23
    2015001192

ISBN: 978-0-415-82973-1 (hbk)
ISBN: 978-1-138-30852-7 (pbk)
ISBN: 978-0-203-40406-5 (ebk)

Typeset in Bembo
by Apex CoVantage, LLC

CONTENTS

Contents

Contents

Contents

NOTES ON CONTRIBUTORS

David L. Andrews is a Professor of Physical Cultural Studies at the University of Maryland, College Park. His research utilizes an interdisciplinary and contextual approach to understanding the social, cultural, political, economic and technological relations shaping the contemporary structure and experience of sport and physical culture. Principal publications include *Sport and Neoliberalism* (with M.L. Silk, 2012) and *The Blackwell Companion to Sport* (with B. Carrington, 2013).

Michael Atkinson is Professor in the Faculty of Kinesiology and Physical Education at the University of Toronto. Michael's central areas of teaching and research interests pertain to the experiences of human suffering in/as physical cultures, the cross-national study of biopedagogical practices, radical embodiment, issues in bioethics within global and local physical cultures and ethnographic research methods. He is author/editor of eight books, and his research has appeared in diverse academic journals, including *International Review for the Sociology of Sport, Body & Society, Sex Roles, Sport in Society, Journal of Sport and Social Issues, Qualitative Research on Sport, Exercise and Health, Field Methods, Youth & Society, Deviant Behavior, Third World Quarterly, The Sociology of Sport Journal and Health.* He is Editor of the *Sociology of Sport Journal* and has served on editorial boards, including those of *Deviant Behavior, Sport in Society, Qualitative Research in Sport, Exercise and Health,* and *Qualitative Sociology Review.*

Susan J. Bandy is a Senior Lecturer in Sport Studies at The Ohio State University. Her expertise is in the cultural study of sport with particular emphasis on sport literature; the participation of women in sport; and gender and the body. She has published several books related to sport literature, including *Coroebus Triumphs: The Alliance of Sport and the Arts* and *Crossing Boundaries* (1988), *An International Anthology of Women's Experiences in Sport* (with A.S. Darden, 1999) and a special issue of *Aethlon: The Journal of Sport Literature* devoted to women, sport and literature (1997). With Annette Hofmann and Arnd Krüger, she published *Gender, Body and Sport in Historical and Transnational Perspectives* (2007), and her most recent book (with V. Bjerre, 2011) is *Litterære fortællinger om idræt i Norden: Helte, erindringer og identitet (Scandinavian Sport Literature: Heroism, Memory and Identity).*

Douglas Booth is Professor of Sport Studies and Dean of the School of Physical Education, Sport and Exercise Sciences at the University of Otago. He is the author of *The Race Game* (1998), *Australian Beach Cultures* (2001) and *The Field* (2005). He serves on the editorial boards of *Rethinking History* and the *Journal of Sport History* and is an executive member of the Australian Society for Sport History.

Ben Carrington teaches sociology at the University of Texas at Austin and is a Carnegie Research Fellow at Leeds Beckett University. His most recent book is *A Companion to Sport* (2013), co-edited with David Andrews.

Jayne Caudwell is Reader in Sport, Gender and Sexualities at the University of Brighton. Her teaching and research take a feminist approach to methodologies, theory and practice. She is editor of *Sport, Sexualities and Queer/Theory* (2006), *Women's Football in the UK: Continuing with Gender Analyses* (2011) and *Sexualities, Space and Leisure Studies* (2011); and co-author of *Sport and the Social Significance of Pleasure* (2015).

Simon C. Darnell is an Assistant Professor in the Faculty of Kinesiology and Physical Education at the University of Toronto. His research focuses on the relationship between sport and international development, the development implications of sports mega-events and the place of social activism in the culture of sport. He is the author of *Sport for Development and Peace: A Critical Sociology* (2012) and co-author of *Sport and Social Movements: From the Global to the Local* (2013). His research has also been published in the *Sociology of Sport Journal*, the *International Journal of Sport Policy and Politics* and *Progress in Development Studies*.

Matthew David teaches sociology at Durham University. His interests are in sharing and digital media. He is the author of *Peer to Peer and the Music Industry: The Criminalization of Sharing* (2010), *Social Research: An Introduction* (2nd edition, with C.D. Sutton, 2011), *Science in Society* (2005) and *Knowledge Lost in Information* (with D. Zeitlyn and J. Bex, 1998). He has also edited the four-volume collection *Researching Society Online* (with P. Millward, 2014). His most recent work in the area of file-sharing, live-streaming and new media has been published in *The British Journal of Sociology*, *The European Journal of Social Theory*, *Sport in Society* and *Crime, Media, Culture*, as well as in the *Oxford Handbook of Internet Studies* (W.H. Dutton, editor, 2013). Research on other aspects of science and technology has been published recently in *Current Sociology*, *International Sociology* and *Sociology Compass*.

Kevin J. Delaney is Professor of Sociology and Vice Provost for Faculty Affairs at Temple University. He has written on sports, economics and politics and is co-author (with R. Eckstein) of *Public Dollars, Private Stadiums: The Battles over Building Sports Stadiums* (2003).

Tim Delaney is Professor and Chair of Sociology at State University of New York at Oswego. He earned his M.A. in Sociology from California State University Dominguez Hills, and a Ph.D. in Sociology from the University of Nevada, Las Vegas. He has published 15 books to date, including *American Street Gangs, Second Edition* (2014), *Beyond Sustainability: A Thriving Environment* (2014), *Classical and Contemporary Social Theory: Investigation and Application* (2013), *Connecting Sociology to Our Lives: An Introduction to Sociology* (2012) and *The Sociology of Sport* (2009). *The Sociology of Sport, Second Edition* will be released in summer 2015. He has published over 100 book reviews, numerous book chapters and journal and encyclopedia articles, and has been published on five continents. He has taught a wide variety of sociology and criminology courses.

Peter Donnelly is Professor in the Faculty of Kinesiology and Physical Education at the University of Toronto and Director of the Centre for Sport Policy Studies. He has served as Editor of the *Sociology of Sport Journal* and Acting Editor of the *International Review for the Sociology of Sport*; two terms as General Secretary of the International Sociology of Sport Association; and a term as President of the North American Society for the Sociology of Sport. He has published widely in the area of sociology of sport, for example, on politics and policy issues (including the area of children's rights in sport), sport subcultures and mountaineering (history). He is currently leading a research team to examine multiculturalism and physical culture in Canada.

Noel Dyck is Professor of Social Anthropology, Simon Fraser University. His research interests span a range of topics, including the use of sport as a means of child-rearing in Canada; the pursuit of athletic scholarships by young Canadians who endeavour to become student athletes in American universities; and the impact of the Olympic games upon child and youth sports in a host city. But his underlying interest is in exploring how anthropological approaches might be applied to elucidate taken-for-granted social and cultural dimensions of sport and, by the same token, how intellectual engagement with sport might contribute to this discipline. His key publications include: *Games, Sports and Cultures* (2000), *Sport, Dance and Embodied Identities* (with E. P. Archetti, 2003) and *Fields of Play: An Ethnography of Children's Sports* (2012).

Mark Falcous is Senior Lecturer in the Sociology of Sport at the University of Otago. His research focuses on the intersections of sport, globalization, national identity and media. His work has appeared in *Sociology of Sport Journal, Continuum: Journal of Media and Cultural Studies, International Review for the Sociology of Sport, Studies in Ethnicity and Nationalism, Soccer & Society, Journal of Sport and Social Issues, Media and Cultural Politics* and *Sites*. He co-edited *Sport and Migration: Borders, Boundaries and Crossings* (with J. Maguire, 2011).

Richard Giulianotti is Professor of Sociology at Loughborough University, and also Professor II at Telemark University College. His main research interests are in the fields of sport, globalization, development and peace, sport mega-events, crime and deviance, cultural identities and qualitative methods. He has headed several projects on these subjects, funded by the UK ESRC, European Commission and Nuffield Foundation. He is author of the books *Football: A Sociology of the Global Game* (1999), *Sport: A Critical Sociology* (2005, revised 2015), *Ethics, Money and Sport* (with A.J. Walsh, 2007), and *Globalization and Football* (with R. Robertson, 2009). He has guest-co-edited special issues of *British Journal of Sociology, Global Networks* and *Urban Studies*, edited a further dozen books and published numerous articles in international journals and edited collections. His work has been translated and published in twelve languages.

Michael Grenfell is Chair of Education at the University of Stirling. He previously held Chairs at Trinity College, Dublin and the University of Southampton. His background is in French Studies and he has a long research association in areas including education; language and linguistics; and cultural studies. He first met Bourdieu in 1979 and collaborated with him for twenty years on various projects. He was three times 'visiting scholar' at the École des Haute Études in Paris. Besides a number of articles on Bourdieu, he is author of *Bourdieu and Education: Acts of Practical Theory* (with D. James, 1998); *Bourdieu: Agent Provocateur* (2004); *Arts Rules: Bourdieu and the Visual Arts* (with C. Hardy, 2007); *Bourdieu, Language and Linguistics* (2012); *Bourdieu: Key Concepts* (2008); *Language, Ethnography and Education: Bridging New Literacy Studies and Bourdieu* (with D. Bloome, C. Hardy, K. Pahl, J. Rowsell and B. Street, 2011); *Bourdieu and Data Analysis* (2014); and *Bourdieu: Education and Training* (2008).

Douglas Hartmann (Ph.D., University of California, San Diego, 1997) is Professor of Sociology at the University of Minnesota. He is the author of *Race, Culture, and the Revolt of the Black Athlete: The 1968 Olympic Protests and Their Aftermath* (2003), and co-author of *Migration, Incorporation, and Change in an Interconnected World* (with S. Ali, 2015). Hartmann's work has also appeared in the *American Sociological Review, Ethnic and Racial Studies*, the *Journal of Sport and Social Issues* and *Social Problems*, and his comments on sport, race, popular culture and multiculturalism have been featured in a variety of media outlets all over the world. He is co-editor and publisher of the award-winning website TheSocietyPages.org, and is currently finishing a book entitled *Midnight Basketball, Race, and Neoliberal Social Policy: The History and Significance of a Sport-Based Innovation.*

Angela J. Hattery (B.A., Carleton College, Ph.D., University of Wisconsin–Madison) is Professor and the Director of the Women & Gender Studies Program at George Mason University. Her research focuses on social stratification, gender, family and race. She is the author of numerous articles, book chapters and books, including *African American Families: Myths and Realities* (2012), *The Social Dynamics of Family Violence* (2012), *Prisoner Reentry and Social Capital* (2010), *Interracial Intimacies* (2009), *Interracial Relationships* (2009), *Intimate Partner Violence* (2008), *African American Families* (2007) and *Women, Work, and Family* (2001). She teaches classes in gender and sexuality, intersections of race, class and gender, gender-based violence and feminist methods. In addition to her academic work, she directs the graduate programs (MAIS and certificate) in Women and Gender Studies.

Hans K. Hognestad is a social anthropologist and an Associate Professor in Sports Sciences at Telemark University College. His main research interests include studies of identity and globalization in football, fan activism and sport and development. He has recently co-edited two books in Norwegian, one on football, identity and power (*Kampen om tribunen*, 2012), the other on gender and power in sport and outdoor life (*Kjønnsmakt i idrett og friluftsliv*, 2014).

Barrie Houlihan is Professor of Sport Policy at Loughborough University and Visiting Professor at the Norwegian School of Sport Sciences. His research interests include the domestic and international policy processes for sport. He has a particular interest in sports development, the diplomatic use of sport and drug abuse by athletes. He has authored or edited twenty books and over fifty journal articles. His most recent books are *Sport Policy in Britain* (with I. Lindsey, 2012) and *The Youth Olympic Games* (co-edited with D.V. Hanstad and M. Parent, 2014). In addition to his work as a teacher and researcher, he has undertaken consultancy projects for various UK government departments, UK Sport, Sport England, the Council of Europe, UNESCO, the World Anti-Doping Agency and the European Union. He is the editor-in-chief of the *International Journal of Sport Policy and Politics*.

P. David Howe is Senior Lecturer in the Anthropology of Sport in the School of Sport, Exercise and Health Sciences at Loughborough University. He is currently also the Vice-President of the International Federation of Adapted Physical Activity (IFAPA) and is a leading figure in the socio-cultural analysis of Paralympic sport. He holds a Visiting Professorship at Katholieke Universiteit Leuven, Belgium and is an adjunct Professorship at Queen's University, Ontario. Trained as a medical anthropologist, he is author of *Sport, Professionalism and Pain: Ethnographies* *of Injury and Risk* (2004) and *The Cultural Politics of the Paralympic Movement: Through the Anthropological Lens* (2008).

William W. Kelly is Professor of Anthropology and the Sumitomo Professor of Japanese Studies at Yale University. His field research and publications have focused on the historical and contemporary anthropology of Japan. The seven books and three dozen articles that he has authored and edited have focused on regional political economy and class formation in Japanese society, the organization of Japanese professional baseball, the place of sports in contemporary Japan, the nature of sports fandom and the Olympic movement in East Asia.

Samantha King is Professor of Kinesiology and Health Studies at Queen's University, where she researches and teaches the embodied dimensions of consumer culture. Her essays have appeared in such publications as *Social Text, Racial and Ethnic Studies*, the *Sociology of Sport Journal* and *Health Communication*. Her book, *Pink Ribbons, Inc.: Breast Cancer and the Politics of Philanthropy* (2006), was the inspiration for a 2011 documentary by the same name. She is currently working on two projects: the first examines the multiple materialities of prescription painkilling, and the second puts interspecies and food studies theories in conversation to explore the ethics and politics of meat consumption.

Frank J. Lechner is Professor of Sociology at Emory University. His publications include *World Culture: Origins and Consequences* (with J. Boli, 2005), *The Netherlands: Globalization and National Identity* (2008), *Globalization: The Making of World Society* (2009) and papers on issues in religion, theory, sports and globalization. His current work focuses on various aspects of American exceptionalism.

Jessica Lee is a Lecturer in Health Promotion in the School of Medicine, Griffith University. Her main research focus is in critical perspectives in health and physical activity promotion, obesity and public health. Key research projects to date are the 'Life Activity Project', a longitudinal qualitative study on young people's experiences of physical activity and health; 'Contradictions and Tensions in the UK's Change4Life'; and 'The Assembling of Healthier. Happier', a Queensland government preventive health campaign. She has published work from these projects in various edited book collections (*Young People, Physical Activity and the Everyday; Boys' Bodies: Speaking the Unspoken; Young People's Voices in Physical Education and Youth Sport*) and peer-reviewed journals (*Sport, Education & Society; Sociology of Health & Illness; Journal of Sport & Social Issues; Journal of Health Psychology*).

Stephen Lyng is a Professor of Sociology at Carthage College. His major areas of interest are the sociology of risk, sociology of the body and sociological theory. He is the author of three books, *Holistic Health and Biomedical Medicine: A Countersystem Analysis* (1990), *Sociology and the Real World* (with D. Franks, 2002) and *Edgework: The Sociology of Voluntary Risk Taking* (2005).

Dominic Malcolm is Reader in the Sociology of Sport at Loughborough University. Empirically his research has focussed upon the socio-historical development of cricket and the intersection between sport, health and medicine. Through this he has sought to apply, examine and extend the theoretical corpus of Norbert Elias and other figurational sociologists. He has authored three books (*The Sage Dictionary of Sports Studies*, 2008; *Sport and Sociology*, 2012; *Globalizing Cricket*, 2013) and has edited a further six (including *The Social Organization of Sports Medicine: Critical Socio-Cultural Perspectives*, 2012; and *The Changing Face of Cricket: From Imperial* *to Global Game*, 2010). He is currently working on two further books: *Sport and Society: A Student Introduction* (3rd edition, with B. Houlihan) and *Sport, Medicine and Health: The Medicalization of Sport and the Sportization of Medicine*.

Wolfram Manzenreiter is Professor of Japanese Studies at the Department of East Asian Studies at the University of Vienna. His research is concerned with the social and anthropological aspects of sports, emotions and migration in a globalizing world. He is author of several books and numerous articles mainly on sport, leisure and popular culture in Japan. As a scholar of globalization, his research also extends into the larger East Asian region and the transnational networks of the Japanese diaspora. Publications of note include *Sport and Body Politics in Japan* (2014) and the co-edited volumes *Migration and Development: New Perspectives* (2014, in German); *Governance, Citizenship and the New European Championships: The European Spectacle* (2011); and *Sports Mega-Events* (2006).

Pirkko Markula is Professor of Socio-Cultural Studies of Physical Activity at the University of Alberta. Her research interests include social analyses of dance, exercise and sport in which she has employed several theoretical lenses ranging from critical cultural-studies research to Foucault and Deleuze. She is a previous editor of the *Sociology of Sport Journal*. She is author of *Qualitative Research for Physical Culture* (with M. Silk, 2011) and *Foucault, Sport and Exercise: Power, Knowledge and Transforming the Self* (with R. Pringle, 2006); and editor of *Feminist Sport Studies: Sharing Joy, Sharing Pain* (2005); *Olympic Women and the Media: International Perspectives* (2009); *Women and Exercise: Body, Health and Consumerism* (with E. Kennedy, 2011); *Critical Bodies: Representations, Identities and Practices of Weight and Body Management* (with S. Riley, M. Burns, H. Frith and S. Wiggins, 2007); and *Moving Writing: Crafting Movement in Sport Research* (with J. Denison, 2003).

Ian McDonald is an activist, sociologist and documentary filmmaker. He is currently Senior Lecturer in Film Practice in the School of Arts and Cultures at Newcastle University. Ian has written widely on the politics of sport. He is the co-editor of *Race, Sport and British Society* (2001) and *Marxism, Cultural Studies and Sport* (2009) (both with B. Carrington).

Kerry R. McGannon is an Assistant Professor in Sport and Exercise Psychology, Laurentian University. Her work seeks to bridge psychology and cultural studies to understand sport and physical activity participation via qualitative methodologies (e.g. critical discourse analysis) and critical interpretations of sport and exercise. Her scholarship includes empirical and theoretically driven contributions through more than 60 national and international presentations and more than 60 publications in refereed journals and scholarly books. She is co-editor of the books *The Psychology of Subculture in Sport and Physical Activity: Critical Perspectives* (2014); *Community Based Research in Sport, Exercise and Health* (2014); and *The Routledge International Handbook of Sport Psychology* (forthcoming). She is the Associate Editor of the *Journal of Applied Sport Psychology* and also serves on the boards of *Psychology of Sport and Exercise* and *Qualitative Research in Sport, Exercise and Health*.

Brad Millington is a Lecturer in the Department for Health at the University of Bath. His research is broadly focused on physical culture, with specific interests in sport's relationship with the environment and the promotion of health and fitness through interactive technologies. His research appears in a range of peer-reviewed journals, including *The Sociological Quarterly, Critical Studies in Media Communication, New Media & Society* and *International Review for the Sociology of*

Sport. His forthcoming book, written with Brian Wilson, is titled *The Greening of Golf: Sport, Globalization and the Environment*.

Peter Millward is Reader in Sociology at Liverpool John Moores University. His research interests largely focus on football supporters (often in connection to the football industry) to discuss issues such as socio-cultural exclusions; popular protests, social movements and mobilizations; theories and realities of 'globalization'; notions of crime and 'criminality'; and the connections between consumption and identity. He has published widely and is the author of *The Global Football League: Transnational Networks, Social Movements and Sport in the New Media Age* (2011), amongst other outputs.

Verner Møller is Professor of Sport and Body Culture at Aarhus University. His main research interest lies in elite sport and body cultural extremes. He is founder of The International Network of Humanistic Doping Research and he has over the past fifteen years devoted much of his time to the study of doping in sport. His books include *The Doping Devil* (1999); *Doping and Public Policy* (2004); *Elite Sport, Doping and Public Health* (2009); *The Ethics of Doping and Anti-doping: Redeeming the Soul of Sport?* (2010); *Doping and Anti-doping Policy in Sport: Ethical, Legal and Social Perspectives* (2011); *The Scapegoat – About the Expulsion of Michael Rasmussen from the Tour de France 2007 and Beyond* (2011); and *Routledge Handbook of Sport and Drugs* (2015).

William J. Morgan, (Ph.D., University of Minnesota, 1977) is Professor in the Division of Occupational Science and the Annenberg School for Communication and Journalism at the University of Southern California, Los Angeles. He has served as editor of the *Journal of the Philosophy of Sport* and has published extensively in sport studies and philosophy journals. He has authored two books, *Why Sports Morally Matter* and *Leftist Theories of Sport: A Critique and Reconstruction*, and edited several anthologies focusing on the philosophy of sport and sport ethics. He is a former president of the International Association of the Philosophy of Sport and was a recipient of its Distinguished Scholar Award in 1994. In the same year, he was elected active fellow of the American Academy of Kinesiology. In 1988, he was awarded a Fulbright Senior Professor and Research Award to teach and conduct research at the University of Marburg, West Germany.

Gertrud Pfister has had a long academic career, which began with a Ph.D. in History, followed by another Ph.D. in Sociology. From 1980 to 2000, she was employed as Professor at the University of Berlin, and was then appointed to a professorial position at the University of Copenhagen in 2001. She has received two honorary doctorates. She has conducted several large national and international research projects, and has published more than 200 articles and 20 books. Playing a leading role in various sport-related scientific communities, she has been President of the International Society for the History of Sport (1983–2001) and Head of the International Sociology of Sport Association (2004–2008). Currently, she is a member of the Executive Board of Women Sport International. Throughout her life, she has been active in sport, in particular in skiing, tennis and long-distance running.

Raffaele Poli holds a Ph.D. in Human Sciences from the University of Neuchâtel and Franche-Comté. He heads the Football Observatory at the International Centre for Sports Studies (CIES) in Neuchâtel. Twice a year, the CIES Football Observatory publishes reports on European professional football. In January, the Demographic Study presents an in-depth analysis of club composition and player characteristics in 31 top European football divisions. In June, the Annual Review analyses clubs and players in the "big 5" European leagues from a demographic, economic and pitch performance perspective. Since 2005, the CIES Football Observatory has been mandated to undertake original research by several prestigious institutions such as, but not limited to, FIFA, UEFA, European Club Association (ECA), European Professional Football Leagues (EPFL) and Swiss Football League (SFL), as well as top-flight European clubs in several countries.

Loïc Ravenel holds a Ph.D. in Geography from the University of Avignon and is Senior Assistant at the University of Besançon. Since 2011, he has worked as a scientific collaborator at the International Centre for Sports Studies (CIES) in Switzerland on the Sports Observatory and Football Observatory projects. Ravenel has almost 20 years of experience studying the geography of sport and applies data analysis methodologies to provide a better understanding of sports, in particular football.

Ian Ritchie is Associate Professor in the Department of Kinesiology at Brock University. He received his Ph.D. in Sociology from Bowling Green State University, where he studied classical and contemporary sociological theory. He teaches courses in sport sociology and sociology of the modern Olympic Games, and his research interests include performance-enhancing drug use in sport and the history of anti-doping prohibitions, media, gender and general aspects of the Olympic Games. His publications have been included in several journals and edited volumes; he also co-authored the book *Fastest, Highest, Strongest: A Critique of High-Performance Sport* (with R. Beamish, 2006). He is currently writing a book on the history of the modern Olympic Games. A former varsity rower and coach, he lives in Fenwick, Ontario, with his wife and three children.

Ken Roberts is Professor of Sociology at the University of Liverpool. His major research areas throughout his career have been the sociology of leisure and the sociology of youth life stage transitions. He was a founding member of the Leisure Studies Association and has been Chair of the World Leisure Organization's Research Commission and President of the International Sociological Association's Research Committee on Leisure. After 1989 he coordinated a series of research projects in East-Central Europe and the former Soviet Union. His current research is into youth in North Africa and the East Mediterranean during and since the 'Arab Spring'. Professor Roberts' recent books are *Key Concepts in Sociology* (2009), *Youth in Transition: Eastern Europe and the West* (2009), *Class in Contemporary Britain* (2011) and *Sociology: An Introduction* (2012). His latest book, *The Business of Leisure*, will be published in 2015.

Kimberly S. Schimmel is a Professor of the Sociology of Sport in the School of Foundations, Leadership and Administration at Kent State University, where she teaches sport and domestic diversity, sport in global perspective and sport and sociological theory courses. Her research related to sport and local/global urban development, the political economic impact of major sport events and urban securitization in the post-9/11 era has been published in numerous scholarly journals and anthologies and has been translated into five languages, including a monograph in Brazilian Portuguese (*Os Grandes Eventos Sportivos: Desafios E Perspectivas*, 2013). She currently serves as the Vice President of the International Sociology of Sport Association and is a past Associate Editor of the *Sociology of Sport Journal*.

Michael Silk is a Professor in the Department of Sport and Physical Activity in the Faculty of Management at Bournemouth University. His research focuses on the relationships between sport and physical activity (physical culture), the governance of bodies, sporting spectacle and urban space. He is author of numerous journal articles, and his books include *The Cultural Politics* *of Post 9/11 Sport: Power, Pedagogy and the Popular* (2013); *Qualitative Research in Physical Culture* (with P. Markula, 2011); *Sports Coaching Research: Contexts, Consequences and Consciousness* (2013, with H. Lauder, A. Bush and D. Andrews); *Sport & Neoliberalism* (2012, with D. Andrews); *Sport & Corporate Nationalisms* (2005, with D. Andrews & C.L. Cole) and *Qualitative Research for Sports Studies* (2005, with D. Mason and D. Andrews).

Barry Smart is currently Professor of Sociology in the School of Social Historical and Literary Studies at the University of Portsmouth. He has long-standing research interests in the fields of critical social theory, political economy and philosophy. Major publications of relevance to this volume include *Consumer Society: Critical Issues and Environmental Consequences* (2010) and *The Sport Star: Modern Sport and the Cultural Economy of Sporting Celebrity* (2005), as well as two essays, 'Global Sporting Icons: Consuming Signs of Economic and Cultural Transformation' in the *Black-well Companion to Sport* (2013) and 'Global Sport and the Cultural Economy of Late Capitalism: Play, Spectacle, and Profit' in *Being Cultural* (2011). He has also edited *Post-Industrial Society* (2011) and *Observation Methods* (2013, with K. Peggs and J. Burridge). Current research interests include sportsmanship and economy, neoliberalism and the transformation of higher education, and a collaborative project on veganism, ethics, and lifestyle (with Kay Peggs and Joseph Burridge).

Brett Smith leads the psycho-social health and well-being strand in the Peter Harrison Cen-tre for Disability Sport at Loughborough University. Working at the intersection of sociology and psychology, his research focuses on disability, sport, physical activity, well-being and the advancement of qualitative methods. This research has resulted in over 100 publications, appear-ing in journals like *Health Psychology, Psychology of Sport & Exercise, Sociology of Health & Illness, Sociology of Sport* and *Qualitative Health Research*. He is founding Editor of the award-winning international journal *Qualitative Research in Sport, Exercise, and Health*. He actively serves on eight editorial boards, and is the first person to simultaneously sit on leading sport sociology and sport psychology journal editorial boards. He is co-author of the book *Qualitative Research Methods in Sport, Exercise, and Health: From Process to Product* (2011, with A. Sparkes). He is currently co-editing the *International Handbook of Qualitative Methods in Sport and Exercise*.

Earl Smith is Emeritus Professor of Sociology and Rubin Distinguished Professor of American Ethnic Studies at Wake Forest University. Dr. Smith is the author of numerous books, research articles and book chapters. Several books are sports related, including *Sociology of Sport and Social Theory* (2010) and *Race, Sport and the American Dream* (3rd edition, 2014).

Ramón Spaaij is Associate Professor in the Institute of Sport, Exercise and Active Living (ISEAL) and the College of Sport and Exercise Science at Victoria University, and Special Chair of Sociology of Sport at the University of Amsterdam. He is also Visiting Professor in the Utre-cht University School of Governance. Major publications include *Sport and Social Exclusion in Global Society* (2014, with J. Magee and R. Jeanes), *Sport and Social Mobility: Crossing Boundaries* (2011) and *Understanding Football Hooliganism* (2006). He also edited *The Olympic Movement and the Sport of Peacemaking* (2013, with C. Burleson) and *The Social Impact of Sport: Cross-Cultural Perspectives* (2010). Current research interests include the sociology of sport and the sociology of terrorism.

Jan Ove Tangen is Professor in the Department of Sport and Outdoor Life Studies at Telemark University College (TUC). He has a Ph.D. in Sociology from University of Oslo. His main research areas are sport as a social system, inclusion and exclusion mechanisms in sport and the use of doping in organized sports and fitness. From 1998 to 2008 he was coordinator of the joint research initiative of TUC and Telemark Research Institute (TRI) with grants from the Research Council of Norway. These institutions were nationally responsible for carrying out research on two main topics: sport participation and sport facilities, and sport policies and politics. His recent books are *How Is Sport Possible? Sketch of a Sociology of Sport* (2004, in Norwegian) and *The Struggle for Sport Facilities*, (2009, edited with K. Rafoss and O.G. Ballo, in Norwegian). He has published other scientific papers, reports and book chapters which cover both theoretical and empirical matters.

Ansgar Thiel is Professor for Sport Sociology and Director of the Institute of Sport Science at the Eberhard Karls University Tübingen. His main research interests are in the sociology and psychology of sports, health and the body. He has published many books, journal articles and book chapters. Some of his key publications include recent papers in the journals *Sociology of Sport Journal*, *PLoS ONE*, *BMC Public*, *Psychology of Sport and Exercise* and *Computers in Human Behavior*; and the books *Sportsoziologie* (2013; with J. Mayer and K. Seiberth) and *Soziale Konflikte* (2003).

Lawrence A. Wenner is Von der Ahe Professor of Communication and Ethics at Loyola Marymount University. He obtained his Ph.D. from the University of Iowa. He is editor of the journals *International Review for the Sociology of Sport* and *Communication and Sport*, and was formerly editor of the *Journal of Sport and Social Issues*. His books on sport include *Media, Sports, and Society* (1989); *MediaSport* (1998); *Sport, Beer, and Gender* (2008, with S.J. Jackson); and *Fallen Sport Heroes, Media and Celebrity Culture* (2013). His current work critically engages the moral contours of narrative constructions of gender, race and ethnicity in promotional culture.

Brian Wilson is a sociologist and Professor in the School of Kinesiology at the University of British Columbia. He is author of *Sport & Peace: A Sociological Perspective* (2012), *Fight, Flight or Chill: Subcultures, Youth and Rave into the Twenty-First Century* (2006) and the forthcoming *The Greening of Golf: Sport, Globalization and the Environment* (with Brad Millington), as well as articles on sport, social inequality, environmental issues, media, social movements and youth culture. His recent work focuses on how the sport of running is used for peace promotion in Kenya and on responses to golf-related environmental concerns. He currently leads a project funded by the Social Sciences and Humanities Research Council of Canada entitled 'Fostering "Sport-for-Peace Journalism" and a Role for Sociologists of Sport.'

Nicholas Wise is Lecturer in International Sport, Events and Tourism Management at Glasgow Caledonian University. His research focuses on sport and geography with a particular emphasis on transnational migration and community identity. He has spent time in the Dominican Republic researching football and how Haitians are using the sport to forge a sense of place in the country. He trained as a geographer and earned his Ph.D. in 2012 from Kent State University. His recent publications in the area of sport and geography appear in *International Review for the Sociology of Sport*; *Soccer & Society*; *Geographical Research*; *Journal of Sport & Tourism*; *International Journal of Sport Communication;* and in a number of edited book collections focusing on events and interdisciplinary approaches to football and migration.

INTRODUCTION

Richard Giulianotti

Over the past few decades, sport has grown very rapidly in terms of social importance and prominence. In economic terms, the 'sport industry' has mushroomed, particularly as leading professional sport leagues and competitions sell television rights to their events for increasingly prodigious sums. Politically, leading sport officials mingle more frequently among political elites, while cities and nations seek to market and 'brand' themselves through hosting sport teams and events. In cultural terms, sport has been a key driver in the fast expansion of the mass media, particularly subscription television services at national and transnational levels. And socially, sport dominates much of everyday public discourse and anchors many of our social identities. Sport itself is a field of interaction for a growing variety and volume of interested parties and associated 'stakeholders', including athletes, officials, teams, administrators, governing bodies, media companies, sport-related corporations, athlete agents and unions, governmental organizations and community-based and non-governmental organizations. In sum, its growing scale and significance demonstrates that, more than ever, sport demands the full attention of sociologists and other social scientists.

The discipline of sociology is ideally placed among the social sciences to pursue the detailed and rigorous investigation of sport. Institutionally, the sub-discipline of the sociology of sport has secured long-standing and diverse international foundations. The International Sociology of Sport Association (ISSA) was founded in 1965, and has gone on to hold its annual conventions in venues across the world; its house journal, the *International Review for the Sociology of Sport*, began publication a year later, in 1966. The *Journal of Sport and Social Issues* was founded in 1977 and has since been characterized by a distinctive sociological voice and focus. The North American Society for the Sociology of Sport (NASSS), founded in 1978, started publishing its *Sociology of Sport Journal* in 1984. More recently, the European Association of Sport Sociology (EASS), founded in 2001, began publishing the *European Journal for Sport in Society* in 2004. Other notable forces include the various national and regional associations for the sociology of sport in Scandinavia, Latin America, East Asia, and other European nations; and a wider pool of associated journals that regularly publish sociology of sport papers, such as *Sport in Society*, *Leisure Studies*, *Society and Leisure* and *Quest*. Moreover, a growing number of sociological papers on sport have been published in the most established mainstream sociology journals, such as the *American Journal of Sociology*, *American Sociological Review*, *Social Forces* and *British Journal of Sociology*.

Given these foundations, the sociology of sport has gained a strong transnational purchase and cross-disciplinary presence. The sub-discipline is practiced most prominently in the UK, mainland Europe, North America, Australasia, Latin America, East Asia and southern Africa. Branching consistently into other major disciplines, sociologists of sport have been particularly conversant with anthropologists, economists, historians, human geographers, philosophers and political scientists. In addition, the sub-discipline reaches into cross-disciplinary 'studies' fields, notably leisure studies, cultural studies, ethnic and racial studies, gender studies, global studies and media studies.

Like the master discipline of sociology *per se*, the sociology of sport is itself a diverse, complex and contested realm of academic inquiry. Among many scholars working within the sub-discipline, it is possible to discern a common, underlying commitment to exercising what the great American sociologist C. Wright Mills (1959: 3) referred to as the 'sociological imagination'; that is, 'the vivid awareness of the relationship between personal experience and the wider society'. At its best, the emphasis is on 'imagination' here, as sociologists of sport exercise creative intellectual energy in exploring new theories, methods and issues within books, journal papers and research projects.

As a field of academic inquiry, the sociology of sport has a long history: indeed, the first substantial sociological discussion of sport was provided by the German writer and cultural critic Heinz Risse in his book *Soziologie des Sports*, published in 1921. However, excepting some occasional essays (such as Stone [1955]), the detailed sociological analysis of sport remained largely dormant until the 1960s, whereupon social science expanded quickly within higher education, thereby enabling a fresh and large influx of scholars to pursue a wider range of research activity on sport and to convene early international meetings on the subject.

Subsequently, the research questions and agendas within the sociology of sport came to be influenced and shaped by the major theoretical paradigms across sociology and other social sciences. In the 1960s and much of the 1970s, structural-functionalist approaches were prominent, probing the extent to which sport contributed to the smooth functioning of societies (Lüschen 1967; Pooley 1976; Stevenson and Nixon 1972). Alternatively, Weberian and other interpretive approaches, such as symbolic interactionism, have been directed towards exploring sport identities, meanings, symbols and forms of rationalization (Fine 1987; Guttmann 1978; Ingham 1979). Marxist and neo-Marxist perspectives have had a deep and enduring impact, underpinning the sociological analysis of sport within capitalist societies with respect to class divisions, ideologies and conflicts (Gruneau 1983; Hargreaves 1986; Rigauer 1981). Rooted in neo-Marxist approaches, multidisciplinary cultural studies perspectives have explored the contradictions of sport, as in other fields of popular culture, in serving both to empower and to disempower relatively weak, marginal or dominated social groups (Andrews and Loy 1993; Clarke and Critcher 1985; Rowe 1995). Different waves of feminist theory have been directed towards the critical analysis of women's dominated position within sport and wider society, and in turn to investigate the role of physical culture in the making of dominant and other masculine identities (Hall 1996; Hargreaves 1993; Messner 2007). Theories of 'race', ethnicity, colonialism and postcolonialism have also critically examined the position of minority communities within sport (Carrington 2010; Hylton 2008; Jarvie 2004). Latterly, the contemporary cultural studies perspective has buttressed the 'physical cultural studies' standpoint advanced by one group of scholars, primarily in the North American context (Andrews and Silk 2011). Since the 1970s, the figurational sociology of Norbert Elias and his followers has had significant influence, notably in examining the long-term historical development of sporting disciplines (Dunning and Sheard 1979; Dunning 1999). The critical perspective of the late French sociologist Pierre Bourdieu has enabled sociologists to examine systematically how the field of sport produces and reproduces forms of social domination and 'distinction' within and between different social groups (Bourdieu 1984; Kay and Laberge 2002; Stempel 2005). Poststructuralist and postmodernist social theories have been widely utilized since the early 1990s, particularly to examine the body, media and cultures of consumption in sport (Markula and Pringle 2006; Rail 1998). And, in recent years, the system theory of Niklas Luhmann, long influential in Central European sociology of sport, has reached English-speaking readers (Tangen 2004; Wagner *et al.* 2010). Thus, the sociology of sport has been strongly shaped by the construction and interplay of these theoretical frameworks, and the discipline of sociology continues to produce new theories that should be mined further by sociologists of sport in future research.

Throughout its development within the academic field, the sociology of sport has also generated a growing variety of substantive themes and issues for research. Areas of inquiry have included, for example, the social divisions of class, gender, 'race', ethnicity and disability in sport, particularly focusing on processes of marginalization and exclusion along and through these social contours; spectator cultures and identities, notably studying fan subcultures and forms of violence; broader civic, national and other forms of identity construction within sport; the body in sport, regarding issues such as pain, risk-taking and doping; the staging of sport mega-events; media discourses and other such representations of sport; and globalization, migration and sport's usage to promote development and peace in different locations across the world. While clearly diverse in content, these substantive research areas often harbour a common concern with 'social problems' in sport, notably on issues of social conflict and division.

This Handbook aims to capture this theoretical and substantive diversity within the sociology of sport. Somewhat surprisingly, given the multitude of academic handbooks published in recent years, this text represents the first named handbook or companion in the sociology of sport to be published. Previous academic publications on this scale either have featured a wider social scientific focus (cf. Andrews & Carrington 2013; Coakley and Dunning 2000; Lüschen and Sage 1981); or engaged with other disciplinary areas (cf. Henry and Ko 2014; Pedersen 2013); or explored more specific topics within sport (cf. Hargreaves and Anderson 2014; Houlihan and Green 2011). Thus, while the sub-discipline is suitably serviced by a good range of textbooks and some multi-volume sets, the sociology of sport has waited a long time for the production of a dedicated handbook on this scale.

The Handbook features forty main chapters written by world leading experts in their respective research areas. As editor, my broad intention has been to enable these experts to explore the appropriate mix of relevant theories, social processes, public issues and/or academic debates within the relevant research areas. The Handbook is intended to reach a wide audience, with the aim of offering a valuable resource to undergraduate and postgraduate students, academics and a much-targeted 'general readership' with an interest in the social aspects of sport.

The chapters are organized into four parts. Part One covers the main theories and approaches within the sociology of sport. We open with a chapter on research methods in the sub-discipline, and then turn to explore a full array of strongly influential social theories within the sociology of sport, specifically functionalism, interpretivism, Marxism and neo-Marxism, physical cultural studies, poststructuralism and postcolonial perspectives, as well as the theoretical frameworks advanced by Elias (figurational sociology), Bourdieu and Luhmann (system theory).

Part Two addresses the collaborations, continuities and differences between sociology and those other social sciences with research interests in sport. Other disciplines featured here are anthropology, economics, geography, history, leisure studies, philosophy, political science and psychology.

Part Three examines how core social divisions impact upon sport. The chapters here consider the key sociological research fields of class, gender, race, sexuality and disability.

Part Four explores the many substantive issues that are investigated by sociologists of sport. In broad terms, these sport-centred issues encompass the body, physical activity and health, risk-taking and doping; the public issues of sport fandom, violence and sport-based social interventions; sport and the urban, mega-events, and environmentalism; media and new media; and national and transnational issues with respect to the nation, athlete migration, the corporate world, international development and peace and globalization. These explorations of transnational issues and problems represent an appropriate conclusion for the Handbook, given the growing scale and significance of sport at the global level.

References

Andrews, D. and J. Loy (1993) 'British Cultural Studies and Sport: Past Encounters and Future Possibilities', *Quest*, 45: 255–276.

Andrews, D.L. and B. Carrington (eds) (2013) *A Companion to Sport*, Oxford: Wiley.

Andrews, D.L. and M. Silk (eds) (2011) *Physical Cultural Studies*, Philadelphia: Temple University Press.

Bourdieu, P. (1984) *Distinction*, London: Routledge.

Carrington, B. (2010) *Race, Sport and Politics*, London: Sage.

Clarke, J. and C. Critcher (1985) *The Devil Makes Work: Leisure in Capitalist Britain*, Basingstoke, UK: Macmillan.

Coakley, J. and E. Dunning (eds) (2000) *Handbook of Sport Studies*, London: Sage.

Dunning, E. (1999) *Sport Matters*, London: Routledge.

Dunning, E. and K. Sheard (1979) *Barbarians, Gentlemen and Players*, Oxford: Blackwell.

Fine, G. A. (1987) *With the Boys: Little League Culture and Preadolescent Culture*, Chicago: University of Chicago Press.

Gruneau, R. (1983) *Class, Sports and Social Development*, Amherst: University of Massachusetts Press.

Guttmann, A. (1978) *From Ritual to Record: The Nature of Modern Sports*, New York: Columbia University Press.

Hall, M.A. (1996) *Feminism and Sporting Bodies*, Champaign, IL: Human Kinetics.

Hargreaves, J. (1986) *Sport, Power and Culture*, Cambridge: Polity.

Hargreaves, J. (1993) *Sporting Females*, London: Routledge.

Hargreaves, J. and E. Anderson (2014) *Routledge Handbook of Sport, Gender and Sexuality*, London: Routledge.

Henry, I. and L. M. Ko (eds) (2014) *Routledge Handbook of Sport Policy*, London: Routledge.

Houlihan, B. and M. Green (2011) *Routledge Handbook of Sport Development*, London: Routledge.

Hylton, K. (2008) *'Race' and Sport: Critical Race Theory*, London: Routledge.

Ingham, A. (1979) 'Methodology in the Sociology of Sport: From Symptoms of Malaise to Weber for a Cure', *Quest*, 31(2): 187–215.

Jarvie, G. (ed.) (2004) *Sport, Racism and Ethnicity*, London: Taylor and Francis.

Kay, J. and S. Laberge (2002) 'The "New" Corporate Habitus in Adventure Racing', *International Review for the Sociology of Sport*, 37(1): 17–36.

Lüschen, G. (1967) 'The Interdependence of Sport and Culture', *International Review for the Sociology of Sport*, 2: 127–139.

Lüschen, G. and G. Sage (eds) (1981) *Handbook of Social Science of Sport*, Champaign, IL: Stipes.

Markula, P. and R. Pringle (2006) *Foucault, Sport and Exercise*, London: Routledge.

Messner, M. (2007) *Out of Play*, Albany: SUNY Press.

Mills, C.W. (1959) *The Sociological Imagination*, Oxford: Oxford University Press.

Pedersen, P. M. (2013) *Routledge Handbook of Sport Communication*, London: Routledge.

Pooley, J. (1976) 'Ethnic Soccer Clubs in Milwaukee: A Study in Assimilation', in M. Hart (ed.) *Sport in the Sociocultural Process*, Dubuque, IA: Brown.

Rail, G. (ed.) (1998) *Sport and Postmodern Times*, Albany: SUNY Press.

Rigauer, B. (1981) *Sport and Work*, New York: Columbia University Press.

Risse, H. (1921) *Soziologie des Sports*, Berlin: Reher.

Rowe, D. (1995) *Popular Cultures: Rock Music, Sport, and the Politics of Pleasure*, London: Sage.

Stempel, C. (2005) 'Adult Participation Sports as Cultural Capital', *International Review for the Sociology of Sport*, 40(4): 411–432.

Stevenson, C. and J.E. Nixon (1972) 'A Conceptual Scheme of the Social Functions of Sport', *Sportwissenschaft*, 2: 119–132.

Stone, G. (1955) 'American Sports: Play and Display', *Chicago Review*, 9 (Fall): 83–100.

Tangen, J.O. (2004) 'Embedded Expectations, Embodied Knowledge and the Movements That Connect', *International Review for the Sociology of Sport*, 39(1): 7–25.

Wagner, U., R.K. Storm and J. Hoberman (eds) (2010) *Observing Sport: Modern System Theoretical Approaches*, Schorndorf: Hofmann.

PART ONE

Major theories and approaches

1

INTRODUCTION TO PART ONE

Richard Giulianotti

In Part One of this Handbook, our attention turns to how social theories are utilized by sociologists of sport. In broad terms, social theories enable sociologists and other social scientists to research and explain sport and other fields of social life. These theories may be understood and used in different ways by sociologists. Relatively 'objectivist' or scientific approaches argue that social theories should consist of a systematic arrangement of specific premises or propositions about the social world; these theories should be fully testable, and should enable social scientists to make specific predictions on future social actions, developments or trends. A second set of approaches is much less stringent and rather more sociological. Here, social theories are understood to include those conceptual approaches or sets of arguments which have been widely applied by social scientists to study diverse social issues over a significant period of time (cf. Ritzer 1996: 4).

This second, more sociological approach to social theories is favoured in Part One of this Handbook. This approach invites us to consider theories which may have lost influence within sociology, or whose status as theories may have been disputed along 'scientific' lines by other social scientists. Adopting this broad approach also enables us to reflect on how different social issues and problems within sport may be theorized in a wide diversity of sociological ways. At their best, these sociological theories are not only built upon logically consistent premises; they are also able to provide critical insights on power relations in sport, and to envision how sport might be understood, organized and experienced in more just, inclusive and democratic ways. Additionally, we should note that the Handbook's consideration of sociological theories is not confined to this opening part. By way of registering their centrality to how sociologists study sport, many theoretical frameworks, problems and debates are explored in detail in the other parts of this Handbook.

Turning to the contents of Part One, chapters 2 through 11 examine different social theories of sport. Chapter 2, by Michael Atkinson, sets the scene by discussing the broad theoretical and methodological principles which undergird sociological research. For Atkinson, sociologists tend to adopt two main approaches when combining theory and evidence: first, 'sport sociologists' draw on pre-determined theories in order to collect and to interpret data; second, 'sociologists of sport' are more adventurous in developing research questions, data collection and new theory-building through a continuous dialogue with each other. While the former approach dominates in sociological research into sport, the latter is more attractive for facilitating original theory-building and innovative research activity. Accordingly, Atkinson observes that sociological studies of sport tend to be 'methodologically flat', in being largely guided by a few very familiar theoretical influences (Bourdieu, Foucault, Elias and Harvey are highlighted here). Conventional ethnographic research with 'risky' subcultures (such as ticket touts or football hooligans) has declined markedly, while interview research has mushroomed, notably for pragmatic reasons, such as relatively low cost and rapid accumulation of data. Atkinson concludes with a powerful, persuasive call for a critical sociology of sport which finds ways of intervening directly in social life in order to facilitate actual social change.

We turn next to examine specific social theories within the sociology of sport on a theory-by-chapter basis. We begin with three theoretical traditions that derive respectively from the 'founding fathers' within sociology, Durkheim, Weber and Marx. First, functionalist social theories, associated with Durkheimian approaches, have lost traction within sociology since the 1960s. However, as Tim Delaney demonstrates in his chapter, the functionalist approach may still be fruitfully applied in order to identify and explain several major social themes within sport, relating in particular to collective solidarity and social order. For example, modern sport is stuffed with references to 'teamwork' and 'playing systems', and how both should 'function' efficiently to produce winning outcomes. As Delaney points out, functionalist theories tend to focus primarily on the reproduction of the social order, on how systems are maintained over time; hence, these theories are most commonly criticized for paying too little attention to social conflicts and social change, for example when athletes challenge their sporting employers or when playing systems are discarded. Nevertheless, functionalist arguments continue to help explain the strong social bonds that are inspired in and through sport, for example in how community members experience greater forms of collective solidarity through identifying with their sport teams (e.g. Bain-Selbo 2012; Serazio 2013).

In substantial contrast to functionalist perspectives, interpretivist sociological approaches focus on everyday human interaction and on how people continuously interpret, negotiate and shape their social relations and environments. Interpretivist sociologies have strong roots within the *verstehen* (meaningful understanding) perspective advocated by Weber in particular. In their chapter, Peter Donnelly and Michael Atkinson explore the very diverse range of interpretivist perspectives within sociology, featuring for example classic approaches associated with the Chicago School or Goffman's 'dramaturgical model', alongside more critical standpoints in the cultural studies tradition. Interpretivist approaches have exercised particular influence on the methods used to study sport. For example, hermeneutic methods are deployed to interpret mass media narratives and themes on sport (e.g. Messner *et al.* 2000), while observational and ethnographic techniques facilitate direct studies of different sport subcultures (e.g. Armstrong 1998; Fine 1987). While criticized in more recent times, interpretivist approaches retain significant currency in sociological studies of sport, for example through auto-ethnographic methods that promote researcher reflexivity on relationships with diverse research groups.

Marxist and neo-Marxist perspectives have had a deep and enduring influence within the sociology of sport since the 1960s. As Ian McDonald explains in his chapter, these diverse approaches are underpinned by the method of 'critique', which enables scholars to expose existing relations of domination to criticize regressive social forces (such as fascism), and to explore alternative ways in which society may be organized. McDonald identifies three broad phases in the development of Marxist standpoints within the sociology of sport. First, 'activist Marxism' in the 1960s and 1970s viewed sport within capitalist societies in essentially negative terms, as shot through with exploitation and alienation (e.g. Hoch 1972). Second, 'cultural Marxism' in the late 1970s and 1980s explored how, within sport, different social groups might resist or contest their domination (e.g. Hargreaves 1986). Third, 'post-Marxism' from the late 1980s onwards has engaged with postmodernist and poststructuralist theories in particular to explore how the politics of identity and recognition are played out within sport (e.g. Andrews 2001). For McDonald, the way ahead for a Marxist sociology of sport is to pursue critique and creativity, to both denounce and celebrate sport, while advancing real 'constructive change'.

Many modern social theories may be understood with respect to where they are positioned in relation to a familiar array of conceptual dualisms, such as structure and action; macro and micro; and the global and the local. For those theories discussed above, functionalist and Marxist positions are commonly associated with structural and macro-level standpoints, whereas interpretivist approaches prioritize human action and micro-level studies. We turn next to consider two theorists sometimes associated with a 'post-dualist' theoretical impulse, in terms of seeking to move beyond the either/or basis of dualist theorizing.

The figurational perspective of Norbert Elias has had perhaps its strongest influence across the discipline of sociology in relation to the study of sport. In examining this contribution, the chapter by Dominic Malcolm explores in particular Elias's post-dualist perspective on, for example, macro- and micro-processes; psychogenesis and sociogenesis; and the routinization and de-routinization of everyday life. Elias's most influential theory centered on the 'civilizing process', which detailed how greater levels of physical and emotional restraint have developed within Western societies over several centuries. For Elias, sport is substantially engaged within this civilizing process, for example through the long-term 'controlled decontrol' of restraints on the emotions, so that the excitement of contemporary sport participation or watching should not spill over into real battle or violence (Elias and Dunning 1986). Other influential Eliasian theories have included his 'established-outsider' concept, which helps to explain social differentiation and the dynamics of power relations; and figuration, which refers to the interdependencies of individuals and social groups. As Malcolm indicates, Elias's focus on the interdependencies of 'nature' and 'nurture' has also provided the basis for figurational studies of the body in sport, for example with respect to fitness regimes or pain and injury among athletes (Mansfield 2010; Roderick 1998).

The theories of the French sociologist Pierrre Bourdieu have had a substantial and enduring influence on the sociology of sport, particularly in facilitating a critical analysis of power relations within different sporting fields. In his chapter, Michael Grenfell indicates how Bourdieu's theories and methods spotlight a host of sociological dualisms, such as subjectivity-objectivity, elite-popular, or amateur-professional; yet, for Grenfell, Bourdieu's perspective seeks to 'break with and to go beyond' the 'issues of theory and practice' that arise from these dualisms. For Grenfell, sport constitutes a 'perfect exemplar' for the application of Bourdieu's perspective. Central to Bourdieusian theory are the concepts of habitus, which explains how we are strongly socialized into making particular 'choices' or acquiring specific cultural tastes (in sport or elsewhere), and field, which refers to the social spaces (such as sport) in which different groups struggle to distinguish themselves and to gain dominance vis-à-vis other social groups. Thus, we find dominant groups being 'at home' within certain sports; more, these groups also claim cultural distinction for their favoured sports, such as golf, sailing and equestrianism (Bourdieu 1984). Physical education classes provide one significant learning space in which teachers and pupils train the body according to particular class and gender habitus (in the plural), and within specific sporting fields (Brown 2005). Overall, for Grenfell, a fully Bourdieusian mapping of the field of sport – including the 'field' of sociological perspectives on sport – should provide for a 'more authentic understanding' of sport *per se*.

In recent years, the 'system theory' of the German social scientist Niklas Luhmann has come to exercise a significant influence within the sociology of sport, particularly in central Europe and Scandinavia. As Ansgar Thiel and Jan Ove Tangen explain in their chapter, Luhmann understands the social system as consisting of a diversity of subsystems, such as the economy, polity, education and sport. Systems and subsystems operate through forms of communication (for example, in terms of what is understood as acceptable or unacceptable in playing sport); these systems and subsystems also serve to structure expectations, for example through the provision of facilities that enable education or sport to occur. In the most advanced societies, subsystems are relatively complex and are usually differentiated in functional ways from one another. Each subsystem is largely defined by a binary code, such as profit/loss in the economy or win/loss in sport (Schimank 2005). However, secondary binary codes also arise, such as improvement/ regression in sport, which reflects the substantial focus on whether individual or team play is 'getting better' (Tangen 2004). In addition, 'structural couplings' occur between subsystems: for example, sport appears to couple closely with business, politics, media, education and other subsystems. As Thiel and Tangen demonstrate, Luhmann's system theory has been used to examine manifold sport issues and problems, such as the organization of elite sport teams, doping in sport, sport environments and the links between sport and educational subsystems. Given their broad applicability and scope for creative adaptation by social scientists, Luhmann's theories might be expected to gain further influence, notably in other, English-speaking communities within the sociology of sport.

In the Anglo-American context, one significant development in the sociology of sport in recent years has been the emergence of 'physical cultural studies' (PCS), which is rooted in the cultural studies tradition and draws substantially on the perspective of David Andrews. In their chapter, Andrews and co-author Michael Silk set out the main aspects of the PCS approach. For them, PCS is concerned with 'physical culture, and more specifically the way specific forms of physical culture are organized, disciplined, represented, embodied, and experienced in relation to the operations of social power.' PCS is presented as harbouring a wide range of qualities, such as being contextual, transdisciplinary, self-reflexive and committed to the transformation of individuals, groups, sports and wider society (cf. Andrews and Silk 2011; Giardina and Newman 2011). Drawing on Paulo Freire's concept of 'conscientization', Andrews and Silk argue that one important feature of PCS involves promoting awareness of forms of oppression in order to shape meaningful social change.

Poststructuralist social theory has had very substantial influence within the sociology of sport since the early 1990s, specifically through the use of Michel Foucault's social theory. In her chapter, Samantha King examines the main arguments and concepts within the diverse field of poststructuralist literature, and their relevance to the sociology of sport. King argues that structuralist scholars such as Ferdinand de Saussure, Claude Lévi-Strauss and Roland Barthes prepared the ground for poststructuralist perspectives, for example by highlighting the relational basis of language. Inevitably, Foucault's contribution requires extensive consideration, particularly on how discourses and technologies of 'biopower' serve to construct frameworks of (self-)knowledge and regimes of discipline and control. These concepts help us to explain how athletes and spectators experience forms of disciplinary power, such as coach-monitored training regimes or the installation of CCTV and other surveillance systems in sport stadiums (Giulianotti 2011; Shogan 1999). In turn, different social groups within sport come to exercise forms of discipline and self-regulation upon themselves, without necessarily having authority figures overlooking their practices. On the other hand, Foucault's work highlights the proliferation and ubiquity of power relations, which individuals and social groups have sought to navigate in creative, resistant and self-fulfilling ways. Sport illustrations of these more optimistic, empowering insights are perhaps evidenced by the Gay Games or the critical perspectives of women on their gender identities in sport.

The final chapter, by Ben Carrington, examines postcolonial theories – or, as he writes, post/colonial theories – in relation to the sociology of sport. These diverse theories have significant continuities with poststructuralist, neo-Marxist and cultural studies perspectives, and seek to make sense of the power relations and everyday impacts of colonialism, the subsequent drive to 'independence' in colonized societies and the emergence of the 'postcolonial' epoch. A core concern here must be for the sociology of sport to resist reproducing the racialized discourses and frameworks of knowledge that have dominated the colonial and postcolonial periods. Drawing on postcolonial theory, Carrington critiques the claims of other sport scholars, that modern Western sports are more civilized, rational and sophisticated than 'primitive' forms of physical culture in colonized and developing societies. These claims both underplay the violence and exploitation within much Western sport, and pay little attention to the cultural meanings of physical culture in non-Western contexts. Overall, this chapter reflects several of the core points within Part One of the Handbook, in terms of registering the diversity of social theories that may be utilized by sociologists of sport, and also the critical importance of questions of social power and domination for the process of sociological theorizing.

References

Andrews, D.L. (ed.) (2001) *Michael Jordan, Inc.*, Albany: SUNY Press.

Andrews, D.L. and M. Silk (eds) (2011) *Physical Cultural Studies*, Philadelphia: Temple University Press.

Armstrong, G. (1998) *Football Hooligans: Knowing the Score*, Oxford: Berg.

Bain-Selbo, E. (2012) *Game Day and God*, Macon, GA: Mercer University Press.

Bourdieu, P. (1984) *Distinction*, London: Routledge.

Brown, D. (2005) 'An Economy of Gendered Practices? Learning to Teach Physical Education from the Perspectives of Pierre Bourdieu's Embodied Sociology', *Sport, Education and Society*, 10(1): 3–23.

Elias, N. and E. Dunning (1986) *Quest for Excitement*, Oxford: Blackwell.

Fine, G.A. (1987) *With the Boys: Little League Baseball and Preadolescent Culture*, Chicago: University of Chicago Press.

Giardina, M.D. and J.I. Newman (2011) 'What Is This "Physical" in Physical Cultural Studies?' *Sociology of Sport Journal*, 28: 36–63.

Giulianotti, R. (2011) 'Sport Mega-Events, Urban Football Carnivals and Securitized Commodification: The Case of the English Premier League', *Urban Studies*, 48(15): 3293–3310.

Hargreaves, J. (1986) *Sport, Power and Culture*, Cambridge: Polity.

Hoch, P. (1972) *Rip Off the Big Game*, Garden City, NY: Doubleday.

Mansfield, L. (2010) '"Fit, Fat and Feminine": The Stigmatisation of Fat Women in Fitness Gyms', in E. Kennedy and P. Markula (eds) *Women and Exercise: Qualitative Research on the Body, Health and Consumerism*, London: Routledge.

Messner, M.A., M. Dunbar and D. Hunt (2000) 'The Televised Sports Manhood Formula', *Journal of Sport and Social Issues*, 24(4): 380–394.

Ritzer, G. (1996) *Modern Sociological Theory*, New York: McGraw-Hill.

Roderick, M. (1998) 'The Sociology of Risk, Pain and Injury: A Comment on the Work of Howard Nixon II', *Sociology of Sport Journal*, 15: 64–79.

Schimank, U. (2005) 'The Autonomy of Modern Sport: Dangerous and Endangered', *European Journal for Sport and Society*, 2(1): 25–33.

Serazio, M. (2013) 'The Elementary Forms of Sports Fandom', *Communication and Sport*, 1(4): 303–325.

Shogan, D. (1999) *The Making of High-Performance Athletes: Discipline, Diversity, and Ethics*, Toronto: University of Toronto Press.

Tangen, J.O. (2004) 'Embedded Expectations, Embodied Knowledge and the Movements That Connect', *International Review for the Sociology of Sport*, 39(1): 7–25.

2

RESEARCHING SPORT

Michael Atkinson

The definitional terrain

For nearly twenty years I struggled to understand why hundreds of researchers refer to the social-scientific study of sport as the 'sociology of sport' while others refer to the sub-discipline as 'sport sociology'. For whatever reason, European and Canadian researchers tend to utilize the former whereas Americans more liberally employ the latter. Over the course of time, I ascribed the subtle divergence in academic vernacular to something as banal as unexplainable cultural habit or preference. But the difference in language potentially suggests a much more subtle division of research agendas in the study of sport in society.

A 'sociology of sport' denotes the systematic, empirically grounded, and theoretically/conceptually driven analysis of sport and physical culture. Sport is studied, that is, as a vehicle for developing, refining, and, dare I add, testing, sociological theory and the concepts welded together to form its undergirding. A sociologist of sport is predominantly obsessed with sport as a context for further illuminating how generic social processes (both contemporary and long-term) unfold, how complex institutions operate and change, the machinations of power, culture, and ideology in society, and basic issues regarding the human condition such as the formation of personal/group identities, shared meaning structures, the experience of embodiment, and the unfolding of personal roles, statuses, and emotions. The sociologist of sport might be described, then, as incredibly selfish toward the discipline itself; excavating the intricacies of sport and other physical cultural practices as a means to a higher sociological (read *analytic*) end. Here, the context and practices of sport are approached as ideal terrain for theoretical interrogations of how social change occurs, how social formations of human interdependence both facilitate and constrain human agency, the political economic aspects of embodied cultural practices, the complicated interplay between selves in society, and the role of (new) collective movements, both locally and internationally.

'Sport sociology' implies a different form, content, and perceptual tack on the nature of academic research. Sport sociology, one might argue, is often underpinned by either an almost evangelical fascination with sport (including its policies and its global management), or an intense critique of sport as an institution rife with social problems (i.e. discrimination and inequality along gender, race, ethnic, sexuality, class, national, or other cultural lines; structural corruption; or violence, abuse, and exploitation). Projects embedded in a sport sociology framework are generally flavoured with keen sociological insight and argument, but thematic emphasis in them may lean more heavily toward substantive articulations of sport's cultural significance in society rather than as theoretical/conceptual excursions into sport. Contributors to the recent spate in sport policy studies, categorical analyses of sport participation around the globe, and the mass mediation of identity through sport might be criticized by traditional sociologists of sport for attending less to intensive *theorization of society through sport-oriented research* and more to the cataloguing of sport's importance in society – even toward the fetishization of sport itself.

In thinking, then, about how to structure a chapter on 'Researching Sport' in a volume such as this, we must first accept and reconcile (for ourselves as well as for students and colleagues) how the act of research is paradigmatically, ideologically, pragmatically, technically, and substantively both organized and characteristically messy – and, quite likely, exists between the ideal type sociology of sport (the term and approach I tend to prefer) and a sport sociology described above. To this end, one simply cannot delineate an exhaustive list of topics truly required to grapple with the complexity and diversity of contemporary studies of sport in society within the confines of a single chapter. Indeed, the many chapters in this volume devote a considerable space to even briefly cover the substantive terrain. In what follows, then, I engage several core issues in researching sport (and physical culture) with a particular emphasis on central questions and topic areas in the sub-discipline, research ethics in sport studies, the usual (and emergent) methodologies in the field, the role of theory and its application in sport studies, and concluding with reflection on both praxis and public academic work in the sociology of sport.

May I ask you a question?

There is likely no aspect of the research process in contemporary practice receiving less attention and therefore shorter shrift than the very nature of our research questions. Depending on one's area of research interest and the paradigm from which one operates, sociologists of sport have historically asked *four main types* of research questions. The first two were much more common in sociological research on sport until the late 1980s and early 1990s, whilst the latter two are dominant today.

(i) *Descriptive*: These questions focus on identifying and outlining common patterns, events, characteristics, or trends in bodies, minds, and societies relevant to sport. Descriptive questions in the sociology of sport often pertain to participation patterns, such as who plays sport, how often, where, and when. They generally focus on demographic characteristics in organized sport around the globe, sport's potential relationship with population health (and injury/illness), state-based investment in sport (measured along any number of lines), and, more recently, the personal and social costs of sport in society. Examples include 'How many people living in Surrey (UK) from working-class backgrounds participate in a sports clubs?'; 'What is the growth rate of coaching certifications in the United States?'; 'How many girls play organized tennis in Canada in comparison to boys?'; or 'What is the risk rate of ankle injury in minor league football for children aged 13–14?'. Descriptive questions and the studies they lead to, while often theoretically 'lean', provide sociologists of sport with important information about the distributional or categorical nature of a phenomenon of interest.

(ii) *Explanatory*: These questions are the hallmark of deductive-positivistic inquiry in the sociology of sport. An explanatory question is ideally derived from an extant theory, whereby the axioms and principles of a theory are used to predict an outcome in the 'real world' of sport and physical culture. Explanatory questions, or *hypotheses*, have focussed on wide-ranging phenomena in sport such as the aetiology of sports violence, whether class is a robust predictor of player ideologies, spectator practices and preferences in sport, and the social determinants of exercise participation. For reasons too detailed to debate in this chapter, explanatory questions and their associated quantitative techniques of data collection and analysis have fallen rather sharply out of favour in the discipline for being overly modernist, techno-scientific, deterministic, apolitical, and Western-hegemonic (Atkinson 2012).

(iii) *Exploratory*: Exploratory questions form the basis of classic inductive sociological inquiry in the sub-discipline, and initiate a programme of investigation intended to 'flesh out' a tentative or working understanding (not explanation) of a phenomenon in the study of sport and physical culture. Here, we might only have a general theoretical or substantive clue about what is going on with respect to a sport-related phenomenon (no past theories or studies accurately account for it or provide us with direction), and therefore a researcher embarks on a very loosely structured programme of data collection and analysis to arrive at a tentative understanding. Examples of exploratory questions include 'Is there a relationship between gender and violence in sport?'; 'What is it like to be an athlete with an injury?'; or 'How do people construct and understand barriers to physical activity participation?'.

Whereas the role of theory in descriptive and explanatory research is quite clear, the role of theory in so-called exploratory sport research (which the lion's share of contemporary qualitative research in the areas claims to be) is much more murky. Exploratory research questions are often undertaken in the pursuit of 'grounded' theoretical conceptualizations of sport's meaning to people. But the term 'grounded theory' is bandied about rather liberally and conceptually misapplied in contemporary sport research like no other (Atkinson 2011, 2012). Grounded theory, in methodological terms, is most accurately described as a technique of question formation, data collection, and data analysis in which the eventual conceptualizations or theoretical understanding of people, small groups, or other social formations one 'discovers' is developed from the data, rather than the other way around. Here, data collection, analysis, and theory formulation are undeniably connected in a reciprocal sense, and the grounded theory approach incorporates *explicit* procedures to guide this process (see Charmaz 2003; Glaser 2001; Strauss and Corbin 1998).

Yet, as noted above, the term 'grounded theory' has become rather lazily applied to a full range of exploratory/qualitative/interpretive questions and the studies they spawn. Indeed, the term is at once generally conflated with the notion of interpreting qualitative data and employed *as a default slogan describing data collection/analysis methods in a qualitative study;* often, one that sounds convincingly scientific to research ethics boards, granting agencies, more quantitatively oriented colleagues, and those fervently convinced that the social sciences must indeed be perceived as 'proper' sciences. We must question, through careful scrutiny of the methods-data-theory link in each study, if research projects flying under the banner of grounded theory within the sport and physical culture literature are most likely ventures in what we might call *concept elaboration* or straight *theory application* (Atkinson 2012). Here, a researcher commences with pre-configured conceptual or theoretical ideas in mind (or their preferred theoretical explanations of the world) and then expands them or even uncritically 'applies' them, in whole, to emergent qualitative data. The sheer volume (and indeed one might suggest overwhelming preponderance), for example, of Foucauldian or Bourdieuisian interpretations of sport and physical activity in the current sociological literature ostensibly produced through 'grounded' readings of data hint to the profuse abandonment of exploratory/grounded theoretical research in the sociology of sport. The result may very well be a theoretical and conceptual flatness in contemporary research in sport wherein a small handful of theorists now dominate in the field (Foucault, Bourdieu, Elias, Deleuze, and Butler, for example). Our concepts might be expanded, contracted, tightened, or partially redefined through so-called exploratory inquiry, but very rarely are new theoretical systems or sets of interconnected conceptually driven questions produced.

(iv) *Evaluative*: These questions can be descriptive, explanatory, or exploratory in nature. These questions address whether or not a sport-based programme or policy developed to produce a result in the world is actually operating as intended. Indeed, evaluative questions are of growing importance in the sociology of sport (Okada and Young 2014). Evaluation-based questions are frequently posed at the request of a public or private group or institution seeking the systematic assessment of one of their initiatives. For instance, does the creation of a staff exercise facility promote physical activity participation at the worksite? A city council might seek to examine the effects of hosting major games like the Olympics or Commonwealth Games on healthy, active living in the city. Another researcher might ask whether or not a sport for development programme in rural Ghana actually improves community health as intended.

If we believe that a research question is a statement that identifies the parameters of the phenomenon to be studied, sociologists of sport must be our own harshest critics and ask whether or not our questions are sociologically relevant, neatly defined, and timely. Students routinely have difficulties in narrowing down their interests into manageable questions, and express frustration over the difference between substantive research questions and sociological problems, or commence so substantively, ideologically, and theoretically opinionated that any data in the study could be interpreted before it is even gathered. Here is where a critical fault line dividing the sociology of sport and sport sociology is most evident. The sport sociologist, tends to favour substantive questions and reads data through somewhat pre-determined theoretical foci, whilst the sociologist of sport formulates questions from core sociological problems and tests/dialogues with/generates new theory through the act of research.

Wait, is it actually okay to ask?

Research in the sociology of sport that involves human subjects or participants raises unique and complex ethical, legal, social, and political issues. This goes almost without saying. From my institutional experience, there are three objectives in research ethics that sociologists of sport must encounter at the forefront of our research efforts. The first and broadest objective is to protect human participants from being 'harmed' in the research process. Given that sport research (especially qualitative studies of embodiment, power, youth, marginalization, discrimination, and so forth) involves vulnerable populations quite frequently, potential participant harm is front and centre as an ethical question. The second objective is to ensure that research is conducted in a way that actually serves the interests of individuals, groups, and/or society as a whole (this, while a lofty and idealistic goal, is difficult to achieve). This often may be difficult to establish in front of research ethics board, as research in the sociology of sport can be seen as somewhat of a 'hobbyist' pursuit by colleagues in the hard sciences (Andrews 2008). Finally, the third objective is to examine specific research activities and projects for their ethical soundness, looking at issues such as the management of risk, protection of participant confidentiality, and the process of informed consent.

Every study undertaken in a university by a student or professor in the sociology of sport must pass ethics review by at least one (but normally two or three) ethics review committee. In many cases, members review protocols outside of their fields of expertise, disciplines, and, for all intents and purposes, life experiences. This is critical to remember. Research in the sociology of sport is typically institutionally assessed by members of social sciences, health, or kinesiology departments who may not understand sociological research on sport, its thrust, and/or purpose.

On the one hand, sociologists often do not understand the fascination with sport, and on the other, health scientists (particularly those with biomedical preferences) may see little value in sociological research on matters pertaining to health, physical activity, and exercise.

The most important issue arising in the ethical review of scientific research involving human participants is risk of harm. Notions of risk and harm in human participant research have evolved from a biomedical tradition, having been borne out of atrocities such as medical experimentation carried out by Nazi physicians in the Second World War and the Tuskegee Syphilis Study alongside tragic events such as the Sonoma State Radiation experiments and the experimental use of thalidomide in the 1950s and 1960s in North America. Today, research ethics boards are routinely criticized for being 'out of touch' with the real world, erring too heavily on the side of caution and thus creating a 'cotton wool' climate in universities. Here is an example. In the mid-1990s I conducted an ethnographic project on ticket scalpers in Canada. I lived with a couple of them, hung out with them on a daily basis, and went to sports contests to watch them in action. This was the first ever sociological study of ticket scalping, and the research helped to question and reshape social policy in Canada regarding the 'after market' selling of tickets. Over the course of time I witnessed quite a bit of criminal behaviour, some violence, and found myself in more than a few troubling situations in the field. The nearly-two-year project taught me a hundred valuable methodological and theoretical lessons. Today, the study would never even pass the 'laugh test' in ethics review because of the inherently 'dangerous' nature of the group, the research questions, and the supposed harm posed to both the research participants and me.

Okay, I will find an answer

If there is a methodological *lingua franca* in the sociology of sport and physical culture, it is certainly *interviewing*. From the early 1990s onward, and dovetailing with the waning popularity of historical and quantitative methods, there has been simply no other research method as popular as interviewing in the sociology of sport. The boom in the method's popularity is perhaps owing in large part to the collective interest sociologists of sport share in substantively examining the meanings of sport to people, how individuals experience sport, and how power, inequality, and injustice are 'felt' through/in sport. Indeed, interviewing is also viewed as less ethically challenging than, say, traditional ethnographic research or experimental designs; there is an abundance of people around to be interviewed on most research topics; interviewing is more economically viable than other field methods; and it can be performed flexibly around one's own schedule.

Interviewing is a research technique with many faces and varieties, including life history interviewing, phenomenological interviewing, focus group interviewing, structured and unstructured interviewing, peer interviewing, active interviewing, and others. What is generally referred to as 'semi-structured interviewing' is, however, at the methodological forefront in the sociology of sport (Markula and Silk 2011; Sparkes and Smith 2014; Thorpe 2012). What constitutes 'semi-structured' is open for methodological debate. Semi-structured interviewing traditionally refers to a question-asking process underpinned by an interpretivist/constructivist ontology and epistemology; that is, one in which the interviewer has a 'loose' set of substantive questions to ask respondents, but the process of conceptual and theoretical development through the data collection process remains relatively open. Today, and as discussed earlier in this chapter, semi-structured interviewing often takes shape as the use of a set of theoretically informed (if not pre-determined) questions; what Stebbins (2001) refers to as the practice of *guided theoretical exploration*. For example, interview-based research commencing from Bourdieu's (1984) understanding of habitus, Foucault's (1979) notions of biopwer and governmentality, Elias's (1978) description of the civilizing process, or Harvey's (2007) position on neo-liberalism abound in the sociology of sport. The sheer popularity of theoretically guided interviewing in the sociology of sport is facilitating a condition of relative 'methodological (let alone theoretical) flatness' in the sub-discipline. While there is apparent methodological diversity in contemporary research practice, even a cursory glance at published research in the *Sociology of Sport Journal; The Journal of Sport and Social Issues; International Review for the Sociology of Sport; Qualitative Research in Sport, Exercise and Health; Sport in Society;* and other leading journals attests to the method's hegemony.

The condition of current methodological flatness is amplified by the additional popularity of *media-based research* in the sociology of sport. Today, few social practices or concerns (save, perhaps, for war, crime, or international politics) are as globally mass mediated as sport or health matters. From the Olympic Games to the study of race in society to the World Cup to obesity, the representation of the active/sporting body is a universally 'weighty' cultural matter (Young and Atkinson 2012). Sport and physical culture researchers find good cause to question what people are producing and consuming through sport and health media, and what are the impacts (Kennedy and Hills 2009). Studies of the representation of gender, sexuality, race, nationhood, religion, and other forms of identity continue to mushroom (Hundley and Billings 2009). Analyses of the audience reception of sport media are growing slowly in popularity (Millington and Wilson 2012), the audience reception of sport media (both online and offline) is a developing research area, and perhaps the fastest growth area in media research is, of course, the use of social media in sport and physical cultures (Hutchins and Rowe 2013). Media-based or -oriented research emerges quite importantly out of the field of discourse analysis, and ascended in prominence in the sociology of sport in the mid-1990s.

Discourse analysis – as inspired by French structuralists including Ferdinand de Saussure, Jacques Lacan, and Roland Barthes, and critical post-structuralists including Judith Butler, Julia Kristeva, and Michel Foucault – is globally popular in the sociology of sport. Discourse analysis, like interviewing, is not a single method, but rather a series of complementary techniques focusing on the interpretive reading of a sample of media texts in order to expose the dominant *episteme* (knowledge), assumptions, ideologies, or values underwriting them. Another way of describing discourse analysis is to call it the study of the dominant or 'preferred meanings' (Hall 1973) or ideologies in media texts that frame how audiences are supposed to understand and use them. Discourse analysts in the sociology of sport and physical culture envision mass media texts as connected through and composed by socially diffuse systems of language encoded with dominant ideologies. Rich and Miah's (2009) research on the medicalization of cyberspace illustrates, for example, how governmental ideologies of self-surveillance and associated neo-liberal discourses of healthism abound online and reach millions. Rich and Miah (2009) highlight how the Internet has become a zone for spreading dominant, conservative, and self-blaming sport, exercise, and health messages, and how they systematically blur real material differences in people's access to quality, state-provided sport, exercise, and health care schemes and styles of healthy living.

Contemporary sociology of sport researchers have diversified the form, content, and purpose of qualitative means of knowing (Markula and Denison, 2005). *Auto-ethnographic* methods have grown in popularity within the study of sport and physical culture. Auto-ethnography is a method in which the investigator develops a research question pertaining to a particular social process, experience, or reality and then creates an ethnographic description and analysis of his/ her own behaviour, attempting to develop an objective understanding of the behaviours and work context under consideration by casting the investigator as both the informant 'insider' and the analyst 'outsider'. For example, a spate of running auto-ethnographies has been published within the recent past (e.g. Hockey 2006). These ethnographies, almost always written in a story or aesthetic narrative form rather than as a traditional academic/journal article, illustrate that by knowing one's own self and exploring how one's own life takes meaning (for instance, as a runner), we learn a great deal about the processes by which social life unfolds.

A relatively new mode of inquiry, *sensory ethnography*, is described by sociologist Sarah Pink (2009) as a way of thinking about and doing sociological research that takes, as its starting point, the multi-sensoriality (e.g. hearing, seeing, smelling, tasting, and touching) essence of human experience, perception, knowing, and practice. Pink describes sensory methods as an outcropping of a traditional form of qualitative inquiry that further accounts for how people's experiences with multi-sensoriality in social life are integral both to the lives of people who participate in our research and how to practice field methods themselves.

Performance (or '*performative*') *methodology* is an emerging arts-based method of enquiry and representation that presents a tangible opportunity to bridge the gap between scholarly activity and community teaching and learning. After spending time in the field with a group of (usually marginalized) others, the ethnographer, generally in conjunction with key informants from the group under study, writes and produces a dramatic play, vignette, or short film representing the culture. By using the theatre or the screen as a place of research representation, performance ethnography transforms the site from a place of entertainment to a venue for participatory action research that extends beyond the performance itself (Alexander 2005; Finley 2005). As a forum for cultural exchange, the power of performance-based interpretation lies in its potential for illumination and engagement of involved researchers, participants, and audience. Thrift (2007) pushes boundaries even further, suggesting that the next stage in the evolution of embodied research might very well be non-representational – meaning that representational practices which portray embodied realities must themselves emerge from written texts and evolve into fully embodied and visceral performance pieces.

Making substantive grounds in interviewing circles is what Smith and Osborn (2009) describe as *interpretive phenomenological analysis* (IPA). IPA is now gaining traction in the psychology of sport, but also in the sociology of sport, among qualitatively inclined researchers and practitioners. The aim of IPA is to explore, in detail, how people make cognitive and cultural sense of their personal and social worlds, and the embodied experience of life in their social worlds. Smith and Osborn (2009) argue that the main 'currency' for an IPA study is the meanings particular experiences, events, and states hold for participants. To this end, IPA-based excursions into sport focus on intense idiographic inspections of people's experiences on selected subjects of inquiry. The approach is 'phenomenological' in that it involves detailed examination of the participant's lifeworld and the emotional experience of that lifeworld. At the same time, IPA emphasizes that the research exercise is a dynamic process with an active role for the researcher in that process.

Finally, the increasing prominence of the sport for development and peace research in the sub-discipline has rekindled an interest in evaluation (or monitoring and evaluation) methods amongst researchers (see Atkinson and De Lisio 2014). Evaluation research is a type of applied research geared towards determining if a programme, policy, intervention, or some intended plan is achieving its desired outcomes. Common sociological 'things' evaluated by sociologists of sport, exercise, and leisure include the effectiveness of sport as a social development 'lever' in places plagued by poverty, illness and disease, crime, war, violence, or discrimination and exploitation; public and private physical activity and fitness practices and policies; pedagogy and coaching techniques; delivery of health services inside and outside of sport; lifestyles of (un) healthy living; and legislation designed to eliminate inequality in sport participation (Atkinson 2012). Evaluation research can be conducted through a range of data collection techniques and forms of analysis such as interviewing, ethnography, document analysis, surveys, and even social experimentation. The small scale and esoteric nature of evaluation projects tends to raise criticisms regarding the broader (theoretical and conceptual) merits of the research. On these grounds and others, sport for development research has often been challenged as being concerned more with social policy than sociological theory generation, testing, or refinement. From a different perspective, however, the rising prominence of sport for development and peace research may signal a shifting generational sensibility that research only for the sake of sociology (of sport) is pointless, unsustainable, socially irresponsible, and the least useful means to illustrate the importance of sociological thought in identifying and addressing social problems, inequalities, and injustices.

Concluding thoughts: further contextualizing research in the sociology of sport

On the heels of the burgeoning sport for development and peace research cluster in the sociology of sport, there has been a renewed, and certainly contested, argument that the research act in the sociology of sport must become more 'politically and socially engaged' to retain its utility. Such an argument, coming perhaps most openly from advocates of physical cultural studies as a contender to the sociology of sport throne (Atkinson 2011; Giardina and Newman 2011; Silk and Andrews 2011), or proponents of a more public sociology of sport (Donnelly, Atkinson, Boyle, and Szto 2011), hinges upon the related premises that not only does theoretically driven sociological research on sport offer much insight into a spectrum of social problems, but that the future of the discipline is likely contingent upon research that 'matters' in the 'new university'.

To be sure, both the context and culture of academic research on sport and physical culture has changed rather immensely over the two past decades. Given the rise of audit cultures within universities and colleges; the crumbling of traditional university business models and upsurge of neo-liberal practices of fund raising; a groundswell in conservative ideologies across many Western landscapes; the ongoing redesign of sport, exercise, and health faculties/departments along kinesiological (in the preferred North American argot) and neo-positivist lines; and a proliferating scepticism about the public utility of social research in Canada, the United States, and United Kingdom (as evidenced, for example, by the sweeping funding cuts to social scientific teaching and research in British universities in 2010); a re-visitation of the *whats, whys*, and *hows* of researching sport and physical culture is not only timely, it is long overdue. The pursuit of sociological knowledge for the sake of sociological knowledge has most likely gone the way of the academic dinosaur, and social scientific units around the world are forced to justify their existence, daily operation, staffing, funding, and future along lines of outcomes, deliverables, products, or other empirical means-to-an-end rationales. Bairner (2009) remarks how the late modern university, as a prison of measured time, both disrespects and allows for little in the way of traditional sociological work. Yet those interested in advocating the practical/translational aspects of the sociology of sport, or applying sociological work to problems facing groups in society, must remember first and foremost that those interested in public, interventionist academic work face considerable internal pressures from above to publish in top-tier academic journals, encounter yearly metrics designed to assess very traditional academic roles and responsibilities, and socialize with colleagues who often express minimum concern for socio-cultural research, and whose subversive and interventionist orientations jibe tangentially at best with the privatized timbres of our late modern, corporate universities.

Andrews (2008) in particular is critical of the transformation of kinesiological, physical activity, sport and health science, and human movement departments by neo-positivist health agendas, research protocols, and pushes toward traditionally 'scientific' (and privately funded) research. Even more micrologically, within sub-disciplinary space (the study of sport, sport policy studies, or the sociology of sport more broadly) questions concerning the over-reliance on preferred critical theoretical readings of social life, non-empirically-driven accounts of sport and leisure and mass media research have done little to engender a public-oriented zeitgeist among colleagues. These trends are further amplified by critical sociologists of sport's pervasive disregard for, or perhaps ambivalence toward, 'knowledge-exchange' research efforts and meaningful engagement with other disciplines (i.e. political science, economics, history, anthropology, philosophy, classics, media studies and communication, human geography, criminology, and others) through research acts. As such, a gloomy forecast is easily predicted for sociological research on sport in an academic world demanding a far less esoteric or 'siloed' engagement with the world.

Atkinson and Donnelly (2010) argue that the traditional sociology of sport runs the very real risk of routinely resting on its own intellectual laurels – emerging far too often as an exercise in the philosophical reading of sport, physical culture, power within social formations, or hegemonic representations of moving bodies and identities, and too infrequently as a concerted and unapologetic ritual of transformative praxis. Critical sociological theories and related research, in their most spirited manifestation, attend to and underscore the politics, problems, and possibilities of research as a lever of engaged praxis; as Tomlinson (1989: 7) comments, a '. . . praxis in both the sense that human agents are the architects of the world that they inhabit, and the sense that such agents can become the architects of renewal, reform and change'. Critical theorizing, from this perspective, is more than the deployment of acerbic thought, comments on the inequities of cultural domination, a detailed analysis of structured inequality, or a rhetoric demanding social change. Relevant sociological theory and the research it inspires must be a vehicle of engaged, committed, irreverent, and passionately charged interventionist work (Atkinson and Donnelly 2010; McDonald 2002).

Much of the current definitional writing in the sociology of sport and physical culture emphasizes the need for politically engaged, interventionist, and transformative research. Yet little evidence is ever given of the actual manifestation of such work. Carrington's (2007) and others' 'calls' for interventionist and political work beyond identity politics have potentially run their course. A forward-thinking sociology of sport and physical culture, it would seem, is essentially the physical cultural study of social life manifesting into and engaging with, as Burawoy writes (2004), the possibility/existence of 'better worlds'. It requires sociologists of sport to break new ground, transgress disciplinary boundaries, pursue theoretically driven policy research with much vigour, and research beyond the comfortable subjects so regularly studied. It may require, only as a small list of possible topics, an invested and concerted interest in matters of sport and physical activity for/as social development, movement cultures as potential solutions to broad gauge social problems, human rights in sport and leisure contexts, visions of democratic humanism across physical cultures, physical cultural 'pastimes', post-sport physical cultures, issues in bioethics and technology, youth development through mainstream and non-mainstream physical activities, experiences of health, wellness, varied (dis)abilities, and illness as/in physical culture, global sport, leisure and recreation management, and the sensual aspects of physical culture.

References

Alexander, B. (2005) 'Performance Ethnography: The Re-Enacting and Inciting of Culture', in N. Denzin and Y. Lincoln (eds) *Handbook of Qualitative Inquiry*, Thousand Oaks, CA: Sage.

Andrews, D. (2008) 'Kinesiology's "Inconvenient Truth" and the Physical Cultural Studies Imperative', *Quest*, 60: 45–62

Atkinson, M. (2011) 'Physical Cultural Studies [Redux]', *Sociology of Sport Journal*, 28: 135–144.

Atkinson, M. (2012) *Key Concepts in Sport & Exercise Research Methods*, London: Sage.

Atkinson, M. and De Lisio, A (2014) 'Mega Events, Sport Legacies and Sociologically Informed Impact Assessment', in C. Okada and K. Young (eds) *Sport, Social Development and Peace*, London: Emerald Group.

Atkinson, M. and Donnelly, P. (2010) 'Sport, Social Intervention and Public Sociology', paper to the Chicago Seminar on Sport and Culture, Newberry Library, Chicago, March 19.

Bairner, A. (2009) 'Sport, Intellectuals and Public Sociology: Obstacles and Opportunities', *International Review for the Sociology of Sport*, 44: 115–130.

Bourdieu, P. (1984) *Distinction: A Social Critique of the Judgment of Taste*, Cambridge: Harvard University Press.

Burawoy, M. (2004) 'Public Sociologies: Contradictions, Dilemmas, and Possibilities', *Social Forces*, 82: 603–618.

Carrington, B. (2007) 'Merely Identity: Cultural Identity and the Politics of Sport', *Sociology of Sport Journal*, 24: 49–66.

Charmaz, K. (2003) *Constructing Grounded Theory: A Practical Guide Through Grounded Analysis*, London: Sage.

Donnelly, P., Atkinson, M., Boyle, S. and Szto, C. (2011) 'Sport for Development and Peace: A Public Sociology Perspective', *Third World Quarterly*, 32: 589–601.

Elias, N. (1978) *The Civilizing Process*, Oxford: Blackwell.

Finley, S. (2005) 'Arts-Based Inquiry: Performing Revolutionary Pedagogy', in N. Denzin and Y. Lincoln (eds) *Handbook of Qualitative Inquiry*, Thousand Oaks, CA: Sage.

Foucault, M. (1979) *Discipline and Punish*, New York: Random House.

Giardina, M. and Newman, J. (2011) 'What is the "Physical" in Physical Cultural Studies?', *Sociology of Sport Journal*, 28: 36–63.

Glaser, B. (2001) *The Grounded Theory Perspective*, Mill Valley, CA: Sociology Press.

Hall, S. (1973) 'Encoding and Decoding in the Television Discourse', Birmingham: University of Birmingham Centre for Cultural Studies (CCS Stencilled Paper no. 7).

Harvey, D. (2007) *A Brief History of Neoliberalism*, New York: Oxford University Press.

Hockey, J. (2006) 'Sensing the Run: Distance Running and the Senses', *The Senses and Society*, 1: 183–202.

Hundley, H. and Billings, A. (2009) *Examining Identity in Sports Media*, London: Sage.

Hutchins, B. and Rowe, D. (2013) *Sport Beyond Television: The Internet, Digital Media and the Rise of Networked Media Sport*, London: Routledge.

Kennedy, E. and Hills, L. (2009) *Sport, Media and Society*, London: Bloomsbury.

Markula, P. and Denison, J. (2005) 'Sport and the Personal Narrative', in D. Andrews, D. Mason and M. Silk (eds) *Qualitative Methods in Sports Studies*, New York: Berg.

Markula, P. and Silk, M. (2011) *Qualitative Research for Physical Culture*, New York: Palgrave Macmillan.

McDonald, I. (2002) 'Critical Social Research and Political Intervention: Moralistic *versus* Radical Approaches', in J. Sugden and A. Tomlinson (eds) *Power Games: A Critical Sociology of Sport*, London: Routledge.

Millington, B. and Wilson, B. (2012) 'Media Analysis in Physical Cultural Studies: From Production to Reception', in K. Young and M. Atkinson (eds) *Qualitative Research on Sport and Physical Culture*, London: Emerald.

Okada, C. and K. Young (eds) (2014) *Sport, Social Development and Peace*, London: Emerald Group.

Pink, S. (2009) *Doing Visual Ethnography*, London: Sage.

Rich, E. and Miah, A. (2009) *The Medicalization of Cyberspace*, London: Routledge.

Silk, M. and Andrews, D. (2011) 'Toward a Physical Cultural Studies', *Sociology of Sport Journal*, 28: 4–35.

Smith, J. and Osborn, M. (2009) 'Pain as an Assault on the Self: An Interpretative Phenomenological Analysis', *Psychology & Health*, 22: 517–534.

Sparkes, A. and Smith, B. (2014) *Qualitative Research Methods in Sport, Exercise and Health: From Process to Product*, London: Routledge.

Stebbins, R. (2001) *Exploratory Research in the Social Sciences*, Thousand Oaks, CA: Sage.

Strauss, A. and Corbin, J. (1998), *Basics of Qualitative Research: Grounded Theory, Procedures and Techniques*, Newbury Park, CA: Sage.

Thorpe, H. (2012) 'The Ethnographic Interview in the Sports Field: Toward a Postmodern Sensibility', in K. Young and M. Atkinson (eds) *Qualitative Research on Sport and Physical Culture*, London: Emerald Group.

Thrift, N. (2007) *Non-Representational Theory: Space, Politics, Affect*, London: Routledge.

Tomlinson, A. (1989) '"Whose Side Are They On?" Leisure Studies and Cultural Studies in Britain', *Leisure Studies* 8: 97–106.

Young, K. and Atkinson, M. (2012) *Qualitative Research on Sport and Physical Culture*, London: Emerald Group.

3

THE FUNCTIONALIST
PERSPECTIVE ON SPORT

Tim Delaney

The defending Stanley Cup champion Los Angeles Kings were trailing 3–2 late in the third period of their Game 2, 2013 second-round playoff series against the San Jose Sharks and were without two star players (Jarret Stoll and Anze Kopitar) due to injuries sustained earlier in the game when suddenly the Kings rallied to score two goals in a 22-second time span as the clock wound down. In the post-game interview with the NBC Sports Network, Kings captain Dustin Brown was asked how it was possible for the team to persevere without two integral players. Brown replied, 'It's stick with the system. When top guys go down it's an opportunity for guys to step in.' Brown was promoting an adage common in sports – play within the system and good things will happen. A further implication of Brown's comment and the systems approach to sport (and life in general) is the idea that players are replaceable as long as every player on the team plays within the system. Playing within the system is reflective of the functionalist perspective, especially the system analysis (to be discussed later) promoted by Talcott Parsons.

In this chapter, we will explore the functionalist perspective of sport. We will find that while functionalism and its variations are mostly out of vogue in contemporary social science, the theory, especially the concept of a social system, is actually quite applicable to the study of sport.

The functionalist perspective

Our look at the functionalist perspective begins by highlighting the 'functional' component of the theory, followed by a definition of functionalism and then an examination of its application to the social institution of sport.

The 'functional' component

The basic premise of the functionalist perspective is that people, social institutions, social systems, and nearly every aspect of society is evaluated according to its functionality; that is to say, 'Is it functional?' Consider, for example, these everyday scenarios: we replace consumer items when they stop working or are outdated; we switch banks, phone carriers, and the like when the original vendor's service is poor (dysfunctional); we may end relationships (personal and professional) when they are no longer positive (functional); civil works projects (e.g. road, bridge, and airport construction) are evaluated based on their functionality; and we evaluate government agencies and social institutions on their ability to meet their goals, an indicator of functionality.

Sports teams are also evaluated on their ability to meet their goals. Team owners evaluate everyone in their organization based on their functionality. Sports fans and spectators evaluate players, managers, and even owners on their ability to field a winning team. Many fans prefer a certain style (e.g. defensive-minded, offensive-minded, entertaining performances, 'flair players') from their favourite team. However, even if the team does not play in the preferred style, fans will continue to cheer for their team so long as they keep winning. The implication of the sport cliché – 'It's better to win ugly than to lose pretty' – is that any victory, even a dull one, is preferred to an entertaining defeat. In this manner, the ends justify the means. Thus, any sport performance that yields a victory is functional and preferred over the alternative (a defeat). And so it goes with most scenarios in life. If something is functional, it provides a victory, of sorts, and that is what most people are content with: functional and successful outcomes.

We seem to expect, perhaps even take for granted, that items (e.g. consumer products) and people will behave in a functional manner. Even if we are not conscious of it, most people seem to prefer a certain amount of predictability. We are certainly reminded of this idea any time something dysfunctional, such as a power outage or act of terrorism, occurs in our lives. It is during times of dysfunctional interruptions to the social system that people seem to crave stability the most. We want to get back to 'normal'. These cravings for stability and equilibrium in the social system are among the fundamental aspects of functionalism.

The functionalist perspective was promoted by the earliest sociologists, including Auguste Comte (the person who coined the term 'sociology'), Herbert Spencer, Emile Durkheim, and Max Weber. Of particular relevance here is Comte's (1851) *organic analogy* wherein he compared society to an organism because each consisted of many parts, all functioning for the survival of the whole entity. Spencer (1860) also utilized an 'organic analogy' and promoted the idea that societies, like organisms, have many system needs; if these needs are not met, the system (organism or society) risks dissolution. It is up to the social system then, to find from the environment, the necessary materials to survive. Spencer termed this process *requisite functionalism* (Turner 2003).

Durkheim viewed society as a social system with its parts (social institutions) contributing to the functioning stability of the whole (society). Each part struggles to maintain stability. When all parts reach stability, the system is stable and therefore functional. Durkheim, like Comte, pointed out, however, that societies, as social systems, are not static and are therefore subject to change at any time. All of the parts of a social system are interconnected and each individual part, as well as the social system as a whole, attempts to meet its respective goals in order to function effectively and efficiently. Durkheim's (1973/1914) view on functionalism is summarized in this quote: 'A great number of our mental states, including some of the most important ones, are of social origin. In this case then, it is the whole that, in a large measure, produces the part; consequently, it is impossible to attempt to explain the whole without explaining the part – without explaining, at least, the part as a result of the whole' (1973/1914: 149).

Max Weber had a significant influence on Talcott Parsons's development of structural functionalism (to be discussed later). Weber had emphasized the role of social systems on human interactions. Parsons (1966) agreed, and concluded that an action system had to be incorporated into any grand theory designed to explain human behaviour and any analysis of how society exists. A social action theory applied to sport would examine the social structure of the sport in question, the network of entities found within the sport (e.g. a sport league or sport team), and also the behaviour of participants within the social system. Functionalists would point out, for example, that when players agree to 'play within a system', they do so at the expense of their own individual style of play for the sake of the whole (the team).

Defining functionalism

While early sociological theory was dominated by the thoughts and concepts of individual social thinkers, grand theories or 'schools of thought' have dominated the field since the mid-twentieth century. Comte, Spencer, Durkheim, and Weber influenced the creation of the first major sociological school of thought, initially, and generically, known as *functionalism*. With a focus on social systems and entire societies, it is clear that functionalism is a macrosociological theory. At its core, functionalism has two basic assumptions. The first is the idea of interdependent parts, where all of society's social institutions (e.g. religion, politics, economics, education, family, sport, and leisure) are linked together and function independently but with the greater good of the whole in mind (Delaney 2014). As Levin (1991: 76) explains, 'Functionalism begins with the idea that any stable system (such as the human body) consists of a number of different, but interrelated, parts that operate together to create an overall order.' Any change in one institution inevitably leads to changes in other institutions. In order to function properly, the system seeks equilibrium, or stability. Equilibrium allows for a smoothly running system that can function at peak levels. Thus, when one team player falls to injury, the next player must be ready to step in. Coaches who implement a 'system' will have back-up players with similar styles to starters in the hope that the team can 'function' in a stable fashion (equilibrium) even without all of its starting players. Of course, such an approach only works if the back-up players are as good as the starters, but this is not always the case.

The second fundamental aspect of the functionalist approach involves the shared 'culture' (basic values and norms) across people in a society, system, or sports team. Functionalists propose that a general agreement on basic values and morality issues allows systems to function properly. In an attempt to maintain equilibrium and reduce the risk of dissolution, members of social systems are encouraged to conform to these core values and norms (Delaney 2014). On sports teams, players are expected to follow the rules and norms dictated by management and the coaching staff. When players lose faith in the system, they challenge the prevailing culture. In professional sports it is often coaches or team officials who lose their jobs when their team is losing and dissent takes place. There are occasions, of course, where individual players are singled out as violators of the prevailing culture, and they may find themselves traded, released, or with playing time dramatically reduced.

Functionalism applied to sport

Sport, as a social institution composed of social systems with interrelated parts and a plurality of individual and group actors interacting with one another, lends itself to functionalist analysis (Delaney and Madigan 2009). Interestingly, in the early 1970s, just as functionalism was being overtaken by other sociological theories such as conflict and feminist approaches, Harry Edwards was playing a critical role in creating the field of sport sociology (Edwards 1973). Many of the first sport sociologists (for example, Allardt 1970; Wohl 1970; Lüschen 1970; Gruneau 1975; and Sage 1979) described sport 'in functionalist terms as supportive of the social order' (Figler and Whitaker 1991: 28). Stevenson and Nixon (1972) detailed five general functions by which sport helps the social system maintain equilibrium and operate smoothly and efficiently:

1   Socio-emotional function – Sport provides opportunities for conflict and tension management and release, camaraderie and community bonding, and ritualistic behaviours that people find comforting.

2   Socialization – People learn society's expectations through the socialization process, and cultural values are transmitted from one generation to the next. Sport serves as a significant agent of socialization.

3   Social integration – A commonly cited function of this is its ability to provide opportunities for diverse groups and individuals to interact with one another. Functionalists ignore, however, sport's ability to create 'us versus them' allegiances, which also sow the seeds of conflict between different factions of fans (as well as players).

4   Political functions – The role of politics and sport is both functional and dysfunctional. The singing of the national anthem before sporting events is among the more obvious manifest functions of politics in action within the sports world. Political leaders routinely utilize opportunities to associate themselves with winners and champions in an effort to bask in the glow of victorious others.

5   Social mobility – Functionalists argue that sport provides individuals with opportunities to improve their socio-economic status. Sport does provide for social mobility that is both direct (through professional sport participation) and indirect (such as through college scholarships for young athletes, leading to better job market opportunities).

The functionalist argument is generally endorsed by those who support sport and sport participation. Sport, as a social institution, is reinforced in many other social institutions such as the family, education system, workplace, community associations, and so on. For example, friends and family find that sport provides valuable bonding opportunities. Playing catch with a parent is almost like a rite of passage for most Americans. Playing soccer serves this role for many parents and children across the globe. Functionalists claim that sport fans bond with one another and form a sense of a collective, inclusive community. Volger and Schwartz (1993: 6) argue that sport is so strongly endorsed by most people in American society that it has been given nearly 'sacred status' and that the majority of people feel that sport is 'compatible with American values'. As a result, sport is viewed as having a positive function in society. Among other things, sport:

1   Transmits cultural values.
2   Is educational.
3   Provides a release for physical and psychological pressures.
4   Provides a feeling of group membership.
5   Provides a means of social mobility.
6   Generates a sense of personal competition.

(Volger and Schwartz, 1993: 6)

The idea that sport serves as a means of uniting diverse people, provides opportunities to reaffirm camaraderie and bonds of friendship, can unite people as an inclusive community, and is a valued social institution, is still touted today by a wide variety of sport adherents, including those who use the functionalist perspective. In 2010, Kofi Annan, former United Nations Secretary-General, wrote an opinion piece in *The Guardian* (26 April 2010) wherein he promoted the ability of sport to transform nations, communities, and individuals. Annan was referring specifically to South Africa, the host for the 2010 World Cup, when he wrote, 'At a time when war, violence and ethnic and religious tensions continue to obscure our common humanity, the World Cup has the real potential to break down barriers and challenge stereotypes.' There are countless numbers of people and organizations that also utilize the functionalist perspective on the value of sport as a social institution.

With a general functionalist perspective established, we can shift our attention to structural functionalism, a specific variation of functionalism created in the 1950s by Harvard professor Talcott Parsons.

Structural functionalism

A basic element of the sociological perspective in general involves the notion that humans reflect the social environment in which they were raised. That is to say, we are all products of our upbringing, life experiences and circumstances, and learning opportunities both formal (education) and informal. Social theories also reflect the climate of their times. The structural functionalist approach of Parsons certainly reflects the era in which he lived. The United States, like other Western nations, enjoyed relative societal calm and prosperity during the post–World War II era. 'Structural-functional sociology mirrored these real-life developments. It emphasized societal stability and the match between institutions like the economy, the family, the political system, and the value system' (Garner 2000:312).

Parsons's structural functionalist perspective has a dual focus on the structural forces that shape human behaviour and the means and ways that the social system addresses societal needs. Parsons proposed that social systems strive for stability like functionalism at its core. 'Parsons argued that the overall system and subsystems of which it is composed work together to form a balanced, stable whole and that the system naturally tends toward stability rather than toward disorder' (Levin 1991:77). Parsons argued that societies must strive for stability or equilibrium if they are to stand the test of time. Individual athletes, sport leagues, franchise sport teams, and college and university athletics all seek this same goal – successful longevity. At the societal level, structural functionalists argued that there must be some sense of social order and interdependence among society's various social institutions. The relative socio-political conservative nature of American society during the 1950s provided the perfect backdrop for Parsons to create his theoretical approach and to witness its flourish, before the general civil unrest of the mid- to-late 1960s changed Americans' outlook on society.

Social action theory and sport

Human behaviour within the social system is addressed in Parsons's social action theory. He made clear his commitment to empirical research as the guiding force behind his theory: 'This body of theory, the "theory of social action", is not simply a group of concepts with their logical interrelations. It is a theory of empirical science, the concepts of which refer to something beyond themselves. . . . True scientific theory is not the product of idle "speculation", or spinning out the logical implications of assumptions, but of observation, reasoning and verification, starting with the facts and continually returning to the facts' (1949/1937: v). Parsons acknowledged the subjective nature of human activity and therefore wished to make clear the distinction between the concepts of *action* (an active, creative response) and *behaviour* (a perfunctory response to stimuli). Action options depend upon the actor's knowledge of her situation, which includes knowledge of the probable effects of the available choices (Delaney 2014). Parsons (1949/1937) insisted that in order to qualify as an action theory, the subjective aspect of human activity cannot be ignored.

When applied to sport, the subjective nature of social action addresses the issue of why sport is appealing to some, but not to all people. In sport-crazed nations, in most parts of the world, there are millions of people who passionately follow their favourite athletes and sport teams; and yet, others have little to no interest. But this is true for all social institutions. Religion and spiritual belief, for example, provide comfort and meaning to their adherents, while others view such faith as irrational ways of looking at the world.

Parsons's *social action theory* involves two essential components, the *actor* and the *act*. The actor is viewed as a human individual and the most reducible component of a social system. The purpose, or function, of the actor is to strive and attain a goal (Parsons 1949). The pursuit of a goal generally involves the actor making choices. As Bourricaud (1984) explains, the actor does not make random choices; instead, these choices are governed by logical considerations, which may vary from case to case. Logical considerations are made within the context of operating within a specific social system; therefore, what may be logical in one setting may not be in another. The actor must heed and anticipate possible system constraints (as spelled out in Parsons's four functional imperatives, discussed below) in the pursuit of goals. The actor needs to be aware that the social system, because it seeks stability and equilibrium, requires (or desires) that actors work within a structured framework. Structured behaviour creates a *normative orientation* among actors which results in patterned behaviour. Over time, structured, normative behaviour leads to the establishment of a *system of culture* wherein normative behaviour becomes routine.

The second component of the social action theory is the 'act' which, for Parsons, (1949/1937) has four basic components. First, an act involves actors engaging in some sort of behaviour. Second, actors organize their activity in order to reach an intended goal. Third, the action engaged in by actors is predicated on given situations at the time of the behaviour. Fourth, there exists the possibility of randomness in any given social act that may lead actors to change their course of action as they strive to meet a goal.

Parsons (1949/1937) explained that an act is always a process in time, and that the concept *end* always implies a future reference to a state (or situation) that does not yet exist. Actions consist of the structures and processes by which human beings form meaningful intentions and more or less successfully implement them in concrete situations (Parsons 1966).

Parsons's theory of social action also involves four steps: motivation, means, overcoming conditions that impede progress, and working with the social system. We can apply his social action theory to sport participation with an end goal of becoming a financially successful professional athlete. Step one involves the actor being motivated to work hard enough to become a professional athlete. Furthermore, because it is very difficult to become a financially successful athlete, the motivation should begin at an early age. Finding the means to reach the desired goal will also be challenging as money for equipment and travel, sufficient free time for sport training, and a support system are among the many variables that may hamper attempts to reach this goal. The third step involves dealing with the conditions, or obstacles that may hinder reaching the goal. These could include the freedom from other obstacles (e.g. raising a family), the ability to work with coaches, trainers, and teammates, and the potential lack of skill elite enough to make the actor into a professional athlete. And finally, the actor must be able to work within the social system, such as following administrative rules and procedures, passing drug tests, and meeting eligibility requirements. Working within the social system is often quite challenging and helps to explain why many people may not attain their desired athletic goals.

Functional imperatives (AGIL) and sport

I stated earlier that, for Parsons, the actor must heed and anticipate possible system constraints as spelled out by his four *functional imperatives*. These four imperatives are often referred to simply as AGIL.

The functional imperatives are a set of conditions that Parsons believed must be met if systems of action are to be stable and effective. Functional imperatives may be viewed as potential problems to the social system, and as such each must be addressed to secure the stable operation of the social system. The four imperatives are: Adaptation (A); Goal attainment (G); Integration (I); and Latency (L). The AGIL principle can be applied to the sports world:

1   Adaptation – Social systems must secure sufficient resources from the environment and distribute them throughout the system. In the sports world, sport league, franchise sport teams, and colleges and universities must generate more revenue than they spend. Professional sport teams must find a way to balance very high salaries for a few elite athletes while leaving enough money for the remaining team members. In addition, while social systems seek stability, change does occur; consequently, members of social systems must learn to adapt to changes.
2   Goal Attainment – The social system must clearly establish the goals that individual members are expected to pursue. Sport teaches participants that working hard leads to victory, and therefore success, the ultimate goal of nearly every social system. Sport is consumed with tracking and recording the successes and failures of its participants, particularly through statistics that provide empirical evidence.
3   Integration – This functional imperative involves the regulation and coordination of actors and subsystems within the greater social system in order to keep it functioning properly (Delaney 2014). Sport leagues must regulate and coordinate all of the participating sport franchises; team managers and coaches must do the same with players (actors); and sporting events provide people with the opportunity to bond as a group and reaffirm a sense of community. Sport also provides actors with a sense of social identification and personal identity.
4   Latency – This consists of two related problems: tension management (internal tensions and actors' sense of strain) and pattern maintenance (displaying 'appropriate' behaviour). Proper socialization is supposed to solve these problems. In sport, athletes and fans are taught to accept well-defined authority structures, such as coaches, team management, and security personnel in stadiums. Sport also provides spectators and participants with socially approved venues for venting their aggression and excessive energy. Very few work environments involve workers being booed, or cheered, as they perform their duties, but such is life in the sports world.

This concise review of social action theory and functional imperatives demonstrates their relevancy to the sport world. Our next topic, the social system, represents the cornerstone of structural functionalist thought and it, too, is quite relevant to the study of sport.

The social system

As articulated by Parsons's structural functionalist perspective, the *social system* is a network of inter-related parts, or subsystems, arranged in such a way as to accommodate the interaction of a plurality of individual actors who are oriented to a given situation and striving to achieve goals.

Parsons and the social system

In his book *The Social System*, Parsons (1951) attempted to expand and clarify his social action theory by integrating the role of structure and processes of social systems and their effect on the actor. Parsons believed it was necessary for social systems to have a sound *social structure* that strives for stability in order to function at peak levels in its attempt to coordinate subsystems efficiently.

'Parsons argued that the overall system and subsystems of which it is composed work together to form a balanced, stable whole and that the system naturally tends toward stability rather than toward disorder' (Levin 1991: 77). In addition to subsystems, a social system consists of the interaction of a plurality of individual actors oriented to a situation (e.g. a sport team consisting of players, coaches, and staff). 'Reduced to the simplest possible terms, then, a social system consists in a plurality of individual actors interacting with each other in a situation which has at least a physical or environmental aspect' (Parsons 1951: 5). It is important to recognize that social systems are designed to continue to exist even as individual actors leave. For example, as members of a university sports team graduate, transfer, or drop out, they are replaced by other individuals. The same scenario is played out in nearly every social system, including universities, corporations, offices, and so on. This cycle of individuals coming and going continues year after year and yet the social system (the team, the league) manages to maintain itself (with varying degrees of success).

Although social systems are quite diverse (some are small, some large; some are complex, others relatively simplistic), a number of general assumptions about social systems can be made:

1   Systems are made of order and the interdependence of parts.
2   The system and all the subsystems strive for equilibrium (normal activity, a self-maintaining order).
3   Systems are generally static or move in a progressively deliberate manner.
4   A disruption in the 'normal flow' of one subsystem can cause a disturbance throughout the whole system.
5   Systems have boundaries, which may involve actual physical space or time and distance.

(Delaney 2005:48–49)

Social actors represent a critical element of social systems as they are the ones who actually operate, coordinate, and supervise the processes involved in order to assure maximum functionality.

Sport and the social system

The social system concept is very relevant to sport. In fact, the more common clichés expressed by coaches and players alike involve some variation of 'playing within the system'. (Note: In May 2013, a Google search of 'Sports: Buy into the System' yielded more than 3.7 billion results.) The introductory story in this chapter, regarding the Los Angeles Kings 'sticking with the system', provided one such example.

Coaches routinely attempt to implement a system. This system is generally the one they feel most confident in, although there are times when a coach may change his or her system to fit the particular talent on the team. The coach will introduce the system to players and then proceed to teach the system to the team. In team sports, systems require that all players act together. There are times when if just one person steps outside the system it can become ineffective, dysfunctional. Systems rely on the collectivity, the whole, not individual stars (parts). In sports, like any other situation, a system is all about its people and the willingness of those involved to 'buy in'. Clemson University head football coach Dabo Swinney's system involves his players concentrating on their explicit tasks while downplaying the specific opponent at hand. Swinney's system is more about his own team, how they prepare and execute, and less about the opponent. Swinney said, 'Everybody is a faceless, nameless opponent' (Bradley 2012).

Team players are likely to see more playing time and greater success when they buy into a coach's system. Such was the case for Kosta Koufos of the Denver Nuggets (NBA).

A benchwarmer for much of the 2012–13 season, Koufos began to dominate toward the end of the season. When asked about this success, the 7-foot-tall Koufos explained, 'The biggest thing is just playing within the system. . . . I feed off our guards. They do such a great job, pushing the ball, driving and dishing off to the big guys. That's the biggest thing' (*Denver Post*, 18 April 2013).

A coach's system will work if it is based on sound principles and so long as players work as a team. All systems, in team sports, require teammates to work together as a functioning whole, rather than as a collection of individuals. There are times when players refuse to buy into the system. The results are almost always negative: the team loses, players and coaches may lose their jobs, and fans become discouraged and upset. By the end of the 2011–12 NBA season, it had become clear that the New York Knicks players had lost faith in coach Mike D'Antoni's system. Feeling the heat, D'Antoni resigned before the end of the season. The following day, when asked for his opinion about why his coach resigned, Amar'e Stoudemire claimed, 'Everyone wasn't buying into this system' (*New York Daily News*, 15 March 2012). In a controversial move (Lakers fans and players were unhappy with the decision), D'Antoni was hired by the Los Angeles Lakers early in the following season when their season-opening coach was fired. Once again, players complained about D'Antoni's system and the Lakers had a miserable season (for them), losing in the first round of the 2013 NBA playoffs.

Some coaches utilize a system that emphasizes offense, while other coaches focus on defense. In American team sports it is often stated that offense sells tickets (because offense is deemed more entertaining) but defense wins championships (the ability to stop other teams from scoring is often the key to success). Thus, as discussed earlier in this chapter, fans may prefer an offensive-minded team (because the games are more exciting), but they will cheer for a defensive-minded team so long as they win (winning 'ugly'). Dave Arseneault, a men's basketball coach at Grinnell College (Iowa), provides us with an extreme example of an offensive-minded system. Grinnell's goal is to have a player shoot within 12 seconds of getting the ball; the style demands fresh legs, and the Pioneers typically substitute every 60 seconds or so (Meredith 2012). This system worked out well for Jack Taylor as one night in November 2012 he set the record for points in a game with 138. Taylor hoisted a mind-boggling 108 shots, one every 20 seconds; he missed 56 shots (Meredith 2012). In defensive-minded systems, the offensive players are generally asked not to lose the game, rather than to try and win. Such was the case at North Carolina State when football coach Dave Doeren asked his quarterback (during the 2013 spring training) to manage the game by making sure he did not put the team in positions to hurt the defense. When asked about his quarterback, Coach Doeren stated that he needed him to 'play within the system' and not to 'screw things up' (Adelson 2013).

The social system requires stability and equilibrium among all of its parts; as a result, a disruption in one subsystem may cause a ripple effect of problems in others. For example, if a head coach at a major university abruptly and unexpectedly quits to take a new position with another team during the height of the time period when incoming recruits (e.g. college transfers and high school seniors) are expected to sign their 'letter of intent' (a written commitment to attend and play for a particular college the following season), chaos may ensue. Such was the case at Syracuse University in January 2013 when head football coach Doug Marrone quit his post in order to coach the NFL team Buffalo Bills, taking with him many of his assistants. Some of the university's proposed student-athlete recruits, who had given verbal commitments to play at Syracuse, changed their minds citing the uncertainty of the football program. (Realizing he was about to lose many more recruits, the athletic director, Daryl Gross, moved quickly and hired a coach who would continue to implement Syracuse's high-powered, offensive-minded playing system, known as a spread/West Coast hybrid, a wide-open, pass-first philosophy of football, that had just set a school record for offensive scoring the previous season). Upon introducing the new head football coach, Scott Shafer, Gross informed the media (and de facto potential recruits), 'We have put our focus on the system we're running and not so much the guy running it. We will not have a new guy with a new system. Scott is committed to the current system. It will continue to be fast, up-tempo, spreading it out at times, going West Coast at times and running the ball when that is working' (*The Post-Standard*, 10 January 2013). At Syracuse, the system remained and actors were deemed replaceable. Time will determine whether that strategy worked or not.

These short case-studies represent a mere sampling of the nearly endless examples of the systems approach to sport. If any one aspect of the functionalist perspective stands above the rest to demonstrate the relevancy of this theoretical approach, it is the social system component.

Criticisms of the functionalist perspective

The functionalist perspective has been attacked by proponents of nearly every other theoretical perspective. Among the criticisms of this theory are its conservative nature and perceived inability to explain social change. The functionalist focus on how social systems attempt to maintain equilibrium leads its proponents to ignore conflict. People do not agree on all the values and beliefs of the dominant society and as a result, functionalism is criticized for failing to acknowledge socio-economic inequalities that lead to different perspectives of the social system (Delaney 2014). Because of its conservative nature and focus on the status quo, functionalism is also criticized for ignoring such social patterns as 'discrimination, exploitation, and political dominations by elites or ruling classes who have a vested interest in maintaining their power and prestige' (Nixon and Frey 1996: 10). The functionalist approach also ignores the reality that sport, like all social institutions, is a social construct amenable to change. Despite these criticisms, the staying power of functionalism as a prominent sociological theory cannot be denied and its relevancy to sport is equally intact.

Although grand theories are not currently in vogue, functionalism is an approach that helps to explain large social institutions like sport. As a proponent of the dominant culture of a given society, functionalism is a relevant theory to the study of sport because this institution generally reflects the key values and norms of a given society. That sport's governing bodies are generally intolerant of individualist behaviours – those athletes who go against the norms of the social institution – is a testament to the status quo emphasis of functionalism. Perhaps the most compelling aspect of the functionalist perspective is its explanation of the social system and the manner in which players and coaches work within a social system.

References

Adelson, A. (2013) 'NC State Coach Dave Doeren Talks QB Race', *ESPN.com*, 19 March. Available at: http://espn.go.com/blog/acc/post/_/id/53415/nc-state-coach-dave-doeren-talks-qb-race.

Allardt, E. (1970) 'Basic Approaches in Comparative Sociological Research and the Study of Sport', in G. Lüschen (ed.) *Cross-Cultural Analysis of Sport and Games*, Champaign, IL: Stipes.

Bourricaud, F. (1984) *The Sociology of Talcott Parsons*, Chicago: The University of Chicago Press.

Bradley, S. (2012) 'Tigers Focused on "Task at Hand" for Furman', *My Orange Update*, September 2012. Available at: http://www.myorangeupdate.com/2012/09/tigers-focused-on-task-at-hand-for-furman-game/.

Comte, A. (1851) *System of Positive Polity, Vol. 1*. New York: Burt Franklin.

Delaney, T. (2005) *Contemporary Social Theory: Investigation and Application*, Upper Saddle River, NJ: Prentice Hall/Pearson.

—— (2014) *Classical and Contemporary Social Theory: Investigation and Application*, Upper Saddle River, NJ: Prentice Hall/Pearson.

Delaney, T. and Madigan, T. (2009) *The Sociology of Sports: An Introduction*, Jefferson, NC: McFarland.

Durkheim, E. (1973/1914) 'The Dualism of Human Nature and Its Social Condition', in K. Bellah (ed.) *Émile Durkheim: On Morality and Society*, Chicago: University of Chicago Press.

Edwards, H. (1973) *The Sociology of Sport*, Homewood, IL: Dorsey.

Figler, S. and Whitaker, G. (1991) *Sport and Play in American Life*, 2nd edition, Dubuque, IA: Wm. C. Brown.

Garner, R. (ed.) (2000) *Social Theory*, Orchard Park, NY: Broadview.

Gruneau, R.S. (1975) 'Sport, Social Differentiation, and Social Inequality', in D. Ball and J. Loy (eds) *Sport and Social Order*, Reading, MA: Addison-Wesley.

Levin, W.C. (1991) *Sociological Ideas*, 3rd edition, Belmont, CA: Wadsworth.

Lüschen, G. (1970) 'Cooperation, Association and Contest', *Journal of Conflict Resolution*, 14(1): 21–34.

Meredith, L. (2012) 'Taylor Kept on Shooting', *The Post-Standard*, November 22: B-1, B-5.

Nixon, H.L. II and Frey, J.H. (1996) *A Sociology of Sport*, Belmont, CA: Wadsworth.

Parsons, T. (1949) *Essays in Sociological Theory: Pure and Applied*, Glencoe, IL: The Free Press.

—— (1949/1937) *The Structure of Social Action*, Glencoe, IL: The Free Press.

—— (1951) *The Social System*, Glencoe, IL: Free Press.

—— (1966) *Societies*, Englewood Cliffs, NJ: Prentice Hall.

Sage, G.H. (1979) 'Sport and the Social Sciences', *The Annals of the American Academy of Political and Social Sciences*, 445: 1–14.

Spencer, H. (1860) *The Social Organism*, London: Greenwood.

Stevenson, C.L. and Nixon, J.E. (1972) 'A Conceptual Scheme of the Social Functions of Sports', *Sportwissenschaft*, 2: 119–132.

Turner, J. (2003) *The Structure of Sociological Theory*, 7th edition, Belmont, CA: Wadsworth.

Volger, C. and Schwartz, S. (1993) *The Sociology of Sport: An Introduction*. Englewood Cliffs, NJ: Prentice Hall.

Wohl, A. (1970) 'Competitive Sport and Its Social Function'. *International Review of Sport*, 5: 117–125.

4

INTERPRETIVE APPROACHES IN THE SOCIOLOGY OF SPORT

Peter Donnelly and Michael Atkinson

Writing at the end of the twentieth century, Donnelly noted that 'interpretive sociology has recently come to be what many consider the predominant approach in the sociology of sport' (2000: 85). The last 15 years have only served to confirm that impression. In this chapter, we locate interpretive sociology within the larger field of sociology, and then focus on the two main expressions of interpretive sociology in the sociology of sport: hermeneutic analyses and ethnographic analyses. An examination of the range of work and insights that resulted from these overlapping ways of studying sport is followed by a note of caution regarding the forms of analysis, and some suggestions regarding future research and analysis.

Interpretive sociology

The processes of careful observation and systematic interpretation are, of course, fundamental to all of the sciences – what are data?; what do the data mean?; how are we to understand them?; how do they relate to our current knowledge, and our theoretical interpretations of that knowledge? The term *interpretive* takes on a more specific meaning in sociology proper – it refers to a range of 'sociologies' broadly concerned with the micro-processes of human interaction and social interchange, and the production, reproduction, and transformation of the meanings people construct about what they do and what others do within situated cultural contexts, settings, places, and fields. In the 1960s and 1970s, this approach to sociology was referred to as the 'action' approach to interpretive analysis, in contrast to the broader (macro-structural) 'systems' approach prominent in the era (Dawe 1970).[1]

The emergent 'action' sociologies, including 'Chicago School sociology', American pragmatism redefined by Mead's social psychology/behaviouralism, Blumer's symbolic interactionism, and Goffman's dramaturgy, generally promoted an anthropological (ethnographic) approach to data collection, and 'close' hermeneutic readings of gathered data. Observation, participant observation, and interviews were employed as mainstay methods, and data were interpreted often in a rather apolitical/uncritical manner via what would later become accepted as 'grounded' analytics. The research generated by action sociologies forms some of the most fundamental conceptual building blocks of contemporary social theory. For example, Cooley's (1902) concept of the *looking glass self*, identifying the way people come to understand themselves based on their understanding of how others perceive them, subsequently informed Mead's *role theory*; the latter became the basis of Goffman's (1959) research on *role playing, impression management*, and *the presentation of self*, and is still evident in the more recent shift to performance studies and theories of performativity (e.g. Butler 1990). Mead, Blumer, and Goffman's emphasis on the reflexive aspects of (embodied) social performance is also starkly evident in the social analysis of a wide range of modernist and postmodern theorists including Norbert Elias, Simone de Beauvoir, Pierre Bourdieu, and Michel Foucault.

In another example, Thomas's (1928: 571–72) theorem, 'If men define situations as real, they are real in their consequences,' not only subsequently enabled our understanding of the *self-fulfilling prophecy*, but also became the basis of *labeling theory* and one of the most fundamental concepts in modern sociology, the *social construction of reality* (Berger and Luckmann 1966), to which all of contemporary sociology owes a tremendous debt.

During the 1960s and 1970s sociologists on both sides of the Atlantic began to problematize the ostensible conceptual and empirical division between 'the two sociologies': 'Do the two approaches of social systems [now often referred to as social *structure*] and social action [now often referred to as *agency*] theory simply correspond to our own ambivalent experience of society as something that constrains us and yet also something that we ourselves construct?' (Thompson and Tunstall 1975: 476). Peter Berger anticipated bringing 'the two sociologies' together with reference to 'men producing society [*agency*] and in turn being produced by it [*structure*]' (Berger and Pullberg 1966: 57); and this recognition was developed when Giddens (1976: 160), echoing Marx, argued: 'The realm of human agency is bounded. Individuals produce society, but they do so as historically located actors, and not under conditions of their own choosing.'[2]

The *critical turn* in North American and British sociology saw an increasing emphasis on power and the constraining features of social structure, even in the interpretive approaches to sociology. For example, the Centre for Contemporary Cultural Studies (CCCS) at the University of Birmingham (UK) began to publish a series of ethnographic studies that combined more traditional action theory approaches to research with critical interpretations drawn from more critical approaches to sociology and social structure. Work inspired by the 'Birmingham School' still wrestled with debates between the apparent dualism of structuralism and cultural agency, but nevertheless provided foundational sociological thinking about how interpretive micrological studies of class, youth, race, and gender could inform broader analyses of social history and hierarchies of power in a society.

This convergence of 'the two sociologies' began to be evident in the sociology of sport during the late 1970s. Donnelly (1986: 570) noted how sport subcultures research up to that time 'show[ed] how sports and other leisure practices [we]re socially constructed and defined activities, meaningful only to the extent that meaning [wa]s attached to them by the participants'. The 'critical turn' was signalled in Gruneau's review of Pearson's (1979) book on surfing subcultures; he called for consideration of how 'subcultures, with their various "establishment" and "countercultural" emphases, have been constitutively inserted into the struggles, the forms of compliance and opposition, social reproduction and transformation, associated with changing patterns of social development' (1981: 10). The *cultural turn* in sociology followed shortly after, and began to converge with the *critical turn*. A number of sociologists started to examine sport as a fundamental element of (popular) culture, and *critical cultural studies* took various forms in the sociology of sport. In the US, the sociology of sport tended to follow mainstream social sciences and humanities by focusing on 'textual' (hermeneutic) approaches to critical cultural studies, while in Canada and the UK ethnographic approaches gained ground. Much of the interpretive sociology in the sociology of sport, since the late 1970s, has incorporated a more political structural perspective – generally recognized as critical cultural studies.[3]

An interpretive sociology of sport

Trueman (2012: 31) describes an interpretive sociology of sport that recognizes an articulation between 'the two sociologies': 'big issues, such as equality, power and race, [are approached] through fine-grained study of the small and unusual niches of our society.' Although Trueman refers primarily to ethnographic studies of subcultures, the same point may be made with reference to hermeneutic studies – aspects of sport and recreation are studied and interpreted with regard to the insights they may bring to larger social problems such as social inequality.

Within interpretive sociology, this chapter focuses on these two approaches because they have been most evident in the sociology of sport.[4] Hermeneutic and ethnographic analyses are related, and the research often overlaps; but they are, for the most part, methodologically distinct approaches.

1   *Hermeneutic analyses* involve the interpretation of 'texts'. In hermeneutics' original manifestation and usage, (i.e. in biblical studies), texts were written communications. However, the concept of text has now broadened considerably to include any message systems or signification processes – material, visual, embodied, symbolic, linguistic – developed by humans to communicate meanings to each other. Analyses range from interpretations of television broadcasts to interpretations of clothing styles to decodings of physical gestures and performances. Such analyses have been variously referred to as *content* or *textual* or *discourse* analyses where the texts or discourses are *decoded* or *deconstructed* or *unpacked*. In each case, the text is closely analyzed for the 'intertextuated' social and cultural meaning(s) it may carry and convey.

2   In traditional *ethnographic analysis* (largely imported into sociology from cultural anthropology), a researcher attempts to place him/herself as closely as possible to those being studied in order to achieve the most comprehensive sense of the social formation and cultural practices under study; often, but not always, becoming a full participant in the group under study. Donnelly (1986: 568) argues that 'in subcultural research, all available sources of data should be employed in order to gain as complete an account as possible and the deepest level of understanding of the subculture.' These sources include data from participant observation, observation, and interviews, as well as detailed examination of what the (sub) culture members write about themselves and each other, what videos they might make for each other and for the general public, and any other available materials such as popular and novelistic accounts of the (sub)culture. And none of these make complete sense without a keen knowledge of the historical, geographical, and social structural context in which the (sub)culture exists.[5]

Hermeneutic and ethnographic approaches are quite distinct in terms of the challenges they pose to researchers. The contemporary (pre)dominance of hermeneutic research in the sociology of sport (namely, media studies and the analysis of popular sport discourses) is likely a consequence of the widespread availability of readily accessible data, the relative ease of analysis, and other academic trends and pressures (see Atkinson 2011). Ethnographic research is, by contrast, more time consuming and personally taxing, plagued by methodological hurdles and frustrations; data collection may be expensive, and carrying out such research often involves the need to seek approval from institutional human-research ethics committees. The two approaches converge in their concern with the production and interpretation of meaning. They come together quite specifically in production and audience ethnographies (noted subsequently), and in fieldwork analyses of social formations, such as subcultures, when interviews and overheard data may be subject to discourse analysis, and where the cultural products of subcultures (e.g. videos, written works) are subject to textual analyses. The following provides examples of some of the ways that these forms of analysis have been employed in interpretive approaches to the sociology of sport.

Hermeneutic analyses

In a recent survey of 757 articles published over 10 years in three journals (*International Review for the Sociology of Sport, Journal of Sport and Social Issues*, and the *Sociology of Sport Journal*) the most prevalent category was 'sports media' (161 articles, 21.3%) (Messner and Musto 2014).[6] A significant proportion focus on gender (mostly women/femininity), often combining quantitative analyses of the amount of media space and/or time devoted to women's (and men's) sport with interpretive analyses of the ways in which women's sports and women athletes are represented in comparison to men. Although these studies usually involve single case studies of one sport or event, and one media source, their cumulative effect shed important light on the representation of women athletes and the ways that women's sports are marginalized and trivialized in sports media. Concepts such as *gender marking* and *compulsory heterosexuality* have emerged from this work, as has recognition that sports coverage often infantilizes women, works to emphasize 'appropriate' femininity, and generates ambivalence in sports coverage in which 'positive images and descriptions of women athletes are juxtaposed with descriptions and images that undermine and trivialize women's efforts and successes' (Wensing and Bruce 2003: 388).

More systematic studies, providing regular analyses of gender representation in specific media sources and events, are rare. The series of studies carried out by Michael Messner and his colleagues focused on both sports news coverage (e.g. Cooky, Messner & Hextrum, 2013; Messner and Cooky 2010) and on televised events such as the US Open tennis tournament and the men's and women's interuniversity basketball championship tournaments in the US (NCAA Final Four) (Duncan *et al.* 2000). Their regular analyses, approximately every five years between 1989 and 2009, enable the researchers to see changes in the quantity of media coverage and the quality of representation of women athletes and women's sports. While their research shows the type of marginalization and trivialization identified above, they also note more subtle differences between the coverage of men's and women's sports in terms of, for example, attributions of success and failure – with women's errors and failures far more likely than men's to be attributed to 'nerves' (see also Cluer *et al.* 2001).

Hermeneutic analyses of gender also include studies of media representation of masculinity and violence (e.g. Messner *et al.* 2000; Trujillo 1995; White and Gillett 1994), adding to the idea that it is not only in the practice of sport but also in its mediation that sport is 'a school for masculinity'. There are few studies of media representations of other aspects of identity such as sexuality and race/ethnicity, and even fewer studies of media representations of social class. Hermeneutic analyses extend beyond mediation to include, for example, analyses of sport policy documents (e.g. Green and Houlihan 2005), correctional service policies regarding sport and recreation in prisons (e.g. Norman 2013), university sports media guides (Kane and Buysse 2005), and other 'texts' that may provide insights into the meaning and practice of sports.

Some of the more striking hermeneutic research in the sociology of sport is grounded in the recognition that media construct *frames* (Goffman 1974), employing stereotypes to assign events to categories and failing to capture the complexity of individuals and events. Such frames may be seen as a form of labeling, and the stereotypes resulting from this power to define represent an assertion of the power of some population segments over others. For example, Birrell and Cole (1990) explored media coverage of Renée Richards (formerly Richard Raskind, a 'constructed female transsexual') playing on the women's tennis tour; and the way that sport organizations and media 'problematize' gender identification is still being examined in, for example, the case of Caster Semenya (e.g. Cooky, Dycus & Dworkin, 2013). Douglas (2005) and Schultz (2005) provided critical analyses of media coverage (and gender/racial stereotyping) of tennis champions Venus and Serena Williams. Others have identified the ways that sports media celebrate violence and stereotypical forms of masculinity – Theberge (1989) focused on a major incidence of violence at the World Junior Hockey Championships; and a study of hockey commentator Don Cherry showed how ethnic intolerance was added to the mix of masculine stereotypes and the celebration of violence (Gillett *et al.* 1996). Finally, hermeneutic analyses have been used in large-scale cross-cultural studies incorporating the complexities of race, gender, and international relations (e.g. Kim 2012).

A note of caution: Decoding and critically identifying specific meanings from 'texts' should be seen as only part of the analytical process. Stuart Hall (1973) pointed out that it was necessary also to consider the encoding process – are the 'messages' encoded in texts deliberate, incidental, or unintentional, or part of some standardized cultural or production 'code'? Hesling (1986) reviewed the development of sportscasting codes, and production ethnographies, although rare in the sociology of sport literature, have provided important insights into the encoding process (e.g. Gruneau 1989; MacNeill 1996; Silk 2001). Similarly, it is important to recognize that the critical 'reading' of a 'text' by a researcher is not necessarily the only 'reading' possible – it is more likely to be one among several. In order to capture the potentially partial nature of researcher interpretations, a (very) few researchers have carried out audience ethnographies of television spectators in sports bars and living rooms (e.g. Duncan and Brummett 1993; Eastman and Riggs 1994). Their findings suggest that, while researchers may focus, for example in broadcasts of male contact sports, on emphasized masculinity, martial metaphors, and celebrations of violence, some audiences (e.g. some women, some gay men) may enjoy an ironic 'reading' of a commentator's bombast or engage in a pleasurable objectification of male athletes' bodies.

Ethnographic analyses

This review of ethnographic analyses in the sociology of sport covers two of the main and overlapping types of research – (1) sport subcultures and (2) sport careers and socialization.

Subcultures: Subcultures, defined as 'any system[s] of beliefs, values and norms . . . shared and actively participated in by an appreciable minority of people' (Jary and Jary 1995, p. 665), have generated a rich body of research in both mainstream sociology and in the sociology of sport. However, postmodern shifts in society that have resulted in more fragmented social formations, and the emergence of new types of communities (e.g. on-line communities), have led some scholars to proclaim the 'death' of subcultures. Others argue that, while such social changes have to be taken into account, subcultural research still has merit. For example, Young and Atkinson (2008: 38) argue that 'these sub-communities, however conceptualized, can tell us much about the world and worlds we inhabit, and how group members forge their own behaviours and meanings from their own lived experiences.'

Just as mainstream sociology has tended to focus on 'deviant' and criminal subcultures, and some interesting occupational subcultures, sociology of sport has also tended to focus on the fringes, especially with regard to alternative sport subcultures where participants are more actively involved in the production, reproduction, and transformation of their sport than in the more institutionalized mainstream sport subcultures. These sport subcultures were frequently characterized by their resistance to hegemonies of class, race, and gender, as well as to authoritative voices attempting to determine and define what sport *is* or *should be*. Thus, single researchers or clusters of researchers have produced a rich body of subcultural knowledge about sports such as surfing (e.g. Kent Pearson), climbing (e.g. Peter Donnelly), skateboarding (e.g. Becky Beal), windsurfing (e.g. Belinda Wheaton), snowboarding (e.g. Holly Thorpe), parkour (e.g. Michael Atkinson), and women's roller derby (e.g. Michele Donnelly).

However, as Young and Atkinson (2008: 38–39) note, 'What often begins as [subcultural] resistance and opposition ultimately ends up, if indeed it did not begin as such, co-opted and incorporated into the very forms and values of dominance that were meant to be subculturally resisted in the first place.' Several of the researchers noted above have also documented the processes of commercialization, incorporation, and institutionalization as, for example, sports such as snowboarding and BMX biking have become Olympic sports. Other sports, such as Ultimate Frisbee and women's roller derby, are in the midst of struggles about their future – torn between those who wish to maintain subcultural independence and those who see benefits in incorporation with larger sport institutions.

There are also rich subcultural studies of sports that are less overtly resistant. These include US high school football (e.g. Doug Foley), rugby (e.g. Kevin Young), women's ice hockey (e.g. Nancy Theberge), professional wrestling (e.g. Larry DeGaris), triathlon and fell running (e.g. Michael Atkinson), boxing (e.g. John Sugden; Löic Wacquant), and women's professional golf (e.g. Nancy Theberge; Todd Crosset). Researchers have also focussed on sport subcultures in ethnocultural communities, such as Nakamura's (2008) study of Chinese nine-man volleyball and Joseph's (2010) study of Caribbean cricket; and on fan and hooligan subcultures (e.g. Richard Giulianotti). All of these studies have generated important insights about the meanings attached to the sports, and insights into subcultural relations with the larger society in terms of 'the struggles, the forms of compliance and opposition, social reproduction and transformation, associated with changing patterns of social development' (Gruneau 1981: 10). It is unlikely that such insights could have been achieved with the use of less painstaking methods.

Careers and socialization: Overlapping with ethnographic research on subcultures, and often part of those studies, is research on socialization and career patterns. Coakley (2009: 92) describes socialization, from an interpretive perspective, as an interactive process through which we actively connect with others, synthesize information, and *make decisions* that influence our own lives and the social worlds in which we participate. From this perspective, it is clear that ethnographic research on sport subcultures has much to offer in terms of the processes involved in becoming a member of a sport subculture, and the ways that one progresses as a member of that subculture (e.g. Donnelly and Young 1988).

The concept of a social 'career' is now less often used in ethnographic studies of sport. It was used to describe the patterns of progress during athletes' competitive lives, and the contingencies encountered during those careers. The sociology of sport has produced some rich comparative studies of careers – for example, gymnasts and professional wrestlers (Birrell and Turowetz 1979) and hockey players and Hollywood musicians (Faulkner 1975), and some important insights into the careers (Ingham 1975) and career changes of high-performance athletes (Stevenson 1990). However, interest in career patterns in sport has now become more common in journalistic and biographical work than in ethnographic research.

A note of caution: No form of data collection or its system of representation will capture the full complexity, diversity, or spirit of any subject under investigation. Further, more than 40 years of interpretivist research on sport testifies to the idea that there may be very few, if any, universal, common, and widely held truths about lived experience. Critics have argued that interpretivist accounts/representations of the empirical world must never be read as definitive or neutral (thus authoritative and objectively 'real') renderings of social reality. Giddens's (1984) compelling discussion of the 'double-hermeneutic' establishes an important issue in data representation:

researchers strive to compare and interpret other people's interpretations of the world – to make sense of how people make sense of the world. Any experience under empirical scrutiny and eventually represented in a textual document is multiply layered by a range of subjective interpretations – giving even more credibility to the interpretivist ontological assumption that no experience can be perfectly (*realistically*) represented. All representations are thus narrated approximations of 'some' truth.

If representation is always an imperfect process, then the generalizability and therefore utility of interpretivist findings, discussions, and conclusions is always in question. While quantitative researchers rally behind statistical significance values and large samples sizes to buttress claims of generalizability – and qualitatively oriented colleagues champion generic social concepts in their research in the same pursuit – the inevitably subjective aspects of representational processes raise doubts about any perfectly generalizable conclusions. Thus Rojek (1986), drawing on Norbert Elias, encourages an ideology of methodological pragmatism by suggesting we should strive to produce the most 'reality congruent' theories and analysis possible without fetishizing the need for universal truths.

Future research and analysis

The term 'interpretivism' is rarely used in contemporary sociology of sport. This under-usage is partially due to the fact that there are many debates about the role, goal, and value of 'old school' interpretivism in sport, physical activity, and health research. The primary problem for contemporary sociologists of sport with the traditional notion of interpretivism is that the paradigm is (seemingly) so broad that its lineage, key figures, or even its essence are difficult to comprehend, narrow, or succinctly describe. For example, theory and methods textbooks regularly fail to cite the difference between interpretivism in general and the theories or paradigms influenced by interpretivism, including symbolic interactionism, dramaturgy, critical race theories, queer theories, feminist theories, (new) media theories, post-colonial theories, post-structuralist theories, (neo)Marxist and other political economic theories, existentialist theories, actor-network theories, critical pedagogy theories, identity crisis theories, theories of intersectionality, globalization and cultural fragmentation theories, risk theories, new social movement theories, environmentalist theories, victimologies, postmodern theories, figurational theory, theories of consumption, and a range of theories loosely described as cultural studies.

Questions concerning the merit and generalizability of interpretivist research in relation to the essentially subjective nature of life are at the forefront of other criticisms about intepretivism in the sociology of sport – particularly in an era of 'evidence-based' or policy-driven research. If interpretivist-inspired research attends to subjectivity and the ways in which people commonly define 'things' as real (the process of achieving *inter-subjectivity*), then ultimately one set of findings in an interpretivist study may only relate to that group alone. If we interviewed 25 children in a PE class about their social constructions of 'fatness', for example, there is no guarantee we will produce similar subjective understandings of fatness in other classes. So what is the use of the case-specific data? Even more problematic is that if we went back and re-interviewed the children a month, six months, or a year later, their understandings of the reality of fatness may have changed considerably. The hyper-subjectivism and emphasis on the locally constructed nature of reality in mainstream interpretivist research may discourage researchers committed to the discovery of objective, standard and generalizable patterns across time and space, policy-driven researchers in the sociology of sport, and those critical scholars in the sociology of sport more inclined toward research as a lever of political change. Interpretivists may fuel these criticisms further by failing to articulate the importance of understanding the relevance of multiple subjectivities in the practice of everyday life, or by ignoring the role of translating important ideas gleaned from research efforts into public practice.

'Old school' interpretivism is challenged further by contemporary qualitative researchers in the sociology of sport: in particular, how the act of using reduced and selected stories from research participants' lives to 'improve' sociological theory is somewhat disingenuous. For critics, any academic attempt to portray a culture and its members academically (in a partial, biased, outsider, and ungeneralizable story about that culture) may be viewed as an act of academic deception or thievery (Van Maanen 2001). Voices, critics tell us, are often 'stolen' from the field without compensation, assembled to suit the researcher's theoretical purposes, and disfigured into inaccessible, verbose academic-speak. From this perspective, interpretivist research is, at its worst, an act of cultural colonialism that privileges the powerful researcher as the author(ity) of other people's cultures (Reinharz 1992). This methodological critique is connected to pervasive theorizing in sociology of sport studies about hyper-individualism, ideological implosion in the West, identity-rights movements and associated politics, and the degree to which scholars in the field have called into question (and rightfully so) how minority groups have been systematically excluded from the historical creation of knowledge about sport and society. From these perspectives, methodological preference through intepretivist methodologies must be given to allowing people to speak for themselves through innovative textual means; to eschewing the notion of universal or generic cultural truths; to abdicating one's proclaimed role as a decoder of culture; to performing hyper-reflexivity about the nature of one's 'position' (identities) in the research process; and, to abandoning attempts to represent living, moving cultural processes through standard textual means. These notions have been mimetically distributed throughout the sociology of sport and physical culture for nearly two decades now, without any sustained (or concatenated) critical response from proponents of traditional modes of interpretivism (Atkinson 2011).

Contemporary 'neo-interpretivist' researchers have diversified the form, content, and purpose of qualitative means of knowing in the wake of the relative 'death' of realism. For example, auto-ethnographic (Hockey 2006), sensory (Pink 2009; Thrift 2007), performative (Alexander 2005), and interpretative phenomenological (Smith and Obsborn 2009) methods have grown in popularity within the study of sport, physical activity, and health. Each of these methodologies has altered the form, content, and system of representation in the process of interpreting and communicating the realities of others in the world. Each of these methods has arguably 'opened up' the research act, allowing for different forms of knowing via interpretivist-inspired methods.

In closing, we contend that although the form and content of interpretivism has changed quite significantly in the past four decades of research, the spirit or heart of the paradigm endures in the sociology of sport. Interpretivism's attempt to analytically account for and theorize the nature of everyday life, micrological interaction, and the process of human meaning production in the broader contexts of the cultural and structural environments in which these unfold, remains the mandate of an interpretive sociology (of sport and physical culture). Sensibilities about the theoretical underpinnings, the methodological format, or means of representing 'interpretivist' sociologies shift almost generationally, but the overall approach continues to emphasize the importance of grounding sociological understandings of human realities and the experience of social life from the perspectives of actors entrenched in the milieu of cultural existence.

Notes

1 The 'social action – social systems' binary is generally related to other binaries in the field: human agency vs. social structure; micro- vs. macro-sociology, and qualitative vs. quantitative research methods respectively.

2 Marx declared: 'Men make their own history [*agency*], but they do not make it just as they please; they do not make it under circumstances chosen by themselves, but under circumstances directly encountered, given and transmitted from the past [*structure*]'. (1991/1852: 5).

3 Much of this work is recognizable as quality critical sociology. Some national, regional, and disciplinary variations involving popular cultural aspects of cultural studies involve complex theoretical approaches to relatively trivial matters; they produce a form of cultural studies characterized by a colleague of ours as 'wacky theories about funky stuff'.

4 Other approaches include dramaturgy, ethnomethodology, and phenomenology.

5 In two landmark ethnographic studies, Paul Willis (1978, 1981) employed the following methods: participant observation, observation, just being around, group discussions, recorded discussions, informal interviews, and existing survey data (see also Willis 2000).

6 The second largest category was 'professional sports' with only 81 articles (10.7%).

References

Alexander, B. (2005) 'Performance Ethnography: The Re-Enacting and Inciting of Culture', in N. Denzin and Y. Lincoln (eds) *Handbook of Qualitative Inquiry*, Thousand Oaks, CA: Sage.

Atkinson, M. (2011) *Key Concepts in Sport and Exercise Research Methods*, London: Sage.

Berger, P. and S. Pullberg (1966) 'Reification and the Sociological Critique of Consciousness', *New Left Review*, I/35, January–February: 56–71.

Berger, P. and T. Luckmann (1966) *The Social Construction of Reality: A Treatise in the Sociology of Knowledge*, New York: Anchor Books.

Birrell, S. and C.L. Cole (1990) 'Double Fault: Renee Richards and the Construction and Naturalization of Difference', *Sociology of Sport Journal*, 7: 1–21.

Birrell, S. and A. Turowetz (1979) 'Character Work-Up and Display: Collegiate Gymnasts and Professional Wrestlers', *Urban Life*, 8: 219–246.

Butler, J. (1990) *Gender Trouble: Feminism and the Subversion of Identity*, New York: Routledge.

Cluer, S., P. Donnelly, M. MacNeill and G. Knight (2001) 'Lessons Learned: A Case Study of CBC Television Coverage of Men's and Women's Diving at the Sydney Olympics', paper presented at the North American Society for the Sociology of Sport conference, San Antonio, TX, 31 October–3 November.

Coakley, J. (2009) *Sports in Society: Issues and Controversies* (10th ed.), Boston: McGraw-Hill.

Cooky, C., R. Dycus and S. Dworkin (2013) '"What Makes a Woman a Woman?" vs. "Our First Lady of Sport": A Comparative Analysis of Caster Semenya in U.S. and South African News Media', *Journal of Sport and Social Issues*, 37: 31–56.

Cooky, C., M. Messner and R. Hextrum (2013) 'Women Play Sports, but Not on TV: A Longitudinal Study of Televised News Media', *Communication and Sport*, 1: 203–230.

Cooley, C.H. (1902) *Human Nature and the Social Order*, New York: Scribner.

Dawe, A. (1970) 'The Two Sociologies', *British Journal of Sociology*, 21: 207–218.

Donnelly, P. (1986) 'Sport Subcultures', in R. Terjung (ed.) *Exercise and Sport Sciences Reviews*, Volume 13, New York: Macmillan.

Donnelly, P. (2000) 'Interpretive Approaches to the Sociology of Sport', in J. Coakley and E. Dunning (eds) *Handbook of Sports Studies*, London: Sage.

Donnelly, P. and K. Young (1988) 'The Construction and Confirmation of Identity in Sport Subcultures', *Sociology of Sport Journal*, 5: 223–240.

Douglas, D.D. (2005) 'Venus, Serena and the Women's Tennis Association: When and Where Race Enters', *Sociology of Sport Journal*, 22: 256–282.

Duncan, M.C. and B. Brummett (1993) 'Liberal and Radical Sources of Female Empowerment in Sports Media', *Sociology of Sport Journal*, 10: 57–72.

Duncan, M.C., M. Messner and C. Cooky (2000) *Gender in Televised Sports: 1989, 1993, and 1999*, Los Angeles: Amateur Athletic Foundation of Los Angeles.

Eastman, S.T. and K. Riggs (1994) 'Televised Sports and Ritual: Fan Experiences', *Sociology of Sport Journal*, 11: 249–274.

Faulkner, R. (1975) 'Coming of Age in Organizations: A Comparative Study of the Career Contingencies of Musicians and Hockey Players', in D. Ball and J. Loy (eds) *Sport and Social Order*, Reading, MA: Addison-Wesley.

Giddens, A. (1976) *New Rules of Sociological Method: A Positive Critique of Interpretative Sociologies*, London: Hutchinson.

Giddens, A. (1984) *The Constitution of Society: Outline of the Theory of Structuration*, Cambridge: Cambridge University Press.

Gillett, J., P. White and K. Young (1996) 'The Prime Minister of Saturday Night: Don Cherry, the CBC and the Cultural Production of Intolerance', in H. Holmes and D. Taras (eds) *Seeing Ourselves: Media, Power and Policy in Canada*, Toronto: Harcourt, Brace and Jovanovich.

Goffman, E. (1959) *The Presentation of Self in Everyday Life*, New York: Doubleday Anchor.

Goffman, E. (1974) *Frame Analysis: An Essay on the Organization of Experience*, Cambridge, MA: Harvard University Press.

Green, M. and B. Houlihan (2005) *Elite Sport Development: Policy Learning and Political Priorities*, London: Routledge.

Gruneau, R. (1981) 'Review of *Surfing Subcultures of Australia and New Zealand*', *ICSS Bulletin*, 21: 8–10.

Gruneau, R. (1989) 'Making Spectacle: A Case Study in Television Sports Production', in L. Wenner (ed.) *Media, Sports, and Society*, Newbury Park, CA: Sage.

Hall, S. (1973) *Encoding and Decoding in the Television Discourse*, Birmingham, UK: University of Birmingham Centre for Cultural Studies (CCS Stencilled Paper no. 7).

Hesling, W. (1986) 'The Pictorial Representation of Sports on Television', *International Review for the Sociology of Sport*, 21: 173–191.

Hockey, J. (2006) 'Sensing the Run: Distance Running and the Senses', *The Senses and Society*, 1: 183–202.

Ingham, A.G. (1975) 'Occupational Subcultures in the Work World of Sport', in D. Ball and J. Loy (eds) *Sport and Social Order*, Reading, MA: Addison-Wesley.

Jary, D. and J. Jary (1995) *Collins Dictionary of Sociology* (2nd ed.), Glasgow: HarperCollins.

Joseph, J. (2010) *Cricket as a Diasporic Resource for Caribbean-Canadians*, Unpublished doctoral thesis, University of Toronto.

Kane, M.J. and J.A. Buysse (2005) 'Intercollegiate Media Guides as Contested Terrain: A Longitudinal Analysis', *Sociology of Sport Journal*, 22: 214–238.

Kim, K.Y. (2012). *Producing Korean Women Golfers on the LPGA Tour: Representing Gender, Race, Nation and Sport in a Transnational Context*, unpublished doctoral thesis, University of Toronto.

MacNeill, M. (1996). 'Networks: Producing Olympic Ice Hockey for a National Television Audience', *Sociology of Sport Journal*, 12: 424–453.

Marx, K. (1991/1852) *The Eighteenth Brumaire of Louis Bonaparte*, New York: International Publishers.

Messner, M. and C. Cooky (2010) *Gender in Televised Sports: News and Highlights Shows, 1989–2009*, Los Angeles: USC Center for Feminist Research (Research Report).

Messner, M., M. Dunbar and D. Hunt (2000) 'The Televised Sports Manhood Formula', *Journal of Sport and Social Issues*, 24(4): 380–394.

Messner, M. and M. Musto (2014) 'Where Are the Kids?' *Sociology of Sport Journal*, 31(1): 102–122.

Nakamura, Y. (2008) *Boundaries of Belonging: Overlapping Loyalties and Multiple Attachments: A Study of the North American Chinese Invitational Volleyball Tournament*, Unpublished doctoral thesis, University of Toronto.

Norman, M. (2013) 'Exploring the Politics of Physical Activity in Canadian Correctional Institutions', paper presented at the International Sociology of Sport Association conference, Vancouver, BC, 12–15 June.

Pearson, K. (1979) *Surfing Subcultures of Australia and New Zealand*, St. Lucia: University of Queensland Press.

Pink, S. (2009) *Doing Visual Ethnography*, London: Sage.

Reinharz, S. (1992) *Feminist Methods in Social Research*, Oxford: Oxford University Press.

Rojek, C. (1986) 'Problems of Involvement and Detachment in the Writings of Norbert Elias', *British Journal of Sociology*, 37: 584–596.

Schultz, J. (2005) 'Reading the Catsuit: Serena Williams and the Production of Blackness at the 2002 U.S. Open', *Journal of Sport and Social Issues*, 29: 338–357.

Silk, M. (2001) 'The Conditions of Practice: Television Production Practices at Kuala Lumpur '98', *Sociology of Sport Journal*, 18(3): 277–301.

Smith J. and M. Osborn. (2009) 'Pain as an Assault on the Self: An Interpretative Phenomenological Analysis', *Psychology &Health*, 22: 517–534.

Stevenson, C. (1990) 'The Early Careers of International Athletes', *Sociology of Sport Journal*, 7: 238–253.

Theberge, N. (1989) 'A Feminist Analysis of Responses to Sports Violence: Media Coverage of the 1987 World Junior Hockey Championship', *Sociology of Sport Journal*, 6: 247–256.

Thomas, W.I. and D.S. Thomas (1928) *The Child in America: Behavior Problems and Programs*, New York: Knopf.

Thompson, K. and J. Tunstall (eds) (1975) *Sociological Perspectives*, Harmondsworth, UK: Penguin.

Thrift, N. (2007) *Non-Representational Theory: Space, Politics, Affect*, London: Routledge.

Trueman, T. (2012) 'Interview with Keith Hahn-Harris on Why He Chose to Investigate Aquatic Sports in Luxembourg', *Network* (British Sociological Association), Spring: 31.

Trujillo, N. (1995) 'Machines, Missiles and Men: Images of the Male Body on ABC's *Monday Night Football*', *Sociology of Sport Journal*, 12: 403–423.

Van Maanen, J. (2001) *Tales from the Field: On Writing Ethnography*, Chicago: University of Chicago Press.

Wensing, E. and T. Bruce (2003) 'Bending the Rules: Media Representations of Gender During an International Sporting Event', *International Review for the Sociology of Sport*, 38(4): 387–396.

White, P. and J. Gillett (1994) 'Reading the Muscular Body: A Critical Decoding of Advertisements in Flex Magazine', *Sociology of Sport Journal*, 11: 18–39.

Willis, P. (1978) *Profane Culture*, London: Routledge and Kegan Paul.

Willis, P. (1981) *Learning to Labour: How Working Class Kids Get Working Class Jobs*, New York: Columbia University Press.

Willis, P. (2000) *The Ethnographic Imagination*, Cambridge: Polity.

Young, K. and M. Atkinson (2008) 'Introduction: A Subcultural History', in M. Atkinson and K. Young (eds) *Tribal Plays: Subcultural Journeys Through Sport*, Bingley, UK: JAI Press.

5

MARXIST AND NEO-MARXIST APPROACHES ON SPORT

Ian McDonald

Introduction: the revolutionary Karl Marx

Speaking at the funeral of Karl Marx in 1883, his lifelong friend and collaborator, Friedrich Engels, declared, 'Marx was before all else a revolutionist' (cited in Foot 2004: 14). Theory was, for Marx, a means to understand the social world as a necessary step to transforming the same. 'One cannot accept Marx's scientific theory', asserted sport sociologists Jarvie and Maguire, 'and reject his revolutionary politics' (1994: 110). Marx's life work – the materialist conception of history and the studies of capital – is dedicated to one goal: to do away with the exploitation, suffering and violence that are built into the capitalist system. As Engels continued in his funeral speech, '[Marx's] real mission in life was to contribute, in one way or another, to the overthrow of capitalist society and of the state institutions which it had brought into being, to contribute to the liberation of the modern proletariat' (cited in Foot 2004: 14). The essence of Marxism is rooted in the unity of theory and practice of the proletarian (or workers) revolution. In this sense, the peculiarity of Marxism is that it is both an analysis of 'the laws of motion' of the capitalist system as well as a political programme for overthrowing that system. The scientific and the philosophic, on the one hand, and the interventionist politics, on the other, are distinct but necessary elements of the Marxist totality. This is suggested by Gramsci's phrase 'the philosophy of practice' and stated without any ambiguity in the attack on the idealism of the young Hegelians in the oft-quoted 11th Thesis on Feuerbach: 'The philosophers have only interpreted the world in various ways: the point is to change it' (Marx 1984: 423).

This chapter presents an overview and a critique of the main contours of Marxist sociology of sport that developed in the academy in the USA and western Europe.[1] This is presented chronologically and maps onto three distinct phases in the development, namely: activist-Marxism in the 1960s and 1970s; cultural-Marxism in the 1980s and 1990s; and post-Marxism from the late 1990s onwards. The discussion of Western Marxist sociologies of sport is preceded by an outline of a key concept in Marxian sociological scholarship, namely 'critique'. An assessment of Marxist sport sociology from the point of view of critique and revolutionary praxis is then developed before arriving at some conclusions about the strengths and shortcomings of Marxist sociology of sport. The chapter concludes with a call for more utopian thinking, appropriately conceived, as the basis for a revolutionary Marxist sociology of sport. It is a notion of utopianism that is premised on a critical duality: the irreformable nature of capitalism's exploitative social structures on the one hand (hence the need for social revolution), and an understanding of the social significance of sport on the other (hence the necessity for an engaged critique of sport). The chapter does not address the official state-sanctioned 'Marxist' sociologies of sport that developed in the USSR and the former 'communist' regimes in eastern Europe, as these tend to lack critical content and are little more than expressions of normative ideas about sport and society. This chapter focusses on the contribution of Marxism to the critique of sport.

Marxism and the critique of sport

The study of sport, as the Marxist sport sociologist Richard Gruneau notes, 'is haunted by a fundamental paradox' (1999/1983: 21). Gruneau argues that rules in sport act to separate the activity from reality but at the same time have the effect of deeply embedding them in prevailing social relations. Depending on how it is structured, sporting practice can be enabling, by 'opening pathways for various freedoms, pleasures, forms of disciplinary mastery, social bonding, and identity', or constraining, by 'directing pleasures and the meanings associated with them into social and cultural forms that sustain relations of domination' (1999/1983: 115). Thus the very act of creating the autonomy of sport serves to undermine that autonomy. For a Marxist critique of sport, paradox plays the same role as contradictions in wider society. Thus, while paradoxes, as non-dialectical formations, tend not to produce their own 'gravedigger' (as Marx called the working class due to their role as the agents of revolutionary change in capitalist society), they do pave the way for a radical critique. 'Critique', explains Marxist sociologist Alvin Gouldner (1980: 70/1), 'throws light on the hidden, repressed, unspoken, possibilities, the possibilities that they may be hostile to "what is," indicating what they are, why they have been hidden, and by whom'. So what is 'critique' and what is its relationship to the Marxist sociology of sport?

Essentially a product of the Enlightenment, critique signalled the displacement of revelation as a criterion of truth with rational thought. By the mid-nineteenth century, critique was associated with oppositional thinking as an activity of unveiling or debunking in Marx's theoretical method. 'The idea of critique', notes Gouldner, 'originally rooted in Kant's critique of pure and practical reason, was transmitted and reshaped by Marx' (1980: 8). Marx explicitly developed Kant's critique of dogmatic theological and metaphysical ideas into the critique of ideology and linked it with the practice of social revolution. Marx did not conceive of his theory simply as a social science designed to understand the world, but also as a force to actively mobilize the proletariat to change the world.

In the twentieth century, scholars from the different theoretical traditions, most notably the Frankfurt School (Critical Theory) took the Marxist notion of critique as their point of departure in articulating an emancipatory theory. In his essay 'Traditional Theory and Critical Theory', written in 1937, Max Horkheimer argued that while traditional theory was content to understand and explain, critical theory seeks to unveil how things came to be the way they are, what they might be in the future and, ultimately, 'to liberate human beings from the circumstances that enslave them' (Horkheimer 1982: 244). Indeed, critique does not simply legitimate partisan scholarship but insists upon it. Others within the tradition of western sociology have followed suit in rejecting the positivistic assumptions of value-neutrality; 'the question is not whether we should take sides', claimed Howard S. Becker, 'since inevitably we will, but rather whose side are we on?' (1971: 123). Marxism, as Gouldner (1980: 55) noted, 'intervenes to change the world. . . . To make a critique of something is thus to state its limits in terms of a set of values; a critique implies – if it does not state outright – that what is ought to be otherwise'.

Critique is rooted in what already exists but is not restricted by the fact of existence. In *Reason and Revolution*, Marcuse (1973/1941) cites Hegel's distinction between existence and essence as crucial, in which the former refers to what exists, while the latter refers to what has yet to come into being, a potentiality. It is the gap between the dialectic of existence and essence that is the sphere of critique. 'Critique', explains Gouldner, 'throws light on the hidden, repressed, unspoken possibilities, the possibilities that they may be hostile to 'what is,' indicating what they are, why they have been hidden, and by whom' (1980: 70–71). It is premised on the ineluctable disjuncture between rhetoric and practice, existence and essence, and the ever-present relations of power (which can be cultural, ideological and institutional) in (for example) sporting policies and practices. For Alan How, 'critique seeks to pull reality towards what it ought to be, what is immanent to it and what, if all other things were equal, it would become' (2003: 4–5).

Critique emerges from the interventionist nature of social research as part of the attempt 'to pull reality towards what it ought to be'. This notion of critique derives from the strategy of 'immanent critique' associated with the Frankfurt School in the 1930s. Immanent critique takes the values of existing society as the starting point of critique and either uses them to expose the failure of dominant groups to realize these values, or uses them to criticize an attack on the existing order by reactionary forces, as with the Frankfurt School use of immanent critique against fascism in the 1930s (Kellner 1989).

Such an approach requires the critic to be theoretically engaged with actual social practices in the real world. For it is within the existing social practices and the surrounding discourses that both the material and the conceptual resources exist to conduct a critique. In Morgan's schema, what gives such an approach a critical dimension is the ability of the critic to appeal 'to the deep, reflectively secured, critical norms of a culture (such as the present belief in equality and fairness) that form a background repository of beliefs that can be tapped to criticize its dominant beliefs' (1994: 190). It is then the job of the critic to deploy the normative standards against the conventional norms, 'looking for inconsistencies, contradictions and argumentative gaps . . . evaluating whether they measure up to the reasoned ideals brought to bear on them' (1994: 191).

An overview and critique of the Marxist sociology of sport

The starting point for a Marxist critique is to locate sport within capitalist social relations, to adopt a materialist analysis of the way in sport is positioned within class society. In a recent essay, the Marxist political theorist Budd (2013) argued that while capitalism takes various historical and national forms, the core is founded on two key sets of social relations that express, more or less precisely, what are sometimes called capitalism's twin separations. The first is the separation of the working class from the means of production, where workers are forced to sell their labour-power as a commodity to a class of owners of means of production simply in order to live. The second is the separation of individual capitals from each other, where capital only functions as capital when there are relations of competitive accumulation between firms. It is intra-class competition (between firms) that is the driver behind inter-class exploitation (of the dominant economic class over the working class). Exploitation is the root source for the alienation (a sense of being a mere extension of the 'bosses' machinery') of the working class. For Budd, capitalism's core relations of exploitation and competition frame all other social relations, including professional and elite sport. Spontaneity and the development of a holistic character are constrained as sporting workers are compelled to accept narrowly specialized roles that maximize productivity and rationalize technique in the pursuit of victory. The overriding drive to victory serves to diminish the pleasurable aspect of sport as sporting activity becomes merely a means to an end with damaging consequences for the alienated body. Although a small elite of sports workers is compensated for its alienation, this represents a tiny fraction of those who set out with aspirations of sporting success. Budd contrasts the exploited and alienated body of high-achievement competitive professional sport with the experience of childhood play, which he argues is a means towards personal integration and an expression of all the faculties and abilities of mind and body.

The exploitative and alienating culture of sport extends to recreational sport as well as to spectatorship in sport. As capitalism developed and the working class became increasingly concentrated in cities and large workplaces, so the significance of state regulation deepened and dovetailed with moves by capital to exercise an increasingly rigid control over routinized labour (Collins 2013). In relation to industry, sport became:

> a way of filling leisure time with brief, but exhilarating periods of uncertainty. . . . The spell of physically competitive activity, far from being broken, was strengthened by the need for momentary release from a colourless world dominated by the monotonous thuds and grinds of machinery.
>
> (Cashmore 1990: 62)

In so far as this 'momentary release' soothed accumulated work-related tensions, sport also functioned as a preparation for a return to work. As capitalism developed then, working-class leisure activities were subject to a variety of constraints, becoming codified and bound within tighter structures, rules and spaces, such as pitches and rings. And as Andrews (2009: 213) notes, the development of capitalism on a global scale merely replicates a global capitalist sporting culture: 'virtually all aspects of the global sport infrastructure (governing bodies, leagues, tournaments, teams and individual athletes) are now driven and defined by the interrelated processes of: commercialization (the exploitation of an object or practice for capital gain); corporatization (the rational structuring and management of sporting entities according to profit motives); and spectacularization (the production of entertainment-driven experiences)'. Far from being separate from society, and far from being outside the political sphere, sport is an integral and not insignificant element of global capitalist (that is class) society.

Sport, then, is part of capitalist society (Collins 2013). Exactly how it is so, and identifying the limits and possibilities for resistance, change and even social transformation certainly preoccupied the first generation of theorists and activists whose concern with sport and the body went against the grain of traditional Marxist theorizing.

Marxist sociology of sport emerged in the wake of the cultural and political radicalism of the mid-to-late 1960s. The 1960s was the 'high point' for forms of anti-colonial resistance and Third Worldist nationalism that had emerged during the 1950s. This was a period marked by worldwide student revolt, civil rights protests, workers' strikes, anti-war movements and general civil unrest. In many areas of society, millions of people were actively engaged in exposing exploitative social structures, values and ideologies, in critiquing different forms of power, in searching for strategies of resistance and debating alternatives (Harman 1989). It was out of this political ferment that the radical critique of sport emerged, led by North American academic sport activists such as Harry Edwards (1969), Jack Scott (1971), and Paul Hoch (1972), and European Marxists such as Jean-Marie Brohm (1978) and Bero Rigauer (1981).

Variously labelled as 'neo-Marxism' (McKay 1986), 'Frankfurt Marxism' (Morgan 1994), 'Structural Marxism' (Young 1986) or what I prefer to call 'activist Marxism', writers from this tradition produced a significant body of work that paved the way for a Marxist critical sociology of sport to emerge in the academy. First and probably most important, they debunked the complacent idea that sport was simply and only a positive force in society. Indeed sport was condemned as ideological, divisive, alienating and exploitative. Sport was the culturally and historically specific expression of physical culture under the conditions of capitalism, and as such, few redemptive qualities were present in sport. As Rigauer asserted, capitalist sport was analogous to work, and had been transformed into what the French Marxist Jean-Marie Brohm evocatively called 'A Prison of Measured Time'. According to John Hargreaves, capitalist sport evinces 'specialisation and standardisation, bureaucratized and hierarchical administration, long-term planning, increased reliance on science and technology, a drive for maximum productivity, a quantification of performance and, above all, the alienation of both producer and consumer' (Hargreaves 1982: 41). Sport is big business and driven by the same logic as the wider system of which it is a part. And it is an ideological state apparatus that cannot be reformed but completely transformed by the revolution.

The limiting and damaging culture of sport was contrasted with the expansive and liberating qualities of play. These writers eschewed the false neutrality of extant positivist paradigms, and sought to connect sport to the radical movements that were confronting traditional, oppressive and imperialist structures of power. However, save for the ongoing struggles of black athletes for civil rights in the US colleges, culminating in the genuinely heroic 'black gloved' salute by Tommie Smith and John Carlos at the 1968 Mexico City Olympic Games (Edwards 1969), the culture and institutions of sport were relatively untouched by the spirit of radicalism (Brohm 1978). The political conservatism of modern sport is not surprising. As numerous historians of sport have established, sport from the beginning was more a form of catharsis than a challenge by the dominated classes to the dominant class (Hargreaves 1986; Holt 1989; Collins 2013). While many commentators have discussed the question of an alternative culture of sport consistent with the principles of socialism (see, for example, Whannel 1983; Hammond 1993; Collins 2013), there has not existed a serious movement for the socialist transformation of sport. The short-lived workers' sports movement of the inter-war years, which vacillated between being a weapon in the international class war and a less politicized, healthy alternative for workers' leisure time (Kruger and Riordan 1996), failed to offer a significant challenge to the institutional structures of modern sport. The history of previous attempts by socialists to intervene systematically in the culture of sport demonstrates the limited contribution that sport can make to advancing the socialist movement (Jones 1986). 'Sport has been a forum for at best reformist politics', concludes John Horne, 'rather than cultural revolution' (2006: 168). At most, it seems that all that can be done are rearguard and defensive strategies such as exposing relations of power, engaging in campaigns for equality and formulating critiques. Sport, it seems, does not have the equivalent of avant-garde artistic movements or revolutionary cinematic and literature movements.

John Hargreaves argues that sport has been a vital tool in the construction and maintenance of bourgeois hegemony over the working class. It has allowed national bourgeois culture to connect to working-class culture in important ways (through securing consent for ideologies such as nationalism and compulsory heterosexuality). However, Hargreaves does not reject the empowering possibilities for subordinate groups. This recognition of the potentially empowering, expressive and creative experience of sport alongside a concern with the exploitative and oppressive aspects constitutes the key duality at the heart of the shift from activist Marxism theorizing to cultural Marxism.

If activist Marxism identified the fundamentally exploitative and ideological nature of sport in capitalist society, then cultural Marxism was more concerned with the limits and possibilities of resistance and transformation of these exploitative and ideological structures. Spanning a period of two decades from the late 1970s to the late 1980s, this was the formative phase in the establishment of the critical sociology of sport within the academy in the West. Scholars outlined the case for a Marxist theorization of sport as culture. In particular, theorists such as

Rob Beamish (1981, 1982, 1985), Alan Ingham (1982), and Hart Cantelon and Rick Gruneau (1982) set about comprehensively challenging the tradition of positivism and functionalism that were characteristic of approaches to studying sport. Influenced by debates on classical Marxism in the social sciences, these scholars turned their attention to a critical analysis of the state and sport, highlighting the rootedness of sport within social relations of power, its ideological potency, its alienating effects and questioning its place in the project for social transformation. The perspective was shaped by an approach to critique that is distinctly Gouldnerian: that is the critique was partly a 'lapidary act' and partly an engagement with contemporary theoretical adversaries (Gouldner 1980: 8). Thus the Marxist theories of sport that emerged during this period were formed out of an attempt to polish earlier, 'cruder' neo-Marxist theories of sport by seeking to erode their flawed and erroneous parts, and against the dominant tradition of positivist-functionalism in sociology. The tendency in activist Marxism to articulate sport as a mirror of society, or as corresponding to the needs of society, was challenged in favour of understanding the mutually constitutive nature of sport as culture and social relations of power.

Yet, crucially, due to the nature of Marxist theorizing, sport was still seen as ultimately a product of dominant interests in society, as more ideologically incorporating than challenging. The key task was to develop a Marxist perspective that placed sport in the structural realities of capitalist society yet was attuned to the creative role of human agency. As Alan Ingham mooted, Antonio Gramsci provided a way of synthesizing the dynamics of structure and agency:

> A dialectical Marxism would require both a theoretical concern for the logic of capital and an empirical concern for experience. The logic, surely, is ever present and cannot be relegated to some last instance of determination and experience, the mediator of culture, is not purely independent of the logic. Is not a concern for the relationships between capital's logic and lived experience integral to an adequate analysis of social formation, social being and social consciousness? Is this concern not the crux of Gramsci's contribution?
>
> (1982: 205–06)

Overlapping but also developing out of, and in key respects arguing against, the early materialist theorists of sport as culture, scholars looked increasingly to the work of Gramsci in the analysis of sport to 'purge' Marxist theorizing of these problematic residues. 'Gramsci's humanism', argues David Rowe (2004: 102), 'appealed especially to those Left-leaning social scientists and cultural critics made uneasy by the dismissal of the working class for being insufficiently revolutionary. Gramsci encourages intellectuals to "feel" as well as to "know" . . . therefore licences critical analysts of sport to share – with reservations – the thrill of the sports stadium and the frisson of sports fandom'. Key here were scholars such as John Hargreaves (1986), Jim McKay (1986), Alan Tomlinson (1999, 2005), Garry Whannel (1983, 1992) and Jennifer Hargreaves (1994). They and others argued that the class reductionism and a simplistic one-dimensional view of the reproductive role of sport under capitalism characteristic of activist Marxists (such as Brohm (1978), Rigauer (1981) and Vinnai (1973)), was still discernible in the early attempts to develop a materialist theory of culture. Thus, referring to the works of Rob Beamish and Rick Gruneau, Jim McKay noted that 'issues of gender domination generally have been treated as afterthoughts or footnotes, which are addressed once the important questions of class have been discussed' (1986: 264). Such class determinism led McKay to conclude:

> Lacking in this neo-Marxist literature on sport is the theorizing of gender and class oppression in a broader social theory of power. . . . It is crucial both theoretically and

politically that neo-Marxists do not view feminist and black critiques of sport as residual, epiphenomenal, or superstructural derivations of class inequality.

(1986: 264)

Gramscian concepts like 'hegemony' and 'cultural contestation' that seemed to overcome the
perceived structural determinism of 'vulgar' Marxism were used to re-theorize the sport-society
relationship as part of the contested terrain of capitalist culture in the war of position between
different social groups and blocs. The key concerns related to understanding relations of power,
exposing forms of domination and highlighting spaces of resistance.

The emergence of Gramscian Marxism in the critical sociology of sport can be seen as part
of a general theoretical shift in the academy towards 'post-Marxism', an expansive and contested
field of Marxist thought that refutes the centrality of the working class as the agent of revolutionary change. The publication in 1985 of *Hegemony and Socialist Strategy* by Ernesto Laclau and
Chantal Mouffe was hugely influential in making this shift. Described as a 'war of manoeuvre'
on classical Marxist theory (Townshend 2004), *Hegemony and Socialist Strategy* argued for a reori-
entation of Marxism so as to take account of the apparent failure of the working class to play
its revolutionary role and the marginal impact of Marxist politics on the burgeoning new social
movements (such as the women's movement, the environmentalist movement, the struggles of
gays and lesbians and of ethnic minorities). For Marxism to remain relevant, it was necessary to
make the shift from the politics of production to the politics of recognition. In short, an apparent
radical embrace of difference concealed a political retreat from the question of workers' struggle
(Jacoby 1999). It was the incarcerated Gramsci of the obscure Prison Notebooks rather than
the revolutionary Gramsci of the Lyon Theses that was capitalized on in post-Marxist theory.
Whereas the Lyon Theses left no doubt about the revolutionary commitment of Gramsci, and
his admiration of the Lenin and the Bolsheviks, the Gramsci of the Prison Notebooks permitted
plenty of room for interpretation. As Terry Eagleton (2003: 31) has argued, Gramsci came to be
used as a means of jettisoning the revolutionary kernel of Marxism in the name of Marxism:
Gramsci's contribution 'came to mean theories of subjectivity rather than workers' revolution'.
In the hostile intellectual climate and political context of the mid-1980s, with postmodern
theories in the ascendancy and new-right governments in office, the discourse of post-Marxism
served to reinforce the isolation of an activist and revolutionary politics of Marxism.

The impact of this post-Marxist moment on the critical sociology of sport was by no means
direct, but it was discernible. It attempted to rework and develop cultural Marxism by drawing
on non-Marxist perspectives in contemporary social theory while maintaining a grounded and
engaged critique of relations of power in sport. This is exemplified in the various writings of
the new generation of cultural studies scholars, who declared their openness to developments
in contemporary social and political theory, while stressing the need for grounded analysis in
keeping with the interventionist 'spirit' of Marxism (for example, see Andrews 2002; Howell,
Andrews, and Jackson 2002). This latest theoretically eclectic phase is certainly an ambitious
attempt to stride contrasting epistemic and metaphysical positions, around for example the
post-Marxist problematic of language and subjectivity, as well as the critical issues of political
change and social agency.

An assessment and conclusion

This brief overview of Marxism in the critical sociology of sport reveals three problematic
positions. The activist-Marxism of Brohm, Hoch and Rigauer at best offered a useful starting
point for the analysis of sport. But its denunciation of sport leaves space only for rhetoric and

polemic rather than serious analysis. In the one-dimensional stress on the repressive culture of sport, activist-Marxism denounces sport as irredeemably capitalistic, exploitative, oppressive and ideological, in which there is little space for political action. The revolution remains, but sport dissolves into insignificance. Cultural-Marxism offers important insights into the shifting ideologies and the cultural significance of sport. However, theorists have tended to overplay the emancipatory potential of sport by exaggerating the political significance of oppositional and resistant acts. Here, sport takes centre stage: opposition, resistance and contestation of sporting cultures are celebrated, but in this schema, reform has replaced revolution as the goal of politics. Post-Marxism meanwhile concedes so much of the theoretical ground to postmodern theories and identity politics that it has distanced itself almost completely from a classical Marxist paradigm based on partial or fundamental social transformation.

The fundamental characteristic of a Marxist sociology of sport is the dialectic of interpretation and transformation of cultures, institutions and practices. The development of a Marxist sociology of sport that is faithful to its revolutionary kernel needs to navigate a form of scholarship that justifies the study of sport as a significant socio-cultural form while understanding the structural limitations placed on sport in capitalism. It is an approach that is committed to the necessity and possibility of limited reforms in our sporting culture while insisting that fundamental transformation can only occur as part of a revolutionary transformation of capitalist society. It lies in using the concept of the revolution as a heuristic device from which to construct a critique of modern sport. The concept of revolution is based on an understanding of the deleterious impact of capitalism and the necessity for fundamental social transformation that starts with practical interventions, which are by definition reformist and progressive in nature. A revolutionary critique is not, then, a justification for political quietude and passivity, but on the contrary, a call for politically engaged scholarship, while recognizing what a well-established Marxist historiography has demonstrated, that sport has tended to play a conservative and incorporating function in society.

The leftist sports-philosopher William Morgan argues that effective social criticism of sports must avoid the twin dangers of hypercriticism and excessive romanticism: 'social critics who do their jobs well are debunkers ... however, a feature of social criticism no less important is getting people to sit up straight and take one's criticisms to heart.... This approach requires giving people some hope ... that there is good reason to believe that they can make a difference' (Morgan 2006: 5–6). There are echoes here of Raymond Williams's (1983) oft-cited adage that to be truly radical is to make hope convincing rather than despair convincing. To make 'hope convincing' requires a vision of a different future for sport.

I would argue that what is lacking in the Marxist sociology of sport is precisely that: a vision of a different future, what Jacoby (1999: 35) has called a 'transformative social imagination ... the utopian spirit – a sense that the future could transcend the present'. As many radical thinkers have been quick to underline, utopianism is not to be confused with a proclivity for fantasy and otherworldly abstraction that distracts from the practical demands of organizing and resisting (Panitch and Leys 1999; Cooke 2004). The task of creating a utopian horizon would offer an opportunity for the Marxist sociology of sport to shift from an exclusively critical and reactive stance based on 'resisting', 'subverting', 'transgressing' or 'deconstructing' dominant forms of social power to a more creative consideration of long-term strategies for constructive change.

The inherent utopian dimension of sport set alongside the essentially conservative role played by sport vis-à-vis revolutionary change, points towards the need for a dialectical approach to sport in modernity. Fredric Jameson has outlined such an approach in relation to culture in general. Jameson argues that the methodological conclusion to be drawn is 'that we must denounce culture (as an idea but also as a phenomenon) all the while we continue to perpetuate it, and perpetuate it while continuing tirelessly to denounce it' (Jameson 1990: 47–48). Based on the notion of radical critique, I suggest that a properly dialectical approach involves denouncing sport all the while continuing to perpetuate it. It is the idea that sport must be simultaneously preserved and overcome: preserved because its paradoxical nature contains within it an inherent criticality that we can articulate as the utopian dimension of sport; overcome because sport contributes to the legitimacy of extant social relations of power, and serves to incorporate us into a system that causes immense human suffering. So, to return and this time to amend Marx's Eleventh Thesis on Feuerbach: sociologists have hitherto only interpreted the world of sport – the point is to denounce and perpetuate it. The social institution of sport does not exist on a level playing field. The forces favouring social reproduction far outweigh social transformation. The communicative, empowering and expressive approach to the game will always be pressed back on the defensive by the power play of the instrumental, alienating and commercial logic of the sporting pragmatists and entrepreneurs. 'Our' side may never win the match in global capitalist society, but neither can they be beaten. A perpetual score-draw in this game of winners and losers: such is the paradox of sport.

Note

1 The ideas presented here were first explored in McDonald (2007), Carrington and McDonald (2009) and McDonald (2009).

References

Andrews, D.L. (2002) 'Coming to Terms with Cultural Studies', *Journal of Sport & Social Issues*, 26(1): 110–117.

Andrews, D.L. (2009) 'Sport, Culture and Late Capitalism', in B. Carrington and I. McDonald (eds) *Marxism, Cultural Studies and Sport*, London: Routledge.

Beamish, R. (1981) 'Central Issues in the Materialist Study of Sport as Cultural Practice', in S. Greendorfer and A. Yiannakis (eds) *Sociology of Sport: Diverse Perspectives*, New York: Leisure Press.

Beamish, R. (1982) 'Sport and the Logic of Capitalism', in H. Cantelon and R. Gruneau (eds) *Sport, Culture & the Modern State*, Toronto: University of Toronto Press.

Beamish, R. (1985) 'Understanding Labor as a Concept for the Study of Sport', *Sociology of Sport Journal*, 2: 357–364.

Becker, H.S. (1971) *Sociological Work: Method and Substance*, London: Allen Lane.

Brohm, J.M. (1978) *Sport: A Prison of Measured Time*, London: Ink Links.

Budd, A. (2013) 'Sport and Capitalism', in M. Lavalette (ed.) *Capitalism and Sport: Politics, Protest, People and Play*, London: Bookmarks.

Cantelon, H. and Gruneau, R. (eds) (1982) *Sport, Culture & the Modern State*, Toronto: University of Toronto Press.

Carrington, B. and McDonald, I. (2009) 'Marxism, Cultural Studies and Sport: Mapping the Field', in B. Carrington and I. McDonald (eds) *Marxism, Cultural Studies and Sport*, London: Routledge.

Cashmore, E. (1990) *Making Sense of Sport*, London: Routledge.

Collins, T. (2013) *Sport in Capitalist Society: A Short History*, London: Routledge.

Cooke, M. (2004) 'Redeeming Redemption: The Utopian Dimension of Critical Social Theory', *Philosophy and Social Criticism*, 30(4): 413–429.

Eagleton, T. (2003) *After Theory*, London: Allen Lane.

Edwards, H. (1969) *The Revolt of the Black Athlete*, New York: Free Press.

Foot, P. (2004) 'Karl Marx: The Best Hated Man', *Socialist Review*, 282: 14–16.

Gouldner, A. (1980) *The Two Marxisms: Contradictions and Anomalies in the Development of Theory*, London: Macmillan.

Gruneau, R. (1999/1983) *Class, Sports, and Social Development* (2nd edition), Champaign, IL: Human Kinetics.

Hammond, D. (1993) *Foul Play: A Class Analysis of Sport*, London: Ubique.

Hargreaves, J.A. (1994) *Sporting Females: Critical Issues in the History and Sociology of Women's Sport*, London: Routledge.

Hargreaves, J.E. (1982) 'Sport, Culture and Ideology', in J.A. Hargreaves (ed.) *Sport, Culture and Ideology*, London: Routledge and Kegan Paul.

Hargreaves, J.E. (1986) *Sport, Power & Culture*, Cambridge: Polity Press.

Harman, C. (1989) *1968: The Fire Last Time*, London: Bookmarks.

Hoch, P. (1972) *Rip Off the Big Game*, London: Anchor Books.

Holt, R. (1989) *Sport and the British: A Modern History*, Oxford: Oxford University Press.

Horkheimer, M. (1982) *Critical Theory: Selected Essays*, New York: Seabury Press.

Horne, J. (2006) *Sport in Consumer Culture*, Basingstoke, UK: Palgrave Macmillan.

How, A. (2003) *Critical Theory*, Basingstoke, UK: Palgrave Macmillan.

Howell, J.W., Andrews, D.L., & Jackson, S.J. (2002). 'Cultural and Sport Studies: An Interventionist Practice', in J. Maguire, J. & K. Young (eds) *Theory, Sport and Society*, Oxford: JAI Press.

Ingham, A. (1982) 'Sport, Hegemony and the Logic of Capitalism: Response to Hargreaves and Beamish', in H. Cantelon & R. Gruneau (eds) *Sport, Culture & the Modern State*, Toronto: University of Toronto Press.

Jacoby, R. (1999) *The End of Utopia: Politics and Culture in an Age of Apathy*, New York: Basic Books.

Jameson, F. (1990) *Late Marxism: Adorno, or, the Persistence of the Dialectic*, London: Verso.

Jarvie, G. and Maguire, J. (1994) *Sport and Leisure in Social Thought*, London: Routledge.

Jones, S. (1986) *Workers at Play: A Social and Economic History of Leisure 1918–1939*, London: Routledge and Kegan Paul.

Kellner, D. (1989) *Critical Theory, Marxism and Modernity*, Cambridge and Baltimore: Polity Press and Johns Hopkins University Press.

Kruger, A. and Riordan, J. (eds) (1996) *The Story of Worker Sport*, Champaign, IL: Human Kinetics.

Laclau, E. and Mouffe, C. (1985) *Hegemony and Socialist Strategy: Towards a Radical Democratic Politics*, London: Verso.

Marx, K. (1984) *Early Writings*, London: Penguin.

Marcuse, H. (1973/1941) *Reason and Revolution*, London: Routledge & Kegan Paul.

McDonald, I. (2007) 'One Dimensional Sport'. Available at: http://www.idrottsforum.org/articles/mcdonald/mcdonald071212.html (accessed 20 July 2014).

McDonald, I. (2009) 'One Dimensional Sport: Revolutionary Marxism and the Critique of Sport', in B. Carrington & I. McDonald (eds) (2009) *Marxism, Cultural Studies and Sport*, London: Routledge.

McKay, J. (1986) 'Marxism as a Way of Seeing: Beyond the Limits of Current "Critical" Approaches to Sport', *Sociology of Sport Journal*, 3(3): 261–272.

Morgan, W. (1994) *Leftist Theories of Sport: A Critique and Reconstruction*, Champaign: University of Illinois Press.

Morgan, W. (2006) *Why Sports Morally Matter*, London: Routledge.

Panitch, L. and Leys, C. (eds) (1999) *Necessary and Unnecessary Utopias: Socialist Register 2000*, London: Monthly Review Press.

Rigauer, B. (1981) *Sport and Work*, New York: Columbia University Press.

Rowe, D. (2004) 'Antonio Gramsci: Sport, Hegemony and the National-Popular', in R. Giulianotti (ed.) *Sport and Modern Social Theorists*, Basingstoke, UK: Palgrave Macmillan.

Scott, J. (1971) *The Athletic Revolution*, New York: Free Press.

Tomlinson, A. (1999) *The Game's Up: Essays in the Cultural Analysis of Sport, Leisure and Popular Culture*, Aldershot, UK: Arena.

Tomlinson, A. (2005) *Sport and Leisure Cultures*, Minneapolis: University of Minnesota Press.

Townshend, J. (2004) 'Laclau and Mouffe's Hegemonic Project: The Story So Far', *Political Studies*, 52(2): 269–288.

Vinnai, G. (1973) *Football Mania*, London: Ocean Books.

Whannel, G. (1983) *Blowing the Whistle: The Politics of Sport*, London: Pluto Press.

Whannel, G. (1992) *Fields in Vision*, London: Routledge.

Williams, R. (1983) *Towards 2000*, London: Chatto and Windus.

Young, T.R. (1986) 'The Sociology of Sport: Structural Marxist and Cultural Marxist Approaches', *Sociological Perspectives*, 29(1): 3–28.

6

NORBERT ELIAS AND THE SOCIOLOGY OF SPORT

Dominic Malcolm

Was Elias 'one of the pioneers of the sociology of sport' (Dunning 2002: 213)? He certainly attended some of the initial meetings in the mid-1960s. He also wrote some early papers which helped scope the area, provide important empirical substance and add theoretical rigour. Indeed, reflecting on his collaboration with Dunning, he even stated that 'we helped a little' to make sport a respectable subject for academic study (Elias 1986a: 19). But as I have argued elsewhere (Malcolm 2012), even in comparison to Bourdieu, who saw himself as 'virtually alone among major sociologists . . . to have written seriously on sports' (Bourdieu and Wacquant 1992: 93), Elias was unique among major social theorists in that he developed both a sociology *of* sport, and his sociological theory *through* sport.

The importance of this distinction is that it relates to the premise of Elias's sociological approach which forms the central organizing concept of this chapter. For Elias can be located – most notably alongside Bourdieu and Giddens – as a 'post-dualist' sociological theorist; someone who has systematically challenged the dichotomies traditionally drawn within the discipline. Specifically, Elias sought to develop ideas which helped re-conceptualize sociological debates over macro- and micro-sociology; objectivity and subjectivity; structure and agency; nature and nurture. This list, however, does scant justice to the degree to which post-dualist thinking infused Elias's general sociological orientation. For example, Elias rejected the relevance of distinctions between past and present and hence history and sociology, saw violence and civilization as radically interdependent rather than oxymoronic, and explored the 'social construction' of human psychology (though he preferred the terms 'sociogenesis' and 'psychogenesis' due to the voluntaristic and rationalistic connotations of the former). It was therefore fundamentally characteristic of Elias's approach to argue that (his) sport-related research was 'as significant to our understanding of the development of European societies as it is for that of sport itself' (Elias 1986b: 127). His aim was to study humans 'in the round', free from disciplinary silos or empirical specialisms. Consequently this chapter is organized around five core sociological dualities, with empirical studies used to illustrate how figurational sociological speaks, sometimes distinctively, to those debates. The central aim is to present theoretical ideas as inherently linked to, or in Elias's terms highly interdependent with, their sport-related application, rather than in abstracted form.

In turn, an aspect of Elias's work which some find particularly frustrating is thrown into sharper relief; namely his very specific use of language. Elias routinely proposed new terms to re-conceptualize familiar problems – e.g. process rather than historical sociology (see Dunning *et al.* 2004 for a discussion), involvement and detachment instead of subjectivity and objectivity, and so forth. This can be off-putting for the newcomer required to invest a relatively large amount of time in coming to terms with Elias's concepts, and indeed such innovative terms are not necessarily without their flaws (Malcolm 2011), but they are often intellectually fundamental to Elias's work, inherent to an approach which seeks to re-configure the way humans think. Challenging false dualisms is one aspect of this broader ambition.

In the following sections I examine Elias's orientation towards the dualisms of macro- and micro-sociology, objectivity and subjectivity, structure and agency, past and present, and nature and nurture. This heuristic division runs the danger of disconnecting theoretical concepts which are fundamentally interdependent, so frequent cross-referencing will occur. The chapter concludes by demonstrating the potential applicability of Elias's theoretical principles to some of the major future research challenges for sociologists of sport.

Macro- and micro-sociology: the theory of civilizing processes

As van Krieken (1998: 353) has summarized, Elias undertook an 'analysis of the historical development of emotions and psychological life ... in relation to the connections ... with larger scale processes such as state formation, urbanisation and economic development'. Fundamental to this project, therefore, was an attempt to bridge what has frequently been called the macro–micro sociological divide, or research which focusses upon a particularly high generality of understanding – consider the feminist concept of patriarchy, or Foucault's use of discourse – and research which focusses on the minutiae of everyday life. For Elias the goal had to be a sociology which drew connections between, as opposed to falsely dichotomized, these aspects of human existence. It underpinned Elias's desire, noted above, to develop both a sociology of sport and sociology through sport. It required the development of 'central theories ... theories based on meticulous, detailed and sensitive empirical observations couched at a level of synthesis sufficiently high to be applicable to a range of topics yet sufficiently down to earth to be clearly related to ... the real-life experiences of humans' (Dunning and Hughes 2013: 77). Elias's central theory, and one of the clearest illustrations of his rejection of the macro–micro dichotomy, is the theory of civilizing processes.

Elias's (2000) *The Civilizing Process* (TCP) was first published in 1936. It describes the process by which people in western Europe *came to view themselves* as (more) civilized (than others). The emphasis here is important as Elias did not wish to address the philosophical or moral dimensions of this claim, but rather to understand the intermingling of a range of social processes (conventionally described as macro and micro) which helped explain this outcome. Elias therefore sought to chart how manners and customs in relation to bodily functions, food consumption, sexual relations and the expression of violence have changed over time. His conclusion was that these aspects of social life become increasingly regulated through the internalization of external social controls. This involves greater rationalization, the use of forethought and the habitual adoption of acts previously prescribed to us. Social etiquette (relative to violence) comes to exert a greater influence on social status. Moreover we increasingly hide these things away from public view and are, at times, physically repulsed by the failure of others to conform to social norms regarding these behaviours.

Specifically Elias argues that this psychogenesis is directly linked to sociogenesis. As states become more extensive and complex, concurrently developing monopolies over taxation and violence (i.e. both the police/military organizations which can coerce citizens and the means by which to pay for such bodies), so the personalities or psychology of people within those states changes. At this point discussions of Elias's theory of civilizing processes frequently get bogged down in empirical questions about the direction of change: are society and sport becoming more or less violent (Collins 2005)? Can one explain periods of heightened violence in terms of a shift in the balance between affective and instrumental violence (Dunning 1986), civilizing and de-civilizing processes (Sheard 1997), or 'informalisation' (Sanchez Garcia and Malcolm 2010)? These debates tend merely to reinforce opposing views. Consequently it is more productive here to focus on Elias's more general point that, over time, people come to perceive and evaluate similar acts in different ways, and come to experience and exhibit differing emotional responses to those acts. These changes – and Elias pre-empted Bourdieu's use of *habitus* as a concept – are not *ad hoc* and individualized but contoured by the broader social context.

This 'central' theory allows/compels Elias to ask two questions which no other major social theorist has broached: what is distinctive about, and what explains the social significance of, sport in contemporary societies? His answers appear in *Quest for Excitement: Sport and Leisure in the Civilising Process* (Elias and Dunning 1986a). In relation to the first, Elias (1986c) looks at the process by which medieval folk games became transformed into their modern sport forms – a process he calls 'sportisation'. Sportization involves the development of more precise and explicit rules, which are written down (codified) and enforced more strictly. Because sports rules invariably restrict the means by which individuals can achieve sporting success, this development is in line with the trends identified in TCP towards stricter personal emotional and corporeal self-control, developed through greater self-reflection.

This relatively discrete social development again has to be understood in relation to macro-social processes, and specifically what Elias calls the 'parliamentarization of political conflict' (defined as the development of parliamentary rules which enable the peaceful transference of political power). Elias did not argue that parliamentarization *caused* sportization; rather, that these concomitant processes involved the *same people* for whom the ideas (i.e. knowledge) which structured the way they organized their working lives similarly informed the way they structured their leisure time. Elias (1986c) initially demonstrated this in relation to the development of fox-hunting, but it has subsequently been demonstrated in relation to boxing (Sheard 1997) and cricket (Malcolm 2002).

In relation to the second, the essay 'Quest for Excitement in Leisure' (Elias and Dunning 1986b), extends Elias's argument in TCP that one could empirically observe a change in the *habitus* of people in western European societies. In line with Elias's broader rejection of dualisms, the essay challenges ideas about the mutual exclusivity of work and leisure and examines sport within a 'spare-time spectrum', the various elements of which are distinguished by their degree of de-routinization. De-routinization leads to emotional stimulation. This, Elias and Dunning argue, is the excitement for which we quest. It is a socially produced psychological need. Thus the popularity and social significance of sport in contemporary societies stems from being one of the few spheres of social life in which relatively high degrees of emotional spontaneity are afforded relatively high degrees of tolerance.

Elias and Dunning point out that their use of 'unexciting' is somewhat ironic, for contemporary societies offer a wide range of opportunities for pleasure seeking. But they note that the 'excitement' people tend to seek in leisure is a mimetic version of emotions – fear, anxiety, anger, sadness – which are otherwise avoided in 'real life'. A delicate balance between routinization (providing security) and de-routinization (generating insecurity and playful risk) is key. The result is a 'controlled and enjoyable de-controlling of restraints on emotions', enhanced in collective activities which make the sport/leisure experience meaningful, distinctive and central to identity formation (Maguire 1992).

Subsequently these ideas have been developed through their application to subjects as diverse as a) the development of mixed martial arts (Sanchez Garcia and Malcolm 2010) and competitive forms of birdwatching called 'twitching' (Sheard 1999), in response to the increasing routinization of their respective antecedents; b) the behaviour of sports spectators such as football hooligans for whom the generation of particular forms of excitement is a central motivating force (Dunning *et al.* 1988), and American professional wrestling devotees drawn towards a 'double mimetic ... a mock sport within a make-believe world of professional sport ... [which] seeks to de-routinize the now "mundane" mimesis created by professional sport' (Atkinson 2002: 62); and c) triathlon participation which provides 'intense social and emotional stimulation through "suffering" athletically' (Atkinson 2008: 165). This, in turn, is a key part of the self-realization aspect of identity formation in the sport.

Objectivity and subjectivity: towards a sociology of knowledge

Although Elias's epistemological position is frequently viewed (within the sociology of sport at least) as an essentially modernist adoption of the primacy of objectivity, his sociology of knowledge is infused with the broader post-dualist principles identified above. Specifically, Elias rejected the dichotomy of 'truth' and social construction (and therefore falsehood) by emphasizing that knowledge cannot be divorced from its social and processual character. In particular, Elias argued that over time human knowledge has become less influenced by immediate self-interest, egocentrism and strong emotions and, correlatively, humans have increasingly enhanced their capacity to distance themselves from their objects of study and become reflexive about their role as producers of knowledge. Philosophical questions about how best to generate knowledge (epistemology) and what constitutes reality (ontology) are sociologically tangential. Rather knowledge, concepts and ideas exist/persist if they survive 'reality testing ... in the crucible of experience' (Elias 1987: 56). Thus Elias 'sidesteps' the objectivity-subjectivity dualism and talks instead about the historic and context specificity of the balance/blend of involvement (self-interest, emotion, etc.) and detachment (distanciation, reflexivity, etc.) which characterizes all human knowledge. This balance varies over time, is shaped by the broader social context and thus relates directly to TCP.

Perhaps one reason why Elias's epistemological position is frequently misunderstood is that these ideas have rarely been explicitly discussed in relation to sport. The main exception is Malcolm's (2011) work, which uses Elias's sociology of knowledge to explain the existence of a 'risk-pain-injury paradox' in sport (Nixon 1992). Specifically Malcolm argues that the occupational insecurity of athletes leads to relatively involved forms of thinking. This combined with contextual factors which advantage lay understanding over clinical medical knowledge, culminates in the prioritization of shorter-term competitive goals (risk) over longer-term health issues (precaution). Malcolm further explains the relative lack of influence of sports medicine knowledge in relation to Elias's arguments about the degree of autonomy of 'applied' as opposed to 'pure' science, the positioning of sports clinicians as simultaneously both subjects and objects – as creators (through diagnosis and prognosis) and resolvers (through treatment) of injury 'problems' – and in relation to Elias's theory of established-outsider relations.

Elias's theory of established-outsider relations has been used more frequently by sociologists of sport. Initially discussed in TCP, it is most explicitly formulated in Elias and Scotson's (1994) study of two working-class communities distinguished by their relative group cohesion and length of association (hence 'established'), but especially in relation to perceptions (i.e. knowledge) about their respective characteristics. Elias and Scotson argue that 'collective fantasies' frequently persist, with the broader context of power relations explaining why the established tend to be characterized by a 'we-group' image abstracted from the 'charismatic' behaviour of the 'minority of the best', while the outsiders are defined by the 'group disgrace' of the 'minority of the worst'. This group disgrace often centres upon beliefs about deviant, 'uncivilized' behaviour. Both the group disgrace of the outsiders and the charisma of the established tend to be accepted, indeed internalized, by all. Note how Elias is disinterested in dualistic philosophical concerns about truth/reality, exploring instead the social conditions in which knowledge is generated and developed through application.

As Bloyce and Murphy (2007) have pointed out, the theory of established–outsider relations rests upon a somewhat un-Eliasian formulation of an oppositional dualism between two groups. However, and despite that apparent flaw, the importance of this concept lies in the breadth of its application (and thus Elias's sociology of knowledge) by figurational sociologists of sport. For instance, Dunning (1999) draws on this model to examine race relations in the USA and, with Waddington, the relationship between sport and drugs (Dunning and Waddington 2003). Most frequently, however, figurational sociologists have applied the theory of established–outsider relations in the analysis of gender relations. While a key division exists between the established males and outsider females, such that one can identify male dominance over resources and administrative networks (Liston 2005), or refer to the 'patriarchal' norms which create the context for the pursuit of the feminine bodily ideal (Maguire and Mansfield 1998), one can also see how outsider groups become fragmented, and how blame gossip pathologizes outsiders' behaviour. For example, Maguire and Mansfield (1998) note how a dominant group of women in an aerobics class exclude and marginalize other women through their fitness/ability, physical positioning in the exercise space and display of feminine ideals through dress and body shape. Similarly, Liston (2005) notes how 'sporty women' are critical of other women for their lack of interest in sport, Velija and Flynn (2010) identify female jockeys' internalization of beliefs about the inherent and universal relative weakness of women, and Velija (2011) describes how female cricketers blame a generalized notion of 'butch/manly/lesbian cricketers' for the negative image, and therefore low status, of their game. Crucial in all cases is not the objective/subjective nature of knowledge but the social processes which lead to its internalization and perpetuate social inequalities.

Structure and agency: figuration

Elias's response to the structure–agency dualism is to introduce a concept – figuration – which would come to be synonymous with his broader sociological approach. Elias argued that this dualism, and especially the value attributed to agency, stems from a perception of individual uniqueness which is distinct to certain societies (i.e. a particular form of human knowledge generated in a particular time and space, relative to TCP). More accurately, Elias (2000: 482) noted, 'Since people are more or less dependent upon each other first by nature and then through social learning . . . and socially generated reciprocal needs[,] they exist . . . only in pluralities'. At the same time Elias warned against the reification of social structures, for this assigned essentially human qualities to abstract conceptualizations, e.g. the tendency to present concepts such as society or capitalism as having 'needs'. Rather, Elias's sociology stresses *interdependence*. All social relations are both enabling and constraining. Any notion of power is thus meaningless without identifying multiple parties and a particular context. For Dunning and Hughes (2013: 52), figuration 'invokes "the individual", "agency", "society", "social change", "power" and "structure" simultaneously but purposely without being reducible to any of these components'.

Elias's first excursus into sport, 'The Dynamics of Sports Groups with Special Reference to Football' (Elias and Dunning 1966), explored the conceptual advantages of 'figuration'. Elias and Dunning point out that the term 'football match' essentially refers to groups of people in constant and ever-changing interdependence, continually adjusting their actions according to the movements of teammates and opponents, at once in cooperation and conflict with each other. This analogy demonstrates the fallacy of the agency-structure dualism for, as in social life more broadly, players' agency can only be understood in relation to the broader structure of the game (e.g. the rules). Whilst on the one hand Elias sees us as active thinking beings with certain freedoms, these freedoms are both created, indeed can *only* be expressed, within the realms of the broader structure of social relations.

The research of figurational sociologists of sport is replete with examples of the use of the concept of figuration. The contrast between Maguire's (1999) notion of a global sport figuration and Waddington's (2000) use of figuration to depict the different health consequences of participation in exercise and sport illustrates the multi-level applicability of this concept. Murphy and Sheard's (2008) use of figuration in charting developments in participant safety in boxing illustrates through the notion of 'unplanned social processes' the relatively limited ability of human agents to purposefully effect social change. Comparing Maguire and Mansfield's (1998) reference to the 'exercise–body beautiful complex', Bloyce *et al.*'s (2008) figurational analysis of sports development policies and Malcolm's (2009) examination of how the relationship between sport clinicians' face-to-face interactions and the broader network of relations (e.g. rugby administrators, the community of sport medicine researchers) mediates the implementation of concussion regulations, shows the breadth of applicability of the concept. Students are frequently confused by a term which can be so flexibly applied, but then the term is specifically designed to simultaneously capture and be applicable to all aspects of social relations.

Perhaps the most extensive sport-related examination of Elias's understanding of structure and agency appears in Roderick's (1998) critique of Howard Nixon's work on risk, pain and injury in sport. Nixon uses the concept of 'sportsnet' which he defines as the 'webs of interaction that directly or indirectly link members of [sports-related] social networks' (Nixon 1992: 128). Roderick argues that Elias's notion of figuration provides greater scope for the analysis to incorporate changes over time (see below) and, if the primacy of face-to-face relations in Nixon's research is indicative, better sensitizes the researcher to the impact of a wider span of inter-relations (i.e. including with people we never meet). Perhaps most significantly in this context, Roderick notes that the use of 'sportsnet' leads Nixon to falsely abstract – or construct a dualism between – a 'culture of risk' and 'athletes' personal relationships' rather than considering them as fluid in their interdependence.

Past and present: the primacy of process

Elias's orientation towards 'diachronic' or historical/developmental research is a particularly noticeable aspect of his general approach. For instance, early works examined the common perception that ancient Greek sports represent something of the pinnacle of 'civilized' sporting achievement (Elias 1971), and the relatively violent characteristics which distinguished folk football from its modern counterpart (Elias and Dunning 1971). Indeed, figurational sociologists have continued to research in this vein (epitomized by Dunning *et al.* 2004), and historians of sport have engaged much more thoroughly (though not to say uncritically) with figurational sociologists than they have with other sociologists of sport (Mansfield and Malcolm 2010).

This diachronic orientation stems from a further rejection of conventional dualisms – namely past and present – which Elias saw as an asociological and therefore erroneous distinction. It is asociological because it conceives of time in abstraction from humans. Rather, Elias argued, time (like knowledge) needs to be understood in its social context; in other words, as 'a symbolic means of orientation, a human construct by means of which we use observable natural sequences . . . to control our relations with each other and with events and processes in the socio-physical universe in which we live' (Dunning *et al.* 2004: 3). For instance, our contemporary conceptions of history are fundamentally different to those of the Victorians because our tools for examining and recording human events over time have altered (NB the continued emphasis on the sociology of knowledge which in turn is linked to TCP). It is erroneous because all sociological research is either located in the past or immediately becomes so. Therefore history and sociology do not constitute a dualism; their difference is a matter of degree. Both, Elias argued, could/should be orientated to the study of *processes*.

Elias argued, however, that we live in societies in which humans are not well equipped to understand the fundamentally processual nature of human life. This is reflected in our language (consider, for example, the concept of climate change, which reduces the inherently dynamic climate to a static entity undergoing a period of change), and our fears of mortality, which obscure the essentially processual character of ourselves and other humans (who are born, age and die). Rather, the high valuation of individualism in contemporary societies leads us to perceive human 'history' as a series of unique and unrepeatable events. Yet uniqueness and repeatability are fundamentally relative; a questions of the level of analysis (humans will codify rugby/football only once, but they repeatedly engage in status-rivalries which foreground notions of 'civilized' behaviour). Crucially, without appreciating these different levels of understanding – in other words distanciation, reflexivity – we cannot see what is unique about the events in which we are entangled. Seemingly narrow studies of historical aspects of the development of sport are thus central to a sociological project to understand how social life changes. Inherent in this emphasis on process is a stress on the fundamentally relational character of social relations (interdependence), and hence on figurations rather than structure and agency.

Consequently, some of the most significant figurational studies of sport adopt a diachronic approach. Dunning and Sheard's *Barbarians, Gentlemen and Players* (2005) explores the development of rugby and association football, providing a theoretical framework for the understanding of how modern sport came to take its contemporary form. Addressing the development of the British class structure (and particularly the role of public schools), the trend towards the increasing seriousness and competitiveness in sport, and sport's increasing centrality in contemporary culture, the text argues that the development of rugby football entailed a 'civilising spurt' (i.e. sportization entails a reduction in the tolerance of violence). Maguire's *Global Sport* (1999) explores how the structures and practices of global sport result from a historical interweaving of societies and individuals over centuries of international relations. The long-term sportization processes underpinning the global development of regulated, competitive and masculinized performance sport are entwined with national/state formation processes, an emphasis on individual achievement, and the development and domination of science; ideas which are in turn consistent with Elias's demonstration of the increasing prominence of rationality and forethought as part of TCP. Finally, Malcolm's *Globalizing Cricket* (2013) undertakes a developmental overview of cricket from the eighteenth to the twenty-first century. In line with van Krieken's description of TCP (see above) it explores the rules and customs of cricket (as an expression of attitudes towards violence), and its role in the expression of social identities (predominantly national and ethnic) in relation to the British state formation, colonialism and post-colonialism. It concludes by exploring aspects of continuity and change in the relationship between cricket and notions of Englishness, with the game both fundamentally rooted in the past and responsive to contemporary changes. It illustrates the belief that it is only by examining how things have come to be that we can adequately understand their contemporary form.

Elias's commitment to post-dualist thinking therefore leads to a perspective which emphasizes a) an understanding of the contemporary world which is inherently relational to previous periods of time; and b) the greater adequacy of focussing on process rather than de-contextualized 'snapshots' of static aspects of social life. The advantages of this approach became particularly evident in challenging ideas that football hooliganism was a temporally specific phenomena, highlighting the varied role of the media in amplifying (and de-amplifying) the scale of hooligan activity over time, and in formulating strategies to address this social issue in the 1970s and 1980s (Dunning *et al*. 1988). It can be seen in relation to the more contemporary-focussed, but nonetheless processually oriented, studies of sport, such as Waddington's analysis of the impact of medicalization and commercialization on the use of performance-enhancing drugs in sport (Waddington and Smith 2009), or Malcolm and Sheard's (2002) analysis of the impact of professionalization on risk, pain and injury in rugby union. A diachronic approach is therefore fundamental to, and logically demanded by, Elias's broader sociological approach. It stems from an advocacy, and a desire to demonstrate the value, of foregrounding process in the analysis of social relations.

Nature and nurture: the hinge

Implicit throughout this chapter has been Elias's rejection of the tendency to perceive nature and nurture as a dualism. We have already seen how Elias stressed the interdependence of psychogenesis and sociogenesis in TCP, and how his emphasis on knowledge as a social process entailed a rejection of 'the idea of an unchanging mind shared by all people and all classes in all historical periods' (Dunning and Hughes 2013: 113). But while Elias's argument that humans can only be understood in relation to the figurations which they form logically entails an emphasis on 'nurture', his desire to develop a combined bio-psycho-social study of humans 'in the round', and preoccupation with emotions, violence and bodies, sensitizes us to his interest in incorporating an understanding of human 'nature'.

Consequently, a distinctive element of Elias's sociology is that he locates humans relative to other animal species. He describes the human self, society and nature as the 'triad of basic controls' (Elias 1978). He notes, for instance, that 'it is one of the specific peculiarities of the societies formed by human beings that their structure, the form of individual interdependencies, can change without a change in the biological organization of human beings' (Elias 1983: 13). He argues that humans have biologically evolved to a) exhibit (and need) close affective relations with each other; b) communicate using complex vocal and body languages; and c) be able to convey knowledge across generations with unprecedented sophistication. The rationale for his focus on bodily functions in TCP is that concerns about the regulation of 'animalistic' instincts, such as sexual desires and appetite, are uniquely human concerns, while human concerns with cleanliness and hygiene are qualitatively distinct. Indeed the very notion of 'civilized' that humans invoke includes, but is not limited to, the way these phenomena are routinized, and the degree to which they distinguish our 'we-group' from both other humans and animals. Elias introduces the notion of the 'hinge' to convey this nature-nurture relationship. The hinge evokes the sense that nature and nurture are always fundamentally linked, and could not exist in separation, whilst alerting us also to the processual nature of the relationship, varying from tightly 'closed' to more widely 'open'.

As a consequence of Elias's conceptualization of nature and nurture, figurational sociology was somewhat re-invigorated by the emergence of a 'sociology of the body' in the late 1980s and early 1990s. Featherstone (1987) drew on Elias in his study of leisure and ageing, and Shilling (1993), in particular, found the work of Elias particularly valuable in developing a theoretical framework for an embodied sociology. Maguire (1993) further argued that an embodied sociology held out the promise of shedding the sociology of sport's marginal disciplinary status. He drew on TCP and the idea that, over time, people became increasingly expected to exercise greater control over their bodies, with manners, emotional expression and bodily deportment increasingly important to social status contests, to develop a typology for an embodied sociology of sporting bodies. With the importance of social distinctions foregrounded in 'stratifying bodies', Maguire suggested the need to consider the subtle blending together of biomedical, disciplined, commodified and symbolic bodies in sport. Subsequently, and as evident throughout this chapter, figurational sociologists have been prominent in researching aspects of sports pain and injury (Malcolm and Sheard 2002) and sports health care (Malcolm and Scott 2011), as well as the stigmatization (disciplined bodies) of fat in women's gyms (commodified bodies) (Mansfield 2010).

Conclusion

Throughout this chapter I have tried to demonstrate the interdependence of Elias's post-dualist sociological perspective and the study of sport, and how these ideas have since been developed. It needs to be re-emphasized that the organization of this chapter is a heuristic device which runs the risk of falsely compartmentalizing Elias's ideas whereas, befitting of a perspective which foregrounds ideas about interdependence, each needs to be seen in relation to the others.

It is also befitting for a perspective which identifies the primacy of process to conclude with some comments about future application. There was a time when even those relatively sympathetic to the approach were critical of the degree to which violence and TCP dominated figurational sociological research (Stokvis 1992). While not necessarily agreeing with that critique, two decades on it is clear that research is now less explicitly informed by Elias's 'central theory' and instead elaborates Elias's broader theoretical toolkit. This is evident in imminent developments in the figurational sociology of sport which include some of the most significant social concerns of our time. First, figurational sociologists (e.g. Waddington 2000; Malcolm 2011) have been at the forefront of research on sport and health, driven by an interest in issues of bodily control, the relationship between external regulation of bodies and internalized self-control of behaviour and emotion. Second, figurational sociologists (e.g. Mansfield 2009) have turned their attention to the relationship between sport and the environment, utilizing the centrality of inter-species relations and interdisciplinary synthesis in Elias's work. Finally, the post-dualist character of Elias's sociology enables researchers to stay attuned to many of the most recent developments in the sociology of identity politics. For instance, it can be used to foreground heterogeneity (e.g. of gender), or emphasize people's multiple and overlapping identities. It can also be used to understand beliefs about the distinctiveness of national characters, amidst a variety of supportive and contradictory evidence (Malcolm 2013; Malcolm *et al.* 2010) akin to Said's (1978) concept of *Orientalism*. The inherent fluidity of 'process' sociology and the contextual and relational emphasis in the notion of figuration bears comparison with contemporary developments towards the consideration of diaspora in ethnic and migration studies. It looks, therefore, as though Elias's influence upon the sociology of sport will continue for some time to come.

References

Atkinson, M. (2002) 'Fifty Million Viewers Can't Be Wrong: Professional Wrestling, Sports-entertainment and Mimesis', *Sociology of Sport Journal*, 19: 47–66.

Atkinson, M. (2008) 'Triathlon, Suffering and Exciting Significance', *Leisure Studies*, 27(2): 165–180.

Bloyce, D. and Murphy, P. (2007) 'Involvement and Detachment, from Principles to Practice: A Critical Reassessment of *The Established and the Outsiders*', *Irish Journal of Sociology*, 16(1): 3–21

Bloyce, D., Smith, A., Mead, R. and Morris, J. (2008) '"Playing the Game (Plan)": A Figurational Analysis of Organizational Change in Sports Development in England', *European Sport Management Quarterly*, 8(4): 359–378.

Bourdieu, P. and Wacquant, L. (1992) *An Invitation to Reflexive Sociology*, Cambridge: Polity Press.

Collins, T. (2005) 'History, Theory and the "Civilizing Process"', *Sport in History*, 25(2): 289–306.

Dunning, E. (1986) 'Social Bonding and Violence in Sport', in N. Elias and E. Dunning (eds) *Quest for Excitement: Sport and Leisure in the Civilizing Process*, Oxford: Blackwell.

Dunning, E. (1999) *Sport Matters: Sociological Studies of Sport, Violence and Civilization*, London: Routledge.

Dunning, E. (2002) 'Figurational Contributions to the Sociological Study of Sport', in J. Maguire and K. Young (eds) *Theory, Sport and Society*, Oxford: Elsevier Science.

Dunning, E. and Hughes, J. (2013) *Norbert Elias and Modern Sociology: Knowledge, Interdependence, Power, Process*, London: Bloomsbury Academic.

Dunning, E. and Sheard, K. (2005) *Barbarians, Gentlemen and Players: A Sociological Study of the Development of Rugby Football*, Abingdon, UK: Routledge.

Dunning, E., Malcolm, D. and Waddington, I. (2004) *Sport Histories: Figurational Studies in the Development of Modern Sports*, London: Routledge.

Dunning, E., Murphy, P. and Williams, J. (1988) *The Roots of Football Hooliganism: An Historical and Sociological Study*, London: Routledge & Kegan Paul.

Dunning, E. and Waddington, I. (2003) 'Sport as a Drug and Drugs in Sport', *International Review for the Sociology of Sport*, 38(3): 351–368.

Elias, N. (1971) 'The Genesis of Sport as a Sociological Problem', in E. Dunning (ed.) *The Sociology of Sport: A Selection of Readings*, London: Frank Cass.

Elias, N. (1978) *What Is Sociology?* London: Hutchison.

Elias, N. (1983) *The Court Society*, Oxford: Blackwell.

Elias, N. (1986a) 'Introduction', in N. Elias and E. Dunning, *Quest for Excitement: Sport and Leisure in the Civilizing Process*, Blackwell: Oxford.

Elias, N. (1986b) 'The Genesis of Sport as a Sociological Problem', in N. Elias and E. Dunning, *Quest for Excitement: Sport and Leisure in the Civilizing Process*, Blackwell: Oxford.

Elias, N. (1986c) 'An Essay on Sport and Violence', in N. Elias and E. Dunning, *Quest for Excitement: Sport and Leisure in the Civilizing Process*, Blackwell: Oxford.

Elias, N. (1987) *Involvement and Detachment*, Oxford: Blackwell.

Elias, N. (2000) *The Civilizing Process* (revised edition), Oxford: Blackwell.

Elias, N. and Dunning, E. (1966) 'Dynamics of Sports Groups with Special Reference to Football', *British Journal of Sociology*, XVII, 4: 388–402.

Elias, N. and Dunning, E. (1971) 'Folk Football in Medieval and Early Modern Britain', in E. Dunning (ed.) *The Sociology of Sport: A Selection of Readings*, London: Frank Cass.

Elias, N. and Dunning, E. (1986a) *Quest for Excitement: Sport and Leisure in the Civilizing Process*, Blackwell: Oxford.

Elias, N. and Dunning, E. (1986b) 'Quest for Excitement in Leisure', in N. Elias and E. Dunning (eds) *Quest for Excitement: Sport and Leisure in the Civilizing Process*, Oxford: Blackwell.

Elias, N. and Scotson, J. (1994) *The Established and the Outsiders*, London: Sage.

Featherstone, M. (1987) 'Leisure, Symbolic Power and Life Course', in J. Horne, D. Jary and A. Tomlinson (eds) *Sport, Leisure and Social Relations*, London: Routledge and Kegan Paul.

Liston, K. (2005) 'Established-Outsider Relations between Males and Females in Sports in Ireland', *Irish Journal of Sociology*, 14(1): 66–85.

Maguire, J. (1992) 'Towards a Sociological Theory of the Emotions: A Process Sociological Perspective', in E. Dunning and C. Rojek (eds) *Sport and Leisure in the Civilizing Process*, London: Macmillan.

Maguire, J. (1993) 'Bodies, Sportscultures and Societies: A Critical Review of Some Theories in the Sociology of the Body', *International Review for the Sociology of Sport*, 28(1): 33–51.

Maguire, J. (1999) *Global Sport: Identities, Societies, Civilizations*, Cambridge: Polity.

Maguire, J. and Mansfield, L. (1998) '"No-body's Perfect": Women, Aerobics and the Body Beautiful', *Sociology of Sport Journal*, 15(2): 109–37.

Malcolm, D. (2002) 'Cricket and Civilizing Processes: A Response to Stokvis', *International Review for the Sociology of Sport*, 37(1): 37–57.

Malcolm, D. (2009) 'Medical Uncertainty and Clinician-Athlete Relations: The Management of Concussion Injuries in Rugby Union', *Sociology of Sport Journal*, 26: 191–210.

Malcolm, D. (2011) 'Sports Medicine, Injured Athletes and Norbert Elias's Sociology of Knowledge', *Sociology of Sport Journal*, 28: 284–302.

Malcolm, D. (2012) *Sport and Sociology*, London: Routledge.

Malcolm, D. (2013) *Globalizing Cricket: England, Empire, Identity*, London: Bloomsbury Academic.

Malcolm, D. and Scott, A. (2011) 'Professional Relations in Sport Healthcare: Workplace Responses to Organisational Change', *Social Science and Medicine*, 72: 513–520.

Malcolm, D. and Sheard, K. (2002) '"Pain in the Assets": The Effects of Commercialization and Professionalization on the Management of Injury in English Rugby Union', *Sociology of Sport Journal*, 19(2): 149–169.

Malcolm, D., Bairner, A. and Curry, G. (2010) '"Woolmergate": Sport and the Representation of Islam and Muslims in the British Press', *Journal of Sport and Social Issues*, 34(2): 215–235.

Mansfield, L. (2009) 'Fitness Cultures and Environmental (In)Justice?', *International Review for the Sociology of Sport*, 44: 345–362.

Mansfield, L. (2010) '"Fit, Fat and Feminine": The Stigmatisation of Fat Women in Fitness Gyms', in E. Kennedy and P. Markula (eds) *Women and Exercise: Qualitative Research on the Body, Health and Consumerism*, London: Routledge.

Mansfield, L. and Malcolm, D. (2010) 'Sociology', in S. Pope and J. Nauright (eds) *Routledge Companion to Sports History*, London: Routledge.

Murphy, P. and Sheard, K. (2008) 'Boxing Blind', in D. Malcolm and I. Waddington (eds) *Matters of Sport: Essays in Honour of Eric Dunning*, London: Routledge.

Nixon, H.L., II (1992) 'A Social Network Analysis of Influences of Athletes to Play with Pain and Injury', *Journal of Sport and Social Issues*, 16: 127–135.

Roderick, M. (1998) 'The Sociology of Risk, Pain and Injury: A Comment on the Work of Howard L. Nixon II', *Sociology of Sport Journal*, 15: 64–79.

Said, E. (1978) *Orientalism*, New York: Pantheon.

Sanchez Garcia, R. and Malcolm, D. (2010) 'De-Civilizing, Civilizing or Informalizing? The International Development of Mixed Martial Arts', *International Review for the Sociology of Sport*, 45(1): 1–20.

Sheard, K. (1997) 'Aspects of Boxing in the Western "Civilizing Process"', *International Review for the Sociology of Sport*, 32(1): 31–57.

Sheard, K. (1999) 'A Twitch in Time Saves Nine: Birdwatching, Sport and the Civilizing Process', *Sociology of Sport Journal*, 16(2): 181–205.

Shilling, C. (1993) *The Body and Social Theory*, London: Sage.

Stokvis, R. (1992) 'Sports and Civilization: Is Violence the Central Problem?' in E. Dunning and C. Rojek (eds) *Sport and Leisure in the Civilizing Process: Critique and Counter-Critique*, Basingstoke, UK: Macmillan.

Van Krieken, R. (1998) *Norbert Elias*, London: Routledge.

Velija, P. (2011) '"Nice Girls Don't Play Cricket": The Theory of Established and Outsider Relations and Perceptions of Sexuality and Class Amongst Female Cricketers', *Sport in Society*, 15(1): 28–43.

Velija, P. and Flynn, L. (2010) '"Their Bottoms Are the Wrong Shape": Female Jockeys and the Theory of Established Outsider Relations', *Sociology of Sport Journal*, 27: 301–315.

Waddington, I. (2000) *Sport, Health and Drugs: A Critical Sociological Perspective*, London: E. & F. Spon.

Waddington, I. and Smith, A. (2009) *An Introduction to Drugs in Sport: Addicted to Winning?*, London: Routledge.

7

PIERRE BOURDIEU ON SPORT

Michael Grenfell

Introduction

The intellectual reputation of the French social theorist *cum* sociologist Pierre Bourdieu has gone from strength to strength since his death from cancer in 2002. It is now not uncommon to find his ideas quoted in a very wide range of disciplines within the human sciences – journalism, art, law, economics, philosophy, architecture, geography, religion. Yet, during his own lifetime, he was best known as a sociologist of education and culture; this stemming from his work on schools, universities, museums and taste from the 1960s onwards. Despite sporadic discussion and application of his work from those involved in the sports sciences, he has never been known particularly as a sociologist of sport. This is a curious oversight for a number of reasons. First, Bourdieu did write quite a lot explicitly about sport: for example, 'How Can One Be a Sportsman?' from his 1984 publication *Questions de Sociologie* (1993/1984);[1] 'Programme for a Sociology of Sport' from *Choses Dites* (1994/87); and 'The State, Economics and Sport' (2007/1998); not to mention frequent references to sport in his study of cultural habits in France (e.g. *Distinction*, 1984/1979). Second, Bourdieu himself was a keen sportsman, and had a special affinity for rugby, a particularly popular game in South-west France from whence he originated. Combat sports also fascinated him: indeed, one of his closest collaborators published a study of boxing (Wacquant 2000), and the title of his of his 2001 biographical documentary following a year in the life of the sociologist is *La sociologie est un sport de combat*. The allusion is a telling one and conjures up the picture of sociological engagement being a kind of hand-to-hand encounter and sociology as a martial art with which one can protect oneself. Third, and somewhat consequently therefore, Bourdieu often saw social processes as 'a game,' and refers to them as such played out according to strict 'rules',[2] and in terms of positioning, a sense of play and outcome in 'winning' and 'losing'. As noted above, Bourdieu has indeed been used by those interested in the academic study of sport; for example, Williams (1995), Stempel (2005), Seippel (2006), Thorpe (2009), Brown (2010), Hunter (2010), Noble and Watkins (2010), Warde (2011). However, what follows is a more systematic consideration of just how sport can be understood from a Bourdieusian perspective; this, not in order to argue for orthodoxy in the use of such a viewpoint to sport but to encourage a wider application and appreciation of this theory to a larger scope of sporting activities and their associated practices when set against the other contributions in this volume. There is a second motive in offering an account of Bourdieu and sport; namely, that it can be considered as a perfect exemplar of Bourdieusian epistemology and practice in that it includes all the salient aspects of what Bourdieu called a metanoia, or 'new gaze' on the world, and I shall take this as my *point de depart.*

Constructing sport

In encouraging greater conformity in using Bourdieu's theory of practice in social science research, I have elsewhere argued for a three-phase methodological approach, including a three-level field analysis (Grenfell 2012: chapter 13). The three phases are: Construction of the Research Object, Field Analysis and Participant Objectivation. The three levels of Field Analysis are: The Field and the Field of Power, The Field Itself, and The Habitus of Those in the Field. I propose to use this approach to structure the narrative of this chapter since it is one which is equally useful and applicable for anyone looking to 'think sport' in this way.

At one point, Bourdieu calls the 'construction of the research object' the 'summum of the art' of the social scientist (1989: 51) as it is here that the epistemological ground rules are set. One approach would be to take the research object in its given, everyday, empirical sense. Obviously, such would be facile since social science aims for greater analysis and objectivity. However, for Bourdieu, to take an object of research – in this case sport – as it is represented in a particular academic field is hardly less misleading since such comes in a pre-constructed form, and thus imports with it a whole world view and set of presuppositions and implicit understandings, more often than not dehistoricized and thus misrepresented as the thing itself. Indeed, the very language we use to talk about a research object often implies a reality beyond the thing itself; such is the logic of thought where 'the things of logic become more real than the logic of things'. 'Beware of words', thus warns Bourdieu, as the very way we talk about things shapes the way we think about them. What is the alternative? Clearly, Bourdieu wants to break with the everyday, commonsensical, empirical understanding of social reality – sport in its unreflexive state in our present case – however, he also wants to break with conventional academic approaches to the same; for example, ultimately arguing that his brand of sport sociology offers a truer version than any other. This is a radical stance, and the language of 'rupture' and 'break' from and 'refusal' of the 'pre-given' is everywhere apparent in Bourdieu's work. Moreover, he insists that this is not a once and for only act but something that is constantly returned to in the course of research practice. Such a stance, of course, is immediately confrontational to an academic space – the study of sport – which is already set with its own orthodoxy of theory and practice. Furthermore, it risks discarding established and dominant modes of thought; resistance can therefore be expected. But, for Bourdieu, this fundamental necessity is a prerequisite to undertaking his brand of sociological analysis. Anything else – to accept conventional thinking – amounts to an intellectual act of bad faith. Ultimately, argues Bourdieu, 'the truth is that truth is at stake' (Bourdieu 1994/1987: 185). So, how to do this?

Bourdieu is clearly most closely associated with a conceptual set of thinking tools which he offers as instruments for analysis; of these, the two most basic and important are *habitus* and *field*.[3] *Habitus* is used to designate individuals' systems 'of acquired schemes objectively adjusted to the particular conditions in which it is constituted' (Bourdieu 1977/1972: 95), and is thus intended to represent the subjective side of human action; whilst *field* describes the objective as 'a network, or configuration, of objective relations between positions objectively defined . . . by present and potential situations in the structure of the distribution . . . of power' (Bourdieu and Wacquant 1992: 72–73). *Habitus* and *field* need therefore to be understood as going beyond simple descriptions of agency/biography and context, and instead seen as mutually constituted; indeed, at one point, Bourdieu discusses their 'ontological complicity' (Bourdieu 1982: 47), since for Bourdieu, his epistemology *is* an ontology. A *relational* rather than *substantialist* view is central to this perspective; thus, aiming to arrive at 'a science of dialectical relations between objective structures . . . and the subjective dispositions within which these structures are actualized and which tend to reproduce them' (Bourdieu 1977/1972: 3). In this sense, Bourdieu might be seen as 'post-dualist' (sic); except, of course, he would argue against this rubric as well. At one point in his work, Bourdieu refers to the 'opposition' between subjectivism and objectivism as dividing the social sciences and as being 'the most fundamental, and the most ruinous' (1990/1980: 25). He goes on to refer to them as 'modes of knowledge' and declares a necessity to go beyond their mutual antagonism whilst preserving what has been gained from each. Both are essential, yet both offer only one side of an epistemology necessary to understanding the social world. The world cannot be reduced to phenomenology or social physics; both must be employed in order to constitute an authentic 'theory of practice'. This is why his approach has been termed a 'science of existential analytics'. Such a 'post-dualist' science is predicated on epistemological *breaks*: from empirical knowledge – the common-sense view of sport (see above) – but also from subjective knowledge – hermeneutics and phenomenological interpretation, and objective knowledge – nomothetical laws and 'knowledge without a knowing subject'.

Structure is key to this perspective, but structure as both *structured* and *structuring*, as both subjective and objectively constituting. So, when a child is born he engages in the 'primary cognitive' act – at a cognitive level of establishing inten*s*ional (sic) (the 's' is italicized to signify the *structural* nature) relations with self, others and objects as a series of control strategies in order to build up individual psychic equilibrium. However, such structures of thought and action to be found in the social environment do not come as value-free entities but, on the contrary, are saturated with preset values, interests and orthodoxies.

All aspects of sport can be thought of in these ways: as a relationship to the body; as an activity; as a source of consumption; as an official institution – and the shared structures that both constitute and are constituting of them. Its whole epistemology is predicated on a sense of 'embodiment' in a sense derived from the phenomenologist Merleau-Ponty. For Bourdieu, this is *hexis*; in other words, an imbibed set of generating structures expressing an entire relationship to the world. To engage in a sporting activity is, then, implicitly to affirm, or otherwise, a whole way of being. Sport involves training the body in the rules of the sporting *ethos*; already a relationship that presupposes a certain degree of leisure in an individual's engagement; one also of deferred gratification as one trains to win, to stay healthy, and so forth. Even in this simple dichotomy, totally distinct relationships are possible: for example, is sport *an end in itself* (style of life (what Bourdieu (1984/1979: 212) calls 'an ascetic exaltation of sobriety')) or *means to an end* – to win competitively (instrumental) (Bourdieu 1993/1984: 129)? Bourdieu also counterposes a hedonistic stance to a more ascetic one; of immediate physical expression to detached casualness. Similar dichotomies can be found in choice of sport: is it a contact sport or team sport? Is it based on sheer physical strength or more intellectual calculation? The answers to these questions literally reveal ways of being for Bourdieu. By way of illustration, he sees gymnastics as expressing 'training for training['s] sake', an activity of 'self-acceptance', or even 'unselfconsciousness' in the very act of practising sport; one which removes oneself from the gaze of another, except where carried out under competitive conditions. One's choice of sport therefore reveals a different order of value signification with respect to the body: 'down to earth' versus 'aerial'; 'virile' versus 'light'; 'hand-to-hand' versus 'distanced'; 'direct' versus 'gracious' (Bourdieu 1994/1987: 157), which is nothing other than a whole way in which the body is 'put into action' with degrees of formality, form, aesthetics and function in the world, which are then equally applied and revealed elsewhere in life activities.

Choice of sport can never therefore be arbitrary, but rather is shaped by any one individual's position in the social hierarchy. The incidence of regular sporting activity itself can be related to social providence: 1.9% for farm workers compared to 32% for the liberal professions according to Bourdieu's statistics at the time in France (1984/1979). Moreover, not all sports are equal in terms of the *symbolic capital* they bestow on those who engage with them. So, bridge is the natural 'sport' of the bourgeoisie whilst the working class prefer football. However, even here, one needs to take a social historical reading of such conclusions. In fact, games like football, rugby, wrestling and boxing were all once aristocratic sports; indeed, by dint of the fact that only those who had the leisure time could pursue them. But, now they seem to represent what the aristocrat would despise – strength, endurance, violence, sacrifice, docility and submission to collective discipline, in short everything contrary to the bourgeois role distance (Bourdieu 1984/1979: 214). In these stances, the vulgar and popular are juxtaposed to the elite and refined; an *ethos* that permeates the whole of any one individual's being and thus style of life. Moreover, such needs to be understood both historically and transnationally. So, just as aristocratic games evolved into institutionalized sporting associations, with their own internal structures of organization and authority to manage the sport, so do differences apply across sporting nations – 'the exaltation of "manliness" and the cult of "team spirit" that are associated with playing rugby – not to mention the aristocratic ideal of "fair play" – have a very different meaning and function for bourgeois or aristocratic adolescents in English public schools than for the sons of peasants or shopkeepers in South-west France' (Bourdieu 1993/1984: 126). In other words, it is not just the nature of specific sporting activities that one needs to take account of but the objective potentialities of different institutionalized practices, and the related social uses that such practices encourage through the way it distributes and is distributed by value and thus symbolic power. This leads us to a consideration of the *field* of sport.

The *field* of sport

As noted above, to regard sport as a *field* is to view it in terms of three levels: the *field* and the *field* of power, the *field* itself and the *habitus* of those involved in the *field*. This section looks at sport in terms of these.

The field *and the* field *of power*

For Bourdieu, sport needs to be understood in just the same way as any other *field*, and thus ultimately as a *field* of production, which itself implies specific conditions of possibilities. So, we need what Bourdieu called a 'historical sociology' of the past and a 'sociological history' of the present in understanding the sports *field* as a *social space* in which a range of sports are *positioned*, each with respect to each other and, ultimately, themselves.

For Bourdieu (2007/1998), the sporting *field* – at every level – needs to be seen first and foremost in relation to the state. This is particularly important in France where, since the great revolution of 1789, the state has upheld a moral and legalistic responsibility towards both national and individual public interest. This position stems from Enlightenment choices: solidarity over individuality and individualism; social security against the private individual; the collective over insular individual. For writers such as the French sociologist Durkheim, no less than German romantic philosophers such as Hegel, the state is society's 'self-awareness', where society 'thinks for itself', goes beyond conflict and acts in the public service. No surprise, therefore, to see sport featuring in a number of state-sponsored initiatives in France: for example, the 'Peuple et Culture' movement of the immediate post–Second World War era rebuilding programme that had a humanistic view of society and the individual, and the role of the state in cultivating the 'educated Frenchman' (see Cacérès 1967). Bourdieu describes (1993/1984: 126) how, in France, sport was organized by a range of social associations – village clubs, churches, trade unions, political parties – for the mobilization of the masses into a 'morality of health'; indeed, how these different associations in effect competed for the physical 'souls' of the French people and for the underlying values they each represented. Not unlike in other countries, many sports were rooted in local organizations: clubs, training centres, sports charters and regulating bodies committed to their social mission in framing sport both at an amateur and professional level; indeed, the latter was seen as an extension of the former. The educative value of sport was thus seen as part of a universalistic project in protecting the public good. However, Bourdieu argues that in later decades of the twentieth century, this take on sport was undermined by neo-liberal economics, which redefined the role of the state and, as part of this process, moved sport away from its social cohesive role and saw it instead as a source of commercial exploitation. Again, a transnational perspective is useful. So, in English football, second, third and fourth division clubs have been detached from the elite league; the latter offering the most commercial potential. Teams, therefore, no longer recruit locally, from amateur clubs, but buy in star players from abroad. As a result, commitment to developing local talent has been destroyed, breaking the link of career development for players as everything is played out in terms of selling the best players to the highest bidder. For Bourdieu, France at first lagged behind this evolution; so, well into the 1980s, football still operated according to practices which were seen as outmoded elsewhere – sport as public service, commercially light, and with a commitment to the links between clubs and local communities/schools. However, since then the neo-liberal rot has set in and, with it, the suspicion of corruption associated with sport as a media dominated *ethos*. For Bourdieu, it is the state which has led the way in this change of outlook; the relationship between the sports *field* and the *field* of power has thus radically been altered. Bourdieu sees this new morality of sport as nowhere better illustrated than in the way the Olympic Games has developed in recent years; again with state powers being instrumental in what occurs in its name. Here, an essentially amateur raison d'être has been replaced by a fierce form of international commercialism; even hosting the games is seen in terms of the economic gain from increased tourism and associated commercial opportunities. Even what is included and excluded in the games, what takes place (and when and where), what is shown and what is not, is all decided according to a logic of sport commercialism, itself determined by sponsoring organizations – TV broadcasters, sportswear manufacturers, advertising agencies, and so forth. The whole way the games are presented is, therefore, shaped by global sports politics; a form of industrialization of the production of sport, condoned by the *field* of power – political, commercial, financial – which has its parallel in the international arts market, with its associated players (agents, critics, gallery owners, curators, artists). For Bourdieu, it is not simply the change in the form of structural relations which is significant in this analysis, but the underlying shift in rationality which has given rise to it: one from universalistic and social to one that is commercial and individual. The result is often more sport: more matches, more TV, more payment, higher salaries, more transfer, and with it more corruption, drug-taking and commercial interference – over which presides a media oligarchy, bloated and drunk by the scope of its own domination. Of course, the effects are differential according to different sports. In order to understand how, we need to look at the structure of the sports *field* itself.

The sports field

In order to understand sport in terms of it being a *field*, it is firstly important to conceive of society as a multidimensional *social space* (see Hardy 2012: 229–249). From this Bourdieusian perspective, we each pass through a range of contexts, some of which are *fields* – cultural, educational, professional, and so on – others are not. The *social space* that includes sport is clearly a very large and diffuse entity, involving both sport consumption and production, and varies from the personal and amateur – private even – to large-scale conglomerates. There is a methodological challenge here as to how to therefore 'make sense' of sport in its particularity and entirety. The aim is to construct the structure of space of sporting practice. It might not be possible in every analysis to include the totality of sporting activities. However, in choosing one area it is possible to say something indicative about all the others. In this way, one can move from the particular to the general and back: 'Methodological problems disappear when one invests a large-scale theoretical problematic within an empirical object well constructed with reference to both overall space in which it is situated, and capable of being mastered by means available' (Bourdieu 1994/1987: 160). What results is a kind of 'mapping of the field', a 'structural framework' capable of illustrating the relational structures both within and between sports constituted as *fields*. For Bourdieu, we can only understand space as structure, and therefore change in structural terms. One of the conditions of all *fields* is their search for autonomy, and we can see this in the public and private associations which are set up to manage individual sports and sporting activities. In other words, it is necessary to take account, not simply of the nature of the sporting activity, but the 'objective potentialities' (Bourdieu 1984/1979: 217) of different institutional practices, and the social uses that such can be put through positional and distributed *symbolic power* within the overall structure. Indeed, for Bourdieu one of the functions of sport is to maintain a certain *social space*, one which links sporting practice (modalities of practice) and positions in that space. There is, then, a kind of homology between sport production and consumption – supply and demand – models of practice, rules, equipment, and so on, and the dispositions individuals hold to make use of them. This is a dual structure between the space of possible practices and the space of dispositional practice: technical properties, body relations, and so on, and relational, structural properties. In a way, the space of producers (*field* agents and institutions that contribute to supply) therefore reproduces the space of consumers: 'they are predisposed to give voice to the more or less conscious expectations of corresponding fractions of the lay public and by objectifying these expectations, realize them' (Bourdieu 1993/84: 131). How all this evolves over time is also accountable for in terms of historical struggles, both within and between sports, and those who practice or watch them. Another way of looking at sport would be as a synchronic structure symptomatic of a certain social hierarchy and the diachronic evolution over time with respect to its dispositional needs. Bourdieu wants to avoid a direct correlation between social position and aesthetic/sporting position and instead move to one of social position and dispositions. This is what is institutionalized in professional and amateur associations charged with managing the supply of various sports in terms of such dispositional demands. Clubs, associations, institutions and federations of sport then all act in terms of their own protected *interest* (see Grenfell 2012: 151–168), which itself is based on a certain physical/intellectual *ethos*. Such associations confer their own *legitimacy* and systems of *consecration* in controlling what is valued and recognized – *doxa* – within each particular sport. Clearly, not all sports are the same – the golf club is not the football association, pétanque is not bridge – but they all conform to this same logical necessity to manage the interests of their sub-field according to a common logic of *field* practice. They do this by institutionalizing 'rules', 'laws' and 'regulations' of the game; in other words, a common code of practice for both individual sports and their public management. Again, it is worth stressing that 'not all sports are equal', and there is literally a world of difference between small minority sports with their restricted audiences and the large-scale game of international significance and mass appeal. For Bourdieu, such differences need to be seen in terms of their structural relationship to each other – a kind of social hierarchy of value constituted in terms of the volume and configuration of various forms of *capital* (cultural, economic and social) – and the homologous structures present in consumption and practice to be found in society as a whole, which themselves are a reflection of the overall structure of the social class–based world. This leads us to the individual subjectivities to be found in sport.

The sporting habitus

As noted above, the third level of any '*field* analysis' from a Bourdieusian perspective would be to consider the *habitus* of those occupying positions in the – in this case sporting – *field*; that is *habitus* in terms of patterns of individual subjectivities and the principled *dispositions* of practice manifest in occupying certain positions in the *field* (and the subsequent *capital* holdings) and their underlying logic of practice. In sport, it is again useful to think of this in terms of various forms of *relations* or structural engagement; for example, those managing sports, those practicing sports and those consuming sports. So, it would not be surprising if, as is often the case, individual sporting associations were managed by individuals whose *habitus* included extensive experience in the sport itself – ex-professional players, for example, or those who have attained recognizable success in the sport (ex-champions). This is particularly so in the case of minority sports with restricted audiences. But even in a sport like football, managers are generally former players with established pedigrees on the *field*. Similar champions of the sport may sidestep to other positions within the sporting *field* – coaches for example – or indeed shift to parallel associated *fields* such as media – as 'expert' commentators – or the *field* of power (the ex-Olympic British runner Sebastian Coe now sits in the House of Lords and directed the British Olympic Games of 2012). Such overlaps between the sporting *field* and other *fields* in terms of the *habitus* of those who manage therein become more apparent the larger and more successful the sport is in terms of public appeal and therefore financial revenue. For example, after a certain threshold of size is gained, it is not uncommon to bring in experts from the media and financial sectors to manage the *field* associations; indeed, such "Trojan horses" act as the vehicle for importing a whole different business *ethos* to the game, and one which can have significant consequences in terms of the way it is played and managed.

As previously noted, sport itself is of interest only to those with a certain amount of leisure on their hands – either as players or consumers – or at least until a sportsman or -woman goes professional. As such, sporting activity of any sort implies a break from an empirical imperative to work and live. Sport is always in some ways 'for sport's sake' to a certain degree; whether in the training of the individual body, or in the simple act of sporting entertainment. However, to re-emphasize, such makes it no less susceptible to social derivation in terms of choice of sport and how it is pursued. As stated above, active involvement in some form of regular sporting activity increases as we ascend the social hierarchy and the empirical imperative to simply live and work decreases. There is also a social distinction between 'elite' sports – bridge, polo, hunting – and mass sports such as football (positions, we must keep in mind, are constantly in flux). Engaging with sport – either as a consumer or a practitioner – is never the single disposition within an individual *habitus* but is part and product of an entire world view. In *Distinction* (1984/1979) Bourdieu offers a social critique of the judgement of taste. In it, and somewhat following on from these previous lines, Bourdieu demonstrates how differences in the consumption of sport – either watching it or playing it, along with a whole host of other cultural pursuits – are a homologous reflection of the social hierarchy. There is, then, a further philosophical argument that needs to be appreciated in order to understand why and how this is so. Bourdieu's main philosophical critique in *Distinction* is with Kant's view of aesthetics. Kant can be seen as the founding father of contemporary aesthetics, defined in his terms as 'transcendental', or a 'pure', 'disinterested' gaze. This subjective position (although of course 'objectively' shared with others similarly positioned in *social space*) is juxtaposed to the immediate sensual pleasure of the senses. Bourdieu sees this opposition in the way refined classical music or art stands somewhat in a contrary position to popular music and painting. For Bourdieu, the former is a mark of distinction, or limited membership, and restricted to the upper echelons of the social hierarchy. Ipso facto, we expose and reveal our social provenance in what we like and dislike in art and music. Of course, this extends to sport where, in theory at least, the popular is expressed in playing and watching sports of mass appeal as opposed to the opposite. Again, such choices also reveal an entire relationship to the body and mind; sensational or contemplative, immediate or deferred, hedonistic or ascetic. The point is that ultimately such predispositions are embedded (embodied in) and shaped by individual *habitus* which itself is a product of social positioning and formation along the lines of the *interest* and *ethos* associated with particular trajectories. So, we can understand that the way we play and consume sport is also an expression of our entire ontology, or being. A sense of fair play, the ethics of leadership, self-help, the power of brute force, discipline and training versus natural talent, the physical versus the intellectual; all are a dispositional expression of *habitus* as a kind of social karma constituting what we do and why. Indeed, for Bourdieu, it is no less than a reflection of two distinct relations to the social world, which itself reflects two distinct relations to the natural: one wild and natural, the other organized and cultivated (1984/1979: 220).

Sport and participant objectivation

I began this chapter by suggesting that a Bourdieusian approach to sport needed to be seen in terms of a 'metanoia', a new gaze, or way of seeing it. Subsequently, I have set out a framework for such a 'gaze' in terms of methodological issues of constructing sport as a research object and *field* analysis. At certain points, I have stressed the way Bourdieu's theory of practice needs to be appreciated in terms of underlying epistemology, one that encourages us to 'break' not only from the pre-given in terms of common sense, but common traditions in the social sciences, including the subjective and phenomenological/interpretative and the objective/nomothetic. Yet, there is a fourth 'break' which Bourdieu insists upon – from scientific knowledge itself – and it is at this point that participant objectivation plays a critical role. No less than the sportsman or sports viewer, the enquiries of researchers into the nature of sport involve, for Bourdieu, a certain relation to the empirical world – one of distant, scientific gaze, which itself implies a degree of leisure – what he terms *skholè*. Such a positional relation justifies and legitimizes itself in terms of 'objective, scientific knowledge'. However, according to Bourdieu's own epistemological tenets and theory of practice, this cannot be so since any activity includes its own systems of orthodoxy and *interests*. Consequently, 'knowledge without a knowing subject', as proposed by the philosopher of scientific knowledge Karl Popper, would be anathema to Bourdieu. He eschews any claim to universal knowledge. Instead, there is the necessity to 'objectify the objectifying subject' in their presumption of objectivity. The way to do this is for the knowledge claimant to *disarm* themselves by turning the very tools of analysis – *habitus*, *field*, *capital*, and so on – back on themselves. In so doing, Bourdieu claims, one consequently avoids the 'scholastic fallacy' of presuming universal knowledge by laying bare the presuppositions at heart of their endeavour, and therefore the limits of truth. Research activity – the scholastic gaze – necessitates three key presuppositions. First, there is the presupposition associated with a particular position in the *social space*: the particular *habitus* of the researcher as constituted by life trajectory and consequent cognitive structures which have shaped their thought and action. Second, there is the orthodoxy of a particular *field* site of enquiry – and its own *doxa*, or conventional ways of thinking – which encourages the researcher to think in these specific terms (the different contributions to this volume are a good example of these). Third, there is the said relation of *skholè* which itself implies a certain 'non-empirical' relation to the world. The danger here is to see the research practice itself as substantively constructed rather than relationally praxeologic.

Such participant objectivation may be included in our enquiries on individual sports themselves and, already, we see that Bourdieu's radical epistemology, as embedded in the three-phase methodology and three-level field analysis, can be brought to bear on the other chapters to this volume in terms of a critique of the way sport is constructed and thought about in each contribution, and thus the consequent knowledge of the same. However necessary as participant objectivation is for the would-be researcher of sport, it is not simply a scholarly endeavour, one which aims to construct a 'science of sport'. The metanoia of which we write is just as available to those involved in the *field* – or sport – as those who study it. Indeed, from his earliest work, Bourdieu writes that 'sociology would be not worth an hour's trouble . . . if it did not restore to people the meaning of their action', and, of course, in so doing alter their relationship to it: to objectify and thus understand the social forces which act on individuals and oneself. This is true for sportsmen and -women themselves, as well as those involved in managing and administering sport. For Bourdieu, sport is ultimately about the production of value, and individual sports are successful in their own terms in affecting a twofold social production: first, as an actual public event in a stadium or sports field involving participants, trainers, judges/referees and doctors; and second, in images created for their communities and spectators. Participants at all levels could take control through the instruments offered by Bourdieu – *habitus*, *field*, *capital* and so forth – and, in so doing, bring to light the mechanisms behind this two-step social construction of sport and how it operates through subjective/objective relations involving sport, the media and commercialism found and in *field* manoeuvres through *capital* configurations and transformations. Such would constitute a reflexive objectivity *of* sport, or indeed a reflexive subjectivity *towards* it, somehow 'torn out' of what passes as the 'commonsensical' view of sport. This would allow the collectivity to maximize the potential of universalism offered by such an epistemological stance, activated in practice. However, literally, there is no *interest* in doing so: for the successful, since they benefit and are therefore content that a non-reflexive relationship to sport should continue; and for the unsuccessful, since their lack of success removes the right and power of speech – the *legitimacy* – to describe sport in this way or indeed any way publicly. As such, for both researcher and successful sportsman, this level of understanding implies disarming themselves of the very things that have made them successful. Why, then, should they do it? Bourdieu: 'We should seek the truth without hesitation; and if we refuse it, we show that we value the esteem of men more than the search for truth' (Bourdieu 2000/1997: 239).

Conclusion

This chapter has sought to offer a brief account of Bourdieu on sport. In so doing, it has stressed issues of construction, thus definition, and methodology, and I have used a three-phase framework and three-level *field* analysis to show how the same epistemological principles are actualized in different – but congruent – ways throughout any enquiry about sport. Looked at another way, we can see that a Bourdieusian approach to sport immediately comes up against a series of dualisms, each implying one of several levels of actualization: aristocratic versus bourgeois; cultural capital versus physical capital; elite versus popular; physical versus intellectual; conscious versus unconscious; individual versus group; contemplative versus sensual; amateur versus professional; player versus spectator; producer versus consumer; religious versus secular; young versus old; instrumental body versus style life; immediate versus deferred gratification; interested versus disinterested; change versus stasis; subjectivity versus objectivity; empirical versus reflexive, and so on. Each of these, individually and as a group, raises issues of theory and practice which Bourdieu's praxeological perspective seeks both to break with and to go beyond. Critical to adopting such a perspective with respect to sport is to set it within *Field Theory* and to use the conceptual tools that Bourdieu developed to navigate within it. What we then end up with is a kind of Bourdieusian topography of sport, an epistemological mapping of the *field* in all its manifestations. The promise of such a 'new gaze' on sport is that a more authentic understanding of it results. Clearly, such potential needs to be held up and read against the other chapters of this book in understanding sport, its causes and consequences and the value a Bourdieusian perspective finally has over any other.

Notes

1 It is my practice to quote the date of publication of Bourdieu's works citing the English translation first, followed by the original date of French publication; this in order to encourage a 'socio-genetic reading' of Bourdieu (see Bourdieu 1993/1984). It allows ease of access to English texts for cross-checking and reference whilst keeping in mind the original date of derivation and thus both the socio-historical context of individual works as well as particular stages in the development of Bourdieu's thinking.

2 Since Bourdieu is often accused of determinism, I need immediately to point out that although Bourdieu did indeed argue that social contexts exist with their own orthodoxy and, in effect, this constituted 'rules of the game', the greater part of human action took place for him in terms of *strategic* action; in other words, semi-conscious manoeuvres, anticipations, behaviours formulated in terms of consequential advantageous positioning within the social hierarchy in terms of distributed *capital*.

3 It is my habit to use these in their italicized form as an aid to remembering that such terms come with a specific epistemological basis as distinct from their everyday usage.

References

Bourdieu, P. (1977/1972) *Outline of a Theory of Practice*, Cambridge: Cambridge University Press.
Bourdieu, P. (1982) *Leçon sur une leçon*, Paris: Les Editions de Minuit.
Bourdieu, P. (1984/79) *Distinction*, (trans. R. Nice). Oxford: Polity. - *La Distinction. Critique sociale du jugement*. Paris: Editions de Minuit.
Bourdieu, P (1990/1980) *The Logic of Practice*. Oxford: Polity Press.
Bourdieu, P. (1993b/1984) *Sociology in Question*, (trans. R Nice). London: Sage. - *Questions de sociologie*. Paris: Les Editions de Minuit.
Bourdieu, P. (1994/1987) *In Other Words: Essays Towards a Reflexive Sociology* (Trans. M Adamson). Oxford: Polity. - *Choses dites*. Paris: Les Editions de Minuit.
Bourdieu, P. (1994) *Choses dites*. Paris: Les Editions de Minuit.
Bourdieu, P. (2000/1997) *Pascalian Meditations* (trans. R. Nice). Oxford: Polity Press. - *Méditations pascaliennes*. Paris: Seuil.
Bourdieu, P. (2007/1998) 'The State, Economics and Sport', *Sport in Society*, 1(2): 15–21.
Bourdieu, P with Wacquant, L (1989) 'Towards a Reflexive Sociology: A Workshop with Pierre Bourdieu', *Sociological Theory*, 7(1): 26–63.
Bourdieu, P. (with L. Wacquant) (1992) *Réponses. Pour une anthropologie réflexive*. Paris: Seuil.
Brown, D. (2010) 'An Economy of Gendered Practices? Learning to Teach Physical Education from the Perspective of Pierre Bourdieu's Embodied Sociology', *Sport, Education and Society*, 10(1): 3–23.
Cacérès, B. (1967) *Histoire de l'éducation populaire*. Paris: Seuil.
Hardy, C. (2012) 'Social Space', in M. Grenfell (ed.) *Pierre Bourdieu: Key Concepts*, Stockfield, UK: Acumen.
Hunter, L. (2010) 'Bourdieu and the Social Space of the PE Class: Reproduction of Doxa through Practice', *Sport, Education and Society*, 1(2): 175–192.
Grenfell, M. (ed.) (2012) *Pierre Bourdieu: Key Concepts*, Stockfield, UK: Acumen.

Noble, G. and Watkins, M. (2010) 'So, How Did Bourdieu Learn to Play Tennis? Habitus, Consciousness and Habituation', *Cultural Studies*, 17(3): 520–539.

Seippel, O. (2006) 'The Meanings of Sport: Fun, Health, Beauty or Community', *Sport in Society*, 9(1): 51–70.

Stempel, C. (2005) 'Adult Participation Sports as Cultural Capital: A Test of Bourdieu's Theory of the Field of Sports', *International Review for the Sociology of Sport*, 40: 411–441.

Thorpe, H. (2009) 'Bourdieu, Feminism and Female Physical Culture: Gender Reflexivity and the Habitus-Field Complex', *Sociology of Sport Journal*, 26: 491–516.

Wacquant, L. (2000) *Corps et Âme: carnets ethnographiques d'un apprenti boxeur*. Marseille: Agone.

Warde, A. (2011) 'Cultural Capital and the Place of Sport', *Cultural Trends*, 15(2/3): 107–122.

Williams, S. (1995) 'Theorising Class, Health and Lifestyles: Can Bourdieu Help Us?', *Sociology of Health and Illness*, 17(5): 577–604.

8

NIKLAS LUHMANN, SYSTEM THEORY AND SPORT

Ansgar Thiel and Jan Ove Tangen

Introduction

Sociological system theory is closely linked with Niklas Luhmann, a renowned sociologist, who published countless books and articles on this subject, mostly in German. Luhmann was influenced by the phenomenologist Edmund Husserl and the sociologist Talcott Parsons, but also by authors and thinkers like Herbert Simon, Robert K. Merton, Erving Goffmann, Humberto Maturana, Gregory Bateson, George Spencer-Brown and Fritz Heider (Stichweh 2011). When Luhmann joined the University of Bielefeld, he was reportedly asked about his research plans. His answer was: 'Theory of society, term of 30 years, no costs'.

For a long time, system theory was almost unknown in international sociology, but in recent years the interest in system theory has continuously increased. Nevertheless, most system theoretical analyses of sport are still found in German-speaking or Scandinavian countries.

System theory differs from other sociological approaches at least in three fundamental assumptions. First, in methodology, system theory is 'radically anti-humanistic, radically anti-regional, and radically constructivist' (Luhmann 1997: 12).[1] System theory 'no longer speaks of objects but of distinctions' (1997: 28). In this regard, system theory focuses on the observer who 'is defined by the scheme on which he or she bases his or her observations, and thus on the distinctions he or she uses' (1997: 83). The blind spot (or contingency) of an observation can only be reflected (as a relativized reflection) from the perspective of a second-order observer (who might be a social scientist).

Second, 'the system of society is [. . .] not characterized by a specific 'nature', let alone a specific morality, but solely by the operation that produces and reproduces society: communication' (1997: 35). Through communication the social system constitutes its elements and its basic operations for itself (Luhmann 1984: 25, 1986, 1990). It produces, reproduces and organizes the elements of which it consists. Everything that functions as an element cannot be determined independently from the system.

Third, the universal medium of all psychic and social systems is meaning (Luhmann 1997: 23). Meaning constitutes the boundary between a system and its environment. 'Yet what is won with the differentiation between system and the environment is the possibility to understand the individual as part of the social environment who is at the same time more complex and free than he or she would possibly be by considering him or her as a part of society. This is because the environment in comparison to the system is the very field of differentiation, which indeed shows higher complexity and less regulated order' (Luhmann 1984: 289).

Methodologically, concepts provide the basis for research in system theory. Scientific knowledge is understood to be always based on the construction of terms, which differentiate an observed object from everything else. In this sense, the methodological paradigm of system theory is to draw distinctions.

On empirical research, Luhmann (1997) not only criticizes the traditional mindset of causality by stressing that every effect could have an infinite amount of causes, and that every cause can have an infinite amount of effects. Luhmann also argues that the conventions of quantitative empirical research have fundamental shortcomings. Empirical observations must draw distinctions in order to name the phenomenon that they want to observe. Nevertheless, with this differentiation, only one side, namely the inner side, is identified. Consequently, the other side of the differentiation, the remainder, will always be carried along through this distinction without being identified. This means that the entity of difference within any personal observation is the blind spot of empirical research. This also holds true for the observations of empirical social scientists. For Luhmann, empirical research through the use of variables cannot unveil reality. Rather, this research only validates the researcher's constructions, because there is only one side included, while the other, excluded, side is given no further attention (Luhmann 1997: 41). Thus, for the system theoretical perspective, the coincidence of empiricism and reality is empirically indeterminate and so 'has to be treated as random' (1997: 41). Systematic empirical research by using variables may notwithstanding be useful for elaborating theory. But then the researcher must understand the results of empirical research as questions which stimulate theory, rather than as 'answers in the sense of a secured knowledge from that point onwards' (1997: 41).

From the outset, the use of functionalist methods played a central role in Luhmann's long-term project (Luhmann 1970). Luhmann's version of this particular methodology differs from the ways in which functionalism and the functionalist method had been otherwise defined and utilized in the social sciences (Knudsen 2010). The functionalist method is an observational technique that produces observations by means of the distinction between problems and solutions (Knudsen 2010). As a comparative and heuristic perspective, it enables us to ask 'expansive questions' about how society solves its problems. In this regard, Luhmann does not ask about causal relations between problems and solutions. From an evolutionary perspective, society does not plan to change from, for example, a nomadic to a settler lifestyle. Instead, evolution involves waiting on useable coincidences (Luhmann 1997: 417). Coincidences develop from deviance to differentiation mostly without intention. Consequently, it is impossible to find definite causes for evolutionary achievements, such as agriculture, writing, print or telecommunications (1997: 508). Luhmann accordingly states that for every effect there are always many possible causes. Solutions therefore are always contingent, so that for every solution there is a functional equivalent. For example: functional systems are functional equivalents to solving the problem of social complexity; trust and distrust are functional equivalents to the problem of establishing expectations about the future.

In the following, we shall discuss some of the core assumptions of system theory before providing an overview of system theoretical research in sport.

Social systems in Luhmann's theory

Communications as basic elements of social systems

Importantly, unlike action-theoretical approaches, system theory argues that the social system does not account for the differentiation of people, but rather for the contexts of communication

(Luhmann 1981: 35). Indeed, system theory is a theory of communication. However, unlike a common-sense understanding of communication, system theory understands communication, not as a simple sender-receiver relation, but as a processing of selections (Luhmann 1984: 194). Forms of communication consist of three integral selections: information, message and understanding (1984: 196). First, information means selecting something that is intended to be communicated out of an infinite range of possibilities. Second, the sender of the information (named 'Alter' by Luhmann) has to choose a behaviour with which she communicates information to the receiver ('Ego'). Third, the receiver ('Ego') has to understand the difference between information (the informative value of a message) and the manner of communication (the reasons why a message was given in the specific way). Understanding is the basis of follow-up communication (1984, 198).

In system theory, social systems are defined as consisting of meaningfully connected communications. Social systems are found at all levels of social relationship: society, organization and interaction. The function of social systems in general lies in the reduction of world complexity. The structures of social systems (as 'expectation structures') lead perception by selection. They give meaning to communication in a specific social context by including a certain understanding of communication while all other possible understandings are excluded. This selection of meanings makes social situations predictable: social systems create regularity between individuals, who can act regularly despite their individuality (Luhmann 1984).

Social systems for Luhmann are autopoietic systems, like cognitive or biological systems (Luhmann 1984, 1995a). Autopoietic systems operate autonomously. Although they obtain energy from their environment, they are organizationally and informationally closed. This means that they cannot be determined by environmental influences. A system's environment can only *irritate* the system. Sustainable system–environment relations are established on the basis of a so-called structural coupling. This means that the respective systems establish structures of expectation, which make them susceptible to specific irritations. However, each system creates meaning for this irritation (that is the 'content of information') with reference to the system's own logic. Hence, a system's state is created by the system itself, and not by its environment.

Individuals and social systems

Helmut Willke, another renowned German system theorist, described Luhmann's depiction of communications as the basic operators of society as a 'communicative turning point' within sociology (Willke 2000). Neither actions nor persons constitute a social system. Rather, actions constitute a person's attributable, special case of communication. Persons (with their cognitions) participate in (but do not completely merge into) diverse social systems. The experiences and actions of people are consequently allocated to the environment, more precisely the 'inner environment', of a system, because neither is entirely controllable by any social system.

The position that social systems are constituted not by persons but by communication, is a common criticism of system theory. Critics often say that in 'inhumane' system theory, the person and her acts are ignored. However, this is based on a misunderstanding: persons are not ignored, but they do not constitute social systems by acting on the basis of their thoughts. System theory does not doubt that individuality, and individual values and needs, exist. However, it is not the persons themselves, with their individual consciousness, who constitute the social world, but rather something that establishes order between individuals. Therefore the focus of system theoretical analysis is on the structures and processes which create order between individuals, or respectively, which are responsible for individuals to act according to social rules and conventions.

Luhmann (1995b: 166) states that a sociology which, in fact, has the social as its object of study, has to accept that no individual (as a complex actor in multiple social contexts) can be integrated entirely in social systems. At the same time, the individual 'is not the measure of society anymore. This idea of humanism cannot continue' (Luhmann 1984: 289). Luhmann states that one cannot seriously claim that society could be formed on the model of a human being (with the head on the top etc.).

Functional systems

Luhmann (1984) distinguishes between three types of society that are differentiated along segmental, stratified and functional lines. The increase in levels of social complexity reflects different degrees of social development (Luhmann 1984; see also Cachay and Thiel 2000). First, segmentally differentiated societies are, as a rule, archaic societies, consisting of small social units such as households, families or tribes. These units may be of different size and are usually interconnected with each other. Segmentally differentiated societies are characterized by oral communication, and role differentiation is low; role specialization does exist, but only on a low level, such as in the positions of patriarch, warrior or shaman. Second, stratified societies are found especially in ancient and medieval times, and feature higher degrees of differentiation. They are hierarchically organized, based on clearly separated layers, and the forms of communication in these societies changed over time, through the development of writing and the invention of printing. Third, functional differentiation is associated with the most complex, modern forms of society. They develop functional systems, which take over socially important functions by specializing in dealing with specific societal problems such as curing diseases, ruling behaviour through law or educating people. Functional systems are operationally autonomous, which serves to increase levels of complexity. They establish their own developmental logic as well as a specific structure, more precisely specific rules and a characteristic differentiation of roles and organizations. Due to the autonomy of functional systems, modern society has no definite central coordinating mechanism. Not even the political system, which is responsible for delivering collective goods, is dominant, and therefore cannot determine the development of other functional systems.

Functional systems separate themselves from their environment by means of binary codes, and in this way they maintain the process of self-reproduction. Binary codes are nothing more than basic orienting differences, disjunctions to enable the understanding of communication, against the background of an infinite quantity of possible meanings for any act of communication (Luhmann 1975: 172f.). Codes therefore reduce complexity regarding the content of information, which enables meaningful follow-up communication to occur (1975: 173).

The form of the binary code is always 'two-sided'. Binary codes provide two versions for all existing information, that is to say a positive and a negative version, respectively (Luhmann 1975: 172). Codes promote understanding of meaning between the participating parties in communication. Communication is in principle poly-contextual and may be understood differently depending on context. Lastly, the purpose of binary codes is to allow communication to be understood as belonging to a specific context of meaning. A communication belonging to the legal system, for example, is recognized as such a communication only with reference to the guiding binary code of 'legal/illegal'.

Codes are operationalized by 'programmes'. While the binary code allows it to recognize communication as a part of the social system, programmes offer 'additional semantic criteria, under which a positive or a negative value may be assigned correctly' (Luhmann 1997: 362). For example: the abstract code 'legal/illegal' is implemented in practical contexts by correspondent programmes, such as statutes, treaties, agreements and so on.

Organizations

In system theory, an organization is a specific form of social system in which decisions form the basic unit of communication (Luhmann 2000). Organizations develop and reproduce themselves by communicating decisions. The structures of any organization are built upon so-called decision premises; in other words, decisions about decisions (Luhmann 2000). Decision premises, such as rules of conduct in an organization, define how following decisions have to be made or which decisions are allowed and which are not. Luhmann differentiates two basic types of decision premises: decidable and undecidable. Decidable premises are decision programs, communication channels and personnel decisions. Decision programs define the objectives of the organization and the methods used to achieve them. Communication channels define positions, hierarchies and decision-making procedures, and distribute tasks. Personnel decisions comprise, for example, decisions about how positions are filled, including recruitment and role assignment (Luhmann 2000). Undecidable premises are bundled into the so-called organizational culture. Organizational culture comprises the organization's tacit assumptions, or, in other words, the unspoken rules of decision-making that are not voiced or written down.

Interactions

Interactions – as the third basic form of social systems according to Luhmann (1984: 551–592) – have their own operations and structures, different from both 'society' and 'organizations'. This kind of social system differs from the other two in particular with regard to 'time'. Interaction systems are temporary systems in which persons meet and communicate face to face. Luhmann uses the concept of 'episode' to illustrate an important difference between 'society', 'organization' and 'interaction'. Interactions are episodes in the ongoing processes of society. Interactions are discontinuous; they are concerned with the 'here and now' (Kieserling 1999). The start and end of an interaction are like *caesurae* in the autopoiesis of society. For example, a vast amount of lectures are given simultaneously in different universities across the society. But every lecture starts and ends at a given time. Lectures do not last as long as the universities in which they take place, nor is a lecture as long-lived as the local community that hosts the university.

In interaction systems, all that can be considered 'present' is included; sometimes interaction systems will determine among the participating persons what shall be considered present. The participants' bodies acquire a prominent position in order to distribute relevance and possibilities for communication. With 'presence' as the main criterion, processes of perception become prominent in the creation of the interaction system. Luhmann argues that perception, even if it is first and foremost a psychological way of acquiring information, can be a social phenomenon. The interaction system sorts out events or occurrences on whether or not these are perceived by others. Interaction becomes an articulation of double contingency as a person does not know the consciousness of the other nor vice versa, but the person sees that the other sees, and, possibly, the person sees what the other sees. Accordingly, interaction systems are very sensitive to disturbances on the level of perception.

Studying sport from a system theoretical perspective, all three forms of social system are relevant for close examination: sport as a functional system, sport as an organization and sport as interaction. It would also be of interest to study how each kind of system relates to the others, as well as to both society at large and the individual. In fact, there are already some studies that have taken steps in that direction.

System theory and sport

The system theoretical perspective on sport has had growing influence in the sociology of sport since the late 1980s (Bette 1999). Key contributions to the development of German sport sociology were forwarded by Klaus Cachay (1988) on sport and society and Karl-Heinrich Bette (2005 [orig. 1989]) on the role of the body in modern society. Both works claimed to develop a theory of the evolution of sport in modern society. Cachay's analysis starts with the so-called take-off of the health and education systems, arguing that physical activity played a central role in subsequent medical and educational theories of the eighteenth century. The invention of 'artificial bodily practices' such as medical and educational treatments led to structural formations at the social, temporal and factual levels, such as facilities for gymnastic exercises, curricula of physical education or teachers for physical education: what in consequence led to the development of an autonomous functional system. Bette (2005) examines the role of the body in modern societies. From a system theoretical perspective, he states that the simultaneity of body repression and body appreciation was a generative mechanism for the development of sport in the context of a wider civilizing process within society. Bette views 'the modern citation of the body in sport as a counter strategy against the gradual fragmentation of reality in modern society' (2005: 255). Sport, for Bette, represents the concrete and familiar in an abstract world. In modern society, social interactions are often de-individualized (e.g. bureaucracy, payment transactions, work organization), and individual 'life worlds' are compartmentalized and 'over-routinized' (Bette 2005: 254). This leads to a fragmentation of identity and to a loss of body awareness. By offering physically based social interactions and allowing sensual experiences, sport can help to compensate for these deficiencies.

Later analyses also take into consideration the differentiation of the sport system. The sociologist Rudolf Stichweh (1990) characterizes sport in modern society as a unity of the three fields of 'athletics, physical education and sports' that is internally divided into subsystems like elite sports, competitive sports and leisure sports. Tangen (1997) analyzes how sport developed into a functionally differentiated subsystem in 'modern' society to be 'the sport of the society'. Tracing the 'roots' of the sport system back to the time of the Mesopotamian king Gilgamesh (circa 2500 BC), Tangen describes how communication about 'who is the best' unfolded and was accepted in segmented, stratified and functionally differentiated societies. Using the functional analysis described earlier, he claims that sport solved different problems in these different forms of society. In functionally differentiated society, sport solves the problem of how society may assess the consequences and advantages of 'progress' without proposing significant risks for the society at large. How 'new' sports develop is analyzed by Bette (2004) through the example of extreme sports. According to Bette, risk sports provide 'parallel milieus' in an 'over-routinized' world that is restricted by an extensive set of rules. Risk sports are thus to be regarded as a 'homage to life' because they create a feeling of vitality, a sort of pleasant horror.

Many system theoretical publications on sport deal with the question of which binary code characterizes the sports system. In the late 1980s, Uwe Schimank (1988), a German sociologist, introduced the term 'code victory/defeat' to characterize sport. In principle, Schimank means competition-oriented sport, whose developmental dynamics are characterized by competing for victory (cf. Tangen 1997, 2004b; Cachay and Thiel 2000; Bette and Schimank 1995; Schimank 2005). Stichweh (1990: 379) contradicts this construction by stressing expressly that there is 'a multitude of performed actions in modern sports which are in no way structured agonally'. For Stichweh, sport is the functional system that comprises all actions that give meaning in order to communicate physical performance (1990: 379f.). Stichweh therefore identifies the code performing/not performing as the distinguishing mark of sport, whereby 'new' leisure activities, such as inline skating or parkour, are described as well as traditional competitive sports, such as football or basketball. Tangen (1997, 2004b) suggests that modern sport has a secondary code of improvement/decline in addition to the primary code of win/lose. This forces the system to reflect continuously on how its performance relates to both codes win/lose and improve/decline, and all possible combinations of these values: for example, how to win next time since we won (or lost) this time and were well (or badly) prepared? By using two codes, the sport system operates more successfully with regard to its autopoietic organization.

Tangen (2004a, 2004c) analyzes how 'expectations structure communication' in ways that take material form: for example, as buildings, roads, parks and so forth. According to Tangen, sport facilities are nothing but 'embedded' expectations. The lines painted on the bottom of the swimming pool, the poles on the slalom course, the white lines around the football field, the ski track; these are all embedded expectations. Most people 'understand' the meaning of these embedded expectations and 'answer' them either by swimming along the lines in the pool, throwing the ball in when it has passed the sidelines and following the ski track; or by refusing to participate in these kinds of communication.

In a later study Tangen (2010) shows that sport participation has to be seen as a mechanism of inclusion/exclusion. On the one hand, the sport system selectively includes those actions that are relevant to the double code of win/lose and improve/decline, and excludes all others by demanding membership, offering training and coaching, looking for talents and producing beneficial internal milieus for potential participants. On the other hand, the individual decides (mainly unconsciously on the basis of his or her embodied experiences with sport) whether to meet or reject the sport system's expectations.

The problems caused by the increasing grade of inclusion in the German sport system is discussed by Schimank (1992). In a very influential paper, he discusses the 'inclusion dilemma' of voluntary sports organizations in Germany. German sport organizations differentiated their offers in order to be open for the entire population (health sports, trend sports, physical activity for the elderly). This strategy led to more societal relevance but, at the same time, to a loss of systemic unity.

In recent years, research has been conducted into what happens when two social systems engage in mutual contact. Cachay and Thiel (2000) analyze the structural couplings of the sport system with other functional systems. They argue that the sport system not only benefits from other functional systems of society, such as economy, politics, mass media or education, but also fosters their development by providing entertainment, news, images, business markets and so on. In a series of papers, Storm (2010, 2013) addresses the relationship between economic and sport systems. In his analysis he documents how traditional economic thinking about making profits does not quite fit the operations of professional sports clubs. Often such clubs struggle with low profitability and high costs. Storm shows that the main goal is to win, not to make profit. All resources are 'plowed into' the system, like buying players to better the teams' performances. Teubert *et al.* (2006) examine the structural coupling of elite sport and schools, specifically the extent to which network structures help athletes to cope with both sport- and school-related demands. With a comparable approach, Borggrefe, Cachay and Riedl (2009) evaluate the coupling of elite sport and universities.

Hansen (2010) uses the system theoretical perspective to analyze the relationship between the sport and political systems in regard to elite sport development in Norway; or, more precisely, the 'structural coupling' between Norwegian elite sport and its environment. He argues that the development of a new sport organization (Olympiatoppen), the development of an educational program for elite athletes, and hosting the Winter Olympics in Lillehammer in 1994, were important elements in the differentiation process of elite sport in Norway.

Ronglan (2000, 2010) followed the national Norwegian female handball team over a year in their preparation for the 1996 Olympic Summer Games in Atlanta, Georgia. Ronglan argues that the communication theoretical perspective makes it possible to see that a sports team does not consist of just one social system but a multiplicity of social interaction systems; mainly, 'the performance group', 'the group of friends' and 'the trade union'. One major finding is that even if the performance system is most important, the context of the other subsystems is equally important for understanding team dynamics. In a later work, he uses Luhmann's perspective to analyze coaching as communication (Rongland and Havang 2011).

Riedl and Cachay (2002) study the effects of the 'Bosman verdict' on the organization of team sports in Europe. Their focus here is on how the logic of a specific system may be hindered by the political system through the adoption of new laws. On 15 December 1995, in its 'Bosman verdict', the European Court of Justice confirmed the freedom of movement (without transfer fees) for out-of-contract players, and lifted all national restrictions on the recruitment on EU players in professional team sports. Riedl and Cachay state that this verdict had different effects, depending on context. Players gained more freedom of movement, while clubs lamented rising salaries. At the same time, clubs tended to recruit experienced foreign players, which led to decreasing chances for young professionals to compete at the top level.

A relatively new branch of system theory in sport is about the development of (voluntary) sports organizations (for example Thiel and Meier 2004; Thiel and Mayer 2009; Borggrefe, Cachay and Thiel, 2012). In these studies, voluntary sports clubs are defined as social systems based on their specific decision programmes, communication channels, their specific recruitment and assignment of personnel and specific forms of organizational culture. Voluntary sport clubs have specific charters, which define the club's purpose and membership rules. They have a specific differentiation of roles and functions, which are mainly based on voluntary engagement, and they have specific ways of finding officials, for example by searching among experienced members. The preservation of a specific club history plays a very important role in binding members to the club. By developing structures, the club's identity becomes independent of the concrete individuals who are members of the club. This allows voluntary sports clubs to cope with the entry and exit of members, although all clubs are widely dependent on and determined by individual engagement.

A very influential contribution in the German sociology of sport was advanced by Bette and Schimank (1995) through their system theoretical analysis of doping. In this study, doping behaviour is considered to be a result of social constraints. Bette and Schimank identify deviant behaviour as a structural effect of elite sport's social conditions. Athletes, who have to ultimately focus on their athletic career within a limited time frame in order to reach their athletic goals, are permanently at risk of engaging in deviant behavior. Focusing on training and competition leads to a 'biographical trap': the more athletes invest in their career, the more they have to lose if someone else performs better than them. The fact that doping is marked as a common behaviour by mass media makes deviance a strategy for avoiding disadvantages. Athletes expect other athletes to be doped, while doping by themselves becomes a dominant strategy. Considering the structural constraints of elite sport, Bette, Kühnle and Thiel (2012) are very skeptical about doping prevention strategies, such as education programmes or codes of ethics. In their system theoretical analysis, the expectation of being caught could lead to a reduction in doping cases. However, this would not only require a very tight control system, but also specific marketing strategies which brand that system as definitely effective. In Denmark, Wagner (2009) looked into the struggle for clean sport and the development of anti-doping strategies between 1960 and 2009. Combining Luhmann's theoretical perspective with Norbert Elias's game model and Michel Foucault's power and discourse analysis, Wagner advances a new and interesting view of how sport and society may try to cope with doping in sport.

System theoretical analyses are also used to study conflicts in sport. While early analyses (e.g. Cachay and Fritsch 1983) focus on the relevance of social structures for the genesis of conflicts, later studies of social conflicts in sport (e.g. Thiel 2002; Borggrefe 2008) rather ask for the mechanism of conflict processes. In the latter, conflicts are – based on Luhmann's conflict theory (1984) – defined as communicated contradictions. This decision allows us to focus on empirically observable processes of communication and to exclude non-communicated dissent. Social conflicts are considered as everyday social phenomena. They start with a communicated 'no', which answers a previous communication (Luhmann 1984: 530). Whether this 'no' is communicated verbally or nonverbally (as it can be in the case of fights or wars), or loudly or quietly, are all irrelevant issues (Thiel 2003). What counts is if the previous communication is understood as a 'no' by 'the other'. Lasting conflicts are considered to be social systems which are defined as meaningfully connected rows of communicated contradictions. Conflicts in sport are often provoked by so-called conflict potentials, which are built into the structures of the sport system, such as the rules of sport, the opportunities to exchange players, the co-existence of team and individual goals and so on. However, conflicts in sport can also be catalyzed by lasting political or ethnic conflicts (for example, in the former Yugoslavia, or the Rangers/Celtic rivalry in Scottish football). From a system theoretical perspective, such phenomena could be considered as a specific form of structural coupling, as conflicting expectation structures in the sport system's environment constitute conflict potentials in sport.

System theory is the basis for many more sociological analyses of sport. In this discussion, we have only been able to present a small segment of system theoretical analyses and authors. All of these studies have contributed to a new understanding of sport that otherwise could not have been observed.

Conclusion

Between 1963 and his death in 1998, Niklas Luhmann published over 50 books and hundreds of articles, all about particular aspects of society. The implications of his theory are both promising and frightening. The universalistic relevance of the concepts and the comparative demands of the functionalist method open up a research program so huge that many scholars refrain from using Luhmann's approach. The issue of whether system theory is indeed applicable to every sociological problem cannot be answered yet. However, the paradigm of 'systemic thinking' is gaining more and more attention in scientific circles, not only in sociology but also in pedagogy, psychology, management theory and even engineering. The future will show if this also holds true for international sport sociology.

Note

1 Translations of German citations have been made by Ansgar Thiel, Jan Ove Tangen and David Götz.

References

Bette, K.H. (1999) *Systemtheorie und Sport*, Frankfurt: Suhrkamp.
Bette, K.H. (2004) *X-treme. Zur Soziologie des Abenteuer – und Risikosports.* Bielefeld: transcript Verlag.
Bette, K.H. (2005/1989) *Körperspuren*, Berlin: Walter de Gruyter.

Bette, K.H., Kühnle, F. and Thiel, A. (2012) *Dopingprävention*, Bielefeld: transcript Verlag.

Bette, K.H. and Schimank, U. (1995) *Doping im Hochleistungssport*, Frankfurt: Suhrkamp.

Borggrefe, C. (2008) *Kommunikation im Spitzensport*, Schorndorf: Hofmann.

Borggrefe, C., Cachay, K. and Riedl, L. (2009) *Spitzensport und Studium, Eine organisationssoziologische Studie zum Problem dualer Karrieren*, Schorndorf: Hofmann.

Borggrefe, C., Cachay, K. and Thiel, A. (2012), 'Der Sportverein als Organisation', in M. Apelt and V. Tacke (eds) *Handbuch Organisationstypen*. (307–326) Wiesbaden: Springer.

Cachay, K. (1988) *Sport und Gesellschaft: Zur Ausdifferenzierung einer Funktion und ihrer Folgen*, Schorndorf: Hofmann.

Cachay, K. and Fritsch, W. (1983), 'Überlebensprobleme von Gruppen im Hochleistungssport', in F. Neidhardt (ed.) *Gruppensoziologie. Sonderheft 25/1983 der KZfSS*, Opladen: Juventa.

Cachay, K. and Thiel, A. (2000) *Soziologie des Sports*, Weinheim: Juventa.

Hansen, A.O. (2010) 'A System Theoretical Perspective on Elite Sport Development: The Case of Norway', in U. Wagner, R.K. Storm and J. Hoberman (eds) *Observing Sport: Modern System Theoretical Approaches*, Schorndorf: Hofmann.

Kieserling, A. (1999). *Kommunikation unter Anwesenden: Studien über Interaktionssysteme*, Frankfurt: Suhrkamp.

Knudsen, M. (2010) 'Surprised by Method: Functional Method and Systems Theory', *Forum Qualitative Sozialforschung/Forum: Qualitative Social Research*, 11(3); available at: http://www.qualitative-research.net/index.php/fqs/article/view/1556/3067.

Luhmann, N. (1970) *Aufsätze zur Theorie sozialer Systeme*, Opladen: Westdeutscher.

Luhmann, N. (1975) *Politische Planung: Aufsätze zur Soziologie von Politik und Verwaltung* (2. Aufl.), Opladen: Westdeutscher.

Luhmann, N. (1981) *Politische Theorie im Wohlfahrtsstaat*, München: Olzog.

Luhmann, N. (1984) *Soziale Systeme: Grundriss einer allgemeinen Theorie*, Frankfurt: Suhrkamp.

Luhmann, N. (1986) 'The Autopoiesis of Social Systems', in F. Geyer and J. van der Zouwen (eds) *Sociocybernetic Paradoxes*, London: Sage.

Luhmann, N. (1990) *Essays on Self-Reference*, New York: Columbia University Press.

Luhmann, N. (1995a) *Social Systems*, Stanford, CA: Stanford University Press.

Luhmann, N. (1995b) *Soziologische Aufklärung. Bd. 6: Die Soziologie und der Mensch*, Opladen: Westdeutscher.

Luhmann, N. (1997) *Die Gesellschaft der Gesellschaft. Bd. 1 und 2*, Frankfurt: Suhrkamp.

Luhmann, N. (2000) *Organisation und Entscheidung*, Opladen: Westdeutscher.

Riedl, L. and Cachay, K. (2002) *Bosman-Urteil und Nachwuchsförderung: Auswirkungen der Veränderung von Ausländerklauseln und Transferregelungen auf die Sportspiele*, Schorndorf: Hofmann.

Ronglan, L.T. (2000) *Gjennom Sesongen: En Sosiologisk Studie av det Norske Kvinnelandslaget i Håndball på og Utenfor Banen*, Oslo: Norges idrettshøgskole.

Ronglan, L.T. (2010) 'Grasping Complexity in Social Interaction', Schorndorf: Hofmann.

Ronglan, L.T., and Havang, Ø. (2011) 'Niklas Luhmann: Coaching as Communication', in R.L. Jones (ed.) *The Sociology of Sports Coaching*, London: Routledge.

Schimank, U. (1988), 'Die Entwicklung des Sports Zum Gesellschaftlichen Teilsystem', in R. Mayntz, B. Rosewitz, U. Schimank and R. Stichweh (eds) *Differenzierung und Verselbständigung. Zur Entwicklung gesellschaftlicher Teilsysteme*, Frankfurt: Campus.

Schimank, U. (1992) 'Größenwachstum oder soziale Schließung? Das Inklusionsdilemma des Breitensports', *Sportwissenschaft*, 22(1): 32–45.

Schimank, U. (2005) 'The Autonomy of Modern Sport: Dangerous and Endangered', *European Journal for Sport and Society*, 2(1): 25–33.

Stichweh, R. (1990) 'Sport: Ausdifferenzierung, Funktion, Code', *Sportwissenschaft*, 20: 373–389.

Stichweh, R. (2011) 'Niklas Luhmann' in G. Ritzer and J. Stepnisky (eds) *The New Blackwell Companion to Major Social Theorists*, Hoboken, NJ: Wiley.

Storm, R. (2010) 'Professional Team Sports Clubs and Profits: An Irreconcilable Combination?', in U. Wagner, R.K. Storm and J. Hoberman (eds) *Observing Sport: Modern System Theoretical Approaches*, Schorndorf: Hofmann.

Storm, R. (2013) *Kommercielle Sportsklubber: Følelser eller Forretning?*, Ph.D. thesis, Odense: Syddansk Universitet.

Tangen, J.O. (1997) *Samfunnets Idrett: En Sosiologisk Analyse av Idrett som Sosialt System: Dets Evolusjon og Funksjon fra Arkaisk til Moderne Tid*, Bø: Høgskolen i Telemark, Avdeling for allmenne fag.

Tangen, J.O. (2004a) 'Embedded Expectations, Embodied Knowledge and the Movements That Connect: A System Theoretical Attempt to Explain the Use and Non-Use of Sport Facilities', *International Review for the Sociology of Sport*, 39(1): 7–25.

Tangen, J. O. (2004b) *Hvordan er Idrett Mulig? Skisse til en Idrettssosiologi*. Kristiansand: Høyskoleforlaget.

Tangen, J. O. (2004c) 'Making Space: A Sociological Interpretation of Sport and Its Facilities', *Sport and Society*, 7(1): 25–48.

Tangen, J. O. (2010) 'Observing Sport Participation – Some Sociological Remarks on the Inclusion/Exclusion Mechanism in Sport', in U. Wagner, R.K. Storm and J. Hoberman (eds) *Observing Sport: Modern System Theoretical Approaches*, Schorndorf: Hofmann.

Teubert, H., Borggrefe, C., Cachay, K. and Thiel, A. (2006) *Spitzensport und Schule. Möglichkeiten und Grenzen einer strukturellen Kopplung in der Nachwuchsförderung*, Schorndorf: Hofmann.

Thiel, A. (2002) *Konflikte in Sportspielmannschaften des Spitzensports. Entstehung und Management*, Schorndorf: Hofmann.

Thiel, A. (2003) *Soziale Konflikte*, Bielefeld: transcript Verlag.

Thiel, A. and Mayer, J. (2009) 'Characteristics of Management in Voluntary Sport Clubs: A Sociological Perspective', *European Journal of Sport Management*, 9(1): 81–98.

Thiel, A. and Meier, H. (2004) ,'Überleben durch Abwehr. Zur Lernfähigkeit des Sportvereins', *Sport und Gesellschaft*, 1(2): 103–125.

Wagner, U. (2009) *The Struggle for Clean Sports: Anti-Doping Strategies from 1960 to 2009* (Unpublished doctoral dissertation). University of Copenhagen, Denmark.

Willke, H. (2000) *Systemtheorie I: Eine Einführung in die Grundprobleme* (6th edition), Stuttgart: Fischer UTB.

9

PHYSICAL CULTURAL STUDIES ON SPORT

David L. Andrews and Michael L. Silk

Over the past decade or so, there has been a noticeable shift toward physical culture as a field of study in the sociology of sport. This growing trend incorporates a relational and pluralistic approach to, and understanding of, physical culture, whose various expressions of active embodiment (including, but certainly not restricted to, exercise, fitness, health, movement, leisure, recreation, dance, and sport practices), are approached as constituent elements of the broader conjunctural formation out of which they were constituted. Furthermore, this understanding is based on the assumption that the very nature of physical culture renders it a complex empirical site incorporating numerous interrelated aspects that can experienced, and thereby examined, from a variety of levels, including the socio-structural, discursive, processual, institutional, collective, communal, corporeal, and subjective. Hence, and whether acknowledged or not, it is our contention that the sociology of sport community has, in parts, taken a physical cultural *turn*, an occurrence indivisibly associated with the emergence of physical cultural studies (henceforth PCS) as a complement – as opposed to an alternative – to the sociology of sport.

Herein we offer an unavoidably personal and, some may argue, parochial genealogy of PCS, recognizing there are as many motivating factors behind people's turn to physical culture as there are discrete expressions of PCS in practice. Rather than speaking from any sort of authority, we eschew any ascribed or achieved intellectual status and/or influence we may have accumulated, and instead position ourselves as offering but one contribution to the on-going PCS dialogue. According to our understanding, PCS is a collective and democratic project, incorporating a productive tension of divergent foci, viewpoints, and opinions (very) loosely united by a common concern with contextualizing the complex field of physical culture. With such critical dynamism at its generative core, PCS fights off the inertia created by the all-too-easy adoption of empirical, theoretical, and/or methodological certainties. Differently put, and in a Freirean sense (Freire 2000), we contend that PCS is a dialogic learning community, in that its committed members are in critical and constructive conversation, or dialogue, with each other as a core part of the learning process (as opposed to having knowledge and understanding imposed on them). Hence, we advance our particular understanding of PCS with the intention of stimulating debate, rather than stifling it. Dialogue is thus understood as 'never an end in itself but a means to develop a better comprehension about the object of knowledge' (Macedo 2000: 18). PCS's objective is thus to nurture dialogic 'reflection and action upon the world in order to transform it' (Freire 2000: 51). The on-going PCS conversation, to which this chapter looks to contribute, aims to co-produce consciousness related to the field's object of knowledge: namely, physical culture in general, and, more specifically, the manner in which specific sites, forms, and/ or expressions of physical culture are organized, disciplined, embodied, represented, and experienced in relation to the operations of social power.

Promptings

The burgeoning field of physical cultural studies represents a response to a number of perceived intellectual (and institutional) threats, ambiguities, and/or inadequacies. The seemingly unrelenting (bio)scientization of kinesiology (and the accompanying devaluing of the humanities and social sciences of kinesiological thought) has been identified as a major contributory factor to the genesis and development of PCS (Andrews 2008; Andrews *et al.* 2013; Ingham 1997; Silk *et al.* 2013). However, not all PCS exponents are located within kinesiology departments and/ or have backgrounds within the field. Thus, it is important to acknowledge other factors that prompted the inception of PCS.

Although both authors of this chapter were trained in the sociology of sport, it would be equally true to say that this nomenclature has proved, at best, to be an increasingly vague and imprecise descriptor of our research practice and object of study. Informed by a variety of intellectual influences (most notably, in our case, cultural studies, body studies, and urban studies), the unfolding transdisciplinary, transtheoretical, and transmethodological nature of our work placed it at odds with sociology, as understood in the traditional sense of the discipline. Additionally, our initial empirical focus on, and understanding of, high profile, prolympic, or corporate *sport* (Andrews 2006; Donnelly 1996), was complicated by the recognition of the universality, yet imprecision, of 'sport' as a collective noun. Thus, as our research ventured more into the realms of leisure, fitness, recreation, and health, we came to question the conceptual pertinence of sport as a means of capturing the empirical breadth of our work. Not that we were by any means alone in this regard. Although the sociology of sport's main journals have always incorporated a degree of disciplinary and empirical diversity, this increased from the early 1990s onwards, rendering 'the sociology of sport', at best, a term of relevance to only a segment of this diverse intellectual community, and, at worst, an anachronistic flag of convenience (Harris 2006).

From our vantage point, rather than an 'expressive totality' coalescing around sport, the sociology of sport is in actuality characterized by a 'unity-in-difference'; the unifying element being a commitment toward understanding various and varied cultures (institutions, iterations, experiences) of the *physical* (of which sport is but one element, albeit a significant one) (Clarke 1991: 17). While numerous scholars have been drawn to physical culture as a site of critical investigation, to date, the most considered and concerted contributions to the physical culture debate are arguably the varied contributions that comprise Jennifer Hargreaves and Patricia Vertinsky's (2007) edited anthology *Physical Culture, Power, and the Body*, and those within the *Sociology of Sport Journal* special issue on physical cultural studies (Silk and Andrews 2011). Evidenced within these works, the turn to physical culture is closely linked to – indeed, it has arguably been propelled by – an increased focus on the body and issues of embodiment within sociology of sport research. Furthermore, and as illustrated by numerous journal articles, conference foci, and conference presentations, once the sociology of sport acknowledged its unavoidably embodied emphasis, the field gradually broke away from its narrow preoccupation with the sporting and broadened its empirical scope to include a wider range of physical cultural forms.

Not that all the promptings responsible for the instigation of PCS are internal to the sociology of sport. The concurrent turn to the body within the wider academic community (specifically within cultural studies and allied fields such as gender studies, health, social and cultural geography, leisure studies, media studies, queer studies, racial and ethnic studies, urban studies, youth studies, etc.), and the attention paid to the processes, practices, and politics of embodiment, have spurred a rethinking of physical culture (in its myriad guises) as a relevant and resonant empirical domain. From displaying a palpable academic disdain, numerous scholars located outside the extant sociology of sport community have come to acknowledge physical culture as a legitimate, and indeed significant, avenue for critical intellectual inquiry into the relationship between the body, power, and culture. Over the past decade or more, there has been a discernible *physical culture creep*, whereby the inalienable social, cultural, political, and economic significance of physical culture has infiltrated even some of the most intransigent academic minds. Coupled with the breakdown (indeed, one could consider it almost to be an inversion) of traditional academic distinctions between high and low culture forms as legitimate objects of analysis, physical culture (including organized sport, dance, exercise, health, leisure, movement, recreation, and rehabilitative-related practices) has occupied the critical gaze of scholars from fields as diverse as American studies, anthropology, architecture, gender studies, geography, Latin American studies, media and communication studies, race and ethnic studies, and urban studies (c.f. Latham 2015; Paradis 2012; Probyn 2000; Trimbur 2013; Woodward 2009). While many of these researchers may be blissfully unaware of the field as they gleefully *discover* physical culture – oftentimes with little or no recognition of the work that preceded theirs – they nonetheless are making contributions to the body of knowledge. Yet, the recognition of physical culture as the central object of research was but a first (albeit an important) step towards imagining, and legitimating, PCS as an approach to studying the politics of (in)active embodiment.

Raising our heads

Defining cultural studies is a risky business. Lots of people are claiming to do cultural studies while others, nervous about its rather sudden success, are attacking it. Yet the fact is that few people working in cultural studies would agree on a definition, and that many who claim to "do" cultural studies might not recognize themselves in such a definition.

(Grossberg 1997: 245)

Lawrence Grossberg's characterization of the issues raised by attempts to define cultural studies has considerable relevance for PCS, and not simply because *some* advocates of PCS see its derivation, constitution, and focus as being closely aligned to those of cultural studies more generally. While by no means claiming any 'sudden success' for PCS – or indeed any real presence outside a relatively sparse, yet expanding, number of (intellectually and geographically) dispersed advocates – PCS has certainly generated considerable ire within certain circles. This palpable mix of defensiveness, hostility, and outright disdain is on one level wholly unsurprising (given the personal investments of committed intellectuals), yet on another level we find PCS's cool reception in certain circles rather perplexing since, in our estimation, many of those agitating against PCS most vehemently would seem to be natural allies of this burgeoning intellectual project.

One is tempted to state that those attacking PCS have failed to engage the diversity and complexity of the project as it is understood and practiced by those working within it. Certainly, the various criticisms leveled at PCS depict a model of PCS many of whose elements (although by no means all of them, since some of the criticisms are incontrovertibly valid) we do not recognize. Nonetheless, rather than blaming the critiques for their misreading of the PCS project, a more productive strategy is to acknowledge that we are presently situated within something of a *knowledge delay* when it comes to PCS. While there is considerable intellectual chatter regarding the merits, or otherwise, of PCS, very little of this has been transposed into published expli- cations or condemnations (for notable exceptions, see Atkinson 2011; Giardina and Newman 2011; King-White 2012; Newman and Giardina 2014; Thorpe *et al.* 2011). In terms of outlining the constituent dimensions of the PCS project, the scant number of empirically, theoretically, methodologically, or axiologically delineating published works leaves PCS vulnerable to mis- understanding and misconception. Currently, PCS is little more (a few published pronounce- ments more) than a vague and ambiguous idea, floating without discernible direction within the academic ether. We think we know what it is, but do we really? If those of us who locate ourselves within this burgeoning intellectual enterprise display such inconclusiveness, how are those observing from outside able to engage it, even if critically, from any informed position?

PCS does not need to be wedded to the impossible pursuit of an absolute definition of what is a fluid and changeable enterprise. Yet it is, surely, compelled to an adherence to the process of definition. PCS is committed to developing ever-more-acute explanations of its focus, struc- ture, and purpose. Otherwise PCS is liable to fall foul of the indeterminacy that has hampered the growth of cultural studies more generally. The collective unwillingness to delineate the parameters of the cultural studies project has created a situation wherein "the refusal to define it becomes the key to understanding what it is" (Grossberg 1997: 253). For PCS, this is simply not a sensible, strategic, or in any way sustainable state of affairs.

Up to this point, PCS has failed to delineate any coherent or consistent sense of its own parameters. This can be partly attributed to the criticism that unavoidably attends any defini- tional effort. Generally speaking, this takes two forms. The first is the anticipated, and indeed greatly welcomed, criticisms occasioned by the outlined definition. Any attempt to define an intellectual phenomenon is bound to elicit disagreement and counter-definition of a particular element or elements (empirical, theoretical, methodological, or axiological), or, indeed, of the definitional effort *in toto*. Definitional efforts are thus the starting points, and subsequent stim- ulants, for the dialogic engagements through which the PCS project can begin to take shape and consequently mature. Hence, those in any sense committed to the development of PCS are compelled to raise their head above the parapet, and offer definitions and counter-definitions. They need to be sufficiently bold to articulate their own definitional thoughts, recognizing that critique is the inevitable corollary but dialogic advancement is the ultimate result. The second form of critique attending any definitional effort is linked to the position of authority that appears to be assumed by the definer(s). This leads to the interrogation of precisely what gives an individual, or collection of individuals, the right to speak for, in this case, a burgeoning intel- lectual project? What misguided sense of intellectual entitlement encourages such definitional efforts? This type of criticism is valid, but only if the definitions offered are positioned as being absolute and incomparable. Should they – as in this case – be framed as, hopefully, suggestive catalysts for considered deliberation, they cannot be critiqued for any totalizing ambitions. Oth- ers may read such assumed authority into the definitional effort, but it is not necessary there. Of course intellectual life is structured in such a way as to afford primacy and privilege to the voices of figures whose status and influence is derived from their accrued intellectual capital. Although understandable in more established fields, PCS's recent emergence means it is a less hierarchical intellectual space, and one *presently* more open to a multitude of generational influences.

Definitions tend to divide as much as they unite, and clearly the following working defini- tion of PCS incorporates numerous points of contestation that could alienate as much as they interpellate potential proponents. This is unavoidable, since PCS cannot and should not, be all things to all people. It should not be reduced to a generalist approach to the study of physical culture, and has to incorporate specific empirical, theoretical, methodological, and axiological dimensions through which researchers either do, or do not, recognize themselves and their work within it. That is not to say that any definition of PCS is fixed or inalienable, rather, the self-reflexivity inherent within the project demands constant critical reflection and revision. Hence, those involved and invested in PCS are charged with the responsibility for – they are the custodians of – its very being. It is in this sense that PCS should be considered a dialogic learning community, (re)generated through critical and constructive conversation (or dialogue), as opposed to being characterized by the imposition of externally derived knowledge (Freire 2000). Dialogue being a collaborative

> act of creation; it must not serve as a crafty instrument for the domination of one person by another. The domination implicit in dialogue is that of the world by the dialoguers; it is conquest of the world for the liberation of humankind.
>
> (Freire 2000 89)

Any definitional effort (such as that offered in the following section) should be considered generative as opposed to being definitive. It is intended to be a stimulus for dialogue, rather than an act of intellectual domination. It is not written from any misguided sense of PCS authority or omnipotence. Rather, it is offered by people who self-identify as members of the PCS learning community, yet who continue to struggle to adequately conceptualize the PCS project. We thus offer the following as a necessarily imperfect and far-from-inalienable definition as a catalyst to encourage others to invest themselves within the definitional process.

A definitional effort

Having made the case for the importance for PCS of on-going definitional practice, we are thus compelled to offer the following:

> PCS is a dynamic and self-reflexive interdisciplinary intellectual project, rooted in qualitative and critical forms of inquiry. Its research object is the diverse realm of physical culture (including, but not restricted to, sport, fitness, exercise, recreation, leisure, wellness, dance, and health-related movement practices).
>
> PCS is concerned with a process of theorising the empirical, in identifying, interpreting, and intervening into the ways physical culture–related structures and institutions, spaces and places, discourses and representations, subjectivities and identities, and/or practices and embodiments are linked to broader social, economic, political, and technological contexts.
>
> By contextualising physical culture in this way, PCS looks to explicate how active bodies become organised, disciplined, represented, embodied, and experienced in mobilising (or corroborating), or at times immobilising (or resisting), the conjunctural inflections and operations of power within a society.
>
> As a form of critical pedagogy, the aim of PCS is to generate and circulate the type of knowledge that will enable individuals and groups to discern, challenge, and potentially transform existing power structures and relations as they are manifest within, and experienced through, the complex field of physical culture.

From this definitional effort, we briefly expound upon what we consider to be the key elements of the PCS project.

Empirical

PCS focuses on physical culture, and more specifically the way specific forms of physical culture are organized, disciplined, represented, embodied, and experienced in relation to the operations of social power. While acknowledging the human body as the subject and object of physical culture, PCS cannot be reduced to phenomenological studies of bodily movement. Physical culture, and therefore PCS, encompasses a breadth of empirical sites and a depth of empirical dimensions/scales. Within its empirical reach, PCS includes activities ranging from sport through fitness, exercise, recreation, leisure, wellness, dance, and health-related movement practices. Furthermore, the empirical dimensions/scales at which these physical cultural forms can be engaged range from the macro through the micro: from structure and institution, to discourse and representation, subjectivity and identity, to experiential practice and embodiment.

Contextual

PCS offers an approach to the study of physical culture that is necessarily contextual in both form and objective. It is anti-reductionist in that any physical cultural expression cannot be reduced to singular or simple effect (i.e. the social, economic, political, or technological). Rather, physical cultural phenomena are the aggregates of multiple and intersecting determinant relations and effects. Mapping the context (the aggregate of determinant relations) in which physical cultural expressions are structured, made meaningful, and experienced represents the contextual imperative and outcome of PCS. Moreover, PCS's contextuality is based on a dialectic assumption that, however minutely, physical cultural practices act as constitutive elements of the larger context through which they are simultaneously constituted.

Transdisciplinary

PCS cannot be considered, nor should aspire to being, an academic discipline. Rather, its breadth of empirical engagement – focussed as it is on a wide range of physical cultural forms and dimensions/scales – necessitates a truly transdisciplinary approach. As such, PCS selectively borrows from various field/disciplinary-based research objects, methods, and theories (such as those drawn from body studies, cultural studies, economics, gender and sexuality studies, history, media studies, philosophy, political science, race and ethnic studies, sociology, and urban studies). PCS's transdisciplinary formations are thus fluid and wholly contingent on the form and dimension/scale of physical culture under scrutiny.

Theoretical

PCS is characterized by a commitment to social and cultural theory as important frameworks informing empirical engagement and interpretation. However, this does assume a slavish adherence to a singular theoretical position, since the empirical diversity of the PCS project precludes the adoption of such a totalizing approach. PCS research requires a critical engagement with theory: a grappling with specific theories to see what is useful and appropriate within a particular empirical site, and discarding/re-working that which is not. Hence, PCS requires the development of a broad-ranging and flexible theoretical vocabulary able to meet the extensive interpretive demands of its diverse empirical remit.

Political

PCS is a political project, in that it is committed to the advancement of the social formations in which it is located. As such, PCS researchers adhere to an unequivocal understanding of politics of intellectual practice as being concerned with discerning the distribution, operations, and effects of power and power relations. PCS is based on the assumption that societies are fundamentally divided along hierarchically ordered lines of differentiation (i.e. those based on class, ethnic, gender, ability, generational, national, racial, and/or sexual norms), as manifest within the existence of socio-cultural inequities or injustices; advantages or disadvantages; enablements or constraints; empowerments or disempowerments. For this reason, and as part of their broader commitment to progressive social change, PCS researchers critically engage physical culture as a site where such social divisions and hierarchies are enacted, experienced, and at times contested. The sites of political struggle – or problem spaces – within physical culture, through which social power becomes manifest and operationalized, are changeable and necessitate an equal dynamism in PCS's strategic emphases.

Qualitative

PCS is a predominantly (yet not necessarily exclusively) qualitative project, which seeks to interpret and understand (as opposed to predict and attempt to control) the diverse realm of physical culture as a social, cultural, political, economic, and technological construct. Acknowledging the value of considered quantitative work, PCS nonetheless provides a largely qualitative counterpoint to the blinkered positivist quantitative dogma that informs many swathes of academic life. Qualitative research encompasses a diverse array of interpretive (as opposed to predictive) methods designed to elicit representations of the social world, through which that world, and experiences of it, are interpreted. PCS's value-laden approach to qualitative inquiry is rooted in a humanist intellectualism – a pathway paved by many who have put their heads above the parapet in a variety of disciplines – motivated by the identification and elimination of disparities and inequities, the struggle for social justice, and the realization of universal human rights.

Self-reflexive

PCS research and researchers are motivated by subjective moral and political commitments, made explicit within and through the choices and enactment of research. Hence, PCS eschews the purported value-free objectivism implicitly and explicitly espoused by many positivists, in favour of a value-laden subjectivism, rooted in a critical approach guided by explicitly humanist goals. The self is thus unavoidably situated within research practice, and needs to be reflected upon as such. The variously located iterations of the PCS project are also more broadly reflexive, in that they recognize the need to be attentive to, and sometimes transform themselves in response to, the specific institutional, societal, and/or historical conditions they confront.

Pedagogical

PCS represents a form of public pedagogy designed to impact learning communities within the academy, in the classroom, and throughout broader publics. Whether teaching, writing, presenting, consulting, advocating, protesting, agitating, mass communicating, and/or mentoring, PCS scholars utilize the products of their research labours in circulating knowledge to – and often-times co-producing knowledge with – wider constituencies. This pedagogical commitment is motivated by the aim of enabling individuals and groups to discern, challenge, and potentially transform existing power structures and relations, as they are manifest within, and experienced through, the complex field of physical culture.

Impact

As we have emphasized, the various dimensions of physical culture are changeable and dynamic moments through which social divisions are imposed, experienced, and at times contested. PCS, as a political project, is thereby driven by the need to *understand* and *expose* the complexities, experiences, and injustices of the physical cultural context it confronts (particularly with regard to the relations, operations, and effects of power). PCS thus becomes centrally concerned with issues of power and justice and the ways the economy, class, race, gender, ideologies, discourses, education, religion, and other social institutions and cultural dynamics interact to create an unjust social system. PCS can, and should, be contributing to a range of conversations (about, for example, gender-based violence and sexual health for disadvantaged women in the global south, health care provision among 'excluded' or 'marginalized' populations, the neoliberal governance of the body, the pathologized or abject body, immigration, racisms, personal identity, citizenship, freedom, patriotism, justice, democracy, perpetual war, violence, terror, global social relations, political struggle, sporting bodies, class relations, bodies in (urban) spaces, (trans)gender bodily politics, and so on, in a necessarily abbreviated list). PCS scholarship needs to ensure it is *meaningful* through connecting private troubles and public concerns, extending its critical, performative, and utopian impulses to address urgent social issues in the interests of promoting social change (Giroux 2001). Hence, at its most fundamental level, PCS seeks to 'construct a political history of the (physical cultural) present' (Grossberg 2006: 2; parentheses added), through which it becomes possible to construct politically expedient physical cultural possibilities out of the historical circumstances it confronts. Yet, and as political theorist Jodi Dean (2000: 5) remarked: 'Cultural studies risks non-intervention by *presuming* its political purchase in advance' (emphasis added). It is for this reason that we, as PCS scholars, are compelled to develop a socio-historic imagination that enables a 'quality of mind that will help [individuals] to use information and to develop reason in order to achieve lucid summations of what is going on in the world and of what may be happening within themselves' (Mills 1959: 11). The *promise*, then, of PCS, like the promise of the socio-logical imagination, and indeed of those who have, in various guises in academe, taken up the sociological imagination as a motivation for their academic work, is as a source of empowerment that can enable individuals to discern the nature of the society around them and their location within it. PCS, then, as a project, is grounded within the trajectories of academe that have an unequivocal 'commitment to progressive social change' (Miller 2001: 1) and aims to *expose and render visible* unequal (physical cultural) power relations and produce the type of knowledge that can enable intervention into the broader social world. PCS, then, is unembarrassed by the label 'political', and, like others before, is unafraid to consummate a relationship with an emancipatory consciousness; a pragmatics of hope in an age of cynical reason (Kincheloe and McLaren 2005).

So what of the civic, pedagogic, and political responsibilities of PCS scholars? In recent years it has been PCS students who have clearly led the way in demanding that PCS research does more than describe the *objects of PCS knowledge*. However, despite such protestations, if truth be told, there are, as of yet, but a few examples of a PCS praxis that has *acted upon the world* in the manner that some individuals have argued for so passionately. Clearly, there is a need for a humility that recognizes (and certainly does not exaggerate) the transformative potential of PCS research. Doubtless prompted by enthusiasm for their research endeavours, some PCS scholars have spoken in hyperbolic terms regarding their approach and the potential influence upon the world; others have exercised greater caution (although institutional drives to *measure* 'impact' sit uneasily alongside humility). The reality is that we can never do enough, and more often than not, our projects, no matter how well meaning, do not make as much of a difference as we would like. Freire's notion of *conscientization* may then point to a more central form of PCS praxis. Differing from 'consciousness raising' in that the latter may involve transmission of pre-selected knowledge, conscientization refers to breaking through prevailing mythologies to reach new levels of awareness. In particular, it involves creation of an awareness of oppression being an 'object' of others' will rather than a self-determining 'subject'. The process of conscientization involves identifying contradictions in experience through dialogue and becoming part of the process of changing the world (Goldbard 2006: 243).

Thus, with Giroux (2001: 7), we press for cultural workers and intellectuals engaging in inter-textual negotiations across different sites of production to assume their roles as engaged critics and cultural theorists, for 'border crossing', for critical educators and cultural scholars to break down the artificial barriers, the separate spaces, and the different audiences that are supported through the infrastructure of disciplinary and institutional borders that 'atomize, insulate and prevent diverse cultural workers from collaborating across such boundaries.' But grandiose claims are perhaps better left to history; judgement over time will give a better indication of the ability of PCS scholars and scholarship to make a meaningful difference. Therefore, and despite the pressure for self-aggrandizement within 'impact metrics', more modest tones when describing how our research praxis leads to a specific form of change are preferable. Achievable action and transformation (however incremental, modest, and/or minuscule) derived from research is surely more beneficial as an outcome than unrealistic, unachievable, and unconvincing radical or activist posturing.

While there are a multitude of ways that praxis can potentially transform, it is perhaps in our educative work we can most clearly take strides. The echoes of Ball (2012), who suggests that the roughest of neoliberal beasts has created a new, soulless, academic performativity that makes us *more calculable than memorable*, ring loudly, yet we need in our educative work to ensure we offer more than 'bare pedagogy' which deems compassion a weakness, scorns moral responsibility given that it places human needs over market considerations, and 'strips education of its public values, critical contents and civic responsibilities as part of its broader goal of creating new subjects wedded to the logic of privatization, efficiency, flexibility, the accumulation of capital and the destruction of the social state' (Giroux 2010: 185). Building on the work of Brophy and Hladki (2012) and Titchkosky (2012), PCS scholars can enact change through a corporeal curriculum (see Silk *et al.* 2013) that recognizes the realities of our fleshly nature and examines the possibilities and constraints that flow from it (Rose 2013). With Garbutt and Offord (2012), our pedagogic practices (in the classroom, with communities, with publics), as a form of praxis, are activated by ethical imperatives and concerns; forms of pedagogy that can consider relations of freedom, authority, democratic knowledge and responsibility (Stevenson 2010). We thereby view all aspects of PCS, whether referring to researching, teaching, writing, presenting, consulting, public engagement, mentoring, and/or nurturing, as acts of potential liberation through the process of collective and/or collaborative conscientization and the transformative acts it may engender in the lives of those involved.

Conclusion

In summation, from our viewpoint, PCS is a critical intellectual endeavor committed to the realization of progressive social change through the generation and dissemination of physical culture–related knowledge enabling individuals and groups to discern, challenge, and potentially transform existing power structures and relations. Yet, and while disconcerting for some, PCS's commitment to an ontological and epistemological conjuncturalism is at the root of its per-petual dynamism; its unremitting commitment to the future through the dialogic generation of ever more acute understandings of the present. At any given moment, the struggle over defining PCS – over deciding what is the most prescient definition and formation of the project – has to be waged. Uncomfortable conversations and confrontations need to be had in order to ensure that PCS retains its intellectual dynamism and political relevance (for fear of falling into the sci-entific method's trap of moribund knowledge generation resulting from adherence to the twin positivist pillars of replication and incrementalization). As the 'problem–spaces' that confront PCS change over time, so the project is compelled to reshape and refocus itself in order to be able to meet the interpretive and political demands of the new conjuncture (Grossberg 2010: 1). PCS has to constantly reinvent itself in response to ever-changing institutional, societal, and/or historical conditions. The last generation's PCS may not be this generation's – something that has provoked, and will surely continue to fan, *stimulating* debates.

This intellectual conjuncturalism renders PCS an anti-relativist project: relativism understood as the uncritical embracing of any PCS project as being an equally valid and/or credible inter-pretation as any other. Adopting a relativist stance would open up PCS to charges of an absence of intellectual coherence and credibility. While it may be an open and fluid project continually *in process*, at any given time, and in regards to any specific project, PCS research needs to be subject to sustained challenges as to whether it adopts the most appropriate object of study, method, theory, and politics. This anti-relativism is not rooted in a realist assumption of the existence of a singular and truthful reality that PCS researchers are driven to discover. No, this approach acknowledges a multiplicity of truth claims, yet equally establishes that some truth claims are more methodologically sound, theoretically informed, and politically prescient – they are more interpretively insightful – than others, based on established criteria for assessing the rigour, relevance, and quality of qualitative research. While advancing a temporal *authority of knowledge* claims, it is important to acknowledge their incompleteness and deficiencies, whilst (hopefully) demonstrating how they realize understandings more interpretively and politically insightful than their antecedents. PCS is not a discipline, but it must be disciplined (it must self-reflexively police the rigour and relevance of its research through the establishment of generally accepted, though dynamic, criteria of evaluation). Only then will it be in a position to produce the 'best knowledge and understanding' of physical culture within the context at hand; knowledge and understanding to be used within the public pedagogical process of what is the 'daunting task of transforming the world' (Grossberg 2010: 1) in whatever way possible.

References

Andrews, D.L. (2006) *Sport-Commerce-Culture: Essays on Sport in Late Capitalist America*, New York: Peter Lang.

Andrews, D.L. (2008) 'Kinesiology's *Inconvenient Truth*', *Quest*, 60: 46–63.

Andrews, D.L., Silk, M.L., Francombe, J. and Bush, A. (2013) 'McKinesiology', *Review of Education, Pedagogy, and Cultural Studies*, 35: 1–22.

Atkinson, M. (2011) 'Physical Cultural Studies [Redux]', *Sociology of Sport Journal*, 28: 135–144.

Ball, S.J. (2012) 'Performativity, Commodification and Commitment', *British Journal of Educational Studies*, 60: 17–28.

Brophy, S. and Hladki, J.T. (2012) 'Introduction: Pedagogy, Image Practices, and Contested Corporealities', *Review of Education, Pedagogy and Cultural Studies*, 34: 75–81.

Clarke, J. (1991) *New Times and Old Enemies*, London: HarperCollins.

Dean, J. (2000) 'Introduction: The Interface of Political Theory and Cultural Studies', in J. Dean (ed.) *Cultural Studies and Political Theory*, Ithaca, NY: Ithaca University Press.

Donnelly, P. (1996) 'Prolympism', *Quest*, 48: 25–42.

Freire, P. (2000) *Pedagogy of the Oppressed*, New York: Continuum.

Garbutt, R. and Offord, B. (2012) 'A Scholarly Affair', *Review of Education, Pedagogy, and Cultural Studies*, 34: 3–7.

Giardina, M.D. and Newman, J.I. (2011) 'What Is This "Physical" in Physical Cultural Studies?' *Sociology of Sport Journal*, 28: 36–63.

Giroux, H. (2001) 'Cultural Studies as Performative Politics', *Cultural Studies <=> Critical Methodologies*, 1: 5–23.

Giroux, H. (2010) 'Bare Pedagogy and the Scourge of Neoliberalism', *The Educational Forum*, 74: 184–196.

Goldbard, A. (2006) *New Creative Community*, Oakland, CA: New Village Press.

Grossberg, L. (1997). 'Cultural Studies: What's in a Name? (One More Time)', in L. Grossberg (ed.) *Bringing It All Back Home: Essays on Cultural Studies*, Durham, NC: Duke University Press, 245–271.

Grossberg, L. (2006) 'Does Cultural Studies Have Futures? Should It? (Or What's the Matter with New York?)', *Cultural Studies*, 20: 1–32.

Grossberg, L. (2010). *Cultural Studies in the Future Tense*. Durham, NC: Duke University Press.

Hargreaves, J. and Vertinsky, P. (eds) (2007) *Physical Culture, Power, and the Body*, London: Routledge.

Harris, J.C. (2006) 'Sociology of Sport', *Quest*, 58: 71–91.

Ingham, A.G. (1997) 'Toward a Department of Physical Cultural Studies and an End to Tribal Warfare', in J. Fernandez-Balboa (ed.) *Critical Postmodernism in Human Movement, Physical Education, and Sport*, Albany: SUNY Press.

Kincheloe, J. and McLaren, P. (2005) 'Rethinking Critical Theory and Qualitative Research', in N.K. Denzin and Y.S. Lincoln (eds) *The Sage Handbook of Qualitative Research*, Thousand Oaks, CA: Sage.

King-White, R. (2012) 'Oh Henry!', *Sociology of Sport Journal*, 29: 385–408.

Latham, A. (2015). 'The History of a Habit: Jogging as a Palliative to Sedentariness in 1960s America'. *Cultural Geographies*, 22(1): 103–126. doi: 10.1177/1474474013491927.

Macedo, D. (2000) 'Introduction to the Anniversary Edition', in P. Freire, *Pedagogy of the Oppressed*, New York: Continuum.

Miller, T. (2001) 'What It Is and What It Isn't', in T. Miller (ed.) *A Companion to Cultural Studies*, Malden, MA: Blackwell.

Mills, C.W. (1959) *The Sociological Imagination*, Oxford: Oxford University Press.

Newman, J.I. and Giardina, M.D. (2014) 'Moving Biopolitics', *Cultural Studies <=> Critical Methodologies*, 14(5): 419–424

Paradis, E. (2012) 'Boxers, Briefs or Bras?', *Body & Society*, 18: 82–109.

Probyn, E. (2000) 'Sporting Bodies: Dynamics of Shame and Pride', *Body & Society*, 6(1): 13–28. doi: 10.1177/1357034x00006001002

Rose, N. (2013) 'The Human Sciences in a Biological Age', *Theory, Culture & Society*, 30: 3–34.

Silk, M.L. and Andrews, D.L. (2011) 'Toward a Physical Cultural Studies', *Sociology of Sport Journal*, 28: 4–35.

Silk, M.L., Francombe, J. and Andrews, D.L. (2013) 'Slowing the Social Sciences of Sport', *Sport in Society*, 17: 1266–1290.

Stevenson, N. (2010) 'Critical Pedagogy, Democracy and Capitalism', *Review of Education, Pedagogy & Cultural Studies*, 32: 66–92.

Thorpe, H., Barbour, K. and Bruce, T. (2011) '"Wandering and Wondering"', *Sociology of Sport Journal*, 28: 106–134.

Titchkosky, T. (2012) 'The Ends of the Body as Pedagogic Possibility', *Review of Education, Pedagogy, and Cultural Studies*, 34: 82–93.

Trimbur, L. (2013) *Come Out Swinging*, Princeton, NJ: Princeton University Press.

Woodward, K. (2009) 'Body Matters', in *Embodied Sporting Practices*, New York: Palgrave Macmillan.

10

POSTSTRUCTURALISM AND THE SOCIOLOGY OF SPORT

Samantha King

Poststructuralism emerged as a primary epistemological orientation in the sociology of sport in the last decade of the twentieth century, bringing with it a profound shift in the content and approach of much scholarship in the field. The rise of poststructuralist thinking is most clearly indicated by a shift in popular vocabulary as scholars have added terms such as 'deconstruction', 'discourse', 'normalization', and 'biopower' to critical frameworks that were previously domi- nated by concerns with 'ideology', 'hegemony', 'the state', and 'power elites'. Whereas in some instances new words have been deployed while the analyses remain essentially the same, overall, the field has witnessed a move away from a focus on the realities behind sporting myths, on class as the primary category of athletic identity and thus scholarly investigation, and on power as owned and embodied by sporting actors and institutions. Instead, influenced especially by the work of French philosopher Michel Foucault, scholars have taken up notions of compet- ing truths, multiple and fragmented subjectivities, and dispersed and microphysical relations of power.

Existing overviews of poststructuralism elaborated by sociologists of sport (Andrews 2000; Rail 1998) and others (Belsey 2002; Finlayson and Valentine 2002; Peters 2001) locate its origins in post–World War II France and explain its emergence as a diffuse set of responses to a range of modes of thought: structuralist, Marxist, and existentialist, primarily. Given that poststructur- alism is an umbrella term used to categorize a diverse range of theoretical and methodological perspectives, such overviews encompass considerable variety in the conceptual aspects they choose to highlight and the authors they select as their primary protagonists. At the most gen- eral level, however, definitions of poststructuralism proffer that it challenges traditional theories of language and culture, what it means to be a human being, and what it is possible to know (Belsey 2002).

My rendition of this theoretical orientation begins with a brief reflection on the emergence of structuralism and the work of Ferdinand de Saussure and Claude Lévi-Strauss, followed by a discussion of the rise of poststructuralism and the work of Roland Barthes and Jacques Derrida. The bulk of the chapter explores the writings of Michel Foucault, by far the most used and referenced poststructuralist figure in the field.

In view of their complex intellectual trajectories and (largely) shared suspicions about reduc- tionism, it is important to note that neither Barthes, Derrida, nor Foucault self-identified as 'poststructuralist'. Barthes made his aversion to such labels clear in his 1955 essay 'Am I Marxist?', where he writes in response to a conservative critic's challenge to him to declare his political allegiances: 'What business is it of his? Ordinarily, this sort of question only interests McCarthyists. . . . Yes, I know, it would be more reassuring if one could catalog writers according to their 'simple' declaration of faith . . . more reassuring but less rigorous' (1993: 499). Taking Barthes's caution seriously, this essay avoids rigid definitions of poststructuralism and assessments of the extent to which particular authors adhere to this approach; instead, it explores a number of key ideas understood to be poststructuralist in nature and how they have been taken up within the sociology of sport.

From structuralism to poststructuralism

Ferdinand de Saussure

Swiss academic Ferdinand de Saussure (1857–1913) is most well known for his posthumously published the *Course in General Linguistics* (Saussure 1983), in which he helped shift the focus of linguistics away from the historical study of the evolution of languages towards an engagement with the centrality of the linguistic system in understanding knowledge and behaviour. Saussure viewed language not simply as a neutral tool or label for communicating a preexisting order of things but as a product of social interaction that is central to constituting human experience and sociality.

Saussure sought to construct a science of systems of representation based on the key claim that the relationship between the signifier (an image, word, or sound) and the signified (the referent for the image, word, or sound) must be understood as arbitrary (Saussure 1983). By 'arbitrary', Saussure did not mean that individuals could make up words at will and be comprehended, but rather that the relationship between the signifier and the signified – known as the 'sign' – is not natural, or immanent, as earlier theorists had assumed. Instead, Saussure argued, meaning resides in the phonetic difference between words, or signifiers.

To illustrate, we can look to English-speaking cultures that have agreed upon the word 'referee' to signify the official who ensures that the rules of a sport are adhered to during the playing of a game. There is nothing inherent to the combination of letters or sounds that connects them to this role, a point illustrated by the fact that the word for this official is *scheidsrechter* in Dutch and *wasit* in Indonesian. Meaning is thus relational and differential – signs make sense only in relation to other signs. Signs gain meaning through what they are not (a player, a fan, a ball; a judge, a moderator, an arbitrator) rather than what they are (a referee). It is Saussure's ideas about the relationality of language that came to be most influential in the emergence of structuralism and poststructuralism as theoretical orientations.

Claude Lévi-Strauss

Saussure's work was particularly important for French anthropologist Claude Lévi-Strauss (1908–2009), who is recognized as a central figure in the development of structuralism as a dominant theoretical paradigm in the mid-twentieth century. In developing what he called a 'structural anthropology' (1968), Lévi-Strauss 'took Saussure's insight that language and society are coextensive to its ultimate conclusion' by making the claim that society is structured in the same way as language (Finlayson and Valentine 2002: 11). Building upon Saussure's ideas about the importance of language in shaping the human mind, Lévi-Strauss argued that all the signifying and material systems that comprise human societies are based on a set of universal binary oppositions such as nature/culture, life/death, sacred/profane, and male/female (Andrews 2000).

In his work on myths, kinship, totems, exchange, and other staples of anthropological research during that period, Lévi-Strauss (1961, 1966) sought to map this universal logic in order to explain how the structures that reproduce relations of power and order in a society are maintained over time.

While inspired by Saussure, Lévi-Strauss also developed his ideas in response to the existentialist philosophy of Jean-Paul Sartre (1905–1980), which was hugely important in France at the time (Sartre 1948). Arguing that existentialism was too introspective, subjective, and focused on human intention as an engine of history (Blackledge 2006), Lévi-Strauss, like his other major inspiration, Karl Marx, leaned towards a determinist theory of the subject. The major legacy of Lévi-Strauss's work for poststructuralism thus lay in his belief that the subject was constituted and directed by objective universal structures (such as language) that exist beyond the subject's consciousness, a stance which helped undermine modernists' notion of individual autonomy and agency.

Roland Barthes

The work of another French critic, Roland Barthes (1915–1980), is often recognized as representing a key shift, or a bridge, from structuralism to poststructuralism. In his early work Barthes drew strongly on Saussurean linguistics to explore the making and meaning of modern myths in popular cultural forms such as wrestling and the Tour de France (Barthes 1972). Later, however, Barthes became a leading figure in the turn away from what he saw as the constraints and formalism of structuralist thought.

In one of his most famous essays, 'The Death of the Author', Barthes (1977) extended the structuralist proposition about the socially constitutive function of language to analyze the role of the writer, but in so doing crystallized a key poststructuralist insight about the interpretation of texts: that the author is not in possession of a unique genius that is then expressed in textual form, but is more akin to a craftsperson who is skilled at deploying a preexisting code (Robinson 2011). The structuralist impetus here is clear; as Andrew Robinson (2011) phrases it: 'Writing occurs within a functional process which is the practice of signification itself', thus, 'the real origin of the text is not the author, but language'. To understand the meaning of a piece of writing, Barthes suggests, we must look not for something that exists behind the words that we imagine provide a clue to the text's authentic meaning (an all-knowing, authoritative, intending writer, for example), but at the text itself. He wrote: 'To give an Author to a text is to impose upon that text a stop clause, to furnish it with a final signification, to close the writing' (1977: 5). By calling for the liberation of the text from the author, Barthes helped draw attention to the possibility of multiple and competing interpretations of the signifiers that comprise a text – an insight that was to become a central tenet of poststructuralist thought in the latter half of the twentieth century.

Jacques Derrida

It should be clear from the preceding discussion that the 'post' in poststructuralism suggests not that this perspective has somehow superseded an obsolete structuralism but rather that the array of theories that travel under the poststructuralist banner emerged chronologically subsequent to structuralism and represent a prolonged engagement with its legacies. Indeed, the paper that is often celebrated as announcing poststructuralism's arrival on the global theoretical scene – Jacques Derrida's (1930–2004) 'Structure, Sign and Play in the Discourse of the Human Sciences', delivered at Johns Hopkins University in 1966 – is precisely an engagement with, rather than a repudiation of, structuralism (Derrida 1970). In this piece of work and in those that followed (1976, 1978, 1981), the Algerian-born French philosopher used the deconstructive method with which he would become synonymous to engage with Lévi-Strauss, Saussure, and a range of other linguists and philosophers to identify and undo the phono- and logocentrism that he argued characterized their work, and indeed the entire tradition of Western thought.

Phonocentrism, according to Derrida, is the primacy given to speech over writing through the ascription to speech of a presence and immediacy that is assumed to guarantee meaning in a way that writing, which is understood as secondary and derivative – little more than a transcription of authentic oral dialogue – does not (Derrida 1976). Derrida disputed this hierarchy by arguing that speech is equally derivative: meaning is not stable or immediately present in any sign (spoken, written, or otherwise communicated), but is instead in the process of constant change, made and remade in the absence of the author. Operating alongside phonocentrism, logocentrism posits a realm of objective universal truth prior to and independent of its representation through language (Derrida 1976). As an alternative, Derrida built on Saussure's ideas about the arbitrariness of signs to offer the groundbreaking suggestion that there exists no pure and free-standing signified, truth, or reality that acts as the foundation of human language, thought, and experience and which is expressed through the 'self-presence of full self-consciousness' (Spivak 1976: xviii). Instead, Derrida argues, our worlds are given meaning through an infinite and multiple chain of contested and dynamic signifiers. Any search for a truth that transcends language will thus ultimately fail (Derrida 1981).

While Derrida understood meaning as fragmented and shifting, his point was not to suggest that language is empty of political import. Like Lévi-Strauss, Derrida understood binaries, such as speech/writing, reality/myth, presence/absence, natural/unnatural, masculine/feminine to be based on a 'violent hierarchy' in which the latter term is subordinate to the former (1981: 41). Unlike Lévi-Strauss, whom Derrida viewed as caught up in a 'kind of nostalgia' for an (absent) centre or a universal structure, Derrida sought to show, through his deconstructive method, that binaries are arbitrary, inherently unstable, and ultimately tend to dismantle themselves 'from within' (Davis and Schleifer 1998). Although deconstruction has been explicitly used only sparingly within the sociology of sport (Cole 1998; Helstein 2005; Pringle and Pringle 2012), Derridean sensibilities have become integral to much work in the field as scholars seek to interrogate and dismantle taken-for-granted assumptions about athletic bodies and subjectivities.

Michel Foucault

Like his former pupil Derrida, Michel Foucault was fundamentally concerned with the politics of language, knowledge, and truth. Whereas Derrida's focus was largely linguistic and textual, however, Foucault took a more historical and institutional approach, exploring the emergence of a range of medical and social sciences and reconstructing genealogies of the modern prison and contemporary and ancient sexualities, among other sites of social and moral regulation.

Foucault's interest in the body and in the health of the population as sites of power has made his work particularly useful to sociologists of sport (especially those trained in North America) who have produced numerous manifestos (Andrews 1993; Cole 1993; Theberge 1991), reviews (Cole, Giardina and Andrews 2004; Rail and Harvey 1995; Smith Maguire 2002), comparative essays (Miller 2009; Pringle 2005), and books (Markula and Pringle 2006; Shogan 1999) advocating his approach, evaluating his influence, and exploring his arguments. Empirical research that takes up Foucault's ideas can be approximately categorized under three conceptual umbrellas: discourse; subjectivity, disciplinary power, and normalization; and technologies of the self.

Discourse

Central to Foucault's framework was the concept of 'discourse', which he used to describe historically and culturally located systems of thought and meaning which constitute and govern individual bodies and minds, both consciously and unconsciously (Foucault 1971; Weedon 1997). For Foucault, discourse was not a synonym for language, but a way of indicating how orders of truth are established through social practices and power relations.

It would be hard to overestimate the impact of Foucault's theory of discourse on the sociology of sport field, although this impact is evidenced not for the most part in voluminous or deep engagements with his writing on this subject but in the ubiquity of textual analyses focused on the production of truth about sporting bodies. Two recent exceptions to this trend – exceptions in that they explicitly engage with Foucault's writing on discourse – include Clare Mackay's (2012) investigation of the London Olympic Bid Committee's effort to garner support for its effort to bring the games to the British capital and Danielle Peers's (2012a) analysis of the role of Paralympic histories in inciting and reproducing problematic notions of disability.

Mackay and Peers both draw upon Foucault's (1972) archaeological method to analyze statements (the units through which discourses are assembled) and how they are 'repetitively articulated' (Mackay 2012: 411), modified and challenged, by a variety of subjects – a public relations professional and a number of newspaper journalists in Mackay's essay, and seventeen historians in Peers's essay. They then explore how these statements are analyzed across a variety of sites – eighteen months of *Sun* newspaper coverage for Mackay and fourteen histories of the Paralympics for Peers. Taken together, their essays clearly echo Foucault's premise that archaeological analysis should displace the primacy of the conscious subject in shaping what can be expressed at any given period within any particular cultural context and instead focus on the conditions of existence of particular discursive formations and the fields in which they operate.

Subjectivity, disciplinary power, and normalization

Although Foucault sought to dislodge the subject as the originator of discourse, the recruitment of subjects *through* discourse, the formation of the subject through norms and values, and the incitement of the subject to be accountable and responsible – that is disciplined – was a major preoccupation of his work. Foucault built on the ideas of Lévi-Strauss, Barthes, Derrida, and others to suggest that individuals are subject to structures and meanings that exist outside their control or awareness. Hence Catherine Belsey's claim that poststructuralism's account of the liberal humanist subject who freely and rationally authors her life's meaning and destiny is its most 'scandalous' and 'radical' contribution to social theory (2002: 65).

Foucault's thinking about subjectivity was largely developed in two books: *Discipline and Punish: The Birth of the Prison* (1977) and *The History of Sexuality, Volume I: An Introduction* (1978). In these volumes Foucault also developed his genealogical method by which he sought to write histories that were not linear and progressive but plural and discontinuous. Foucault explained in an interview that genealogical histories account for the 'constitution of knowledges, discourses, domains of objects, etc., without having to make reference to a subject which is either transcendental in relation to the field of events or runs in its empty sameness through the course of history' (1980: 117).

Such thinking is clearly evident in *Discipline and Punish*, where Foucault explored the shift from a society organized primarily through what he calls 'sovereign power' to a society organized primarily through what he calls 'disciplinary power', or 'normalization'. This text is designed in part to question the assumption that modern penal regimes and related mechanisms of social control are more humane than their predecessors, as linear and progressive histories suggest. Sovereign power, in Foucault's parlance, involves obedience to a central and highly visible authority, such as a king, and ensures compliance through spectacular, public forms of punishment, such as the execution. In contrast, disciplinary power, which Foucault argued came to hold sway over the course of the eighteenth and nineteenth centuries, is anonymous, dispersed, and discreet, operating largely through the internalization of social norms by individual subjects.

Foucault used the schematic of the Panopticon, British philosopher and reformer Jeremy Bentham's 1791 design for a modern prison, to illustrate how internalization occurs. The Panopticon consists of a central tower surrounded by a circle of cells. The tower is visible to the occupants of the cells at all times, but they can never be sure if and when they are being observed. This dynamic produces a constant state of anxiety and a guarantee of appropriate behaviour among the surveilled: The prisoner becomes, in Foucault's words, 'the principle of his own subjection' (1977: 203). Importantly, Foucault did not view the exercise of disciplinary power as confined to the prison, or even to institutions in general, but as dispersed throughout the social body, shaping every aspect of human existence.

The Panopticon has proven a popular motif for sociologists of sport seeking to highlight the intense (self)surveillance to which athletes are subjected and, in some instances, the racial and gendered inflections of such control (Foster 2003; Peers 2012b; Robidoux 2012). Margaret Duncan's (1994) analysis of *Shape* magazine as a panoptic mechanism through which women relate to their bodies has been particularly influential in the body of feminist literature detailing the gendered dynamics of the fitness industry (Duncan and Robinson 2004; Dworkin and Wachs 2009; MacNeill 1994; Markula 1995; Markula 2001).

Debra Shogan's (1999) *The Making of High-Performance Athletes: Discipline, Diversity, and Ethics* offers perhaps the most elaborate and accessible exploration of the production of high-performance athletes through mechanisms of disciplinary power. Explicitly writing against a conceptualization of power as possessed (by coaches, owners, managers) and oppressive (towards athletes) in its function, Shogan is 'interested in understanding whether what counts as ethical and what is conceived as moral agency might be altered when power is seen not as oppressive or repressive but as productive of situations, problems, and possibilities' (1999: x). Shogan offers a detailed analysis of the technologies of docility, 'correct training', panopticism, and the confessional – all concepts drawn from Foucault's oeuvre – that help to produce a normalized high-performance athlete. Shogan is also keen to demonstrate how the diversity and hybridity of athletes and the constraining *and* enabling effects of power open up new ways to understand and practice ethical sport, beyond established accounts that construe participants as 'caught in an either/or choice between meeting the demands of sport or following the rules' (1999: ix).

The theoretical ideas underpinning Foucault's account of the technologies through which the body becomes a locus of control in disciplinary societies were further developed in *The History of Sexuality, Volume 1*. Here, Foucault traces how various forms of knowledge about sexuality become mechanisms for producing and maintaining notions of normal and abnormal sexual identity, practice, and desire. Writing against the idea that modern regimes of power simply repress or constrain sexuality, Foucault claimed that the very idea of sexuality – as an object of study and a form of identity – is a product of power relations; that power, in fact, proliferates sexual identities, practices, and desires. These ideas became central to the emergence of queer theory in the 1980s and 1990s, which in turn shaped the work of sociologists, especially feminist sociologists (King 2008; McDonald 2006; Sykes 2006), who have explored how sexualities are produced, regulated, and transformed across various sporting contexts, including men's figure skating (Adams 2011), tennis (Birrell and Cole 1990), and the Gay Games (Davidson 2013).

Although sexuality formed the major empirical focus of *The History of Sexuality, Volume 1*, theoretically the book is much wider in scope. It is here that Foucault suggested that the population, alongside the individual body, emerges as a key site for the exercise of modern power in the eighteenth and nineteenth centuries. He used the term 'biopower' to describe the mechanisms that work to maximize individual bodily forces on the one hand, and those of the species body on the other. To emphasize, once again, the distinction between modern (bio)power and the sovereign power that he claimed it had largely displaced, Foucault wrote:

> The setting up, in the course of the classical age, of this great bipolar technology – anatomic and biological, individualizing and specifying, directed toward the performances of the body, with attention to the processes of life – characterized a power whose highest function was perhaps no longer to kill, but to invest life through and through.
>
> (1978: 139)

Because Foucault used biopower to explain how the health of individuals and populations emerges as an object of knowledge and a site of management and intervention, this concept has seen more widespread use in sociological analyses of health, fitness, and physical activity, than of sport per se. Shannon Jette's (2006) analysis of the operation of biopower in an *Oxygen* magazine column on exercise tips for new and expectant mothers is typical of work in this area. Judy Davidson's (2014) historical study of the Gay Games is one of the few pieces to use a biopolitical framework to explore a sporting context and to do so, moreover, by highlighting the centrality of racialization and racism to the constitution of normal – and thus abnormal – sexuality. Davidson's piece argues for the necessity of moving beyond celebrations of lesbian and gay identity associated with the games to consider how normalization has actually produced the games as a 'biopolitical technology of whiteness, class privilege and racism' (2014: 357).

Technologies of the self

In his later work (*The History of Sexuality, Volume 2: The Use of Pleasure*, 1990; *The History of Sexuality, Volume 3: The Care of the Self*, 1988; and a number of interviews and lectures in 2010 and 2011), Foucault shifted his focus away from how subjects are constituted through discourse and power (what fellow French philosopher Gilles Deleuze calls the 'outside' of the subject) towards the ethical work that subjects perform upon themselves as a way to negotiate power-knowledge relations (that is, the 'inside' of the subject) (Deleuze 1988; Markula 2003). In his turn towards Greek and Roman philosophy and to self-constitution – or 'subjectification' – as sites of study, Foucault surprised many commentators who saw his new interest as challenging, if not entirely contradicting, his earlier critiques of modern subjectivity.

For a variety of reasons, including a preference, perhaps, for this earlier approach, sport studies scholars have not made extensive use of Foucault's later work. The field as a whole has tended to give primacy to documenting the structural forces – in Foucauldian parlance, disciplinary and normalizing power – that organize modern sport and exercise, an unsurprising and worthwhile commitment given the exalted place of athletic individualism and self-responsibility for health in many societies. As a result, however, how subjects care for themselves, engage in self-stylization, and practice critical self-awareness have not been principal concerns within the sociology of sport (Markula 2003).

Pirkko Markula (2003, 2014), Pirkko Markula and Richard Pringle (2006), and Holly Thorpe (2008) have offered the deepest engagements with Foucault's later work, sharing in common a desire to redirect attention away from what they view as pessimistic representations of modern sport towards its 'creative possibilities, freedoms, ambiguities, and contradictions' (Markula and Pringle 2006: 48). Before turning to a discussion of their ideas, it is important to note that Foucault did address resistance within earlier works, most notably in *The History of Sexuality, Volume 1*, in which he penned perhaps his most oft-quoted claim, which was designed to highlight the futility of the search for a space outside of power from which subjects might resist and revolt: 'Where there is power, there is resistance, and yet, or rather consequently, this resistance is never in a position of exteriority in relation to power' (1990: 95). For Foucault this meant that resistance is not merely a secondary reaction to power, but rather that power and resistance exist in a strictly relational dynamic, each constituting the shape and trajectory of the other. Occasionally resistive forces connect, proliferate, and grow into something bigger, such as a revolution, but more often than not they are contingent, fleeting, and diffuse (Thorpe 2012). In Simon Thorpe's words, Foucault prompts us to ask not how we can abolish power altogether but rather 'what forms of power do we want to live with and which forms do we wish to limit or prevent?' (2012).

In turning to questions of ethics in his later work, Foucault stressed that he was not abandoning politics; instead, as Pringle argues, he saw ethical work as 'inherently political' (2005: 271). Critical awareness about one's self and how that self is constituted through subjectifying discourses provides the conditions for transgression and thus transformation, according to Foucault. Moreover, caring for the self implies caring about how the self relates to others such that introspection and self-awareness become essential for participation in social and political life.

It is a focus on self-awareness that characterizes late Foucauldian work in the sociology of sport. This literature can be understood as a response to the huge feminist sport sociology literature documenting the operation and effects of objectifying and pathologizing discourses around women's participation in sport and physical activity. Both Markula (2003) and Thorpe (2008) wish to identify and theorize the ways that women athletes might engage with and ultimately change 'practices of domination' (2003: 87). Markula's essay is largely theoretical and draws on close readings of extant sport studies texts focused on technologies of the self, subjectification, and gender negotiation, which variously demonstrate how hard it is to practice and identify resistance in women's sport, particularly if using a Foucauldian framework. Markula proceeds to make an argument for the need for feminist researchers to analyze and nurture 'athletes' awareness of the discursive construction of their training practices and performance standards' in order to create positive change in women's sport (2003: 105).

Thorpe's essay, which draws significantly on Markula's analysis, explores the 'ways in which power operates within everyday relations between people (snowboarders) and institutions (the media)' (2008: 224) in order to make the case that apparently sexist representations in snowboarding media are not inherently oppressive, but rather that the effects of the images depend on the discursive frameworks of their viewers and their critical self-awareness. In some cases, Thorpe argues, critical reflection leads to what Foucault called 'ethical conduct' or 'practices of freedom', concepts she illustrates through reference to the self-stylizing practices of women snowboarders who question discourses of femininity in snowboarding media and the production of all-women snowboarding videos.

Conclusion

As the research discussed here suggests, almost a quarter-century after it was first introduced, Foucauldian thought remains a vital force in the sociology of sport, giving shape to both how and what scholars study. Because the work of Foucault, Derrida, and other theorists labeled as poststructuralist refuses grand narratives, universal truths, and definitive conclusions, it often raises more questions than it answers (and is, it must be said, especially ill suited to overviews such as the one I have constructed here!). While the provisional and fragmented nature of poststructuralist criticism can be frustrating for the reader seeking neatly packaged solutions to all that ails contemporary sport, it is also the source of this perspective's vitality and durability: poststructuralist truths, like all truths, are contingent and multiple, proliferating new problems to address, ideas with which to wrestle, and political possibilities to assess.

References

Adams, M.L. (2011) *Artistic Impressions: Figure Skating, Masculinity, and the Limits of Sport*, Toronto: University of Toronto Press.

Andrews, D.L. (1993) 'Desperately Seeking Michel: Foucault's Genealogy, the Body and Critical Sport Sociology', *Sociology of Sport Journal* 10(2): 148–167.

Andrews, D.L. (2000) 'Posting Up: French Post-Structuralism and the Critical Analysis of Contemporary Sporting Culture', in J. Coakley and E. Dunning (eds) *Handbook of Sport Studies*, London: Sage.

Barthes, R. (1972) *Mythologies*, New York: Hill and Wang.

Barthes, R. (1977) *The Death of the Author*, Available at: http://www.tbook.constantvzw.org/wp-content/death_authorbarthes.pdf.

Barthes, R. (1993) 'Suis-je marxiste?', in E. Marty (ed.) *Oeuvres Complètes, Tome 1, 1912–1961*, Paris: Éditions du Seuil.

Belsey, C. (2002) *Poststructuralism: A Very Short Introduction*, New York: Oxford University Press.

Birrell, S. and Cole, C.L. (1990). 'Double Fault: Renee Richards and the Construction and Naturalization of Difference', *Sociology of Sport Journal*, 7: 1–21. (On my copy of the essay, there is no issue number listed, though I have seen others list it as 1).

Blackledge, P. (2006) *Reflections on the Marxist Theory of History*, Manchester: Manchester University Press.

Cole, C.L. (1993) 'Resisting the Canon: Feminist Cultural Studies, Sport and Technologies of the Body', *Journal of Sport and Social Issues*, 17(2): 77–97.

Cole, C.L. (1998) 'Addiction, Exercise, and Cyborgs: Technologies of Deviant Bodies,' in G. Rail (ed.), *Sport and Postmodern Times*, Albany: SUNY Press.

Cole, C.L. Giardina, M.D., and Andrews, D.L. (2004) 'Michel Foucault: Studies of Power and Sport', in R. Giulianotti (ed.), *Sport and Modern Social Theorists*, London: Palgrave Macmillan.

Davidson, J. (2013) 'Sporting Homonationalisms: Sexual Exceptionalism, Queer Privilege, and the 21st Century International Lesbian and Gay Sport Movement', *Sociology of Sport Journal*, 30(1): 57–82.

Davidson, J. (2014) 'Racism against the Abnormal? The Twentieth Century Gay Games, Biopower and the Emergence of Homonational Sport', *Leisure Studies*, 33(4): 357–378.

Davis, R.C. and Schleifer, R. (1998) *Contemporary Literary Criticism: Literary and Cultural Studies*, New York: Longman.

Deleuze, G. (1988) *Foucault*, Minneapolis: University of Minnesota Press.

Derrida, J. (1970) 'Structure, Sign, and Play in the Discourse of the Human Sciences', in R. Macksey and E. Donato (eds), *The Languages of Criticism and the Sciences of Man*, Baltimore, MD: Johns Hopkins University Press.

Derrida, J. (1976) *Of Grammatology*, Baltimore: Johns Hopkins University Press.

Derrida, J. (1978) *Writing and Difference*, Chicago: University of Chicago Press.

Derrida, J. (1981) *Dissemination*, Chicago: University of Chicago Press.

Derrida, J. (1982) *Positions*, Chicago: University of Chicago Press.

Duncan, M. and Robinson, T.T. (2004) 'Obesity and Body Ideals in the Media: Health and Fitness Practices of Young African-American Women', *Quest*, 56(1): 77–104.

Duncan, M.C. (1994) 'The Politics of Women's Body Images and Practices: Foucault, the Panopticon, and *Shape* magazine,' *Journal of Sport and Social Issues*, 18(1): 48–65.

Dworkin, S.H. and Wachs, F-L. (2009) *Body Panic: Gender, Health and the Selling of Fitness*, New York: NYU Press.

Finlayson, A. and Valentine, J. (2002) (eds) *Politics and Poststructuralism: An Introduction*, Edinburgh: Edinburgh University Press.

Foster, K.M. (2003) 'Panopticonics: The Control and Surveillance of Black Female Athletes in a Collegiate Athletic Program', *Anthropology & Education Quarterly*, 34(3): 300–323.

Foucault, M. (1971) 'Order of Discourse', in R. Young (ed.), *Untying the Text: A Post-Structuralist Reader*, Boston: Routledge and Kegan Paul.

Foucault, M. (1972) *The Archaeology of Knowledge*, New York: Pantheon Books.

Foucault, M. (1977) *Discipline and Punish: The Birth of the Prison*, New York: Pantheon Books.

Foucault, M. (1978) *The History of Sexuality, Volume 1: An Introduction*. New York: Random House.

Foucault, M. (1980) *Power/Knowledge: Selected Interviews and Other Writings, 1972–1977*. New York: Random House.

Foucault, M. (1988) *The History of Sexuality, Volume 3: The Care of the Self*, New York: Vintage.

Foucault, M. (1990) *The History of Sexuality, Volume 2: The Use of Pleasure*, New York: Vintage.

Foucault, M. (2010) *The Government of Self and Others: Lectures at the Collège de France 1982–1983*, New York: Palgrave Macmillan.

Foucault, M. (2011) *The Courage of Truth: Lectures at the Collège de France 1983–1984*, New York: Palgrave Macmillan.

Helstein, M. (2005) 'Rethinking Community: Introducing the "Whatever" Female Athlete', *Sociology of Sport Journal*, 22(1): 1–18.

Jette, S. (2006). 'Fit for Two? A Critical Discourse Analysis of Oxygen Fitness Magazine', *Sociology of Sport Journal*, 23(4): 331–351.

King, S. (2008) 'What's Queer About (Queer) Sport Sociology Now?: A Review Essay', *Sociology of Sport Journal*, 25(4): 419–442.

Lévi-Strauss, C. (1961) *Tristes Tropiques*, New York: Criterion Books.

Lévi-Strauss, C. (1966) *The Savage Mind*, Chicago: University of Chicago Press.

Lévi-Strauss, C. (1968) *Structural Anthropology*, London: Allen Lane The Penguin Press.

Mackay, C. (2012) '"Back the Bid": The London Olympic Bid Committee and the Sun newspaper', *Journal of Sport and Social Issues*, 36(4): 410–421.

MacNeill, M. (1994) 'Active Women, Media Representations, and Ideology', in S. Birrell and C.L. Cole (eds), *Women, Sport and Culture*, Champaign, IL: Human Kinetics.

Markula, P. (1995) 'Firm but Shapely, Fit but Sexy, Strong but Thin: The Postmodern Aerobicizing Female Bodies,' *Sociology of Sport Journal* 12(4): 424–453.

Markula, P. (2001) 'Beyond the Perfect Body: Women's Body Image Distortion in Fitness Magazine Discourse', *Journal of Sport and Social Issues*, 25(2): 158–179.

Markula, P. (2003) 'The Technologies of the Self: Sport, Feminism, and Foucault', *Sociology of Sport Journal*, 20(2): 87–107.

Markula, P. (2014) 'Embodied Subjectivities: Intersections of Discursive and Critical Psychology with Socio-cultural Exercise Research', *Sociology of Sport Journal*, 31(2): 139–161.

Markula, P. and Pringle, R. (2006) *Foucault, Sport and Exercise: Power, Knowledge and Transforming the Self*, London: Routledge.

McDonald, M.G. (2006) 'Beyond the Pale: The Whiteness of Sport Studies and Queer Scholarship,' in J. Caudwell (ed.), *Sport, Sexualities and Queer/Theory*, London: Routledge.

Miller, T. (2009) 'Michel Foucault and the Critique of Sport,' in B. Carrington and I. McDonald (eds) *Marxism, Cultural Studies and Sport*, New York: Routledge.

Peers, D. (2012a) 'Patients, Athletes, Freaks: Paralympism and the Reproduction of Disability', *Journal of Sport and Social Issues*, 36(3): 295–316.

Peers, D. (2012b) 'Interrogating Disability: The (De)Composition of a Recovering Paralympian', *Qualitative Research in Sport, Exercise, and Health*, 4(2): 175–188.

Peters, M.A. (2001) *Poststructuralism, Marxism and Neoliberalism: Between Theory and Politics*, Lanham, MD: Rowman & Littlefield.

Pringle, R. (2005) 'Masculinities, Sport, and Power: A Critical Comparison of Gramscian and Foucauldian Inspired Theoretical Tools', *Journal of Sport and Social Issues*, 29(3): 256–278.

Pringle, R. and Pringle, D. (2012) 'Competing Obesity Discourses and Critical Challenges for Health and Physical Educators', *Sport, Education & Society*, 17(2): 143–161.

Rail, G. (1998) 'Seismography of the Postmodern Condition: Three Theses on the Implosion of Sport', in G. Rail (ed.) *Sport and Postmodern Times*, Albany: SUNY Press.

Rail, G. and Harvey, J. (1995) 'Body at Work: Michel Foucault and the Sociology of Sport', *Sociology of Sport Journal*, 12(2): 164–179.

Robidoux, M. (2012) *Stickhandling through the Margins: First Nations Hockey in Canada*, Toronto: University of Toronto Press.

Robinson, A. (2011, October 14) 'Roland Barthes: Death of the Author.' *Ceasefire*. Available at: http://ceasefiremagazine.co.uk/in-theory-barthes-4/ (accessed 4 July 2014).

Sartre, J-P. (1948) *Existentialism and Humanism*, London: Methuen.

Saussure, F. de. (1983) *Course in General Linguistics*, C. Bally and A. Scheheye (eds), R. Harris (tr.), London: Duckworth.

Shogan, D. (1999) *The Making of High-Performance Athletes: Discipline, Diversity, and Ethics*, Toronto: University of Toronto Press.

Smith Maguire, J. (2002) 'Michel Foucault: Sport, Power, Technologies and Governmentality', in J. Maguire and K. Young (eds), *Theory, Sport and Society*, London: Elsevier.

Spivak, G. (1976) 'Translator's Preface', in J. Derrida, *Of Grammatology*, Baltimore, MD: Johns Hopkins University Press.

Sykes, H. (2006) 'Queering Theories of Sexuality in Sport Studies', in J. Caudwell (ed.), *Sport, Sexualities and Queer/Theory*, London: Routledge.

Theberge, N. (1991) 'Reflections on the Body in the Sociology of Sport', *Quest*, 43: 148–167.

Thorpe, H. (2008) 'Foucault, Technologies of the Self, and the Media: Discourses of Femininity in Snowboarding Culture', *Journal of Sport and Social Issues*, 32(2): 199–229.

Thorpe, S. (2012) 'In Defence of Foucault: The Incessancy of Resistance', Critical Legal Thinking. Available at: http://criticallegalthinking.com/2012/02/07/in-defence-of-foucault-the-incessancy-of-resistance/ (accessed 10 July 2014).

Weedon, C. (1997) *Feminist Practice and Poststructuralist Theory*, Oxford: Blackwell.

11

POST/COLONIAL THEORY AND SPORT

Ben Carrington

. . . no one colonizes innocently.

Aimé Césaire, Discours sur le colonialism

Modern imperialism was so global and all-encompassing that virtually nothing escaped it; besides, as I have said, the nineteenth-century contest over empire is still continuing today. Whether or not to look at the connections between cultural texts and imperialism is therefore to take a position *in fact taken* − either to study the connection in order to criticize it and think of alternatives for it, or not to study it in order to let it stand, unexamined and, presumably, unchanged.

Edward Said, Culture and Imperialism

Introduction

What is post/colonialism? This seemingly innocuous question prompts at least four further lines of enquiry. First, *what* is the actual phenomenon that the 'post' in post/colonialism has somehow gone beyond? Second, and intimately related, *when* is post/colonialism? What temporal markers are used to differentiate, to mark, the colonial period from the post/colonial? Third, *where* is post/colonialism? Which regions, nations or cities of the world are − or claim to be − post/colonial and in what ways? And fourth, *who* is post/colonial? Which people or groups are post/colonial and are they post/colonial in the same way? Whilst the line of distinction between the colonized and the colonizer was, historically speaking, usually clear, in the current moment which subjects might be understood as 'post/colonial' is less immediately obvious. These deceptively simple questions cut to the core of the conceptual, temporal, geographic and, above all, political problematics that have animated theoretical discussions concerning post/colonialism and are the central concerns for what is called 'post/colonial theory' (Childs and Williams 1997).

In order to see how post/colonial theory might help us to make better sense of sports, I first define a number of key terms, attempting to clarify these *what, when, where* and *who* questions, before outlining some of the arguments from prominent post/colonial writers. Although post/colonial theorists have tended to overlook sport as a subject for critical enquiry, I briefly examine how sociologists of sport have recently tried to engage post/colonial studies by focussing attention on the problematic of the body. I conclude by highlighting future possibilities and approaches for sociologists of sport wanting to better understand the question of 'the post/colonial' and related debates concerning 'diaspora' and 'multiculturalism'.

Defining the post/colonial

If post/colonial theory is an intellectual framework concerned to understand the socio-economic, political and ideological conjunctures that shape our contemporary era, then what is the 'colonial' at the heart of this project? *Colonialism* can be defined as the mechanisms that allow one country to control and exploit another. More specifically, colonialism denotes the *practice, policies and institutions of direct governance*, wherein administrators and state officials from the colonizing nation oversee the affairs of the colonized. Robert Young (2001) suggests that initially, colonization, as Europeans originally used the term, referred to the movement of populations or 'settlers' seeking a better life (economic, religious, political) to new areas and wanting to maintain an allegiance to their original culture. Only latterly did the concept extend to include the 'geographic violence' in exploiting and extracting the wealth from those lands whilst either overseeing or exterminating indigenous populations – and, of course, in the context of transatlantic slavery, extracting and exploiting those peoples too. Colonialism is *racialized* to the extent that 'race' becomes a signifying system that is used to mark particular bodies as 'not European' and therefore as 'not white'. *Racial difference*, that is the ability to draw (allegedly) sharp racial lines of ontological distinction, becomes both a mechanism and an effect of colonial power. 'The objective of colonial discourse', notes Homi Bhabha, 'is to construe the colonized as a population of degenerate types on the basis of racial origin, in order to justify conquest and to establish systems of administration and instruction' (1994: 70).

In contrast, *imperialism* refers to a set of power relations (political, economic and cultural) between countries, relations that are often underpinned by military force or the threat of force, in which one country comes to assert itself over another. In this sense we could suggest that imperialism is the name given to the process of influence, domination and exploitation of one country over another and colonialism is the practice. Thus there can be imperialism without colonization but rarely colonization without imperialism. In a context where one sovereign state, monarch or geo-political entity manages to exert such control over a number of countries, simultaneously, over an extended period of time, and with some sense of shared cultural or ethnic affinity, then we can perhaps suggest that such an entity has an *empire* as in the usage of terms such as the Ottoman, Roman and British Empires.

The term *post/colonialism* is generally understood to mark, and emerge from, the post–Second World War period after the formal demise of western European colonial regimes, which we can date variously from the independence of India from Britain in 1947, through to the formation of independent north African countries in the 1950s, such as Tunisia and Morocco in 1956. By the early 1960s, west and central African countries such as Nigeria and the Ivory Coast had similarly gained independence, followed shortly after by Caribbean nations such as Jamaica, Trinidad and Tobago and, a little later, in 1966, Barbados. In other words, in a period of about two decades, two centuries of direct European governance had been challenged and overturned. This was a remarkable and profound change in international relations and the global order. Post/colonial *theory*,[1] then, is an attempt to make sense of and comprehend these significant changes, to understand why colonial regimes first emerged and how they were sustained and resisted. It also seeks to trace colonialism's effects on the culture, language and identity of 'non-Western' nations, an imposition often reinforced through violence, and to map how the centre, or 'metropole', was also shaped by colonial discourses.

But post/colonial theory is not simply an exercise in historical mapping of facts and figures, events, peoples and places. It interrogates the foundations of Western thought, the belief systems of the West – and in its more deconstructionist guise, seemingly descriptive terms such as 'the West and the Rest' – that made colonialism possible in the first place. Post/colonial theory tries to unpack and rethink 'the West' from the inside, to subject to critical scrutiny the self-professed claims of Western superiority and universal progress in order to show the violence that lies just beneath the surface. As such, we might think of post/colonial theory as a critique of the West's *ideological apparatus*, an apparatus that sustained the bloodshed and violence that was the European colonial project,[2] especially as that enterprise came to be subsumed under the powerful political and cultural rhetorics of 'democracy', 'capitalism' and 'civilization'. Young is instructive here when he notes that if 'colonial history, particularly in the nineteenth century, was the history of the imperial appropriation of the world, the history of the twentieth century has witnessed the peoples of the world taking power and control back for themselves. Postcolonial theory is itself a product of that dialectical process' (2001: 4).

Clearly there were and are many forms of colonial governance, underpinned by different ideological justifications. French imperialism operated with a different ideology than its British counterpart (and indeed from its German, Spanish, Dutch, Belgium and Portuguese equivalents) and even the British Empire was heterogeneous and far from monolithic. Many South American colonies, for example, became independent before the formation of some European states, thus some scholars argue that the appropriate frame to challenge Eurocentric theorizing should come from *decolonial* thought. This approach utilizes indigenous forms of theorizing as a way to reject the imposition of Western temporal schemas and concepts in order to produce alternatives *to* modernity rather than *alternative* modernities (Mignolo 2011). We need to be careful, then, about invoking a singular global 'colonial history' that post/colonial theory can map and explain. The colonial condition is in fact a series of colonial encounters suturing multiple histories, some overlapping, some distinct, a plural and not singular phenomena.

Many of the authors and thinkers who might be called 'post/colonial theorists' rarely use that term to describe their own works or projects, precisely because they are sceptical of claims that we have moved beyond the period of Western economic, militaristic and political domination into a new historical epoch. Organizations such as the International Monetary Fund (IMF) and the World Trade Organization (WTO), the practices of Western-based nongovernmental organizations (NGOs), the sovereign debt owed to European nations by the formerly colonized, the power of Western and particularly American corporations, and the ongoing use of military force, including war, extrajudicial executions via drone strikes, human experimentation and torture via 'renditions' to so-called black sites, can all be seen as constituting a continuing form of US-backed Western imperialism (Johnson 2004; Harvey 2005; Mann 2005; Hajjar 2014). This 'new' imperialism is occurring at the same time as China's global economic strength increases, as sporadic forms of resistance (often violent) to American influence across much of the Middle East grow, and as alternative, socialist-influenced models of economic and social development across much of Latin America flourish. Absolute breaks or ruptures are rare within history, if they can be found at all. Understanding the continuing effects of colonialism on contemporary societies and culture, including sports cultures, is post/colonial theory's problematic.

Civilization, colonialism and the idea of the West

Two important anti-colonial critics whose writings have influenced later post/colonial theorists are the Martinique-born revolutionary intellectuals Aimé Césaire and Frantz Fanon – especially through writings such as Césaire's 'third world manifesto' (Kelley 2000) *Discourse on Colonialism* and Fanon's (1952/2008) *Black Skin, White Masks*, which focuses on the dehumanizing effects of colonial racism on both the colonizer and the colonized. Césaire shows how the European bourgeoisie's claims of an enlightened and benevolent colonialism merely served to hide the atrocities carried out against the colonized; colonialism being a 'campaign to civilize barbarism' (1955/2000: 40). Césaire demonstrates that the devastation Germany's Nazi Party brought to Europe in the 1940s was a continuation and not a break with what Europeans had been doing elsewhere; Hitler was applying procedures to white Europeans that were only previously permissible when done to the colonized. Hitler gave racism a bad name, as Césaire provocatively puts it. The true barbarians, Césaire holds, are those who torture and murder and plunder under the banner of an enlightened humanism. The colonizer who gets into the habit of seeing the colonized as savage, 'accustoms himself to treating him like an animal, and tends objectively to transform *himself* into an animal' (1955/2000: 41). The origins of fascism, in other words, are not to be found in the peculiarities of the Third Reich, the membership of the German Nazi Party or the culture of Germany, but in colonialism and therefore within the centre of the European liberal state. 'Europe' is indefensible, bluntly states Césaire.

Whilst the texts of Césaire and Fanon are regularly cited within post/colonial theory, it is the work of Gayatri Spivak, Homi Bhabha and Edward Said that is seen as foundational to post/colonial theory (Childs and Williams 1997). All three thinkers are concerned with the subjective and not purely materialist effects of colonialism as well as with mapping the broader politics of subaltern resistance, the agency of the colonial subject, and the possibilities for anti-colonial struggle that may produce different or alternative visions of Western modernity. Briefly, Spivak's writing has been central to debates within post/colonial theory regarding the extent to which the voices of the subaltern and the lives of the colonized can be recognized within the theoretical frameworks used to make sense of colonialism (Spivak 1993). Bhabha's (1994) work on questions of race, hybridity, stereotypes and mimicry pursues a similarly deconstructionist approach to the question of identity. The alleged uniqueness of European culture (or any 'national' culture) as separate, pure and inherently superior to all others is challenged as Bhabha deconstructs the binaries that produce the 'The West' and 'The Rest' as essentially different and discrete cultural entities.

However, if there is a single 'foundational text' for the field of post/colonial studies, then Edward Said's *Orientalism* is probably it. Originally published in 1978, and continually reprinted ever since, the book almost single-handedly forged an intellectual space for thinking about the discursive and material consequences of European imperialism and how the social sciences and humanities were complicit with the colonial project. Said argues, in effect, that 'the Orient' is not a stable, objective reality, an inert fact of nature that the Western explorer, artist or scientist 'discovers', but, rather, the Orient is discursively produced through the very act of writing about it. The Western eye constructs what it wants to see. The Orient is almost entirely an invention of the West, the Other to the Occident. Thus, accounts of the mystical, sensual, seductive (and often dangerous) Orient tell us more about the Europeans themselves than the supposed exotic beings of the Orient.

The study of the Orient, or 'Orientalism', is not a neutral exercise. The attempt to 'better understand' the Orient is at one and the same time also an attempt to dominate and have power over it. In short, the system of knowledge about the Orient serves particular Western interests. Said shows that 'what we know to be true' about the Orient, even and especially amongst experts, is often a mixture of fact, falsehoods, partial truths and fantasies. Said is clear that the problem of Orientalism is not confined to the tall tales of nineteenth-century fiction writers, or the anthropological writings of the early twentieth century, or 'the caricatures propagated in the popular culture' (1978/2003: 290), but in how politicians and so-called experts on the Middle East continue to use these frameworks as the basis for foreign policy decisions, Orientalist frameworks that are underpinned by erroneous perceptions of the backward 'Arab mind' and their developmentally truncated culture. This white colonial frame (Carrington 2010), of course, makes it possible for 'us' to torture and murder, and then to excuse such acts as not murder or torture at all, because our moral superiority and claims to civility are inherent in being Western. 'They' are savages who torture and murder; 'we' are civilized and use legitimate 'enhanced interrogation techniques'. The discourse produced (from the academies, by writers and explorers, by state bureaucrats and others) by the West about the West and its Others, these 'supreme fictions' (1978/2003: xii) as Said puts it, are part of the same techniques of colonial power as military intervention, occupation and governance, and, in a fundamental sense, *enable* such modalities of oppression and exploitation.

This Foucauldian-inspired focus on the ideological fictions produced by discourses of power has been taken up by other authors, beyond Said's original focus on Orientalism. J. M. Blaut (1993) in *The Colonizer's Model of the World* develops these ideas and focusses more generally on the reproduction of Eurocentrism within the social sciences. Blaut demonstrates how 'rationality' as a discourse was a central justification for colonialism. Far from being a neutral description of objective social relations and ways of thinking, the invocation of rationality operated as an ideological framework for explaining European economic and political progress, or what Blaut calls the myth of the European miracle, compared to the 'primitive' ways of the rest of the world. This way of understanding world events was not just an account of colonialism but a part of the colonial project; it was, as Blaut's title puts it, *the colonizer's model of the world*. This white colonial frame assumes that Europeans are the makers of history, that Europe shapes and drives forward social change while the rest of the world stagnates and is dragged along. The world is thus imagined as having a centre and a periphery, an Inside and Outside. The Inside leads, the Outside follows, the Inside innovates, the Outside imitates (Blaut 1993: 1). The key characteristics of the European Inside are believed to be inventiveness, rationality, abstract thought, theoretical reasoning, discipline, adulthood, sanity, science and progress. In contrast, the non-European periphery gets defined in terms of imitativeness, irrationality, emotion, instinct, practical reasoning, spontaneity, childhood, insanity and stagnation (1993: 17). Europe's internal qualities and unique characteristics are seen to have enabled it to achieve its dominant world position, thus Europe's 'modernization' starts from within (unique innovation) and spreads outwards (diffusion). Within this narrative, modernity becomes a singularly European achievement, such that modernity is European, Europe is modernity. Colonialism is seen to be exterior to this formation, therefore 'colonialism must mean, for the Africans, Asians, and Americans, not spoliation and cultural destruction but, rather, the receipt-by-diffusion of European civilization: modernization' (1993: 2).

Echoing Césaire and Said, Blaut argues that the unexamined implicit beliefs held by scholars about the marvellous uniqueness of Western development, the supposed inherent incompatibility of Western and non-Western civilizations, and the 'obviousness' of racial and cultural differences allows them to conform to and reproduce erroneous dominant ideologies even as they claim to be engaged in rigorous, objective scholarship. Colonial tropes saturate the concepts of the social sciences, such as Weberian accounts of Western rationality, action and social development, concepts that have been foundational to contemporary sociological approaches to understanding the emergence of the nation-state system, the international division of labour, the spread of globalization and even modernity itself.

As a discipline premised upon studying the West's Others, anthropology was forced by the mid-twentieth century anti-colonial struggles to re-evaluate its relationship to coloniality[3] and its methods of representing the subaltern. In contrast, other social science disciplines, and especially sociology (and by extension, therefore, the sociology of sport), have largely failed to interrogate their own complicities with colonialist ways of thinking and seeing. The post/colonial challenge requires that we do more than simply note the congruence between the emergence of sociology as a discipline and the formation of colonial nation-states. Instead, it initiates a more radical agenda, namely to challenge the notion that the conceptual categories of sociology are timeless and universal (as opposed to seeing them as inherently Eurocentric), and to contest the idea that racism is somehow exterior and not constitutive of the social formations of the West (Bhambra 2007; see also Steinmetz 2013). As Barnor Hesse puts it, 'Is it unreasonable to recall that the modernity of our worldly interdependence was imperial in its formal contours and remains globally racialized in its specular provenance? Failure to recall this leads to an inability to understand the formative role of European racism in Western societies' (1999: 123).

Post/colonial theory *and* sport?

Given that modern sport was born in the age of colonialism and the centrality of sports to the cultural project of Western imperialism, as well as certain imperialist notions of muscular Christianity (Mangan 1986; Guttmann 1994), it might be expected that critical work on colonialism would have much to say about sport. This is not so. Homi Bhabha's influential *The Location of Culture*, for example, has no location for anything resembling sport. In the 400-plus pages of Said's (1993) *Culture and Imperialism*, sport hardly surfaces. And Spivak has never written on sports. On the rare occasions when sport is directly discussed by post/colonial theorists, this is usually via an all-too-brief discussion on C.L.R. James and his work *Beyond a Boundary*. In that book, James (1963) skillfully demonstrates how the game of cricket became a site for West Indian independence struggles, and therefore a space of anti-colonial politics. For this reason it can be seen as one of the foundational texts for the critical study of race and sport, and an important starting point for any post/colonial theory of sport (Carrington 2013). But clearly there is more to be said on this topic than a single book (however significant) published over fifty years ago, focussed almost entirely on cricket in the middle of the twentieth century. It may be that post/colonial theory's over-reliance on reading culture as text and treating literary texts as the sum of culture, perhaps because the field is so dominated by literary theorists, means that 'culture' often gets reduced to a linguistic frame, rendering forms of *physical* culture problematic and hence largely ignored. Thus, despite Bhabha's observation that modes of 'popular rebellion and mobilization are often most subversive and transgressive when they are created through oppositional *cultural* practices' (1994: 20), sport has rarely been seen as a cultural practice worthy of extended consideration.

Sport studies has replicated this problem. Otherwise excellent and comprehensive sociology of sport introductions invariably have index entries as well as substantive chapters on a plurality of theoretical perspectives, including postmodernism and poststructuralism, for example, but rarely on post/colonial theory (see, for example, Jarvie and Maguire 1994; Coakley and Dunning 2000). However, there is some indication that over the past decade sport studies scholars have slowly become more aware of the important contributions that post/colonial theory can offer in helping us to rethink some of the established narratives of sport. More recently the ideas and contributions of Césaire, Fanon, Bhabha, Said and Spivak, among others, have at least been engaged in survey texts (Said's *Orientalism* is the most likely to be cited and discussed) (see, for example, Giulianotti 2005; Hughson *et al.* 2005). In seeking to correct what they call the 'lacuna' within post/colonial studies and its lack of work on sport, John Bale and Mike Cronin's (2003) edited collection *Sport and Postcolonialism* is a welcome and important text. The book addresses the body's centrality to both sport as practice and discourse, and post/colonial theory's interest in racial alterity and identity. The editors map out an agenda for a post/colonial theory of sport that includes unveiling the complicity of sports with colonial regimes of domination; considering the role of sport as a form of subaltern resistance; the examination of the representation of sport (photography, writing practices of authors and such) within colonial discourse; delinking sport from what they call 'metropolitan theory' and its 'totalizing systems of generalizations' (or what I would simply call Eurocentric thought); and the recovery of hidden histories of alternative forms of physical culture and bodily practices that generate different meanings to those of the dominant competitive sports cultures of the West (Bale and Cronin 2003: 8).[4]

Whilst this recent work represents a significant development (see also Farred 2004; Falcous 2007), it remains the case that too many within the sociology of sport use the term 'postcolonial' in a largely descriptive sense that simply refers to analyses of sport in societies that were once formally colonized (see, for example, Wagg (2005), Chappell (2008)). This, unfortunately, negates a deeper deconstrunctionist and comparative rethinking of sports discourses, structures and practices that would require examining the ways in which particular societies are 'post/colonial' in different and significant ways. This suggests that the engagement of post/colonial theory *and* sport, which challenges the epistemological claims of both sport and sport theory as produced in the West – that is the serious intellectual work of decolonizing ways of understanding sport – has yet to fully arrive.

Rethinking how we conceptualize sport might be a useful place to start the project of a post/colonial sports studies. Allen Guttmann's (1978) Weberian typology, first expounded in *From Ritual to Record*, defines sport not so much in terms of meaning but rather by a set of inter-related formal-structural characteristics and has become the standard, if occasionally contested, definition within sport history and beyond. Drawing on anthropological work on the relationship between play and social structure, it is suggested that 'primitive' societies are marked by simple forms of spontaneous play, whereas advanced societies develop more complex forms of rule-bound play. Historical change occurs through a latent evolutionary progression from the primitive to the ancient and medieval and eventually to the modern. Thus, as societies become more complex, so do their forms of play. This structuralist account is then used to provide a set of seven core characteristics that are claimed to distinguish 'modern sport' from that which came before, namely secularism, equality of opportunity, specialization of roles, rationalization, bureaucratic organization, quantification and the quest for records (1978: 16).

Guttmann's typology, a framework that has been foundational to much sociological work on sport, rests on a series of problematic binaries. These operate to distinguish the rational civilized moderns contrasted against the irrational violent primitives who, we are told, can barely even speak the language of sport. It could be argued that the history of sport (as dominant narrative) and sports history (as discipline) are indebted to a model of Eurocentric diffusionist thought and logic. In tautological fashion, Europe is seen as the unique incubator of all forms of meaningful physical activity that can be properly understood as sport, and sport is defined in such a way as to preclude other forms of physical culture from being sport. Europe is the place where sport 'starts' and then 'spreads' on the wings of colonialism. There is little cross-cultural diffusion (Blaut 1993: 167) in the development of sports, and the influence of sporting forms from outside of Europe on 'modern' sports is either downplayed or ignored altogether. Binaries, often invoked unproblematically, of modernity/tradition, the rational/irrational and the civilized/primitive, work to structure how modern sport is conceptualized.

We might better formulate sport as embodying not so much the reason and order of European modernity and its self-declared properties – secularization, rationality, meritocracy and so on – but rather the *incomplete, partial and paradoxical* elements of competing modernities that refuse to be disavowed. Rather than attempting to locate the timeless, supposedly objective characteristics of modern sport – the subtitle to *From Ritual to Record* is *The Nature of Sports* – we would enquire, instead, into the transitory, ethical and above all, political contexts within which 'sport' is given meaning and the uses to which sport is put (Booth 2013). Much ideological work has been necessary to hide modern sport's supposedly pre-modern, anti-rational tendencies – sexual, racial, gender and class discrimination, gratuitous violence, unpredictability, emotional excess – all the while these very attributes are actually *constitutive elements* that help to create sport's appeal and sustain its very possibility. Sport, like the claims of liberal democracy – tolerance, civic freedoms and citizenship, deliberative philosophical reason and so on – should be conceptualized more as a particular physical manifestation and representation of European myths ('fair play' rules, masculine codes of 'good sportsmanship' and meritocratic 'level playing fields') born of colonial conflict than as the actual objective embodiment of the 'truth' of such claims. Just as the idea of an enlightened Europe is dependent on the creation of the 'savage' Other in order to make itself, so too are modernist definitions of sport reliant upon the non-sporting 'primitive', or what might be better called the Myth of Modern Sport (Carrington 2010).

Conclusion: Towards a post/colonial theory *of* sport

Post/colonial theory represents an important advance in understanding how the modern world has been shaped and particularly how Western societies and their economic, political, technological and cultural development cannot be understood outside of or separate from colonialism. Key sociological concepts such as 'the state', 'modernization' and 'globalization' and even socio-philosophical terms such as 'freedom', 'liberty' and 'democracy', terms that have enabled the West to view itself as more advanced and civilized than the rest of the world, are complicit with Europe's violent colonial histories. Post/colonial theory is important precisely because (alongside Marxism) it interrogates the West's self-produced claims to superiority that have often been used to ignore or cover up the darker side of European modernity (Mignolo 2011), a modernity founded, in part, upon transatlantic slavery and the dispossession of indigenous peoples, and which also created the conditions and techniques that made the Holocaust possible (Gilroy 1993; Bauman 2000).

Unlike disciplines such as anthropology, sociology has largely failed to fully interrogate its own continuing complicities with coloniality. A reflexive, post/colonial sociology (and therefore, a sociology of sport), needs to do more than acknowledge the coeval emergence of sociology as a discipline with the high point of Western imperialism. It would consider how its categories of thought and analysis emerged *as a result of* and were *produced by* those colonial encounters. As Gurminder Bhambra puts it, 'What, for example, are the consequences of thinking colonialism and empire as entangled within the discipline? It cannot be for the discipline to continue as usual with a few new case studies at its disposal. It must be to radically reconfigure the discipline, to account for the narratives that were missing in dominant ones, and to rewrite them on the basis of acknowledging our shared histories and the inequalities with which they are associated' (2014: 3).

For example, what happens to our frames of analysis and our claims about the legitimacy of the use (and decline) of violence as a modality of state control if we conceptualize the birth of the modern 'liberal democratic' nation-state as, instead, a *colonial state* predicated upon the subjugation of subaltern struggles for freedom? If we avoid theorizing globalization as a purely Western-centred phenomenon that expanded civilizing tendencies and processes outwards from Europe, and instead interrogate the inherently racialized dimensions of globalization? What if our *starting* point for understanding 'society' was premised on the ubiquity of Western imperialism and we viewed the distinctive forms of racial alterity, economic exploitation and colonial governance as axiomatic (and not exterior) to the emerging Atlantic economy and the rapid industrialization of Western Europe? Such an approach would lead us to consider how racism, as a form of 'racialized governmentality' (Hesse 1999), is in fact central to processes of modernization and globalization and cannot be treated as epiphenomenal to the core conceptual frameworks frequently used within the sociology of sport.

A post/colonial sociology of sport would also avoid being locked into a narrow nation-state framework for analyzing society. The concept of diaspora is important in this context because it contests, disrupts and draws attention to the mirage that national borders and identifications are fixed and natural, allowing subaltern voices and discrepant histories to be mapped and traced. Diaspora also helps us to understand why questions concerning multiculturalism have generated such heated political and public debate in recent years. This is because the 'multicultural question' reveals the hidden underbelly of imperial nation-state formations that tried to disavow their own inherent ethnic heterogeneity and racial hybridity. European states were, from their inception, dependent upon the labor, bodies and resources of the colonized, bodies which now, due to the very same imperial circuits, are increasingly located, living in and claiming belonging to the post/colonial metropoles. These changes are nowhere more visible than within the sporting spaces of Europe, and especially across its football fields and athletic arenas, wherein the racial and ethnic composition of city, regional and national teams (and by extension the identities attached to them), have been radically altered over the past two to three decades. As Said reminds us, 'The construction of identity is bound up with the disposition of power and powerlessness in each society' (1978/2003: 332), thus the symbolic and social significance of these changing post/colonial sporting identities, reshaping what it means to be European in the process, should not be underestimated.

Does sports studies, broadly defined, need its own revolution, especially given its ability to produce expert knowledge on the body, arguably the foundational category for racial discourse? Post/colonial studies pushes us to consider the extent to which the institutional and disciplinary spaces we work within, the epistemological assumptions we make and the forms of enquiry and 'facts' produced thereafter, are themselves implicated in the reproduction of Eurocentric forces of oppression and coercive forms of domination. Nineteenth-century racial science and the Western academy made the idea of race meaningful and helped to service the colonial project, but what of our own teachings, writings, concepts and institutional spaces today? Are they spaces of intervention against the new forms of imperialism or, through acquiescence, docile and complicit? That, in the end, is the urgent challenge facing a genuinely post/colonial theory of sport.

Acknowledgement

Parts of this chapter draw substantially on arguments first published in my *Race, Sport, and Politics* (2010). For their critical comments and useful feedback on an earlier draft I'd like to thank Simone Browne, Minkah Makalani and Richard Giulianotti.

Notes

1 My use of the virgule (post/colonial) instead of the standard rendering, either *postcolonial* or *post-colonial*, is deliberate and used to signal that the current conjuncture is caught in ambivalent tension between the surpassing of formal colonial governance and the continuance of neocolonial relations. The virgule can be used with correlative conjunctions (and/or) to mean 'and', implying a strong association, and it can also be used to mean 'or', as in an exclusive divide between two different words. Another way to put this is that even the meaning of the *neocolonial* (*continuing* economic domination) and the *postcolonial*

(after, relative autonomy) shifts from one geographical and historical location to another, just as the virgule's formal linguistic usage implies that either side of the division (and indeed both) can be used to complete the meaning of the sentence.

2 Despite denials from apologists for Western imperialism, systemic violence was central to European colonial regimes – especially as independence movements grew – well into the twentieth century, such as the mass killings carried out by the Belgians in the Democratic Republic of the Congo and the systematic torture of Algerians by the French. On the use of concentration camps, executions, sexual violence and torture of and on Kenyans by the British, see Elkins (2005) and Anderson (2005). On the more recent use of torture on Iraqis by British soldiers, see Finn and Raphael (2014).

3 'Coloniality names the underlying logic of the foundation and unfolding of Western civilization from the Renaissance to today of which historical colonialisms have been a constitutive, although down-played dimension. . . . Coloniality, in other words, is constitutive of modernity – there is no modernity without coloniality' (Mignolo 2011: 2–3).

4 Malcom's (2012) recent sociology of sport textbook does have a separate index entry on 'post-colonialism' and a discussion of post/colonial theory, perhaps indicating a more developed engagement compared to similar texts of even a decade ago.

References

Anderson, D. (2005) *Histories of the Hanged*, New York: Norton.
Bale, J. and Cronin, M. (eds) (2003) *Sport and Postcolonialism*, Oxford: Berg.
Bauman, Z. (2000) *Modernity and the Holocaust*, Cambridge: Polity Press.
Bhabha, H. (1994) *The Location of Culture*, London: Routledge.
Bhambra, G. (2007) *Rethinking Modernity*, Basingstoke, UK: Palgrave Macmillan.
Bhambra, G. (2014) 'Postcolonial Entanglements', *Postcolonial Studies*, doi: 10.1080/13688790.2014.963926.
Blaut, J.M. (1993) *The Colonizer's Model of the World*, London: Guilford Press.
Booth, D. (2013) 'Constructing Knowledge: Histories of Modern Sport', in D. Andrews and B. Carrington (eds) *A Companion to Sport*, Oxford: Blackwell.
Carrington, B. (2010) *Race, Sport and Politics*, London: Sage.
Carrington, B. (2013) 'The Critical Sociology of Race and Sport: The First Fifty Years', *Annual Review of Sociology*, 39: 379–398.
Césaire, A. (1955/2000) *Discourse on Colonialism*, New York: Monthly Review Press.
Chappell, R. (2008) 'Sport in Postcolonial Uganda', *Journal of Sport and Social Issues*, 32(2): 177–198.
Childs, P. and Williams, P. (1997) *An Introduction to Post-Colonial Theory*, London: Prentice Hall.
Coakley, J. and Dunning, E. (eds) (2000) *The Handbook of Sports Studies*, London: Sage.
Elkins, C. (2005) *Imperial Reckoning*, New York: Henry Holt.
Falcous, M. (2007) 'The Decolonizing National Imaginary: Promotional Media Constructions During the 2005 Lions Tour of Aotearoa New Zealand', *Journal of Sport and Social Issues*, 31(4): 374–393.
Fanon, F. (1952/2008) *Black Skin, White Masks*, New York: Grove Press.
Farred, G. (2004) 'The Double Temporality of *Lagaan*: Cultural Struggle and Postcolonialism', *Journal of Sport and Social Issues*, 28(2): 93–114.
Finn, P. and Raphael, S. (2014) 'Dogs, Water and Coffins: An Untold Story of British Torture in Iraq', *Open Democracy*, December 16. Available at: https://www.opendemocracy.net/peter-finn-sam-raphael/dogs-water-and-coffins-untold-story-of-british-torture-in-iraq (accessed 20 December 2014).
Gilroy, P. (1993) *The Black Atlantic*, London: Verso.
Giulianotti, R. (2005) *Sport*, Cambridge: Polity Press.
Guttmann, A. (1978) *From Ritual to Record: The Nature of Sports*, New York: Columbia University Press.
Guttmann, A. (1994) *Games and Empires*, New York: Columbia University Press.
Hajjar, L. (2014) 'The CIA Didn't Just Torture, It Experimented on Human Beings', *The Nation*, 16 December. Available at: http://www.thenation.com/article/193185/cia-didnt-just-torture-it-experimented-human-beings# (accessed 20 December 2014).
Harvey, D. (2005) *The New Imperialism*, Oxford: Oxford University Press.
Hesse, B. (1999) 'Reviewing the Western Spectacle: Reflexive Globalization through the Black Diaspora', in A. Brah, M. Hickman, and M. Mac an Ghaill (eds) *Global Futures*, Basingstoke, UK: Macmillan.
Hughson, J., Inglis, D. and Free, M. (2005) *The Uses of Sport*, London: Routledge.
James, C.L.R. (1963) *Beyond a Boundary*, London: Serpent's Tail.
Jarvie, G. and Maguire, J. (1994) *Sport and Leisure in Social Thought*, London: Routledge.

Johnson, C. (2004) *The Sorrows of Empire*, New York: Henry Holt.

Kelley, R. (2000) 'A Poetics of Anticolonialism', in A. Césaire (1955/2000) *Discourse on Colonialism*, New York: Monthly Review Press.

Malcolm, D. (2012) *Sport and Sociology*, London: Routledge.

Mangan, J.M. (1986) *The Games Ethic and Imperialism*, London: Frank Cass.

Mann, M. (2005) *Incoherent Empire*, London: Verso.

Mignolo, W. (2011) *The Darker Side of Western Modernity*, Durham, NC: Duke University Press.

Said, E. (1978/2003) *Orientalism*, London: Penguin Books.

Said, E. (1993) *Culture and Imperialism*, London: Vintage.

Spivak, G. (1993) *Outside in the Teaching Machine*, London: Routledge.

Steinmetz, G. (ed.) (2013) *Sociology and Empire*, Durham, NC: Duke University Press.

Wagg, S. (ed.) (2005) *Cricket and National Identity in the Postcolonial Age: Following On*, London: Routledge.

Young, R. (2001) *Postcolonialism*, Oxford: Blackwell.

PART TWO

Sociology, social sciences and interdisciplinary studies of sport

12

INTRODUCTION TO PART TWO

Richard Giulianotti

In Part Two of the Handbook, we examine the interdisciplinary links that do or should exist between the sociology of sport and other social scientific disciplines and sub-disciplines. Inter-disciplinary work has long been positively valued and widely practiced by many social scientists, and strongly favoured by universities and other institutions that fund social research. Sociology has maintained and extended particularly strong ties and orientations towards social sciences such as anthropology, human geography, and political science, and these links have provided an effective basis for undertaking interdisciplinary work. A key impetus for such activity lies in the various theories, methods, and substantive research questions that derive at least in part from sociology, and which are influential in these and other disciplines.

The sociology of sport has featured significant interaction and collaboration with some social sciences, while also displaying some curious gaps in ties with other disciplines. These issues are addressed in Part Two, alongside how specific social sciences other than sociology approach the study of sport. The eight chapters which follow cover respectively the disciplines of anthropology, economics, geography, history, leisure studies, philosophy, political science, and psychology.

We begin by exploring the anthropological approach to the study of sport, and its continuities and differences with sociology. As Noel Dyck and Hans Hognestad explain in their chapter, anthropologists have tended towards an 'unabashed eclecticism' in embracing diverse concepts and research issues in order to investigate sport. Certainly, anthropologists have lacked the formal journals, associations, and critical mass of numbers that appear to be an advantage for the sociology of sport. On the other hand, as Dyck and Hognestad indicate, a smaller scale may bestow a disciplinary advantage, enabling anthropologists to extend constantly the boundaries of their field, to work 'outside the box', and to avoid sliding into what Eduardo Archetti referred to as 'sportology' – that is social research which is focused purely on sport. In terms of method, anthropological approaches tend to share rather more consistent ground, particularly in the use of ethnographic methods that bring alive the meanings, identities, and lifeworlds within, for example, the Balinese cock-fight, Canadian children's sport, or Norwegian football supporters (Dyck 2012; Geertz 1973; Hognestad 2009). A strongly comparative dimension runs through much of anthropology, reflected in how particular aspects of sport (such as spectator subcultures or youth sports) are interpreted with reference to different cultural settings. Closer disciplinary ties between anthropologists and sociologists would inspire the latter towards greater conceptual and substantive openness, and to draw on the rich ethnographic and comparative methods which characterize the anthropological approach.

Collaborative research between economists and sociologists on sport has been relatively limited. However, as the chapter by Kevin Delaney demonstrates, there are common issues for scholars in these disciplines to investigate, particularly in the broad field of the sport market. For economists, sport market activities tend to be viewed as reflecting individual or collective interests, whereas for sociologists there is greater focus on how these preferences are socially constructed, for example through socialization, marketing impacts, and the wider influence of consumer culture. As Delaney points out, both disciplines are interested in how political interests shape the sport market in specific ways: for example, in the United States, in how privately owned sport teams secure huge public subsidies, such as through stadium construction or tax concessions; or on the questionable contribution of sport mega-events towards boosting economic development in host cities (Baade 2006; Delaney and Eckstein 2003). Both disciplines are also interested in the cost of gaining access to sport in market contexts, and subsequent sport participation across different social classes. Again, it might be reasonably argued that these common research issues should inspire greater levels of economics-sociology collaboration than has been evidenced hitherto.

Much more significant links have arisen between geography and sociology in the study of sport. As Nicholas Wise explains in his chapter, foundational work in sport geography was provided by John Rooney (1974) and, in particular, John Bale (1994). Subsequently, much of the work in sport geography that is of interest to sociologists has centred on the interrelated themes of space, landscape, community, and identity. For example, sport stadiums within specific communities are associated with particular senses of place and forms of socio-cultural identity. When sport teams 'move home' – for example, when North American sport 'franchises' relocate to new cities – fans may lose interest in the team and experience significant senses of loss with respect to their personal and social identities. Geographers are also interested in the transnational aspects of sport with regard to many broadly sociological themes and processes, such as the worldwide migration of leading athletes, the global marketing of sport clubs and league systems, and the socio-spatial aspects of hosting sport mega-events.

The history of sport is one of the most established sub-disciplines within sport studies, as reflected in its long-standing international journals and associations. Accordingly, there has been substantial interplay between the historical and sociological analysis of sport. Douglas Booth and Mark Falcous argue in their chapter that a common critical stream within both disciplines – focusing on 'social justice, relations of power, social conflict and social change' – provides the best way ahead for the collaborative and complementary analysis of sport. In tracing the history of these links and ties, Booth and Falcous highlight the significant influence of different social theories and perspectives on both disciplines, notably various strains of Marxism, cultural studies standpoints, and postmodernism or poststructuralism. These critical standpoints have enabled strong historical and sociological accounts of, for example, class, gender, and sexuality within the sport context (e.g. Gruneau 1999; Hargreaves 1994). In reflecting on future areas of interest for the sub-discipline of sport history, and which are of direct relevance for sociologists, Booth and Falcous note that the ethical components of critical inquiry need to be addressed, including how the past is to be written and to be judged in normative terms.

The chapter by Ken Roberts examines the complex and often close relationships between the transdisciplinary field of leisure studies and the sociology of sport. For Roberts, the latter is a relatively established and secure sub-discipline, whereas leisure studies has far looser disciplinary roots. Leisure studies grew particularly out of the rapid expansion of the 'leisure industries' (such as media, tourism, and music, as well as sport), and its academic departments and programmes contributed to the expansion of the higher education sector, initially in the United States from the 1950s onwards. As Roberts notes, active sport accounts for a very small proportion of leisure time and leisure spending, although much more of both is directed towards 'following' sport, particularly through media. Sociological approaches enable leisure studies scholars to examine major social divisions in sport participation, particularly along the lines of age/life-cycle, gender, class, and ethnicity/nationality (Critcher *et al.* 1995; Roberts 2015). Moreover, as Roberts points out, sport's historical development was far more gender-biased than the wider leisure field, in being shaped by a focus on men (particularly young men); sport was also unduly slow in responding to new innovations in mass media, particularly television. Latterly, sport and the wider leisure sphere have continued to grow, despite the global economic downturn; indeed, despite much contradictory evidence, major sport events are often viewed as potential vehicles for providing financial boosts to cities and nations.

While the philosophy of sport has become an established sub-discipline in sport studies, its interactions with the sociology of sport have been relatively circumscribed, despite regular calls to the contrary. In his chapter, William Morgan argues that such collaboration is itself 'critically important' if social scientists are to generate a critical analysis of sport. For Morgan, the social theory of Michel Foucault, despite its epistemological twists and turns, provides a potentially vital basis for such work. Foucault's theory of *epistemes* postulates that frameworks of knowledge or world-views are distinct from each other, being based on different rationales and principles, hence there is deadlock in argument when any one confronts the others. In sport, such an impasse occurred when the proponents of amateurism and professionalism clashed with each other at different points in sport history, as neither side recognized a 'rational' basis for the 'discourses' of the other. Morgan in turn proposes that a proper social criticism of sport – which would engage both sociology and philosophy – needs to be founded on a mix of rational argument and transgression, enabling other possibilities and visions of sport to be explored. For example, new sports for women may be developed which move beyond masculine models and ideals of physical culture (see Marion-Young 1979).

While there are a significant number of political scientists with research interests in sport, collaborative work with sociologists has been relatively circumscribed. In his chapter, Barrie Houlihan indicates that part of the reason for non-communication may lie in the fragmentation of the respective disciplines, as registered by diverse theoretical moves and switches in substantive research problems. However, as Houlihan argues, the two disciplines do share underlying interests in the nature and exercise of power, and in the making and influence of political ideas or ideologies. Political science contributes a range of theories with regard to the making of sport policies, governance, and modernization which may be positively harnessed by sociologists. For Houlihan, the Foucauldian theory of governmentality, which explains how neo-liberal self-regulating subjects are constructed, offers one analytical framework which the two disciplines may share (cf. Barry *et al.* 1996). At the same time, as Houlihan argues, further research should be undertaken into the influences of global institutions in shaping national sport policies and structures, and into the role of sport for smaller states in shaping their identities and influences.

Further interdisciplinary gaps, which must be filled in the study of sport, are identified by Brett Smith and Kerry McGannon in their chapter with respect to psychology and sociology. Several reasons for this absence of activity are suggested, such as different disciplinary vocabularies, ontologies, methods, and approaches to critical inquiry, along with wider institutional factors within academe. Yet, the authors argue, clear benefits would derive from mixed sociological and psychological approaches. For example, scholars should not ignore the actual influence of both psychological and socio-cultural processes on social actions. Collaborative work may also generate original methods and theories for social research. 'Concept analysis' and 'narrative inquiry' may provide the methodological bases for cross-disciplinary research. In addition, the method of 'discursive psychology' has significant continuities with established sociological approaches such as ethnomethodology and conversation analysis, along with Foucauldian post-structuralist theory. Such an approach also enables analysis of the 'subject positions' that are taken up by individuals through their discourses on sport and other subjects. Thus, in line with the arguments elsewhere in Part Two of this Handbook, Smith and McGannon highlight the substantial benefits to be drawn from interdisciplinary research, not least in enabling sociologists to learn fresh concepts and methods through engaging with alternative disciplines.

References

Baade, R. (2006) 'The Economic Impact of Mega-sporting Events', in W. Andreff and S. Szymanski (eds) *Handbook on the Economics of Sport*, Cheltenham, UK: Edward Elgar.

Bale, J. (1994) *Landscapes of Modern Sport*, London: Leicester University Press.

Barry, A., T. Osborne and N. Rose (eds) (1996) *Foucault and Political Reason*, Chicago: University of Chicago Press.

Critcher, C., P. Bramham and A. Tomlinson (eds) (1995) *Sociology of Leisure: A Reader*, London: E. & F.N. Spon.

Delaney, K. and R. Eckstein (2003) *Public Dollars, Private Stadiums*, New Brunswick, NJ: Rutgers University Press.

Dyck, N. (2012) *Fields of Play: An Ethnography of Children's Sports*, Toronto: University of Toronto Press.

Geertz, C. (1973) *The Interpretation of Cultures*, New York: Basic Books.

Gruneau, R. (1999) *Class, Sports and Social Development*, 2nd edition, Urbana, IL: Human Kinetics Press.

Hargreaves, J. (1994) *Sporting Females*, London: Routledge.

Hognestad, H.K. (2009) 'Transglobal Scandinavian? Globalization and the Contestation of Identities in Football', *Soccer & Society*, 10(3/4): 358–373.

Marion-Young, I. (1979) 'The Exclusion of Women from Sport: Conceptual and Existential Dimensions', *Philosophy in Context*, 9: 44–53.

Roberts, K. (2015) 'Social Class and Leisure during Recent Recessions in Britain', *Leisure Studies*, doi: 10.1080/02614367.2013.855939.

Rooney, J.F. (1974) *A Geography of American Sport: From Cabin Creek to Anaheim*, Reading, PA: Addison-Wesley.

13

ANTHROPOLOGICAL PERSPECTIVES AND THE SOCIOLOGY OF SPORT

Noel Dyck and Hans Hognestad

Anthropological treatments of sport differ from their sociological counterparts by virtue of their underlying disciplinary orientation. This is especially evident in how practitioners of the two disciplines tend to define and demarcate their respective inquiries within this field. From a sociological perspective, the modernization and institutionalization of sport that exploded especially in Britain during the nineteenth century reflected the impacts of industrialization and urbanization upon existing games and athletic practices, as well as the integration of these reworked forms into new ways of life. The rapid spread of these 'new' sports to elsewhere in Europe, North America and beyond established their status both as popular leisure activities and exemplars of modernity. Yet it was precisely this latter dimension that rendered sport a problematic subject for investigation within anthropology, a discipline initially positioned as the science of the non-modern and 'primitive' (Archetti 1998). Nevertheless, anthropologists conducting fieldwork in aboriginal communities and non-Western societies continued to stumble across athletic competitions and pastimes that, for want of a better term, appeared to be 'sport-like' in one or another respect.

Within sociology, attention focused on the ways in which modern sport had evolved beyond the forms and purposes of pre-modern games and athletic contests. This gave rise to a generally shared disciplinary understanding of the characteristics of modern sport. A recent iteration of this perspective defines sport as 'institutionalized activities that involve rigorous physical exertion or the use of relatively complex physical skills by participants motivated by internal and external rewards' (Coakley and Donnelly 2009: 4). Essential to this rendering of sport are competition; standardized rules of play; accentuation of the organization and technical development of sport; formalized learning of sport techniques; quantification of results; construction of records; and the secularization of sport (Coakley and Donnelly 2009: 3–5; Guttmann 1978). Activities that fall outside this working disciplinary consensus about what modern sport comprises may, nonetheless, attract the attention of individual sociologists (e.g. Vertinsky, McManus and Sit 2010).

In contrast, early anthropological reports of games and athletic contests appeared sporadically and tended to be regarded as tangential to more categorically 'indigenous' social arrangements and cultural beliefs. Aside from detailed ethnological descriptions of traditional Native American games (e.g. Culin 1907/1992; Mooney 1890), athletic contests and 'sports' were seldom treated as central concerns within ethnographic reports (e.g. Firth 1930; Fox 1961). But this disciplinary indifference to sport began to erode in the latter part of the twentieth century in the wake of a far-reaching rethinking of socio-cultural anthropology, which promoted the adoption of more processual and performance-oriented analytical perspectives. Accounts of the Balinese cock-fight as a site of 'deep play' (Geertz 1973), the use of Trobriand cricket as an 'ironic' response to colonialism (Leach 1976), and the political implications of the Afghani equestrian sport of *buzkashi* (Azoy 1982) marked a turning point for the discipline. This belated acknowledgement of games and sporting contests that clearly mattered to peoples who had long figured within anthropological accounts served to undercut any abiding disciplinary inclination to steer clear of the study of sport as a matter of principle.

Another factor contributing to this nascent anthropological appreciation of sport ensued from reassessing the merits of making room within the discipline for inquiries conducted within modern and Western settings previously ceded to other social sciences. This opened the door to anthropological publications on, for example, American baseball (Gmelch 1972) and football (Arens 1975; Dundes 1978) as well as MacAloon's study of the modern Olympic games (1981). These and other works brought the examination of professional sports, as well as of traditional athletic contests and other forms of what Mauss termed 'techniques of the body' (1973), inside the fold, if not necessarily to the centre, of anthropological inquiry. By the end of the twentieth century there existed a corpus of anthropological writings on sport, including accounts of traditional forms of wrestling (Alter 1992), sports in post-Maoist China (Brownell 1995), cricket in India (Appadurai 1995), baseball in the Dominican Republic (Klein 1991) and along the Mexico-Texas border (Klein 1997), the Winter Olympic Games in Lillehammer (Klausen 1999a), capoeira in Brazil (Lewis 1992), football 'hooligans' in England (Armstrong 1998), and football, polo, and tango in Argentina (Archetti 1999a).

Anthropological treatments of games and sports – as well as of embodied practices like dance that have much in common with sport (Dyck and Archetti 2003) – have not, however, given rise to a separate disciplinary subfield. Instead, anthropologists are usually at pains to demonstrate how their accounts of particular games, sports, or embodied cultural forms fit within and contribute to anthropological scholarship more generally. What has emerged is a variegated but original literature that examines a dizzying array of sport and sport-like activities from differing analytical perspectives. What these works share is not a singular research agenda but a robust appreciation of the exploratory possibilities presented by ethnographic approaches. This predisposition valorizes the preparation of detailed accounts and analyses of particular sporting activities, relationships, and passions that occur within specified contexts. Equally important is the priority within contemporary anthropology of elucidating similarities and differences revealed when accounts such as these are juxtaposed. Comparative analyses of differing types of athletic and embodied activities offer sturdy means for surveying the myriad practices, purposes, relationships, and meanings brought into play within this teeming sector of human endeavour.

Leaving open the issue of whether any given set of practices does or does not 'count' unambiguously as sport permits anthropologists broad leeway to delve into any activities that it might seem useful to view as being sport-like. This permits anthropologists to examine sports and sport-like practices as they would any other form of social or cultural practice. By noting the definitional schema placed by sportsmen and some sociologists around the concept of sport, yet ranging freely beyond these, anthropologists fashion an intellectual space within which these activities can be interrogated in novel ways. Nor are they entirely alone in this: individual sociologists have also observed that play, games, and sports are 'not abstract "things" to be concretely defined; rather they are complex processes and relationships that can never be adequately encapsulated into rigid definitional schemes or formulas' (Gruneau 1999: 132).

Traditionally identified as the backbone of anthropological endeavour, comparison also looms large in anthropologists' inquiries into sport and sport-like activities. But the internal critique of the discipline mounted in the latter part of the twentieth century not only triggered renunciations of positivistic anthropology but also prompted a fundamental re-assessment of cross-cultural comparison as a means of description and generalization. This led to revision of disciplinary purposes and methodological practices: henceforth, social facts were deemed constructions rather than things, and comparison comprised not a singular method but a set of overlapping dimensions (Holy 1987). The first and most basic of these dimensions recognizes comparison as an essential element of human life and cognition:

> Humans always compare. . . . Since anthropologists study humans and are themselves human, the question can no longer be whether or not anthropologists should pursue comparison. Rather, the question is *what kind of recognition* scholars give to this basic human activity.
>
> (Fox and Gingrich 2002: 20)

By way of illustration, note how few of the rules and accoutrements of professional or amateur ice hockey figure within street hockey games played year-round by children and youths in communities across Canada (Dyck 2000: 23). Nevertheless, participants in these informally organized matches often enthusiastically 'broadcast' their own vocalized 'play by play' commentary about their exploits as they move down the street, before imagined audiences, to score or prevent goals. In doing so, they playfully present their feats as being *just like* those of their heroes and 'counterparts' in the National Hockey League.

A second and largely implicit dimension of anthropological comparison involves the incidental 'translation' routinely required within a discipline whose practitioners typically seek to explain particular forms, practices, and beliefs to 'others' residing within quite different contexts. Even the most elementary socio-cultural translation of such practices entails the use of terminologies from both contexts since performing this task involves undertaking at least a minimum amount of comparison between them (Fox and Gingrich 2002: 20). How better, for instance, to render explicable to non-Indian readers the distinctive action featured within the Indian sport of *kabbadi* than to identify it as a game inflected by yoga that is, nonetheless, played by participants divided into two teams (Alter 2000: 85, 94).

Beyond these two dimensions rest more explicit modes of comparison that anthropologists approach in varying ways. A well-selected case can, in the hands of a skilled analyst, reveal a plurality of distinguishable modes and levels of participation within a single event, as Ronsbo (2003) demonstrates in an account of a particular football match played in a Salvadorean village following that country's civil war. The two teams that took the field that afternoon engaged in not just an organized athletic competition but also a re-enactment of the violent relations that exploded in that region during the early 1980s. The wealthy organizers of this particular football match, who assembled a team of paid semi-professional players to represent them, had years before served as *ladino* patrol members who were supported by outside army and police forces. These forces had killed male relatives of members of the indigenous team that turned up some years later to play in this particular match. Therefore, as well as exhibiting contrasting playing styles, the two sides athletically restaged a conflict that continues to separate these communities on and off the field of play.

Anthropological authors also draw comparisons between differing actualizations of similar sport forms. Swyers's (2010) study of a set of Chicago Cubs fans who choose to sit together year after year in certain sections of the outfield bleachers at Wrigley Field examines what sets them apart from the tens of thousands of other fans who frequent that ballpark. These 'Wrigley regulars' celebrate their commitment to their small and self-selected baseball community. They contrast their stylized expressions of allegiance to the team and to one another to the presumed inferiority or absence of such sentiments among the 'others' who arrive to watch the Cubs. In contrast, Kelly notes the manner in which baseball fan clubs at the legendary Koshien Tigers stadium in Japan reflect, among other things, the medium- and small-business character of the local economy (Kelly 2004: 99). Meanwhile, baseball in Cuba evokes passionate debates amongst fans about the nature of Cuba, of *cubanidad* (the quality of being Cuban) and the inescapable presence of the Cuban state in sport (Carter 2008).

Anthropologists sometimes juxtapose ostensibly dissimilar phenomena or forms that upon closer analysis may be shown to share previously unrecognized commonalities. Sport and dance are conventionally separated from one another in typologies of leisure activities that circulate in the West. Nevertheless, both forms of practice revolve around the acquisition, organization and performance of physically demanding techniques of the body (Wieschiolek 2003; Wulff 1998). What is more, these activities can be pursued at any number of levels of intensity, reaching from the recreational, within which participants seek primarily to satisfy themselves, to more highly accomplished levels, where dancers or players strive to demonstrate their accomplishments and technical superiority over other practitioners. Without needing to reduce dance to sport or vice versa, ethnographers have enlarged our ethnographic appreciation of both types of activities by considering the telling similarities that these share, despite their differences. Setting aside categorical presumptions and paying close attention to particular practices has also served to disclose why football and tango have long been intimately associated with one another in Argentina (Archetti 2003) and how and why the Tanzanian concept of *michezo*, a term that likens dancing, football and many other expressive physical activities to one another, so steadfastly denies the categorical boundaries that underpin Western notions of sport and physical education (Leseth 2003). Recognizing the heuristic value that explicit comparison of a broader range of phenomena potentially offers has opened the door to appreciating the sport-like dimensions of chess, while simultaneously providing an articulated model of the tactics of 'counterplay' that could be profitably applied to any number of sport activities (Desjarlais 2011).

Thinking outside the box of 'sportology'?

The study of sport is a well-established and institutionalized sub-field within sociology, which is anchored by organizations such as the International Sociology of Sport Association (ISSA), the North American Society for the Sociology of Sport (NASSS) and the European Association for Sociology of Sport (EASS). Although these professional bodies include researchers based within general sociology departments, a great many of the members and conference delegates at events hosted by these organizations consist of scholars employed at various sports science departments or research units where sport studies is the common focus for teaching and research. This arrangement serves to draw the sociology of sport towards the larger field of sport sciences, and, in so doing, to focus its range of inquiry upon institutionalized sport policies, events and interests structured by organized modern sport. While the pursuit of health benefits or gold medals may serve effectively as strategic themes for legitimating public spending on mass or elite level sport within a nation, slipping into a narrow research concentration on sports policy runs the risk of ignoring more fundamental questions about how sport is socially situated, improvised and experienced. The late Eduardo Archetti, one of the pioneers of anthropological studies of sport, jokingly, yet critically, characterized academic work that focuses almost exclusively on the study of sport as 'sportology'.

While the lack of such institutionalization of anthropological studies of sport may be disempowering in some respects, it does allow for intellectual approaches to be developed 'outside the box' laid out by organized sport. Anthropologists tend to locate sport within wider social, political and cultural contexts that are not limited to the institutional structures of modern sport organizations and businesses. This permits greater independence than may be available to sport researchers who are more directly tied to the interests prioritized by stakeholders in sport clubs or sport federations. An example of this disciplinary freedom is provided by a team research project initiated in 1989 in advance of the 1994 Winter Olympic Games held in Lillehammer, an undertaking led by the Norwegian anthropologist Arne Martin Klausen. The volume that presented the findings of this project, *Olympic Games as Performance and Public Event* (Klausen 1999a), included contributions from six anthropologists and one media scientist. The introduction to this volume positioned it as a contribution to the practice of 'anthropology at home', equating it to other anthropological studies conducted in contemporary Western societies (Klausen 1999b: 1). In Klausen's view, not the least of their achievements had been to conduct ethnographic fieldwork on a global sporting event despite 'the difficulties [of] conducting conventional fieldwork in an Olympic context' (Klausen 1999b: 4).

The studies carried out by Klausen and his colleagues (including one conducted during the preceding 1992 winter games in Albertville) presented, among other things, detailed analyses of the interplay between ritual and drama in the preparations for and performance of Olympic competitions and ceremonies. By situating their accounts within the complex social, cultural and political contexts that frame the staging of a global event within a particular national setting, this team of anthropological researchers transgressed the boundaries normally observed by 'sportologists'. They also scrutinized some of the locally controversial measures forced on Norwegian organizers by the International Olympic Committee (IOC), one of the most powerful governing bodies in modern sport (Klausen 1999d). Klausen's (1999c: 27–48) account of 'Norwegian Culture and Olympism' took an insider's perspective on the working relations and conflicts that developed between the various Norwegian, Olympic and corporate agencies involved in preparing and managing the Lillehammer Games. Invoking a classical anthropological dichotomy between traditionalism and modernism in his analysis, Klausen concluded that these games 'became an occasion for revitalising traditional Norwegian identity . . . while, at the same time, it became an arena for presenting Norway's modernity' (Klausen 1999c: 46).

Archetti's account of skiing competitions staged during the 1992 Albertville Games, the precursor to the games hosted two years later in Lillehammer, explored the practical and theoretical challenges involved in studying a time-limited phenomenon such as the Olympics. As Archetti explained it, his enquiry accumulated data and insights that 'were a mixture of the seen, the lived, the said, and the written' (Archetti 1999b: 199). In the course of several visits to forthcoming Olympic venues in the Savoie region near the Italian border prior to the Albertville Games, Archetti established contacts with a range of people engaged in winter sports. Opportunities for observing the Winter Olympics are restricted to just a few weeks of competitions that occur in venues scattered across what are often distant rural areas. Since it was impossible for Archetti to attend and observe all or even most of the skiing competitions, he decided to concentrate his fieldwork in the town of Mégève, where the men's cross-country skiing competitions took place. Thus, during the short and intense period of competition, he made observations and 'hung out' largely with French and Norwegian supporters and practitioners of cross-country skiing. Out of this experience he constructed an ethnographically grounded analytical account that compared the performances and personae of the Italian alpine skier Alberto Tomba and the Norwegian cross-country skier Vegard Ulvang. These two came to play key roles in Archetti's research, which dissected the widely differing public perceptions of their respective performances of heroic masculinity. This ethnographically inspired inquiry subsequently led Archetti to his acclaimed studies of masculinities and nationalism in Argentina, which he framed in terms of the performative body practices of football, polo and tango (Archetti 1999a).

The particular fieldwork that informed Archetti's analysis of Tomba occurred during a single desperate day spent with a group of Italian supporters in the town of Les Menuires during the slalom competition. What was truly remarkable was Archetti's deft balancing of a set of unfolding fieldwork relations with simultaneous analysis of the Italian fans' expressions of their experiences that day. Grounded analyses of the type produced by Archetti remain difficult to imagine, let alone to obtain, by means of methodological approaches which might be simpler to apply, but which also remain distant from relationships and opportunities such as these. Archetti reflected upon how this fieldwork made him aware of the manner in which the Olympic games carry quintessential elements of modernity, specifically in the way competitions and disciplines are streamlined both to accommodate new disciplines and shed more archaic ones. Overall, his comparative analysis of Tomba and Ulvang led Archetti to an innovative account of diverging masculinities that 'touch the individual imagination and the collective sensibility in a different way and represent different bodily performances and sport traditions' (Archetti 1999b: 200). This imaginative comparative exegesis enabled him to pursue certain complexities of sport heroism in ways which have implications for examining and understanding social, cultural and political contexts that extend far beyond the sporting activities summed up by the modern Olympic motto *citius, altius, fortius* (i.e. quicker, higher, stronger).

Ethnographic studies of sport frequently exhibit capacities that reach beyond more conventional ones, such as testing the validity of a particular hypothesis or collecting data that tends to support the presumptions of a given body of social theory (Dyck 2012: 9). What anthropological fieldwork at its best brings to notice are unanticipated practices, problems and possibilities. Thus, in an extended ethnographic study of community sports for Canadian children and youths, Dyck (2012) explored the shape and tenor of social relationships between parents, children, coaches and other sport practitioners, and, in so doing, began to encounter more complicated issues than are usually reported in depictions of children's sport. Observing the dynamics of child and adult participation in everyday community sport activities uncovers the extent to which parental concerns about the future educational and career prospects of their offspring surreptitiously shape the conditions and meanings of boys' and girls' participation in these activities. Especially notable is what a son's or daughter's accomplishments on the fields of play may be commonly presumed to disclose about any given mother or father's capacities as a parent (Dyck 2012). Similarly, Hognestad's (1997, 2003, 2009) ethnographic studies of football supporters in Scotland and Norway illustrate how a global sport can furnish distinctive personal identities that equip individuals to navigate otherwise confining social and domestic situations (Hognestad 2009). Particularly evocative is Hognestad's (2003) account of the deliberately constructed undertakings of those Norwegians who opt to support English club teams rather than local football teams. What Hognestad explains is the stance adopted by these Norwegian football enthusiasts in order to distance themselves symbolically from cloying aspects of Norwegian cultural nationalism.

Disciplinary overlaps and conflicts

It has been argued that the philosophical and ethical issues raised by anthropology's reliance upon participant observation continues to give the discipline its critical edge towards various 'mainstream orthodoxies' seen as repressing the interests, passions and experiences of marginalized groups and individuals (Atkinson and Hammersley 1994: 249). Of course, some sport sociologists do utilize ethnographic methods in their research, but only infrequently do their works rely solely on extensive fieldwork (Giulianotti 1999). Ethnographic inquiry remains one of many alternative methodological approaches within sociology, while within anthropology fieldwork continues to constitute an integral aspect of the ethos of the discipline. Close and often unpredictable encounters with research subjects and the landscapes in which they operate remain underlying expectations for anthropological research. This set of disciplinary preferences continues to leave quantitative approaches and positivistic modes of analysis in a fairly marginalized position for most anthropologists.

While overlaps between sociological and anthropological studies of sport are, perhaps, more common than enforcements of disciplinary frontiers, a case of the latter arose in a special issue on football hooliganism published in *The Sociological Review* in 1991. An essay by Gary Armstrong and Rosemary Harris (1991) challenged what they saw as a lack of fieldwork data in works about football hooliganism produced by a leading research unit based at Leicester University. It was, in short, claimed that members of this group had ignored 'the social relationships typically generated by the life experiences of people in communities of this sort' (Armstrong and Harris 1991: 430). In response to these criticisms, Dunning, Murphy and Waddington (1991) argued that anthropological approaches were too commonsensical, particularistic and subjective. They concluded that their own figurational sociological approach, based on Norbert Elias's theory of *the civilizing process* (Elias 1978, 1986), constituted 'a better means than ethnography on its own or any other one-dimensional approach for penetrating empirically and theoretically to the core of phenomena such as football hooliganism' (Dunning, Murphy and Waddington 1991: 476). Nevertheless, this counter-critique, which suggested that ethnography constituted a more 'one-dimensional' approach than one which filters all collected data through a single theoretical paradigm, is not particularly illustrative of the current state of relations between sociological and anthropological approaches to the study of sports and games. Contemporary sociologists and anthropologists share a number of common concerns and may commonly value proximity and *einfühlen* (i.e. the ability to empathize with) as presuppositions for understanding social life (Geertz 1974). It may, therefore, sometimes be easier to identify differences *within* the practice of either of these disciplines than *between* anthropology and sociology per se, as has been suggested by the American cultural anthropologist H. Russell Bernard (2011: 2).

Concluding remarks

Like a number of other substantive fields of study (e.g. youth, dance, embodiment) that have gained more concerted attention in recent research, sport has actually made appearances in ethnographic accounts within anthropology for some time. For the most part, these appearances were serendipitous. The anthropologist was not setting out to find examples of sporting practices but discovered them in the course of an investigation of other matters within a particular context or setting. To an important extent, this kind of emergent discovery is still a significant feature of contemporary anthropological accounts of sport. But in the course of a broader rethinking of anthropology that commenced during the last third of the twentieth century, sport has gradually emerged as a more substantial and significant field of investigation in its own right. As a field of study, sport has drawn strongly on key and longstanding epistemological orientations within social and cultural anthropology. First, it places an emphasis on studying particular sporting practices within their larger social and cultural *contexts*, which might variously entail places, networks (whether mediated, deterritorialized and/or localized), institutions, organizations, infrastructures and fields. Second, it is *comparative*, with comparisons drawn through use of examples that are often extended across space and time.

These orientations have helped anthropologists avoid the kind of definitional preoccupations that have sometimes exercised scholars of sports in other social science disciplines. In valuing cross-cultural comparisons, anthropologists have been sensitive to the wide variety of possible forms and contexts in which sports and games may appear around the world. This, in turn, has allowed them to take note of overlaps and pursue comparisons with other types of activities and forms of embodiment (as in comparisons of sport and dance). Attention to context has also made anthropologists aware of the myriad ways in which sport may be implicated within a wider range of ostensibly 'non-sport' practices, events, ideology and aspirations. The result is an unabashed eclecticism that continues to shape anthropological investigations of sport. This enterprising scope of inquiry also offers promise for future investigations because it allows anthropologists continually to open up the range of issues and contexts that can be associated with sport.

One example of this kind of future-oriented unwrapping is conveyed by recent anthropological research that examines the neurobiological implications of sport. In his studies of capoeira, Greg Downey has systematically examined the articulation of the socio-cultural, biophysical and neurological facets of this distinctive Brazilian form of embodied practice (Downey 2005, 2010). In doing so, he has ventured into intellectual territory that socio-cultural anthropologists have long been reluctant to enter for fear of becoming entangled in biologically deterministic explanations of human and social development. What Downey has demonstrated, however, is the manner in which thoroughly documented ethnographic accounts of the distinctive features of an undeniably 'sport-like' practice can be combined with unexpected comparisons to achieve penetrating insights.

Not the least of these concerns is the manner in which any given 'skill-shaped body' displays distinctive patterns of both competence and incompetence (Downey 2010: 298). Working from his chance discovery of the startling ineptitude of otherwise remarkably skilled Brazilian practitioners of capoeira to throw objects with anything approaching the routine dexterity of amateurs who play baseball or softball at the lowest of competitive levels, Downey seized upon the implications of comprehending the biocultural processes that produce ineptitude as well as athletic mastery. To understand these processes, he concludes, 'places us in a much better position to understand patterns of bodily proficiency in different societies' (Downey 2010: 304). Far from stumbling into biological determinism, Downey has raised the intriguing prospect that biology is likely shaped by the types of cultural preferences that are manifested in athletic practices:

> The point is not that athletes are unique, but that activity patterns and programs of skill acquisition – influenced by cultural norms, shaped by social structures – are constantly cultivating all human tissue, conditioning our neurological systems and sculpting our skeletons, even if this is through neglect or sedentariness. Our ways of life shape our bodies. Athletes make that process more obvious, exaggerated, and better scrutinised, but we are all subject constantly to similar processes through which our culture helps to determine the conditions in which our physiology and psychology develop.
>
> (Downey 2010: 318)

The history of anthropological inquiry into sport has, therefore, been a history of repeated extensions of the concept and field. We haven't finished drawing the boundaries of the field and hopefully we never will.

References

Alter, J.S. (1992) *The Wrestler's Body: Identity and Ideology in North India*, Berkeley: University of California Press.
Alter, J.S. (2000) 'Kabaddi, a National Sport of India: The Internationalism of Nationalism and the Foreignness of Indianness', in N. Dyck (ed.) *Games, Sports and Cultures*, Oxford; New York: Berg.

Appadurai, A. (1995) 'Playing with Modernity: The Decolonization of Indian Cricket', in C.A. Brecken-ridge (ed.), *Consuming Modernity: Public Culture in a South Asian World*, Minneapolis; London: University of Minnesota Press.

Archetti, E.P. (1998) 'The Meanings of Sport in Anthropology: A View from Latin America', *European Review of Latin American and Caribbean Studies*, 65: 91–103.

Archetti, E.P. (1999a) *Masculinities: Football, Polo and the Tango in Argentina*, Oxford; New York: Berg.

Archetti, E.P. (1999b) 'The Spectacle of Heroic Masculinity: Vegard Ulvang and Alberto Tomba in the Olympic Winter Games of Albertville', in A.M. Klausen (ed.) *Olympic Games as Performance and Public Event: The Case of the XVII Winter Olympic Games in Norway*, New York: Berghahn Books.

Archetti, E.P. (2003) 'Playing Football and Dancing Tango: Embodying Argentina in Movement, Style and Identity', in N. Dyck and E.P. Archetti (eds) *Sport, Dance and Embodied Identities*, Oxford; New York: Berg.

Arens, W. (1975) 'The Great American Football Ritual', *Natural History*, 84: 72–81.

Armstrong, G. (1998) *Football Hooligans: Knowing the Score*. Oxford; New York: Berg.

Armstrong, G. and Harris, R. (1991) 'Football Hooligans: Theory and Evidence', *The Sociological Review*, 39(3): 427–59.

Atkinson, M. and Hammersley, M. (1994) 'Ethnography and Participant Observation', in N.K. Denzin and Y.S. Lincoln (eds) *Handbook of Qualitative Research*, Thousand Oaks, CA; London; New Delhi: Sage.

Azoy, G.W. (1982) *Buzkashi: Game and Power in Afghanistan*, Philadelphia: University of Pennsylvania Press.

Bernard, R.H. (2011) *Research Methods in Anthropology: Qualitative and Quantitative Approaches*, Lanham, MD: AltaMira.

Brownell, S. (1995) *Training the Body for China: Sports in the Moral Order of the People's Republic*, Chicago: University of Chicago Press.

Carter, T.F. (2008) *The Quality of Home Runs: The Passion, Politics, and Language of Cuban Baseball*, Durham, NC; London: Duke University Press.

Coakley, J. and Donnelly, P. (2009) *Sports in Society: Issues and Controversies*, 2nd Canadian edition, Toronto: McGraw-Hill Ryerson.

Culin, S. (1907/1992) *Games of the North American Indians*, vol 2, Lincoln; London: University of Nebraska Press.

Desjarlais, R. (2011) *Counterplay: An Anthropologist at the Chessboard*, Berkeley; Los Angeles; London: University of California Press.

Downey, G. (2005) *Learning Capoeira: Lessons in Cunning from an Afro-Brazilian Art*, Oxford: Oxford University Press.

Downey, G. (2010) 'Throwing Like a Brazilian: On Ineptness and a Skill-Shaped Body', in R.R. Sands and L. Sands (eds) *The Anthropology of Sport and Human Movement: A Biocultural Perspective*, Lanham, MD: Lexington Books.

Dundes, A. (1978) 'Into the Endzone for a Touchdown: A Psychoanalytic Consideration of American Foot-ball', *Western Folklore*, 37: 75–88.

Dunning, E., Murphy, P. and Waddington, I. (1991) 'Anthropological versus Sociological Approaches to the Study of Soccer Hooliganism: Some Critical Notes', *Sociological Review*, 39(3): 459–79.

Dyck, N. (2000) 'Games, Bodies, Celebrations and Boundaries: Anthropological Perspectives on Sport', in N. Dyck (ed.) *Games, Sports and Cultures*, Oxford; New York: Berg.

Dyck, N. (2012) *Fields of Play: An Ethnography of Children's Sports*, Toronto: University of Toronto Press.

Dyck, N. and Archetti, E.P. (2003) 'Embodied Identities: Reshaping Social Life through Sport and Dance', in N. Dyck and E.P. Archetti (eds) *Sport, Dance and Embodied Identities*, Oxford; New York: Berg.

Elias, N. (1978) *The Civilizing Process*, Oxford: Basil Blackwell.

Elias, N. (1986) 'The Genesis of Sport as a Social Problem', in N. Elias and E. Dunning (eds) *Quest for Excitement: Sport and Leisure in the Civilizing Process*, Oxford: Basil Blackwell.

Firth, R. (1930) 'A Dart Match in Tikopia: A Study in the Sociology of Primitive Sport', *Oceania* 1: 64–97.

Fox, R. (1961) 'Pueblo Baseball: A New Use for Old Witchcraft', *Journal of American Folklore*, 74: 9–16.

Fox, R.G. and Gingrich, A. (2002) 'Introduction', in A. Gingrich and R.G. Fox (eds) *Anthropology, by Comparison*, London; New York: Routledge.

Geertz, C. (1973) 'Deep Play: Notes on the Balinese Cockfight', in C. Geertz (ed.) *The Interpretation of Cultures*, New York: Basic Books.

Geertz, C. (1974) '"From the Native's Point of View": On the Nature of Anthropological Understanding', *Bulletin of the American Academy of Arts and Sciences*, 28(1): 26–45.

Giulianotti, R. (1999) *Football: A Sociology of the Global Game*, Cambridge: Polity Press.

131

Gmelch, G. (1972) 'Magic in Professional Baseball', in G.P. Stone (ed.) *Games, Sports and Power*, New Brunswick, NJ: Dutton.

Gruneau, R. (1999) *Class, Sports and Social Development*, revised edn, Champaign, IL: Human Kinetics Press.

Guttmann, A. (1978) *From Ritual to Record: The Nature of Modern Sports*, New York: Columbia University Press.

Hognestad, H. (1997) 'The Jambo Experience: An Anthropological Study of Hearts Fans', in G. Armstrong and R. Giulianotti (eds) *Entering the Field: New Perspectives on World Football*, Oxford; New York: Berg.

Hognestad, H. (2003) 'Long-Distance Football Support and Liminal Activities Among Norwegian Fans', in N. Dyck and E.P. Archetti (eds) *Sport, Dance and Embodied Identities*, Oxford; New York: Berg.

Hognestad, H. (2009) 'Transglobal Scandinavian? Globalisation and the Contestation of Identities in Football', *Soccer & Society*, 10(3–4): 358–373.

Holy, L. (1987) 'Description, Generalization and Comparison: Two Paradigms', in L. Holy (ed.) *Comparative Anthropology*, Oxford: Basil Blackwell.

Kelly, W.W. (2004) 'Sense and Sensibility at the Ballpark: What Fans Make of Professional Baseball in Japan', in W.W. Kelly (ed.) *Fanning the Flames: Fans and Consumer Culture in Contemporary Japan*, Albany: State University of New York Press.

Klausen, A.M. (ed) (1999a) *Olympic Games as Performance and Event: The Case of the XVII Winter Olympic Games in Norway*, New York: Berghahn Books.

Klausen, A.M. (1999b) 'Introduction', in A.M. Klausen (ed.) *Olympic Games as Performance and Event: The Case of the XVII Winter Olympic Games in Norway*, New York: Berghahn Books.

Klausen, A.M. (1999c) 'Norwegian Culture and Olympism: Confrontations and Adaptations', in A.M. Klausen (ed.) *Olympic Games as Performance and Event: The Case of the XVII Winter Olympic Games in Norway*, New York: Berghahn Books.

Klausen, A.M. (1999d) 'The Torch Relay: Reinvention of Tradition and Conflict with the Greeks', in A.M. Klausen (ed.) *Olympic Games as Performance and Event: The Case of the XVII Winter Olympic Games in Norway*, New York: Berghahn Books.

Klein, A.M. (1991) *Sugarball: The American Game, the Dominican Dream*, New Haven, CT; London: Yale University Press.

Klein, A.M. (1997) *Baseball on the Border: A Tale of Two Laredos*, Princeton, NJ: Princeton University Press.

Leach, J. (dir.) (1976) *Trobriand Cricket: An Ingenious Response to Colonialism*, 54 min, Media Resources Center, University of California, Berkeley.

Leseth, A. (2003) 'Michezo: Dance, Sport and Politics in Dar-es-Salaam, Tanzania', in N. Dyck and E.P. Archetti (eds) *Sport, Dance and Embodied Identities*, Oxford; New York: Berg.

Lewis, J.L. (1992) *Ring of Liberation: Deceptive Discourse in Brazilian Capoeira*, Chicago: University of Chicago Press.

MacAloon, J.J. (1981) *This Great Symbol: Pierre de Coubertin and the Origins of the Modern Olympic Games*, Chicago: University of Chicago Press.

Mauss, M. (1973) 'Techniques of the Body', *Economy and Society*, 2(1): 70–88.

Mooney, J. (1890) 'The Cherokee Ball Game', *American Anthropologist*, 3: 105–32.

Ronsbo, H. (2003) 'The Embodiment of Male Identities: Alliances and Cleavages in Salvadorean Football', in N. Dyck and E.P. Archetti (eds) *Sport, Dance and Embodied Identities*, Oxford; New York: Berg.

Swyers, H. (2010) *Wrigley Regulars: Finding Community in the Bleachers*, Urbana: University of Illinois Press.

Vertinsky, P., McManus, A. and Sit, C. (2010) 'Dancing Class: Schooling the Dance in Colonial and Post-Colonial Hong Kong', *Sport, Education and Society*, 12(1): 73–92.

Wieschiolek, H. (2003) '"Ladies, Just Follow His Lead!": Salsa, Gender and Identity', in N. Dyck and E.P. Archetti (eds) *Sport, Dance and Embodied Identities*, Oxford; New York: Berg.

Wulff, H. (1998) *Ballet across Borders: Career and Culture in the World of Dancers*, Oxford; New York: Berg.

14

ECONOMIC AND SOCIOLOGICAL APPROACHES TO SPORT

Kevin J. Delaney

Two major academic fields of study that have contributed significantly to our understanding of the sporting world are sociology and economics. Unlike in some areas of inquiry in which sociology and economics have acted primarily as theoretical competitors, in the study of sports, they have been largely complementary to one another. In this article, I highlight the ways that these two fields have contributed important perspectives to more fully address and satisfactorily understand issues in sport. I also highlight areas where they have not overlapped as much as perhaps they should, concluding with some ideas on ways that economics and sociology might fruitfully align future research agendas in the study of the sporting world.

The market for sport

Economists and sociologists are both interested in understanding the size and operation of sports markets (Fort 2011; Leeds and von Allmen 2008; Li, Hofacre, and Mahony 2001; Quirk and Fort 1999; Sandy, Sloane, and Rosentraub 2004). There is a market for sport that is worth estimating, understanding, and describing for theoretical, policy, and practical reasons. As economists see it, the market for sports might be understood as the appetite that consumers have for sport, ranging from their own participation in sport, to their consumption of sport as spectators, to the goods and services they purchase connected to sport. Economists have spent considerable effort estimating the size of various markets while sociologists have tended to study the ways in which producers and suppliers of sport work to increase market interest, increase the demand for sport, and shape the market for sport (some critical approaches might even say 'manipulate' the market to ensure monopoly profits).

While significant work has been done estimating national and local markets, Humphreys and Ruseki (2009) caution that much of the data on the size and scope of the sports market have problems in measurement, and this becomes increasingly problematic as we start to estimate global markets. For starters, defining 'sport' differs from one culture to the next. Even within a single country there may not be agreement on what counts as sport (do we include darts, petanque, and competitive ballroom dancing as sports, for example?). In addition to these basic definitional questions, sport activities usually occur across a number of economic categories and measurements, involving participating, in-person spectating, consuming licensed products and sports equipment, and listening and watching across a wide range of media. This diversity makes it quite tricky to tease out the direct and indirect market for sport; assumptions about what will be included end up driving the final data even more so than in most other measures of economic activity. Since estimates of markets in various sports sometimes differ by factors of 2 to as many as 10, scepticism about assumptions and measurement is probably warranted. Moreover, since economic data on size of markets are not directly available in many cases from government data but are produced by those with an interest in presenting the largest market possible (e.g. team owners, cities in search of support for an Olympic bid, proponents of a new sports franchise), it increases the importance of carefully examining claims of current or potential market size.

As sport becomes a consumption product, a status marker, and a global export, any one particular sports organization must now view its competition not only as other teams in the same league or the same sport but also as sports enterprises in entirely different sports or from entirely different regions of the world (Giulianotti and Robertson 2007). From this perspective, basketball competes with European football for global supremacy, American football competes with American baseball in a race to globalize, and we could even say that the New York Yankees compete with Manchester United while the Dallas Cowboys compete with Real Madrid in their expansion of their fan bases worldwide as they develop their worldwide brand (Carter 2011; Westerbeek and Smith 2003).

While economists view the market for sports as a representation of the public's collective appetite for sports, sociologists question whether 'appetites' simply exist within individuals or whether they are socially constructed. In the arena of sport in particular, markets are manipulated, shaped, and constrained in very significant ways. For example, in professional sports, the supply of sport is controlled and restricted through the cartel-like operations of sports leagues. In the United States, tying sports participation to scholarships for athletes drives up interest in competitive sport as a way to afford the high cost of a university education, particularly for those of limited financial means. Professional sports facilities across the world have been subsidized with public resources, sometimes in the face of strong opposition from the general public. Each of these examples suggest we not take 'appetite for sport' as an intrinsic desire residing within individuals that once aggregated may be considered 'the market demand for sport'.

While estimating the size of the market for sport has taken considerable work, both sociologists and economists have also been interested in the actual operation of those markets, and recognize the perversities in sports markets (Noll and Zimbalist 1997; Zimbalist 1998, 2010). In many professional leagues, for example, team owners control the supply of sports, owing to their position as oligopolists (restricted number of sellers of a product or service). Whether they have official exemptions from antitrust (antimonopoly) laws or not, team owners have found effective ways to limit new entrants through high entrance fees and other financial requirements (including, for example, making it a requirement that a potential ownership group must have an agreement in place for a new stadium). This restriction in the supply of sports allows for monopoly profits (or more accurately oligopoly profits) and all that flows from that. With this restriction of supply in place, many parts of society – not just team owners – work to heighten demand for professional sports. Sports teams get plenty of free coverage in the daily newspaper and television news programs. Politicians and other public figures may join in the frenzy as well. In sum, professional sports teams are in an enviable position – tightly restricted supply with great pressures on the demand side for sport. This structural advantage goes a long way toward explaining many of the features we see in the operation of markets for professional sports, including high player salaries and soaring club or team-franchise values.

More research certainly needs to be done on understanding the potential of the global market for sport as many sports have now moved beyond national boundaries (PricewaterhouseCoopers

2011). This seems to be a particularly fruitful area for interdisciplinary collaboration. If some sports become truly global in nature, there are opportunities for revenue of geometrically higher proportions as sports move into untapped markets. In addition, the market for a particular sport can broaden significantly. The National Football League in the United States has been working overtime to extend the reach of American football into Europe, hosting more and more games in England and entertaining the possibility of locating a franchise in London (something current players appear much less enthusiastic about). On the other hand, globalized sports can eat into the market share of indigenous local sports and can introduce new competition into formerly stable and oligopic markets. It will be fascinating to watch the breakdown and re-establishment of stability and oligopoly in global sports markets over the coming decades, and this should prove a fruitful area for research between sociologists, economists, and political scientists.

Player salaries, team profitability, and the market for athletes

What flows from the advantageous market position of sport may seem obvious: high ticket prices, parking and concession fees, licensing revenues, broadcast revenues, lucrative player salaries, high player transfer fees, ever-escalating entrance fees for potential new franchises and owners, a tight limitation on the number of slots in professional sports for new athletes, and soaring team values in the vast majority of cases and certainly for established sports and leagues (this is less true in newer sports and less established leagues) (Carter 2011; Kessene 2007; Team Marketing Report 2013; Zimbalist 2010). Not all teams turn high operating profits year after year. If poorly managed, teams can overspend on player salaries or fail to attract a large fan base if they perform poorly on the pitch or the court year after year. However, even in cases like this, owners may realize a profit on the sale of a franchise if the league itself remains healthy (Fort 2011; Quirk and Fort 1992).

At the league level, executives are concerned with maintaining the overall profitability of a sport (as opposed to a particular team's profitability), and this presents a different set of challenges. One of the biggest is maintaining competitive balance among teams. If one team has significantly higher earnings than another, there is the possibility that one team can dominate others in performance or that teams in smaller markets are unable to compete with teams with high payrolls. Leagues have combatted this problem with all sorts of revenue-sharing schemes, 'luxury taxes' for payrolls above a certain amount, or salary caps, sometimes even agreed to through collective bargaining (Zimbalist 2010). Because team owners are very competitive with one another, achieving such agreements can be as difficult among owners as it is between players and owners. Some smaller-market teams with less revenue have turned to forms of statistical analysis and economic modeling to introduce new advantages in competing (Berri and Bradbury 2010). In the United States, this approach was popularized through the book and film version of *Moneyball*, which followed a baseball executive's attempt to use statistical analysis to determine how much each player contributes to winning and then to try to 'purchase' players who are 'undervalued' by traditional market mechanisms (Lewis 2003; *Moneyball* 2011). This approach has been copied by other teams and sports executives and the jury is still out on its long-term success.

Of sociological interest, this statistical market-driven approach has sparked a debate between sport traditionalists who believe in scouting players and having a feel for latent and emerging talent, versus pure quantitative analysis of measurable performance variables. This debate shares similarities with other contemporaneous societal trends accompanying the increasing availability and accessibility of large amounts of numerical data. So, for example, we see similar debates occurring between pure quantitative traders in stock markets who trade based solely on mathematical models and the traditionalist traders who claim to have a feel or instinct for markets through accumulated experience. What we seem to be seeing in sport is another front in the battle over the quantification and commensurability of complex social processes that we have seen in other venues, like the 'rankings' of educational institutions or new measures of 'return on investment' of a college or university degree or a particular major course of study (Espeland and Stevens 2008; Ruiz, Pastor, and Pastor 2013). Future research combining sociological and economic expertise could help us understand the role of culture, professional judgement, and quantifiable measures in the approach of sport executives in search of building winning teams. Such research might provide interesting theoretical insights into how and when 'big data' is employed in activities that encompass talent, potential, and measurable performance outcomes.

Although benefiting for decades from oligopoly advantages, there are many clear signs that professional sports may be reaching a saturation point within their own national markets. In order to maintain or increase profits, teams and leagues have begun – with varying success – to move across global boundaries (Millward 2011). Football (or soccer in the United States) has led the way in establishing global teams and global markets. Football has developed a system of transfer fees that allows players to move across national boundaries to play on teams outside of their home country more easily than in most other sports. If one of the hallmarks of globalization is the movement of capital and human labour more easily across national boundaries, and the decline in barriers to such movement, sport has been affected by the trend as much as other industries. If a by-product of globalization is the movement of culture across boundaries (with attendant cultural clashes, disputes between local culture and global culture, and the like), then sport, too, has experienced those same by-products.

Sociologists, for their part, have made important contributions in understanding the ways that markets have not been free and open for athletes and teams. Racial and gender barriers have kept athletes from fair and equal participation in athletic labour markets. Professional sports have gone through long battles over integrating players of races that are not the majority race into sport. Remnants of racism may still be found in sociologists' research into what they call 'racial stacking'. A host of research has shown that in many sporting contexts, members of certain racial groups dominate a particular position on the field while being underrepresented at other positions. Debates rage over whether this is a result of deliberate or unconscious discrimination by coaches, or a result of role modeling and other socialization factors, or perhaps of differential access to specialized coaching. Racial imbalance among coaches and front office management staff is even greater in most sports than it is among the players (see, for example, the annual racial and gender 'report cards' issued by TIDES 2013). Some economic research suggests subtle processes of discrimination in pay for professional athletes along racial lines (Gill and Brajer 2012; Groothuis and Hill 2013; Mitchell, Stavros, and Stewart 2011; Yang and Hsuan 2012). Gender parity in sport markets has come a long way in many countries, but this progress is uneven and still has quite a distance to travel before anything approaching gender equality is reached. More female youth are playing sport than ever before and opportunities, including professional ones, are improving. Prize money, scholarships, and spending on sport, however, still lag behind men's athletics (Shulman and Bowen 2001).

Other structural and legal constraints have important effects on the operation of athletic markets. In the United States, for example, controversies rage over whether college athletes should receive compensation for their playing. Currently, rules in the United States only allow college athletes to receive scholarships that cover tuition, room and board, and a small per diem stipend for travel away. However, the top coaches of American university teams in high-profile sports like men's basketball and American football earn as much as several million dollars per year (and often earn more than the president of their own university). In order to maintain non-profit status, not to mention more noble ideals of amateurism, universities defend vigorously the status quo whereby athletes are not paid for their athletic endeavours.

Economic development through sport

One of the most fertile areas for research combining economic and sociological analysis is the study of stadium subsidies and the economic development that may accompany new stadiums. In the United States, most professional baseball and American football teams have built new stadiums since 1980, often with significant public subsidies (Baade 1994, 1996; Baade and Dye 1990; Rosentraub 1996, 1997, 2009). The arguments in favour of providing public money to new stadiums have fallen into two general categories: economic arguments and social arguments. The economic arguments stress the potential economic benefit of a new stadium, including the direct benefits of construction wages and the taxes on those wages and the longer-term jobs provided within the stadium. The taxes on professional player salaries can also be a potential benefit, depending on the rules of the local taxing authority. Indirect benefits may include potential development that occurs around a new stadium. The majority of economists have concluded, however, that there are limits to the direct and indirect economic benefits of a new stadium that make large subsidies difficult to justify on economic grounds alone. Those limits include: the rather small number of jobs created by stadiums, the substitution effect which implies that a large amount of stadium spending is simply spending that is transferred from one part of a city or region to another, limiting any increases in tax revenues, and the multiplier effect, which demonstrates that spending on professional sports tends to have a lower multiplier than other types of spending done in a city (Baade and Sanderson 1997; Coates and Humphreys 2000; Danielson 1997; Euchner 1993). This latter point is because money spent at a sports stadium often goes to player salaries (which in large part may eventually be spent elsewhere) and national food and beverage companies.

Arising alongside the economic arguments are a set of social arguments that became more popular beginning in the 1990s, in part because of the discrediting of the economic justifications (Eckstein and Delaney 2002; Keating 1997, 1999; Weiner 2000). The social arguments include the proposition that stadiums provide an improved image to tourists and outsiders and make local residents feel better about their city (Fainstein and Stokes 1998). Some allege that cheering for the home team helps bring residents together across racial and social class lines. Critics of this position counter that new stadiums tend to separate social classes owing to their increased prices for seating or discourage the poor and working class from attending live professional sporting events.

Many observers ask why a lucrative business like professional sports requires public subsidy at all. This can only be understood through the oligopoly power of sports. Given the severe restriction on the availability of professional sports franchises, and the high demand for sport, professional team owners gain significant bargaining leverage over their cities. Combine this with the high visibility of professional sports teams and the reluctance of local politicians to be blamed for the exit of a local team and you have an unbalanced bargaining relationship between team and city.

While there is often general dismay over the fact that municipal governments are asked to subsidize sports stadiums, recent research suggests that there is enough variance in subsidy level and local economic and social conditions that each new stadium proposal, and eventual stadium brought to fruition, must be examined on its own merits. For example, if a city sits on the border of another state and attracts a large number of people from outside the taxing authority to the stadium, the increased tax revenue to the local authority will be greater than if the stadium sits in the middle of a vast taxing authority attracting mainly people from within the taxing authority who would have spent the same money on other activities within the authority. This is just one example of how stadium location can have a significant impact on the likelihood of additional tax revenue being brought into a city or state. There are similar differences in the likelihood of development occurring around a new sports facility (Agha 2013; Austrian and Rosentraub 1997; Blair and Swindell 1997; Rosentraub 2009).

Similar in tone, debate also occurs over the economic development that may come from hosting sports mega-events like the Olympics, the World Cup, or the Super Bowl (Coates and Depken 2011). Following the 1976 Olympics, the host city of Montreal declared a significant financial deficit, incurred hosting the games, that increased reluctance on the part of some cities to seek serving as host. The citizens of Los Angeles voted against public support for the city's hosting of the 1984 games, making it the first to be primarily financed through non-public (i.e. mainly corporate) means. Critics complained of the commercialization that resulted in the 1984 Olympics, but the result should not have been surprising. Despite the criticism, the Los Angeles Games were considered a financial success and spawned new models of public-private support for mega-events.

Cities can sometimes take advantage of the impending pressure of hosting the Olympics to significantly upgrade transportation systems and other forms of infrastructure like information systems. While mega-events attract many tourists to host cities, they also drive away locals, so the net increase in spending is partially blunted. Overall, there is mixed evidence on the long-term benefits of having hosted the games. Some argue that there is a discernible post-game slowdown that must be accounted for and weighed against pre-game and event spending (Maennig and Richter 2012; Rose and Spiegel 2011)

Both sociologists and economists sharpen their analyses by understanding that debates over hosting mega-events like the Olympics or over providing public financing for new sport stadiums are not only about economic impact narrowly conceived. They also reflect larger ideological battles over the view of cities and the beliefs about how to create vibrant cities (Delaney and Eckstein 2003). Those who believe in a top-down, trickle-down approach to economic growth tend to favor investment in large, visible projects, whether those are stadiums, convention centers, or luxury hotels. The hope from this vantage point is that this will attract tourist spending and keep businesses in cities that are perceived as vibrant. Those favoring a more grass-roots, bottom-up approach to urban development favor investment in neighborhood infrastructure, roads and public transport, schools, and local small business development. From this vantage point, the hope is to develop an exciting, vibrant, livable city from the bottom up that will then make hotel developers, professional sports teams, and convention centers want to be in your city owing to the quality of life there (Florida 2003, 2004). Urban growth ideologies intersect with ideas about the role of sport in regional economic development and the use of sport as a way to attract tourism.

However, professional sport is not the only game in town when it comes to understanding the market for sports and the importance of sport to economic development. In fact, the attention paid to professional sports may be outsized compared to its actual value, and we have not paid enough attention to the market for leisure and recreational sports and the use of recreational sport as a form of economic development. Those who are sports enthusiasts – either as participants or spectators – but are not professional athletes also create sizeable markets in what might be called sports participation and sports tourism. People travel to climb mountains, to compete in marathons or triathlons, to swim or sail in new waters, to watch a football game in every stadium in a European country or attend a baseball game in every baseball park in North America. Families travel to Walt Disney's Wide World of Sports complex to watch their child compete in a range of youth sport. In all of these, one sees see the vast economic and sociological impact of sports participation and sports tourism. Future research might pair sociological and economic perspectives in understanding the size and growth of such markets, along with the factors that propel that growth. Cities and regions in search of economic development through sport might be well served to turn their attention to citizen participation in sport and leisure rather than focusing centrally on the role of professional sport in economic development. Focus on amateur and recreational sport participation could foster a more bottom-up economic development through the support of participatory and recreational sport and leisure opportunities.

The cost of participation and changes in youth sport

Sociologists have led the way in studying changes in youth and childhood sport participation Some sociologists locate these changes in childhood sport experiences within a larger-scale change in the organization of childhood (Lareau 2011). Numerous social analysis have shown the ways in which childhood, particularly in the middle classes and above, has become more controlled, scheduled, and organized by adults. Accompanying these changes is often an increase in the cost of participating in sport. While sports are often lauded as 'leveling the playing field' for people of all social classes, there are subtle ways in which inequality has increased in sport accessibility and the practice of sport in day-to-day life, even while legal restrictions by race, gender, or class have been removed.

For example, the increased organization of childhood and childhood sports differs by social class. Middle- and upper-class childhood is what has become more organized and more costly, while working-class and poorer children are sometimes either left behind or reared in different ways. Lareau (2011) makes the point that in middle-class-dominated, wealthier societies, this compounds disadvantages for poor children who do not gain the same experience navigating middle-class organizational life, including the increasingly organized world of youth sport.

How and where people play competitive sport differs across the globe. In much of Europe, for example, youth play in local sport clubs learning their sport. In the United States, schools and universities have been important sites for the playing of sport (although in the US club sports have been on the ascendancy for several decades and in some sports they may have eclipsed scholastic sports). More comparative work is needed by both sociologists and economists on how childhood and youth athletics are organized in different countries. In many sports, the United States has colleges and universities as one major training ground for professional athletes. This American exceptionalism has not been fully and satisfactorily compared to Europe's use of sports clubs as training grounds for future professionals. Economists and sociologists have done limited research on the differences this makes to sport's role in society. Clearly, the playing of sport at the college and university level has led to a big-money arms race to build sports programs with attendant critics who argue this has warped the educational values of these institutions. Despite the loud cries of critics, this trend shows little sign of abatement. Because there are so many university and college options in the United States, some universities have come to see sports as a major drawing card for students. Many universities argue that sports are – to use a phrase often heard on American campuses – the front porch to the university. This means that it is often through the athletic teams that prospective students and their families first become familiar with the names of particular universities.

Conclusion

Generally speaking, when sociology and economics have approached an issue in the field of sport with the strengths of their complementary perspectives, we often achieve a more satisfying understanding of the issue at hand. The economic perspective helps us see the operation of markets and the dynamics at work between labour and capital while the sociological perspective helps uncover political, cultural, and social issues that often underlie the economic phenomenon or shape the playing surface upon which economic forces operate. As in many other areas of study addressed by economics and sociology, the *ceteris paribus* assumptions of economics allow for a methodological rigour and a relatively sparse elegance in modeling while sociology reminds us that 'all else is rarely equal' when observing social phenomena. Sociologists highlight how changing conceptions of childhood, leisure, and recreation all play a role in shaping sports activities and markets as do the political ideologies at work in creating, maintaining, and fostering sports at both the professional and recreational levels. Working in tandem, sociology and economics better illuminate the complex forces at work in the sporting world.

References

Agha, N. (2013) 'The Economic Impact of Stadiums and Teams: The Case of Minor League Baseball', *Journal of Sports Economics*, 14: 227–52.

Austrian, Z. and Rosentraub, M. (1997) 'Cleveland's Gateway to the Future', in R. Noll and A. Zimbalist (eds) *Sports, Jobs and Taxes*, Washington, DC: Brookings Institute.

Baade, R. (1994) 'Stadiums, Sports and Economic Development: Assessing the Reality', *Heartland Policy Study*, #62, April.

—— (1996) 'Sports as a Catalyst for Metropolitan Economic Development', *Journal of Urban Affairs*, 18: 1–17.

Baade, R. and Dye, R. (1990) 'The Impact of Stadiums and Professional Sports on Metropolitan Area Development', *Growth and Change*, Spring: 1–14.

Baade, R. and Sanderson, A. (1997) 'The Employment Effect of Teams and Sports Facilities', in R. Noll and A. Zimbalist (eds) *Sports, Jobs, and Taxes*. Washington, DC: Brookings Institute.

Berri, D. and Bradbury J. (2010) 'Working in the Land of the Metricians', *Journal of Sports Economics* 11: 29–47.

Blair, J. and Swindell, D. (1997) 'Sports, Politics and Economics: The Cincinnati Story', in R. Noll and A. Zimbalist (eds) *Sports, Jobs and Taxes*, Washington, DC: Brookings Institute.

Carter, D. (2011) *Money Games: Profiting from the Convergence of Sports and Entertainment*, Stanford, CA: Stanford University Press.

Coates, D. and Depken, C. (2011) 'Mega-Events: Is Baylor Football to Waco What the Super Bowl Is to Houston?', *Journal of Sports Economics* 12: 599–620.

Coates, D. and Humphreys, B. (2000) 'The Stadium Gambit and Local Economic Development', *Regulation* 23: 15–20.

Danielson, M. (1997) *Home Team*, Princeton, NJ: Princeton University Press.

Delaney, K. and Eckstein, R. (2003) *Public Dollars, Private Stadiums: The Battle over Building Sports Stadiums*, New Brunswick, NJ: Rutgers University Press.

Eckstein, R. and Delaney, K. (2002) 'New Sports Stadiums, Community Self-Esteem, and Community Collective Conscience', *Journal of Sport and Social Issues* 26: 235–47.

Espeland, W.N. and Stevens, M. (2008) 'A Sociology of Quantification', *European Journal of Sociology* 49: 401–36.

Euchner, C. (1993) *Playing the Field: Why Sports Teams Move and Cities Fight to Keep Them*, Baltimore, MD: Johns Hopkins University Press.

Fainstein, S. and Stokes, R. (1998) 'Spaces for Play: the Impacts of Entertainment Development on New York City', *Economic Development Quarterly* 5: 150–65.

Florida, R. (2003) *The Rise of the Creative Class*, New York: Basic Books.

—— (2004) *Cities and the Creative Class*, New York: Routledge.

Fort, R. (2011) *Sports Economics*, 3rd edition. Boston, MA: Pearson.

Gill, A. and Brajer, V. (2012) 'Wonderlic, Race, and the NFL Draft', *Journal of Sports Economics* 13: 642–53.

Giulianotti, R. and Robertson, R. (eds) (2007) *Globalization and Sport*, Malden, MA: Blackwell.

Groothuis, P. and Hill, J. (2013) 'Pay Discrimination, Exit Discrimination or Both? Another Look at an Old Issue Using NBA Data', *Journal of Sports Economics* 14: 171–85.

Humphreys, B. and Ruseki, J. (2009) 'Problems with Data on the Sport Industry', *Journal of Sports Economics* 11: 60–76.

Keating, R. (1999) 'Sports Pork: The Costly Relationship between Major League Sports and Government', Cato Institute: Cato Policy Analysis No. 339.

Keating, W.D. (1997) 'Cleveland: The "Comeback City": The Politics of Redevelopment and Sports Stadiums amidst Urban Decline' in M. Luria (ed.) *Reconstructing Urban Regime Theory: Regulating Urban Politics in a Global Economy*, Thousand Oaks, CA: Sage.

Kessene, S. (2007) *The Economic Theory of Professional Team Sports: An Analytic Treatment*, Cheltenham, UK: Edward Elgar.

Lareau, A. (2011) *Unequal Childhoods: Class, Race, and Family Life*, Berkeley: University of California Press.

Leeds, M. and von Allmen, P. (2008) *The Economics of Sport*, 3rd edition, Boston, MA: Pearson.

Lewis, M. (2003) *Moneyball: The Art of Winning an Unfair Game*, New York: W.W. Norton.

Li, M., Hofacre, S. and Mahony, D. (2001) *Economics of Sport*, Morgantown, WV: Fitness Information Technology.

Maennig, W. and Richter, F. (2012) 'Exports and Olympic Games: Is There a Signal Effect?', *Journal of Sports Economics* 13: 635–41.

Millward, P. (2011) *The Global Football Leagues: Transnational Networks, Social Movements and Sports in the New Media*, Hampshire, UK: Palgrave Macmillan.

Mitchell, H., Stavros, C. and Stewart, M. (2011) 'Does the Australian Football League Draft Undervalue Indigenous Australian Footballers?', *Journal of Sports Economics* 12: 36–54.

Moneyball (2011) Dir. Bennett Miller, Sony Pictures. Film.

Noll, R. and Zimbalist, A. (eds) (1997) *Sports, Jobs, and Taxes*, Washington, DC: Brookings Institute.

PricewaterhouseCoopers (2011) *Changing The Game: Outlook for Global Sports Market to 2015*, December, available online at: http://www.pwc.com/gx/en/hospitality-leisure/changing-the-game-outlook-for-the-global-sports-market-to-2015.jhtml.

Quirk, J. and Fort, R. (1992) *Pay Dirt: The Business of Professional Team Sports*, Princeton, NJ: Princeton University Press.

—— (1999) *Hard Ball: The Abuse of Power in Pro Team Sports*, Princeton, NJ: Princeton University Press.

Rose, A., and Spiegel, M. (2011) 'The Olympic Effect', *Economic Journal* 121: 652–77.

Rosentraub, M. (1996) 'Does the Emperor Have New Clothes? A Reply to Robert Baade', *Journal of Urban Affairs*, 18: 23–31.

—— (1997) *Major League Losers: The Real Cost of Sports and Who's Paying It*, New York: Basic Books.

—— (2009) *Major League Winners: Using Sports and Cultural Centers as Tools for Economic Development*, Boca Raton, FL: CRC Press.

Ruiz, J., Pastor, D. and Pastor, J. (2013) 'Assessing Professional Tennis Players Using Data Envelopment Analysis (DEA)', *Journal of Sports Economics* 14: 276–302.

Sandy, R., Sloane, P. and Rosentraub, M. (2004) *The Economics of Sport: An International Perspective*, New York: Palgrave Macmillan.

Shulman, J. and Bowen, W. (2001) *The Game of Life: College Sports and Educational Values*, Princeton, NJ: Princeton University Press.

Team Marketing Report (2013) *Fan Cost Index*. Chicago: Team Marketing Report.

TIDES (The Institute for Diversity and Ethics in Sports) (2013) 'Racial and Gender Report Card', available online at: www.tidesport.org.

Weiner, J. (2000) *Stadium Games*, Minneapolis: University of Minnesota Press.

Westerbeek, H. and Smith, A. (2003) *Sport Business in the Global Marketplace*, New York: Palgrave Macmillan.

Yang, C. and Hsuan, Y. (2012) 'Is There Salary Discrimination by Nationality in the NBA?: Foreign Talent or Foreign Market', *Journal of Sports Economics*, 13: 53–75.

Zimbalist, A. (1998) 'The Economics of Stadiums, Teams and Cities', *Policy Studies Review*, 15: 17–29.

—— (2010) 'Reflections on Salary Share and Salary Cap', *Journal of Sports Economics*, 11: 17–28.

15

GEOGRAPHICAL APPROACHES AND THE SOCIOLOGY OF SPORT

Nicholas Wise

Introduction

The study of sports geography has been underexplored in the academic literature until relatively recently. Broadly defined, geography is the study of space, place, movements and human/environmental interactions – and sociological research has much to benefit from particular geographical approaches and understandings. Part of the struggle with geography is many believe the discipline simply refers to identifying geographical features on a map. While knowing where places are located relative to another and associated physical features are important, geographers are interested in how such interrelations suggest why certain sports are played, or invested in and developed in some areas more so than others. Moreover, geographers seek to better understand the significance of a sports team in relation to the culture and political identity of a place or why athletes move to earn their professional salaries (Bale 2003). Such questions of geography become apparent when watching the winter Olympics or understanding politically contested histories, such as when England and Argentina meet in the FIFA World Cup. Alternatively, professional football clubs such as Manchester United, Chelsea, Real Madrid and FC Barcelona over the last several decades have developed extensive fan bases, not only through their brand, but also due to their ability to attract the best footballers from around the world. However, we may see a shift in power in future decades as countries in the East (particularly China) rise as emerging economic powers and seek to attract elite athletes to develop their national competitions. These are all perspectives and questions that concern geographers – whether linked to the physical features or designations of economic power. As I shall argue here, a geographical perspective also offers perceptive insight into the sociological imagination.

The study of sport in the field of geography received only little attention and was not fully integrated into the academic work concerning sport until the early 1980s. The field of sports geography can be traced back to the 1960s, with some of the early (most) relevant literature being published in the 1970s and early 1980s (e.g. Bale 1982; Rooney 1974; Wagner 1981). John Rooney is regarded as the 'father' of contemporary sports geography, but it was John Bale who further developed the niche field from the 1980s onwards – and his writing has been the most influential towards expanding sports geography. Moreover, these early pioneers in the field developed a sport-dedicated geography journal titled *Sport Place: An International Journal of Sports*, but this journal ceased production in 2000 due to a lack of submissions. It is John Rooney's and John Bale's foundational work that much of the recent research refers to, showing how this field has significantly developed/expanded. Recent work on sport geography has since evolved, with new contributions offering more critically informed approaches and case studies to further develop the field. Much of the recent work is relevant to the discipline of sociology, with research assessing social/cultural landscapes, community and identity, through to globalization and migration.

Sport has always been approached holistically; in the 1980s, new understandings began to emerge that required geographically informed insight. During the 1980s, on-going social and political disputes and the impact of economic restructuring were in the headlines of news, and sport was at the centre of much of these then-current affairs. For instance, politically, the Falkland (or Malvinas) War in 1982 led to tensions in the 1986 FIFA World Cup match between Argentina and England. Protests of the Olympic Games erupted between the United States and the Soviet Union during the Cold War when the games were held in Moscow in 1980 and Los Angeles in 1984. Moreover, shifting economic structures saw the rapid emergence of private sector involvement to assist funding stadiums/venues to bid for and host major international events when public sector funds were limited (Smith 2012). Such topics required a particular geographical understanding, but the field of sports geography was only in its early development stage.

Geographically informed research contributes a particular (spatial) understanding to closely related fields, most notably sociology, anthropology, economics, history, philosophy, political science and cultural studies. Moreover, conceptual approaches are rooted in a range of epistemological frameworks such as humanism, Marxism, post-structuralism, post-modernism, post-colonialism and feminism (e.g. Bale and Cronin 2003; Cresswell 2004; Gaffney 2008; Van Ingen 2003; Wise and Harris 2010). Pertinent to geography, being the holistic discipline that it is, much research in the field of sports geography is inherently cross-disciplinary. In outlining a geography of sport, Bale (2003) touches upon several themes, including globalization, diffusion, regional analysis, location, social welfare, place and geographical imaginaries. Sports, while very developed in sociological research, are inherently geographical – with researchers interested in similar phenomena from collective identities, communities and place (Bale 2000; Gaffney 2008; Goksøyr and Olstad 2009; Wise 2011). The focus on geographical understandings of sport with a sociological emphasis has seen increased attention in recent years, and spatial understandings have been blended amongst the sport and sociology literature (e.g. Baller 2007; Conner 2014 Grainger 2006; Shobe 2008a, 2008b; Wise 2013, 2015; Wise and Harris 2014). In particular, other notable geographically focused studies, for example, have concentrated on sports facilities/ stadiums and the landscape (e.g. Bale 2000; Gaffney 2008; Vertinsky and Bale 2004), productions of social and cultural identities (e.g. Conner 2014; Shobe 2008b; Wise 2014) and sports development (e.g. Wainwright and Ansell 2008). An outline of recent work regarding the study of sports geography is outlined below. As this overview indicates, contemporary geographers are interested in how space and place is transformed through globalization and expansive practices, linked to transnationalism, identity, policy and economic development (Gaffney 2010; Harris and Wise 2011; Overton, Murray and Heitger 2013; Wainwright and Ansell 2008; Wise and Harris 2014).

Notions of space and place in sports geography

Geographers and social science researchers (most notably sociologists and anthropologists) have directed much attention towards understanding perspectives of place, relevant to landscape, community and identity. Geographers have approached and debated notions of space and place from several perspectives. It is important to define space and place, as these are the key conceptual and practical constructs upon which this section will be based. Space, which is all around us, is an abstraction of time and distance, locality or dimensions. It has been argued that space becomes place through lived experiences whereby individuals and groups give particular spaces meaning. For example, people commonly recreate and use parks or vacant spaces to play football. The everyday involvement in a space is therefore given meaning by those who use it and define boundaries for sport.

Other perspectives suggest designation and control of space is based upon semblances of power. This limits who can access or use certain spaces, offering insight into inclusion and exclusion based on socio-economic status. Entering a stadium to attend a football match often involves purchasing a ticket; likewise, some recreational facilities come with monthly charges. This also is the case with country clubs that have high membership fees, or sports such as ice hockey that require substantial financial investments by an individual because of high equipment costs along with high facility and maintenance costs of ice rinks. From another perspective, spatial land-use planning for new stadium venues also impacts local populations, through both positive and negative regeneration efforts.

Sociologists are interested in the impacts of particular activities on places. How people use space to forge a sense of community and identity first requires a particular understanding of a place and its history. Place is defined by Agnew (1987) as *location, locale* and *sense of place*. Location widely refers to a place's geographical coordinates, or from a sports mind-set, we associate professional sports teams or stadiums with place locations – such as the Yankees and New York or Old Trafford and Manchester. Locale involves social interactions, and these can relate to community building or division, inclusion or exclusion. Moreover, locales may be linked to particular events, such as how we associate with certain settings that bring people together for a range of reasons to participate in sport or attend and spectate. Youth clubs in rural areas bring people together to reinforce a sense of social capital and encourage active participation among members of the community (Atherley 2006; Koch 2013). Reid (2012) looks at spatial distributions of participation in sports clubs to determine under- or over-representation based on geographical location. Such a study offers perspective, not only into how participation in sport is geographically concentrated, but suggests insight into possible inclusions or exclusions – to determine opportunities or access/availability to sport. In other cases, sport creates clear social divisions. Such meditation may be associated with, or is specific to, particular areas of a city or sports spaces where existing tensions result in how a place is perceived and experienced based on a group's identity (Conner 2014).

The last point, sense of place, refers to belonging, socially and emotionally, through attachment and a collective community identity (Wise 2011). Moreover, 'sense of place' is:

> the phrase used by many geographers when they want to emphasize that places are significant because they are the focus of personal feelings . . . to refer to the significance of particular places for people. These feelings for 'place' are not seen as trivial; geographers argue that senses of place develop from every aspect of individuals' life experience and the senses of place pervade everyday life and experience.
>
> (Rose 1995: 88)

Sense of place is sought and understood vis-à-vis lived experiences and performing identity in everyday settings. Sense of place, then, suggests belonging, socially and emotionally, through attachment and collective community identity. Sport geographers have used Yi-Fu Tuan's (1974) work on *topophilia* and *escapism* as foundations to understand sense of place and identity to consider territory and imaginations (see Bale 1996); however, more recent work has moved beyond simple explanations and descriptions of places to more critical and exploratory trains of thought in order to make 'sense' of places (Potter 2014; Wise 2015). Nascent geographic thought is concerned with social and material constructions, adding validity to the multiplicity of contexts involved in understanding sense of place (Cresswell 2004). More social research is needed to critically acknowledge sense of place and the role sport plays in shaping local community identities. From this suggestion, geographers have been involved with a range of socio-political constructs of space and place, concerning race and ethnicity, gender, social class, nationalism and contested identities. These points are fully explored in the sociology of sport literature, and many contributions from geographical perspectives do exist (e.g. Gaffney 2008; Paton, Mooney and McKee 2010; Shobe 2008a; Wise 2011), but have been limited. To this regard, evolving complexities, heterogeneity and juxtapositions of identity are increasingly involved with sense of place explorations (Vertinsky and Bale 2004; Wise 2013).

Landscape

Social and cultural geographers invest much time in the study of landscapes; therefore, a particular focus on sporting landscapes has been an important area of emphasis in sports geography (see Bale 1994; Gaffney 2008; Griggs 2009; Harrison 2001; Raitz 1995; Wise 2014). Bale (2003: 131) refers to sports landscapes as 'sportscapes', or 'monocultural sites given over solely to sport'. While this notion is limited, early studies looking at sports and geography were descriptive overviews of landscapes. New, and more critically informed, directions in the study of sports landscapes address how interplays of identity add value to the making of sports landscapes by offering more in-depth analyses that explore local interactions or how social identities are forged through cultural or political ties (Shobe 2008a; Wise 2014). Several metaphors have been used to refer to stadiums. According to Raitz (1995: 1) 'a sporting event takes place in a distinctive setting that is a kind of theatre'. In his edited collection, Raitz (1995) brought together detailed accounts into the staging and history of certain landscapes for sports (e.g. baseball, basketball, cricket, golf) and recreational activities (e.g. fox hunting, climbing). While these 'theatres' act to bond and bring people together, more critical insight points to how stadiums also become spaces where social challenges emerge; many of these challenges are rooted in the history and identity of a place. Similarly, Gaffney (2008: 24–25) notes, stadiums have also been called 'temples, shrines, cathedrals, and hallowed ground. This is a sacred space for a diasporic community'. The emphasis here is on how stadiums have become sacred sites, which suggests dedication, trust and comfort. Given the points addressed, sports landscapes also have the power to unite and divide groups of people (Baller 2007; Shobe 2008b; Wise 2015).

Comprehensive analyses of local sports spaces and landscapes have contributed nascent insight to the sport and geography literature (Gaffney 2009; Mitchelson and Alderman 2011; Rosso 2010; Shobe 2008b; Wise 2011, 2014). Stadiums can often define a place, and are significant icons in the landscape. In terms of meanings or complexities associated with stadiums, venues are often associated with regional and/or national identity (Bairner 2001; Bale 2003; Gaffney 2008; Goksøyr and Olstad 2009; Shobe 2008a, 2008b). For instance, in Dublin's Croke Park, the sports of football, rugby and cricket, sports associated with the British Empire, were banned and only Gaelic sports could be played in the stadium until 2007. The Gaelic Games became part of a wider initiative to promote indigenous Irish sports and preserve a sense of Irish national identity through sport (Bairner 2001). Stadiums are also political platforms; Shobe's (2008a, 2008b) longitudinal research on Catalonian identity formation and FC Barcelona addresses how power, politics and nationalistic sentiment are inherently linked to football stadiums and clubs. The challenge for the researcher is addressing how these interplays of identity and political contexts frame social relations and contested meanings embedded in places or specific venues. Since land-scapes are an important concept in geography where interactions and performances of identity are either forged or rooted, further insight in the sociology of sport literature on community and identity brings together geographical and sociological approaches and imaginations.

Baller's (2007) work is inherently social and geographical and addresses how vacant spaces in Dakar, Senegal, are used to bring together communities from across the city. What is created are sporting landscapes in spaces that were regarded as vacant spaces, and through sport, the use of and meaning of such spaces was given social and cultural meaning. Moreover, landscapes take on several layers of meaning, which can be approached from two perspectives. In his work on sport-ing landscapes in the Dominican Republic, Wise (2014) focused on one particular landscape in a rural community that was used by Haitians for football and Dominicans for baseball. A field was designated for Haitians to play football, but since Dominicans consider their country (the Dominican Republic) to be a baseball country, the Dominicans saw a football field as a threat and began using the very same space to play baseball as a way of defending their sense of place and identity (Wise 2013). Additionally, the Dominicans also encouraged Haitians to play base-ball to get them to conform to their national sporting ideals. In this case, one space was utilized differently depending on what group of people was utilizing the space. Related work by Wise (2011, 2013, 2015) is much more concerned with the everyday sporting spaces that people use for recreation and how people create meaningful sporting experiences in the spaces available to them for sport and recreation.

Community and identity

Based on associations alluded to above and in subsequent sections, sports are a way of expressing culture through socializations among community members (Walseth 2006). It is through com-munity involvement that sports establish foundations where groups express a common sense of identity (MacClancy 1996), or act to promote a collective identity (Shobe 2008b). According to MacClancy (1996: 7), sports, addressed from the perspective of community, contribute to 'the creation of new social identities; to give physical expression to certain social values and to act as a means of reflecting on those values'. A shared sense of belonging is sustained through inter-actions in common places, such as locations or geographical reference points, where identities are constructed, staged and performed (Edensor 2002; Rosso 2010; Tonts and Atherley 2010; Walseth 2006). Bale (2000: 91) challenged this approach, suggesting that 'a community of fans is a social network of interacting individuals but it is not necessary for such a community to be concentrated in a defined territory'. While a team is defined to a location, in an era of fluid migration, people move but retain their loyalty to a particular team, but nonetheless continue to be a part of the community of supporters. Hence, across the United States, *Steeler Nation* or *Red Sox Nation* is integral to people who departed Pittsburgh or Boston, respectively, but retain their loyalty to their 'home' city or region. However, this can become more complex when a team decides to change locations, such as the case when the Baltimore Colts moved to Indianapolis or when Wimbledon FC relocated to Milton Keynes. Relocations impact people, specifically the fans or supporters who are attached to the team or club in certain place locations. Affiliations and loyalties are contested when a club moves; the supporters who remain in a location can often no longer associate with the club because the club becomes associated with a new place, which suggests deterritorialization (Potter 2014).

While sports reflect collective identities, involving individuals, groups and communities, numerous subsequent elements of identity are also embedded in sports spaces, such as race, ethnicity, social class and gender. These broader aspects of identity again bring up the notions of inclusion, exclusion and geographical positioning, or how we associate or link sports to particular areas. Basketball is often regarded as a sport that is common in inner-city areas whereas cricket is more of a rural sport because of the expansive amounts of space required. Around the world, sports spaces are perceived as masculine, or male-dominated. Therefore, referring back to Gaffney's (2008) work on Buenos Aires, the stadium is regarded as a social space where boys become men, or places where a father and son can bond. Wise and Harris (2014) also discuss how sports spaces create several layers of exclusion, in terms of ethnicity and gender by addressing Haitians residing in the Dominican Republic. Haitians are often excluded by Dominicans and often have limited access to sports spaces. This is a result of an ethnic and racial divide where Dominicans control and determine the use of space. However, when Haitian men secure a sports space to play football, they exclude women from participating alongside them, adding another social dimension to who can access or use sport/recreational spaces at a given time.

Geographical imaginations and national identities

Bringing the above points together, the concept of geographical imaginations links these understandings. Bale (2003) dedicated an entire chapter to imaginative geographies because our cognitive associations often link certain sports with particular places. Sports are increasingly broadcasted as spectacles through the media (Mitchelson and Alderman 2011). Our knowledge of places is communicated to us through newspapers, television, film, photographs and more recently social media (Shears and Fekete 2014). Nations, regions and cities are each places that are imagined through various cultural elements, political situations or economic bases. Therefore, sports have become an extension of place narratives that often fulfil how people come to know or associate with places because they are so widely publicized through links to particular sports or iconic individuals (Wise and Harris 2010). For instance, rugby is popular in south Wales, Australian rules football is extremely popular in the greater Melbourne area and the Gaelic Games symbolize Irish heritage and nationalism. The same regional or national associations may be found with particular athletes, such as Novak Djokovic and Serbia, Yao Ming and China or Wayne Gretzky and Canada.

Anderson's (1991) notion of nations as imagined communities is widely used in the sociology of sport literature when addressing how people are bound together vis-à-vis *horizontal comradeship*, which in contemporary times extends beyond national borders (Carter 2007; Wise 2011). Furthermore, representations in the landscape act to stage or display symbolisms that connect imagined communities, and while national identity can be staged, it is also performed (Edensor 2002). In this sense, sport becomes a performance of national identity to connect people with their sense of home because people find comfort in familiarity. Meanings associated with being in place or out of place (Cresswell 2004) conceptually situate people's belonging and performances of identity in a foreign place. Also important is Bairner's (2001) discussion of dichotomies that position perspectives of ethnic and civic nationalism in sport. Regarding ethnic nationalism, nations are identified through homogenous ideals (i.e. language or race). In contrast, civic nationalism 'celebrates citizenship within particular political entities as opposed to membership in supposedly natural human associations [and therefore,] civic nationalism is inclusive' (Bairner 2001: 3).

National identity, in this regard, situates how individuals and social actors from a particular nation imprint their unique sense of sporting identity in another country to symbolize their presence. As we reside in an increasingly interdependent world, the independent movement of people and their national identity will continue to have an impact on spatial contestations, heterogeneity and local community interactions. Furthermore, by recognizing the fluidity of national identities, as a result of increased transnational migrations, people will continue to assimilate their ethnic sense of nation(ness) in other countries, and this is seen by how people adapt and transform landscapes to create spaces of familiarity. National unity then generates some semblance of identity that is collectively or homogeneously shared among community participants, by forging new meanings in a different place. Smith (1991) suggests that nations are bounded entities, but in a nascent era of transnational movements, the nation is no longer bounded geographically per se, but is fluid, referring to the interconnectedness of national societies across borders (Carter 2007; Darby and Solberg 2010; Grainger 2006).

Expansion, change and future directions of sports geography

Geographers are concerned with how social, cultural, political, economic and environmental impacts either contribute new meaning or transform perceptions of space and place. In particular the impact of globalization on sports has received much attention in the sociology of sport literature (e.g. Giulianotti and Robertson 2009; Harris 2010; Klein 2006), but more geographical analysis can also help frame how migrations and movements shape the changing characteristics of places (Overton, Murray and Heitger 2013) or result in contestation (Wise and Harris 2014). The global expansion of competitions and major sporting events is changing and challenging the way we think about space transformations and place meanings (see Gaffney 2009, 2010; Smith 2012). This section outlines two timely areas of research that concern geographers and sociologists. The expansion of sport to new markets – referring to transnationalism, and the impact of change or 'regeneration' on places – is influenced by wider processes of globalization. Geographies of transnationalism and regeneration reflect the rapid transformations of space and place. Each of these points relates to the directions of research in geography and sociology by considering the impact of globalization on the expansion and commercialization of sporting clubs, the increased migration of football players around the world or the transformation of cities to host major sporting events. The final point on regeneration not only deals with physical infrastructural changes in the landscape and shifting economic bases, but research is especially concerned with how policy and planning of new spaces has an impact on the local and social identities of places.

As a result of increased movement and migration, such contemporary research is concerned with the notion of transnationalism. Sports here are considered from two perspectives: an expansion (referring to corporate organizational) approach and the migration of athletes. These two approaches to transnationalism are also relevant to economic research on sport (see Delaney, this volume) where dominant markets within the elite sporting competitions attract the most talented athletes from around the world. This explains the movement of high-profile footballers from South America and Africa to clubs in the English Premier League (EPL). EPL clubs such as Manchester United, Manchester City, Chelsea and Liverpool, as examples, are globally recognized brands, and in many developing-world countries it is common to see players celebrated who were recruited by such clubs. The same is with the case of Dominican baseball players moving to the United States (Klein 2006). Major sporting organizations in the United States such as the National Basketball Association (NBA), Major League Baseball (MLB) and the National Football League (NFL) are expansive enterprises that seek to capture a wider commercial market share and global audience. While sports expansions are capital driven, they are still inherently social and geographical. Such expansions are linked to cultural globalization where powerful associations look to expand into new markets. When a sport enters a new market, it is sometimes accepted differently, and takes on a different meaning. This was observed by Kelly (2007), who highlights how baseball takes on different meanings in the United States and Japan.

To position expansion and movement in regards to sport and migration, Bale and Maguire (1994) put together a geographically informed collection to identify the impact of mobility on global sports development. Elliott and Harris's (2014) recent collection revisits many of these key points to acknowledge how continued transnational movements are impacting sport identities at local and global levels. Moreover, migration research builds on work concerning national identity, detailed above, and is challenging academics to further determine the wider social and cultural impacts that transnational expansions and movements have on host populations. Sports clubs used to be concentrated locally, but the need to be competitive required attracting the most talented athletes. Sometimes players are signed on lucrative contracts just to gain exposure or to open new sporting markets. One example is Didier Drogba from Ivory Coast, recruited by clubs in the French leagues before signing a contract with Chelsea in 2004. In an effort to attract high-profile footballers to China, Shanghai Shenhua of the China Super League signed Drogba to further develop China's national football competition. This process has also been witnessed in Major League Soccer (MLS) in the United States, through the recruitment of world-famous players such as David Beckham and Thierry Henry to further promote and commercialize the domestic competition and increase popularity.

Shifting now to a discussion on regeneration (also referred to as change, renewal, revitalization or redevelopment), this is another important focus that will see increased research among social geographers. Newsome and Comer (2000) state that the time and money dedicated to stadium construction reflects the importance of sport in contemporary society, and how stadiums come to define a particular city. Henry and Gratton (2001) outlined concepts which may be used to examine sport-led regeneration in urban areas, although more research is needed to frame the link between sport and interurban renewal among urban geographers as existing studies are now dated (e.g. Newsome and Comer 2000; Turner and Rosentraub 2002) or have been rooted in other related disciplines such as tourism and events (e.g. Smith 2012). Beyond the physical and infrastructural changes to the landscape, there has been a new directive to understand the 'softer' impacts of sport-related urban change, particularly with respect to social benefits (Gaffney 2010; Smith 2012). Investments in the sport industry in post-industrial cities, and across wider regions, have become an integral part of more contemporary regeneration strategies as a result of on-going economic transitions. New social policies are being proposed, implemented and allocated based on access and availability of resources – as part of wider legacy initiatives. Policies are pertinent to strategic investments and specific developments; for instance, in Scotland, sport-led regeneration is not only an attempt to build new facilities but to encourage wider participation (Paton *et al.* 2010). This is especially pertinent to geographers who look at the interactions between developments and impacts on society – as such approaches are framed around the concepts of regeneration. For instance, the 2012 Olympic Games in London focused on three key themes: regeneration, sustainability and legacy. Geographers are especially interested in these themes because they encompass holistic approaches specific to wider societal challenges in order to better understand the nascent role of sport and sports development (Wainwright and Ansell 2008).

Concluding thoughts

The future of sports geography is concerned with social impacts and how sports make a difference. How we understand sport and recreational approaches in different places aligns with the continued transformation of space and attitudes towards sport. Bale's (2003) key text outlining the geography of sport set the agenda for contemporary approaches in the field of sports geography, but it is the spatial perspective that geographers offer to contemporary debates in sociology that will contribute supplemental understanding to the host of impacts concerning globalization, transnational migrations and regenerative strategies on urban and regional social policy. As major sporting events continually seek new markets, countries in the developing world are using sports to redefine themselves to create new associations through commercial exposure to attract investors and attention.

To conclude, geographers have applied the concepts outlined above to numerous case studies around the world to determine the geographical significance of space and place to how sports impact society. The expansion of the global economy and pressures to adapt to transitions and new developments are challenging geographers to rethink the role of sport and social impacts. These will be challenges that will require particular geographical perspectives and analysis, both to understand social patterns and to contribute to changing wider meanings of place and society.

References

Agnew, J.A. (1987) *Place and Politics*, Boston, MA: Allen and Unwin.

Anderson, B. (1991) *Imagined Communities*, London: Verso.

Atherley, K. (2006) 'Sport, Localism and Rural Social Capital in Rural Western Australia', *Geographical Research*, 44: 348–360.

Bairner, A. (2001) *Sport, Nationalism, and Globalization: European and North American Perspectives*, Albany: State University of New York Press.

Bale, J. (1982) *Sport and Place*, Lincoln: University of Nebraska Press.

Bale, J. (1994) *Landscapes of Modern Sport*, Leicester: Leicester University Press.

Bale, J. (1996) 'Space, Place and Body Culture: Yi-Fu Tuan and a Geography of Sport', *Geografiska Annaler, Series B, Human Geography*, 78(3): 163–171.

Bale, J. (2000) 'The Changing Face of Football: Stadiums and Communities', *Soccer & Society*, 1(1): 91–101.

Bale, J. (2003) *Sports Geography*, New York: Routledge.

Bale, J. and Cronin, M. (eds) (2003) *Sport and Postcolonialism*, London: Berg.

Bale, J. and Maguire, J. (eds) (1994) *The Global Sports Arena: Athletic Talent Migration in an Interdependent World*, London: Frank Cass.

Baller, S. (2007) 'Transforming Urban Landscapes: Soccer Fields as Sites of Urban Sociability in the Agglomeration of Dakar', *African Identities*, 5(2): 217–230.

Carter, T. (2007) 'Family Networks, State Interventions and the Experience of Cuban Transnational Sport Migration', *International Review for the Sociology of Sport*, 42(4): 371–389.

Conner, N. (2014) 'Global Cultural Flows and the Routes of Identity: The Imagined Worlds of Celtic FC', *Social & Cultural Geography*, 15(5): 525–546.

Cresswell, T. (2004) *Place: A Short Introduction*, Oxford: Blackwell.

Darby, P. and Solberg, E. (2010) 'Differing Trajectories: Football Development and Patterns of Player Migration in South Africa and Ghana', *Soccer & Society*, 11(1/2): 118–130.

Edensor, T. (2002) *National Identity, Popular Culture and Everyday Life*, Oxford: Berg.

Elliott, R. and Harris, J. (eds) (2014) *Football and Migration: Perspectives, Places and Players*, London: Routledge.

Gaffney, C.T. (2008) *Temples of the Earthbound Gods: Stadiums in the Cultural Landscapes of Rio de Janeiro and Buenos Aires*, Austin: University of Texas Press.

Gaffney, C. (2009) 'Stadiums and Society in Twenty-First-Century Buenos Aires', *Soccer & Society* 10(2): 160–182.

Gaffney, C. (2010) 'Mega-Events and Socio-Spatial Dynamics in Rio de Janeiro, 1919–2016', *Journal of Latin American Geography*, 9(1): 7–29.

Giulianotti, R. and Robertson, R. (2009) *Globalization and Football*, London: Sage.

Goksøyr, M. and Olstad, F. (2009) '"… Far to the North": Geography and Football in Norway', *Soccer & Society*, 10(3/4): 324–340.

Grainger, A. (2006) 'From Immigrant to Overstayer: Samoan Identity, Rugby, and Cultural Politics of Race and Nation in Aotearoa/New Zealand', *Journal of Sport & Social Issues*, 30(1): 45–61.

Griggs, G. (2009) '"Just a Sport Made Up in a Car Park?" The "Soft" Landscape of Ultimate Frisbee', *Social and Cultural Geography*, 10(7): 757–770.

Harris, J. (2010) *Rugby Union and Globalization: An Odd-Shaped World*, Basingstoke, UK: Palgrave Macmillan.

Harris, J. and Wise, N. (2011) 'Geographies of Scale in International Rugby Union: The Case of Argentina', *Geographical Research* 49(4): 375–383.

Harrison, B. (2001) 'Tracks across Vermont: *Vermont Life* and the Landscape of Downhill Skiing, 1946–1970', *Journal of Sport History*, 28(2): 253–270.

Henry, I. and Gratton, C. (2001) *Sport in the City: The Role of Sport in Economic and Social Regeneration*, London: Routledge.

Kelly, W.W. (2007) 'Is Baseball a Global Sport? America's "National Pastime" as Global Field and International Sport', *Global Networks*, 7(2): 187–201.

Klein, A. (2006) *Growing the Game: The Globalization of Major League Baseball*, New Haven, CT: Yale University Press.

Koch, N. (2013) 'Sport and Soft Authoritarian Nation-Building', *Political Geography*, 32: 42–51.

MacClancy, J. (1996) 'Sport, Identity and Ethnicity', in J. MacClancy (ed.) *Sport, Identity and Ethnicity*, Oxford: Berg.

Mitchelson, R.L. and Alderman, D.H. (2011) 'Mapping NASCAR Valley: Charlotte as a Knowledge Community', *Southeastern Geographer*, 51(1): 31–48.

Newsome, T.H., and Comer, J.C. (2000) 'Changing Inter-Urban Location Patterns of Major League Sports Facilities', *Professional Geographer*, 52(1): 105–120.

Overton, J., Murray, W.E. and Heitger, J. (2013) 'Pass the Passport! Geographies of the Rugby World Cup 2011', *New Zealand Geographer*, 69: 94–107.

Paton, K., Mooney, G. and McKee, K. (2010) 'Class, Citizenship and Regeneration: Glasgow and the Commonwealth Games 2014', *Antipode*, 44(4): 1470–1489.

Potter, D. (2014) 'From Merton to Milton Keynes: Wimbledon Football Club Fans and the Impact of Relocation, Ten Years after the Move', in S. Dun, K. Spracklen and N. Wise (eds) *Game Changer: The Transformative Potential of Sport*, Oxford: Interdisciplinary Press.

Raitz, K., (ed.) (1995) *The Theater of Sport*, Baltimore: Johns Hopkins University Press.

Reid, F. (2012) 'Increasing Sports Participation in Scotland: Are Voluntary Sports Clubs the Answer?', *International Journal of Sport Policy and Politics*, 4(2): 221–241.

Rooney, J.F. (1974) *A Geography of American Sport: From Cabin Creek to Anaheim*, Reading, MA: Addison-Wesley.

Rose, G. (1995) 'Place and Identity: A Sense of Place', in D. Massey and P. Jess (eds) *A Place in the World*, Oxford: Oxford University Press.

Rosso, E. (2010) 'From Informal Recreation to a Geography of Achievement: Women's Soccer in South Australia', *Geographical Research*, 48: 181–196.

Shears, A. and Fekete, E. (2014) 'Re-Constructing the Map: NBC's Geographic Imagination and the Opening Ceremony for the 2012 London Olympics', *Sociological Research Online*, 19(1). Available at: http://www.socresonline.org.uk/19/1/7.html (accessed 10 November 2014).

Shobe, H. (2008a) 'Football and the Politics of Place: Football Club Barcelona and Catalonia, 1975–2005', *Journal of Cultural Geography*, 25(1): 87–105.

Shobe, H. (2008b) 'Place, Identity and Football: Catalonia, *Catalanisme* and Football Club Barcelona, 1899–1975', *National Identities*, 10(3): 329–343.

Smith, A. (1991) *National Identity*, London: Penguin.

Smith, A. (2012) *Events and Urban Regeneration: The Strategic Use of Events to Revitalise Cities*, London: Routledge.

Tonts, M. and Atherley. K. (2010) 'Competitive Sport and the Construction of Place Identity in Rural Australia', *Sport in Society*, 13: 381–398.

Tuan, Y-F. (1974) *Topophilia*, Englewood Cliffs, NJ: Prentice Hall.

Turner, R.S. and Rosentraub, M.S. (2002) 'Tourism, Sports and the Centrality of Cities', *Journal of Urban Affairs*, 24(5): 487–492.

Van Ingen, C. (2003) 'Geographies of Gender, Sexuality and Race: Reframing the Focus on Space in Sport Sociology', *International Review for the Sociology of Sport*, 38(2): 201–216.

Vertinsky, P. and Bale, J. (2004) *Sites of Sport: Space, Place, Experience*, London: Routledge.

Wagner, P. (1981) 'Sport: Culture and Geography', in A. Pred (ed.) *Space and Time in Geography*, Lund, Sweden: Gleerup.

Wainwright, E. and Ansell, N. (2008) 'Geographies of Sports Development: The Role of Space and Place', in V. Girginov (ed.) *Management of Sports Development*, Oxford: Butterworth-Heinemann.

Walseth, K. (2006) 'Sport and Belonging', *International Review for the Sociology of Sport*, 41(3/4): 447–464.

Wise, N. (2011) 'Transcending Imaginations through Football Participation and Narratives of the *Other:* Haitian National Identity in the Dominican Republic', *Journal of Sport & Tourism*, 16(3): 259–275.

Wise, N. (2013) 'Maintaining Dominican Identity in the Dominican Republic, Forging a Baseball Landscape in Villa Ascension', *International Review for the Sociology of Sport*, doi: 10.1177/1012690213478252.

Wise, N. (2014) 'Layers of the Landscape: Representation and Perceptions of an Ordinary (Shared) Sport Landscape in a Haitian and Dominican Community', *Geographical Research*, 52(2): 212–222.

Wise, N. (2015) 'Football on the Weekend: Rural Events and the Haitian Imagined Community in the Dominican Republic', in A. Jepson and A. Clarke (eds) *Exploring Community Festivals and Events*, London: Routledge.

Wise, N. and Harris, J. (2010) 'Reading Carlos Tevez: Football, Geography, and Contested Identities in Manchester', *International Journal of Sport Communication*, 3(3): 322–335.

Wise, N. and Harris, J. (2014) 'Finding Football in the Dominican Republic: Haitian Migrants, Space, Place and Notions of Exclusion', in R. Elliott and J. Harris (eds) *Football and Migration: Perspectives, Places and Players*, London: Routledge.

16

HISTORY, SOCIOLOGY AND CRITICAL SPORT STUDIES

Douglas Booth and Mark Falcous

Scholarly interest in the study of sport as a social phenomenon gained momentum in the 1960s with the institutionalization of various subdisciplines – notably sport history, sport philosophy, sport psychology and sport sociology – following soon thereafter. Whilst each field of study generally comprises broad churches of philosophies, methods and theories, clearly defined critical streams concerned with social justice, relations of power, social conflict and social change gained impetus in the late 1970s and early 1980s. In this chapter we discuss the emergence, development and influence of these critical streams, to which we both subscribe, in sport history and sport sociology. Notwithstanding the fact that the critical streams of sport history and sport sociology share common political and ideological ground, we maintain that the traditional disciplinary foci of empirical evidence (history) and theory (sociology) and associated differences in methodological traditions constrain closer subdisciplinary connections. Moreover, we suggest that the recent intellectual turn toward postmodernism and scepticism of realist epistemologies compounds divides between the two subdisciplines. Although anti-essentialism remains a minority position in sport history, largely articulated through a small postmodern historiographical stream, it occupies a conspicuous, albeit contested, position in sport sociology. Thus, we are of the view that closer relationships between the two subdisciplines will remain limited in the foreseeable future.

Our chapter comprises two substantive sections. In the first we examine the differential development and impact of critical sentiments, themes and theories on sport history and sport sociology. In the second, we identify key epistemological turns in the two subdisciplines as responses to intellectual and political conundrums. We conclude with a brief prognosis for the future.[1]

Critical sentiments and perspectives

Under the weight of institutional and disciplinary pressures, and guided by a number of visionaries, physical education began to fragment in the 1960s into research-grounded academic fields. Although fragmentation coincided with a radical cultural *Zeitgeist* in which nationalist, class, gender and social movements coalesced against Western and capitalist institutions, the primary context for the formation of sport history and sport sociology was an academic vision rather than social critique. The critical sentiments and perspectives associated with the radical cultural

Zeitgeist were yet to surface in either historical or sociological investigations of sport which continued to be framed by positivist methodologies, value-neutral theories and conservative politics. History, at this juncture, remained a primarily empirical endeavour to reconstruct the past as it actually existed, and historians refrained from overt political, ideological or moral assessment.

Sociology, especially dominant Parsonian sociology in the United States, underscored grand theory and privileged systems of classifications and societal institutions over lived experiences. In the economic boom following the Second World War, sociological investigations of sport favoured structural-functionalist theories that accentuated social equilibrium. Using metaphors of the physical world to visualize human societies as wholes or totalities, structural-functionalism likened societies to organisms whose components – institutions – ensured relative social stability. These theories connected logically with objective methods and writing styles. For example, sport sociologist Gunther Lüschen (1969) used structural-functionalism and quantitative techniques to explore the relationship between preferences for certain sports and social class among German youth. Lüschen (1969: 276) found that sport functions to ensure 'the security and advancement of social life', a conclusion that accentuated social equilibrium and predictably reflected the structuralist-functionalist paradigm.

Structural-functionalism guided several early histories of urban sport in North America which advanced sport as a social stabilizer in nineteenth-century cities. Although few sport historians explicitly expounded their versions of structural-functionalism, this theoretical framework gained a foothold in the field through the influential modernization approach to social change. Modernization focused on the transformation of rural and agrarian societies into urban and industrial forms, with sport reflecting this transition (e.g. Adelman 1986; Guttmann 1978). Modernization theory and its concomitant conservative political ideology persisted in sport history into the 1990s.

Ideological, political and theoretical critiques of modernity infused the emerging fields of sport sociology and sport history in a piecemeal fashion in the 1970s. (Although the remit of this chapter privileges history, in our view historians of sport lagged as much as a decade behind sociologists of sport in the reception of critical ideas and approaches.) Marxist and feminist influences proved especially significant in these shifts.

European scholar-activists articulated a Marxist analysis of sport and advocated intervention. Jean-Marie Brohm (1978), for example, organized teachers' unions to call for a boycott of the 1978 football World Cup and to protest against the Olympic Games, and he wrote about the commercial exploitation and oppressive nature of high-performance sport in the popular media. Collectivelly, politically charged texts such as Brohm's highlighted the capacity of sport to create and entrench social divisions and inequalities, and questioned its traditional conservatism. Such influences constituted the vanguard of a critical, politically committed framework within which to evaluate sport. Contingent to this shift, left-leaning sociologists increasingly railed against structural-functionalist explanations of sport whether they emanated from historians or sociologists. They claimed that structural-functionalism glossed over disparities in different sporting contexts, exaggerated social stability and harmony and ignored inequality in consensus-building initiatives whether at the community, regional or national levels; some also critiqued the absence of political action. Critics also opposed the political passivity and lack of structural analysis in the emerging symbolic interactionist approaches that emphasized the formation of individual identity through sporting subcultures.

Despite evoking political sympathy, the structural Marxism of the European scholar-activists rapidly became a target of academic critics. The structuralist suppositions of Marxism, which rendered sport an economically determined social practice and which removed free-thinking and acting agents from the past, drew heckles from both historians and sociologists of sport who critiqued their deterministic foundations. Among historians, the primary tenet of structural Marxism – that economic, political and social structures determine daily life – repeatedly faltered under the weight of evidence. The notion that sport engenders reactionary political views or that it forestalls oppositional class consciousness appeared ludicrous to scholars conversant with the likes of the workers' sports movement, the athletic revolution of the 1960s or the range of lived cultures enjoyed by the working classes.

Simultaneously, feminist approaches in North America constituted a new voice with a critical bent. M. Ann Hall's (1978) *Sport and Gender: A Feminist Perspective on the Sociology of Sport* and Mary Boutilier and Lucinda San Giovanni's (1983) collection *The Sporting Woman* reflected the impetus for more radical feminist approaches to sport sociology. These works challenged the prevailing male domination of the field, the male-centrism of research topics, and hitherto liberal-leaning feminism. But, illustrating the lag in critical thinking in sport history, critical feminist perspectives only began to emerge in the mid- to late 1980s.

In the 1970s social historians increasingly questioned the hitherto narrow assumptions and themes of traditional history and its privileging of 'great men' and political and military milestones over culture and the lives of ordinary people. Turning their attention to the latter, social historians found society ridden with inequities and inequalities; several also envisaged themselves as emancipationists. Social historians not only gave ordinary people, and particularly minority groups, a voice, they incorporated political and moral judgements around discrimination, exploitation and abuse into their narratives. Social history attracted the attention of some sport historians who opened sport as a window into everyday lives and experiences. For example, in his pioneering and acclaimed social history of English football (soccer), Tony Mason (1980) revealed a distinct working-class sporting culture and consciousness. The working classes may not have been the legal or commercial owners of football, but they oversaw the culture of the game – playing and watching with parochial pride and spontaneity. Social historians of sport also found sport to be a site of racial and gender conflict.

Not even shared critical sentiments and perspectives could prevent skirmishes over methods, theories, politics and paradigms within and between sport history and sport sociology. Indeed, they have remained a source of endless ferment. Theory is an enduring thorn for many historians and presented an immediate problem for those working within a social history context. For most sport historians, alignment with social history meant placing sport into broader social, economic and political contexts. As we have noted, however, a few explicitly turned to theory to explain the relationship between sport and society. While most of the criticisms directed at these early theoretical explanations of sport focused on their conservative political content, theorization also raised epistemological concerns about predetermined interpretations and the privileging of abstraction over fact. Historians also objected to sociologists who shied from the archives and relied on secondary sources; indeed, there is an irony in sociologists who uncritically appropriate evidence gathered by historians while variously dismissing them as antiquarians or accusing them of subconscious biases in the gathering and presentation of their evidence. Advocates of theory insist that historians invariably impose their beliefs on the evidence; theory, they argue, helps to identify historical patterns and brings to the fore interrelations between the components of human experiences.

Interestingly, while theory triggered divisions among historians of sport, left-leaning sociologists of sport took historical contextualization for granted. C. Wright Mills's *The Sociological Imagination* (1959) played an influential role. Mills (1959) defined good sociology as historical sociology: history, he insisted, is 'the shank of social study' (143) while theory 'generates general conceptions about society' in the service of specific problems (48). Richard Gruneau (1983), Jennifer Hargreaves (1997) and Alan Ingham and Peter Donnelly (1997) explicitly refer to Mills's influence on their work. Eric Dunning and Kenneth Sheard's (1979) *Barbarians, Gentleman and Players* and Norbert Elias and Dunning's *Quest for Excitement* (1986) are oft-cited examples of historical sociology. However, the figurational approach to historical sociology held little sway among sport historians who objected to its conceptualization of progress. Similarly, some sociologists queried the conceptual foundations of figurationalism and its silences with respect to social change and political intervention. In our view, the lack of explicit commitment to social critique by figurationalists offers a stronger explanation for the limited reception of the figurational approach within sport sociology.[2]

Despite acknowledging the limitations of structural Marxism, historians and sociologists of sport remained receptive to the idea that sport reproduces many of the 'repressive constraints inherent in capitalism' (Gruneau 1983: 36). The problem was to unshackle sport studies from economically deterministic Marxism(s) and to incorporate notions of agency. Some critical sociologists turned toward the nascent field of cultural studies that conceptualized sport as a contested cultural practice and emphasized social conflict without economic determinacy. It was a significant shift in theorizing sport and signposted new post-Marxist critical perspectives.

The post-Marxist critical transition emerged in a number of texts. Jennifer Hargreaves's (1982) edited collection *Sport, Culture and Ideology* interrogated power dynamics and inequality in sport across the multiple axes of class, gender and race. Richard Gruneau's *Class, Sports and Social Development* (1983) and John Hargreaves's *Sport, Power and Culture* (1986) further consolidated the turn toward cultural studies in sport sociology and sport history. While acknowledging the constraints imposed on the sporting and working masses by macro-economic and political structures and forces, Gruneau and John Hargreaves found that these groups possessed considerable agency. The concept of hegemony provided the theoretical key to this conclusion. 'A dominant class has advantages' and 'superior resources', Gruneau (1983: 69) contended, 'but it cannot prevent human beings from thinking on their condition, from wanting to expand their powers, or from continually constituting their identities now in one way, now in another'. Hegemony became the tool of choice among many sport sociologists who analyzed sport as a contested cultural practice.

Some historians of sport explicitly advanced a concept of hegemony as an ongoing political process characterized by conflict, struggle and negotiation. But most historians, and indeed sociologists, conflated hegemony with ideology (as a set of false ideas) and viewed it as a force that conceals systems of domination by persuading the subordinate of the naturalness of the social order and life. In this way, hegemony became, at times, shorthand for what was effectively a preoccupation with structures and relationships of domination and power, and scepticism of agency and real social change. Although such conceptualizations provided easy targets for critics, hegemony signposted critical directions that re-shaped the theorizing of sport in Australia, Britain, Canada and the United States.

The critical turn comprised diverse theoretical directions which frequently shared little in common other than an analytical focus on power and social conflict and oft-stated, yet vague, visions of social equality. The cross-disciplinary field of cultural studies was significant here. Cultural studies channelled attention to the relationship between power and (sport as) culture, the contested reproduction of power relations, and the narratives of marginal groups while allowing for theoretical diversity. This theoretically eclectic framework, which emphasized context, ultimately re-shaped approaches to analyzing sport and was in turn informed by a series of injunctions from feminists who argued for a specifically feminist-informed cultural studies. Furthermore, cultural studies encouraged sports scholars to look beyond their immediate disciplinary confines, ultimately leading toward cross-disciplinary fertilization of methods and theorizations.

Critically informed approaches also infused the study of race and sport. Sport sociologists initially focused on the United States but they quickly extended their work to Australia, Britain, Canada, New Zealand and South Africa. Similarly, historians of sport examined racism in Australia, Britain, Canada, New Zealand and South Africa. In recent times sport sociologists have adopted more explicit and systematic theorizations of race, and have also drawn upon 'whiteness' studies.

French theorist Pierre Bourdieu inspired a further thread of critical thought in sport studies. Bourdieu analyzed the historical resonance of particular sporting practices and styles which he described as entangled in a continual quest for different types of capital (e.g. cultural, social, corporeal) as a basis for class-based distinctions. Bourdieu's landmark *Distinction* (1984) was preceded by a paper given at the International Congress of the History of Sports and Physical Education Association in Paris (Bourdieu 1978). It was sometime, however, before his influence manifested among English-speaking sport historians and sport sociologists. In keeping with the trend of cross-fertilization, sociologists extended their Bourdieu-influenced analyses beyond class to multiple axes of identity and incorporated gender and ethnicity.

While competing schools and disciplinary traditions marked critical analyses of sport, by the turn of the twenty-first century a broader consensus around the complexity of sport accompanied a wariness of reductionist and determinist theories that focused on single categories of power. Richard Gruneau (1999: 114) called for a 'synthetic, multidimensional' approach to sport that conjoined 'history and theory, interpretive cultural analysis, and political economy'. Pamela Grundy's *Learning to Win* (2001) encapsulated the synthetic, multidimensional approach in history. Examining physical activity and organized games in nineteenth-century North Carolina, Grundy intertwined three distinct theoretical concepts – structure (i.e. capitalism), human action (i.e. agency) and culture (i.e. sport) – into her narrative. Simultaneously, a plethora of theories and approaches – arising from sociology, urban studies, geography, history, cultural studies, gender theory, media studies, postcolonialism, queer theory, poststructuralism, post-Marxism and anthropology – permeated an increasingly diffuse sports sociology.

In a landmark assessment of new directions in sport sociology, Mary McDonald and Susan Birrell (1999) captured the essence of an emerging multiperspectivalism. As they put it, approaches that analyze ageism, sexism, racism, classism and heterosexism as 'independent forces' risk silencing the ways in which they 'interact' (McDonald and Birrell 1999: 284). Importantly, McDonald and Birrell (1999: 284) stressed history and local context. Every event or incident, they reminded their readers,

> offers a unique site for understanding specific articulations of power. The importance of using particular incidents as points of analytical access is precisely their particularity. Because power operates differently in different places and times, we should avoid the reductive tendencies of arguments over primacy: We cannot settle once and for all which relation of power is always and everywhere most important. What we can say as cultural critics is that at this historical moment, in this particular place, these discourses on race, sexuality, age, ability, and nationality are produced around this particular incident. Thus these analyses traverse the boundaries between lived experience, knowledge production, and political practices.
>
> (McDonald and Birrell 1999: 284)

In critical sport history a broader cultural turn tended to overshadow multiperspectivism. Historians of sport began to embrace cultural topics in the second half of the 1980s. This trend strengthened in the 1990s with the recognition that sport provided a medium for forming and expressing all types of collective identities (see especially Allison 1993; Jarvie and Walker 1994; Nauright and Chandler 1996). Historians cite numerous causes of the turn to culture. Allan Megill (2007: 188) refers to the new cultural history as both 'an extension of, and a rebellion against, the dominance of social history'. As well as new 'questions about the status of "the social"', Victoria Bonnell and Lynn Hunt (1999: 6) highlight 'methodological and epistemo- logical dilemmas' and the 'realignment of the disciplines (including the rise of cultural studies)'. Notwithstanding what she described as sport historians' commitment to social history, Catriona Parratt (1998: 4) identified 'postmodernist assaults on history's epistemological claims, empiricist certainties and the modernist credo of progress' as significant contributions to developments in the field.

Epistemological turns

Modernist, scientific and objective, sport history and sport sociology proceeded from faith in analytical empiricism to produce and verify knowledge. Critical ideas and thoughts introduced subjective/ideological components into the two subdisciplines which nonetheless remained committed to realist epistemologies in the form of emancipatory meta-narratives. Critically influenced historians, for example, adopted a practical realist epistemology (Appleby, Hunt and Jacob 1994). Practical realists define themselves as 'inquiring subjects' and admit their personal biases, values, emotions and cultural preferences; nonetheless, they insist that they can apply standards of objectivity when examining historical materials (i.e. 'external objects'). While prac- tical realists concede that 'it is impossible to know the "truth" about the social past in any abso- lute sense', they maintain that their 'propositions' about the past are 'reliable to varying degrees' (Fairburn 1999: 6). Practical realism effectively propped up both conservative modernist and critical social and socio-cultural history. Indeed, practical realism found expression in the inau- gural edition of the *Journal of Sport History* when Marvin Eyler (1974: 75) wrote that 'selectivity, a necessary tool of the historian, does not necessarily indicate bias ... unless the historian selects *only* the evidence that will support his [sic] contentions' and that 'objectivity' is always condi- tional on 'the purpose which the historian has in mind'. However, in the late twentieth century, postmodernism introduced new questions for both conservative and critical socio-cultural his- tory and issued profound challenges to their foundations.

Postmodernism is a highly contested notion that explicitly evades a unified essence and is manifest across a range of contexts. Genevieve Rail (1998), for example, identifies five forms of postmodernism: as artistic representation, as style, as epochal transition, as a method centred on literary theory and as theoretical reflection. We discuss postmodernism here as an epistemology grounded in notions of anti-essentialism and anti-foundationalism that rejects universal and/or objective knowledge. Radical feminist sports scholars most readily embraced postmodernism. Especially influential here were the conceptualizations of power and knowledge advanced by the French philosopher and social theorist Michel Foucault (1991; Rabinow 1991). Foucault conceived power as diffuse, ubiquitous, embodied and productive. In so doing he shifted atten- tion away from longstanding views of power as something applied by dominate classes and rul- ing groups in a coercive manner. Foucault also embraced knowledge as a fundamental form of power. These ideas contributed to an epistemological shift in sport sociology and sport history and the turn from notions of absolute 'knowledge [and] understanding, and (thus) mastery of the social and natural world' toward 'diversity and fragmentation, contingency and fluidity, [and] constructedness and self-interestedness' (Parratt 1998: 5).

Postmodern thought, however, did not sweep all before it in either sport history or sport sociology. Scepticism preceded (a level of) accommodation in both subdisciplines. In sport sociology, William Morgan (1995) describes the accommodation in terms of postmodern vocabulary 'seeping' into pre-existing critical theories and leading to 'hybrid' treatments. Morgan's (1995: 26) examples include John Hargreaves's attempt in *Sport, Power and Culture* (1986) to conjoin Foucault's concept of power with Gramsci's concept of hegemony, and Juhu Heikkala's (1993) 'effort to mesh Foucault's accounts of "technologies of power" and "techniques of the self" with [Anthony] Giddens' accounts of structuration and human agency'.

In sport history, Parratt (1998: 13) similarly identifies an 'accommodation between postmodernist and more conventional approaches'. She cites Susan Cahn's *Coming on Strong* (1995) and Patricia Vertinky's *The Eternally Wounded Woman* (1989) as exemplars, and refers to the use of 'discourse to examine the cultural production and policing of women, gender, sexuality, physicality, and bodies' (Parratt 1998: 12). While Parratt (1998: 13) suggests that most sport historians are 'probably quite comfortable' with such ideas, she also points to a significant epistemological break in at least some quarters of sport history which followed the path trodden by sport sociologists.

Today, postmodernist influences have a firm foothold within sections of the sociological study of sport. Evidence of postmodern sport sociology includes 'alternative' methods of presentation that favour juxtaposition and irresolution over neatness, linearity and coherence (e.g. Denison and Markula 2003), auto-ethnographies (e.g. Allen-Collinson 2012), and creative performances (e.g. Rinehart 2010). Yet, notwithstanding these postmodern frameworks, modernist linear narratives continue to dominate the presentation forms.

Although postmodernism has not permeated sport history to the same degree as sport sociology, key elements are nonetheless evident. Historians of sport have referred to elusive sources, indeterminate sources and affective sources. They have classified facts as 'beliefs' (e.g. Bale 2004) and concepts as 'negotiated meanings' (e.g. Hill 2006), and they have conceptualized sporting practices as cultural texts grounded in multiple voices and perspectives. Sport historians have also conceptualized archives as sites of power, photographs as productive processes in the creation of history, myths as functions of social power and vested interests, memory as a process of construction and historians as authors. They have embraced reflexivity and experimented in presenting history in new ways.

As well as advocating these aspects of postmodern epistemology, a few sport historians subscribe to a more radical notion of history as a representation, rather than a reconstruction, of the past. The philosopher of history Alun Munslow places the concept of reference at the heart of the difference between a representation of the past (i.e. a historical narrative) and the past:

> [H]istories can, and invariably do, contain referential sentence-length descriptions. But to then assume willy-nilly that we can now 'tell the truth' in a narrative is akin to saying that we can 'tell the truth' of *The Rocky Mountains* as a painting, or that we can 'tell the truth' about *Macbeth* as a play. Descriptions allow historians to refer and attribute properties, but not at the level of representations. . . . [R]epresentation is not reference; it is *about* its subject. That history contains references does not authorize our access to the past's meaning.
>
> (2006: 223)

In one sense, the idea of history as a representation of the past emerges directly from the cultural turn. 'As historians learn to analyze their subjects' representations of their worlds', Lynn Hunt (1989: 20) predicted, 'they inevitably begin to reflect on the nature of their own efforts to represent history; the practice of history is, after all, a process of text creating and of "seeing", that is, giving form to subjects'. Indeed, this process fuelled the interest of several historians of sport in historiography.

Critically, this historiographical turn transforms the historian from a scientist who reconstructs the past into an author who represents the past. The potential for this transformation to fundamentally shift the nature of history is profound, as Emily Rosenberg explains:

> History is inevitably selective, mediated, and structured, [arising] situationally from particular times, places, and interpretive communities: empirical evidence is essential, but its selection and interpretation remain so contingent, so dependent upon questions asked, and upon diverse narrative and metaphorical frames [that closure is an illusory goal]. History and other forms of public memory are not avenues to some authentic version of the past but ever-changing and inevitably mediated fields of contestation over how to structure the past's representation.
>
> (cited in Finney 2008: 117)

The recent interest among sport historians in different forms of representation such as statues, stamps and museums reflects the dynamic nature of historical representation.

Postmodern approaches and agendas in sport sociology and sport history have not been without critique. Morgan (1995: 31), for example, criticized what he called the political and cultural relativism of postmodernism, that is, its alleged tendency 'to junk normative evaluation and reasoning and replace them with a partisan, and rather trendy championing of the beliefs of certain social groups'. According to Morgan (1995), this predisposition potentially neutralizes social criticism. He regards the lack of guidelines for classifying 'normatively privileged' narratives and acceptable beliefs as serious political shortcomings (Morgan 1995: 37).[3] In reference to feminist politics, Jennifer Hargreaves (2004) questions the political impact of postmodernism which, she argues, 'does not prioritize praxis' (199) and 'distances itself from politics' (200). Specifically, she cautions that the emphasis on personal stories in the 'new narrative research methods' (199) may not always link with the 'wider social circumstances' (199) that she believes are critical to the political potency of feminist activism.

Historians of sport are yet to produce a cogent critique of postmodernism of the calibre offered by the mainstream historian and historiographer John Arnold (2007). This may be simply because historians remain wedded to searching the archives for facts and have little desire to engage the concepts and philosophical ideas propagated by the social sciences. Certainly there is a large cohort that has yet to embrace different forms of interpretivism, let alone postmodernism.

Conclusion

Although often only implicitly understood by scholars committed to realist epistemologies, critical sentiments and perspectives have had wide-ranging impacts on sport history and sport sociology. They constituted an important shift from apparently politically neutral analyses of sport toward explicitly ideologically committed frameworks; they also precipitated new methods, theories and paradigms. Despite the explicit political rhetoric of the emancipatory approach to sport, the subsequent critical turn in sport history and sport sociology witnessed a shift from intervention and application toward a greater emphasis on theoretical/intellectual arguments. A content analysis of the *International Review for the Sociology of Sport*, for example, revealed a dramatic growth in the use of critical qualitative and anti-positivist approaches in the late 1980s, and simultaneously 'a drop in practice-orientation and application' (Heinemann and Preuss 1990: 11). Indeed, 'over the past decade or more, as critical theory travelled from neo-Marxism, via Gramscianism, to the hegemonic influence of post-Marxism, critical sport sociology has been noticeably detached from a significant leftist politics' (McDonald 2009: 41). It is somewhat ironic that the turn toward critical paradigms helped bestow institutional legitimacy on sport sociology and that, today, political engagement seems to have receded in preference to theorizing. Today, we observe applied sport sociologists gravitating toward sport management and marketing, fields which some critics believe are hindered by conservative ideas and approaches.

Debates about the connection between social criticism and application in the sociology of sport occurred as part of the post-Marxist critical turn and have been reprised in recent attempts to recast sport sociology as physical cultural studies and reassertions of emancipatory agendas. In advocating for 'physical cultural studies' in preference to 'sociology of sport', David Andrews (2008) and his colleagues conceptualize the former as 'a civic, participatory, collaborative project . . . that joins the researcher with the researched in an ongoing moral dialogue' (Silk and Andrews 2011: 14). (For a full explication, see the chapter on physical cultural studies in this volume.) Some critics have labelled attempts to couch physical cultural studies within an amplified critical pedagogy as 'faux radicalism' (e.g. Sugden *et al.* 2012).

Similarly, the historiographic turn in sport history has sparked questions about ethics. Critical social and socio-cultural historians of sport conveyed ethical positions in their narratives by passing judgements on human values and propriety (i.e. identifying, sympathizing and empathizing with their subjects, whom they imply are inherently ethical), critiquing structures and relations of power and advocating for social and political change. One of the implicit goals of critical history was to induce self-reflection among readers as a prerequisite for social change. But while critical historians frequently marry their empirical evidence with ethical narratives, this marriage contradicts the empirical-analytical tenet of history as an objective reconstruction of the past. Indeed, Keith Jenkins (1999) says historians should concede the incommensurability of reconstructing the past and ethics. In contradistinction, Munslow (2006: 95) proposes that historians encompass ethics by acknowledging 'the moral choices they make as they construct the past as a representational narrative'. Reinforcing the notion of history as a narrative construction, Munslow (2006: 95) argues that 'it is how we choose to write history that allows us to take up certain political options and uphold preferred moral standards and moral ideals'. Moral lessons do not emerge from the past per se; historians build those lessons into their narratives.

The effect of physical cultural studies on sport sociology and the influence of critical historiography on sport history are still to be determined. Nonetheless, both movements are powerful reminders that the criteria for assessing fields of scholarly enquiry are neither universal nor fixed. Richard Pringle (2013: 132) is correct when he states that 'legitimate' research is always the product of 'negotiation and modification' and that any evaluation must include the subjective positions, including the 'politics and paradigmatic beliefs', of those producing the critique.

Acknowledgement

Sincere thanks to John Loy and Richard Pringle for their helpful comments on an earlier version of this chapter.

Notes

1 Academic fields are hotly contested and highly complex, and we are acutely aware of the potential limitations of grand narratives such as the one we espouse here.
2 There are variations in the application of figurational sociology to social change. Maguire (2004), for example, is more explicitly political in contrast to Dunning's (2010) rigid use of Elias.
3 Interestingly, neither sociologists nor historians of sport have engaged Morgan's critique. As of April 2013, Google Scholar listed just three citations of the article; none appeared in sport sociology or sport history journals.

References

Adelman, M. (1986) *A Sporting Time: New York City and the Rise of Modern Athletics, 1820–1870*, Urbana: University of Illinois Press.

Allen-Collinson, J. (2012) 'Autoethnography: Situating Personal Sporting Narratives in Socio-Cultural Contexts', in K.Young and M. Atkinson (eds) *Qualitative Research on Sport and Physical Culture*, Bingley, UK: Emerald Group.

Allison, L. (ed.) (1993) *The Changing Politics of Sport*, Manchester: Manchester University Press.

Andrews, D. (2008) 'Kinesiology's *Inconvenient Truth* and the Physical Cultural Studies Imperative', *Quest*, 60(1): 45–62.

Appleby, J., Hunt, L. and Jacob, M. (1994) *Telling the Truth about History*, New York: W.W. Norton.

Arnold, J. (2007) 'Responses to the Postmodern Challenge; or, What Might History Become?' *European History Quarterly*, 37(1): 109–132.

Bale, J. (2004) *Roger Bannister and the Four-minute Mile: Sports Myth and Sports History*, London: Routledge.

Bonnell, V. and Hunt, L. (1999) *Beyond the Cultural Turn: New Directions in the Study of Society and Culture*, Berkeley: University of California Press.

Bourdieu, P. (1978) 'Sport and Social Class', *Social Science Information*, 17(6): 819–840.

Bourdieu, P. (1984) *Distinction: A Social Critique of the Judgement of Taste*. Cambridge, MA: Harvard University Press.

Boutilier, M. and San Giovanni, L. (1983) *The Sporting Woman*, Champaign, IL: Human Kinetics.

Brohm, J. M. (1978) *Sport: A Prison of Measured Time*, London: Ink Links.

Cahn, S. (1995) *Coming On Strong: Gender and Sexuality in Twentieth-century Women's Sport*, Cambridge, MA: Harvard University Press.

Denison, J. and Markula, P. (2003) *Moving Writing: Crafting Movement in Sport Research*, New York: Peter Lang.

Dunning, E. (2010) 'Figurational/Process-Sociological Reflections on Sport and Globalization: Some Conceptual-Theoretical Observations with Special Reference to the "Soccer" Form of Football', *European Journal for Sport and Society*, 7(3/4): 183–194.

Dunning, E. and Sheard, K. (1979) *Barbarians, Gentlemen and Players*, Oxford: Martin Robertson.

Elias, N. and Dunning, E. (1986) *The Quest for Excitement: Sport and Leisure in the Civilizing Process*, Oxford: Basil Blackwell.

Eyler, M. (1974) 'Objectivity and Selectivity in Historical Inquiry', *Journal of Sport History*, 1(1): 63–76.

Fairburn, M. (1999) *Social History: Problems, Strategies and Methods*, New York: St Martin's Press.

Finney, P. (2008) 'Hayden White, International History and Questions Too Seldom Posed', *Rethinking History*, 12(1): 103–123.

Foucault, M. (1991) *Discipline and Punish: The Birth of a Prison*, London: Penguin.

Grundy, P. (2001) *Learning to Win: Sports, Education, and Social Change in Twentieth-century North Carolina*, Chapel Hill: University of North Carolina Press.

Gruneau, R. (1983) *Class, Sports, and Social Development*, Amherst: University of Massachusetts Press.

Gruneau, R. (1999) *Class, Sports and Social Development*, 2nd edition, Urbana, IL: Human Kinetics Press.

Guttmann, A. (1978) *From Ritual to Record: The Nature of Modern Sports*, New York: Columbia University Press.

Hall, M.A. (1978) *Sport and Gender: A Feminist Perspective on the Sociology of Sport*, Ottawa: Canadian Association for Health, Physical Education and Sport.

Hargreaves Je. (ed) (1982) *Sport, Culture and Ideology*, London: Routledge.

Hargreaves, Je. (1997) 'Speaking Volumes on C. Wright Mills's *The Sociological Imagination*', *The Times Higher Education Supplement*, 21 March.

Hargreaves, Je. (2004) 'Querying Sport Feminism: Personal or Political?' in R. Giulianotti (ed.) *Sport and Modern Social Theorists*, London: Palgrave Macmillan.

Hargreaves, Jo. (1986) *Sport, Power and Culture*, Cambridge: Polity Press.

Heikkala, J. (1993) 'Discipline and Excel: Techniques of the Self and Body and the Logic of Competing', *Sociology of Sport Journal*, 10(4): 397–412.

Heinemann, K. and Preuss, W. (1990) '25 years of the *International Review for the Sociology of Sport*: A Content Analysis', *International Review for the Sociology of Sport*, 25(1): 3–17.

Hill, J. (2006) 'Anecdotal Evidence: Sport, the Newspaper Press, and History', in M. Phillips (ed.) *Deconstructing Sport History: A Postmodern Analysis*, Albany: SUNY Press.

Hunt, L. (1989) *The New Cultural History*, Berkeley: University of California Press.

Ingham, A. and Donnelly, P. (1997) 'The Sociology of North American Sociology of Sport: Disunity in Unity, 1965 to 1996', *Sociology of Sport Journal*, 14(4): 362–418.

Jarvie, G. and Walker, G. (eds) (1994) *Scottish Sport in the Making of the Nation*, Leicester: Leicester University Press.

Jenkins, K. (1999) *Why History? Ethics and Postmodernity*, London: Routledge.

Lüschen, G. (1969) 'Social Stratification and Social Mobility among Young Sportsmen', in J. Loy and G. Kenyon (eds) *Sport, Culture and Society: A Reader on the Sociology of Sport*, New York: Macmillan.

Maguire, J. (2004) 'Challenging the Sports-Industrial Complex: Human Sciences, Advocacy and Service', *European Physical Education Review*, 10(3): 299–321.

Mason, T. (1980) *Association Football and English Society, 1863–1915*, Brighton, UK: Harvester.

McDonald, I. (2009) 'One-dimensional Sport: Revolutionary Marxism and the Critique of Sport', in B. Carrington and I. McDonald (eds) *Marxism, Cultural Studies and Sport*, London: Routledge.

McDonald, M. and Birrell, S. (1999) 'Reading Sport Critically: A Methodology for Interrogating Power', *Sociology of Sport Journal*, 16(4): 283–300.

Megill, A. (2007) *Historical Knowledge, Historical Error: A Contemporary Guide to Practice*, Chicago: University of Chicago Press.

Mills, C.W. (1959) *The Sociological Imagination*. Oxford: Oxford University Press.

Morgan, W. (1995) 'Incredulity toward Metanarrative and Normative Suicide: A Critique of Postmodernist Drift in Critical Sport Theory', *International Review for the Sociology of Sport*, 30(1): 25–43.

Munslow, A. (2006) *The Routledge Companion to Historical Studies*, 2nd edition, London: Routledge.

Nauright, J. and Chandler, T. (eds) (1996) *Making Men: Rugby and Masculine Identity*, London: Frank Cass.

Parratt, C. (1998) 'About Turns: Reflecting on Sport History in the 1990s', *Sport History Review*, 29(1): 4–17.

Pringle, R. (2013) 'Sport History Legitimation: A Historical Examination of What Constitutes "Good" Sport History', in R. Pringle and M. Phillips (eds) *Examining Sporting Histories: Power, Paradigms, and Reflexivity*, Morgantown, WV: Fitness Information Technology.

Rabinow, P. (1991) *The Foucault Reader: An Introduction to Foucault's Thought*, London: Penguin.

Rail, G. (1998) *Sport in Postmodern Times*, Albany: State University of New York Press.

Rinehart, R. (2010) 'Performing Sport: Re-visioning Sport Practices in an Age of Global Discord', *International Review of Qualitative Research*, 2(4): 445–456.

Silk, M. and Andrews, D. (2011) 'Toward a Physical Cultural Studies', *Sociology of Sport Journal*, 28(1): 4–35.

Sugden, J., Tomlinson, A. and Wheaton, B. (2012) 'Joining the Dialogue: Challenging the PCS (Physical Cultural Studies) Positioning within the Sociology of Sport', paper presented at the Association of Cultural Studies Crossroads conference, Paris, July 2–6.

Vertinsky, P. (1989) *The Eternally Wounded Woman: Women, Doctors, and Exercise in the Late Nineteenth Century*, Manchester: Manchester University Press.

17

LEISURE STUDIES AND THE SOCIOLOGY OF SPORT

Ken Roberts

Introduction

This chapter examines a triangle of relationships. Leisure is a field of study to which various disciplines contribute (mainly sociology, geography, politics and psychology). Sport, media, tourism, heritage and the arts are simultaneously sub-fields within leisure studies, but can also be independent fields of study, drawing from leisure studies and all the basic disciplines which include sociology. All these sub-fields, and the wider field of leisure studies, can be specialisms within sociology (and all the other disciplines that contribute to the fields). Teachers and researchers may locate themselves simultaneously within leisure studies, one or more of its sub-fields, and within a discipline such as sociology. The relationships between the disciplines and fields are never stable. They can stimulate and help to develop each other. Or they can divide, compete and decide that strength lies in independence. The following sections review the history of the triangle. We then ask what leisure studies contributes to and gains from one specialism within sociology, namely the sociology of sport.

Background

Leisure studies departments and programmes were first created in the USA in the 1950s and 1960s, and spread quickly into Canada. The subject was launched in the UK in the 1970s, then spread into Australia and New Zealand, and much more thinly throughout the rest of the world. The context was the same everywhere. Higher education systems were expanding, which enabled graduates to be recruited into formerly non-graduate occupations such as managing public leisure facilities. Also, some leisure and recreation services had always been part of and others were being incorporated into the welfare states which were being expanded and strengthened between the 1940s and 1970s. Equally important, leisure was growing in terms of time, rates of participation in many leisure activities and the amounts of money that were being spent on these activities. This led to debates about whether the industrial societies in which work had been at the centre of people's lives were being replaced by societies of leisure (Dumazedier 1967).

In America the first leisure studies courses were created by merging existing syllabuses that trained leaders for the recreation programmes that usually targeted 'at risk' groups (see Pangburn 1940), syllabuses in parks management and also in physical education (see Roberts 2010; Samdahl 2010). Parks which were designated and managed by federal and state governments were the jewels in the crown of America's public leisure services, and were usually prominent in leisure studies programmes. Leisure scholars in the USA have never created a scholarly association but have always held their symposia within the conferences of the National Recreation and Parks Association (Henderson 2011). Despite incorporating physical education syllabuses, sport was never prominent in American leisure studies. This is because sport already had an established academic base. College sport was already playing a more pivotal role in the American sports system than has ever been the case in any other country. Sports sciences (to which sociology contributed) developed within the college departments that managed campus sports facilities and teams, recruited players (on sports scholarships) and acted as feeders into professional leagues. It was different in the UK, and also in Australia and New Zealand, where the physical education departments in former teacher training colleges (which were incorporated into polytechnics or became colleges of higher education in the UK during the 1960s) were often the base from which leisure studies departments and programmes developed. Moreover, their playing fields, swimming pools and also, from the 1960s onwards, their new indoor multi-sports and leisure centres, were the jewels in the crown of the UK's public leisure services. The Sports Council, which was created in 1965, and the Countryside Commission were major funders and users of the research, and employers of the graduates that were produced by UK leisure studies courses, as were local authority departments of leisure and recreation services.

These leisure studies programmes never encompassed the whole of leisure. Media studies developed as a separate academic discipline, closely aligned with cultural studies. Commercial leisure was all but ignored in leisure studies programmes although tourism, which was being promoted by public agencies, was incorporated. Teaching and research focused on the 'good leisure' that was serviced primarily by the public and voluntary sectors.

Sociology was another expanding (and reconstituted) discipline on both sides of the Atlantic in the 1950s and 1960s, and the study of sport and of leisure began to emerge as sub-disciplines within sociology. Until the 1980s these sub-disciplines were tiny. Since then, within sociology, there has been spectacular growth of teaching and research in sport, tourism and consumption (and leisure more rarely). The context has been the expansion of the leisure industries in post-industrial societies, and new opportunities for graduates to embark on careers in these fields (Roberts 2004). Meanwhile, leisure studies programmes and departments have been liable to explode into separate subjects, usually sport or tourism or events. Specialization enables the programmes to attract students who are more likely to be enthusiastic about sport, for example, than about leisure in general. Also, many believe, rightly or wrongly, that the different leisure industries prefer to recruit specialists rather than leisure generalists. Another trend has been towards describing the relevant programmes as leisure, sport or tourism 'management' rather than 'studies', and the specialist departments have often moved away from the social sciences into management and business faculties or, in the case of sport, into health faculties.

Nowadays, sport sociology may be located within a multi-disciplinary department of sport or leisure, or within a sociology department. Leisure studies may be a component of a sport or tourism programme, a sociology programme or a stand-alone specialty. The triangle changes shape constantly. Personnel and ideas flow in all directions, but we now focus on the two-way flows between the sociology of sport and leisure studies.

Knowledge exchanges

The distinctive contributions of leisure studies

Leisure studies will provide a home for scholars from any of its sub-fields but would not die if denied contributions from them all. This is because leisure studies' remit is to scan the whole of the leisure field: uses of leisure time and participation rates in and spending on the various leisure activities. Leisure studies investigates trends over time, which tend to unfold slowly from year to year (Gershuny 2000). It examines differences between socio-demographic groups defined by social class, age, gender, ethnicity, place of residence, nationality and religion. Investigators explore inter-country differences in leisure and levels of economic development, and political and welfare regimes (Gronow and Southerton 2011; Lopez 2011). Another major interest throughout leisure studies' history has been to relate involvement in different leisure activities to various measurements of well-being (Iso-Ahola and Mannell 2004).

What sociology and other disciplines have contributed to leisure studies

Leisure studies has benefitted not so much from inputs from the sociology of sport as from general sociology and other social sciences. In the 1950s and 1960s geography was the discipline which made the strongest contributions to leisure studies. This was on account of the field's interest in spaces and their uses (especially parks), and the spread of car ownership, which was leading to mass 'invasions' of the countryside by trippers. Subsequently sociology (broadly defined) became the strongest contributor to leisure studies. Marxism, feminism and symbolic interactionism became sources of new questions about leisure. Latterly, theories about the economically advanced countries' shift into a post-industrial, digital, globalized, neo-liberal era have refreshed the leisure studies agenda. Economics, psychology and political science have made relatively minor contributions, whereas historians are currently becoming increasingly influential.

The wider leisure context: how is sport different?

Leisure studies compares different uses of leisure in terms of the time and money that they account for, the proportions of the population that participate, and the benefits that they derive. How does sport measure up?

Participant sport accounts for a tiny proportion (around one per cent) of all lifetime in modern societies. Around a half of all leisure time is accounted for by the media, mainly television but also radio, recorded music and the internet. Online time has not diminished time spent attending to other media. Nor has it reduced time devoted to sport and other active uses of leisure. The internet is not turning us into couch potatoes. The uses of leisure that tend to be compressed by other 'compulsory' demands (paid work, study and child care) are watching television and housework. These are the uses of time that tend to expand into whatever time is literally spare. Socializing and relaxing are second (behind the media) in leisure time accounted for. In terms of money spent and employment supported, all other uses of leisure are dwarfed by tourism. Sport is low-to-middle-ranked in terms of the proportion of the population that participates and in the flows of money that are involved. It lags well behind the media, going on holiday and out-of-home eating and drinking.

However, a much higher proportion of the population 'follows' sport without either playing or paying. This is evident in the newspaper pages that sport commands, and the regular sport bulletins in general news broadcasts. Major sports events can command large television audiences, but sport cannot do this as regularly as soap operas. Another distinctive feature of sport is that a minority of its followers are fanatics who simply have to be present at fixtures when their teams are playing or, failing that, in front of a television if the fixture is being broadcast. Sport has surprised the broadcasters. Sport, not blockbuster films, has proved to be television's most compelling content for which viewers will pay channel subscriptions (Hutchins and Rowe 2012). The fans are willing to pay because, unlike movies and music concerts, the value of a sport event perishes immediately it ceases to be live. Hence the willingness of television broadcasters to bid up the prices paid for top sport. They broadcast to much smaller numbers of fans than the audiences that would watch if the broadcasts were free-to-air. Also, needless to say, no sport can regularly attract audiences that match those of soap operas. It is true that most of the world's population has watched some of the recent Olympic Games, but the 'some of' varies from country to country. Every country sees a different Olympics dominated by the onscreen presence of its own competitors, especially when they are within sight of medals.

People are urged to play sport for the health and fitness benefits, but sport is not the sole use of leisure that enhances well-being (which can be measured in various ways). Any form of activity is good for well-being. Even non-energetic leisure leads to improvements in physiological functioning (the causal mechanisms remain unknown) (see Iso-Ahola and Mannell 2004). Spending time in green environments is especially beneficial for mental well-being. Again, the causal mechanisms are unknown (Burls 2010). Paid work, even when people dislike their jobs, is better for well-being than being unemployed. Anything appears to be better than doing nothing, maybe just watching television, especially if the viewer is alone. Watching a film as part of a cinema audience leaves people feeling better, which does not happen if they watch a film on television (Uhrig 2005). Being part of a crowd, whether it is a cinema or theatre audience or a crowd in a sports stadium, is beneficial. The benefits that sport offers are not unique to sport. Sport's special capabilities are attracting very large numbers of weakly engaged followers and a core of fanatics who will pay to watch live top sport on television.

Social divisions

Every sociology of sport course will teach that participation is related to social class, age and gender. A wider leisure perspective will identify which of these relationships are sport effects and which are broader leisure patterns.

Participation in most leisure activities is related to social class. The main exception is television viewing. This is a relationship which can truly be said to be over-determined. The higher social classes have more money. They are more likely than members of other classes to have been reared in leisure-active families. They are the most likely to have received an extended education, which is likely to have widened their leisure experiences. Sports differ in the extent of the class skew. It is steepest in high-money-expenditure sports such as those that involve horses, boats and travel (to ski, for example). Some sports are classless and in some (boxing and other martial arts are the main examples) the lower classes predominate. Initiatives to boost sports participation usually target disadvantaged groups, but it is impossible for sport to countervail against the advantages conferred by high socio-economic status. Wider leisure opportunities are supposed to be a reward for success (merited or not).

Young people are the most active age group in most forms of out-of-home recreation. Participation declines during the 'life cycle squeeze' that accompanies new household and family formation when there are new demands on young adults' time and money (Estes and Wilenski 1978; Gershuny 2003). There are some leisure activities where participation recovers in later life – volunteering, church-going and reading are examples – though there is much steeper growth in later life in television viewing. Sport is not among the leisure activities where there is a later-life surge. In fact, sport is distinguished by how steeply participation drops, and how early the decline begins during youth. The peak age for participation in most economically advanced countries (in terms of time spent and number of sports played) is early teens. Uncharacteristically for out-of-home leisure activities, the trend in sport participation during youth is downwards. In fact, 16–25 is the age group within which decline is steepest. Afterwards decline continues but at a slower pace. Sport has an appallingly low loyalty rate (measured as the percentage of those who have ever taken part in an activity who are continuing to do so). High culture is the opposite. Its loyalty rate is extremely high (Hantrais and Kamphorst 1987; Kamphorst and Roberts 1989). Children who are introduced to the classical arts (usually by their families) and who acquire the tastes when young, are likely to remain involved for the rest of their lives. The drop-out rates from sport vary by social class and gender, and also between countries (see below), but the steepness of the drop requires a sports-specific explanation.

This applies even more so to gender differences in sport participation. Girls and women are not under-represented in most forms of leisure. They are as likely as males to watch television (though for fewer hours), listen to the radio and recorded music, to use the internet, to read, to take holidays and to visit theatres, the cinema, galleries and museums. They are also equally likely to go out to eat and drink (though they consume less alcohol than men). Women do not have less leisure time than men. It is true that their greater shares of housework and childcare result in women having less leisure time than men who spend the same number of hours in paid jobs. However, this is compensated by more women working part time and some still being housewives, and women live longer, thereby enjoying more years of paid work-free retirement. In every country where time budget data has been collected, total workloads (paid and unpaid) of males and females across the entire lifespan have been virtually identical (Bittman and Wajcman 1999). Women tend to earn less than men, so those who live singly are disadvantaged compared with their male counterparts, but most males and females live in homes where the family, not the individual earner, is the unit of consumption. Women's under-representation in sport requires a sport-specific explanation.

All the sport-specifics become easier to explain when we recall that most of our modern sports were invented by men, and were intended to be played mainly by young men. Some sports were invented by and were specifically intended for the socially and economically privileged minority that attended England's nineteenth-century secondary schools and universities.

Sport and leisure differences between ethnic groups are complex and difficult to explain. Within countries leisure practices vary between different ethnic minorities as well as, in most cases, between all the minorities and the host/titular populations. Inter-country differences in sport and leisure practices are partly explicable in terms of levels of economic development (Gronow and Southerton 2011; Lopez 2011). Just like the higher social classes within countries, the most developed countries tend to be the most leisure-active, but some other differences are better explained in terms of geography and climate (more time spent outdoors in southern as opposed to northern Europe for example) and national histories and cultures. Europeans drink more alcohol than Americans. The USA actually prohibited the manufacture and marketing of alcohol products between 1920 and 1933. Scandinavian countries, especially Norway, have unusually high rates of sport participation. This is partly due to class and gender differences in sport participation being narrower than in the rest of Europe, which applies to Scandinavia's class and gender inequalities in the labour market and politics as well as sport. Drop-out rates during young adulthood are relatively shallow in Scandinavia. This seems best explained in terms of the types of sport that Nordic people play, plus where they play. Outdoor family recreation is a leisure norm. It is also normal for parents and children to belong to and attend the same sports clubs (Green *et al.* 2013). These are sport-specific differences. Scandinavians do not lead other Europeans in the frequency with which they go out to eat and drink, in their overall levels of alcohol consumption or attendances at cultural events, or taking holidays away from home.

History

Our understanding of present-day sport and other uses of leisure can be enhanced by setting their histories side by side. Sociologists of sport and leisure have typically been preoccupied with the present day and have left history to historians, but a proper understanding of the present is impossible while ignoring the past. Sometimes developments in sport have occurred in parallel with developments in other areas of leisure. At other times sport has been, and indeed for the greater part of the twentieth century sport was, de-aligned.

Most of our modern sports were invented during the second half of the nineteenth century. England, and more specifically England's secondary schools and universities (all privately funded at that time), were the sites of most of these inventions. England's lead role in sport, and in most other modern uses of leisure (see below), was due to England having become the world's first industrial nation (Cunningham 1980). The urban population was experiencing a new kind of leisure time and also, from the 1870s onwards, increasing prosperity. From the sites of their invention, many of the new sports, but most spectacularly association football, spread throughout the population, then throughout the rest of the world (see Walvin 1975). Only the USA developed its own modern sports (see Markovits and Hellerman 2001; Szymanski and Zimbalist 2005). The take-up of England's new sports was sufficiently rapid for a Frenchman, the Baron de Coubertin, to organize the first of the modern Olympic Games in 1896.

Other new, modern uses of leisure were being invented alongside the modern sports. The modern holiday 'away' was among these inventions. Scores of new hobbies were popularized. Enthusiasts began collecting stamps, coins, butterflies, flora and fauna – almost anything that was collectable. New indoor games were invented, usually played on a board. These games included snakes and ladders, ludo and tiddlywinks. Local governments created urban parks, designated playing fields (for the new sports), opened swimming baths, libraries, concert halls and civic meeting rooms (see Bailey 1978; Meller 1976). Most of the leisure pioneers were not profit-seeking businesses. Sports were invented by enthusiastic amateurs who formed voluntary associations which agreed to rules of play and organized competitions. The modern holiday away was pioneered by churches, philanthropists and progressive employers before being largely taken over by commercial businesses (Walvin 1978). The music hall (vaudeville in North America) was exceptional in that its pioneers were businessmen (Bailey 1986; Crowhurst 2001). Board games were also invented by commercial entrepreneurs, but it was enthusiastic amateur players who turned them into hobbies.

Sports were exceptional not in their amateur roots (see Allison 2001) but in that these games were invented by men and were intended to be played by men (not women). More specifically, the sports were intended for young men. When present-day sociologists of sport puzzle over the persistent sex and age differences in participation rates, they need to recall for whom these leisure activities were designed. Popular entertainments (in music halls and theatres), urban parks and cultural facilities were for men and women, and usually for all age groups. In these respects sports were different from the outset.

Sport missed the main leisure revolution of the twentieth century. This was the birth and rapid rise in popularity of the original mass media. Popular daily newspapers made possible by relatively cheap newsprint, advances in printing technology and railroads for distribution, spread from the end of the nineteenth century (Lee 1976; Williams 2009). After the First World War they were joined by radio, movies and recorded music (Robinson 1996). Actors who had performed in theatres had the opportunity to become national and sometimes international celebrities by becoming movie stars. Music hall entertainers were able to achieve a somewhat lesser celebrity by being broadcast on radio and being recorded for sale on gramophone disks. Meanwhile, new kinds of commercial entertainment were being promoted, usually with young people as the target. The dance palais was the main example. These new leisure options joined the existing leisure industries in making 'going out' the highlight of weekly and sometimes daily leisure (Nasaw 1993). After the Second World War the age of television began, going out became more occasional and all existing forms of entertainment needed to adjust (Briggs and Burke 2005; Hesmondhalgh 2013; Wheen 1985). Increasingly prosperous European populations began taking holidays abroad, usually seeking Mediterranean sun. Throughout all this, sport continued much as before. Spectator events were watched by live crowds. Radio broadcasting of fixtures was for dedicated fans. Outside North America most sports were reluctant to embrace television. They feared that attendance at events would be reduced. Amateurs continued to use playing fields and swimming baths that had been available since the late nineteenth and early twentieth centuries.

Another post-1945 development was that most forms of non-commercial recreation received a boost from the expansion of Western countries' welfare states. These included countryside recreation, which was becoming increasingly popular as car ownership became more widespread. More state funding was channelled to the classical arts. Sport benefitted mainly from the construction of multi-sport indoor facilities, which led to rises in participation. Meanwhile, attendances at professional sports events suffered from the increasingly intense competition. Tourism was a major growth area in terms of leisure spending (see Becker 2013). Also, people were spending more on the media, home furnishings, clothing and on out-of-home eating and drinking. Consumer culture rapidly became the dominant leisure culture (Cross 1993; Miles 1998).

Top sport became part of the media revolution only towards the end of the twentieth century. Sport was then catching up rather than forging ahead. The catch-up was due to the advent of television broadcasting by satellite and cable (in addition to airwaves), and the transmission of digital signals which multiplied the number of channels that viewers could access. Simultaneously in Europe most television ceased to be public service and became commercial (Hesmondhalgh 2013). Broadcasters quickly discovered that live top sport was their most compelling content. It was not the most popular content, but it was the content for which viewers were willing to pay channel subscriptions. The creation of global television networks, which enabled the live broadcasting of events to all parts of the world to become routine rather than exceptional, led to a global competition which has steadily bid up the value of the rights to televise live top sport. This has created new streams of income for the top sports, competitions and clubs, most of which has flowed straight out of sport and into top players' bank accounts. Top players now enjoy similar levels of income and celebrity to those of television and film stars and popular musicians (Giulianotti and Robertson 2009; Millward 2011). By the beginning of the twenty-first century sport had joined the main leisure revolution of the twentieth century and a further revolution had begun.

Sport and leisure since the financial crash of 2008

During the closing decades of the twentieth century, sport re-aligned with broader trends in leisure. These trends have been part of the package of changes that have occurred as economically advanced countries have become post-industrial, assimilated the latest information and communication technologies and integrated themselves into a globalized and financialized economy, and as governments have adopted neo-liberal (free market) economic policies. The replacement of jobs in primary industries (mainly agriculture and fishing) and subsequently jobs in manufacturing with service sector employment has been underway for almost a century. However, during the closing decades of the twentieth century, the decline in manufacturing jobs accelerated and simultaneously some service sectors began reducing their payrolls. Public sector employment, which expanded after the Second World War, ceased to expand. Financial and business services began replacing employees with technology such as automatic cash dispensers. Subsequently retail sales began to move online, thereby reducing jobs in retail parks, high streets and supermarkets. The leisure industries became among the few business sectors where employment continued to grow, mainly in commercial leisure businesses (Roberts 2004).

Many of these businesses continued to grow throughout the recession and austerity that followed the collapse of the international banking system in 2008–09. Top sport continued to increase its revenues from the sale of live broadcasting rights. Global tourism continued its former rise after a slight dip in 2009. Growth in tourist numbers is now mainly from the emerging market economies. These tourists have created additional jobs in hotels, catering and transport in the countries that they visit, which include European and North American countries. Despite high levels of unemployment and declining real wages, Western consumers have continued to spend more on the media (old and new). This has been possible because income inequalities within most countries have continued to widen, which is good for leisure spending. If the better-off are given more money, it is spent on 'luxuries', which include leisure goods and services. If the poor are given more money, it goes on necessities. Narrower inequalities between countries – the result of emerging market economies recording the fastest growth rates – are also good for leisure spending. This creates expanding middle classes in these poorer countries who are able and willing to pay for media content and to travel.

The complementary trend has been more and more austerity in public leisure services. Facilities – many libraries, civic halls, swimming pools and sports centres – have been either closed or continued with reduced opening and staffing levels. Some assets ranging from museum exhibits to playing fields have been sold. User charges have been raised. The costs of playing sport and meetings of drama and other clubs have risen. The management of many public leisure services has been out-sourced with the new service providers – maybe a separate section of a public authority, a voluntary association or a commercial enterprise – expected to deliver better value per unit of spending (see Alexandris 2008). Public leisure services thereby lose their public identities. In participant sport and exercise, public sector cutbacks have created space for commercial fitness gyms. Sport and other leisure activities are now positioned as individual consumer choices, made in the expectation of private gains. The notion of public goods whose simple availability benefits all citizens is at risk if not already lost

Yet suddenly governments find loads of money for sport and other leisure projects where the spending can be treated as investment (see Gratton *et al.* 2005). Sport mega-events are mega-examples, but national and local governments are also willing to invest in bids to become 'capitals of culture' (see Garcia 2005; Garcia *et al.* 2010). The aim is always to attract visitors whose spending will more than compensate for the investment, though the relevant calculations are invariably controversial (see Oxford Economics 2012; Richards and Palmer 2010; Smith 2012; Veal *et al.* 2012). In the emerging market economies state spending on leisure has never been treated as other than a business proposition. Heritage sites are protected and restored for the benefit of outsiders. Similarly, facilities for sport are built and designed for visitors, and sport events themselves are geared to the viewing of the global media audience.

Conclusions

The sociology of sport is now a sturdy sub-discipline. It has two larger and even sturdier hosts: sports studies and sociology. Leisure studies is different. It is inherently fragile. The subject has no natural secure base. It is neither able to pledge loyalty to nor become an essential requirement within a discipline such as sociology or a sub-field such as sport studies. Within sociology 'leisure' competes for attention and space on syllabuses with 'everyday life', 'popular culture' and 'consumption'. Leisure studies (and leisure management) could disappear as department and programme titles. Its complementary strength is leisure studies' ability to lodge in so many disciplines and sub-fields. It can survive and thrive through leisure scholars clustering around symposia and journals. They must draw ideas (theories) from disciplines such as sociology and evidence from sub-fields such as sport. Leisure studies will be sustained while it returns added value, as this chapter has sought to demonstrate.

References

Alexandris, K. (2008) 'Performance Management and Leisure Management', *Managing Leisure*, 13: 137–138.
Allison, L. (2001) *Amateurism in Sport*, London: Frank Cass.
Bailey, P. (1978) *Leisure and Class in Victorian England*, London: Routledge.
Bailey, P. (ed.) (1986) *Music Hall: The Business of Pleasure*, Milton Keynes, UK: Open University Press.
Becker, E. (2013) *Overbooked: The Exploding Business of Travel and Tourism*, New York: Simon and Schuster.
Bittman, M. and Wajcman, J. (1999) *The Rush Hour: The Quality of Leisure Time and Gender Equity*, SPRC Discussion Paper 97, Sydney: University of New South Wales.
Briggs, A. and Burke, P. (2005) *A Social History of the Media*, Cambridge: Polity.
Burls, A.P. (2010) 'The Multifunctional Values of Therapeutic Green Spaces', available at: http://www.hphpcentral.com/wp-content/uploads/2010/09/5000-paper-by-Ambra-Burls.pdf.
Cross, G. (1993) *Time and Money: The Making of Consumer Culture*, London: Routledge.
Crowhurst, A. (2001) 'The Portly Grabbers of 75 Per Cent: Capital Investment in the British Entertainment Industry, 1885–1914', *Leisure Studies*, 20: 107–123.
Cunningham, H. (1980) *Leisure in the Industrial Revolution*, London: Croom Helm.
Dumazedier, J. (1967) *Towards a Society of Leisure*, New York: Free Press.
Estes, R.J. and Wilenski, H. (1978) 'Life-Cycle Squeeze and the Morale Curve', *Institute of Industrial Relations, Reprint 422*, Berkeley: University of California.
Garcia, B. (2005) 'De-Constructing the City of Culture: The Long-Term Cultural Legacies of Glasgow 1990', *Urban Studies*, 42: 1–28.
Garcia, B., Melville, R. and Cox, T. (2010) *Creating an Impact: Liverpool's Experience as European Capital of Culture*, Liverpool: University of Liverpool.
Gershuny, J. (2000) *Changing Times: Work and Leisure in Post-Industrial Societies*, Oxford: Oxford University Press.
Gershuny, J. (2003) *Time through the Lifecourse, in the Family*, ISER Working Paper 2003–3, Colchester: University of Essex.
Giulianotti, R. and Robertson, R. (2009) *Globalization and Football*, London: Sage.
Gratton, C., Shibili, S., and Coleman, R. (2005) 'Sport and Economic Regeneration in Cities', *Urban Studies*, 42: 985–999.
Green, K., Thurston, M., Vaage, O. and Roberts, K. (2013) '"We're on the Right Track, Baby, We Were Born This Way"! Exploring Sports Participation in Norway', *Sport, Education and Society*, doi: 10.1080/13573322.20130769947.
Gronow, J. and Southerton, D. (2011) 'Leisure and Consumption in Europe', in S. Immerfall and G. Therborn (eds) *Handbook of European Societies*, New York: Springer.
Hantrais, L. and Kamphorst, T.J. (eds) (1987) *Trends in the Arts: A Multinational Perspective*, Amersfoort, NL: Giordano Bruno.
Henderson, K.A. (2011) 'A Continuum of Leisure Studies and Professional Specialties: What If No Connections Exist?', *World Leisure Journal*, 53: 76–90.
Hesmondhalgh, D. (2013) *The Cultural Industries*, 3rd edition, London: Sage.

Hutchins, B. and Rowe, D. (2012) *Sport Beyond Television: The Internet, Digital Media and the Rise of Networked Media Sport*, London: Routledge.

Iso-Ahola, S.E. and Mannell, R.C. (2004) 'Leisure and Health', in J.T. Haworth and A.J. Veal (eds) *Work and Leisure*, London: Routledge.

Kamphorst, T.J. and Roberts, K. (1989) *Trends in Sport*, Amersfoort, NL: Giordano Bruno.

Lee, A.J. (1976) *The Origins of the Popular Press, 1855–1914*, London: Croom Helm.

Lopez, M.D.M.-L. (2011) 'Consumption and Modernization in the European Union', *European Sociological Review*, 27: 124–137.

Markovits, A.S. and Hellerman, S.L. (2001) *Offside: Soccer and American Exceptionalism*, Princeton: Princeton University Press.

Meller, H.E. (1976) *Leisure and the Changing City, 1870–1914*, London: Routledge.

Miles, S. (1998) *Consumerism – As a Way of Life*, London: Sage.

Millward, P. (2011) *The Global Football League: Transnational Networks, Social Movements and Sport in the New Media Age*, Basingstoke, UK: Palgrave Macmillan.

Nasaw, D. (1993) *Going Out: The Rise and Fall of Public Amusements*, London: Harvard University Press.

Oxford Economics (2012) *The Economic Impact of the London 2012 Olympic and Paralympic Games*, Oxford: Oxford Economics.

Pangburn, W.M. (1940) 'Play and Recreation', *Annals of the American Academy of Political and Social Science*, 212: 121–129.

Richards, G. and Palmer, R. (2010) *Eventful Cities: Cultural Management and Urban Revitalisation*, Oxford: Butterworth-Heinemann.

Roberts, K. (2004) *The Leisure Industries*, Basingstoke, UK: Palgrave Macmillan.

Roberts, K. (2010) 'Is Leisure Studies Ethnocentric? If So, Does This Matter?' *World Leisure Journal*, 52: 164–176.

Robinson, D. (1996) *From Peepshow to Palace: The Birth of American Film*, New York: Columbia University Press.

Samdahl, D.M. (2010) 'Is Leisure Studies "Ethnocentric"? It Takes More Than Optimism: A View from Athens, Georgia, USA', *World Leisure Journal*, 52(3): 185–190.

Smith, A. (2012) *Events and Urban Regeneration: The Strategic Use of Events to Revitalise Cities*, London: Routledge.

Szymanski, S. and Zimbalist, A. (2005) *National Pastime: How Americans Play Baseball and the Rest of the World Plays Soccer*, Washington, DC: Brookings Institute Press.

Uhrig, S.C. (2005) 'Cinema Is Good for You: The Effects of Cinema Attendance on Self-Reported Anxiety or Depression and "Happiness"', *Institute of Social and Economic Research, Working Paper 2005–14*, Colchester, UK: University of Essex.

Veal, A.J., Toohey, K. and Frawley, S. (2012) 'The Sport Participation Legacy of the Sydney 2000 Olympic Games and Other International Sport Events Hosted in Australia', *Journal of Policy Research in Tourism, Leisure and Events*, 4: 155–184.

Walvin, J. (1975) *The People's Game*, London: Allen Lane.

Walvin, J. (1978) *Beside the Seaside*, London: Allen Lane.

Wheen, F. (1985) *Television: A History*, London: Century.

Williams, K. (2009) *Read All About It: A History of the British Newspaper*, London: Routledge.

18

PHILOSOPHY, SOCIOLOGY, AND THE CRITICAL ANALYSIS OF SPORT

William J. Morgan

Introduction

Theorists in sport sociology and sport philosophy have had little to no interaction with one another thus far, despite the fact they often pursue topics in sport of common interest and concern. This lack of communication is particularly evident in the 'social criticism' of sport, where ethical, social, and political issues in sport are examined. In this chapter, I argue that a serious rapprochement of sport sociology and sport philosophy is critically important. I begin by briefly considering the call for social critics of sport – whether they are in sociology, philosophy, or other disciplines – to work collaboratively in order to subject the ever-growing and ever-menacing capitalized sport industry to the full critical scrutiny warranted. The second, longer part of my chapter builds a case for why critical sociologists and philosophers of sport have much to learn from advances and mistakes in their earlier critical investigations. Foucault's distinctive approach to the critical study of social practices like sport figures in two important ways in this latter regard. The first is as a useful corrective to a main tendency among sport philosophers to ground their criticisms of sport in ahistorical, transcendental norms that supposedly are binding on all rational agents. The second is as an object lesson in why a main tendency among critical social theorists of sport to discount rational argument even of the local and historically contextual kind is a mistake.

A call to critical arms

Despite the lack of serious, sustained dialogue between sport sociologists and sport philosophers, there have been calls, particularly from critical social theorists, for both sides to start talking. In fact, the only philosophical essay advocating such collaboration that I could find is by Hans Lenk (1986), published, interestingly enough, in a sport sociology journal. Lenk's plea for this cross-disciplinary interaction centered on the rather simple, and, from a critical perspective at least, incidental claim that sport philosophers should weave into their inquiries the relevant empirical evidence unearthed by sport sociologists, and that sport sociologists should do the same with philosophic arguments regarding causal claims when evaluating empirical data. By contrast, two main calls for collaboration from critical social theorists of sport were more helpful and to the point. The first, by Richard Gruneau in his important book *Class, Sports, and Social*

Development (1983), prodded sport sociologists to look beyond their own disciplinary problems and intramural concerns, and to concentrate instead on evaluative questions regarding the social development of cultural practices like sport. To do so, he argued, critical theorists should embrace the classical, synthetic tradition of social theory, which integrates philosophical, political and sociological inquiry. The second call for collaboration was made recently by Atkinson (2011).[1] Like Gruneau, Atkinson (2011) argued that such dialogue would broaden the theoretical perspective of social theorists beyond their own internecine disciplinary squabbles. However, Atkinson went one step further by exhorting social theorists and their interdisciplinary counterparts to go public with their critical work on sport, to avoid shying away from 'the moral and ethical debates' on public issues, and to 'take sides' based on their own investigations (140, 142).

In gauging the impact of these pleas for collaboration, it is clear that there would have been little reason for Atkinson to issue his later call had his sociological peers been persuaded by, and acted on, earlier calls by Gruneau or even Lenk. Undoubtedly, Gruneau's book had major influence on critical sport theory at that time, but almost no effect on getting social theorists to expand their theoretical reach, especially into sport philosophy. Given that lack of response, it is likely that Atkinson's recent collaborative gesture will face tough sledding in future years.

Foucault's critical agenda

My own strategy for pushing Gruneau's and Atkinson's cross-disciplinary agendas is to leverage Foucault's approach to social criticism, which has increasingly become a favourite approach of critical social theorists of sport (Markula and Pringle, 2006: Shogan, 1999). Getting a theoretical handle on Foucault's body of work, however, is a daunting task, not least as he changed his mind in at least three important ways.

The first stage of Foucault's work was taken up with his archaeological writings, which focused on discursive practices and their meanings. Foucault's interest in discourse stemmed from what he took to be its important connection to knowledge. For it is only within a particular discursive formation, what he calls the *episteme* of a culture, that we can claim to know anything at all. More specifically, the *episteme* of a society 'sets up a particular space within which certain kinds of things can appear which can then be known in certain ways' (1977a: xxii). So what qualifies as knowledge, reason, truth, and a discipline like science depends entirely on the *episteme* of a society, on the discursive practices used by that society to validate claims to knowledge and truth. That means that a concept or proposition must meet certain discursive conditions before it can be admitted into a discipline like science or medicine.

The publication of *Discipline and Punish* in 1975 and *The History of Sexuality* in 1976 marked the second stage of his critical work that he called geneaology, which prioritized the notion of power. The shift to genealogical analysis signalled his resolve to firmly situate discursive practices within non-discursive practices and institutions such as prisons, schools, military barracks, and the like, where the effects on people's actual lives are most telling. By doing so, the relations of meaning in discourse were embedded in the strategic relations of power in these disciplinary institutions. Foucault coined the term the 'apparatus' to designate this new arrangement, which is 'a *strategic* . . . matter of a certain manipulation of forces, either developing them in a particular direction, blocking them, stabilising them, utilising them, etc.', and 'always linked to . . . knowledge' (1977b). Thus, for Foucault, knowledge and truth are necessary complements of power and not checks against it. Hence, on his view, 'We cannot exercise power except through the production of truth' (1977b).

Crucially, Foucault's turn to genealogical analysis laid the groundwork for how he thought the social criticism of non-discursive social practices like sport should go. Perhaps most revealingly, he begins *Discipline and Punish* with a detailed, gruesome account of the public execution of Damiens for the crime of regicide that occurred in Paris in the mid-eighteenth century. A few pages later, Foucault juxtaposes this horrific account with a dull, dispassionate, bureaucratic timetable and set of regulations for a Paris prison for young offenders. A mere eighty years separates these two events.

Foucault chose this dramatic genealogy to begin his enquiry into practices of punishment for several reasons. First, carrying over from his discursive writings, it demonstrates how our concepts of a social institution change radically from one epoch to another. Second, it reveals how discourse is both a precondition and effect of power. Since power takes different forms depending on the needs of the society in question, it entails that a notion like punishment will mean different things to different people at different times, as observed above, and that the actual behavior and actions that punishment calls for will change as well. Monarchical power required spectacular public executions to ensure that large crowds would toe the line; in its later, modern phase, such cruel punishments were no longer needed as deterrents and were rendered obsolete by new disciplinary technologies such as the famous Panopticon. The aim of these new surveillance techniques was to ensure that every deviation from an instituted norm was met with a specific institutionally relevant punitive measure rather than a generally violent one. The success of prison disciplinary measures spilled over into other institutions like the military and the school, where every non-conforming act was also met by an institutionally specific punishment (1977a: 179).

The third feature of Foucault's genealogical turn, and perhaps the most important for social criticism, holds radical implications for the rational and normative way we assess these epochal changes in our social practices and institutions. To begin, Foucault's genealogical approach dismisses any claim that major changes in our social practices, such as in types of punishment, represent a rational advance in our understanding of and dealings with criminals. We cannot speak of rational progress here because monarchical and modern penal practices cannot be compared, evaluated, or ranked on a common rational scale. The same point may be made about normative assessments of forms of punishment: we moderns are understandably shocked and repelled by the extreme measures used to execute Damiens, but his peers regarded it as an unobjectionable, just punishment for a serious crime, as instructive for avoiding the same fate, and as entertaining to watch. Of course, Damiens's peers would have been equally bewildered and morally disoriented by modern penal devices such as timetables and observation towers, which, for Foucault, 'insert the power to punish more deeply into the social body' (1979: 82).

If Foucault's genealogical take on social criticism commits us to the proposition that human agents have no true self, no essence, independent of some conceptual scheme or vocabulary, and if our social practices and the things we run up against in our dealings in the world likewise have no essence independent of some conceptual scheme or vocabulary, and if, finally, our conceptual schemes and vocabularies are themselves simply the effects of power, then he seems to leave no room for an emancipatory element in his own social criticism. Foucault's response to this apparent dilemma will ultimately prompt him to take his thinking in yet another direction. But in his genealogical period, his response is to concentrate on local forms of knowledge and practice, on what he calls the '*insurrection of subjugated knowledges*' (Foucault's emphasis) (1977b: 81). The basic idea behind the retrieval of such subjugated knowledges is that while the complex machinations of power that drive present disciplinary society cannot be undercut wholesale, they can be destabilized, thereby making it possible to transgress them and create something altogether new. The subjugated knowledges he has in mind here 'have been disqualified as inadequate to their task or insufficiently elaborated; naïve knowledges, located low down on the hierarchy, beneath the required level of cognition or scientificity' (82).

The third, and last, notable change in theoretical course Foucault makes concerns just this issue of the apparent unyielding dominance of disciplinary society. In Foucault's own words, 'When I was studying asylums, prisons, and so on, I insisted, I think, too much on the techniques of domination' (1997: 182). To correct this overemphasis, Foucault turned to techniques of the self, to 'the forms and modalities of the relation of self to self by which the individual constitutes and recognizes himself qua subject' (1985: 6). This led Foucault to a study of sexuality and to the ancient Greek ethical practices of the self in which the goal was not 'to discover a secret reality inside the individual,' an essence waiting to be discovered, but rather to create a new, beautiful self. For Foucault, this aesthetic/ethical ideal of subjectivity stood in marked contrast to the modern notion of the self, anchored in science, specifically, psychology's notion of sexual normalcy. Foucault was under no illusion that such ethical practices of the self could simply be 'reactivated' in a disciplinary society like ours, but he insisted that they 'can be very useful as a tool for analyzing what's going on now – and to change it' (349–50). And the only truly critical way to ply this tool, he further insisted, was to transgress what we have become in order to become something else, something new, something other than what we presently are (1996: 306–07).

Foucault and the social criticism of sport

There have been several recent books and an impressive body of essay literature on sport that bear Foucault's unmistakable influence.[2] Most of this critical work has been of the genealogical variety, since sport, like prisons, schools, and so forth, is a paradigmatic non-discursive practice, notwithstanding the considerable discursive attention it has received. My strategy here is to mine this work in terms of theory and method, highlighting its important contributions to the social criticism of sport, while noting its weaknesses. I will feature a significant normative transition in the conception and practice of modern sport that occurred during the late nineteenth and early twentieth centuries to argue that Foucault's critical approach meets with only mixed success.

This transition in sport came to the fore in the early period of the modern Olympic games, roughly from the 1906 Athens Games to the 1924 Paris Games, when two radically different conceptions of athleticism vied with each other to shape the large and growing international athletic community (Dyreson 1998). The conflict pitted a predominantly English version of gentleman–amateur sport (specifically, of a second wave of British amateurism, which engaged a growing and influential English middle class) against a predominantly American version of professional sport. Enthusiasts of both conceptions openly and bitterly argued over which view best captured the main purpose of competitive sport and its central values. There have been numerous such normative clashes over the purpose and value of elite sport in its long history. However, this epochal shift in our notion of sport is precisely the sort of major normative shift that concerned Foucault, and which thus makes this athletic transition relevant to a critical evaluation of those writings.

Briefly put, proponents of the gentleman–amateur position argued that sport is an intrinsic perfectionist practice that should be pursued foremost for the love of the game itself. Their view was that sport is an avocation rather than a vocation, which accounted for their opposition to taking sport too seriously, to trying too hard to win, whether by athletic specialization or adopting rationalized training methods based on the latest scientific advances, or using professional coaches and strategic tactics (such as pace-makers in races) to succeed (Collier 1898: 382–88). By contrast, proponents of professional sport, while suspicious, like their amateur rivals, of any mercenary design on sport (Rader 2004: 31), argued that sport is a serious endeavour rather than an unserious pastime, hence their emphasis on winning. It is no surprise, therefore, that they gave their unreserved normative support as well to scientific training methods, technically proficient professional coaches, strategic acumen (including in-game tactics and rule-bending), and specialized athletic performance. Thus, wholehearted commitment to athletic victory went from a much maligned vice to a virtuous and normatively exemplary way to engage in sport (Dyreson 1998: 138).

The important question raised by such dramatic normative shifts is what to make of them from a critical perspective. To start with the social side of these issues, what Foucault and his like-minded theorists of sport got right is that any credible rational argument and normative assessment of sport and its values cannot range outside of the discursive boundaries set by the *episteme* of the relevant community or culture in which it is situated. Put simply, rational argument and normative inquiry are always an inside, intramural affair, in which only those conceptual moves licensed by the reigning game of truth of the relevant community will be recognized and treated by its members as reasons or arguments at all.

What this means for the rival amateur and professional conceptions of sport is all too clear and all too deflating: while proponents of each view will be able to persuade fellow members of the rational and normative cogency of their position, they will be manifestly unable to persuade members of the rival athletic community of the cogency of their views. That is because the standard inferential way in which community members justify to one another their particular take on the purpose and value(s) of sport – by satisfying their peers that their rational and normative judgments follow logically from the shared premises from which they began their enquiry – is closed off to them when they take up extramural debates across two or more communities that are armed with different *epistemes*. The problem here, as Foucault helps us to see, is not that one side or the other is unreasonable, but rather that each side holds a radically different conception of sport and plays a different game of truth with different rules of argument. Thus, normative disputes of this extramural kind are simply unwinnable, and can only end in an argumentative impasse.

The moral of Foucault's genealogical story, however, is not just that games of truth and their argumentative moves must fail in such normative conflicts, but that any effort to rationally adjudicate them can only lead to conceptual mischief and normative grief. Any belief that we can assess the rational cogency and normative value of competing conceptions of sport would also assume that there is some other, larger meta-game of truth yet to be played, and some meta-normative vocabulary yet to be tapped, that we can deploy to resolve such thorny normative problems when they crop up. The problem, however, according to Foucault, is that this idea we can go transcendent in our social criticism, that there is some sort of skyhook we can latch onto in order to lift us out of our local games of truth and see sport and the world as it really is, is a rational fantasy.

The danger in indulging this fantasy, however, comes with a heavy normative cost. It can only lead to the hypostatization of the game of truth presently in use, to the dangerous idea that the present game of truth is the only game in town. If members of some athletic or other practice community were to delude themselves into believing this tall tale, then they would criticize opponents for being not just mistaken but also, far more strongly, irrational. They would see this unwinnable argument as a refusal of their rivals to listen to (their) reason. This is precisely what occurred in the early modern Olympic period in which this conflict broke out: each side was sure both that it could win the argument if reason prevailed, and that the other held a mistaken account of sport so wide of the mark that, if accepted, would lead to its ruination. Thus, amateurs accused their professional rivals of taking sport too seriously, of irreparably damaging its intrinsic nobility, while professionals accused amateur rivals of failing to take sport seriously, and irreparably damaging its intrinsic perfectionist character (Dyreson 1998: 163).

The takeaway from Foucault's powerful argument that rational discourse is always an inside game for sport philosophers is to resist the temptation to go transcendent in their own critical probing of sport. Yet the reigning normative theories of sport, despite their differences, all remain firmly wedded to this transcendent approach, to the effort to divine ahistorical, universal, normative principles that can be used to evaluate sport regardless of the social or historical context. It is of little consequence whether in normative terms one follows the hard realist path of John Russell in arguing that sport possesses objective, intrinsic properties that it is the job of philosophic analysis to discover (1999: 35), or the softer, discourse path Simon took in arguing that such normative principles can be determined by a dialogue open to all comers, in which a plurality of viewpoints on what is the purpose of sport can be entertained and subjected to careful scrutiny from all quarters, and the one which wins out is the one we can be confident is the most intellectually meritorious (2004: 135). Both approaches subscribe to the bad idea that the only normative principles of sport that are 'intellectually meritorious' are those 'that have a rational basis independent of cultural, linguistic, or pragmatic considerations' (2004: 125).

Normative inquiry and the social criticism of sport

What, though, of the other philosophic side of the equation: that normative philosophers of sport have not only something important to learn from, but also to teach, Foucauldian social theorists of sport? The answer lies in Foucault's important claim that the different conceptual schemes (*epistemes*) by which we make sense of sport and the larger world are both the conditions of power and the effects of power. This claim has a significant, deflationary impact on the games of truth sanctioned by particular discursive communities, since whatever truths they manage to produce do not and cannot serve as a check on power. For Foucault, nothing eludes the complex micro- and macro-forces of power, least of all the games of truth that inform the way we talk, think, and criticize what goes on in sport.

Shogan's and Ford's claim that the 'constitutive demand[s] of [contemporary] sport discipline' push athletes to ruin their bodies and compromise their health, and that sport ethicists who argue athletes have a moral obligation to obey these constitutive demands, as embodied in their constitutive rules, 'cannot avoid complicity in supporting a sport culture that is often harmful to athletes' (2000: 50), captures precisely Foucault's account both of how power does its work in our disciplinary society and how discourse abets rather than curbs its pervasive effects. Further, by refraining from the temptation to characterize these effects of power on sport as somehow deforming or corrupting what it is and what it is capable of being, Shogan is also importantly seconding Foucault's denial that there is any discursive or non-discursive way to circumvent power, to loosen its hold over social practices like sport. As Foucault repeatedly proclaimed, any suggestion that disciplinary forces deform or degrade sport conveniently glosses over the fact that power goes all the way down, that what it produces it produces without remainder.

That leaves, as previously discussed, essentially two roles for social criticism to play: first, to destabilize power by calling to our attention 'subjugated', discredited knowledges that remind us that what presently 'is' need not be; second, to introduce new games of truth and new ways of talking and thinking about sport and ourselves. However, there are only so many discredited knowledges around that we can resurrect to shake things up, and they have already been discredited, which seriously limits their possible critical effect. Consequently, Foucault came to increasingly rely on the second form of social criticism, on championing efforts to transgress the up and running games of truth in order to generate novel ways of looking at, discoursing about, and doing things. So his view of the social critic is someone who 'detach[es] oneself from what are the received truths and seek[s] . . . other rules of the game' (1998: 275). Rather, then, than working with the normative resources of the prevailing game of truth, Foucault exhorts us 'to produce something that doesn't exist yet, without being able to know what it will be' (1998: 275).

For Foucault, then, social criticism comes down to discursive acts of transgression that provoke radical shifts in social and political practices. Rather than trying to argue for a critical result, Foucault thinks we are better to change the subject by thinking outside the box. But without some clear idea when to give up on the old normative vocabulary and dream up a new one, Foucault's equating of social criticism with transgression, though it might make for a catchy slogan – transgression for transgression's sake – hardly makes for a viable critical ideal or promising critical agenda.

Before I can flesh out this criticism, I first need to entertain an obvious objection, that for Foucault social criticism can't simply be reduced to conjuring up novel redescriptions of sport because it ignores his ethical writings regarding techniques of the self, which were intended to correct his self-confessed previous overemphasis on techniques of domination. This same objection was raised by Markula and Pringle (2006: 48) against Gruneau's criticism that completely buying into Foucault's technologies of domination might 'deflect attention from analyzing the creative possibilities, freedoms, ambiguities, and contradictions also found in sport' (1993: 104), to which they replied that this ignores Foucault's later writings on the technologies of the self. Miller has also taken issue with Gruneau on this very same point, claiming, in another bow to Foucault's ethical writings, that 'the notion of sport as a technique of the self that is equally a technique of domination makes sense . . . [and] looks like a good agenda for the Cultural Studies of Sport' (2009: 190). But I find Markula's and Pringle's response somewhat disingenuous and Miller's twin assurances that sport embodies equally techniques of the self and of domination, and that their co-constitutive commingling makes for a promising critical agenda, as nice thoughts but little more. The problem with both rejoinders is that neither Foucault nor his fellow social theorists of sport actually worked out how to meld these two types of techniques into a coherent critical theory of sport without undermining much of what he claimed about both the subject and power.

The one possible exception is Shogan, who has interestingly argued that the hybrid identities human agents bring to sport as a consequence of their engagement in other disciplinary practices (family, work, diverse occupations, etc.) sufficiently complicate and confound the sense they have of themselves as athletes engaged in sport to provoke them to question their commitment to athletic practice and even perhaps to withdraw their consent to play by rules that deny the value of their subjectivity (1999: 91). This would be a plausible claim, however, if and only if Shogan could show that the hybrid identities human agents acquire by virtue of their engagement in other disciplinary practices not only conflict with their athletic identities but provide some genuinely alternative, anti-disciplinary sense of self denied in sport. But since these other social practices are no less products of disciplinary power than sport is, it is hard to see how the conflicting claims they make on us as subjects could provide some actual critical breakthrough, some sense of self, for example, that Foucault claimed to find in the ancient Greeks' aim to create 'beautiful souls' not rooted in some disciplinary structure.

With this objection behind us, I can return to my original point that in privileging discursive transgressions over discursive argument, Foucault leaves would-be social critics in a lurch over when to argue and when to transgress to get the critical results that they seek. For Foucault, of course, this is a false choice because argument always leads to the same old intractable debates, which make re-imagining the purpose of sport the only genuine critical option. But I think Foucault is simply wrong about the potential critical merits of rational argument, and that it is only when we have run out of arguments, have exhausted our existing games of truth, that discursive and non-discursive acts of transgression can play their rightful critical roles.

There are at least two reasons for hanging on to the rational argument option. First, no matter how skewed the vectors of power might be in a society, rational discourse, like culture itself, is always a joint production. The discursive practice of giving and asking for reasons is itself an integral feature of culture, since its very existence and its development depends on what Walzer calls 'cultural elaboration', an acutely important task that typically falls to 'teachers and sages; story-tellers, poets, historians, and writers generally' (1987: 40). It also includes for Walzer, interestingly enough from a critical perspective, ideologues whose work of cultural elaboration mainly aims to affirm already existing society. All these cultural elaborators insist that the normative authority of their elaboration is based entirely on their claim to be purveyors of the common culture, to be speaking for and to all of its members. What they have to say opens the door for social criticism, for rational argument about the normative standards and cultural ideals embedded in that common culture. This is as true of ideologues as it is of other cultural elaborators, since, as Marx noted, they are obliged to present the ideals and ideas of the ruling class as the universal class, as ideals and ideas of all the people not just those at the top (1976: 40–41). If they are unable to persuade the members of the relevant community that they speak for all of them, then their arguments will lack any normative authority. Thus, these ideologues must present the existing culture in its best possible light, but this in turn gives social critics all the normative ammunition they need to attack society for not living up to its own professed ideals.

The second feature of local games of truth, which explains why they have the argumentative firepower they do to hold the forces of power at bay, directly implicates their local character. It is only when rational discourse, as Rorty was at pains to show, is situated within the interior of a language game that it can be a critical force for the good (1989: 47). It is only within the familiar precincts of such language games that we can be reasonably confident that people will agree on what counts as good reason and argument to believe something because they will agree on the appropriate norms and rules of rational discourse. Once we move beyond such familiar precincts, all rational bets are off, and disputes over the purpose of social practices like sport devolve into, among other things, mere name-calling. Foucault's mistake was in assuming that the micro- and macro-forces of power would neutralize whatever criticisms rational discourse might yield.

That Foucault was wrong to claim that rational discourse can't act as a check on power, but rather is fated to be its complex accomplice, is evident if we recall the dispute between the amateur and professional athletic communities. The anti-technological and anti-scientific bent of the amateur athletic community illustrates how a conception of sport midwifed by a local game of truth is able to pose a critical challenge to the disciplinary technologies of the prison, school, and military that were circulating around the same time in France. Similarly, the more technologically and scientifically disposed professional conception of sport that succeeded it, though obviously not as opposed to disciplinary technologies, was opposed to the growing market fundamentalism of advanced capitalist societies because such intrusion of market forces would imperil its commitment to athletic excellence. If asked how each conception of sport survived in the face of these formidable disciplinary technologies, I would reiterate both Walzer's argument, that those tasked to elaborate the ideals and norms of the relevant athletic community, even its appointed ideologues, have to make their case to all of its social actors if they are to be successful, and Rorty's argument, that rational deliberation rightly situated within the local game of truth is a critical force to be reckoned with.

There is a good case to be made, therefore, against giving up too soon on rational argument in our social criticism of sport. Nothing I have argued thus far should be seen as a direct knock on Foucault's notion of transgression, only on his apparent overreliance on it at the expense of argument. There is no question that when our arguments have run out there is no alternative but to change the subject by trying to come up with something new to upset the status quo. This is precisely what Iris Marion Young (1979) did in her oft-cited essay bemoaning the fact that the going conceptions of sport denied women any genuine place or role in athletic affairs, which prompted her to agitate for a new conception of sport free of masculinist notions of athletic excellence. In my estimation, she was on firm critical footing in advocating for new sports, since the games of truth in these masculine conceptions of sport blocked any path to feminist-friendly conceptions of sport. The critical point, then, is not that transgression has no role to play in social criticism, but that its role appropriately kicks in only when our present argumentative resources have been exhausted.

One final point to be made is that the sort of discursive transgressions called for by Young get their critical purchase not just when our justificatory efforts have been exhausted but when they result in new games of truth. Transgression is a valuable critical tool only if its aim is to continue argument anew by giving it a new charter and set of norms and rules. Marion Young's call for new women's sports would have failed if it had not attracted a sufficient number of adherents to form an athletic community in its own right, who went on to create their own normative vocabulary and rational arguments for such a conception of sport. Discursive transgressions that have no such argumentative goals in mind might suit well the romantic dreamers among us, but they couldn't be more unsuited to those of us who aspire to be social critics.

Conclusion

I have argued that the collaboration of social theorists and normative philosophers would significantly advance the social criticism of sport. Using, as my points of departure, Foucault's theoretical writings on the social theory side and the normative writings of Walzer and Rorty, among others, on the philosophy side, I have argued that by embracing their critical contributions and avoiding their missteps, critical-minded theorists would be better able to steer sport in a more progressive and ethical direction. That will only happen, however, if we start to engage one another's work in a serious and sustained way. Whether that will ever come to pass, of course, I cannot say. All I can say is that for whatever reason we have each been content, to the detriment of our own critical ambitions, to go our separate ways. Perhaps our complacency in this regard will at some point be shaken. It was my intent in writing this chapter to try to start this process.

Notes

1 The ostensible aim of Atkinson's essay, however, was to review the work of various social theorists of sport who claim physical culture studies as their intellectual moniker.
2 Markula and Pringle (2006) and Shogan (1999) are good examples of relevant book literature. The essay literature is much too voluminous to cite specific examples; see Miller (2009) for a nice overview.

References

Atkinson, M. (2011) 'Physical Cultural Studies (Redux)', *Sociology of Sport Journal*, 28: 135–44.
Collier, P. (1898) 'Sport's Place in the Nation's Well-Being, *Outing*, 32: 382–88.
Dyreson, M. (1998) *Making the American Team: Sport, Culture, and the Olympic Experience*. Urbana: University of Illinois Press.
Foucault, M. (1977a) *Language, Counter-Memory, Practice*, Ithaca: Cornell University Press.
Foucault, M. (1977b) *Power/Knowledge*, New York: Pantheon Books.
Foucault, M. (1979) *Discipline and Punish*, New York: Vintage Books.
Foucault, M. (1985) *The Use of Pleasure*, New York: Vintage Books.
Foucault, M. (1996) *Foucault Live: Collected Interviews. 1961–1984*, New York: Semiotext(e).
Foucault, M. (1997) *The Politics of Truth*, New York: Semiotext(e).

Foucault, M. (1998) *Essential Works of Foucault, 1954–1984*, New York: New Press.

Gruneau, R. (1983) *Class, Sports, and Social Development*, Amherst: University of Massachusetts Press.

Gruneau, R. (1993) 'Modernization or Hegemony: Two Views on Sport and Social Development', in J. Harvey and H. Cantelon (eds) *Not Just a Game: Essays in Canadian Sport Sociology*, Ottawa: University of Ottawa Press.

Lenk, H. (1986) 'Notes Regarding the Relationship Between the Philosophy and the Sociology of Sport', *International Review for the Sociology of Sport*, 21(1): 83–91.

Markula, P. and Pringle, R. (2006) *Foucault, Sport and Exercise*, New York: Routledge.

Marx, K. (1976) *The German Ideology, Volume 5, Collected Works*, New York: International Publishers.

Miller, T. (2009) 'Michel Foucault and the Critique of Sport', in B. Carrington and I. McDonald (eds) *Marxism, Cultural Studies and Sport*, New York: Routledge.

Rader, B. (2004) *American Sports: From the Age of Folk Games to the Age of Televised Sports*, Upper Saddle River, NJ: Prentice Hall.

Rorty, R. (1989) *Contingency, Irony, and Solidarity*, New York: Cambridge University Press.

Russell, J. (1999) 'Are Rules All an Umpire Has to Work With?', *Journal of the Philosophy of Sport*, XXVI: 27–49.

Shogan, D. (1999) *The Making of High-Performance Athletes: Discipline, Diversity and Ethics*, Toronto: University of Toronto Press.

Shogan, D. and Ford, M. (2000) 'A New Sport Ethics', *International Review for the Sociology of Sport*, 35 (1):49–58.

Simon, R. (2004) 'From Ethnocentrism to Realism: Can Discourse Ethics Bridge the Gap?', *Journal of the Philosophy of Sport*, XXXI: 142–60.

Walzer, M. (1987) *Interpretation and Social Criticism*, Cambridge, MA: Harvard University Press.

Young, I. (1979) 'The Exclusion of Women from Sport: Conceptual and Existential Dimensions', *Philosophy in Context*, 9: 44–53.

19

POLITICAL SCIENCE, SOCIOLOGY AND THE STUDY OF SPORT

Barrie Houlihan

Whereas the study of sport has stimulated considerable academic interest among sociologists, historians and economists, interest in sport among political scientists has been far slower to develop and arguably remains significantly under-developed. Part of the explanation for this relative neglect lies with the structure of the political science academic community and the relatively narrow focus on government institutions, inter-government relations, and a limited range of policy areas, primarily those concerned with security and trade and those with large budgets such as health and education. However, where political scientists have developed an interest in sport it has often been in areas with significant resonance for sociology, such as identity and globalization, as well as in areas of overlapping theoretical interest, such as organizational stability and change, and the relationship between structure and agency.

The aims of this chapter are, first, to explore the nature of the current relationship between sociology and politics and, second, to consider how the relationship might be developed to the mutual benefit of both social sciences. The chapter begins with a brief discussion of the problems arising from disciplinary fragmentation and the tendency to isolate concept development from theory development. The chapter continues with an exploration of two central concepts within political science – power and ideas – and how they affect the motives of governments and non-governmental policy actors and how they can be integrated into middle-range theories of policy-making. The chapter concludes with a discussion of areas for research where a closer integration of sociology and political science would be beneficial.

Part of the explanation for the lack of dialogue between the two social sciences is the intensification of specialization and increasing dispute over the core object of the disciplines. The conventional definition of sociology, as 'the study of how society is organized and how we experience life',[1] has been challenged by what Wickham (2012: 428) refers to as 'whatever passing theoretical trend it chooses to study' and quotes Cooper's (2009: 9) listing of such trends as 'liquid modernity, information, mobility, the relation between literary and social theory, cosmopolitanization, globalization, governance and postcolonialism'. Whether or not one accepts Wickham's criticisms of the loss of primary focus on society within sociology, many of the 'trends' that Cooper identified resonate with contemporary concerns in political science and in the study of sport. Moreover, the more traditional themes within sociology – such as the ways in which individuals are networked through a wide variety of relationships including family, social class, gender, locality, nationality and ethnicity – link with many current themes in political science.

A similar problem of disciplinary fragmentation has been evident in political science since the discipline's formative years. For Heywood (2013: 2) political science is the study of 'the activity through which people make, preserve and amend the general rules under which they live'. A similar definition of political science as the study of political processes is given by Goodin and Klingemann (1996: 7) who suggest that the focus of the discipline is the 'constrained use of social power . . . [and] the nature and source of those constraints'. The centrality of the concept of power is not only a defining concern of political science but also a concept which links political science to sociology. Even if one adopts a restrictive view of the scope of political science as concerned with the actions of government and the authoritative use of power to make rules and laws that take precedence over other sources of authority in society (Moodie 1984), there still remains the important question of the relationship between the actions of government (in relation to gender and disability discrimination in sport and funding for elite sport development, for example) and social norms, values and attitudes. The adoption of a broader definition of politics which rejects the distinction between the public and the private spheres implicit in the previous definition leads to the view that politics takes place 'wherever conflict exists about goals and the method of achieving those goals' (Renwick and Swinburn 1987: 14). This view offers the political scientist a much broader focus for study as it acknowledges that politics is about the ordering of social affairs and that the 'student of politics cannot in principle exclude the possibility of political activity in any sphere of human life from the smallest groups . . . to the activities of international organizations' (Ponton and Gill 1993: 8). This broader, and increasingly accepted, view of the scope of political science brings the discipline much closer to the concerns of sociologists as it encourages a focus on the internal politics of international organizations, such as the International Olympic Committee (IOC) and international sport federations, as well as on domestic sport organizations, such as national governing bodies (NGBs) and sports lobby groups. It is in relation to these international and domestic sport organizations that political science has much to offer. Putting the emphasis on the use of power acknowledges the wide variety of ways in which power can be manifest and deployed. Of particular interest is the use of power in a covert way to manipulate the formal or informal agendas of sport organizations (Schattschneider 1960), as the internalization of values and norms (Bachrach and Baratz 1963) and as manifest in the 'law of anticipated reactions' and the hegemonic management of people's preferences (Laclau and Mouffe 1985).

The strong complementarity between political science and sociology in the nature and use of power is also evident in the study of the consequences of the use of power. In political science this concern with consequences has been encapsulated in Lasswell's (1950) classic formulation – 'Who gets what, when and how?'. The distribution and redistribution (Lowi 1964) of public resources (for example, between sport and other calls on public funding and between elite and community sport) are the outcome of political processes and have potentially profound consequences for the structure of opportunities in society. However, it is not just the public sector that makes decisions about the allocation of resources; such decisions are also made, though often with guidance from governments, by not-for-profit sport organizations (especially NGBs). Both governments and sport organizations also make decisions about the regulation of participation in sport (for example in the areas of child protection, coaching curriculum and qualifications) and the organizational infrastructure for sport. Governments will decide whether to have a ministry for sport and whether to have specialist administrative units/agencies for elite sport, while NGBs will decide the regional structure for their sport and the remit and responsibilities of individual clubs.

Of the range of factors that affect the prominence of sport as a political issue and also shape the response of the state to sports issues, one of the most significant is ideas and the ways in which they are linked to the broader social structure. Benson (1982), for example, explored the constraints on political action that result from the deep structure of power relations in society. Working within a neo-Marxist paradigm and drawing on the social constructivist ideas of Berger and Luckmann (1975), Benson argued that the deep structure of power (the rules of structure formation) strongly influenced access to the political agenda within a policy sector and the way in which political issues and policy responses were defined. A similar emphasis on the significance of ideas is given by one of the leading contemporary policy analysts, Sabatier (1998), who suggested that policy sectors, for example sport, operate within a hierarchy of beliefs which constrain policy-makers' choices. Equivalent to Benson's notion of 'rules of structure formation' is Sabatier's concept of 'deep core' beliefs, which are fundamental norms and beliefs that apply across all policy areas and might concern gender roles, the social value of sport and the balance between individual freedom and social responsibility. Deep core beliefs are understandably slow to change. At a less profound level are policy core beliefs which are the basic normative commitments and causal perceptions common to a policy area. In relation to sport these might include beliefs about the relative importance of elite sport success, the significance of traditional sports and the age at which young people should take part in elite level international sport competitions. At the shallowest level are 'secondary aspects', which refers to beliefs about the seriousness of problems (for example, lack of success at the Olympic Games or the adequacy of indoor sports facilities).

Any study of the role of ideas in influencing government attitudes towards sport involves the utilization of the basic sociological concept of socialization and an exploration of the mechanisms by which ideas are acquired, maintained and refined. The importance of ideas and ideology in the sociological analysis of the construction of identity, such as gender, national and cultural identity, resonate with the significance accorded ideas in the analysis of public policy. Public choice theorists (Niskanen 1973), for example, promote the idea of rational self-interest (as opposed to public service) as the defining ideology of public officials and consequently reinforce neo-liberal free market ideology and the neo-liberal critique of the state. However, ideas are only one factor which can explain why, and in what ways, governments get involved in sport: other factors would include evidence, scandal, the structure of government and history. The accumulation of evidence, of rising childhood obesity and match-fixing, for example, may prompt intervention even among the more neo-liberal governments. Similarly, major events (such as hosting an Olympic Games) and crises (major doping scandals) will motivate government to intervene in sport policy due primarily to the media attention that such events and crises generate and the need to protect the interests (national brand) of the state and its resources (sporting success). Also significant are the institutional arrangements of government and the significance of civil society organizations. The organization of government has long been a central sociological concern and one that has prompted equal interest among political scientists addressing issues such as the impact of bureaucracy and new public management (Clegg *et al.* 2006), inter-organizational relations (Benson 1982) and the role and significance of civic organizations and interest groups (Bennett and Segerberg 2013). The final major factors influencing the motives for government involvement in sport are the cultural significance of sport and the history of the development of sport in a country. The extent to which communities value sporting success and sport as a productive use of spare time will affect the utility of sport as a political resource, as will the historical development of sport in the country, for example, the association with class divisions and invasion and foreign occupation (Boyne 2002, Polley 2008).

One important debate in the social science of sport concerns the relationship between ideas/ ideologies and interests. The issue here is whether ideas and ideologies are independent variables in the policy process, as suggested by John (2003), or dependent variables in the politics of sport, as neo-Marxists argue, and thereby simply a reflection and rationalization of group or class interests. However, identifying ideas is generally much easier than identifying interests, particularly at the level of a policy sub-sector such as sport. It is also acknowledged that interests and ideas are influenced by the institutionalization of norms and values across time and also by events external to the policy sub-sector, such as the decisions of the IOC (for example, to introduce the Youth Olympic Games) or in relation to sport scandals (for example, due to doping). The interplay between ideas and interests is only one illustration of the overlap between political science and sociological concerns and of the importance of acknowledging the wide range of factors that influence the contemporary motives of government and shape sport policy.

Motives for government involvement in sport

The range of motives evident among governments for involvement in sport is testament not only to the perceived utility of sport as a political resource but also to its malleability. At various times and across a variety of countries sport has been used in pursuit of a wide range of domestic and diplomatic objectives. At the domestic level sport has been used to reinforce/manufacture a sense of national unity, for example in Canada (Thibault and Harvey 2013); to engineer social integration, for example in post-apartheid South Africa (Kiem 2003); to achieve urban regeneration, for example in East London (Davies 2010); and to stimulate the national economy, for example in Japan (MacCormack 1991). At the international level there is an equally broad range of diplomatic objectives for which sport has been considered an appropriate instrument, including improving relations with neighbours, for example between North and South Korea (Merkel 2008); to express disapproval of another state's actions or policy, for example South Africa's policy of apartheid (Keech and Houlihan 1999); to advance claims to sovereignty, for example East Germany (Strenk 1980); to maintain an international presence, for example many small states (Houlihan and Zheng, forthcoming); and to express ideological opposition, for example the Games of the New Emerging Forces (Connolly 2012). However, while governments may have a wide range of motives in relation to the use of sport as a resource it is important to acknowledge that the capacity to operationalize sport as political resource is far from uniform. Major political powers also tend to be major sporting powers and are thus much better placed to use their sporting resources (as hosts or as successful Olympic squads, for example) for both domestic and diplomatic purposes. Nevertheless, as will be argued below, small states are not necessarily excluded from utilizing sport resources.

There are many examples of governments using sport as a crude instrument of international diplomacy, such as the boycott of the Moscow Olympic Games in 1980 by the United States and its allies and the reciprocal boycott by the Soviet Union and its allies of the 1984 Los Angeles Olympic Games; or, more recently, the preference for using the hosting of events to promote the status of a country through conspicuous expenditure, as was the case with the 2008 Beijing Olympic Games and the 2014 Winter Olympics in Sochi, Russia. However, it is not just the major political powers such as China and Russia that are able to exploit international sport for political purposes, as many small states, with populations of 5 million or less, are also able to utilize the malleability and global profile of sport in pursuit of their objectives. Small states are characterized not only by a small population but also often by a small landmass and low per capita GDP, and consequently have limited access to the diplomatic repertoire of the major powers, especially the 'hard power' military and trade resources. However, international sport provides a rare diplomatic resource. International sports events and international sport organizations provide important opportunities for small states to remind their immediate neighbours and the more powerful states of their sovereign status and interests. For example, international sport is an opportunity for small states to project a degree of cultural distinctiveness which reinforces their claim to sovereign status. As Grant (1997: 638) comments, 'Nationals of micro-states are often indistinguishable from nationals of their larger neighbours at least in terms of race, language, religion and tradition'. The concern to project national distinctiveness from near neighbours is, for example, apparent in parts of the Caribbean and the Middle East.

International sport presents a number of high visibility, low risk and low cost opportunities for small states whose claims to statehood are contested, for example Palestine (Sherwood 2012), to act in a manner that is 'characteristically state-like' (Grant 1997: 656). It also presents an opportunity for aspiring states, for example the Kosovo region (BBC 2012), to draw the attention of an international audience to that aspiration. Major international sports events provide small states with the opportunity to share with the major powers a formal equality of status, most evidently in the opening and closing ceremonies. Membership of international sport organizations provides small states with a further opportunity to assert, even if only in a symbolic fashion, their autonomous status. Sport thus provides a relatively rare context within which the often limited tangible resources of small states can be deployed to manage and reinforce the perception of statehood and thereby protect or advance claims to de facto and de jure recognition (Chong 2010). Evidence of the perceived value of elite sport as a domestic and especially a diplomatic resource is provided by the willingness of many governments to invest increasing amounts of tax income in athlete development and in event hosting (Houlihan and Zheng 2013).

Policy regimes: the influence of non-domestic policy actors

The acknowledgement of the utility of sport as a resource prompts questions about how that resource is deployed. While some states have sufficient resources to pursue a relatively independent strategy, most, even the sports powers, are constrained to operate within international policy regimes. The recent interest in the functioning of policy regimes has been prompted by two developments. The first is the perceived decline in the capacity of government. It is argued that policy sectors previously considered to be dominated by the state such as health, welfare and sport are subject to increasing external influence and that power to shape policy is more dispersed. It is suggested that 'government', which implies an authoritative role for the state or its agencies, is no longer an adequate description of policy-making and that 'governance', a concept which implies a wider distribution of power and a more constrained role for the state, is a more accurate description. In relation to sport policy, while government and wider state influence is substantial, power is shared with a number of external commercial and civil society organizations, including the broadcast media, commercial sponsors and NGBs, especially those representing the more commercially successful sports such as football, cricket and rugby union. The second development is the growing influence on sport policy of non-domestic actors. The influence of the IMF, the OECD and the World Bank on the domestic economic policy of many countries has long been recognized. In a similar fashion, it is evident that the policy decisions of the major international federations, event organizers and organizations such as WADA have a significant impact on the domestic policy of many states, particularly in relation to funding decisions, but also, in the case of WADA, an impact on the regulatory framework for sport.

Policy regimes are increasingly acknowledged as independent policy actors explicitly concerned to influence domestic policy decisions. While WADA may be an example of a formal regime (with a secretariat, budget and the support of a legally binding UNESCO convention) other, less formal policy regimes exist, for example the promotion of gender equity in sport (International Working Group on Women and Sport). In an increasing number of areas, policy is made by actors drawn from multiple levels of global politics. As Kooiman (2003: 3) notes in his analysis of contemporary policy-making, 'Governing issues generally are not just public or private, they are frequently shared, and governing activity at all levels (from local to supra-national) is becoming diffused over various societal actors whose relationships with each other are constantly changing'. The globalization of many aspects of sport policy reflected in the expansion in the role and significance of policy regimes is one of the more recent constraints on domestic policy processes, but they are far from being the only constraints.

The constraints on policy choice

The acknowledgement of the impact of non-national actors on domestic sport policy decisions draws attention to constraints on the scope for policy choice by governments. While some constraints reflect patterns of resource dependence (for example, those countries dependent on funding from Olympic Solidarity), other constraints can be a consequence of patterns of decision-making which commit even resource-rich countries to particular policy trajectories (for example, the desire for high-profile elite sporting success at the Olympic Games will influence the funding decisions of many governments to favour the range of sports and disciplines selected by the IOC). Although far less pronounced, there can be influence by non-national actors on school/youth sport (from organizations such as Right to Play and ICCSPE[2]) and on community sport (World Health Organization). In addition to the interplay of domestic and international policy actors, the accumulation of previous domestic policy decisions which both reflect and augment domestic sporting cultural values will constrain the scope for agency in policy-making. Policy, as both objectives and process, can become institutionalized, making significant changes in policy direction difficult to achieve. Institutionalization constrains policy options and resonates with the concept of path dependency, which suggests that 'the trajectory of change up to a certain point constrains the trajectory after that point' (Kay 2005: 553). Referring to the significance of institutionalization, Howlett and Ramesh (1995: 27) argue that institutions, whether defined as cultural values or as organizational arrangements, constitute 'unique patterns of historical development and [impose] constraints . . . on future choices'. Consequently, previous decisions function as institutions in relation to subsequent policy decisions with path dependency capturing the insight that 'policy decisions accumulate over time; a process of accretion can occur in a policy area that restricts options for future policy-makers' (Kay 2005: 558).

The concepts of institutionalism and path dependency are valuable not only as correctives to the more simplistic versions of rational choice theory which seek to explain the behaviour of public officials, for example, in terms of rational self-interest, but they are also valuable in explaining policy continuity in the face of accumulating contrary evidence and in focusing attention on the relationship between structure and agency in sport policy. Sydow *et al.* (2009) provide a useful ideal-typical model of the process of path dependence which they see as moving through three phases: Pre-formation, Formation and Lock-in.

- First, at the Pre-formation stage there is broad scope for policy choice/action and considerable uncertainty about the impact of any particular policy choice. At this stage a small decision may unintentionally set in train a self-reinforcing process. Such a decision can be considered a 'critical juncture' and signifies the end of the Pre-formation phase and the start of the Formation phase.

- Second, in the Formation phase a set of supportive interests coalesce around the emerging policy and a dominant action pattern emerges which narrows the scope for policy reversal. In this phase the path is evolving and narrowing.
- Third, at the Lock-in phase 'the dominant decision pattern becomes fixed and gains a deterministic character, the actions are fully bound to a path' (Sydow *et al.* 2009: 692). Reaching a position of Lock-in can result in inefficiency as the policy sub-sector loses the capability to adopt more efficient or effective alternative policies.

Neither elite sport policy nor competitive school sport policy display all the features of Sydow *et al.*'s (2009) ideal type, but they do effectively prompt questions about the extent to which previous decisions affect the scope of future decisions and also about the influence of broader social factors such as public opinion and the role of the media in shaping issue/problem definition and policy options.

Meso-level analytical frameworks

There are many middle-range analytical frameworks which attempt not only to explain the significance of the possible motives for government involvement in sport (discussed earlier), but which also seek to explain how that influence is operationalized (see John 1998; Sabatier 2007, for reviews of the major frameworks). The multiple-streams framework and policy network theory will be briefly reviewed in order to illustrate the ways in which different analytical frameworks focus attention on different aspects of the policy-making process and give varying weight to the factors and motives identified earlier. More important, the two frameworks illustrate the value of using multiple lenses through which to view policy-making.

As the term indicates, the multiple-streams framework conceptualizes the policy process as comprising distinct streams (Kingdon 1995; Zahariadis 2003). The framework identifies three streams – problem, policy and political – which are relatively independent. Confluence of the three streams occurs during the 'launch window' of the policy, where 'a problem is recognized, a solution is developed and available in the policy community, a political change makes the time right for policy change, and potential constraints are not severe' (Kingdon 1984: 174). Kingdon's framework also emphasizes the scope for agency by drawing attention to the role of policy entrepreneurs. In regard to the factors that shape government motives for sport policy, the multiple streams framework puts relatively low emphasis on the significance of interests and organizations (institutions), and much more attention is paid to the role of ideas, events, culture and contingency. The framework also provides a challenge to the assumptions of path dependency and thus provides the researcher with a valuable corrective to the overly hasty assumption of institutional constraints on policy choice.

In contrast to the pluralist underpinnings of the multiple-streams framework, the policy networks approach conceptualizes policy-making as occurring within clusters of policy actors within particular sub-sectors, such as sport, and interacting on a regular basis. Policy networks vary according to membership, extent of resource control/dependency and, most important, degree of integration (Marsh and Rhodes 1992). The more tightly integrated networks (often the product of the pattern of resource dependence and the prominence of core professions) are considered to form a policy community of which government is a part. As John (2012: 72) notes, 'The word "community" captures the idea of a small number of participants who know each other well and who share the same values and policy goals'. With the emphasis on interests and resource control, the framework suggests the institutionalization of definitions of 'legitimate' problems and of acceptable policy responses. The closed nature of policy communities imposes political constraints on policy choice which might reinforce and be reinforced by the inertia that develops around a policy trajectory as hypothesized by path dependency theorists. In relation to sport policy there has been considerable debate about whether a policy community exists and, if it does, which interests dominate (Houlihan 1997; Houlihan and Lindsey 2013).

The policy community framework is of particular interest in prompting an analysis of the significance of government in shaping policy and in the ways in which governmental power is exercised. It is in this connection that the work of the sociologist Foucault in relation to governmentality is particularly insightful (see, for example, Dean 2007; Rose 1999). The governmentality analysis, which has stimulated as much research among sociologists as among political scientists, suggests that the emergence of policy communities represents not a diminution of government power, but a more subtle exercise of power and indeed an extension of state power.

One consequence of the exploration of the concept of governmentality is that rather than debating whether the power of the state has been hollowed out or dispersed through a plurality of agencies (NGBs, professional leagues/clubs, international federations, national Olympic associations and so on), attention is directed to the strategies adopted by government to shape the behaviour of community members to the extent that they are constituted as self-disciplining subjects. According to this analysis, governmental power in relation to sport is less a matter of imposing constraints upon organizations and their leaders than of constructing or shaping organizations 'capable of bearing a kind of regulated freedom' (Rose and Miller 1992: 174). The enthusiasm of governments of the past fifteen years in the UK for modernization is a good example of attempts to fashion a policy community consistent with their priorities (Houlihan and Green 2009). As Raco and Imrie (2000: 2191) comment, 'Increasingly, government seeks not to govern society per se, but to promote individual and institutional conduct that is consistent with government objectives'. The key aim is to make NGBs and sports clubs fit partners for government. The intended net effect of the bundle of technologies that constitute modernization is to ensure that NGBs and other key partners are instrumental in their own self-government and constitute malleable partners in the implementation of government policy.

Conclusion

While political science places greater emphasis on the institutions of government and on the concept of power, the foregoing discussion should clearly indicate the extent to which political science borrows and adapts concepts and frameworks from sociology and also the way in which the preoccupations of political science are enriched by, but also complementary to, the concern of sociologists with the organization and functioning of society. Political science, especially that element which is concerned with policy analysis, provides a varied and sophisticated repertoire of concepts and theories of which regimes, the multiple streams framework, policy network theory and path dependency are but a small sample. There are three areas in particular where further collaboration between sociologists and political scientists would be fruitful, namely, globalization, identity and governmentality/modernization. Although it is possible to argue that the theorization of globalization as both a social and a political phenomenon is mature, there is still a relative paucity of empirical studies of the mediation of global influences at the domestic and policy-sector levels. Sport provides a fertile field for collaborative research to tackle this gap. The impact of the network of global monopolistic and largely unaccountable international sport organizations and their national counterparts on domestic policy priorities is, with the exception of association football, grossly under-researched. Also at the global level, the role of transnational broadcast media is relatively well researched, while the role and significance for sport production and consumption of new media is largely neglected.

Although the sociological and political-scientific study of identity has generated a rich body of research, it is confined, with a few exceptions, to the richer developed countries. The link between sport and identity for smaller countries, whose prominence in international sports events such as the Olympic Games is often limited to appearing in the opening and closing ceremonies, is seriously neglected. The tendency is either to ignore these countries or else to assume that their interests and motives for involvement in international sport mirror those of the major sports powers. Finally, both sociologists and political scientists have a central concern with the social impact of processes of governmentality and modernization with sport long regarded as both the object of these processes, but also a medium for their realization. The significance of sport as both object and medium has resulted in tensions between tradition and modernization in sport affecting the relationship between fans and their clubs, clubs and their national sport organizations, and national sport organizations and government – all of which deserve closer analysis.

Notes

1 As defined by the British Sociological Association (available at http://www.britsoc.co.uk/WhatIsSoci ology/studyingsoc.aspx; accessed 18 February 2014).
2 For information on Right to Play, see http://www.righttoplay.com/International/Pages/Home.aspx; for the ICSSPE (International Council for Sport Science and Physical Education), see https://www. icsspe.org/.

References

Bachrach, P. and Baratz, M.S. (1963) 'Decisions and Non-Decisions: An Analytic Framework, *American Political Science Review*, 57: 632–42.
BBC (2012) 'London 2012: Judoka's Kosovo Olympic Bid Turned Down', Available at: http://www.bbc. co.uk/sport/0/olympics/18205297 (accessed 10 January 2014).
Bennett, W.L. and Segerberg, A. (2013) *The Logis of Collective Action: Digital Media and the Personalisation of Contentious Politics*, Cambridge: Cambridge University Press.
Benson, J.K. (1982) 'Networks and Policy Sectors: A Framework for Extending Intergovernmental Analysis', in D. Rogers and D. Whetten (eds) *Interorganisational Coordination: Theory, Research and Implementation*, Ames: Iowa State University Press.
Berger, P.L. and Luckmann, T. (1975) *The Social Construction of Reality: A Treatise on the Sociology of Knowledge*, Harmondsworth, UK: Penguin.
Boyne, R. (2002) 'Bourdieu: From Class to Culture. In memoriam Pierre Bourdieu 1930–2002', *Theory, Culture and Society*, 19: 117–128.
Chong, A. (2010) 'Small State Soft Power Strategies: Virtual Enlargement in the Case of the Vatican City and Singapore', *Cambridge Review of International Affairs*, 23(3): 383–405.
Clegg, S.R., Hardy, C., Nord, W.R. and Lawrence, T. (eds.) (2006) *Handbook of Organization Studies*, 2nd edition. Thousand Oaks, CA: Sage.
Connolly, C.A. (2012) 'The Politics of the Games of the New Emerging Forces (GANEFO)', *The International Journal of the History of Sport*, 29(9): 1311–1324.
Cooper, G. (2009) 'The Objects of Sociology: An Introduction', in G. Cooper, A. King and R. Rettie (eds) *Sociological Objects: Reconfigurations of Social Theory*, Farnham, UK: Ashgate.
Davies, L. (2010) 'Sport and Economic Regeneration: A Winning Combination?' *Sport in Society*, 13(10): 1438–1457.
Dean, M. (2007) *Governing Societies: Political Perspectives on Domestic and International Rule*, Maidenhead, UK: Open University Press.
Goodin, R .E. and Klingemann, H.-D. (1996) 'Political Science: The Discipline', in R.E. Goodin and H.-D. Klingemann (eds) *A New Handbook of Political Science*, Oxford: Oxford University Press.
Grant, T.D. (1997) 'Between Diversity and Disorder', *American University International Law Review*, 12(4): 629–686.
Heywood, A. (2013) *Politics* (4th edition), Basingstoke, UK: Palgrave Macmillan.

Houlihan, B. (1997) *Sport, Policy and Politics: A Comparative Analysis*, London: Routledge.

Houlihan, B. and Green, M. (2009) 'Modernisation and Sport: The Reform of Sport England and UK Sport', *Public Administration*, 87(3): 678–698.

Houlihan, B. and Lindsey, I. (2013) *Sport Policy in Britain*, Abingdon, UK: Routledge.

Houlihan, B. and Zheng, J. (2013) 'The Olympics and Elite Sport Policy: Where Will It All End?', *International Journal of the History of Sport*, 30(4): 338–355.

Houlihan, B. and Zheng, J. (forthcoming) 'Sport and Small States: Politics at the Margin', *International Journal of Sport Policy and Politics*.

Howlett, M. and Ramesh, M. (1995) *Studying Public Policy: Policy Cycles and Policy Sub-Systems*, Oxford: Oxford University Press.

John, P. (1990) *Analyzing Public Policy*, London: Pinter

John, P. (2003) 'Is There Life After Policy Streams, Advocacy Coalitions and Punctuations? Using Evolutionary Theory to Explain Policy Change', *Policy Studies Journal*, 31(4): 481–498.

John, P. (2012) *Analyzing Public Policy*, 2nd edition, London: Routledge.

Kay, A. (2005) 'A Critique of the Use of Path Dependency in Policy Studies', *Public Administration*, 83(3): 553–571.

Keech, M. and Houlihan, B. (1999) 'Sport and the End of Apartheid', *The Round Table*, 88(349): 109–121.

Kiem, M. (2003) *Nation Building at Play: Sport as a Tool for Social Integration in Post-Apartheid South Africa*, Aachen: Meyer and Meyer.

Kingdon, J.W. (1984) *Agendas, Alternatives and Public Policy*, Boston, Mass.: Little, Brown.

Kingdon, J. (1995) *Agendas, Alternatives and Public Policies*, New York: HarperCollins.

Kooiman, J. (2003) *Governing as Governance*, London: Sage.

Laclau, E. and Mouffe, C. (1985) *Hegemony and Socialist Strategy*, London: Verso.

Lasswell, H. (1950) *Politics: Who Gets What, When and How*. New York: Peter Smith.

Lowi, T.J. (1964) 'American Business, Public Policy, Case Studies and Political Theory', *World Politics*, 16: 676–715.

MacCormack, G. (1991) 'The Price of Affluence: The Political Economy of Japanese Leisure', *New Left Review* (series 1), 188.

Marsh, D. and Rhodes, R. (eds) (1992) *Policy Networks in British Government*, Oxford: Clarendon Press.

Merkel, U. (2008) 'The Politics of Sport Diplomacy and Reunification in Divided Korea: One Nation, Two Countries and Three Flags', *International Review of the Sociology of Sport*, 43(3): 289–311.

Moodie, G.G. (1984) 'Politics Is About Government', in A. Leftwich (ed.) *What Is Politics? The Activity and Its Study*, Oxford: Basil Blackwell.

Niskanen, W.A. (1973) *Servant or Master: Lessons from America*, London: Institute of Economic Affairs.

Polley, M. (2008) 'History and Sport', in B. Houlihan (ed.) *Sport and Society: A Student Introduction*, London: Sage.

Ponton, G. and Gill, P. (1993) *Introduction to Politics*, Oxford: Basil Blackwell.

Raco, M. and Imrie, R. (2000) 'Governmentality and Rights and Responsibilities in Urban Policy', *Environment and Planning A*, 32(12): 2187–2204.

Renwick, A. and Swinburn, I. (1987) *Basic Political Concepts* (2nd edition) London: Stanley Thornes.

Rose, N. (1999) *Powers of Freedom: Reframing Political Thought*, Cambridge: Cambridge University Press.

Rose, N. and Miller, P. (1992) 'Political Power Beyond the State: Problematics of Government', *British Journal of Sociology*, 43(2): 172–205.

Sabatier, P. (1998) 'The Advocacy Coalition Framework: Revisions and Relevance for Europe', *Journal of European Public Policy*, 5(1): 98–130.

Sabatier, P. (ed.) (2007) *Theories of the Policy Process* (2nd edition), Boulder, CO: Westview Press.

Schattschneider, E.E. (1960) *The Semi-Sovereign People*, New York: Holt, Reinhart and Winston.

Sherwood, H. (2012) 'Gaza's Lone Runner Will Carry the Flag for Palestinian Pride at the London Olympics', *The Guardian*, 1 March 2012.

Strenk, A. (1980) 'Diplomats in Tracksuits: The Role of Sports in the Foreign Policy of the German Democratic Republic', *Journal of Sport and Social Issues*, 4(1): 34–45.

Sydow, J., Schreyögg, G. and Koch, J. (2009) 'Organisational Path Dependence: Opening the Black Box', *Academy of Management Review*, 34(4): 689–709.

Thibault, L. and Harvey, J. (eds) (2013) *Sport Policy in Canada*, Ottawa: University of Ottawa Press.

Wickham, G. (2012) 'The Core Object "Society" and Sociology's Public Relevance', *Journal of Sociology*, 48(4): 427–442.

Zahariadis, N. (2003) *Ambiguity and Choice in Public Policy*, Washington, DC: Georgetown University Press.

20

PSYCHOLOGY AND SOCIOLOGY IN SPORT STUDIES

Brett Smith and Kerry R. McGannon

The aim of this chapter is to promote scholarship that works at the intersection between the psychology and sociology of sport. By 'working at the intersection of these two disciplines', we mean to suggest scholarship that connects or draws from *both* psychological and sociological traditions and literatures to examine a specific topic. Lest we suffer from amnesia and forget our rich disciplinary histories, such scholarship has been suggested for over 100 years. Outside of sport, classical thinkers, such as Mead, Goffman, Garfinkel, Foucault, and Habermas, have stressed connections between sociology and psychology. In so doing, psychological knowledge and the sociological imagination have been greatly enhanced. Despite such benefits, within sport scholarship there is a paucity of work situated at the intersection of psychology and sociology.

While much of our own respective research programmes for over a decade has sought to work at the intersection of sport psychology and the sociology of sport, the journey has not been without, and continues to present, challenges. For example, finding appropriate publication outlets for this work was very difficult early in our careers, and at times still is. On the one hand, research submitted to a psychology journal would be judged as 'excellent work' but rejected simply on the basis it was 'sociology' and thus not 'appropriate' for readers. The *same* research submitted to a sociology journal, on the other hand, would be evaluated as 'excellent psychological work' and then returned because it was not 'appropriate' for sociologists.

In this chapter, we therefore begin by outlining some of the boundaries that exist between sport sociology and psychology and offer some reasons for why this might be the case. Next, we briefly highlight some benefits of why researchers within both disciplines might engage in working across the psychology-sociology hyphen. To begin to realize some of these benefits, the chapter closes by outlining several possibilities for how researchers might work at the intersection of sport psychology and sport sociology.

Boundaries between the sociology and psychology of sport

'Border crossings – a nice idea', one might say; 'pity about the reality.'

(Evans 2012: 3)

Before outlining some possible reasons for the longstanding boundary between sport sociology and psychology, lest we risk either giving the impression that each discipline is homogenized or producing a dichotomy, we acknowledge that not only are there many differences and conflicting relations *within* each discipline, there are also connections *across* disciplines. For example, many researchers in both sport sociology and sport psychology have the goal of developing humanity's fundamental stock of knowledge, influencing policy or practice, and improving human lives. Whilst conceptualized differently within and across disciplines, many researchers in both disciplines accept that our personal lives are socially, culturally, and politically influenced. Given such points of commonality and connection, we do not want to over-inflate or exaggerate a divide between sport sociology and sport psychology. With this point noted, like others (e.g. Ingham, Blissmer and Davidson 1999; McGannon and Mauws 2000), we believe there are boundaries, however massive, paper-thin, or porous, that make intersectionality less frequent or less likely within each discipline. Some possible reasons for this division are as follows.

First, sport sociologists and sport psychologists have tended to tread two different roads in terms of what each primarily attends to and how much critical attention is afforded in research. The former is predisposed to attend to society or culture in ways that display a preference for highly critical forms of understanding of the often taken-for-granted world. In contrast, the latter has a disposition to, and taste for, understanding the mind as a separate and unique entity housed within the individual, which in turn directs and/or is influenced by human behaviour and the social and cultural world. Further, the focus has been largely on performance enhancement[1] in ways that are rarely critical and/or seldom tackle how performances are shaped by the socio-cultural.

A second possible contributing factor for a persistent divide between the disciplines is that, by and large, sport sociologists and sport psychologists tend to use very different academic vocabularies. It can therefore be a challenge to understand what is being said in another discipline and, in turn, be accepted as a 'competent' scholar. It is perhaps unsurprising, then, that each discipline formed, and continues to form, separate journals, handbooks, conferences, specialist associations, ethical guidelines, and research groups and spaces within universities. Whilst these formal boundaries help maintain a professional identity and clear focus of research and practice, such divisions make it even more difficult (or require too much effort) for us to engage in a meaningful dialogue with one another. As a result, boundaries between fields are typically sustained via very 'real' concrete and material constructions, and (inter)disciplinary practices, as well as language and symbolic ones, rather than crossed or blurred.

A third possible reason for why a divide between the fields of sport sociology and psychology exists might be attributed to the differing beliefs each holds about ontology and methods. Psychologists of sport generally believe that there is an objective reality – an external referent – that can be discovered independent from their knowledge of it through the use of appropriate methods. For them, this access and/or explanation of objective reality can be achieved, since it is believed that the scientific method itself is a neutral tool and thus can be used as a repository of procedural objectivity for establishing contact with an external reality and discovering the real world. This real world includes the mind that resides within the individual as a separate entity from the social and cultural realm. Moreover, quantitative methods, and at times even qualitative methods, are predominately positioned and/or used as tools to gain access to the objective realities within and/or reflecting the mind and world (e.g. social, cultural) surrounding that mind. In contrast, qualitative methods prevail in sport sociology, and researchers in this discipline ontologically tend to believe that social reality is constructed and as such, that reality is multiple, subjective, fluid, and interdependent with the researcher and research participants. Sport sociologists also contend that research methods are not neutral but rather are a social construction and practical affair: they are a way of constructing the world in response to the particular interests and purposes of particular people, who are also socially constructed. As such, whereas most sport psychologists tend to suggest theory-free observation or knowledge is possible or a goal worth striving toward, sport sociologists argue it is a chimera (Sparkes and Smith 2014).

Fourth, it might be argued that power relations and the neo-liberal audit culture contribute further to erecting and maintaining boundaries between sport sociology and sport psychology. As Sparkes (2013) notes, the dominant disciplines within most sport science/kinesiology university departments are physiology and psychology. He also suggests that within the climate of an audit culture in academia, how people in these disciplines use power to help consolidate dominance is partly through the systematic application of individualized outcome-based assessment systems for research productivity on bodies that tell us what counts as 'proper/good science' and 'priority research'. These systems include the impact factor of a journal that one's research is published in, the number of citation counts a paper accrues in a year, and grant income generated. For example, the rhetoric goes, the higher the impact factor of a journal the better the quality of the research published within it. Equally, by definition, a low impact factor for a journal means poor-quality research. Such quantified systems of assessment strongly favour sport psychology (and physiology in particular) over the sociology of sport as a partial consequence of how impact factors are constructed and the higher scores available to journals with closer links to (post)positivist methodologies and/or natural sciences. Yet, this favouring can mean that the former is depicted as the 'proper science that should be prioritized' and the latter constructed as 'neither real research nor a priority'. It too can result in the demeaning or culling of sport sociologists in departments. Indeed, and exacerbated by scarce economic resources that are being directed by the powerful at the micro level (e.g. departmental), meso level (e.g. university), and macro level (e.g. government) to certain subjects (e.g. natural sciences) and away from others (e.g. social sciences), this demeaning or culling is not just a possibility, but is already occurring across universities within Europe, North America, and Australasia (Evans 2012; Sparkes 2013).

Given the picture painted above, why would any sport psychologist risk crossing borders into sport sociology? This is especially the case when, in terms of the Bourdieusian ideas of *illusio* and *capital*,[2] many sport psychologists recognize what counts as capital throughout the trajectory of their careers. For example, usually very early on in one's career, through the doctoral process and through interactions with senior mentors, students experience the neo-liberal audit culture in various forms (e.g. being told impact factors count, presenting research at national and international meetings, publishing as many refereed journal papers as possible). As one progresses further in an academic career, the foregoing practices of presenting and publishing continue on, as the neo-liberal audit culture remains (e.g. grants) an ever-present reminder of how the merit's of one's work will be evaluated. In turn, many sport psychology researchers continue to invest in these forms of academic capital (e.g. publishing in high-impact journals and accumulating grant income) and take seriously the rules of the game by which that capital is acquired.[3] Moreover, such *illusio* is in contrast to how many sport sociologists operate. Many cannot invest in, or take seriously, what counts as capital in the audit culture because they critique this culture and illuminate its dangers. Moreover, the process of acquiring capital also represents a distraction from the very lengthy (often years of) work and personally intense embodied process of doing research that sport sociologists often engage in and value. Why, then, would they cross borders into sport psychology and risk turning themselves into what they see as governable subjects of managerial power? Why would they relinquish what they value, change tastes, and submit themselves to a habitus transplant? In any event, ultimately power relations and the audit culture may prohibit or hinder, rather than nurture and encourage, researchers to work at the intersection of sport sociology and sport psychology, thereby resulting in boundary (re)creation, maintenance, or closure.

Benefits of working at the intersection of sport sociology and sport psychology

Although boundary-crossing is no easy task and relatively rare, there are scholars who do cross boundaries and set sail on an adventure to work at the intersection of sport sociology and psychology (e.g. Ingham, Blissmer and Davidson 1999; McGannon, Cunningham and Schinke 2013; Smith 2013a, 2013b; Smith *et al.* 2009; Sparkes, Perez-Samaniego and Smith 2012; Thorpe 2010). But why might this cultural and interdisciplinary turn be the case? One response revolves around the benefits that come with engaging with both sport psychological and sociological literatures which include, but are certainly not limited to, the following four possibilities.

First, although sport sociologists and psychologists have different research foci and divergent interests as outlined above, the influence of the socio–cultural realm on people's psychological and emotional experiences cannot be ignored by either discipline. In this regard, it is useful to return to our earlier point as a reminder of what both disciplines have in common: the fundamental belief that people's lives and experiences are socially, culturally, and politically influenced, with both disciplines seeking to produce knowledge that hopefully understands and/or improves the human condition. By focusing on these similarities and keeping this latter point in mind, sport sociology and sport psychology researchers are afforded the opportunity to expand their understanding and knowledge regarding the intersectionality of the social, cultural, and psychological constructions within sport contexts. An example of this intersectionality can be found in the recent push toward a more culturally inclusive and critical sport psychology (Schinke and McGannon 2015) known as *cultural sport psychology* (CSP). Scholars within this growing genre draw upon developments within cultural studies of sport to challenge mainstream sport psychology's assumptions to facilitate contextualized understandings of marginalized topics and cultural identities (e.g. McGannon *et al.* 2013; Ryba, Schinke and Tennenbaum 2010). As the cultural turn within sport psychology continues to grow, it becomes clear from the mounting research and evidence that sport sociology also has much to gain from incorporating and/or considering the psychological and emotional implications of the socio–cultural and political influences within sport.

Second, by turning to the intersectionality of sociology and psychology, new and different theories and research questions are put forward, which further enhances each discipline's knowledge base and the social-psychological imagination. And with that, the need for an increased repertoire of research methods for collecting, analyzing, and representing data is born. While it may be daunting to master new and/or different theories and research methods, doing so has a larger and bigger-picture 'payoff' for sport sociology and psychology: dialogues (as opposed to debates) and connections are made using theories, methodologies, and research methods that *both* disciplines can harness to understand the intersection of the psychological, social, and cultural realms. A turn to intersectionality within our methodologies also opens the possibility for researcher reflexivity, whereby our own identities, values, and backgrounds are explored in relation to the research process. Reflexivity is an important step toward acknowledging power issues and achieving cultural sensitivity and inclusion of marginalized identities and communities with and for whom we work.

With an emphasis on innovative methods and methodologies, a third benefit is that sport science research continues to move forward, as opposed to remaining stagnant, insular, and/or (re)producing 'the same old'. A fourth benefit of drawing upon theories and methodologies that 'capture' the complexity of intersectionality and the creative imagination of the psychological and socio-cultural world could be that the research silos that often erect boundaries between the disciplines may be opened up and/or made less likely. Below, some of these benefits are illuminated further. Additional benefits are also highlighted.

Working at the intersection of sport sociology and sport psychology: suggestions for consideration

Having briefly offered some reasons as to why working at the intersection of the sociology of sport and sport psychology is beneficial, the question is, 'How and where might we begin to work at the intersection of sport sociology and psychology?' Whilst remaining cognizant of the difficulties and attendant pitfalls of engaging in such work, the following are some possibilities that hold merit as means of encouraging and making modest boundary crossings: concept analysis, narrative inquiry, and discursive psychology.

Concept analysis, as highlighted in Evans (2012), involves tracing the origins and applications of a concept, looking at the differing ways in which it appears both within and outside a particular discipline, and examining the various definitions and representations used to describe it and the consequences. For instance, approached in a principled manner this process might involve a group of researchers in sport psychology and the sociology of sport, or a researcher from one discipline, embarking on research that examines 'coach–athlete relationships' by interrogating how meanings around the individual and social relationships are (and have been historically) configured within both their own and others' research communities, what ideas are used to define relations in different disciplines, and how such definitions might relate to those of others in communities being researched; all the while leaving open the possibility for new understandings (and (re)definitions) of coach-athlete relations to emerge in the research act in the relations between the research community and the populations they research. Such an example can be found in the work of Smith (2013a) who, working at the intersection of sport psychology and the sociology of sport (as well as critical disability studies), argued that when read through the lens of relational sociology as well as social constructionism in sport psychology, how coach-athlete relationships are conceptualized within cognitive sport psychology is best described as a coach/athlete dualism rather than as coach–athlete relations. This is because researchers who conduct research through the lens of cognitivism attend to the coach and athletes as bounded individuals and locate key concepts (e.g. closeness, commitment) for developing relationships within the mind of the individual, not within social relations. Other key concepts, like performance, mental training, health, disability, concussion, and disordered eating, might be subjected to similar scrutiny.

According to Evans (2012), concept analysis holds enormous potential for facilitating crossings of disciplinary borders and research. It is committed to 'expanding the space of the possible' and pursuing new understandings. Rather than suggesting that there are 'simply' other more useful or better concepts to be found 'out there' or 'elsewhere' (among other disciplines), concept analysis has the capacity to draw attention to, and disrupt, thinking about the ways in which knowledge/s are produced via 'relations within' research communities and the social structures that maintain them. Concept analysis also 'can reconfigure the ways in which we think about engagements with the knowledge/s (and key concepts) of those others with whom we "relate to"' (Evans 2012: 9). Moreover, concept analysis does not mean that researchers from differing disciplines dissolve or ignore the tensions and differences between them. Rather, this kind of analysis enables them to acknowledge and embrace these differences and tensions positively and creatively while engaging in dialogue with each other regarding the ways that they can retain strong subject-specific attachments and allegiances while simultaneously searching for heightened and shared understandings on ideational common ground.

Although there are various psychological and sociological approaches to narrative, when both work within sociology (e.g. Frank 2010) and psychology (e.g. Brockmeier 2012) is harnessed, *narrative inquiry* can be described as a psycho-social approach that is distinguished from other approaches (e.g. ethnography or phenomenology) by its focus on stories. There are good reasons for this focus which, in turn, lay the ground for why researchers might turn to narrative inquiry as a means to cross boundaries and work at the intersection of sport psychology and the sociology of sport. These reasons, or 'operating principles of narrative inquiry', are as follows.

First, narrative is a *ubiquitous form of human activity that functions to make meaning and communicate a complex sense of interiority*. People are storytelling creatures. We need and use stories because narrative is our primary medium through which we constitute meaning communally in order to make sense of life experiences and act within our social world. Further, stories are our pervasive and singularly good equipment for communicating our *sense* of an interior, subjective reality. This includes our thoughts, emotions, motivations, identities, sense of self through time, intentions, and individual behaviour. Accordingly, narrative is a particularly useful bridge for connecting the sociological and psychological because it orientates researchers to our storytelling impulse, quest for meaning that guides human action, and belief or claim that we have an inner experience. That is, both stories and meaning-making, which have typically been neglected by sport psychologists, are attended to. At the same time, the 'felt inner life and story' that a person claims is 'within them' is given authenticity in sociological analyses.

Second, *narratives are personal and humans are acting storytellers*. In other words, people act, and one means of them acting – of performing agency – is in and through their storytelling (Gergen 2009). For example, a person can *perform* agency by not only choosing to tell a story, but also through selecting what particular type of story to tell and how to personally compose it in relation to the context, past responses from people, the expectation of a listener, and so on. Moreover, individuals use stories to remember, argue, persuade, justify, entertain, mislead, connect, and motivate. Narrative inquiry thus helps connect sociological work to the psychological realm because, rather than being deleted, the person and agency are honoured and studied; a person *is* an acting subject and a place for the individual is found.

The above point leads to a third premise of narrative inquiry, which is the equal emphasis on *narratives as social actors* (Frank 2010). Whilst stories are actively composed, they are not something to be found in the mind, entirely ever anyone's own, or are a window into the inner world of the individual. This is because the stories we tell about ourselves are constituted relationally: constituted from the menu of narratives our relationships within society and culture makes available at a micro, meso, and macro level. Thus, whilst people depend on and will act to defend what they experience as their interior lives and their personal story, from a narrative perspective our sense of interiority and an inner story as within us derives from outside us. Further, these stories that circulate outside of our bodies are actors – forms of action – in that they do things on people. Narratives don't do everything, but they do act on us by shaping our human conduct, affecting what we think and how we behave.

Accordingly, for researchers who wish to harness the benefits that go with working at the intersection of sport psychology and the sociology of sport, narrative inquiry is one useful way to go because it holds on to the recognition that being human necessarily involves both agency and structure in some balance. The notion that people are active storytellers in that they shape and act on society, whilst at the same time are shaped and acted on by the various narratives that circulate within society, means that both agency and structure are viewed as merging into one another, rather than being distinct. In light of the foregoing, narrative inquiry dissolves any individual/society dichotomy in that it *simultaneously* recognizes that stories are learned from outside us whilst, at the same time, people depend on and will act to defend what they experience as their interior lives and their personal authenticity.

Examples of a sport narrative approach that draws on both sociological and psychological work can be found in Blodgett *et al.* (2011), Carless and Douglas (2009), Phoenix and Smith (2011), Smith and Sparkes (2011), Sparkes and Smith (2009), and Sparkes *et al.* (2012). Another example can be found in the work of Smith (2013b) who critically examined the stories a group of men who became disabled through playing sport told about their health. For him, working at the intersection of sport psychology and the sociology of sport that a narrative approach afforded propelled him across disciplinary borders and legitimized the academic use of both sociological ideas (e.g. habitus, capital, interpellation, and the social relational model) and psychological ideas (e.g. resilience, self-compassion, and psychological well-being) to understand the lives of participants. One upshot of all this was that a more 'truly' psycho-social picture of their lives was produced. Participants in Smith's study were highlighted as meaning makers who configured their experience of a traumatic sporting injury using the narrative resources that their social and cultural world passed down in order to interpret life and do certain things (e.g. care for health, but not too much) whilst pass over other things (e.g. playing disabled sport) in ways that socially oppressed them or positively impacted on their psycho-emotional well-being and cultural status as disabled males. In other words, narrative inquiry helped give a sense of people as individuals and social beings who do perform agency but are also constrained by structural matters. Narrative inquiry in this case further helped re-conceptualize commonly held assumptions in psychology whilst bringing these into the foreground of the sociological imagination. For example, resilience, which is largely a concern of psychology, was re-conceptualized as emerging from within social relations and a resource people actively use to do certain things (e.g. uphold hegemonic masculinities), rather than as being located solely in the individual mind and ultimately separated from the social.

Another useful way to work at the intersection of psychology and sociology is via *discursive psychology* (DP). Grounded in social constructionism and interpretive social psychology, DP theorizes self-identity – which is an important focal point of research in both sport psychology and sport sociology – as the product of individual, social, and cultural discourses, which interact to create particular meanings and associated actions pertaining to selves and identities (McGannon and Spence 2010). In contrast to cognitive approaches within psychology which reduce identities as being within the mind, in DP, identities cannot be understood independent of language and need to be explored within the context of the language practices that create them (Benwell and Stokoe 2006; Potter and Wetherell 1987). DP was introduced into sport psychology by McGannon and Mauws (2000) and then into sociology (McGannon and Mauws 2002) to expand understandings of exercise participation beyond mainstream theoretical approaches (e.g. social cognitive). DP has been extended towards developing qualitative research methodologies in sport psychology (e.g. Locke 2008) as well as enhanced understandings of sport (e.g. Cosh, LeCouteur, Crabb and Kettler 2012) and exercise participation issues (e.g. McGannon and Schinke 2013; McGannon and Spence 2010).

It is important to point out that most of the DP work in sport psychology produced to date has tended to align closely with the sociological traditions of ethnomethodology and conversation analysis and/or an approach that combines discourse analysis with conversation analysis. However, critical health and exercise psychologists have distinguished between DP investigations adhering to this fine-grained analytic approach to action-oriented talk versus investigations concerned with broader discourses, power and subjectivity grounded in post-structuralism, and the work of Foucault. This latter focus on power and discourse is something that sport sociologists have been traditionally interested in, but a focus that holds potential for understanding the human psyche and condition for both sport sociology and sport psychology. Thus, despite these two seemingly different DP 'camps' it is possible for sport sociologists and sport psychologists to place *both* ethnomethodological and post-structuralist analyses in dialogue to benefit both of their interests, rather than in opposition (McGannon and Spence 2010). This 'synthetic/eclectic approach' to discourse draws attention to *both* discursive practices (e.g. how discourse is used to perform specific functions, with specific effects) and broader discursive resources (e.g. how texts and/or talk are informed by wider cultural practices and norms). McGannon and Mauws's DP work outlined earlier provides an example of this dialogue, as it aligns with Garfinkel's ethnomethodological principle of attending to taken-for-granted talk and understandings about psychological concepts (e.g. self-identity) and a Foucauldian post-structuralist approach, whereby DP is also 'concerned with the discourses, the subject positions those discourses confer, and the subsequent use of discursive resources' (McGannon and Mauws 2000: 159).

Both approaches as articulated within a critical, eclectic DP, whether combined or used singularly, have much to offer sport sociology and sport psychology researchers. In this regard, because sport sociologists and sport psychologists are both interested in the behaviours and/ or practices that afford or limit certain identities, within DP as articulated above, discourse can also be understood as providing the meanings that constitute people's everyday practices. Discourses – be they personal, social, or cultural – offer competing and (potentially) contradictory ways of giving meaning to the world and how we construct our identities and view ourselves. Known as *subject positions* for individuals to take up, these positions further offer conditions of possibility for constituting subjectivity (identities, understandings of the world) and vary in terms of the power and agency they afford people. Philosophers/discourse theorists Davies and Harré define a subject position in the following way:

> A subject position incorporates both a conceptual repertoire and a location for persons within the structure of rights for those that use that repertoire. Once having taken up a particular position as one's own, a person inevitably sees the world from the vantage point of that position and in terms of the particular images, metaphors, storylines and concepts which are made relevant within the particular discursive practice in which they are positioned. At least a possibility of notional choice is inevitably involved because there are many and contradictory discursive practices that each person could engage in.
>
> (1990: 46)

People thus acquire a sense of who they are (i.e. an identity) and interpret the world from a particular perspective by participating in discursive practices that allocate meanings to particular categories (e.g. female athlete, male athlete). The self is then positioned and experienced in relation to the story lines articulated around those categories and people have particular psychological and emotional experiences associated with that world view (McGannon and Schinke 2013; McGannon and Spence 2010). While the site of subjectivity one occupies in a discourse carries with it particular conventions as to how one will think, feel, and behave, individuals are not passive and have some choice when positioning themselves in discourses. While people may be constituted in one position or another, in one discourse or another within a story about their lives, they can negotiate new subject positions by refusing the ones articulated, by taking up alternatives within different discourses. The notion of a subject position suggests the potential for human agency, resistance, and change, something that both sport psychology and sport sociology are interested in impacting.

Conclusion

This chapter has promoted scholarship that works at the intersection of the sociology of sport and sport psychology. Although engaging in such scholarship is not easy nor politically neutral, nor the implications of engaging with such intersectionality a panacea, there are benefits that go with such engagement. By explicitly drawing on ideas from both sport sociology and the psychology of sport, and crossing boundaries, researchers can enrich psychological knowledge and the sociological imagination; connect with the social and cultural dimensions of our lives whilst honouring the individual as social agent; dissolve tensions between the macro and micro; expand our repertoire of research methods for collecting, analyzing, and representing data; enhance theoretical creativity and deepen critical thinking; expand the connection of research projects with the fate of our times; and, most important, improve the lives of the various people and communities we work with. We suggested three ways to facilitate working at the intersection of the sociology of sport and sport psychology. These – concept analysis, narrative inquiry, and DP – are not the only ways. Researchers might also consider the additional opportunities that critical psychology, relational sociology/psychology as outlined by Crossley (2011) or Gergen (2009), a Foucauldian approach, or, for example, various strands of phenomenology hold for doing work that crosses boundaries. With such benefits and opportunities in mind, we hope this chapter has encouraged an informed, respectful, and fruitful dialogue among and between sociologists of sport and sport psychologists. As part of this, it is hoped the chapter stimulates researchers from both disciplines to cross boundaries and engage in the adventure of working at the intersection of the sociology of sport and sport psychology.

Notes

1 Social cognitive theories are, of course, popular in sport psychology. But, these theories, like much psychological work on relationships (e.g. coach-athlete relations), end up tracing the 'social' back to the individual mind. The individual unit remains under scrutiny (Gergen 2009; McGannon & Mauws 2000; Smith 2013a).

2 *Illusio* is Bourdieu's term for the tendency of people to engage in the game and believe in its significance; that is, believe that the benefits promised by the field are desirable without questioning these. The considerable investments in the game guarantee its continued existence. Broadly, capital is the resource, command of which enables one to exercise and to resist domination in social relations; or, put another way, to maintain a position in the status hierarchy of society.

3 We recognize that just like there are sport sociologists who do connect with sport psychologists by participating in and legitimating the audit culture, there are some sport psychology scholars who share with sociological colleagues a deep concern about the ideologies and practices that inform this culture.

References

Benwell, B. and Stokoe, E. (2006) *Discourse and Identity*, Edinburgh: Edinburgh University Press.

Blodgett, A. *et al.* (2011) 'Exploring Vignettes as a Narrative Strategy for Co-Producing the Research Voices of the Aboriginal Community', *Qualitative Inquiry*, 17: 522–533.

Brockmeier, J. (2012) 'Narrative Scenarios: Toward a Culturally Thick Notion of Narrative', in J. Valsiner (ed.) *The Oxford Handbook of Culture and Psychology*, Oxford: Oxford University Press.

Carless, D. and Douglas, K. (2009) '"We Haven't Got a Seat on the Bus for You" or "All the Seats Are Mine"': Narratives and Career Transition in Professional Golf', *Qualitative Research in Sport and Exercise*, 1: 51–66.

Cosh, S., LeCouteur, A., Crabb, S. and Kettler, L. (2012) 'Career Transitions and Identity: A Discursive Psychological Approach to Exploring Athlete Identity in Retirement and the Transition back into Elite Sport', *Qualitative Research in Sport, Exercise and Health*, 5: 21–42.

Crossley, N. (2011) *Towards Relational Sociology*, London: Routledge.

Davies, B., and Harré, R. (1990) 'Positioning: The Discursive Production of Selves', *Journal for the Theory of Social Behaviour*, 20: 43–63.

Evans, J. (2012) 'Ideational Border Crossings: Rethinking the Politics of Knowledge within and across Disciplines', *Discourse*, doi: 10.1080/01596306.2012.739466.

Frank, A.W. (2010) *Letting Stories Breathe*, Chicago, IL: University of Chicago Press.

Gergen, K. (2009) *Relational Being*, Oxford: Oxford University Press.

Ingham, A.G., Blissmer, B.J., and Davidson, K.W. (1999) 'The Expendable Prolympic Self: Going Beyond the Boundaries of the Sociology and Psychology of Sport', *Sociology of Sport Journal*, 16: 236–268.

Locke, A. (2008) 'Managing Agency for Athletic Performance: A Discursive Approach to the Zone', *Qualitative Research in Psychology*, 5: 103–126.

McGannon, K.R., Cunningham, S.M. & Schinke, R.J. (2013) 'Understanding Concussion in Socio-Cultural Context: A Media Analysis of a National Hockey League Star's Concussion', *Psychology of Sport and Exercise*, 14: 891–899.

McGannon, K.R., and Mauws, M.K. (2000) 'Discursive Psychology: An Alternative Approach for Studying Adherence to Exercise and Physical Activity', *Quest*, 52: 148–165.

McGannon, K.R., and Mauws, M.K. (2002) 'Exploring the Exercise Adherence Problem: An Integration of Ethnomethodological and Poststructuralist Perspectives', *Sociology of Sport Journal*, 19: 67–89.

McGannon, K.R. and Schinke, R.J. (2013) '"My First Choice Is to Work Out at Work; Then I Don't Feel Bad About My Kids": A Discursive Psychological Analysis of Motherhood and Physical Activity Participation', *Psychology of Sport and Exercise*, 14: 179–188.

McGannon, K.R., and Spence, J.C. (2010) 'Speaking of the Self and Physical Activity Participation: What Discursive Psychology Can Tell Us About an Old Problem', *Qualitative Research in Sport and Exercise*, 2: 17–38.

Phoenix, C. and Smith, B. (2011) 'Telling a (Good?) Counterstory of Aging: Natural Bodybuilding Meets the Narrative of Decline', *The Journals of Gerontology Series B: Psychological Sciences and Social Sciences*, 66(5): 628–639.

Potter, J., and Wetherell, M. (1987) *Discourse and Social Psychology: Beyond Attitudes and Behavior*, London: Sage.

Ryba, T.V., Schinke, R.J., and Tenenbaum, G. (eds). (2010) *The Cultural Turn in Sport and Exercise Psychology*, Morgantown, WV: Fitness Information Technology.

Schinke, R.J. and McGannon, K.R. (eds) (2015) *The Psychology of Sub-Culture in Sport and Physical Activity: Critical Perspectives*, London: Psychology Press, Taylor and Francis.

Smith, B. (2013a) 'Sporting Spinal Cord Injuries, Social Relations, and Rehabilitation Narratives: An Ethnographic Creative Non-Fiction of Becoming Disabled through Sport', *Sociology of Sport Journal*, 30: 132–152.

Smith, B. (2013b) 'Disability, Sport, and Men's Narratives of Health: A Qualitative Study', *Health Psychology*, 32: 110–119.

Smith, B., et al. (2009) 'Dialogue, Monologue, and Boundary Crossing within Research Encounters: A Performative Narrative Analysis', *International Journal of Sport & Exercise Psychology*, 7: 342–358.

Smith, B. and Sparkes, A.C. (2011) 'Multiple Responses to a Chaos Narrative', *Health*, 15: 38–53.

Sparkes, A.C. (2013) 'Qualitative Research in Sport, Exercise and Health in the Era of Neoliberalism, Audit and New Public Management: Understanding the Conditions for the (Im)Possibilities of a New Paradigm Dialogue', *Qualitative Research in Sport, Exercise and Health*, 5: 440–459.

Sparkes, A.C., Perez-Samaniego, V., and Smith, B. (2012) 'Social Comparison Processes, Narrative Mapping, and Their Shaping of the Cancer Experience: A Case Study of an Elite Athlete', *Health*, 16: 467–488.

Sparkes, A.C. and Smith, B. (2009) 'Men, Spinal Cord Injury, Memories, and the Narrative Performance of Pain', *Disability & Society*, 23(7): 679–690.

Sparkes, A.C. and Smith, B. (2014) *Qualitative Research Methods in Sport, Exercise & Health: From Process to Product*, London: Routledge.

Thorpe, H. (2010) 'The Psychology of Extreme Sport', in T. Ryba, R. Schinke and G. Tenenbaum (eds) *The Cultural Turn in Sport and Exercise Psychology*, Morgantown, WV: Fitness Information Technology.

PART THREE

Social divisions and sport

21
INTRODUCTION TO PART THREE

Richard Giulianotti

In Part Three, we examine how fundamental social divisions are manifested and experienced within sport. For the sociologist, social divisions represent a crucial subject of research: they shape the social experiences and life chances of individuals and social groups, and reflect how societies are organized through frameworks of social stratification and unequal distributions of power. Sociological analysis is enhanced by the application of relevant social theories which critique existing power relations and pursue the radical transformation of social divisions. The most important social divisions for sociologists have been social class, gender, and race; more recently, greater recognition has been accorded to other divisions relating, for example, to sexuality and disability. In Part Three, we examine how these five types of social division – class, gender, race, sexuality, and disability – are played out within sport.

Chapter 22, by Ian Ritchie, draws heavily on different sociological theorists in order to examine the intersection of social class and sport. Marx's theoretical framework serves to identify the material foundations upon which social class, and class conflict, are established. Weber's work helps to account for the growing complexity of modern societies, such as in the influence of status groups. Bourdieu accounts for the close ties between social class and the 'habitus' (or dispositions) of individuals. Ritchie notes that the systematic analysis of social class within sport emerged from the 1960s onwards; some early work was particularly polemical, for example in attacking the capitalist exploitation of 'worker-athletes' (e.g. Brohm 1978). Subsequently, the class/sport intersection inspired a substantial volume of sociological and related social scientific analysis (e.g. Kidd 1997). Latterly, scholars have examined how neo-liberal social and economic policies have impact on social class relations within sport, arguing that privatized experiences, lifestyles, and wider cultural values have come to dominate contemporary sport (e.g. Newman and Giardina 2011).

Gender-based divisions in sport are explored in the chapter by Gertrud Pfister and Susan Bandy. Their analysis highlights how our interpretations and understandings of gender, femininity, sex, and sexuality have been critically transformed by different theoretical interventions, such as from liberal, Marxist, and postmodernist feminist theories (see Hargreaves 1993; Markula 2005). Sport provides one important space in which the dominant gender order is socially constructed, such as through different bodily practices and techniques, or in media coverage and discourses that surround (primarily male) sports. Sport thus represents a key space in which young people are socialized into 'appropriate' gender identities and roles. Huge differences remain between men and women in respective levels of sport participation and physical activity, in mass media coverage of elite sport, and in the politics and governance of sport. The fluidity of gender is highlighted by the public emergence of intersex or transsex athletes, and the hotly disputed issue of 'sex verification' testing in elite-level sport (see Sullivan 2011). Pfister and Bandy conclude, and serve to demonstrate through their chapter, that the academic study of sport represents one significant space in which women have managed to make a serious and substantial impact.

The chapter by Earl Smith and Angela Hattery explores the critical significance of 'race' within sport. The actual definition of 'race' is hugely problematic and highly contested; it is socially constructed and thus subject to significant variations and differences in application over time and space. Smith and Hattery examine the structural positions and everyday experiences of African Americans in North American sports as an extended case study of how 'race' plays out within contemporary sport. They consider how, historically, African Americans have endured social marginalization and exclusion in relation to sport, for example by being 'stacked' into particular sport playing positions, often due to racist assumptions regarding intelligence levels or 'natural' sporting prowess, and also in being confronted by acts of individual and group aggression, in physical and verbal ways (Loy and McElvogue 1970; Sailes 1998). The elite socio-economic status of top athletes provides no real buffer from abuse by fellow athletes and wider audiences. Whilst sport organizations make efforts to challenge racism – for example, through rules that require clubs to interview ethnic minority candidates for top coaching positions – Smith and Hattery argue that these initiatives should be buttressed by stronger societal interventions, including legal measures.

Jayne Caudwell's chapter examines the interface of sexualities and sport. Caudwell examines the particular importance of definitions and self-identifications in constructing different sexual identities or statuses. Consequently, categories of sexual identity are diverse, imprecise, and subject to constant change, and thereby extend far beyond the more widely recognized 'LGBT' (lesbian, gay, bisexual, transgender) domain. Sport represents an important field in which the citizen and broader human rights of sexual minorities may be pursued, for example as symbolized by the 'coming out' of elite individual athletes. Yet, in many national jurisdictions across the world, the lingering oppression of sexual minorities takes many forms. In many sports, homophobic abuse is experienced by athletes, by spectators, fellow athletes, and sport leaders and officials (cf. Griffin 1998). In addition, sport mega-events continue to be allocated to cities and nations where the systematic marginalization and criminalization of sexual minorities is still apparent (Lenskyj 2014). Thus, overall, for sexual minorities, as for other social groups at the sharp end of social divisions, the struggle for recognition, equality, and justice continues in sport as it does in wider society.

Focussing specifically and in detail on the Paralympic Games, the chapter by P. David Howe illuminates core issues on the intersection of sport and disability. Howe examines how different physical impairments are classified with the aim of facilitating relatively balanced competition within Paralympic sports. However, classification has significant negative consequences in creating de facto 'hierarchies' of impairment, while discouraging some athletes from maximizing their performance due to the danger of being reclassified into other categories of disability where competition will be tougher. A key goal for much Paralympic sport is 'true integration' for disabled people within mainstream sport and society. Such a laudable objective is difficult to achieve as elite sport is inherently selective. Meanwhile, Paralympic sport is marked by cross-cutting divisions of gender, race, and class. Women with disabilities have low participation rates in sport, as ideologies of 'hegemonic masculinity' prevail, whilst the advanced technologies in Paralympic sport are often only afforded by competitors from the wealthiest nations and regions. Leading Paralympians may have 'captured the public imagination', but, as Howe argues, such adulation reinforces the marginalization of the vast majority of disabled people who appear to have 'failed' to succeed in these exceptional ways.

References

Brohm, J.-M. (1978) *Sport: A Prison of Measured Time*, London: Pluto.

Griffin, P. (1998) *Strong Women, Deep Closets*, Champaign, IL: Human Kinetics.

Hargreaves, J. (1993) 'Gender on the Sports Agenda', in A.G. Ingham and J.W. Loy (eds) *Sport in Social Development*, Champaign, IL: Human Kinetics.

Kidd, B. (1997) *The Struggle for Canadian Sport*, Toronto: University of Toronto Press.

Lenskyj, H. (2014) *Sexual Diversity and the Sochi 2014 Olympics*, Basingstoke, UK: Palgrave.

Loy, J.W. and McElvogue, J.F. (1970) 'Racial Segregation in American Sport', *International Review for the Sociology of Sport*, 5: 5–24.

Markula, P. (ed.) (2005) *Feminist Sport Studies*, Albany: SUNY Press.

Newman, J. and Giardina, M. (2011) *Sport, Spectacle and NASCAR Nation: Consumption and the Cultural Politics of Neoliberalism*, Basingstoke, UK: Palgrave.

Sailes, G. (ed.) (1998) *African Americans in Sport*, New Brunswick, NJ: Transaction.

Sullivan, C.F. (2011) 'Gender Verification and Gender Policies in Elite Sport: Eligibility and "Fair Play"', *Journal of Sport and Social Issues*, doi: 10.1177/0193723511426293.

22

SOCIAL CLASS AND SPORT

Ian Ritchie

Introduction

This chapter builds three themes. First, class is arguably the most important determinant of participation in sport. As Donnelly (2011: 185) states, 'Social class, both on its own and in combination with gender, race/ethnicity, and other social characteristics, is the most important determinant of participation in sport and physical activity'. While Donnelly's comment is with respect to Canada, the same can be said for countries around the world. Class, in short, is a crucial determining factor in terms of participation in and the experience of sport.

Second, in their analysis of class in post-industrial societies, Clement and Myles (1994: 4) make the point that '[c]lasses are not labels people wear on their chests'. In other words, we do not see the effects of class directly, and so when people throw balls, skip, run, play football, watch the Olympic Games on television, or, for that matter, experience sport and physical movement in myriad other ways, rarely do they consider that those experiences are filtered through class. This is a reflection of an issue that lies at the core of sociology: the fact that many social variables have real effects but cannot be seen directly. In his classic *Suicide*, Émile Durkheim (1951) spoke to this point by demonstrating that there are social causes for what most people believed was an individual act – suicide. C. Wright Mills (1959) reinforced the same position when he implored people to use the sociological imagination because they neglect the impact social environment has on their everyday lives.

The final theme is that the institution of sport is particularly conducive to class's 'disappearing act' in accounting for people's experiences because sport itself is typically not taken seriously as a social variable. Cole (1994: 15) put this point succinctly: '[t]he "logic" of the sport/body combination, the seemingly free play of bodies in motion, contributes to an illusion that sport and its bodies are transparent, set apart from politics, culture, and the economy'.

The discussion that follows builds these themes by considering classical and contemporary theoretical perspectives in sociology that have attempted to understand the class dimension of society and people's experiences of class, followed by a summary of some major areas of research specific to sport. Limited space cannot do justice to an immense area of enquiry and as such, what follows is a brief outline of theories and of studies influenced by them. The central point that this chapter makes is that understanding the intersections between sport and class is crucial because virtually every experience of sport and physical movement is infused with class.

Classical and contemporary theories of class

This section summarizes in brief the perspectives of Karl Marx, Max Weber, and Pierre Bourdieu, because the work of these three theorists has been the most influential in terms of understanding class in the parent discipline of sociology. As the summaries are out of necessity so brief, the reader is directed to more thorough contributions elsewhere – for example, Beamish (2002, 2010), Coakley and Dunning (2000), Giulianotti (2005), Maguire and Young (2002). Here, I discuss Marx's insights into the material conditions of capitalist society and the alienation of workers, Weber's contributions on goal-rational action and the complexities of class and power in developing industrial-capitalist societies, and Bourdieu's notions of field and habitus.

Karl Marx

It has often been stated that studies of class in sociology have generally been discussions with 'Marx's ghost', and this statement is not an exaggeration. Theorists after Marx provided analyses regarding many of the complexities and nuances of capitalist society that Marx had not considered, with Max Weber (1958, 1968, and see below), Anthony Giddens (1973), and Pierre Bourdieu (1984, 1990a, and see below) standing out. However, the foundation upon which those theorists stood was Marx, and it is for this reason that his *oeuvre* warrants attention.

Part of the reason Karl Marx's (1818–1883) work has lasted the test of time is the complexity of his own early experiences alongside his lifelong commitment to developing his understanding of capitalist society. It should be kept in mind that generalizations about his work are heuristic strategies that belie both the immensity of Marx's theorizing and the fact that he shifted his focus on matters such as the nature of capitalism, the role of the individual in society, labour, alienation, and class relations (Beamish 2002: 218–239). What set Marx's critique of capitalist society apart from others was his ability to recognize that economic conditions formed the foundation of social life, the expansion of this recognition into a more general theory of society, and his identification of the unique role social conflict played in the history of societies.

At the heart of Marx's theory is that economic conditions lay the foundation of social life. What lay behind the *modes of production* that shaped societies historically was the *material* conditions upon which humans labour to create the essentials of life. *Labour* for Marx was a critical concept that reflected a fundamentally important component of human practice, in which, in his own words, 'Man sets in motion the natural forces which belong to his own body . . . in order to appropriate the materials of nature in a form adapted to his own needs. Through this movement he acts upon external nature and changes it, . . . he simultaneously changes his own nature' (Marx 1977: 283–284). In short, labour is much more than a means towards accomplishing instrumental goals; it is a fundamental practice in which human potential is realized – 'the way humans externalize their unique capacities and actualize human potential' (Beamish 1985: 359).

Marx pointed out that of course humans do not labour in a social vacuum, but instead 'enter into definite relations that are indispensable and independent of their will, relations of production which correspond to a definite stage of development of their material productive forces. The sum total of these relations of production constitutes the economic structure of society, the real foundations, on which rises a legal and political superstructure and to which correspond definite forms of social consciousness' (Marx 1972: 4). Here we see Marx's central point regarding the material foundation of social life and the fact that culture and human thought itself emerge out of that foundation. For Marx, classes emerge during different epochs based on people's ability to gain control over resources and the means of producing goods essential for human life. While he was interested in various modes of production throughout history, the capitalist mode of production received the bulk of Marx's attention.

In his most important work, *Capital*, first published in 1867, Marx attempted to explain that the economic form, in its drive to create profit, produces two separate classes – capitalists (the *bourgeoisie*), who realize the profits and surpluses from the system, and workers (the *proletariat*), who do not. Workers, however, cannot realize their potential because their labour is *alienated*, or, in Marx's (1963: 124–125) words, 'Work is *external* to the worker. . . . His work is not voluntary but imposed, *forced labour*. It is not the satisfaction of a need, but only a *means* for satisfying other needs'.

Two of Marx's main insights summarized here regarding labour as a fundamental element of human life and, relatedly, the production of the class system within the capitalist mode of production, alongside the alienation of the worker, we will soon see, have both been important for sociological accounts of class and sport.

Max Weber

There are two major elements of Max Weber's (1864–1920) work that have influenced the understanding of the interrelationship between class and sport: the concept of goal-rational action and Weber's observations regarding the increasing complexities of class and power in industrial-capitalist societies. Weber derived his knowledge base from a number of different disciplines, including law, economics, philosophy, and history, making him, in the words of Cantelon and Ingham (2002: 64), 'a superior thinker'.

In his classic *The Protestant Ethic and the Spirit of Capitalism*, Weber (1958) demonstrated that a value system which emerged in the seventeenth century in Protestant sects in the north-east of the United States led ultimately to a particularly robust form of capitalism. In line with the sixteenth-century Protestant reformer John Calvin, Puritan sects believed that God had predestined dutiful followers to heaven. The followers could never know whether they were destined for heaven or not, but could prove their loyalty (and thereby seek God's grace) by leading an *ascetic* life of hard work and abstention. The connection between this ascetic value-system and the early capitalist economy came in the form of the *calling*: the development of personal fulfillment through the commitment to work and the re-use of material rewards, including financial gain, back towards work. As Weber (1958: 172) explains, 'Continuous work in a worldly calling, as the highest means to asceticism . . . must have been the most powerful conceivable lever for the expansion of that attitude toward life which we have here called the spirit of capitalism'. Over time, the emphasis on hard, rationalized work became commonly accepted as a way of life even if, as Weber points out, the original religious source of that value system disappeared.

Weber believed that ascetic Puritanism and the economic value system that emerged out of the seventeenth century ultimately led to a greater emphasis on what he termed 'goal-rational action', or human action involving the most calculated means towards achieving a particular end (Beamish 2010: 175–179). Importantly, in emphasizing goal-rational action, Weber was foreshadowing an important development in the understanding of the intersection between class and sport by sport sociologists much later in the twentieth century, namely that class is experienced as a subjective factor and could not be completely explained, as was the case by some Marxists, as solely an objective factor.

A second element of his work that is important to the intersection between sport and class is Weber's recognition of the increasing complexity of capitalist societies. In *Economy and Society*, Weber (1968: 926–940) outlines the increasing fragmentation of classes from the perspective of members' access to resources. However, Weber also points out that the manner in which class positions are exercised, such as through status position and power derived from political associations, is equally important.

The concept of *status groups* (*Stände*) was important for Weber, in that it expressed the fact that it is through one's status that power could be exercised and through which associations of class power and privilege could be reinforced. Defined as the 'social estimation of honour' (Weber 1968: 932), status for Weber is often related to class position defined in the traditional sense of members having access to relative levels of resources, including property and money. But status is not necessarily linked to tangible resources, and in fact Weber points out, 'It normally stands in sharp opposition to the pretensions of sheer property' (932). Interestingly, foreshadowing the work of Bourdieu to some degree, Weber pointed out that status honour 'is normally expressed by the fact that above all else a specific *style of life* is expected from all those who wish to belong to the circle' (932).

Pierre Bourdieu

Reflecting the increasing complexity both of class under capitalist expansion in the twentieth century and the recognition that the subjective experience of class needs to be considered, the work of Pierre Bourdieu (1930–2002) has had an enormous influence on recent sociological accounts of class. Certainly influenced by Marx and Weber, Bourdieu's own *oeuvre* also emanated out of careful consideration of a complex array of sociological, political, and philosophical thought (see Grenfell 2004; Laberge and Kay 2002).

One of Bourdieu's central concerns was how power was exercised through a combination of social structure and human agency. *Field* and *habitus* are the two most important concepts in terms of combining the objectively given and subjectively experienced elements of social structure and everyday life, respectively. A field for Bourdieu is the structured space human agents find themselves in that includes hierarchical distributions or objective relations of people in terms of wealth and symbolic or cultural capital. The capital one can potentially be endowed with includes direct financial resources, certainly, but Bourdieu identified many different delimited spaces in which what counts as capital can vary immensely. In the field of education, for example, family background might play an important role. Or in the field of art, the status of particular artists might influence what 'counts' as legitimate art in the field. Bourdieu preferred *field* to the concept of class because there are a number of forms of capital that exist – economic, social, and cultural.

Habitus is perhaps the most referred-to term with respect to Bourdieu's work in the sociology of sport. He specifically defines it as 'systems of durable, transposable dispositions, structured structures predisposed to function as structuring structures, that is, as principles which generate and organize practices and representations that can be objectively adapted to their outcomes without presupposing a conscious aiming at ends or an express mastery of the operations necessary in order to maintain them' (Bourdieu 1990a: 53). While somewhat convoluted, Bourdieu's main point is that dispositions – the manner in which people conduct themselves, broadly speaking – are worked through in their everyday life but they are also predetermined in the sense that the social milieu organizes dispositional tendencies – it sets the conditions upon which human agents act. Habitus, and the context of the field within which everyday human action exists, sets the stage for what most assume are reflections of active volition. Common elements of habitus include 'body language' and the manner in which people comport themselves; patterns of speech; tastes in food, art, and cultural products as a whole; and of course appreciation for and ways of participating in sport and physical movement. Importantly, the experience of habitus in the various fields reinforces social structure as a whole. Put simply, in terms of understanding class, everyday dispositions themselves reflect but simultaneously reinforce class position.

We will return to a greater consideration of Bourdieu in a moment because, interestingly, he was a rare case of a general sociologist being aware of the importance of sport, and of the experiences of the body and physical movement, as part of the wider social structure and in terms of the roles they play in the construction of class as a whole.

Studies on class and sport

Whilst the perspectives of Marx, Weber, and Bourdieu have been the dominant ones in terms of understanding class in sociology, the previous summary of these figures' positions on class in the discipline of sociology is just that – a summary or a heuristic device that necessarily belies the true complexity of class analysis as a whole. Also, whilst a generalization could be made that as one moves from Marx through to Weber and Bourdieu, one also moves from a consideration of the 'objective' or 'structural' components of class to, increasingly, the 'subjective' or 'experienced' components, this too should be thought of as a heuristic way of thinking about the theorists' perspectives because all were in various ways aware of the intricate ways in which social structure and human agency are combined in the creation, reinforcement, and experience of class. The summary of research on sport and class studies that follows is similarly a summary to guide thinking. While a chronological progression of theories and studies is presented, there is far more blurring between the periods than there are clear and distinct differences in terms of theoretical emphasis.

Interestingly, in what sport sociologists today consider to be one of the pioneering texts in their field, Thorstein Veblen's (1953) *Theory of the Leisure Class* considered leisure pursuits in the United States very much along the lines of both Marx's and Weber's thought. Veblen made the argument that the upper classes used 'conspicuous consumption', or the ability to expend time and financial resources on non-essential leisure goods, in order to demonstrate and reinforce class position. Reinforcing status was important, Veblen (1953: 42) claimed, because 'it is not sufficient merely to possess wealth or power. The wealth or power must be put in evidence'.

After Veblen's work, two other events in the early twentieth century are noteworthy early considerations of class and sport. First, a vibrant and successful international workers' sport movement in the 1920s and 1930s emphasized the role sport could play in international worker solidarity whilst simultaneously opposing conservative and elitist movements. Importantly, organizers and participants actively debated the nature of 'sport' in terms of its ability to reinforce political ideologies and class positions, applying in a sense an early version of 'sport sociology' before the discipline was conceived. Second, in 1923 at the University of Frankfurt, the Frankfurt Institute for Social Research was founded and early developers such as Max Horkheimer and Theodor Adorno used the insights of Marx and Weber to understand elements of culture within capitalist economic systems, including sport. It was a student of Adorno's, Heinz Risse, who published *Die Soziologie des Sports* in 1921, using the name of the discipline in a title for the first time (Risse 1981).

A first phase of more regular and organized critical scholarship into the interrelationship between class and sport came with the advent of the development of sport sociology itself in the post–World War II era. It is important to highlight the political events that spear-headed this scholarship, the development of the discipline, and the framing of the theoretical debates in the context of general sociology, particularly American and European sociology.

International attention to organized sport reached rarefied heights during the early Cold War Olympic Games era. While many in the West assumed politically 'backwards' Communists could not compete in international sport, after the USSR entered the 1952 Helsinki Olympic Games, the country went on to beat the USA 14 out of the 20 times the countries competed in Cold

War Olympic sport. Also, the partitioning of Germany after World War II led to the development of the German Democratic Republic's state-run sport system, which in many ways was the most advanced sport system of modern times. It both accelerated competition around the world and brought heightened awareness to the issue of sport. Various Olympic boycotts during the 1970s and 1980s, alongside the continued growth of professional-commercial sport, especially in the USA, brought attention to the importance of understanding the role of sport in society. Finally, within university settings from the mid-1960s on, there was the gradual recognition that sport and physical activity were culturally and socially contingent practices. This coincided with a process of institutional expansion, leading to an environment in which newly emerging 'sports studies' professors and the programs they developed could flourish (Ritchie 2012).

A first phase of scholarship on class occurred roughly during the 1960s and 1970s, coinciding with the formal foundation of sociology of sport. A reflection of radical social movements internationally but also a reaction against structural-functionalist theoretical tendencies that had dominated the discipline of sociology since the 1930s, critical work during this period revealed, following Marx, the many ways that sport reproduced class divisions and was at times an alienating experience for athletes, and then, following Weber, the many ways in which the body was increasingly treated in a rationalized, machine-like manner.

Important works from this period include Bero Rigauer's (1981) *Sport and Work* (translated from the original *Sport und Arbeit*); Jack Scott's (1971) *The Athletic Revolution*; Paul Hoch's (1972) *Rip Off the Big Game*; and Jean-Marie Brohm's (1978), *Sport: A Prison of Measured Time* (translated from the original *Critiques du Sport*). The theoretical influences varied from the neo-Marxist Frankfurt School on Rigauer's *Sport and Work* to Hoch's Marxist-Leninist approach in *Rip Off the Big Game* to the influence of French Marxism and Louis Althusser's theories of 'Ideological State Apparatuses' on Brohm's *Sport: A Prison of Measured Time* (Beamish 2002: 27–33).

Brohm's text is perhaps the most important because his critique of sport under the class relations of capitalism was far-reaching. Brohm claimed that by instilling people with values and reinforcing practices supportive of capitalist relations, sport, under the direction of the state apparatus, constrains and controls the populace. Ideologically, for example, sport, in Brohm's (1978: 55) words, '*veils* the real structure of production relations which it assumes as "natural". This ideology *masks* class relations by turning the relations between the individuals within the sporting institution into material relations between things: scores, machines, records, human bodies treated as commodities'. Also, following Marx's discussion of alienated labour, *Sport: A Prison of Measured Time* is full of examples of athletic endeavours that, while taken to be a 'natural' part of training and competition, should be highly questioned, including the masochistic celebration of pain during training and competition, the treatment of the body as a machine at the expense of more liberating forms of physical movement, and the reduction of the human body to meticulously timed units and spatially restricted movements (Brohm 1978: 18–29, 56–57, 59–64, 66–76).

Increasing theoretical complexity characterizes the work that took place, roughly from the 1980s to the mid-to-late 1990s. Importantly, US historian Allen Guttmann's (1978) *From Ritual to Record* was released in the transition between the two periods. Guttmann applied Weber's work directly to highlight the highly rationalized and bureaucratized elements unique to modern sport. Other notable titles from this period include John Hargreaves's (1986) *Sport, Power and Culture*, Jennifer Hargreaves's (1994) *Sporting Females*, Alan Tomlinson's (1999) *The Game's Up*, Garry Whannel's (1983, 1992) *Blowing the Whistle* and *Fields in Vision*, and Richard Gruneau's (1983) *Class, Sports, and Social Development*. All represent approaches that move beyond considering class alone to the intersections between class and gender, elements of popular culture, including, increasingly, the media industry, race, and more. The agency of individuals and groups to influence what was previously seen as the overbearing and exploitative aspects of capitalist class structure was generally emphasized in these works, and in fact references to sport as a 'contested terrain' became common during this phase (Carrington and McDonald 2009: 4).

Gruneau's (1983) work stands out and *Class, Sports, and Social Development* has subsequently been republished and updated. In that book and in an often-cited essay entitled 'Modernization or Hegemony: Two Views on Sport and Social Development', Gruneau (1988) makes a strong claim for considering class and power in accounts of sport history. Gruneau pits traditional accounts, or what he refers to as those that fall under the umbrella of the 'theory of industrial society', against newer critical accounts, ones that fall under the umbrella 'theory of capitalist society', inspired by the works of Marx and also other progressive scholars. The latter, Gruneau claims, consider capitalist relations both economically and as a system of social relations, based on Marx's insights into the nature of capitalist society discussed earlier. Accounts of sport history need to always look at class divisions as an important factor in the development of sport, Gruneau claimed, in addition to the manner in which sport reproduces class through such means as reinforcing values appropriate for work under capitalism's system of production, and the alienation experienced by athletes and participants.

Important examples of accounts that consider the intersection of sport, class, and power in the construction of nations and nationalism include Bruce Kidd's (1997) *The Struggle for Canadian Sport* and Richard Holt's (1989) *Sport and the British*.

Kidd's historical account, for example, considers the power struggles of organizations during the period between the two world wars as they attempted to take control of sport in Canada. Class dynamics played a critical role in these struggles, and Kidd demonstrates how the male middle-upper-class leaders of the Canadian Amateur Athletic Union, the middle-upper-class women who promoted girls' and women's sport through the Women's Amateur Athletic Federation, the workers who attempted to build working-class power through the Workers' Sports Association of Canada, and finally the profiteering businessmen of the National Hockey League all fought for the commitment of Canadian people and ultimately to control the meaning of sport in the country. Interestingly, it was the businessmen of the NHL – the interests of a very small handful of capitalists – who eventually won out and set the agenda for Canadian sport at the expense of other traditions. Hockey today is thought of as quintessentially 'Canadian' owing to the events and power struggles dating back to the early twentieth century.

Various works on the class-sport dynamic since (approximately) the mid-to-late 1990s can be characterized by the attempt to bring together traditional Marxist scholarship and many of the radical features of Marx's work, with Weber's and Bourdieu's social theories, alongside other perspectives as well, including post-structuralist theories and varied perspectives in cultural studies.

As mentioned earlier, Bourdieu himself recognized the importance of sport. In *Distinction: A Social Critique of the Judgement of Taste*, in particular in a chapter entitled 'The Habitus and the Space of Life-Styles', Bourdieu (1984) highlights the manner in which sport and physical movement experiences reinforce class position. There is little question that some sports present financial restrictions and become the reserve of the upper classes. But 'economic barriers . . . are not sufficient to explain the class distribution of these activities. There are more hidden entry requirements, such as family tradition and early training, or the obligatory manner (of dress and behaviour), and socializing techniques, which keep these sports closed to the working class . . . and which maintain them . . . among the surest indicators of bourgeois pedigree' (Bourdieu, 1984: 217). Fully recognizing the impact sport has on people's lives and the manner in which its seeming detachment from social affairs makes understanding it so crucial, Bourdieu (1978, 1990b) wrote essays specifically to guide a greater understanding of sport's role in society for sport sociology, including 'Sport and Social Class' in 1978 and 'Programme for a Sociology of Sport' in 1990.

In 1995, the *Sociology of Sport Journal* published a special issue on Bourdieu and sport, representing the shift towards a more comprehensive analysis of sport and its intersection with class. Since then, several studies – far too many to summarize here – have been published, including Booth and Loy (1999), who follow Bourdieu directly and highlight the status-seeking confirmation of sports like riding, sailing, and golf, which usually take place at private, expensive clubs. Wilson (2002) highlights another aspect of habitus: the intersection between spectatorship and class position. He demonstrates that lower classes are more likely to spectate at 'prole' sports such as motorcycle or stock car racing, citing the reproduction of cultural capital as having greater influence than economic capital. In another interesting application of Bourdieu's work, Kay and Laberge (2002) demonstrate the symbolic capital that is derived from adventure racing for management-level corporate personnel. Management-level participants are over-represented in these types of races, the authors show, precisely because of the belief that the skills, knowledge, and experiences derived from adventure racing can be transferred to participants' experiences and dominant values in corporate life.

Recently, several scholars have pointed out the crucial connections between class and sport under the conditions of neoliberalism. Neoliberal economic and public policies are those that have emerged since the 1970s, in which governments have played a decreased role in welfare state services, there has been an emphasis on pro–free market policies including reduced taxation, and, importantly, there has been enhanced emphasis on personal 'accountability' of individuals. Harvey (2005: 2) summarizes neoliberalism as 'a theory of political economic practices that proposes that human well-being can best be advanced by liberating individual entrepreneurial freedoms and skills within an institutional framework characterized by strong property rights, free markets, and free trade'.

An important early work on the intersection between sport and class under the emerging conditions of neoliberalism was Alan Ingham's (1985) essay 'From Public Issue to Personal Trouble: Well-Being and the Fiscal Crisis of the State', in which Ingham argues that conservative pro-market ideologies have led to heightened emphasis on individual citizens 'taking responsibility' for aspects of their lives previously provided by governments and other public agencies. 'Lifestyle', Ingham (1985: 48) shows, became the new social requirement from the 1970s onwards, and a 'pick yourself up by the bootstraps' mentality placed responsibility in the hands of people's personal habits and routines, rendering the perception that those who were 'dependent' on the state were inferior: 'as an ideology of self-discipline continues to define structural impediments as personal troubles . . . being indigent or placing demands on the State to take care of the body are signs of moral weakness'.

Since Ingham's publication there have been countless studies on the effects of neoliberalism on the intersection between sport and class, in particular with respect to the exercise and fitness industry. The studies are far too numerous to mention here, but importantly, a recent contribution by Richard Gruneau (2015) has detailed the manner in which neoliberal policies have affected exercise and sport participation in the Canadian case. With reductions in state expenditures on social programs over the last few decades, an enhanced 'pay to play' environment has emerged in which only those who can afford the fees have access to an increasingly privatized exercise and sport-participation infrastructure, exacerbating the class divide in terms of participation. Importantly, this includes children and their access to programs and facilities, and the influence of class on children's participation in Canada is apparent: household income is directly related to whether kids play, or not, in both formally organized and informal 'pick-up' versions of sport.

Conclusion

The relatively few examples discussed here scratch the surface of what is an evolving interest in the study of the complex intersection between people's everyday experiences and class position, inspired by Bourdieu's work in recent times and, ultimately, by Weber and Marx in their classic works. Generally, studies have applied aspects of theoretical work to unique situations, in part owing to the nature of the journal publication process in which a study must have a specific unit of focus. But more broad-based analyses, like what Bourdieu (1984) himself attempted, remain to be accomplished in the study of sport, and given the almost boundless complexity of class structure combined with the limitless ways in which humans experience the social world around them, it is not difficult to comprehend why a 'Bourdieusian' analysis of the sport-class intersection has not been completed. After all, it would be exceedingly difficult, to put it mildly.

However, that gaining such an understanding is difficult does not by any means suggest that it should not be attempted. As events since the global recession in 2008 and subsequent social movements such as 'Occupy' against entrenched inequalities attest, the potential to recognize class divisions is very real. So while class cannot disappear, what can be brought to light by the discipline of sociology of sport is the largely unrecognized intersection between sport and social inequalities that directly impacts people's lives. Doing so will go a long way to satisfying one of the central goals of sport sociology: to highlight the enriching role that sport and other forms of physical movement and expression can play in people's lives.

References

Beamish, R. (1985) 'Understanding Labor as a Concept for the Study of Sport', *Sociology of Sport Journal*, 2(4): 357–364.

Beamish, R. (2002) 'Karl Marx's Enduring Legacy for the Sociology of Sport', in J. Maguire and K. Young (eds) *Theory, Sport and Society*, Amsterdam: JAI.

Beamish, R. (2010) *The Promise of Sociology: The Classical Tradition and Contemporary Sociological Thinking*, Toronto: University of Toronto Press.

Brohm, J.-M. (1978) *Sport: A Prison of Measured Time*, London: Ink Links.

Booth, D. and Loy, J. (1999) 'Sport, Status, and Style', *Sport History Review* 30: 1–26.

Bourdieu, P. (1978) 'Sport and Social Class', *Social Science Information* 17(6): 819–840.

Bourdieu, P. (1984) *Distinction: A Social Critique of the Judgement of Taste*, New York and London: Routledge.

Bourdieu, P. (1990a) *The Logic of Practice*, Stanford, CA: Stanford University Press.

Bourdieu, P. (1990b) 'Programme for a Sociology of Sport', in P. Bourdieu, *In Other Words: Essays Towards a Reflexive Sociology*, Stanford, CA: Stanford University Press.

Cantelon, H. and Ingham, A.G. (2002) 'Max Weber and the Sociology of Sport', in J. Maguire and K. Young (eds) *Theory, Sport and Society*, Amsterdam: JAI.

Carrington, B. and McDonald, I. (eds) (2009) *Marxism, Cultural Studies and Sport*, London and New York: Routledge.

Clement, W. and Myles, J. (1994) *Relations of Ruling: Class and Gender in Postindustrial Societies*, Montreal and Kingston: McGill–Queen's University Press.

Coakley, J. and Dunning, E. (eds) (2000) *Handbook of Sports Studies*, London: Sage.

Cole, C.L. (1994) 'Resisting the Canon: Feminist Cultural Studies, Sport, and Technologies of the Body', in S. Birrell and C.L. Cole (eds) *Women, Sport, and Culture* (pp. 5–29), Champaign, IL: Human Kinetics.

Donnelly, P. (ed.) (2011) *Taking Sport Seriously: Social Issues in Canadian Sport*, Toronto: Thompson Educational.

Durkheim, É. (1951) *Suicide: A Study in Sociology*, New York: Free Press.

Giddens, A. (1973) *The Class Structure of the Advanced Societies*, London: Hutchinson.

Giulianotti, R. (2005) *Sport: A Critical Sociology*, Cambridge: Polity Press.

Grenfell, M. (2004) *Pierre Bourdieu: Agent Provocateur*, London and New York: Continuum.

Gruneau, R. (1983) *Class, Sports, and Social Development*, Amherst: University of Massachusetts Press.

Gruneau, R. (1988) 'Modernization or Hegemony: Two Views on Sport and Social Development', in J. Harvey and H. Cantelon (eds) *Not Just a Game: Essays in Canadian Sport Sociology*. Ottawa: University of Ottawa Press.

Gruneau, R. (2015) 'Goodbye Gordie Howe: Sport Participation and Class Inequality in the "Pay for Play" Society', in D. Taras and C. Waddell (eds) *How Canadians Communicate V: Sports*. Edmonton: Athabasca University Press.

Guttmann, A. (1978) *From Ritual to Record: The Nature of Modern Sports*, New York: Columbia University Press.

Hargreaves, J. (1986) *Sport, Power and Culture: A Social and Historical Analysis of Popular Sports in Britain*, Cambridge: Polity Press.

Hargreaves, J. (1994) *Sporting Females: Critical Issues in the History and Sociology of Women's Sports*, London and New York: Routledge.

Harvey, D. (2005) *A Brief History of Neoliberalism*, Oxford: Oxford University Press.

Hoch, P. (1972) *Rip Off the Big Game: The Exploitation of Sport by the Power Elite*, New York: Anchor Books.

Holt, R. (1989) *Sport and the British: A Modern History*, Oxford: Clarendon Press.

Ingham, A. (1985) 'From Public Issue to Personal Trouble: Well-Being and the Fiscal Crisis of the State', *Sociology of Sport Journal* 2(1): 43–55.

Kay, J. and Laberge, S. (2002) 'The "New" Corporate Habitus in Adventure Racing', *International Review for the Sociology of Sport* 37(1): 17–36.

Kidd, B. (1997) *The Struggle for Canadian Sport*, Toronto: University of Toronto Press.

Laberge, S. and Kay, J. (2002) 'Pierre Bourdieu's Sociocultural Theory and Sport Practice', in J. Maguire and K. Young (eds) *Theory, Sport and Society* (pp. 239–266), Amsterdam: JAI.

Maguire, J. and Young, K. (eds) (2002) *Theory, Sport and Society*, Amsterdam: JAI.

Marx, K. (1963) 'Economic and Philosophical Manuscripts', in T.B. Bottomore (ed.), *Karl Marx: Early Writings*, New York: McGraw-Hill.

Marx, K. (1972) 'A Contribution to the Critique of Political Economy', in R.C. Tucker (ed.) *The Marx-Engels Reader*, New York: W.W. Norton & Company.

Marx, K. (1977) *Capital, Vol. I*, New York: Vintage Books.

Mills, C.W. (1959) *The Sociological Imagination*, London: Oxford University Press.

Rigauer, B. (1981) *Sport and Work*, New York: Columbia University Press.

Risse, H. (1981) *Die Soziologie des Sports*, Münster: Lit Verlag.

Ritchie, I. (2012) 'Sociology of Sport', in J. Nauright and C. Parrish (eds) *Sports Around the World: History, Culture, Practice*, Santa Barbara, CA: ABC-CLIO.

Scott, J. (1971) *The Athletic Revolution*, New York: Free Press.

Tomlinson, A. (1999) *The Game's Up: Essays in the Cultural Analysis of Sport, Leisure and Popular Culture*, Aldershot, UK: Arena.

Veblen, T. (1953) *Theory of the Leisure Class: An Economic Study of Institutions*, New York: Mentor.

Weber, M. (1958) *The Protestant Ethic and the Spirit of Capitalism*, New York: Charles Scribner's Sons.

Weber, M. (1968) *Economy and Society*, New York: Bedminster Press.

Whannel, G. (1983) *Blowing the Whistle: The Politics of Sport*, London: Pluto Press.

Whannel, G. (1992) *Fields in Vision: Television Sport and Cultural Transformation*, London and New York: Routledge.

Wilson, T.C. (2002) 'The Paradox of Social Class and Sports Involvement: The Roles of Cultural and Economic Capital', *International Review for the Sociology of Sport* 37(1): 5–16.

23
GENDER AND SPORT[1]

Gertrud Pfister and Susan J. Bandy

Introduction

At the end of 2013, a fundamental political decision was made in Germany. Based on the fact that a considerable number of children are born with ambiguous sex characteristics, the law-makers decided to exclude the obligation to indicate the sex of newborns in birth registration documents. Thus, Germany is the first country in Europe where a person can chose which sex to have, if any. It is an open question if and how this new ruling affects the dichotomous gender order in many areas of the society and, specifically, in sport.[2]

In any case, this option is a further step towards gender equality, which is considered to be a human right and has been implemented in many Western countries – at least on paper. Women and men are treated equally in law and have access to all professions, as well as to political power. However, at the same time gender differences and hierarchies are reproduced, for example in politics, employment, fashion, everyday life and in the various fields of sport.

Although today women participate in all Olympic events, in most sports they do not compete with men. With regard to many indicators – such as performances and records, public attention and financial resources – more or less important gender differences can be observed. What are the reasons and the consequences for these gender gaps?

Gender and sport: definitions

In contrast to sex, the biological status of individuals, 'gender' refers to the social construction of women and men in a given society. The term became popular in the 1970s in the wake of the women's movements when feminists adopted the concept of gender in order to emphasize the social construction of femininities and masculinities. Since the 1980s, the dichotomy of sex and gender has been increasingly criticized, and the interdependencies of biology and social construction, the relational quality as well as the ambiguity and fluidity of gender, have been emphasized (Fisher *et al.* 2013).

Numerous discussions on gender, gender identities, doing gender and the gender order in various societies have taken place, and different 'schools' of gender studies have been established. These discussions also had an effect on sport and sport studies whereby the multiple meanings of the term *sport* caused numerous misunderstandings. In some languages, 'sport' includes 'sport for all' activities. In other languages, the term refers to competitive, elite sports. In this chapter, gender is understood as a social construction and *sport* is used as a broad term.

Gendered sports cultures: historical developments

Sport, games, dances and varied forms of physical activity have existed in all societies throughout history from the ancient societies to the present. These activities have typically expressed specific aims and patterns and reflected the values of particular social groups. They have also embodied societal norms and values while reflecting the structures and ideologies of different cultures. Moreover, these activities have been fashioned by prevalent behaviours and tastes that are related to and dependent upon age, ethnicity and social class, but most importantly upon gender (Pfister 2013). Since most societies have been and still are dominated by men, it is hardly surprising that they have taken the leading role in the development of various physical exercises and sports. Nonetheless, in traditional cultures women have often been able to develop their own move-ment cultures, and there may have been some women who have succeeded in their demands to participate in men's sporting endeavours. As in pre-modern societies, men also shaped the landscape of modern physical education and sport. From the beginning of the nineteenth cen-tury, they developed various concepts of physical activity; many of these have been based on the ideas and concepts of Johann Christoph Friedrich GutsMuths (1759–1839), a German educator, who created a comprehensive system of 'gymnastics' (games and exercises) for boys. Not least as a reaction to the Napoleonic wars, in many European countries (in particular Germany, Swe-den and France) various systems of gymnastics that promised to increase the health and fitness of young men were created. This was true for Swedish gymnastics, developed by Per Henrik Ling (1776–1839), and for German gymnastics (*Turnen*), created by Friedrich Ludwig Jahn (1778–1852). Concurrently, English traditional physical pastimes were transformed into what is now recognized as modern sports, focusing on competition, quantitative performances and records. Gymnastics, *Turnen* and sport were invented by men for men and excluded girls and women until the end of the nineteenth century (Pfister 2003).

Although women appeared in the 1900 Olympics (an event organized by French sport organizations), female athletes had to wait until 1928 to be able to compete in athletics, a field of sport that raised particular concerns about the femininity of the participants. In this period, the Olympic Games became a highly visible arena for controversies over the appropriateness and desirability of women's sports, and the history of the games reflects these controversies as well as the attendant exclusion of women from numerous sports for over a hundred years. Since the 1920s, several groups and organizations – such as the Fédération Sportive Féminine Inter-nationale (FSFI) in Europe (founded in 1921 in Paris) and the Women's Sport Foundation in the USA (founded in 1974) – have been devoted to developing gender equality in sports. As a result of these and other initiatives, but also because of general social and cultural developments, the gender gaps in sport decreased, at least in industrialized countries, and female athletes could finally compete in all sports in 2012.[3] However, questions remain: does gender still matter in sport, with regard to participation, media attention, financial resources or leadership? Or, most important, what is gender and why is it an issue?

Understanding gender: theoretical approaches

General considerations

Men and women, masculinities, femininities and sexualities, as well as gender, have been explored and described from various perspectives using several theoretical concepts extending from psy-choanalysis to socialization. Currently, numerous scholars understand gender and sexualities as discursive constructions, embodiments of identities and practices as well as social arrangements and relations of power among individuals with various gender and/or sexual identities. In contemporary studies, constructions of gender and sexuality are often related to and intersecting with other fields of power and difference, for example with ethnicity, race and social class (see the overview in Beasley 2005).

Despite the increasing number of publications on gender issues, studies that cover or integrate the interrelations between femininities, masculinities and sexualities are rare. In addition, many feminists, lesbians and gay men are skeptical about the concept of gender as it seems to ignore their specific issues and situations (Evans 1991; Messner 1997). Debates have also focused on the term *gender*, as it seems to neglect the realities of the biological body and the seemingly natural biological sex differences. Donna Haraway (1988: 591), among others, warned us to 'lose . . . the body itself as anything but a blank page for social inscriptions'. Scholars reacted to this criticism by emphasizing the interactions between sociological and biological influences on sex and gender (Scott 1999). Controversies also emerged about the way in which sex, gender and sexuality interact. Whereas many scholars with a gender perspective assume that sexuality depends on gender identities and practices, scholars with a focus on sexuality tend to emphasize that gender and sexual desire are independent of each other (Rubin 1984).

Beasley (2005) describes the well-known 'waves' of and approaches to feminism and identifies its core issues, particularly its critical perspective on many taken-for-granted facts and figures. For her, 'feminism is a critical stance that decenters the assumptions of the mainstream in terms of center (men)–periphery (women)' (Beasley 2005: 16). Feminisms developed and changed in accord with political and epistemological developments, in particular with the rise of postmodernism. Whereas liberal and Marxist concepts aimed at the 'emancipation' of women according to their political agenda, 'second wave feminists' fought against repressions caused by patriarchy and compulsory heterosexuality (Rich 1981). Despite their different political positions and goals, feminists aimed at an overthrow of male power. More complex approaches to feminism emerged in the 1980s when scholars recognized and appreciated gender differences. Psychoanalyst Nancy Chodorow (1978), for example, re-interpreted the role of mothers in the psychological development of daughters and sons, and psychologist Carol Gilligan (1982) emphasized the specific ways of women's moral development. In the last few decades, it became increasingly obvious that gender, race and ethnicity, as well as social class, intersect, and it is currently the consensus view that each of these categories and their combinations have significant consequences for gender identities, discourses and practices. Since the 1990s, postmodern feminisms have been influential, with Judith Butler (1990, 2004) as one of the icons. From her perspective, the coherence of sex, sexuality and gender is based on internalized norms, produced in ritualized and performative acts and enforced by the heterosexual matrix, the compulsory practice of heterosexuality. It goes without saying that not only the various sex and gender categories, but also the theories referring to them, intersect and reinforce each other.[4]

Constructivist approaches to gender

Sport as a social system, and participation in sport as social interaction in a leisure or a professional context can be explored with reference to numerous theories and conceptual paradigms. Here, constructivist approaches, in particular, are presented as they focus on behavioral aspects and are most pertinent to our examination and discussion of gender and sport. On the basis of a constructivist epistemology, gender can be defined as 'a process of social construction, a system of social stratification, and an institution that structures every aspect of our lives because of its embeddedness in the family, the workplace and the state as well as in sexuality, language and culture' (Andersen & Witham 2011; Lorber 1994: 5). Thus, gender is not something we have or we are, but something we do. Sport, too, is a gendered institution and, at the same time, a gender performance, as playing sports is always also presenting oneself as a woman or a man, that is 'doing gender'. Lorber describes the relations between these three aspects of gender as follows: 'The social reproduction of gender in individuals reproduces the gendered societal structures; as individuals act out gender norms and expectations in face-to-face-interaction, they are constructing gendered systems of dominance and power' (Lorber 1994: 7). Hirschauer (1996) further clarifies that gender is part of collective knowledge and is anchored in culturally defined patterns of interpretation that structure information using a binary code (1996: 242). According to him, gender is a system of classification that divides the population into two groups. Bodily differences are constructed as gender signs, and the identification of gender differences, even before birth, depends on the pre-existence of already defined dichotomous categories. This means that individuals do not 'possess' gender-specific features per se; but 'because they belong to an appropriated category ... they are attributed a specific nature' (Guillaumin 2002: 5). 'Once the differences have been constructed, they are used to reinforce the "essentialness" of gender' (West and Zimmerman 1991: 24).

As a social institution, gender is embedded in societies, and also organizes daily life (Lorber 1994: 15). Social responsibilities and duties are allotted according to the major categories of gender, age, class and ethnic origin, the categorization being legitimized by norms and values and enforced by institutions such as religion and science, law and administration as well as the educational system, the mass media and sport organizations and institutions. In these and numerous other spheres, gendered norms, ideals and scripts that guide thinking and behaviour, as well as the perceptions and interpretations of individuals, are produced. In addition to affecting the formation of individual identities, gender is inscribed on bodies, bodily activities and sport practices. Connell (2002) adds the dimension of the body to constructivist theories with an emphasis on 'social embodiment': 'Bodies are both objects of social practice and agents in social practice. . . . The practices in which bodies are involved form social structures and personal trajectories which in turn provide the conditions of new practices in which bodies are addressed and involved' (Connell 2002: 47).

Lorber and Martin (2001: 230), too, claim that 'bodies are socially constructed in material and cultural worlds, which means they are physical and symbolic at one and the same time'. From this perspective, bodies – as well as related norms and ideals – are created via discourses and practices which conform to the tastes of the dominant groups, but also allow subcultural deviations. Norms, ideals and usages of bodies are produced by cultural practices, in accordance with the gender arrangements and the related 'scripts' of (sub)cultures and societies (Cooky 2009; Klein 1993; Lorber and Martin 2001; Wellard 2006).

Doing gender

The socially constructed and gendered body is the medium for interactions and performances that are crucial to the (unconscious) construction and embodiment of gender. People are categorized as belonging to certain gender and social groups defined by age, social class or ethnicity according to their hairstyles, clothes, postures and ways of moving that reveal gender in every interaction (Butler 1990; Connell 2002; Lorber 1994, 2005). Moreover, this categorization based on various 'bodily practices' further emphasizes the difference between females and males, and, as Lorber and Martin (2001) posit, produces and legitimizes gender hierarchies, that is men's dominance and women's compliance. Gendering processes occur all the time, everywhere and in every interaction, also in the various fields of sport, because individuals must present themselves as males and females. Gender, therefore, is not something we are or have but something we produce and do (West and Zimmerman 1991); it is adopted and internalized in ubiquitous processes of appropriation and (self)socialization. According to Lorber (1994: 13), 'gender is constantly created and re-created out of human interaction, out of social life, and it is the texture and order of that social life [. . .] which depends on everybody constantly doing gender.' Failure to comply with the 'heterosexual matrix' – the coherence of sex, gender and desire – causes conflicts, or, in Butler's (1990) words, creates 'Gender Trouble'.

Process-oriented approaches to gender

Lorber (1994) and other scholars understand gender as a process and a relational (and situational) concept. From this perspective, gender is considered as fluid, a perception that avoids essentialism, also because it allows for the recognition of various genders. Emphasizing the fluidity and changeability of gender allows for the possibility that individuals and cultures may 'degender'; it also enables scholars to identify and evaluate the differences on which society's structures of power are based.

Approaching gender in this way enables us also to understand that 'woman' and 'man' are not homogenous categories because they intersect with individual traits such as sexual orientation or age and other features of identity derived from or related to race and ethnicity, social class, national identity and so on. Recent arguments suggest that the intersections of these features, and the multiplicities of genders leading to gender diversity and gender freedom, would allow people to live outside of the binary sex/gender system. De Lauretis and other scholars advocate that societies should accept intersexuality, transgender queering and sexual fluidity as well as deliberately ambiguous non-gendered presentations of identities (De Lauretis 1991; Jagose 1996). Recently, the term and the notion of 'genderqueer' were developed for gender identities which do not fit in the binary scheme of man and woman or in any other fixed categories (Winter 2010). The acknowledgement of the fluidity of gender has caused sport federations, as well as the International Olympic Committee, to reconsider and change their politics of gender verification.

Gender and sport

Whereas societies in many parts of the world experience an increase of gender integration, competitive sport is one of the social systems which operate with a relatively strict gender segregation. Sport was invented by men and for men in accordance with men's social situations and physical abilities. Women were accepted into the various sport cultures only slowly and reluctantly. Although female athletes can participate (since 2012) in all Olympic events, women and girls are a negligible and invisible minority in some of the extremely popular sports, such as baseball and American football in the USA or sumo in Japan. Men are still excluded from rhythmic gymnastics and synchronized swimming, which both reward and emphasize traditional femininity.

In most sports, men and women compete in different categories and often specific rules apply to male and female athletes. In spite of gender integration, sport, in particular elite sport, provides different opportunities for self-presentations of male and female athletes because it is based on comparisons of performances, which identify differences and create hierarchies among the participants. Highlighting achievements and records, sport reveals and emphasizes performance differences between men and women. Although compliance with the constitutive rules of a sport is enforced in competitions, there are numerous ways to display various masculinities and femininities. In certain sports, power, speed and strength showcase the masculinity of male athletes. In contrast, rhythmic gymnastics demands a display of femininity, for example a slim body and graceful movements. But also in seemingly 'gender neutral' activities, such as athletics, the participants are 'doing gender', such as in their hairstyles, make-up, demeanour or sportswear.

According to Judith Butler's concept of the 'heterosexual matrix' (1990), societies enforce a naturalization of bodies, genders and sexualities as well as the coherence between biological sex, gender identities and sexual desires. It can be argued that sport has been framed with and can be viewed through Butler's matrix. Observations of the performances of women and men, as well as the media representations of male and female athletes, reveal the way in which athletes are 'doing gender' and in which the mass media emphasize their presentations and 'heterosexualize' both sportsmen and sportswomen. The coverage of the women's Football World Cup in 2011 in the German press, for example, provides numerous examples for the 'beautification' and 'sexualization' of players (Pfister 2014).

Socially constructed gender differences and the hegemony of men are incorporated into the structure of sport and into the habitus of its adherents. Bourdieu (1997, 2012) assumes that men acquire the dispositions to strive for domination in social interactions with other men: 'the male habitus is constructed and completed only in connection with the space reserved for men, a space in which the serious games of competition are played' (Bourdieu 1997: 203). Sport, in general, and football, in particular, can be considered as 'social fields' that provide opportunities for men, the players and the fans, to stage their 'serious games' and to gain visibility as well as economic, social and cultural capital (Bourdieu 1997; see also Lenneis & Pfister 2015). This is particularly true for association football (soccer) and for American football, which are among the most popular sports not only with regard to the number of players, but also their media coverage and the size and enthusiasm of their audiences. In both sports, masculinity is prominently displayed and conveys the clear message that 'real' sport is men's sport. This may be one of the reasons why these sports are so attractive to numerous boys and men, as players or spectators. But men are not only beneficiaries but also victims of the gender order, as they have been socialized to perform masculinity on and off the sport field and to prove their manhood so as not to be excluded from the community of men (Bourdieu 2012: 92). The psychological pressure to stay on the team (and to be a 'real' man) induces numerous athletes to participate in sport in spite of injuries, even with serious concussions that could cause brain damage. In contrast to men, women are socialized into a 'disposition to subjugation' (Bourdieu 2012: 90). They unconsciously become men's 'accomplices' and contribute, as 'flattering mirrors', to the reproduction of the hegemonic gender order (Bourdieu 1997: 203). Relatively few women participate in games, although the number of female players in association football is increasing worldwide. However, until now women's football and sport in general do not have the same significance as the 'serious games' of men (Pfister 2014).

The fluidity of gender and the challenges of sex verification

In most sports, men and women compete in different leagues which seem to require a 'gender verification' that aims at determining the eligibility of an athlete to compete in a sport event restricted to male or female participants. Visual examinations of female athletes (since 1966), later replaced by chromatin tests, were instituted at athletic events and the Olympic Games (until 1998), which should reveal the combination of x and y chromosomes. However, it has become obvious that neither sex nor gender can be reduced to a combination of chromosomes.

In the last decade, the 'coming out' of transgender, transsex and intersex athletes has brought new issues to the agenda of sport organizations. How should athletes who do not fit in the gender binary be treated in elite sport? Problems emerged in particular for individuals who had changed from man to woman because the testosterone level has a decisive influence on training effects and on physical performances. After long discussions, the IOC (International Olympic Committee) developed guidelines that regulate the eligibility of athletes for women's competitions. Transgendered athletes can compete as women if their assigned sex is recognized by their government and if they underwent hormonal treatment for a period of two years prior to competition in their newly assigned sex. Gender identities, sex assignments and eligibility are also a matter of gender justice whereby the rights of transgendered athletes may be consistent with the right of women to be compared with individuals who have no performance advantages.

More recently, the issue of eligibility has focused on women with naturally elevated androgen levels ('hyperandrogenism') who seem to have distinct competitive advantages over other women. In 2012, the IOC came to a 'revolutionary' decision and issued its *Regulations on Female Hyperandrogenism*, which were 'designed to identify circumstances in which a particular athlete will be eligible (by reason of hormonal characteristics) to participate in 2012 OG [Olympic Games] Competition in the female category'.[5] Although the test does not focus on the sex of the athlete, it has been argued that it underscores a binary organization of sport (Pieper 2012; Pieper 2014). Further, this test is based on the assumption that androgenic hormones are the primary components of biological athletic advantage, although this is not always the case (Karkazis *et al.* 2012).

Another issue of gender justice is the right to self-identification. Whereas the self-labelling of athletes as men does not seem to cause problems as it does not provide competitive advantages, their identification as women may be contested by sport officials, referees or other athletes. Some scholars, feminists and human rights activists propose that the dual sports structure based on sex should be abandoned (Pieper 2012, 2014; Sullivan 2011). Although some female athletes may be able to beat numerous men in various competitions, the existing records reveal large gender differences, in particular in sports in which strength or speed are at stake. Because women do not have a biological advantage with regard to sporting performances, they should be allowed to compete with men, if they wish to do so. But it would be unfair to give men access to women's contests as this would lessen sporting opportunities for women given the physical advantages of men.

Although gender has become increasingly fluid in everyday life, the world of elite sport enforces conformity with a binary gender order, which is a challenge for many athletes, but also for the sport organizations that must establish gender justice in a field that is dominated by competition for resources and power.

Gender and doing sport: socialization processes

The interrelations between the gender order, on the one hand, and sports-related habits, tastes and practices of women and men, on the other, can be explored by drawing on current concepts of socialization (Heinemann 1998; Horne *et al.* 1999; Hurrelmann 2006). According to Bilden (1991), individuals adopt norms and rules by means of self-training in and through cultural practices. Connell uses the term 'active learning' and integrates the body into her approach to socialization. 'The pleasure involved in learning gender is to some extent a bodily pleasure, pleasure in the body's appearance and in body performance' (Connell 2002: 78). Growing up is connected with changes in the body, such as an increase in physical abilities, however, some changes are ambiguous and may even cause conflicts. Menstruation, for example, is considered in some cultures as a sickness or impurity that may lead to restrictions in girls' and women's lives.

Connell (2002) proposes interpreting the appropriation of gender as a series of projects in which children learn how gender arrangements work and may be managed. They develop patterns of practices and in this way appropriate femininity and masculinity, including male or female identities and behaviour patterns. This approach allows us 'to acknowledge both the agency of the learner and the intractability of gender structures. Gender patterns develop in personal life as a series of encounters with the constraints and possibilities of the existing gender order. In these encounters the learner improvises, copies, creates and thus develops characteristic strategies . . . if the strategies are successful, they become settled, crystallizing as specific patterns of femininity and masculinity' (Connell 2002: 82). Based on the considerations presented above, doing sport, while at the same time doing gender, is learned in 'self-training in and through social practices', and socialization into sport can be described and interpreted as part of a gender project since doing sport and doing gender are intertwined. The dichotomous structure of (competitive) sport 'genders' the participants and reinforces gender duality as it groups individuals into one of the two gender categories. However, growing up also includes resistances and conflicts, as integration into the gendered world of grown-ups can be difficult, in particular for individuals who do not comply with rigid cultural expectations. Boys who want to dance in a ballet and girls who want to become boxers can easily become outsiders.

Drawing on the theoretical considerations presented above, the adoption of sport-related tastes and skills should be understood as a result of socialization processes. Boys and girls are identified as male and female even before birth and immediately treated accordingly, for example by being dressed in blue or pink clothes. Boys are often given cars and balls while girls are given dolls, and both are encouraged and predisposed to move and play in accordance with their gender. Thus, many boys take part in football games while girls – in many countries – dream of ballet or horse-riding. Children learn gendered rules, norms and values as well as the 'scripts' that shall guide their behaviour in everyday life as well as on the sporting ground. They grow up in a gendered world and adopt the dominant discourses including sport skills and practices, but this is not a simple and easy process because socialization is always connected with struggles and ambiguities, but also with multiple opportunities.

Gender and sport: activities and practices

Despite dramatic changes in recent decades, such as in sport opportunities for women, the 'gender gap' has not totally closed. Worldwide, even in industrialized countries, girls and women are less physically active than boys and men, they play different sports than males, and they are underrepresented among the members in sports organizations. Surveys such as the Eurobarometer (European Commission 2010: 12) reveal that the 'gender gap' is already significant among young Europeans: '19% of men aged 15–24 play sport "regularly", as opposed to 8% of women'. This information is confirmed by numerous other studies, such as a survey on the health behaviour of school-aged children (HBSC) developed by the World Health Organization (Iannotti 2005–2006). The HBSC study conducted in 41 European countries and in North America revealed that 25% of boys and 19% of girls aged 13 years and 19% of boys but only 12% of girls aged 15 years were vigorously active for at least 60 minutes on five or more days per week (as advised in health recommendations).[6] Gender differences are also reported by the US Women's Sports Foundation: 59% of girls aged 8–18 participate in sports compared to 80% of boys.[7] According to the US Centers for Disease Control and Prevention (CDC), 'men (52.1%) are more likely than women (42.6%) to meet the 2008 Physical Activity Guideline for aerobic activity'.[8] However, the rates of activity and inactivity vary across states and are dependent on the socio-economic status of families. The CDC also provides information about the types of physical activity of male and female adolescents: 48% of 12–15-year-old boys play basketball, 35% run and 27% play football. The activities of girls include running (35%), walking (28%), basketball (21%) and dancing (21%). Other surveys confirm these gender differences with regard to the amount and the types of sporting activities.[9]

Currently, women can participate in activities once thought to be male domains, such as marathon running, football, rugby, water polo, boxing, weight-lifting and ski jumping. However, men are still more likely than women to engage in sports that require aggressive bodily contact and in high-risk sports such as parkour, skateboarding or kite-surfing. Gymnastics, aerobics and dance continue to attract far more females than males.

Despite the access of women to all sports, female athletes still receive little media coverage. Worldwide, less than 10% of television time or newspaper coverage devoted to sports focuses on women (Bruce, Hovden and Markula 2010; Horky and Nieland 2011). The lack of public interest in female athletes has an impact on the financial resources which are available in women's sports. With the exception of tennis and golf, opportunities for women to earn a living as professional athletes remain scarce. Among the 100 best-earning athletes, only three are female (as tennis players).[10]

Women are rarely to be found in the press box or as commentators on televised sports; they are also drastically underrepresented among coaches and leaders at every level, from the IOC to the local sports clubs. Studies in several European countries revealed that only around 10% of coaches in elite sport are women. Examination of the membership of the IOC, national Olympic committees (NOCs) and the executive committees of national and international sport federations revealed also a stunning underrepresentation of women (see Pfister 2013). Currently, only 25% of the 115 members of the IOC are women, and more than 80% of the members of 204 NOCs governing committees are men.[11] On the boards of more than 70 international sports federations, women are also a small minority: the average percentage of women in those positions of power is less than 10%. Twenty-nine international sport federations do not have a single woman on their executive committees, and in 86% of them the proportion of female members is under 25% (Pfister 2013; World Economic Forum 2014). Only five federations (curling, equestrianism, triathlon, bowling and netball) are governed by a female president. There is, however, one area in which women have made major gains. They have made their voices heard in the academic study of sports, and it is hoped that their findings will make a difference.

Conclusion

We, the authors, grew up at a time when girls still were expected to wear skirts and be well behaved. We both loved sports and dreamed about being a famous tennis player or an excellent gymnast, but it was not even thinkable for us to become a ski jumper, a wrestler, weight-lifter or boxer.

Watching the European athletics championships in 2014, we were amazed at the skills and capabilities of female athletes, and the results of hammer throwers, 10-kilometre runners and pole-vaulters. We admire the 73-year-old woman who climbed Mount Everest, the 14-year-old Dutch girl who sailed around the world – alone – and the astronaut Sally Ride, who showed the world that women have entered new dimensions. Also, the way in which men do gender has changed over time: it is acceptable for them to take child leave or to cry over a movie, while there are men who want to participate in synchronized swimming. However, it is important to recognize that although the ways of doing gender have changed, new norms and rules that continue to emphasize femininities and masculinities have emerged. Sport will continue to be a crucial field in which these norms and rules are constructed – and contested.

Notes

1 We thank Verena Lenneis for many good comments and excellent advice which improved the text considerably.
2 See http://www.sueddeutsche.de/leben/geschlechter-im-deutschen-recht-maennlich-weiblich-unbest immt-1.1747380.
3 See the overview in Pfister (2013).
4 See the interview with Crenshaw on the concept of intersectionality at: http://www.americanbar.org/ content/dam/aba/publishing/perspectives_magazine/women_perspectives_Spring2004CrenshawPSP. authcheckdam.pdf.
5 See http://www.olympic.org/Documents/Commissions_PDFfiles/Medical_commission/2012–06–22 -IOC-Regulations-on-Female-Hyperandrogenism-eng.pdf.
6 Since the last survey, in 2002, the percentage of active children has decreased. The HBSC data provide information on trends but have to be interpreted with caution. Country-specific conditions may not have been taken into consideration satisfactorily.
7 See the Women's Sports Foundation 2008 report *Go Out and Play: Youth Sports in America* (available at: http://www.womenssportsfoundation.org/home/research/articles-and-reports/mental-and-physical-health/go-out-and-play).
8 See *Facts about Physical Activity*, available at http://www.cdc.gov/physicalactivity/data/facts.html.
9 See the Global Health Observatory Data of the WHO on Physical Inactivity, available at: http://apps. who.int/gho/data/node.main.A893.
10 See http://www.forbes.com/athletes/list/#tab:overall.
11 See the *Gender Balance in Global Sport Report. Women on Boards* (July 2014), available at: http://www. womenonboards.co.uk/news/gender-balance-in-sport-report/.

References

Andersen, M.L. and Witham, D.H. (2011) *Thinking about Women*, Boston: Pearson.
Beasley, C. (2005) *Gender and Sexuality*, London: Sage.
Bilden, H. (1991) 'Geschlechtsspezifische Sozialisation', in K. Hurrelmann and D. Ulich (eds) *Neues Handbuch der Sozialisationsforschung*, München: Beltz.
Bourdieu, P. (1997) 'Die männliche Herrschaft', in I. Dölling and B. Krais (eds) *Ein alltägliches Spiel. Geschlechterkonstruktion in der sozialen Praxis*, Frankfurt/Main: Suhrkamp.
Bourdieu, P. (2012) *Die männliche Herrschaft*, Frankfurt/Main: Suhrkamp.
Bruce, T., Hovden, J., and Markula, P. (2010) *Sportswomen at the Olympics*, Rotterdam: Sense.
Butler, J. (1990) *Gender Trouble*, New York: Routledge.
Butler, J. (2004) *Undoing Gender*, New York: Routledge.
Chodorow, N. (1978) *The Reproduction of Mothering*, Berkeley: University of California Press.
Connell, R. (2002) *Gender*, Cambridge: Polity.
Cooky, C. (2009) '"Girls Just Aren't Interested": The Social Construction of Interest in Girls' Sport', *Sociological Perspectives*, 52: 259–283.
De Lauretis, T. (1991) 'Queer Theory: Lesbian and Gay Sexualities', *Differences: A Journal of Feminist Cultural Studies*, 3: iii–xviii.
European Commission (2010) 'Sport and Physical Activity', *Special Eurobarometer*, Brussels: EC.
Evans, M. (1991) 'The Problem of Gender for Women's Studies', in J. Aaron and S. Walby (eds) *Out of the Margins*, London: Falmer, 67–74.
Fisher, L. *et al.* (2013) 'Theories of Gender and Sport', in E.A. Roper (ed.) *Gender Relations in Sport*, Rotterdam: Sense.
Gilligan, C. (1982) *In a Different Voice*, Cambridge, MA: Harvard University Press.
Guillaumin, C. (2002) *Racism, Sexism, Power, and Ideology*, London: Routledge.
Haraway, D. (1988) 'Situated Knowledges', *Feminist Studies*, 14: 575–599.
Heinemann, K. (1998) *Einführung in die Soziologie des Sports*, Schorndorf: Hofmann Verlag.
Hirschauer, S. (1996) 'Wie sind Frauen, wie sind Männer. Zweigeschlechtlichkeit als Wissenssystem', in C. Eifert (ed.) *Was sind Frauen? Was sind Männer? Geschlechterkonstruktionen im historischen Wandel*, Frankfurt: Suhrkamp.
Horky, T. and J.-U. Nieland (2011) *International Sports Press Survey 2011*, Norderstedt: Books on Demand.

Horne, J., Tomlinson, A. and Whannel, G. (1999) *Understanding Sport*, London: Routledge.

Hurrelmann, K. (2006) *Einführung in die Sozialisationstheorie*, Weinheim: Beltz.

Iannotti, R.J. (2005–2006) *Health Behavior in School-Aged Children (HBSC), 2005–2006*. ICPSR 28241-v1, Ann Arbor.

Jagose, A. (1996) *Queer Theory*, New York: New York University Press.

Karkazis, K. *et al.* (2012) 'Out of Bounds?', *American Journal of Bioethics*, 12(7): 3–16.

Klein, A.M. (1993) *Little Big Men*, Albany: SUNY Press.

Lenneis, V., & Pfister, G.U. (2015). Gender constructions and negotiations of female football fans: A case study in Denmark. *European Journal for Sport and Society*, 12(2), 157–185.

Lorber, J. (1994) *Paradoxes of Gender*, New Haven, CT: Yale University Press.

Lorber, J. (2005) *Breaking the bowls: degendering and feminist change*. New York, W.W. Norton.

Lorber, J. and Martin, P.Y. (2001) 'The Socially Constructed Body', in P. Kivisto (ed.) *Illuminating Social Life*, Thousand Oaks, CA: Pine Forge Press.

Messner, M.A. (1997) *Politics of Masculinities*, Thousand Oaks, CA: Sage.

Pfister, G. (2003) 'Cultural Confrontations: German Turnen, Swedish Gymnastics and English Sport – European Diversity in Physical Activities from a Historical Perspective', *Culture Sport Society*, 6: 61–91.

Pfister, G. (2013) 'Developments and Current Issues in Gender and Sport from a European Perspective', in E.A. Roper (ed.) *Gender Relations in Sport*, Rotterdam: Sense.

Pfister, G. (2014) 'Sportswomen in the German Popular Press', *Soccer & Society*. 30 September: 1–18. doi: 10.1080/14660970.2014.963314.

Pieper, L. (2012) 'Mixed Doubles: Renee Richards and the Perpetuation of the Gender Binary in Athletics', *The International Journal of the History of Sport*, 29 (5): 675–690.

Pieper, L. (2014) 'Sex Testing and the Maintenance of Western Femininity in International Sport', *The International Journal of the History of Sport*, 31 (13): 1557–1576.

Rich, A. (1981) *Compulsory Heterosexuality and Lesbian Existence*, London: Onlywomen Press.

Rubin, G. (1984) 'Thinking Sex: Notes for a Radical Theory of the Politics of Sexuality' in C.S. Vance (ed.) *Pleasure and Danger*, London: Routledge.

Scott, J.W. (1999) *Gender and the Politics of History*, New York: Columbia University Press.

Sullivan, C. (2011) 'Gender Verification and Gender Policies in Elite Sport: Eligibility and "Fair Play"', *Journal of Sport & Social Issues*, 35: 400–419.

Wellard, I. (2006) 'Able Bodies and Sport Participation', *Sport, Education and Society*, 11: 105–119.

West, C. and Zimmerman, D.H. (1991) 'Doing Gender', in J. Lorber and S.A. Farrell (eds) *The Social Construction of Gender*, Newbury Park, CA: Sage.

Winter, C. (2010) *Understanding Transgender Diversity: A Sensible Explanation of Sexual and Gender Identities*. Colorado Springs, CO: CreateSpace Independent Publishing Platform.

World Economic Forum (2014) 'Global Gender Gap Report 2014'. Available at: http://reports.weforum.org/global-gender-gap-report-2014 (accessed 11 April 2015).

24

RACE AND SPORT

Earl Smith and Angela J. Hattery

Introduction

Race matters (Feagin 2013; West 2000). Race impacts virtually every aspect of our lives, from the opportunities we have to attend higher education, our access to health care, the foods we eat, the likelihood that we will go to prison and the sports that we play.

In this essay, we examine the centrality of race to sport. We begin with a discussion of race as it is defined by scholars; we then identify several key 'themes' that illustrate the ways that race and racism appear in sports, followed by a focussed discussion of the experiences of African Americans in the US. We conclude with recommendations for addressing the kinds of racism that exist in SportsWorld.[1]

Definitions of race

As sociologists, we understand race to be socially constructed, which we illustrate with our examples below. In contrast, *ethnicity* describes one's cultural background and refers to behaviours such as religious practices, food preferences and language. Most people use the term *race* to refer to inherited physical characteristics like skin complexion, the shape of our nose, eyes, hair texture and hair colour. Furthermore, people commonly use the term *race* to refer to these physical traits as if they are always inherited and consistent (e.g. 'white' people always have light complexions or Asians always have eyelids with no folds). These assumptions reflect a collective ignorance about race; indeed, they have made naked fools of us. Why? The reasons for this ignorance return us to the sociological fact that race is a social construct. Simply put, there is *no coherent, fixed definition of race*, nor is there a single 'race gene' (Garcia 2007: 2) that can be specified as a basis for biological distinction – or, much less, is there such a gene that establishes a scientific basis for ranking different groups into hierarchies (Lombardo 2011) – or for explaining athletic performance. That said, across the world, an athlete's 'race' and their 'ethnicity' become important for a variety of reasons, not least of which is how they are treated within the sports they play.

Based on these assertions, sociologists, legal scholars and others argue that *race is a social construction*; it exists only through social interaction and by the behaviours of social actors; as such, we, as individuals but more importantly as a society, are forced to construct and reconstruct its abstract significance.

The legal scholar Lopez (2000) provides a case study of the social construction of race using his own 'mixed race' family wherein his brother 'chooses' to be White (as does his father) and he chooses to be non–White (as does his mother, who is Hispanic). In providing this portrait, Lopez concludes that, 'in my experience race reveals itself as plastic, inconstant, and to some extent volitional' (2000: 166).

Furthermore, as he states:

> I understand race as a mutable social construction that has been used historically to classify and stratify people based on clusters of physical characteristics. Race is defined by and against whiteness, an unmarked, invisible, and unexamined category that strategically has 'a touchstone quality of the normal, against which members of marked categories are defined', so that all members of marked categories possess race in ways that whites do not.
>
> (2000:144)

As Lopez alludes to, race is socially constructed, specifically for political purposes; and, in the US, access to many social, economic, political, educational and occupational institutions have been and often continue to be limited by race and racial identity.

We might also note the particular and peculiar history of classifying African Americans and other 'races' in the American Decennial Census (Prewitt 2013). For example, in the 1860 census, there were three racial categories: 'white', 'negro' and 'mulatto.' Immediately following the US Civil War, a special census was taken in 1865; those who identified as 'negro' or 'mulatto' were asked again to confirm their racial identity. Part of the purpose of this special census was to offer 'negroes' a chance to be 'returned' to Africa. Never mind the fact that only a small percentage of 'negroes' living in the US at that time had ever been to Africa, as most had been born in the US. The category 'mulatto' disappeared in both terminology and popular usage until 2000.

In the 2000 census, for the first time since the mid-1800s, individuals could choose more than one race. In response, approximately 13% of the US population identified as multi-racial, or deriving from more than one 'racial' category. The 2000 census was also important because it moved the designation 'Hispanic' out of the set of racial categories and into a special designation of 'ethnicity'. Interestingly 'Hispanic' is the *only* ethnic category in the US Census. Providing an illustration relevant to sports of how this single change impacted Hispanics, imagine the position of Dominican baseball players such as Sammy Sosa or Albert Pujols. According to the 1990 census, both men were classified racially as 'Hispanic'; in 2000 and 2010, they had lost that particular racial identity but acquired a new ethnicity. Racially, in the later censuses, they would have to choose to be either White or Black (or Asian/Pacific Islander or Native American/ Native Alaskan) and their ethnicity would be designated as 'Hispanic'.

Each man was the same person in 1990 and 2000. The traits we identify as 'racial' – skin tone, hair texture, facial features – did not change, but their racial identity did! Not surprisingly, in 2000 the majority of 'Hispanics' left the racial category blank. It didn't make sense to them that they were anything other than 'Hispanic'. These examples from the census and from Lopez highlight how race is socially constructed. They also demonstrate how the idea of race is very vaguely defined, and subject to major changes over time (Lopez 2000; Prewitt 2013).

Themes at the intersection of race and SportsWorld

From birth to death the racial or ethnic classification of the individual has direct impacts upon his or her station in life (Smith 2014). Here, we examine some of the ways in which race impacts sport (Fields 1990). To the casual observer, sport represents a level playing field, one in which talent trumps race and even gender. For the scholar of the sociology of sport, the research shows that this is still not the case.

Here we explore two 'themes' in the intersections of race and sport. Specifically, we examine 'exclusion' and 'individual and group level aggression'. Many of our examples in sport are drawn from the particular and peculiar experiences of African Americans in the US. That said, the US has not by any means limited discrimination to just African Americans and thus we include the experiences of other racial/ethnic groups.

Exclusion

As much of my (Smith's) previous research has demonstrated, race and sports are intertwined in many ways in the United States; for example, race shapes access to sports, the 'stacking' of athletes into specific playing positions and coaching opportunities, to list only a few issues (Smith 2014).

In order to best understand the origins of the exclusion of African Americans from various sporting activities, it is instructive to examine the logics that Whites have used to justify these barriers. As we shall see in subsequent examples, Whites applied the same process of 'logical explanation' to justify the exclusion or differential treatment of others as well.

Race has impacted sports participation of African Americans in two fundamental ways: (1) by restricting, either formally or informally, the sports they could participate in, and (2) by shaping the ideological beliefs about African Americans' intellectual and physical abilities in terms of sport participation and post-sport experiences.

The hegemonic ideological beliefs about African Americans – as lazy, shiftless and dumb – have been relatively stable over several centuries. These stereotypes have traction not only among 'rednecks' – a self-identified group of mostly rural, southern Whites who espouse allegiance to the Confederate flag – but by educated White males like Arthur Jensen, an educational psychologist from the University of California at Berkeley, who argued in a 1969 *Harvard Education Review* article, without credible evidence, that Whites were intellectually superior to African Americans. Another educated White male, William Shockley, winner of the 1956 Nobel Prize in Physics for co-inventing the transistor, made claims during a lecture to the National Academy of Sciences that the United States had a 'Negro problem'. Shockley claimed that 'Negroes' were reproducing in greater numbers than 'Caucasians', thus lowering the average intelligence of the American population; he concluded that African Americans should be sterilized to prevent further reproduction of 'defective children'. A good portion of Shockley's views on race, IQ and genetics appears in newspapers and magazines that support these far right perspectives.[2] These ideological beliefs played out in strange ways, such as by preventing African Americans from fighting in World Wars I and II, and from playing in certain positions in American sports.

Ideological beliefs about African Americans lacking intellectual acumen were expanded to incorporate further assumptions about hyper-sexuality and cowardice in warfare. In terms of restricting access to sports, there were commonly held beliefs that African Americans could not swim because they had 'fixed ankles' – which proved to be a comfortable excuse for keeping African Americans out of White swimming pools (Smith 2014) – as well as beliefs that were a direct outgrowth of stereotypes describing African Americans as unintelligent. The latter belief was a powerful tool in positional segregation in sports like baseball and American football. In short, the belief was that in a tight, competitive game – where control of the outcome lies firmly and exclusively with the quarterback or pitcher – African Americans could not make the intellectual decisions needed to secure victories (Smith and Henderson 2000; Smith and

Leonard 1997, Smith and Seff 1990). This is a similar 'logic' to the belief that African Americans would not, when confronted by the threat of an enemy in wartime, be able to make quick and intelligent decisions. As a result, Whites did not want African Americans fighting alongside them in their platoons because they perceived their mere presence as compromising their (Whites') safety.

These beliefs were around in American society in general and in SportsWorld in particular for most of the twentieth century; they may have since abated but are not entirely gone. Nor were (are) these racist beliefs and practices limited to characterizing African Americans in sports. For example, Peter Levine (1992) details the travails of the Jewish athlete in the United States, particularly second-generation migrants in the 1920s and 1930s. While Jews used sports to strengthen their ethnic pride and to ease assimilation into American culture, sports were also seen as a strategy for advancing their social mobility. Yet ironies abound. For the 1936 Berlin Olympics, two top Jewish athletes – Marty Glickman and Sam Stoller – earned places on the United States' 4 × 110 yard men's relay team and traveled to Germany to compete. Prior to the finals, US Olympic Committee Chairman Avery Brundage, a terrifying anti-Semite, and coach Dean Cromwell removed both athletes from the relay team (Levine 1992). Ironically, the replacement athletes were African Americans: Jesse Owens (who would win four gold medals) and Ralph Metcalfe.

Karabel (2005) explains the wider historical context of anti-Semitism in American higher education, which in turn blocked access to sports for young Jewish people (mostly men, as women were largely excluded from participating in intercollegiate sport regardless of their race or ethnic identity) simply because of the interconnectedness of intercollegiate sport in the overall US system of sport. All of the 'Ivy League' colleges, including Harvard, Princeton and Yale, held restrictive policies (implicit and explicit) on the admission of Jews. This, the reader will note, is very similar to the blocked access that African American student-athletes faced in the segregated southern states of the US.

Despite being denied entry to institutions of higher education and thereby access to one venue for developing as an athlete, great Jewish sports stars like Hank Greenberg (baseball), known affectionately as 'The Hebrew Hammer', did emerge. There were many other Jewish athletes who were highly successful during the interwar period, especially in boxing (Levine 1992). A defining moment for Jewish athletes took place in major league baseball in 1965, when Brooklyn Dodgers pitcher Sandy Koufax refused to pitch in Game One of the World Series because it was Yom Kippur, a Jewish holy day. Today there does not seem to be outward animosity towards Jewish athletes, but that is not to say anti-Semitism has ceased to exist.

Individual and group level aggression

Exclusion, as illustrated above, though it can be perpetrated by individuals – the coach who won't put a Black player at quarterback, the team owner who refused to hire a non-White coach – has the greatest impact when it is structural, such as when there is a quota or exclusion system for Jews or African Americans, as occurred with regard to American colleges and universities. We turn now to the kind of racism that readers are more likely familiar with: individual and group aggression. Though the overall impact here is actually much less significant because it involves individuals rather than entire populations, the stories are powerful and their personal impact on individual athletes is demonstrably profound. In many ways, these incidents are disconcerting insights into the wider racial climate and thus are worthy of discussion.

One initial, brief example is provided by one of the most dominant college and professional basketball players in the 1980s and 1990s, Patrick Ewing. Standing 7 feet tall and weighing

240 pounds, Ewing has incredible stature and was one of the first players to bring the current high levels of physicality to the men's basketball game. As an African American, and an extremely powerful and dominant man, he was a constant target for individual and group racial aggressions. His case illustrates not only the pervasiveness and content of the typical racism that African American athletes experience, but also highlights the fear that scholars like Orlando Patterson (1999) claim undergirds much of White male racism, a fear of the power of African American men.

While playing for Georgetown University, Ewing was a 'chief target' for racist abuse by fans. It was not uncommon for fans of opposing teams to hold up signs that said things like: 'Ewing Can't Read' or 'Ewing Kan't Read Dis'. These signs not only invoke the stereotype of African Americans as dumb, but they are particularly powerful in light of the fact that Georgetown University is among the elite academic institutions in the US. Thus, accusing Ewing of not being able to read was an indictment of Georgetown in allegedly treating an African American student athlete differently than the rest of the student body; the implication was that he was admitted for his skills on the court despite his *assumed* intellectual inferiority.

As our next, much more detailed example demonstrates, African American men are not the only targets of individual and group racial aggression; nor is basketball, where they make up approximately 80% of the top-flight NBA, the only arena for such abusive behaviour.

One of the best examples we can provide of this type of individual and group racial aggression is the abuse routinely thrown at Venus and Serena Williams, who have dominated women's tennis internationally for more than a decade. In the twenty-first century, one of the Williams sisters has won the Wimbledon women's singles title in 10 of the first 13 tournaments. In February 2015 Serena Williams won the Austrian Open, and in doing so she passes Chris Evert and Martina Navratilova to become third in the list of women's grand slam tennis championships. To say they have been dominant is an understatement. Yet, their success is even more impressive when one learns of the very painful racism they have experienced at the hands of tennis fans, including the parents of other players, as well as other women on the professional tour. The impact of these acts of individual and group racial aggression is perhaps best demonstrated by their collective decision to boycott Indian Wells, California, after their well-documented experiences in 2001, when they endured racist taunting and booing while on the court and in the stands. Their father, Richard Williams, and their mother, Oracene Price, very publicly discussed the individual and group aggressions that they witnessed against their daughters and themselves, as parents. Richard accused the crowd at Indian Wells of overt racism, stating, 'The white people at Indian Wells, what they've been wanting to say all along to us finally came out: "Nigger, stay away from here, we don't want you here"'. Venus Williams underscored his charge saying: 'I heard what he heard.' Oracene drew parallels with the tennis crowd and the white supremacist Ku Klux Klan, saying 'they [the audience] took off their hoods' (Smith and Hattery 2013). Serena Williams announced in spring 2015 that she would, for the first time in nearly 15 years, return to play at Indian Wells.

Such racially aggressive behavior has not been limited to fans. Venus and Serena have been targeted by other players as well. And the antagonisms have been personal, targeting them *explicitly as African American women*. Certainly some of the motivation for this behavior may be professional jealousy, though that does not offer an adequate explanation. For example, during an exhibition match in Brazil in 2012, Danish tennis player Caroline Wozniacki appeared on court having stuffed towels into her sports bra and her skirt in an attempt to impersonate Serena Williams, who has a body that is not typical among White women tennis players. Yet the Williams sisters have achieved success not only because of the biological characteristics they possess, perhaps most prominent in their strength, but also by pursuing an innovative training regime, both mental and physical, that has equipped them with a much better set of game-day skills than their rivals. In short, the Williams sisters win because they are more committed, successful agents than their opponents.

A recurring question in regard to race and sport relates to social class. Is the aggression more about class location than racial identity? In the case of elite minority athletes, the question is whether wealth insulates them from experiencing individual and group racial aggression. In the next section, we explore these issues a bit more closely.

Race versus class

Sometimes when writing about 'racism in SportsWorld' (Smith 2014) we encounter the beliefs that elite-level African American athletes, because of their fame, are protected from the individual and group racial aggressions expressed by fans. We will argue here that while fame can sometimes provide protection, even the most famous and financially successful are not totally immune.

The legal scholar Phoebe Weaver Williams provides evidence of the hostile work environment that the late Reggie White of the Green Bay Packers encountered at the same time that a spate of African American churches were being attacked by arsonists (Williams 1996: 292). White was a preacher campaigning to stop this criminal activity; indeed, his own church in Knoxville, Tennessee, was burned to the ground. Williams points out that during this period the Green Bay Packers specifically chose not to tell White that they had received threats targeting him because of his campaign. Despite his tremendous popularity, White was not immune to racialized aggressive behaviour. Williams (1996) summarizes the arising issues nicely:

> When seeking social reforms, African-Americans are reminded that our society rewards merit and excellence. Yet, the experiences of Black athletes, whose merits are meticulously, statistically, and publicly documented, undermine arguments that merit alone rather than race matters in our society. If Black athletes still experience racism, what of other African-Americans whose meritorious performances are not so quantifiable, not so public, and not so clearly extraordinary? If the wealth, the performances, and the economic value African-American athletes bring to our economy do not shield them from racism, then what will shield the rest of us?
>
> (1996: 292)

Another illustration can be seen in the treatment of Tiger Woods, undoubtedly the most successful male golfer of the past 30 years, who has been on the receiving end of racial epithets. Twice, other golfers (Fuzzy Zoeller and Sergio Garcia) have made racialized comments about Woods ordering fried chicken – a heavily stereotypical reference to African American food in the southern states. Both players later apologized for their comments. It is interesting to note how, like much of the abuse directed at Ewing and the Williams sisters, the defence of these comments is that they were simply a form of 'humour'.

Conclusion and recommendations

We have argued here that racism in sport unfolds in several ways. In this chapter we highlighted two ways or 'themes' in which racism is expressed: (1) exclusion and (2) individual and group aggression. When we attempt to move forward and identify recommendations for reducing racism in sports, we must have a clear understanding of the differences in these various expressions as each will require different actions.

Exclusion has, for the most part, moved beyond entire classes of people – such as all Jews or all African Americans – but it still exists as a result of both ideology and patterns of social segregation, which are difficult to eradicate. Several prominent African American athletes who play elite 'country club' sports, in which African Americans are grossly underrepresented (Smith 2014), have established development programs for African American youth. These initiatives include the Tiger Woods Learning Center, which focuses on a range of issues including education and golf, and the Legacy Youth Tennis and Education program, which has a similar focus, and in which the late Arthur Ashe was heavily involved. Additionally, one promising approach involves providing funding for under-resourced schools to establish sport programs and teams beyond American football and basketball; the aim here is for boys and girls of all racial and ethnic identities to have the opportunity to play an entire range of sports, including ice and field hockey, football (soccer), volleyball and wrestling.

Another area of significant exclusion is the opportunity to coach in college and professional football and basketball. Despite significant over-representation of African American players at both the college and professional levels, there has been a long-standing under-representation of African American coaches (Smith 2014). In the US there has been a lot of talk, less action, on the implementation of the Rooney Rule in professional sports such as football. The Rooney Rule was introduced in 2003 by Pittsburgh Steelers owner and former US ambassador to Ireland Dan Rooney.

The Rooney Rule stipulates that every time a head coaching position becomes vacant in the American National Football League (NFL), at least one minority candidate must be interviewed. Rooney's rationale was that this process would reveal appointable candidates who might otherwise be overlooked. Empirical research on this attempt to level the playing field has been limited, but in the end many scholars and activists note that it has not been successful in changing the racial landscape of NFL head coaches. One unintended consequence has been the emergence of sham interviews that are held for non-White applicants for posts in which the successful candidate is already identified.

One such example occurred with the Detroit Lions NFL team, when President Matt Millen (2002–2003) let it be known that his next head coach would be his friend Steve Mariucci, even before any of the interviews had been held. As a result, Millen could not keep to the Rooney Rule as no African American 'candidates', of the five contacted for the post, would travel to Detroit for a sham interview. Another example is Art Shell, who did coach for the Oakland Raiders, but after he was fired he became the token Rooney Rule candidate, never winning another coaching opportunity, unlike his similarly situated White colleagues with similar credentials who routinely gained second, third and even fourth chances. There are no minimum quotas for minority recruitment nor are there any penalties for teams that fail to achieve some measure of social diversity in their coaching or managerial staff. Arguably, teams should incur penalties for sham interviews.

If the Rooney Rule were extended into college sport, and had some 'teeth', such as penalties for not achieving an agreed level of diversity or for conducting sham interviews, then we can confidently anticipate that more African American men would have these opportunities. And, when groups that are initially excluded from an activity are offered access, they typically reach an equivalent level of performance and success, as we have certainly witnessed on the fields of play (Smith 2014).

Individual and group aggression is perhaps the most difficult form of racism to identify and to prevent. The lessons from the Civil Rights movement in the United States are a case in point. De facto segregation existed long past the time when laws had been passed against this practice. Changing attitudes is a difficult process and often takes generations to accomplish in any widespread manner. That said, we are optimistic and have one proposal that might be effective. Anti-racism measures and activities – such as the Rooney Rule, or the 'Kick It Out' campaigns in European football – are legitimate efforts to end structural racism in sports, but they are – in and of themselves – not enough to get the job done. We suggest that, certainly in the United States context, the national legal system should criminalize aggressive behaviour inside sport and beyond that has racist aspects. For example, fans caught engaging in aggressive behaviour – verbal or physical – could be detained by the facility security and fined. After a second offence, for example, they could be banned for life from attending future events. Fans could be arrested by the local law enforcement and charged with assault. Ultimately in the US, they could be charged with a hate crime. We wonder just how quickly these kinds of responses might result in reductions in individual and group aggression. We certainly would propose some sort of consequence for bad behaviour to see if it would in fact reduce aggressive acts.

Finally, we must note that we have one example that leaves us optimistic. One form of structured racism in team sports that has died a natural death is 'stacking'. Stacking was the most pernicious form of racism in team sports. As indicated earlier in this chapter, stacking involved coaches placing players into positions according to racial stereotypes, so non-White players were typically excluded from 'intelligent centre' roles, such as pitcher or catcher in baseball and quarterback in American football. Stacking had a long life. But today, we find many African American and non-White players in positions from which they were previously systematically excluded.

Notes

1 SportsWorld is a term coined by Earl Smith (2014). The term SportsWorld refers to the social, cultural, political and economic institutions that make up the sporting enterprise globally.
2 See, especially, http://science.howstuffworks.com/dictionary/famous-scientists/physicists/william-shockley-info.htm and http://www.youtube.com/watch?v=sAszZr3SkEs

References

Feagin, J. (2013) *The White Racial Frame*, New York: Routledge.
Fields, B. (1990) 'Slavery, Race and Ideology in the United States of America', *New Left Review*, 181: 95–118.
Garcia, M. (2007) 'Elmira Express Ernie Davis Runs Again in movie'. *USA Today*. Available at: http://usatoday30.usatoday.com/sports/college/football/2007-07-16-ernie-davis-feature_n.htm (accessed 11 April 2015).
Karabel, J. (2005) *The Chosen: The Hidden History of Admission and Exclusion at Harvard, Yale, and Princeton*, New York: Houghton Mifflin.
Levine, P. (1992) *Ellis Island to Ebbets Field: Sport and the American Jewish Experience*, New York: Oxford University Press.
Lombardo, P.A. (2011) *A Century of Eugenics in America: From the Indiana Experiment to the Human Genome Era*. Bloomington: Indiana University Press.
Lopez, H. (2000) 'The Social Construction of Race', in R. Del Gado and J. Stefancic (eds) *Critical Race Theory: The Cutting Edge*, Philadelphia: Temple University Press.
Patterson, O. (1999) *Rituals of Blood: Consequences of Slavery in Two American Centuries*, New York: Civitas.
Prewitt, K. (2013) *What Is Your Race? The Census and Our Flawed Efforts to Classify Americans*, Princeton, NJ: Princeton University Press.
Smith, E. (2014) *Race, Sport and the American Dream*, 3rd edition, Durham, NC: Carolina Academic Press.
Smith, E. and Hattery, A.J. (2013) 'Venus and Serena Williams: Traversing the Barriers of the Country Club World', in J. Rosen and D. Ogden (eds) *A Locker Room of Her Own: Celebrity, Sexuality, and Female Athletes*, Jackson: University of Mississippi Press.

Smith, E. and Henderson, D. (2000) 'Stacking in the Team Sport of Intercollegiate Baseball', in D. Brooks and R. Althouse (eds) *Racism in College Athletics*, 2nd edition, Morgantown, WV: Fitness Information Technology.

Smith, E. and Leonard, W. (1997) 'Twenty-Five Years of Stacking Research in Major League Baseball: An Attempt at Explaining This Re-occurring Phenomenon', *Sociological Focus*, 30: 321–331.

Smith E. and Seff, M. (1990) 'Race, Position Segregation and Salary Equity in Professional Baseball', *Journal of Sport and Social Issues*, 13: 100–119.

West, C. (2000) *Race Matters*, Boston: Beacon Press.

Williams, P. (1996) 'Performing in a Racially Hostile Environment', *Marquette Sports Law Journal*, 6: 287–314.

25

SEXUALITIES AND SPORT

Jayne Caudwell

In this chapter I offer discussion of sexualities and sport. As with many issues related to social divisions in sporting contexts, the debates and controversies are deep and far reaching. It is impossible to cover all aspects of this topic in one short book chapter, therefore I provide a particular overview of Lesbian Gay Bisexual Transgender Queer Intersex (LGBTQI) sport participation. I start by critically engaging with sexualities-based terminology. This is important because defining and naming are political processes that serve to produce social and cultural divisions. Then, I move to consider some examples of increasing access and participation, and I end with evidence of ever-present social divisions in society and sports that have a negative impact on sexually diverse individuals and communities.

Ontologies of sexualities

> To understand how sexology produced a variety of models of the [*sic*] *homosexuality*, it is necessary to conceive of sexology as a dynamic field that produces knowledge (and related medical practices) about sexuality.
>
> (Crozier 2014)

The origins of the naming of homosexuality are traced to the emergence of sexology in the late 1800s in Europe and the USA (Foucault 1990/1978). This sexological construction, and arguably re-construction of the homosexual and homosexuality (same-sex sex was not a new phenomenon), helped to produce simple and artificial boundaries between people and their sexual activities. Paradoxically, sexual acts and behaviours (oral sex and anal sex, to name the more graphic) between a woman and a man were deemed heterosexual, but identical acts between two women or two men were assigned as homosexual. Through pseudo-scientization, the individual as homosexual was, and continues to be, objectified, pathologized and medicalized (for example, through venereology and psychology). So-called homosexuality was also the focus of moral judgement. And, as I demonstrate later in this chapter, we continue to live with the legacies of these early definitions.

However, in recent history, a variety of terms and acronyms have emerged to help define, describe and explain the vast and complex nature of human sexuality. For example, a cursory glance at the Internet evidences the glorious multiplicity of sexuality-based definitions – see below for a few illustrative examples. As with previous 'models' of sexuality, it is often impossible to separate gender and sexuality. Suffice to say, for many contemporary theorists the inter-relationships between sex–gender–sexuality are inextricable (Butler 1990). With this in mind, the acronym LGBTQI covers a combination of both gender and sexuality. The acronym is by no means exhaustive, and importantly, a multitude of definitions and terms are emerging from within various communities, as evidenced by several websites:

Bigender: a person who fluctuates between traditionally 'woman' and 'man' gender-based behaviour and identities, identifying with both genders (and sometimes a third gender).

Binary gender: a traditional and outdated view of gender, limiting possibilities to 'man' and 'woman'.

Binary sex: a traditional and outdated view of sex, limiting possibilities to 'female' or 'male'.

Same-gender-loving (SGL): a phrase coined by the African American/Black queer communities used as an alternative for 'gay' and 'lesbian' by people who may see those as terms of the White queer community.

Skoliosexual: attracted to genderqueer and transsexual people and expressions (people who aren't identified as cisgender). (http://itspronouncedmetrosexual.com/2013/01/a-comprehensive-list-of-lgbtq-term-definitions/)

Asexual: one who feels no sexual attraction or desire towards any gender identity; free from or unaffected by sexuality.

GSM: an acronym for 'gender and/or sexuality minority'. This is the basic catch-all for people who are not cisgender and/or heterosexual. It is more encompassing than the traditional LGBT and other such acronyms while still including those who don't identify as queer or who are offended by the term. (http://queerdictionary.tumblr.com)

Bisexual: a person who is attracted to two sexes or two genders, but not necessarily simultaneously or equally. This used to be defined as a person who is attracted to both genders or both sexes but since there are not only two sexes (see *intersex* and *transsexual*) and there are not only two genders (see *transgender*), this definition is inaccurate.

Cisgender: a person who by nature or by choice conforms to gender/sex-based expectations of society (also referred to as 'gender-straight' or 'gender normative').

Cisgenderism: assuming every person to be cisgender, therefore marginalizing those who identify as trans in some form. It is also believing cisgender people to be superior, and holding people to traditional expectations based on gender, or punishing or excluding those who don't conform to traditional gender expectations.

Genderqueer: a person whose gender identity is neither man nor woman, is between or beyond genders or is some combination of genders. This identity is usually related to or in reaction to the social construction of gender, gender stereotypes and the gender binary system. Some genderqueer people identify under the transgender umbrella while others do not.

Pansexual: a person who is fluid in sexual orientation and/or gender or sex identity.

Polyamory: the practice of having multiple open, honest love relationships. (http://geneq.berke ley.edu/lgbt_resources_definiton_of_terms#pansexual)

Queer: used as an umbrella identity term encompassing lesbian, questioning people, gay men, bisexuals, non-labeling people, transgender folks and anyone else who does not strictly identify as heterosexual.

Transgender: this term has many definitions. It is frequently used as an umbrella term to refer to all people who deviate from their assigned gender at birth or the binary gender system. This includes transsexuals, cross-dressers, genderqueers, drag kings, drag queens, two-spirit people and others. Some transgender people feel they exist not within one of the two standard gender categories, but rather somewhere between, beyond or outside of those two genders. (http://international spectrum.umich.edu/life/definitions)

Intersex: a general term used for a variety of conditions in which a person is born with a reproductive or sexual anatomy that doesn't seem to fit the typical definitions of female or male. (http://www.isna.org/faq/what_is_intersex)

Explaining, describing and defining sexualities has socio-cultural and political ramifications. Scholars of sexuality (e.g. Foucault 1990/1978; Warner 2000) demonstrate how naming, language and discourse produce dominant notions of sexuality and sex acts, as well as human subjectivity. Within this post-structuralist theoretical scaffold, 'subjectivity' is the preferred term to 'identity' because subjectivity signals the diverse, layered and fluid nature of so-called identity, and it highlights the continuous role of the social, cultural and historic in producing the self as a 'subject'. In contrast, 'identity', as it is often viewed, refers to a fixed way of being. And yet, identity has social and cultural meaning for many people. Regardless of preference for the concept of subjectivity or identity, those who have challenged the linguistic labelling of 'others' – e.g. sexual minorities – have revealed some of the intricate, everyday, subtle mechanisms of domination, subordination and subjugation.

For example, language and discourse are significant to any understanding of abuse, discrimination, harassment, prejudice and persecution. In many cultures and societies, language and discourse bring people and communities into being. Frequently, individual and community identities and subjectivities are produced through language and labelling. Undeniably this occurs within sporting contexts. This is especially the case for LGBTQI, and this hailing into existence is fraught with tension. Despite having hugely pejorative dimensions, terms and acronyms remain important to LGBTQI communities and individuals. The above definitions, gleaned from the Internet, attest to the positively-generative and productive potential of self-naming and self-identification through language.

To compound the issues surrounding the ownership of linguistic definitions, these ontologies of sexualities are complicated by the meanings attached to LGBT as well as LGBTQI. I have discussed this in detail elsewhere:

> LGBT suggests artificial alliances between groups of people who have diverse sexual and gendered identities/subjectivities as well as complex social locations of class, ethnicity, disability and age. Even within these individual groups, experiences of sexuality

and gender are discontinuous. Additionally, the label (LGBT) frequently becomes synonymous with the experiences of lesbian and gay individuals and communities.

(Caudwell 2012b: 4)

LGBT and LGBTQI, along with other acronyms such as LGBPTTQQIIAA+,[1] appear to
denote a number of separate sexuality- and gender-based communities and individuals. For
some, both the separate names and the umbrella terms allow for a politics of identity and the
gravitas that identity politics provides within the political-judicial system (e.g. age of consent,
right to marry). However, these acronyms work from the idea of a stable and fixed identity,
which is not the case for many who belong to a gender and sexual minority (GSM). Additionally, there is concern that these acronyms create hierarchies of visibility.

Within sport studies, 'lesbian' and 'gay' sport experience and sport participation are well
documented. I discuss this further in the next section on in/visibility. In this way, the terms 'lesbian' and 'gay' are easily understood; they represent and reflect same-sex attraction. Both lesbian
studies and gay studies are established scholarly fields within sport studies. They have tended to
develop separately with research and literatures usually focusing on either lesbians (e.g. Griffin
1998) or gay men (e.g. Anderson 2005).

The purpose of a critical engagement with ontologies of sexuality is to make the argument
that within the study of sexualities and sport, certain terms (homosexual, lesbian and gay) are
familiar, they are understood within Western academic circles and they have enabled research,
intervention and transformation of some sporting cultures and practices. However, the point is
that the fixing of same-sex attraction to 'lesbian' and 'gay' forgets the vastness of gendered and
sexualized individuals and communities. It closes down the possibilities to explore the entirety
of sexualities and sport, and it forgets the social divisions that might be faced by bisexual, transgender, queer and intersex as well as questioning and unsure individuals. For example, what do
we know about asexuality, genderqueer sexuality, skoliosexuality, pansexuality and polyamory in
sport? How are attraction, desire, lust, love, romance, sex and embodiment socially sanctioned
and culturally configured for sexual minorities who do not self-define as lesbian and gay?

Visibility of sexualities

Recently, in the UK, we have witnessed – via mass-mediated reports – the 'coming out' of
elite male athletes such as Robbie Rogers, Jason Collins, Tom Daley, Thomas Hitzlsperger
and Michael Sam. Previously, a similar flurry of public 'coming out' narratives involved John
Amaechi, Gareth Thomas, Steven Davies and Anton Hysen. We have received less hype about
elite female athletes, but there has been some coverage of Brittney Griner, Nicola Adams, the
field-hockey couple Helen Richardson and Kate Walsh, and Casey Stoney. Although these stories are not entirely about the white male athlete, there is some evidence that they do tend to
make more visible white male gay and bisexual sexuality. At this juncture, the media institutions
and the UK public at large appear at ease with both the telling, re-telling and hearing of dec-
larations such as Tom Daley's: 'Of course I still fancy girls but right now I'm dating a guy and
I couldn't be happier' (*BBC News*, 2 December 2013).

In amongst this mainstreaming of 'out' LGB-sexuality, and in the aftermath of London 2012,
The Independent provided a 'top 10' of 'the growing numbers of athletes to publicly announce
their sexuality'.[2] Of the 10 featured, only two rankings tell of women. No. 7 is GB boxing gold
medalist Nicola Adams and No. 4 is GB hockey bronze medalists Kate Walsh and Helen Richardson. Nicola Adams declared her bisexuality and Kate Walsh and Helen Richardson shared the
details of their civil partnership (September 2013) with the British media.

Accompanying this seemingly positive attention by the UK media, the Coalition Government (2010–) passed legislation to 'allow' same-sex marriage in England and Wales (July 2013) on 14 March 2014 and thereafter. Scotland followed this move towards sexuality equality on 4 February 2014. Specifically related to sport, the Coalition Government also passed a Charter for Action on 4 March 2011: *Tackling Homophobia and Transphobia in Sport.* These legislative and policy initiatives can operate to support LGBT visibility. However, at the same time as applauding these moves, it is important to take a critical view on what is effectively a right-wing government's involvement with sexuality, and sexuality and sport.

In many ways, it is easy to explain the recent shifts in the UK's media and statutory response to same-sex sexuality through notions of progress, equality and perhaps affect. Those such as the pressure group Stonewall, who have lobbied for same-sex visibility within law and popular cultural activities, might argue that they have achieved some of their aims, for example, for same-sex couples to have the same legal rights as heterosexual couples. This equality has been achieved through sexual identity politics, underpinned by human rights. Surrounding these sexual cultural politics of inclusion there have been sentiments of Pride. Pride is a complicated and contested construct within LGBTQI cultures, not least because it is juxtaposed with Shame and within this binary set-up Pride is viewed as more desirable (Davidson 2006). Clearly, Shame and Pride are more complicated than this (Probyn 2005) because politics and privilege underpin the production, reproduction and experiences of Shame as well as Pride. In this way, emotion and affect become political currency and these arrangements help shape socio-cultural relations of power.

In terms of emotion and affect (cf. Wetherall 2012), mass spectator sports, especially sporting spectacles such as the Olympic games, seek to engage the participants and viewers on an emotional level (Pringle, in press). A critical view of this mass-generated and nationwide production of emotion and affect reveals the operation of dominant ideologies and discourses, and the social significance of Pride in sporting context; we are proud of 'our' medal winners. In the same way, as a nation, we are proud 'we' are not homophobic.

And yet, through increased LGB visibility – both mediated and government-driven inclusion policy initiatives – we learn only that athletes who identify as lesbian, gay or bisexual are sexually attracted to the same sex (as well as the opposite sex in the case of bisexuals). Through these rather simplistic representations of sexuality – same-sex/opposite sex attraction – LGB athletes have been hailed into existence via the media and the state. However, this mainstreaming, and regulation, of LGB sexualities within UK society and sport are shallow and can be aligned with notions of homonormativity[3] whereby athletes who come 'out' are acceptable because they adopt many of the practices of idealized heteronormativity (for example, participating in monogamous relationships, marriage, and child rearing). That is, some LGB sexualities are no longer socially and politically separated as non-normative. This lack of division appears to signal progress for LGB athletes. However, the social divisions have shifted, and it is evident that queer sexualities and messy sexualities – in other words, non-normative sexualities – do not feature positively within public celebrations of sexuality and sport.

There is a silence surrounding sexualities such as genderqueer, skoliosexual, pansexual and asexual. These 'other' sexualities operate outside of the traditional sex-gender-desire binaries that now frame both same-sex and opposite-sex attraction. Consequently, there are emerging social divisions – again producing dominance and subordination – within sexual minority populations.

As I highlight at the start of this chapter, within the various acronyms that help define and celebrate the diversity of sexuality, transgender sexualities receive far less consideration. Transgender and transsexual athletes have received severe scrutiny from the governing bodies of elite competitive sport such as the International Olympic Committee. But the absence of everyday accounts of transgender athletes creates an invisibility that works to further marginalize their active involvement with sport. In most cases, when there is visibility, transgender becomes a gender-based issue almost empty of sexuality.

There are a few known transgender athletes in popular cultural sporting contexts and this has gone some way to enhancing opportunities for transgender sport communities. Recently, for example, there was some positive coverage of Johnny 'Jayiah' Saelua (e.g. Bagchi 2011; Montague 2011). Jayiah played centre-back for American Samoa in the men's FIFA World Cup qualification rounds in 2011. As reported in the press, Jayiah is '*fa'afafine*, biologically male but identified as a third sex widely accepted in Polynesian culture. She . . . is the first transgender player to compete in a World Cup match . . . with . . . Rawlston Masaniai, who along with other team-mates, calls her "sister"'(Bagchi 2011: ¶ 9). A comment from the team coach, Thomas Rongen, furthers this public positioning of Jayiah as female and feminine: 'I've really got a female starting at centre back. Can you imagine that in England or Spain?'.[4] Despite Jeyiah's moment of brief visibility, there is nothing of her sexuality, only her gender identity. Transgender sexuality appears often as taboo and unimaginable.

In comparison with lesbian and gay sport participation, there are few studies of transgender athletes' participation. What we do know tends to explore the circumstances facing individual transgender athletes within teams of cisgender or lesbian athletes (e.g. Travers 2006; Travers and Deri 2011) or elite athletes facing the strict rulings and medical procedures of the IOC (Caudwell 2012a; Cavanagh and Sykes 2006; Sykes 2006). That said, there appear to be sport-participation opportunities for groups of transgender individuals in the UK in the form of swimming. These opportunities include Marlin in Manchester, Out to Swim in Clapham, Tyne Trans Swimming Group and Different Strokes in Edinburgh. In the case of Marlin, the following information is provided:

> Marlin is Manchester's trans swimming group. It is open to all trans people, MTF and FTM. It is FREE due to funding from Pride Sports. We have exclusive use of the pool during this time. Changing facilities are individual cubicles around the side of the pool. You can wear whatever you feel most comfortable in, as long as it's safe to wear for swimming.
>
> The staff in attendance have been specially trained also, so no need to worry about that either.[5]

So far, there are few accounts and/or representations within the sociology of sport of how transgender athletes experience embodiment and sexuality. Swimming is an activity that often involves amplified and diverse embodied sensation. As well as the familiar by-products of physical activity – such as increases in breathing and pulse rates, and skin temperatures – the swimmer's skin is in contact with, and moves through, water. More broadly, we know very little about how this haptic experience links with embodiment, sensuality and sexuality. There is some commentary on runners' bodies and the sensual (Hockey 2006), but it is not related to sexuality, and there is emerging work on lesbian surfers' embodiment, which does connect with sexualities (Roy 2013).

Perhaps martial arts are other forms of sports that allow for sensual embodiments, although these issues continue to be only partially addressed in contemporary culture. In the film *Beautiful Boxer* (2005), we learn of a young Thai person's desire to transcend. The protagonist Nong Toom becomes a muay Thai martial artist in order to make money to achieve these transitions. The boxer's body is central to the film's narrative and the representation of this 'true story'. Despite some disruption and dislocation of traditional notions of gendered and sexual embodiments, not much is disclosed of the sexual dimensions of sporting and transitioning bodies. We do learn something of the gendered dimensions of the boxer's body, but, again, sexuality is largely absent.

Transitioning bodies open new ways to experience body parts and embodied sensuality (see Davy 2012), especially during moments of physical activity. And yet, these potentially queer and queering moments remain unknown within the sociology of sport. Interesting questions might be – do new sensual, erogenous and erotic body zones appear and develop for transgender athletes? If so, how do these new bodily sensations shape sexuality at different levels, for instance at the levels of the personal, interpersonal and cultural?

The social divisions that contain sexualities in many societies and in sport tend to operate on the level of language, definition and the human rights of LGB people. Some long-standing social divisions in some Western nations have been dissolved and there are notable shifts to increasing the visibility of LGB athletes, albeit centred upon sexuality as same-sex attraction and concomitant legal rights. Notably, there is little by way of exploration of embodied sensuality and how this might impact on breaking down social divisions in sport. Significant social divisions persist in sport and these involve transgender, transsexual and queer individuals and communities. Such divisions are not benign; they carry significant sanctions and brutalities. In some countries these consequences are targeted at the LGBT community as a whole.

The brutalities of social divisions

In sharp contrast to positive representations of LGBT athletes – and perhaps some of this juxtapositioning is partially created by Western media – the brutalities of homophobia in Russia surrounded political discussion and media coverage of the Sochi Winter Olympics 2014. At this writing, Russia's so-called Anti-Gay Laws continues to face fierce opposition and legitimate calls for amendment.[6] These laws, enacted in 2013 to a wave of international criticism, banned what is referred to as 'propaganda of non-traditional sexual relationships'. Western journalists have produced hard-hitting – sometimes sensationalist – accounts of how LGBT individuals in Russia are persecuted as a consequence of an increasing focus on anti-gay legislation (for example, in the UK Channel 4 documentary 'Hunted' for the *Dispatches* series, 31 January 2014).

If the Russian government heeds the significant concerns of human rights campaigners – for example, Amnesty International, Human Rights Watch and others advocating for equality and anti-discrimination – and changes the blatantly 'Anti-Gay' Law, then the desired repeal might be relatively swift. However, it is too early to tell whether international campaigns and critical media reports will have an impact, in the long term, on the Russian legislation. In many ways, now that the Winter Olympics is over the issue has faded from the global limelight.

Repeal of regressive legislations takes considerable time, and we have to look only as far as the UK for a prime example. The renowned 'Section 28' legislation, which was introduced by the Conservative Government, took 15 years to repeal (1988–2003), and the repeal process was not straightforward. Section 28 had specifically prohibited local government, under the 1986 Local Government Act (prohibition of political publicity), from 'the promoting of homosexuality by teaching or by publishing material'. There are many similarities between this past UK legislation and current Russian (and Ugandan) legislation, the main similarities being the criminalization of so-called promotion of homosexuality; the political, legislative and legal denial of recognition of same-sex relationships and same-sex sexual acts; and the defining of homosexuality as non-traditional, 'pretend' and diseased. On a fundamental level, Section 28 and other 'anti-gay' legislation serves to produce political and legal demarcations of sexual difference, and countries that adopt such laws are in effect creating statutory social divisions that are set in law.

Sporting mega-events such as the Olympics have received critical scrutiny from a range of global commentators, including the media, social justice campaigners and human rights activists. Issues surrounding sexuality join a lengthening list of human rights abuses relating to indigenous peoples, local residents and migrant workers. Sochi is not the only mega-event host city or nation that may be deemed homophobic, as this editorial points out:

> Enthusiastically backing Hitzlsperger seemed like an open goal for the organization [FIFA], particularly with its recent patchy record on gay rights. The 2018 World Cup will be held in Russia, which has introduced laws to ban gay 'propaganda'; four years later, the tournament moves to Qatar, where homosexuality is still punished with a prison sentence. There is genuine speculation that players and spectators will be vetted by a Kuwaiti-engineered 'gay test' in 2022.
>
> When Sepp Blatter, the Clouseau-esque president of Fifa, was asked in 2010 about the issue, he smiled and suggested that homosexual football fans would just have to 'refrain from sexual activity' in Qatar. Pushed further last June, he deflected: 'What you are speaking about . . . this is going into ethics and morals.'
>
> ('Fifa's Stance' 2014)

Ethics and morals are a reminder of the politico-religious discourses set up during the initial era of sexology in the West (late nineteenth century). Within these discourses, heterosexuality is positioned as the only viable expression of sexuality and sex acts. In other words, sexual activity available to almost all human adults must only take place between a woman and a man. If this convention is breached in the slightest, the sex act is positioned as illegal and absolute sanctions prevail in some nation-states. These sanctions are not only imposed through a legal-judicial framework (e.g. UK in the period 1986–2003), they are often enforced at the level of the personal. The rapes of South African women soccer players Mvuleni Fana, Tumi Mkhuma and Eudy Simelane are chilling reminders.

In 2008, 'soccer star' Eudy Simelane was raped and murdered by a group of men in Kwa Thema, Gauteng, South Africa. Simelane, a midfield player for South Africa and the national team Banyana Banyana, lived openly as a lesbian (Diesel 2011; Msibi 2009). She was a gay rights activist and a coach and referee as well as a player. In short, she was well known for her involvement in football and for her lesbian sexuality (Meises 2009; Msibi 2009). It is widely acknowledged that she was 'gangraped [sic], beaten and stabbed to death for her perceived flouting of conservative/traditional gender stereotypes' (Diesel 2011: xvi).

The way Eudy Simelane was killed has become known as 'corrective rape', an atrocious crime perpetrated by men. Kelly, in *The Guardian*, cites campaigners when she writes: '"corrective rape" [is] committed by men behind the guise of trying to "cure" lesbians of their sexual orientation' (2009, ¶ 2). Corrective rape is often associated with South Africa; however, there is evidence of corrective rape in Russia, Ecuador and in other African states (e.g. Nigeria and Uganda). Human rights organizations such as Amnesty International have warned of a rise in this type of homophobic crime in countries that have criminalized same-sex acts and relationships. In regard to Africa, Amnesty argue that existing (homophobic) legislation and penal codes can be traced back to a colonial past and the imposition of Christian moral values. India provides a recent example of this colonial legacy. In January 2014, India's parliament refused to consider abolishing an 1861 law passed under British colonial rule, which gives police the power to arrest anyone suspected of homosexuality. The now 153-year-old law mandates 10-year prison sentences for homosexual acts.

And yet, there are recent socio-cultural histories that continue to engender brutal homophobic crimes against women (and men), such as corrective rape and murder, especially in parts of Africa. I noted earlier the legislation in Uganda. Elsewhere, on 13 January 2014 President Goodluck Jonathan authorized a severe tightening of Nigeria's existing anti-gay laws.

Countries that boast gender and sexual egalitarianism are not exempt from the brutalities that occur in public spaces and involve individual LGBT campaigners and activists. On 8 March 2014 (International Women's Day), Showan Shattak, a 25-year-old gay activist who helped set up Sweden's 'Football Supporters Against Homophobia', was stabbed several times by neo-Nazis during a rally against sexism. Importantly, Malmö FF, one of Sweden's leading men's professional football clubs, has publicly declared their support and concern for Shattak. We are yet to hear of the criminal consequences facing the perpetrators of this heinous attack.

Addressing social divisions in sport does not happen within a vacuum; broader and dominant historical, social, cultural, political and judicial configurations must be taken into consideration. In terms of the brutalities of social divisions based on sexuality, many LGBT activists within sport are activists in their communities, thus reflecting the need for connections between sport and wider society.

Conclusions

In this chapter, I have emphasized the importance of language and definition in the production of sexual subjectivity. In particular, I highlight the importance of self-definition and self-identification for and by sexual minorities. As a way to illustrate this point, I display a range of terms that come from within gender and sexual minority communities. The quantity of defining terms and phrases is irrelevant, but some have acquired more cultural currency than others. Within mainstream sport, 'lesbian', 'gay' and, increasingly, 'bisexual', are coherent descriptors of sexuality. Within the sociology of sport, lesbian studies and gay studies are established fields of inquiry and we appear to grasp and accept same-sex attraction. In many ways, the divisions between heterosexual and LGB athletes have lessened in some sports and some societies. Often, this acceptance is based on notions of a stable and fixed sexuality, and the production of homonormativity.

Naming continues to produce social divisions, and in some societies and cultures the human rights of sexual minorities are improving. These social divisions, which bolster calls for human rights, are productive. In sport in the UK, we might measure this through public 'coming out' stories and celebrations of Pride. However, for others around the world, LGBT human rights are either ignored or obliterated. Crimes against LGBT people are based on politically and legally instigated discourses of illegitimacy and the production of powerful state-supported homophobia. This context has a profound effect on sport and sport participants, and I have provided some examples of violent and bloody crimes against sexual minorities.

During this chapter, I have raised the issue of the lack of research and literature, within sport studies, on transgender, transsexual, queer and messy sexualities (non-normative sexuality). Despite increasing examples of transgender and transsexual athletes and their sporting opportunities, there is little that explores transgender and transsexual sexuality. For these individuals and groups, gender identity appears to be the main focus of inquiry. Such an approach can operate to make transgender and transsexual athletes and participants falsely asexual. Additionally, given the close connections between transgender, transsexuality and embodiment, it is surprising that there is little on the links between sport, the body, sensuality and sexuality. Perhaps the transitioning body is used to a hidden and silent presence because of prejudice and discrimination. If so, we are missing a potential wealth of embodied narratives that might help change the nature of physical activity and sport. At present – within the LGBTQI collective – T, Q and I remain largely unknown sexual subjectivities and this oversight functions to maintain layers of social division.

Finally, my overriding questions (which I have been unable to answer in this chapter), in relation to the brutalities of social divisions are: What is at stake by producing, maintaining, reinforcing and reproducing social divisions of sexuality? Is it a simple case of policing the assumed illegitimacy of certain anatomical sexual acts? In other words, is the issue here simply how body parts fit together during sensual and sexual intercourse? Or, are there deeper issues involving the affectual and emotional dimensions of sexualities? As yet, the sociology of sport has not explained the role of affect and emotion in the study of social divisions based on sexuality. Such a discussion might extend the human rights agenda, which is fundamental to any discussion of the negative impacts of social divisions and divided societies.

Notes

1 This acronym refers to lesbian, gay, bisexual, pansexual, transgender, transsexual, queer, questioning, intersex, intergender, asexual, ally identities. See http://itspronouncedmetrosexual.com/2013/01/a-comprehensive-list-of-lgbtq-term-definitions/ (accessed on 30 April 2014).
2 See http://www.independent.co.uk/sport/general/others/tom-daley-olympic-diver-should-not-feel-alone-after-he-joins-a-growing-number-of-athletes-to-publicly-announce-their-sexuality-8977860.html?action=gallery&ino=3 (accessed on 22 July 2014).
3 Duggan (2002: 179) understands this in terms of 'a politics that does not contest dominant heteronormative assumptions and institutions, but upholds and sustains them, while promising the possibility of a demobilized gay constituency and a privatized, depoliticized gay culture anchored in domesticity and consumption'.
4 As quoted in Different Trains (2011), 'American Samoa Football Team Third Gender/Transgender Player'. See http://forum.transgenderzone.com (accessed on 22 July 2014).
5 See http://marlin.org.uk (accessed on 2 July 2014).
6 Additionally, on 24 February 2014, Ugandan president Yoweri Museveni signed an anti-gay bill, thus compounding the existing criminalization of homosexuality in Uganda. The bill includes life imprisonment for gay sex and same-sex marriage. It also criminalizes the 'promotion' of homosexuality. As many have reported, this legislation is deeply and disturbingly homophobic; according to Amnesty International, it 'will institutionalize hatred and discrimination against LGBTI people in Uganda' (http://www.amnesty.org.uk/ugandas-anti-homosexuality-bill-becomes-law#.U7QvAha4klI; accessed on 2 July 2014).

References

Anderson, E. (2005) *In the Game: Gay Athletes and the Cult of Masculinity*, Albany: SUNY Press.
Bagchi, R. (2011) 'Amazing Transformation of American Samoa from Whipping Boys to Winners', *The Observer*, 26 November. Available at: http://www.theguardian.com/football/2011/nov/26/american-samoa-first-victory (accessed 30 March 2015).
Butler, J. (1990) *Gender Trouble: Feminism and the Subversion of Identity*, London: Routledge.
Caudwell, J. (2012a) 'Sex Watch: Surveying Women's Sexed and Gendered Bodies at the Olympics', in J. Sugden and A. Tomlinson (eds) *Watching the Games: Politics, Power and Representation in the London Olympiad*, London: Routledge.
Caudwell, J. (2012b) '[Transgender] Young Men: The Physically Active Body and Gendered Subjectivities', *Sport, Education and Society*, doi:10.1080/13573322.2012.672320.
Cavanagh, S. and Sykes, H. (2006) 'Transsexual Bodies at the Olympics: The International Olympic Committee's Policy on Transsexual Athletes at the 2004 Athens Summer Games', *Body & Society* 12(3): 75–102.
Crozier, I. (2014) 'Sexology and Homosexuality'. Available at: http://www.academia.edu/2020002/Homosexuality_and_Sexology_-a_draft_of_an_encyclopaedia_entry (accessed 2 July 2014).
Davidson, J. (2006) 'The Necessity of Queer Shame for Gay Pride: The Gay Games and Cultural Events', in J. Caudwell (ed.) *Sport, Sexualities and Queer/Theory*, London: Routledge.
Davy, Z. (2012) 'Bodily Aesthetic Affects in Trans Erotica: Towards a Wider Spectra of Desire', paper presented at British Sociological Association Annual Conference, 11–13 April, Leeds University, UK.
Diesel, A. (ed.) (2011) *Reclaiming the L-word: Sappho's Daughters Out in Africa*, Athlone, SA: Modjaji Books.

Different Trains (2011) 'American Samoa Football Team Third Gender/Transgender Player'. Available at: http://forum.transgenderzone.com/viewtopic.php?f=8&t=2593#.U7QnVRa4klJ (accessed 2 July 2014).

Duggan, L. (2002) 'The New Homonormativity: The Sexual Politics of Neoliberalism', in R. Castronova and D.D. Nelson (eds) *Materializing Democracy: Towards a Revitalized Cultural Politics*, Durham, NC: Duke University Press.

'Fifa's Stance on Homophobia Is Failing Gay Footballers: Thomas Hitzlsperger's Announcement Should Spur Football's Governing Body into More Positive Action' (2014) *Observer*, 12 January. Available at: http://www.theguardian.com/commentisfree/2014/jan/12/fifa-gay-footballers-thomas-hitzlsperger (accessed 30 March 2015).

Foucault, M. (1990/1978) *The Will of Knowledge. The History of Sexuality: 1*, London: Penguin.

Griffin, P. (1998) *Strong Women, Deep Closets. Lesbians and Homophobia in Sport*, Leeds, UK: Human Kinetics.

Hockey, J. (2006) 'Sensing the Run: The Senses and Distance Running', *The Senses and Society*, 1(2): 183–201.

Kelly, A. (2009) Raped and killed for being a lesbian: South Africa ignores 'corrective' attacks. Online. Available at HTTP: http://www.guardian.co.uk/world/2009/mar/12/eudy-simelane-corrective-rape-south-africa (accessed 27 June 2013).

Mieses, A. (2009) 'Gender Inequality and Corrective Rape of Women Who Have Sex with Women', *Gay Men's Health Crisis Treatment Issues* (December). Available at: http://www.gmhc.org/files/editor/file/ti-1209.pdf (accessed 11 April 2015).

Montague, J. (2011) 'A First in Cup Qualifying for a Player and a Team', *The New York Times*, 25 November. Available at: http://www.nytimes.com/2011/11/26/sports/soccer/jonny-saelua-transgender-player-helps-american-samoa-to-first-international-soccer-win.html?_r=0 (accessed 30 March 2015).

Msibi, T. (2009) 'Not Crossing the Lines: Masculinities and Homophobic Violence in South Africa', *Agenda*, 23(80): 50–54.

Pringle, R. (in press) 'The Pleasurable Is Political: An Affective Analysis of Viewing the Olympics', in R. Pringle, R.E. Rinehart and J. Caudwell (in press) *Sport and the Social Significance of Pleasure*, London: Routledge.

Probyn, E. (2005) *Blush: Faces of Shame*, Minneapolis: University of Minnesota.

Roy, G. (2013) 'Women in Wetsuits: Revolting Bodies in Lesbian Surf Culture', *Journal of Lesbian Studies*, 17(3–4): 329–343.

Sykes, H. (2006) 'Transsexual and Transgender Policies in Sport', *Women in Sport and Physical Activity Journal*, 15(1): 3–13.

Travers, A. (2006) 'Queering Sport: Lesbian Softball Leagues and the Transgender Challenge', *International Review for the Sociology of Sport*, 41(3–4): 431–446.

Travers, A. and Deri, J. (2011) 'Transgender Inclusion and the Changing Face of Lesbian Softball Leagues', *International Review for the Sociology of Sport*, 46(4): 488–507.

Warner, M. (2000) *The Trouble with Normal: Sex, Politics, and the Ethics of Queer Life*. Cambridge, MA: Harvard University Press.

Wetherell, M. (2012) *Affect and Emotion: A New Social Science Understanding*, London: Sage.

26

DISABILITY AND SPORT

The case of the Paralympic Games

P. David Howe

This chapter will outline what I believe to be the key issues for a robust sociological under-standing of disability in sport, with specific reference to the Paralympic Games. Those who are interested in sociological issues related to sport and disability are more than likely to have come across media images related to the Paralympic Games. For this reason, the relatively high-profile event that is the Paralympic Games will be the focus of this chapter. Therefore, it is important that the issues raised in regards to the Paralympic Games also have a social impact upon disability sport at the grassroots level. To begin this sociological discussion I will first focus on a brief out-line of the structure of Paralympic sport organization before turning my attention to exploring the relevance of the socio-political field of disability studies to Paralympic research. This will be followed by the issue of integration of athletes with disabilities into 'mainstream' sports and the sociological interpretation of athlete classification. Paralympic bodies will be the final focus of the chapter because it is at the level of the individually impaired body where we are best placed to explore issues of agency of the athletic body in which issues related to degree of impairment, gender, and technology will be highlighted.

Before the establishment of the International Paralympic Committee (IPC) in 1989, sport for the disabled was organized internationally by a number of sporting federations. Each of these federations had a responsibility to a constituent body of member nations and structured a sport-ing calendar for impairment-specific groups, from grassroots to international level (DePauw and Gavron 1995). The federations, namely the Cerebral Palsy International Sport and Recrea-tion Association (CP-ISRA), International Blind Sport Association (IBSA), International Sports Federation for Persons with Intellectual Disability (INAS-FID), and the International Wheel-chair and Amputee Sport Association (IWAS),[1] were established with the explicit intention of creating opportunities for people with disabilities and using sport as a vehicle for their empow-erment. Collectively these federations are known as the International Organizations for Sport for the Disabled (IOSDs). It was the IOSDs and their predecessors that helped to organize the Paralympic Games from 1960 through to 1988. Early games were organized and run on a much smaller scale than those under the influence of the IPC. The rapid growth of the IPC in the last few years has enabled it to establish an extensive network of 164 national affiliates that in some cases replicate or replace the national governing bodies of the federations.

The IPC currently organizes and administers both the Paralympic Games and the quadren-nial World Championships for individual Paralympic sports, such as swimming and athletics.

Using the resources of the four federations listed above (including athletes, volunteer administrators, and classification systems) the IPC has arguably turned the Paralympic Games into the most recognizable and possibly most influential vehicle for the promotion of sport for the disabled. The Paralympics is well organized with a relatively high profile that attracts significant media coverage and commercial sponsorship like many other modern sporting spectacles. Some 4,237 athletes from 164 nations competed in the 2012 Paralympic Games in London, making the Paralympic Games unquestionably the main international sporting forum for athletes with varying degrees of impairment. I now turn to discuss the field of disability studies before exploring research into the specific area of Paralympic sport.

Socio-political disability studies and Paralympic research

It is only in the last decade and a half that, with a few exceptions (see DePauw 1997), those sociologists of sport who have chosen disability as the focal point of their research have actively embraced the extant literature in the field of disability studies. This corpus of work, which is a direct product of a political movement led by people with disabilities themselves, has given researchers whose focus is the Paralympic Games an ability to explore more deeply the importance of the disability sport movement.

Disabled activists and theorists make the distinction between impairment, an acquired or born trait, and disability, the wider impact of the social context of these impairments; the sociological literature on Paralympic sport has increasingly adopted this approach. The view that disability is a social construction is known in the field of disability studies as the 'social model' of disability (Oliver 1990). This model is seen as being in direct opposition to the so-called medical model that highlights disability as a medical problem. To those who advocate the social model, impairment is a functional trait, or what is physically different from the norm, which often has the social consequences of imposing a disability on the person. It has been suggested that '[i]mpairment does not necessarily create dependency and a poor quality of life; rather it is a lack of control over the physical help needed which takes away people's independence' (Morris 1996: 10). Within the field of disability studies, then, the choice of words used to discuss individual athletes who engage in Paralympic sport is also seen to have political relevance (see Oliver 1990). When the phrase 'sport for the disabled' is used instead of 'disability sport', it becomes clear that sporting provision for the disabled is part of what might be labelled a 'disability industry' (Albrecht 1992). By extension, it appears that 'sport for the impaired' might be a more appropriate term than 'sport for the disabled', yet the former lacks the overt political connotation that is culturally relevant within sociological approaches to Paralympic sport. The difficulty in sociological interpretations of Paralympic sport is that the practice of sport for the disabled is closely linked to medical taxonomic systems; therefore, these interpretations can be related to the medical model which is directly linked by scholars to the social oppression of the impaired population.

Classifying bodies in Paralympic sport

Classification in Paralympic sport is simply a structure for competition similar to the systems used in the sports of judo and boxing where competitors perform in distinctive weight categories, except for the fact that athletes are able to diet themselves out of or eat themselves into such categories. Within Paralympic sport, competitors are classified in an attempt to minimize the impact of impairment on the outcome of competition. Therefore, it is important that the classification process is robust, achieves equity across the Paralympic sporting practice, and enables athletes to compete on a 'level playing field'. As Sherrill (1999: 210) suggests, one 'basic goal of classification is to ensure that winning or losing an event depends on talent, training, skill, fitness, and motivation rather than unevenness among competitors'.

The bodies of athletes with impairments are categorized according to the degree of functional difference and placed on a continuum where one trait may make one individual less marginalized than someone else who exhibits another (different) trait. Whilst categorization is often seen as unproblematic within the Paralympic movement, it has negatively impacted upon the wider disabled community by placing various impairment groups in a hierarchy of acceptability where some impairments are more marginal than others. The practice of classifying for sport is largely a medical one that can lead to stigmatization and alienation because it ultimately creates a hierarchy of bodies. It creates a hierarchy of impairment on activity limitations or on competitive outcome. Such hierarchies may have a negative impact upon the identities of people with disabilities involved in sport and throughout life more generally (Deal 2007). There is a problem with seeing people with disabilities as being entirely marginalized, since this suggests that the social position of the disabled community hinges upon the type and severity of impairment; however, the culture of Paralympic sport is not so clear cut (see Howe 2008). In other words, identification is a social construction which is never a completed process. The establishment of a disabled identity is not something that is concrete. It will be continually transformed. Identification is important, since through the process of classification that all athletes undergo within the practice of the Paralympic Games, they will be forced to accept their place within the organizational structure of the sport and begin to draw similarities and differences between themselves and those individuals both inside and outside their categorization. Hence, athletes with a disability are controlled by the process of classification that is a requirement for participation within the sporting practice.

The notion of the categorization of impairments that leads directly to a marginal position in society stems from the work of Erving Goffman (1963). Goffman was one of the first scholars to draw attention to the nature of the problem of stigmatization for people with impairments. Some critics of disability research have argued that the role of studies of stigma was as an attempt to 'medicalize' disability in order to classify it with respect to the predominant views that are expressed by society at large. For this reason, Goffman's work on stigma is useful when exploring the classification of athletes with impairment within Paralympic sports.

The IOSDs were on the front line in offering expertise on disability and sport when the IPC was established in 1989. Many of the first officials of the IPC had previously held posts within the IOSDs. Consequently, there was initial carte blanche acceptance of the IOSD's classification systems in the early days of the Paralympic movement. Yet very early in the history of the IPC there had been a desire to streamline classification, and over the years there have been various classification systems favoured by the IPC, all designed to reduce the number of classes in each sport (Tweedy and Howe 2011). While the athletes may be seen to be controlled through classification, it is important to note a number of key factors in establishing a complete sociological picture. First of all, the process of classification 'belongs' to the sport. Only a few sports are still under the umbrella of the IPC, hence, the IPC cannot control all systems in place. Secondly, many sports, such as swimming, are not impairment based (Howe and Jones 2006). The IPC also has recently developed the Classification Code to make the classification process as consistent as possible (Tweedy and Vanlandewijck 2011). The IPC suggests, 'The classification code will aim to synchronize all sport specific classification processes and procedures, in much the same way that the World Anti-Doping Code has done for international anti-doping rules and regulations' (IPC 2004: 11). In this manner, the classification code has acted as a catalyst for various sports to make their classification system more robust. In the sports that it does maintain, like athletics, the IPC has a role to play in policing the fair use of the classification system, though it did not have a direct hand in developing the systems themselves.

The culture that surrounds the practice of Paralympic sport and the knowledge participants have of their bodies and their self-identity means that to work towards achieving goals on an individual level is just as important as the work done through and by institutions, such as the IPC. Through work on and with the body, athletes experience, establish, and extend their limits and abilities, while placing themselves in the context of a number of rules and styles that make up their social circumstances. This is not simply a matter of doing exercises, but of monitoring and refining, keeping training records and making confessions, giving up and taking up different behaviours (Howe and Jones 2006).

In this regard the world of contemporary Paralympic sport is indistinguishable from the sporting mainstream except for the impact of the process of classification. This is, in part, why classification may be seen as central to a sociological investigation of Paralympic sport. As noted earlier, other sporting practices have forms of classification such as age and weight because the general population varies across these categories, but these are less restrictive than the protocols established within Paralympic sport. Classification within Paralympic sport has been one of the main areas of disagreement between the IOSDs and the IPC, since the latter feels that new methods of classification advantage some impairment groups over others (Howe 2012). Specifically, the system may be more difficult to classify because of the need to consider a great number of impairments simultaneously, and many of the tests used have not been statistically validated. A decade and a half ago there was even fear that athletes would 'cheat' the system by fooling the classifiers because the classification tests have not been validated statistically. According to Wu and Williams (1999), this has been a problem within the sport of swimming:

> Misclassification is an interesting and perennial problem in disability sport. As with many others, it is the root cause of much frustration and anger (a) among swimmers who feel they have been disadvantaged by losing to a competitor who should be in a higher class and (b) among coaches and swimmers who may believe that they have been disadvantaged by being placed in a higher class than their impairment warrants.
>
> (1999: 262)

Perhaps more important, athletes may be penalized for enhancing their own performances as the training of an elite athlete is central to the culture and identity of the majority of Paralympians. If athletes train and improve their technique in swimming (or any sport that adopts an integrated functional classification system), they may be reclassified based on their new ability, with the result that some of their desire to achieve athletic excellence is undermined (Vanlandewijck and Chappel 1996). In the current era with the IPC Classification Code, an evidence-based approach and ICF terminology, the problems highlighted in swimming above can be eliminated and not simply replaced by other matters of concern. In practice, the determination of sporting potential is almost impossible to achieve through any classification system. Yet the aim of achieving as fair a competition as possible is still the goal of the classification process and the place one's body occupies within a category may impact significantly upon identity. How well a given body will be integrated into mainstream sport will also impact on identity issues.

Mainstreaming sport for the disabled

The integration of athletes with a disability that is being undertaken by mainstream sporting organizations in many Western nations is seen as important if an inclusive society is to be achieved. Integration, broadly speaking, is the equal access and acceptance of all in the community. Some scholars have distanced themselves from discussion of integration since the concept implies that the disabled population are required to change or be normalized in order to join the mainstream (Ravaud and Stiker 2001). In other words, the concept of integration requires members of the disabled community to adopt an 'able' disposition in order to become members of the mainstream. However, some scholars working within the social scientific investigation of Paralympic sport have adopted a concept of integration that is useful in the current overview of this field. Sørensen and Kahrs (2006), in their study of integration of sport for the disabled within the Norwegian sport system, developed a 'continuum of compliance' which aims to explore the success of their nation's inclusive sport system. In this study, the situation in which both athletes with disabilities and those from the mainstream adapt their cultural systems is referred to as *true* integration. The situation in which athletes with a disability are forced to adopt the mainstream culture without any attempt at a reciprocal action is seen as assimilation. On the continuum, the least integrated model is seen as segregation, where neither group is willing to transform its core cultural values in spite of being jointly managed within the sport system.

Those working and researching in Paralympic sport would be most content if integration was *true* in the sense discussed above. If sport, and by extension society, is going to become more inclusive, 'it is necessary for existing economic, social and political institutions to be challenged and modified. This means that disabled people [sic] are not simply brought into society as it currently exists but rather that society is, in some ways, required to change' (Northway 1997: 165). In the long term, this might ultimately mean that the IPC and the International Olympic Committee (IOC) become equal partners, as this would be an overt indication that *true* integration had taken place.

This conceptualization of integration reflects recent work which argues that integration can be effectively understood as an outcome of an inclusive society. More specifically, it is argued that '[i]ntegration occurs through a process of interaction between a person with a disability and others in society' (Ven *et al.* 2005: 319). In other words, it is the process of interaction between an individual with a disability, who possesses his or her own attitude toward integration, strategies and social roles, and others in society, who adopt certain attitudes towards and images of people with disabilities. As a result, factors that influence the success of the integration process are personal as well as social, but also include an element of support provision that will be distinct depending on the severity of the individual's disability.

It is possible, for example, to see *true* integration as a literal intermixing that entails the culture of both groups adapting to a new cultural environment. Dijkers (1999) uses the term 'community integration' to articulate a similar conceptualization as *true* integration. Community integration, according to Dijkers, 'is the acquiring of age, gender, and culture-appropriate roles, statuses and activities, including in(ter)dependence in decision-making, and productive behaviours performed as part of multivariate relationships with family, friends, and others in natural community settings' (1999: 41).

True integration, therefore, is 'a multifaceted and difficult process, which although it could be defined at a policy level rhetoric, [is] much less easy to define in reality' (Cole 2005: 341). The difficulty when exploring the success of integration policies is that the balance between the philosophical position and the reality (in this case a sporting context) is not always clear. Simply exploring the policy landscape means that any interpretation of the sporting context is devoid of explicit cultural influences, though all policy is a cultural artefact. This being said, the ultimate aim of integration should be to allow people with disabilities to take a full and active role within society. The ideal would be

> [a] world in which all human beings, regardless of impairment, age, gender, social class or minority ethnic status, can co-exist as equal members of the community, secure in

the knowledge that their needs will be met and that their views will be recognised, respected and valued. It will be a very different world from the one in which we now live.

(Oliver and Barnes 1998: 102)

In the context of high-performance sport, this aim is hard to achieve. By its very nature, elite sport is selective, as Bowen suggests: 'Within professional sport, though, all but the super-able "suffer" from "exclusion or segregation" and "sport isolates individuals, but only those who are *super*-able. The rest *are* left to the realm of the minor leagues, masters' leagues, local tournaments, or backyard pick-up games' (Bowen 2002: 71). This understanding of sport makes it difficult to address the issue of integration. It is believed to be important, however, that international sporting organizations achieve *true* integration at the high-performance end of the spectrum in order to send a clear message regarding the positioning of people with disabilities within wider society.

Paralympic bodies

The bodies of impaired athletes have continually been judged in relation to an able-bodied 'norm', whilst the standards of play and performance are compared with those of mainstream competitions. This can have an adverse effect on participation rates in sport for the disabled as these bodies do not match up to the able-bodied norm.

> It is through the study of the body in the context of, and in relation to, sport that we can understand sport as one of the sites for the reproduction of social inequality in its promotion of the traditional view of athletic performance, masculinity, and physicality, including gendered images of the ideal physique and body beautiful.
>
> (DePauw 1997: 420)

Sport is an embodied practice, and as such many people who possess atypical bodies may shy away from the masculine physicality associated with sport. In sociological terms, the bodies of athletes can be seen to take centre stage in their lives. Following Seymour, 'embodiment is our life-long obsession. Eating, sleeping, washing, grooming, stimulating and entertaining our bodies dominate our lives' (1998: 4). For sportsmen and women with a disability, the manner in which they are embodied often marks them out for 'special' treatment in society as their bodies highlight these individuals in a meaningful way as imperfect and therefore inadequate. This is because a lack of a physical impairment is seen as normal. The imperfect body highlights the opposite – a lack of normality.

In the context of Paralympic sport, there are two broad types of bodies that are of concern, those with either congenital or acquired impairments. Both broad types of bodies will have travelled different roads before they got involved in Paralympic sport. Individuals with congenital impairments traditionally would have attended what in the West are commonly referred to as 'special' schools. Congenitally impaired Paralympians would have perhaps gotten their first exposure to sport through adapted physical activity classes at their school. These early experiences will have been instrumental in shaping the sporting experiences of these individuals. Today, in many cases congenitally impaired individuals are schooled in inclusive environments, but depending on the nature of the impairment, they may or may not engage in a segregated physical education environment. Regardless of the type of access they have to organized sport, the socialization of these young people will be distinct from those who attended special schools.

Those who come to Paralympic sport as a result of a traumatic accident, such as a car crash, are often socialized differently than congenitally impaired individuals. If the traumatic injury occurred in their youth, these individuals may also have attended a special school or had adapted physical activity classes as their introduction to sport. If the traumatic injury happens after the age when young people attend school, there is bound to be a period of transition to the new bodily circumstances. These individuals, regardless of age, go through a process of rehabilitation where their bodies need to be retrained often in the most basic tasks such as the management of daily hygiene regimes. After these individuals have relearned basic tasks they in essence become re-embodied, that is learning some of what their 'new' body can and cannot do in an adaptive physical activity setting where sport will be featured.

Both congenitally and acquired impaired bodies that make up the major sub-groupings within the Paralympic games can be further subdivided into athletes with severe disabilities. In 2005, the IPC Athletes with a Severe Disability Committee (ASDC) produced a revised definition that includes a specific list of sport classes where persons with a severe disability compete. The current definition is:

> An athlete who requires assistance during competition, based on the rules of the sport and/or an athlete who requires support staff in the sport environment, including for daily living functions, travel/transportation, transfers, etc.
>
> (IPC 2005: 10)

The ASDC was established to increase involvement of the most severely impaired athletes in the Paralympic movement. For these athletes, the sports in which they compete have to be the most adapted and their physical prowess is the least acknowledged within the Paralympic movement. This should not be a surprise, because even Paralympic sport is ultimately about physicality. In an environment where the body is essential such as sport, imperfection becomes evident. DePauw (1997) examines how sport marginalizes the disabled and argues that sport authorities need to re-examine the relationship between sport and the body with respect to disability.

> Ability is at the centre of sport and physical activity. Ability, as currently socially constructed, means 'able' and implies a finely tuned 'able' body. On the other hand, disability, also a social construction, is often viewed in relation to ability and is, then, most often defined as 'less than' ability, as not able. To be able to 'see' individuals with disabilities as athletes (regardless of the impairment) requires us to redefine athleticism and our view of the body, especially the sporting body.
>
> (DePauw 1997: 423)

This is a laudable goal. However, to redefine athleticism would require an overhaul of sport itself. The point that DePauw makes is an important one in relation to the ASDC, and this is only one of the key issues for the IPC – to ensure that these athletes are celebrated for their physical prowess.

It is not just the ASDC athletes that are marginalized through the practice of sport, because, as DePauw (1997) suggests, masculinity, physicality, and sexuality are integral aspects of sport and each of these is a social construction. Social constructs are generally understood to be the by-products of countless interactions between humans instead of laws resulting from divine will or nature. Therefore, these three components have socially ascribed definitions and together these elements marginalize bodies that do not fit into society's definition of sport. Athletes that are part of the remit of ASDC have traditionally been marginal to the practice of sport.

Women have also been traditionally marginalized in the context of sport and therefore it is not surprising that the IPC has a committee to give voice to female Paralympians (DePauw 1997). In the Paralympic Games in particular, low numbers of women competing in events is seen by some as a result of the double bind that women with disabilities must face. As Seymour (1998) suggests, because of the connotations of masculinity, it is a strong male body that resonates with the re-embodied image of a high-performance athlete.

> A winning wheelchair athlete is seen as the epitome of rehabilitative success. The vision of the strong male bodies competing for honours on the sports field is an image that has currency in the able-bodied world. Bravery in overcoming the catastrophe of a damaged body is a quality everyone can admire.
>
> (Seymour 1998: 119)

Of course, not everyone can match up to this image. Even a male who has used a wheelchair all his life does not have the heroic tale to go with his achievement in the same way as someone impaired in an accident might. Those with more severe impairments may never be able to achieve the image of the successful wheelchair hero. Such images can be counter-productive to the equitable treatment of people with disabilities, as not everyone can achieve this form of re-embodiment. The use of role models with a particular physicality due to spinal cord injury 'may disenfranchise the very people who most need its services. The creation of sporting heroes as rehabilitative triumphs obliterates from view the many severely damaged people for whom such activities will always be an impossibility' (Seymour 1998: 120). In other words, social issues like gender and degree of impairment are subjects of concern that in a more detailed sociological account should not be treated in isolation (Howe 2012).

The muscularity that makes the highly functioning male wheelchair body cause for celebration will lead some women with the same physique to be seen as lacking femininity. Pressure for those with severe impairments to conform to able-bodied norms is great, but it also has a gendered component. A physical or intellectual impairment can be seen as a threat to masculinity. Some gender scholars have suggested that control over senses and physical and mental toughness are attributes that have traditionally lead to hegemonic masculinity (Connell 1995). Hegemonic masculinity implies that more often than not, men are in positions of control within society, which is a reflection of their strong masculine identity. The presence of impairment undermines this social order. According to Connell, 'The constitution of masculinity through bodily performance means that gender is vulnerable when the performance cannot be sustained – for instance as a result of physical disability' (Connell 1995: 54).

Since sport embodies hegemonic masculinity, it has been popular with men with disabilities as a vehicle for reclaiming and re-embodying themselves. Like men, women can regain body function through rehabilitation regimes that may have sport as a constituent part, but 'such activities do not have the same powerful effect for women as they do for men since such bodily attributes are associated with masculinity and are considered to be contradictory aspects of femininity' (Seymour 1989: 114). This is in part because women are influenced by the dominant gender ideology, which holds that, though some may perform in sport at a high level, many women with disabilities choose to avoid sport because of its close association with masculinity and the non-athletic images of desired femininity (Hargreaves 2000).

It must be remembered that women with impairments fall into the broad categories of acquired and or congenitally disabled, as highlighted above. In the former category, some may consider themselves too old to reinvent themselves after a disabling injury, whilst the latter may not have been actively encouraged into physical activity in the home or school settings where they were socialized. Notably, sport for the disabled has mirrored the gender inequalities that have been inherent in modern sport since its inception in the nineteenth century. It is heavily male dominated, with fewer female participants than male and a lower proportion of women than men in senior administration. Ultimately, both disability and gender can be seen to negatively impact and limit choices and opportunities for disabled women and girls to participate in sport (Hargreaves 2000).

Some high-profile sportswomen with disabilities have begun to exhibit the ability to empower themselves by embracing the narratives of 'ability over disability' each time they compete (Howe and Parker 2012). These women Paralympians can exhibit the aesthetics of high performance – the skill, strength, and coordinated movement that comes from a highly trained athletic body. There are an increased number of women with disabilities using the agency of their bodies in a confident manner which suggests they understand themselves in relation to the culture of Paralympic sport and their own identity. Of course, not all women with disabilities are in a position to challenge the widely held views that disability precludes women's involvement in sport, but this would be a fruitful area for more robust sociological research.

Before closing, it is important to briefly discuss the social implications of movement technologies such as wheelchairs and prosthetic limbs as they relate to sport. The development of mobility technologies that are specifically designed for sport represents a response to the desires of the athletes to perform with greater proficiency. Today, many of the top athletes work with leading wheelchair and prosthesis suppliers to ensure that their future success is based not only on their detailed and comprehensive training regimes but on the synergy between their bodies and the competitive technologies. Athletes who use mobility technologies such as racing chairs and prosthetic limbs are to a large extent the public face of the Paralympic Games. These technologies have traditionally been symbols of weakness, of dependency, of neediness, but when used in a sports context they transcend these notions and celebrate power, speed, and muscularity. To the outside world, the Paralympics are celebrated for the 'cyborg' athlete, that is the marriage of human and machine that is embodied in figures such as Oscar Pistorius and David Weir. Because of the high profile of these athletes, technology may be seen as literally pushing the Paralympic Movement forward (Howe 2011a).

Able-bodied high-performance athletes rely on technology in their day-to-day training, yet when these athletes perform in sports like athletics, the technology that has enabled them to reach the sporting arena may be completely absent from view. An able-bodied athlete takes technology with him or her to the start of an Olympic final, as their clothing and footwear are products of advanced technology. However, specialist clothing and shoes appear less like advanced technology in comparison to racing wheelchairs and space-age prosthetic limbs as they are not explicitly aids for mobility. Shogun (1998) has suggested:

> When persons with disabilities use technologies to adjust the participation in 'normal' physical activity, the use of these technologies constructs this person as unnatural in contrast to a natural, nondisabled participant, even though both nondisabled participants and those with disabilities utilize technologies to participate.
>
> (Shogun 1998: 272)

While the debate about naturalness highlighted in the quote above is still ongoing in discussions within the field of the philosophy of sport, sociologically the greatest importance is that mobility technologies crafted for Paralympic athletes make the public more aware of Paralympic performances. The technology and the incredible things that athletes can do with it has to a limited extent captured the imagination of the general public (Howe 2011b). Technology such as racing wheelchairs and flex-feet (artificial legs biomechanically designed for running) have enhanced the performances of athletes whose impairments benefit from their use and are central to the identity of the Paralympic movement. These bodies that are able to successfully adapt to technology (which wherever possible normalizes their movements on the field of play and within society) are in general the hallmark of disability sport.

These technologies should be celebrated, but within limits. Not all Paralympians are able to take advantage of this technology, and some may be in danger of being marginalized as a result of the fact that they do not engage in the use of mobility technologies. Seymour (1998) suggests that we need to avoid the pitfalls of assuming that involvement in high-performance sport impacts all people with disabilities in a similar fashion.

> It is undeniable that sport and physical activities provide a context for enjoyment, self-identity and competence, but unless the conditions and ideology of sport are challenged, women, and indeed many men, will continue to operate in a context that compounds their disadvantage.
>
> (Seymour 1998: 126)

This chapter has attempted to highlight how sociologists of sport can explore issues that are central to disability with specific reference to the Paralympic Games, using integration, classification, and 'the' Paralympic body as exemplars. Understanding structural issues, such as classification, is central to acquiring a detailed sociological knowledge of sport for the disabled and the Paralympic Games; the latter, because of its relative high visibility, is a good place to start this discussion. It is also vital sociologically to study the individuals or agents within the Paralympic Games and sport for the disabled more generally, the most important of whom are the athletes.

Note

1 This is a federation that was launched in September 2004 at the Athens Paralympic Games. It is the result of a merger of two federations, the International Stoke Mandeville Wheelchair Sports Federation (ISMWSF) and the International Sport Organisation for the Disabled (ISOD), that have been part of the Paralympic movement since its inception.

References

Albrecht, G.L. (1992) *The Disability Business: Rehabilitation in America*, London: Sage.

Bowen, J. (2002) 'The Americans with Disabilities Act and Its Application to Sport', *Journal of the Philosophy of Sport*, 29: 66–74.

Cole, B.A. (2005) 'Good Faith and Effort? Perspectives on Educational Inclusion', *Disability & Society*, 20: 331–344.

Connell, R. (1995) *Masculinities*, Cambridge: Polity.

Deal, M. (2007) 'Aversive Disablism: Subtle Prejudice toward Disabled People', *Disability & Society*, 22(1): 93–107.

DePauw, K. (1997) 'The (In) Visibility of DisAbility: Cultural Contexts and "Sporting Bodies"', *Quest*, 49: 416–430.

DePauw, K. and Gavron, S. (1995) *Disability and Sport*. Leeds, UK: Human Kinetics.

Dijkers, M. (1999) 'Community Integration: Conceptual Issues and Measurement Approaches in Rehabilitation Research', *Journal of Rehabilitation Outcome Measurements*, 3(1): 39–49.

Goffman, E. (1963) *Stigma: Notes on the Management of Spoiled Identity*, London: Penguin.

Hargreaves, J. (2000) *Heroines of Sport: The Politics of Difference and Identity*, London: Routledge.

Howe, P. D. (2008) *The Cultural Politics of the Paralympic Movement: Through the Anthropological Lens*. London: Routledge.

Howe, P.D. (2011a) 'Cyborg and Supercrip: The Paralympics Technology and the (Dis)empowerment of Disabled Athletes', *Sociology*, 45(5): 868–882.

Howe, P.D. (2011b) 'Sociology and Paralympic Sport', in Y. Vanlandewijck and W. Thompson (eds) *The Paralympic Athlete*, Oxford: Wiley-Blackwell.

Howe, P.D. (2012) 'Children of a Lesser God: Paralympics and High-Performance Sport' in Sugden, J. and Tomlinson, A. (eds.) *Watching the Olympics: politics, power and representation*. London: Routledge. pp. 165–181.

Howe, P.D. and Jones, C. (2006) 'Classification of Disabled Athletes: (Dis)empowering the Paralympic Practice Community', *Sociology of Sport Journal*, 23: 29–46.

Howe, P.D. and Parker, A. (2012) 'Celebrating Imperfection: Sport, Disability and Celebrity Culture', *Celebrity Studies*, 3(3): 270–282.

IPC (2004) *The Paralympian: Official Newsletter of the International Paralympic Committee*, Issue Number 1.

IPC (2005) *Annual Report*, IPC: Bonn. Available at: http://www.paralympic.org/sites/default/files/document/120201081616846_2005_annual_report_web.pdf at p. 10.

Morris. J. (1996) *Encounters with Strangers: Feminism and Disability*, London: Women's Press.

Northway, R. (1997) 'Integration and Inclusion: Illusion or Progress in Services for Disabled People?', *Social Policy and Administration*, 31(2): 157–172.

Oliver, M. (1990) *The Politics of Disablement*, London: Macmillan.

Oliver, M. and Barnes, C. (1998) *Social Policy and Disabled People: From Exclusion to Inclusion*, London: Longman.

Ravaud, J.-F. and Stiker, H-J. (2001) 'Inclusion/Exclusion: An Analysis of Historical and Cultural Meaning', in G.L. Albrecht, K.D. Seelman, and M. Bury (eds) *Handbook of Disability Studies*, London: Sage.

Seymour, W. (1989) *Body Alterations*, London: Unwin Hyman.

Seymour, W. (1998) *Remaking the Body: Rehabilitation and Change*, London: Routledge.

Sherrill, C. (1999) 'Disability Sport and Classification Theory: A New Era', *Adapted Physical Activity Quarterly*, 16: 206–215.

Shogun, D. (1998) 'The Social Construction of Disability: The Impact of Statistics and Technology', *Adapted Physical Activity Quarterly*, 15: 269–277.

Sørensen, M. and Kahrs, N. (2006) 'Integration of Disability Sport in the Norwegian Sport Organizations: Lessons Learned', *Adapted Physical Activity Quarterly*, 23: 184–203.

Tweedy, S. and Howe, P.D. (2011) 'Introduction to the Paralympic Movement', in Vanlandewijck, Y. and Thompson, W. *The Paralympic Athlete*. Oxford: Wiley-Blackwell p. 3–30.

Tweedy, S. and Vanlandewijck, Y.C. (2011) 'International Paralympic Committee Position Stand – Background and Scientific Principles of Classification in Paralympic Sport', *British Journal of Sports Medicine*, 45: 259–269.

Vanlandewijck, Y.C. and Chappel, R.J. (1996) 'Integration and Classification Issues in Competitive Sports for Athletes with Disabilities', *Sport Science Review*, 5(1): 65–88.

Ven, L. van de, Post, M., Witte, L. de, and Heuvel, W. van den (2005) 'It Takes Two to Tango: The Integration of People with Disabilities into Society', *Disability and Society*, 20(3): 311–329.

Wu, S.K. and Williams, T. (1999) 'Paralympic Swimming Performance, Impairment, and the Functional Classification System', *Adapted Physical Activity Quarterly*, 16(3): 251–270.

PART FOUR

Central issues in the sociology of sport

27

INTRODUCTION TO PART FOUR

Richard Giulianotti

In Part Four, we turn to examine many of the major substantive issues and problems that are addressed by sociologists of sport. These topics fall into five broad, overlapping categories. First, we consider physical and experiential issues relating to the body, health, risk-taking, and doping. Second, we explore the public aspects of sport, with regard to sport fandom, sport violence (which has involved substantial focus on spectator-related violence), and the use of sport to deal with identified social problems such as youth-related crime. Third, we address social geographical issues in sport, relating to urban politics and policy, the staging of sport mega-events by cities and nations, and environmental problems associated with the installation of sport facilities. Fourth, we examine communication issues in regard to sport media and new media. Fifth, we conclude by exploring the transnational aspects of sport, on the sporting nation in the global context, athlete migration, aspects of global sport's commercialization, the sport for development and peace sector, and the interface of sport and globalization.

We begin with a chapter by Pirkko Markula on the body: a subject of extensive social research in sport since the 1980s, particularly by scholars influenced by gender studies and post-structuralist theory. Accordingly, a substantial has been on the intersection of the body, gender, fitness, and consumerism, and on how this bundle of issues serves largely to reinforce hegemonic forms of male and female identity (e.g. Dworkin and Wachs 2009). However, Markula recognizes that sociologists have also interpreted 'embodied identities' and subjectivities as complex and contradictory, in combining dominated and resistant aspects within sport contexts. For example, women football players or kick-boxers may emphasize or reproduce some aspects of 'conventional' feminine identity, while also challenging others (e.g. Cox and Thompson 2000). The critical theories of Bourdieu, Foucault, and Gramsci help in particular to underpin analysis of these cultural political issues in relation to the body. Overall, Markula argues, the sociology of sport has marshalled a wider diversity of perspectives in order to advance the study of the body as a moving social entity.

In recent years, most nations have witnessed substantial political and medical discussion on the body in terms of using sport and physical activity to avert impending 'health disasters' over obesity, and growing levels of diabetes and other non-communicable diseases. In her chapter, Jessica Lee draws particularly on Bourdieu's social theory to explore the interface between physical activity, sport, and health. Lee notes that 'public health campaigns' on obesity are far more alarmist than is warranted by the limited scientific evidence which links ill health to body mass (cf. Rich *et al.* 2010). Gender relations shape popular perceptions of health, with many women defining 'physical activity' with respect to male sports and recreation rather than their own corporeal practices. The implication here for Lee is that social policies on physical activity need to recognize and to promote a wider range of practices and experiences, including more playful forms of recreation.

In social science, 'risk' has been a major theme within social analysis and research since at least the 1980s. The chapter by Stephen Lyng explores the growing importance of questions of risk and uncertainty within contemporary sport. Lyng notes the roles of biography and history in igniting sociological interest in risk – in his own case, early student encounters with a group of skydivers inspired his initial research and theory of 'edgework' (Lyng 1990). More broadly, from the late 1960s onwards, new types of 'risk sport' (such as rock climbing, caving, or sky-diving) have grown rapidly, particularly among the professional middle classes (Fletcher 2008). Ironically, as Lyng notes, the limited data available suggest that traditional sports such as rugby and cycling carry far greater risk in producing injuries that are fatal or seriously disabling. But what sets contemporary 'risk sports' apart is how they embrace rather than reduce uncertainty in risk-taking. For Lyng, the appeal of these risk sports lies in achieving 'a form of self-discovery and transcendence that is rarely attained in human experience'. As such, as Lyng concludes, it might be better to refer to risk sports as 'voluntary uncertainty-seeking' rather than 'voluntary risk-taking' activities.

Doping has been arguably the most important public issue within sport over the past three decades, particularly since the 1988 Olympics in Seoul when the Canadian sprinter Ben John-son was found to have taken performance-enhancing drugs, and the string of scandals in cycling since the late 1990s, culminating in the exposure of seven-time Tour de France champion Lance Armstrong. In his chapter, Verner Møller seeks to extend sociological understanding of dop-ing by critically examining the question of reliable evidence on the subject, and by exploring potential avenues for future research. For Møller, a key moment for doping in sport occurred at the Tour de France in 1998, when the Festina cycling team were investigated and found to have been heavily involved in systematic doping of competitors. Møller argues that much prior research on doping has been founded on shaky empirical foundations, including popular 'myths' that specific cyclists have died directly due to taking performance-enhancing substances. Møller is particularly concerned that these stories are repeated as fact by 'doping idealists' who have political agendas to pursue. To challenge these tendencies, Møller argues that should draw on the insights of the great sociologist C. Wright Mills (1959), particularly in recognizing the complex conditions within which people (including doping athletes) are 'historical and social actors'.

Sport fans play a critical role in the making of sport clubs and events both at elite and grass-roots levels. In his chapter, William Kelly explores in detail how sport fans have been studied by social scientists. Kelly argues that sport fans share several key characteristics with other mass consumer fans, including knowing and caring more about their cultural focus; being engaged in 'fandom as serious play'; and walking a 'fine line between the pleasure of fantasy and the pathol-ogy of fanaticism'. Kelly explores how the historical development of sport fandom since at least the nineteenth century has been characterized by the interplay of 'identity and commodifica-tion', whilst still being capable of evading or surviving powerful forces of consumerism. Much sociological research since the 1970s has concentrated on fan violence and hooliganism, whilst significant insights have been drawn from exploring the emotions, rituals, and social psychology of fandom, which connect experience to identity (e.g. Armstrong and Giulianotti 2001; Kelly 2004). Kelly also notes that, in regard to gender, women are drawn to sport in much the same way as men, while being confronted with 'greater obstacles' before being recognized fully as fans. Perhaps the most intriguing field of research in the future will lie in the interrelationships between fandom, media, and fantasy. Transnational media allow many fans to have long-distance love affairs with sport teams, seemingly irrespective of proximity. Moreover, as fans participate more in fantasy sport leagues, the distinctions in sport between production and reception, or doing and watching, begin to break down.

Violence in sport has been a subject of recurring interest for sociologists. In his chapter, Ramón Spaaij examines some of the diverse forms of violence within sport, and how these have been studied by sociologists. The actual definition of violence is, as Spaaij emphasizes, highly contested and problematic, ranging from minimalist through to widely inclusive under-standings. In sport, as Smith (1983) indicated, there may be a 'sliding scale' of violence among players in regard to perceived levels of legitimacy, ranging from 'brutal body contact' through to actual 'criminal violence'. Spaaij examines four main sociological arguments which seek to explain sport violence. First, the figurational position of Norbert Elias and his followers explains sport-related violence with reference to his theory of the civilizing process. Second, the collective behaviour approach examines the specific social conditions (such as breakdowns in social control, or precipitating flashpoints) that are required for major disturbances and riots to occur. Third, the 'microsociology of sport violence', advanced by Randall Collins, enables analysis of sport-related violence with reference to 'dramatic tensions', shared emotions among teammates, and 'emotional energy' between opponents. Fourth, 'masculinity perspectives' examine violence with respect to dominant masculine identities alongside the denigration of women.

From social disorder we turn to examine how sport has been harnessed with the aim of reproducing and restoring the social order. The chapter by Douglas Hartmann provides a critical sociological assessment of how sport is used as form of social intervention in the United States. Hartmann highlights how these sport programmes – such as the crime-prevention initiative Midnight Basketball – have long since been directed at poor, lower-class males who are often otherwise unable to afford sport facilities, while also being represented as major 'threats' to bourgeois and 'respectable' city life. Notably, such initiatives promise that they can offer quick, effective, targeted solutions to specific social problems. Critical studies of such interventions, however, point to a wide range of potential weaknesses, notably in terms of being difficult to justify or to prove their efficacy (Hartmann 2001; cf. Kelly 2011). These programmes also tend to reinforce the simplistic assumption that 'the problem' lies specifically with the minority groups rather than with deeper structural forces and processes (such as unemployment, deindus-trialization, lack of educational opportunities, and so on). Moreover, these initiatives do not offer their 'user-groups', particularly from poor locales, either an at-a-stroke solution to structural problems, nor a sufficient entry point into facilities that provide for sport and physical activity.

The relationship of sport to the urban context is examined in the chapter by Kim Schim-mel. Schimmel points to how political economy perspectives have highlighted both the role of entrepreneurs in shaping commercial sport in cities, and the contributions of stadium con-struction and hosting of sport mega-events towards urban (re)development. More socio-cultural perspectives examine how sport, as a 'dominant cultural form', contributes to the making and remaking of community life (cf. Bale and Moen 1995). Latterly, sociologists have explored how sport venues are integral to new urban landscapes that centre on consumption-laden 'specta-cles' (Friedman and Andrews 2010). Social divisions are redoubled here as poorer populations are excluded from these venues, despite having contributed substantially to their construction through taxation and cuts in spending on front-line services such as health and education. In the post-9/11 context, there is a growing focus on the vast security measures that envelop major sport events such as the Olympics or Super Bowl. Schimmel echoes earlier calls for future research to examine urban sport in the global South, where most the world's population is located and where many mega-events are now being staged (Giulianotti and Klauser 2010).

Sport mega-events such as the Olympic Games and football World Cup finals are examined in depth in the chapter by Wolfram Manzenreiter. The scale and significance of these events have grown very rapidly since the 1980s. They are the site for powerful forms of community-building and identification, most obviously in the construction and promotion of national identities before global audiences (Roche 2000). Following the 1984 Los Angeles Olympics, cities and nations have entered into fervent bidding competitions to secure the rights to host these events, although the resulting political and economic benefits are hard to identify. The aura, spectacle, and 'magical moments' of sport mega-events allow for the suspension of the mundane, every-day world. Wrapped in global media and consumer cultures, these events enable spectators in and around stadiums to be 'active performers' in making the spectacle. As Manzenreiter notes, substantial protests and conflicts surround the hosting of these events over a mix of local and transnational issues, such as the displacement and disempowerment of local people, the high financial costs of hosting, and the international policies and human rights records of the host and competing nations (Lenskyj 2000).

The environment has become a significant issue in the hosting of sport mega-events, and in the development of sport facilities and landscapes. In their chapter, Brian Wilson and Brad Millington examine how specific environmental issues in sport are politically contained and neutralized within broader contexts that are 'post-political' (Swyngedouw 2009). Wilson and Millington consider the particular role of 'sport management environmentalists' (SMEs), who recognize the potentially harmful impacts of sport on the environment, but who are also incorporated into the wider sport system, and thus pursue practical, accommodating solutions. Thus, for example, SMEs tend to assume that new scientific innovations will be found to repair the damage done by pesticides on golf courses or even to create new cooling technologies that will obviate high humidity and heat levels at major sport events. For Wilson and Millington, SMEs favour post-political contexts, where stakeholders build partnerships that reproduce neoliberal capitalist interests, rather than acknowledging differences and conflicts that have deep political roots. In this way, the environmental politics of sport lose their 'public issue' status, and are reduced to the realm of a narrow consultative managerialism.

We turn next to examine a variety of sociological issues that are generated by media and new media within sport. Sociologists have an extensive track record of research for investigating media in sport. The chapter by Lawrence Wenner examines in extensive detail the broad field of sport media studies which, in being heavily influenced by the British cultural studies tradition, has passed through four main phases. First, running up to the late 1980s, social scientists sought to confirm sport media as a legitimate subject for research, while including a mix of studies on specific events, audiences, and media 'texts'. Second, through the 1990s, research focused more on power issues in sport media, notably how sport media institutions reproduced dominant ideologies (e.g. in the portrayal of ethnic minorities), and how sport audiences generated resistant interpretations of media texts and discourses. Third, sport media research up to the mid-2000s was marked by a mix of theoretical perspectives, and by a continuing focus on ideologies and power relations. Fourth, up to the present point, sport media research has explored more diverse issues, such as media-dependent fandoms, globalization, and mega-events, as well as new fields such as digital media and gaming. Wenner indicates that future sociological studies of sport media will likely focus on issues such as social divisions and commodification, and should be well placed to contribute to policy debates.

The field of 'new media' encompasses cable and satellite television, the internet and mobile telephony. In their chapter, Matthew David and Peter Millward draw on the works of the sociologist Manuel Castells (2000) to examine the impact of such new media upon contemporary sport. They identify two digital revolutions within sport. First, from the early 1990s onwards, subscription television channels and networks started to spend increasingly large sums to buy live television rights to major sport tournaments. Second, there has since been a growing volume of global sharing and streaming of live sport through the internet, which offers improving visual quality, and without requiring viewers to make illegal copies of content. Such new media offer a potential commercial challenge to major sport leagues and subscription television networks by enabling sport followers globally to watch events free on the internet or through other new media sources. Television networks have struggled to combat these threats, either through blocking transmission or dissuading viewers from seeking access. Yet, despite the global economic downturn since 2007, the value of television rights for elite global sport remains remarkably high, suggesting that any 'creative destruction' of the sport–corporate media partnership continues to be a long way off.

The final set of chapters explores further themes on the transnational aspects of sport. We begin here by examining the relationship of sport to national identity in the global age. The chapter by Frank Lechner argues that these sport-nation ties may take diverse paths. Thus, some nations have adapted sports to develop distinctive forms of national (largely male) identity, for example for Indians in relation to cricket, and Argentinians in football (e.g. Appadurai 1995; Archetti 1998). Latterly, the influence of sports upon national identity can depend significantly on competitive success or failure: for example, when Greece or France won major championships in football, the connection intensified; but as West Indian cricket fell into decline, such ties also fell away. The United States provides a study in transnational sporting exceptionalism, as uniquely American sports (baseball, American football) were created to encapsulate national identity; despite the rapid grassroots growth of association football and some notable performances in the World Cup finals, the 'global game' has still to grab the full national interest (Dyreson and Mangan 2007).

The international migration of elite athletes represents one of the most substantial and fastest-growing aspects of globalization within sport. In their chapter, Raffaele Poli and Loïc Ravenel draw on their extensive empirical research to examine football as a detailed case study for understanding the contemporary contours of elite athlete migration. They argue that, in some contrast to popular assumptions, greater levels of player migration in football have not adversely affected forms of local identification at many clubs, while the jury is still out on the impacts of this process on the reproduction of national identities. The authors explore how the international flow of players has increased very substantially since the early 1960s, with nations such as Brazil and Argentina exporting large numbers, particularly into European nations with strong historical, cultural, and linguistic ties, such as Portugal or Spain respectively (cf. Lanfranchi and Taylor 2001). Poli and Ravenel also utilize a relational perspective to examine the transnational movement of players across multiple nations. This approach enables examination of the different social networks that influence the migration of players, including player agents, club officials, and 'investors' who acquire different types of 'ownership' of players, particularly in developing nations. Poli and Ravenel argue that the various political and legal authorities within football and beyond need to exercise their powers of regulation in the context of a rapidly expanding global market for top athletes.

Elite-level sport has experienced substantial levels of long-term commercialization. The chapter by Barry Smart explores the sport–corporate interlinks while drawing largely on the modern Olympics as a case study. Smart highlights how the founder of the modern Olympic movement, Baron Pierre de Coubertin, was inspired in part by the staging of grand exhibitions and fairs, and was later concerned that commercialism rather than the philosophy of amateurism was coming to dominate the initial Olympic Games. Early signs of global sport's commodification were provided by significant commercial advertising (at the 1908 London Olympics), exclusive corporate deals for the marketing and sale of specific products (1912 Stockholm Olympics), and the later business partnership with Coca-Cola, which began in 1928. Such commercial activity entered a new level from the 1984 Los Angeles Games onwards, notably through the arrival of a much wider pool of global corporate sponsors and rising television revenues (cf. Tomlinson 2005). Subsequently, London 2012 featured twenty five commercial partners including widely criticized corporations such as Dow Chemical, Rio Tinto, and BP. As at earlier mega-events, corporations such as Nike which lacked Olympic partnership deals have still been able to launch 'ambush marketing' campaigns – thereby redoubling the ties between global commerce and elite sport (cf. Preuss *et al.* 2008).

The field of 'sport for development and peace' (hereon SDP) has grown very rapidly since the mid-1990s, and has generated substantial interest across the sociology of sport (see Schulen-korf and Adair 2014). SDP involves the use of sport to pursue non-sporting social goals such as peace-building, gender empowerment, and health education, particularly in developing nations and regions. In his chapter, Simon Darnell explores SDP in regard to its emergence and devel-opment, its sociological study, and how a critical perspective might contribute to its possible transformation. Prior research in the field has identified, for example, some contextual benefits of SDP for gender empowerment, economic development, and health promotion. However, sociological research also must explore how the SDP sector often connects closely to neoliberal socio-economic policies, which underpin many of the everyday social problems that are the focus of sport-based initiatives (Hartmann and Kwauk 2011). Darnell notes that future research should include examination of how SDP work is monitored and evaluated, and critical assess-ment of the extent to which sport contributes to development and peace.

The final chapter is on the globalization of sport, which has been a major research theme in the sociology of sport since at least the early 1990s. In my chapter on this subject, I build on prior collaborative work with the major globalization theorist Roland Robertson to explore how global sport has been constructed with reference to historical, political, economic, and socio-cultural dimensions (see Giulianotti and Robertson 2004, 2007, 2009). Globalization is thus understood as a long-term and multi-dimensional process. The historical 'take-off' of global sport occurred in the late nineteenth and early twentieth centuries, particularly as British sports such as football and cricket were codified and spread across the world. The global politics of sport have become increasingly multipolar, in being characterized by a growing diversity and complexity of stakeholders and prospective actors. The global economy of sport has become more and more tied to the interests of leading sport and corporate institutions in the global North, for example through the flows of top athletes into Europe and North America. In turn, some scholars have also argued that global sport is marked by cultural imperialism, for example as elite sports competitions (such as English or Spanish football, or American basketball) from the global North are televised globally, to the detriment of local sport cultures in the global South. Yet, the socio-cultural dimensions of global sport indicate that power relations are rather more blurred and two-way at the everyday level. For example, transnational sport cultures are created, both by migrant groups who maintain allegiances to their 'home' sports, and by wider social groups who engage selectively with the global media in order to follow their favoured sports and teams. More broadly, global sport enables fans in the global North to become 'banal cosmopolitans', by routinely encountering 'other' cultures through sporting competitions. Thus, overall, study of the globalization of sport serves to crystallize the deeper dilemma that con-fronts sociologists of sport in many research fields, in requiring to account for both top-down structures and relations of domination, and the bottom-up critical creativity of social actors at the everyday level.

References

Appadurai, A. (1995) 'Playing with Modernity: the Decolonization of Indian Cricket, in C.A. Breckenridge (ed.) *Consuming Modernity*, Minneapolis: University of Minnesota Press.

Archetti, E. (1998) *Masculinities*, Oxford: Berg.

Armstrong, G. and Giulianotti, R. (eds) (2001) *Fear and Loathing in World Football*, Oxford: Berg.

Bale, J. and Moen, O. (eds) (1995) *The Stadium and the City*, Keele, UK: Keele University Press.

Castells, M. (2000) *The Rise of the Network Society*, Oxford: Blackwell.

Cox, B. and Thompson, S. (2000) 'Multiple Bodies: Sportswomen, Soccer and Sexuality', *International Review for the Sociology of Sport*, 35: 5–20.

Dworkin S.L. and Wachs, F.L. (2009) *Body Panic: Gender, Health, and the Selling of Fitness*, New York: New York University Press.

Dyreson, M. and J.A. Mangan (2007) (eds) *Sport and American Society*, London: Routledge.

Fletcher, R. (2008) 'Living on the Edge: The Appeal of Risk Sports for the Professional Middle Class', *Sociology of Sport Journal*, 25(3): 310–330.

Friedman, M.T. and Andrews, D.L. (2010) 'The Built Sport Spectacle and the Opacity of Democracy', *International Review for the Sociology of Sport*, 46(2): 181–204.

Giulianotti, R. and Klauser, F. (2010) 'Security Governance and Sport Mega-Events: Toward an Interdisciplinary Research Agenda,' *Journal of Sport and Social Issues*, 34(1): 49–61.

Giulianotti, R. and Robertson, R. (2004) 'The Globalization of Football: A Study in the Glocalization of the "Serious Life"', *British Journal of Sociology*, 55(4): 545–568.

Giulianotti, R. and Robertson, R. (2009) *Globalization and Football*, London: Sage.

Giulianotti, R. and Robertson, R. (eds) (2007) *Globalization and Sport*, Oxford: Wiley.

Hartmann, D. (2001) 'Notes on Midnight Basketball and the Cultural Politics of Race and At-Risk Urban Youth', *Journal of Sport and Social Issues*, 25: 339–371.

Hartmann, D. and Kwauk, C. (2011) 'Sport and Development: An Overview, Critique, and Reconstruction', *Journal of Sport and Social Issues*, 35(3): 284–305.

Kelly, L. (2011) '"Social Inclusion" through Sport-Based Interventions', *Critical Social Policy*, 31 (1): 126–150.

Kelly, W.W. (2004) 'Sense and Sensibility at the Ballpark: What Fans Make of Professional Baseball in Modern Japan', in W.W. Kelly (ed.) *Fanning the Flames: Fans and Consumer Culture in Contemporary Japan*, Albany: SUNY Press.

Lanfranchi, P. and Taylor, M. (2001) *Moving with the Ball: The Migration of Professional Footballers*, Oxford: Berg.

Lenskyj, H. (2000) *Inside the Olympic Industry*, Albany: SUNY Press.

Lyng, S. (1990) 'Edgework', *American Journal of Sociology*, 95(4): 851–886.

Mills, C.W. (1959) *The Sociological Imagination*, Harmondsworth, UK: Penguin.

Preuss, H., Gemeinder, K., and Séguin, B. (2008) 'Ambush Marketing in China: Counterbalancing Olympic Sponsorship Effects', *Asian Business and Management*, 7: 243–263.

Rich, E., Monaghan, L. and Aphramor, L. (eds) (2010) *Debating Obesity: Critical Perspectives*, Basingstoke, UK: Palgrave.

Roche, M. (2000) *Mega-Events and Modernity*, London: Routledge.

Schulenkorf, N. and Adair, D. (ed.) (2014) *Global Sport for Development*, Basingstoke, UK: Palgrave.

Smith, M.D. (1983) 'What Is Sports Violence? A Sociolegal Perspective', in J.H. Goldstein (ed.) *Sports Violence*, New York: Springer-Verlag.

Swyngedouw, E. (2009) 'The Antinomies of the Postpolitical: In Search of a Democratic Politics of Environmental Protection', *International Journal of Urban and Regional Research*, 33(3): 601–20.

Tomlinson, A. (2005) 'The Commercialization of the Olympics: Cities, Corporations, and the Olympic Commodity', in K. Young and K. Wamsley (eds) *The Global Olympics: Historical and Sociological Studies of the Modern Games*, London: JAI Press.

28

SPORT AND THE BODY

Pirkko Markula

Introduction

The body has been of major interest to social scientists for more than two decades. Dovetailing Brian Turner's (1984) seminal text *The Body & Society*, sport sociologists were awakened to the need to include examinations of the body in their research agendas. For example, in their influential article, Loy, Andrews, and Rinehart (1993) called for bringing the body into the sociology of sport. Almost a decade later, Cole reviewed the state of body studies in the sociology of sport. Somewhat contrary to Loy, Andrews, and Rinehart (1993), Cole (2000) argued that the body has, in fact, appeared in social science research, including sport sociology, for some length of time despite the perception of its absence. This type of research demonstrated how the normalization of desirable bodies was part of the stabilization of the modern state. Against the construction of the normalized body, there was also literature that focused on the destabilizing effect of deviant bodies. For example, consumer culture normalized, but also produced, 'transcendent' celebrity bodies. Cole further referred to the increasing prominence of the commodified fitness industry that, by its individualized focus on body shaping, served to depoliticize feminist concerns over women's oppression through an excessive focus on appearance. Cole's review concluded with a concern regarding the absence of 'corporeality' – the muscles, nerves, genes, and blood – in favour of abstract thought, structures, and power, in the social analysis of the body.

If the issues of normalization, deviance, celebrity identity, and consumer culture were some of the central concerns of sport sociological study of the body in the 1980s and 1990s, have new directions developed during the new millennium of research into sporting bodies? In this chapter, I continue to develop some of the themes identified by Cole (2000) to sketch the current state of body studies within the sociology of sport. The interest in the body continues to flourish and consequently, similar to Cole, I do not claim to offer a definite review of all possible perspectives, but I do focus on what I consider to be the current body-related research themes within sport sociology.

Body studies in sport sociology have now diversified beyond sport to include other types of physically active bodies. Based on my reading of this field, I have divided the discussion into four sections: the physically active body as representation of identity construction; examinations of 'embodied subjectivities'; Foucauldian studies of disciplinary body techniques; and, finally, calls for the inclusion of the material body within social analysis. I explore how each of these themes encompasses diverse theoretical approaches and methodological stances, while highlighting the main innovations and limitations of these sociological understandings of the body in sport, coaching, and exercise.

The physically active body as the representation of identity

The body as a 'symbol' (Hargreaves and Vertinsky 2007: 8) of identity construction persists as one of the dominant themes in sport sociological discussions. Sociologists of sport place significant attention on gendered, transgendered, racialized, classed, and sexualized sporting and exercising bodies in order to critique inequality that is enforced by current physical activity practices. Consequently, I will first discuss how identity is constructed in the representations of the 'mediated' sporting and/or fit body in order then to examine how 'personal' body experiences in physical activity have been read to symbolize identity.

Mediated bodily identities

Since at least the 1990s, sport sociology has been dominated by analysis of the 'desirable' body identity and/or its deviations (Cole 2000; Wenner 2013). For example, through a content analysis, Dart (2014) found that issues related to race/ethnicity, sex/sexuality, and to a lesser degree, class, dominated the main sport sociology journals. The construction of these identities was often located within the media and illustrated through celebrity bodies to demonstrate normalization and/or resistance through sport and exercise.

While acknowledging the increased visibility and success of black sporting bodies, including such celebrity American athletes as Venus and Serena Williams (Schultz 2005; Spencer 2004) and Tiger Woods, sport sociologists continue to problematize racism in the media representations of these bodies. Carrington (2010: 177), for example, asserting that 'Black athletes have re-made sports, but not under conditions and rules of their own choosing', identified sport as a place to resist racism. As a result, there has been broad interest in race and ethnicity in men's soccer around the world – too numerous, however, to provide a comprehensive account here. In addition to blackness, the emergence of critical race theory has necessitated an interrogation of whiteness as a part of the complex social formation that grounds the logic of race 'in the realm of visibility as apparently locatable in the body' (McDonald 2005: 248).[1] This line of research concludes that the sporting body, despite the increased visibility of a variety of ethnic and racial bodies, continues to be a site of racism.

If critical race theorists demonstrate how racism continues to be maintained through athletes' bodies, critical masculinity studies aim to illustrate how the dominant male ('raced') body is sustained in sport (Montez de Oca 2013). From this perspective, racism continues in sport because challenges to (white) men's privilege and authority create crises of masculinity over what it means to be a man. To avoid such anxieties, the media continues to construct the male athletic body as naturally powerful. A central characteristic of this powerfulness is tolerance and even celebration of pain and violence in men's sport (e.g. Young 2005, 2012). These tough sporting bodies are commodified by the media as the ideal representation of masculinity, which also comes to represent the nation through international sporting competitions (e.g. Montez de Oca 2013). Critical masculinity studies, thus, focus on how masculinity is constructed in relations of power, patriarchy, and exclusion, as a dominant, yet continually unstable identity category (Messner 2002; Montez de Oca 2013).

Parallel to critical masculinity scholars, critical feminists locate sport within a patriarchal system in which a feminine body is constructed according to an ideology of masculinity that reinforces male superiority (often justified by men's superior physical performance) over women. Media representations continue to marginalize, trivialize, and sexualize women athletes (Markula 2009; Wensing and Bruce 2003). For example, successful women athletes' bodies are sexualized in media representations of such sports as swimming (Elling and Luijt 2009), action sports (Thorpe and Wheaton 2013), diving (Wu 2009), or tennis (Harris and Clayton 2002). A sexy, feminine image has, nevertheless, benefitted certain female athletes, such as tennis player Anna Kournikova (Harris and Clayton 2002), who have attracted media attention and consequent lucrative sponsorship based on their looks. Consequently, women who take part in traditionally 'male' sports (such as ice hockey, rugby, soccer) have to negotiate their display of gender in relation to the aggressive physicality in these sports and the requirements for the 'normalized,' 'heterosexy' feminine body (Scraton and Flintoff 2013). In a media context that favours heterosexually attractive women's bodies as appropriate bodies, the lesbian image is problematic and thus, almost invisible (Caudwell 2006; Wensing and Bruce 2003). Heterosexually attractive feminized images dominate also the fitness media.

Several critical scholars of fitness have examined the media's obsession with the ideal, feminine fit body with respect to the oppressive ideological forces of consumer culture (Kennedy and Pappa 2011). For example, Dworkin and Wachs (2009: 162) argued that women's fitness magazines promote white, heterosexual, middle-class notions of '"emphasized femininity" shaped in relation to hegemonic masculinity' that are typical in consumer culture. Smith Maguire (2007) added that the ideal feminine body provided a starting point to market an entirely consumerist fitness lifestyle.

Recently, Foucault's concept of governmentality has been employed to understand the images of the (feminine) (un)healthy (obese) body (King 2003; McDermott 2011; Rail 2012). The fitness media operate as a force for the contemporary bio-political control of bodies, within the context of neoliberal governance, which presents the individual as a rational economic actor who is 'free' to take responsibility for his/her self-care (Jette 2006; Markula 2001). Accordingly, exercise practices are marketed and sold by appealing to the individual's responsibility to 'self-care' for his/her body. Francombe (2010) and Millington (2014) have illustrated how 'new media' such as exergames (video-based exercise games such as Nintendo Wii Fit and We Cheer), rather like 'old' types of media workout, target neoliberal consumer citizens who are responsible for their bodies. Heywood (2007) observed that the 'normal' feminine body ideal has shifted slightly to further accommodate such consumerism.

The acceptable heterosexual feminine body now embraces (a certain level) of athleticism and has become normalized as the ideal role model: the 'can do girl' who has 'got it right' (Heywood 2007: 113). This body is also the ideal image of the self-determining consumer who takes responsibility for constructing her own body, success, and happiness 'in the neo-liberal ideology of the DIY lifestyle' (2007: 114). Several researchers (Capon and Helstein 2005; Giardina and Metz 2005; Lucas 2000) have read Nike advertisements as a similar sign of involving women more deeply within the post-Fordist, post-feminist, neoliberal consumer culture, in which the female athlete 'is both "girly-girl" and "athlete"' (Giardina and Metz 2005: 75). However, these readings focus on mediated images, not audience reactions that might include critical receptions. For example, Thorpe and Wheaton (2013: 347), using a Foucauldian perspective, indicated that some men and women adopt critical views of media constructions of snowboarding bodies.

Intersectionality

While the gendered body continues to occupy a central position within sport sociological analyses, it has been intersected, particularly by critical sport feminist scholars, with analyses of other forms of oppression such as racism, nationalism, and/or heterosexism that also normalize or exclude sporting bodies. Scholars such as Birrell and McDonald, 2000, Lock (2003), and McDonald (2008) have read how male dominance is constructed in the intersections of gender and sexuality in women's sports (for intersections of sporting masculinity and whiteness, see Kusz 2007). The construction of sexual identity is further problematized in analyses of trans-sexual bodies in the sporting context (Hargreaves and Anderson 2014).[2] Several sport feminist researchers have articulated how the power lines (Birrell and McDonald 2000) of nationalism, gender, race, and class cross the media to produce relations of dominance and subordination that are embedded in women athletes' bodies (Cooky, Wachs, Messner, and Dworkin 2010; Douglas and Jamieson, 2006; Elder, Pratt, and Ellis 2006; Elling and Luijt 2009; Hills and Kennedy 2009; Koh 2009; Lippe 2002; Stevenson 2002). These readings highlight the contradictions and ambiguities in representations of some bodies: although commonly aligned with hegemonic masculinity, their representations also open up possibilities to negotiate multiple meanings and thus diversity. In addition, new body identities such as disability (Duncan and Aycock 2005; Silva and Howe 2012) and ageing have been added to the selection of stereotypes that normalize the sporting bodies. Regardless of further recognizable identity categories, some sport scholars note an absence of analysis on how these identities are lived into existence by individual athletes and exercisers.

Embodied identities

Despite this growing interest in how individual identities are constructed through sport, several scholars continue to critique the lack of focus on embodied experiences of physical activity. Hockey and Allen-Collinson (2007: 116) looked for research that is 'truly grounded in the carnal realities of the lived sporting body' and used a phenomenological perspective to examine their own experiences of running with injuries. In their phenomenological study, Synne Groven, Solbrække and Engelsrud (2011) emphasized the role of an active exercising self in the intercorporeal and intersubjective world of interactions. Although phenomenological researchers acknowledge the impact of social interaction, they focus on the individual 'agent' whose subjectivity is undetectable through any analysis of language use (textual or interpersonal). Consequently, Hockey and Allen-Collinson (2007) emphasized how phenomenological inquiry can articulate physical activity experiences at multiple sensory levels (e.g. touch, olfactory, visual). Research writing, they added, has to bring the multiple layers of body experience alive; thus, they advocated representational techniques such as autoethnography. A related strand, narrative research, has emphasized the centrality of individual bodily experiences in the construction of coherent self stories (Jones, Glintmeyer, and McKenzie 2005; Smith and Sparkes 2009). Other sport sociologists have employed additional theoretical tools to infuse individual experiences within various models of social construction.

Embodied subjectivities

Several researchers have explicated the role of individual body experiences in the social and cultural construction of identity. Using such diverse theoretical perspectives as Bourdieu's reflective sociology, Gramscian-inspired hegemony theory, and Foucault's notion of self as constructed within power/discourse, advocates of this type of approach aim to demonstrate that the individual's gendered, raced, and/or sexualized identity is constructed through lived bodily experiences. Furthermore, while each individual body is considered to be socially constructed, it is also understood as a resistant agent. This dualism has been captured in the term 'embodied subjectivity' that accounts for the individual's ability to exercise power through his/her bodily actions. From this point of view, identity categories are socially constructed, but the researcher must account for how these are formed through embodied experiences in the micro context of the individual's life. Therefore, while focusing on embodied experiences similar to phenomenological research, these scholars consider how power relations enable certain meanings of sporting and exercising bodies to turn into dominant meanings.

The theme of sport (and fitness), as a simultaneously normalizing and resistant bodily practice, dominates the discussion of embodied subjectivities. For example, several feminist researchers have investigated how women have resisted dominant forms of heterosexual femininity by engaging in traditionally masculine sports such as rugby (Broad 2001; Chase 2006), soccer (Caudwell 2006; Mennesson 2012), ice hockey (Theberge 2002), or action sports (Rinehart and Sydnor 2003; Thorpe and Wheaton 2013) that require strong, aggressive, and powerful bodies. At the same time, Cox and Thompson (2000) demonstrated from a Foucauldian perspective that New Zealand women soccer players struggled to negotiate the contradictory demands of the soccer body, feminine identity, and sexuality. Similarly, Markula and Pringle (2006) concluded that the New Zealand male rugby body was negotiated according to multiple discourses of ethics, health, violence, and feminism. Drawing on Bourdieu, Mennesson (2000) demonstrated how women boxers simultaneously conformed to socially acceptable femininity yet engaged in aggressive contact sport. Research in women's bodybuilding (Bolin 2003; McGrath and Chananie-Hill 2009; Roussel *et al.* 2003; Wesely 2001) reveals a contradictory feminine body that, despite its visible muscularity, is built by following the ideologically dominant forms of emphasized femininity. Thorpe and Wheaton (2013: 1063) defined action sports as a commercial subculture that, nevertheless, enables resistance 'at the levels of the everyday and in the body.' Several scholars ascertained that women exercisers often construct normalized feminine identities which follow dominant mediated consumerist fitness discourses, yet also reject such ideals as unrealistic (Craig and Liberty 2007; Haravon Collins 2002; McGannon, Johnson, and Spence 2011).

Contradictions also characterize athletes' experiences with pain and violence in sport: pain tolerance is celebrated, thus bodies are commonly exposed to injuries, but at the same time, they are cared for and protected in order to secure winning performances (Howe 2004; Pike and Maguire 2003; Young 2005). Young (2012) observed that the celebration of hegemonic masculinity is at the core of continued sport-related violence leaving some players to negotiate their contradictory feelings of fear of (future) pain and/or disability (Markula and Pringle 2006). Women and men athletes' relationships to pain and injury, nevertheless, appear very similar (Malcolm 2011; Pike and Maguire 2003). An interest in athletes' lived experiences of physical pain has also sparked an interest in the medicalization of injury care in sport (Malcolm 2011; Safai 2013; Theberge 2007). Theberge (2007), who recorded accounts by administrators, medical practitioners, and physiotherapists, observed that the medicalization of the sporting body is a form of disciplinary power exercised over athletes by the clinical practice of sport medicine.

Although identity is central to the examinations of embodied subjectivities, gender politics tend to dominate the discussion with less emphasis on the construction of sexuality (Broad 2001; Caudwell 2006; Ravel and Rail 2006) or on racial identities through embodied, lived, everyday sporting activities. Nevertheless, embodied experiences construct forms of subjectivity that align with dominant identities, but can be resisted by using individual agency. Although providing insights into the contradictory construction of identity through contemporary body management practices, this research has not effectively demonstrated how these oppressive gender, racial, or sexual identities can be changed. Some of these examinations have combined a focus on ideological identity construction with a Foucauldian perspective; however, another strand of Foucauldian scholarship, based on his analysis of dominance through bodily discipline, has further examined the construction of the body within dominant power relations.

Foucauldian readings: docile sporting bodies

Several Foucauldian body scholars analyze how disciplinary techniques can be used as a tool of dominance. From this perspective, sport and fitness practices act as extensions of ubiquitous, invisible power relations that normalize a certain type of body and bodily conduct: they are a part of the 'panoptic' power arrangement whereby an invisible gaze ensures that athletes and exercisers self-survey their bodily flaws and continually work towards externally defined normalcy. Such control is implemented through disciplinary techniques of space distribution, effective time use, and the organization of exercises to produce successively longer and more complex segments that progress towards continuous improvement. For example, Markula and Pringle (2006) demonstrated how a health club serves as a space for strictly timed, continually progressive exercise regimes; and Barker-Ruchti and Tinning (2010) explored how women gymnasts' specific distribution within the gymnasium space, the strict and specific time-tabling of gymnastics training, and learning progressions, all acted as disciplinary techniques. Disciplinary exercises require precise command by a fitness leader or coach who easily observes, controls, and regulates the athletes or clients in an enclosed gymnasium (Barker-Ruchti and Tinning 2010), but who has also internalized the culture of panoptic control. The result is useful, efficient, obedient, and unquestioning docile bodies that operate effectively in a purpose-built space such as the gymnasium, athletics track (Denison, Mills, and Jones 2013), fitness studio (Markula and Pringle 2006), and society at large. In the sporting context, disciplinary training culminates in an exam, the actual competition event, wherein each individual's aptitude is visibly compared to the others. Visible comparisons, exams, and organization into seamlessly moving units all serve to construct certain type of behaviour and body as normal. As a result, individuals unquestioningly accept someone else's idea of normalcy. The Foucauldian approach tends to demonstrate the tight control of these disciplinary techniques and offers little hope for escaping the inevitable docility-utility of the physically active body, a body that is productive, but at the same time normalized into docility.

The material body in socio-cultural research

Several scholars, inspired by various theoretical perspectives, advocate an understanding of the body concomitantly as a material and social, cultural, and political entity. For example, Brown (2006: 169) employed Bourdieu's concept of (gender) somatization 'to consider how the material body is worked upon within relations of social domination'. Somatization, Brown argued, provides a theoretical device to articulate how gender relations operate both at somatic and symbolic levels. Somewhat parallel to the Foucauldian analyses of disciplinary techniques, he proposed an analysis of how gendered postures, gestures, and physical expressions are repeated but also enhanced when combined with certain (gender specific) equipment, clothing, or language use in social (sporting) space.

Acknowledging previous Bourdieusian and Foucauldian works, Thorpe (2011) observed that these explorations have nevertheless ignored accounts of the biological body. In her own appeal, Thorpe (2012: 15) engaged with feminist researchers Burke and Grosz to critically examine female exercisers' lived experiences of their biological bodies through an engagement 'in trans-disciplinary dialogues with scholars and professionals across the social and biological sciences.' Parallel to Brown and Thorpe, Evans, Davies, and Rich (2009) advocated an approach that treats the body as a 'real' material entity without ignoring its location within cultural meanings. Following Bernstein, they suggested the term 'corporeal device', which accounts for embodied action and somatic and kinetic meaning-making. In addition to the theoretical treatises by Brown (2006), Thorpe (2011) and Evans, Davies, and Rich (2009), there have been further calls, from poststructuralist perspectives, to include, not only the biological body, but the moving body within the social and cultural analysis of physical activity.

Larsson and Quennerstead (2012) observed that the body, instead of movement, has been of interest to researchers in physical education and sport sociology. Drawing from Butler and Barad's work, they advocated an exploration of how movement occurs, and how it is organized and systematized within certain historically, culturally, and socially constituted series of events and actions, as well as in relation to who is moving. They argued, similar to Brown (2006), Evans, Davies, and Rich (2009), and Thorpe (2014), that an examination of the moving body necessitates combining bio-scientific and socio-cultural knowledges within one project. Another poststructuralist line of thought advocating the inclusion of the moving body features Deleuzian-inspired research into the physically active body.

Deleuze's concept of 'rhizome' offers a poststructuralist alternative to the modernist 'tree model' philosophy where all knowledge stems from one root. The 'rhizome' that multiplies in all directions accounts for the multiplicity of everyday life, for the immanence, where the possibilities for change can be detected. Deleuze's philosophy highlights how the body, currently dominated by the capitalist regime, can act as an agent of social change. Bodily practices – what the body can do – provide one avenue out from the knowledge beds of capitalism and towards social change. The doing body, then, has the potential to reveal new ways of thinking, operating, and functioning in the world. Following Deleuze's philosophical path requires a major departure from the examination of the body as a representation or embodiment of dominant/subordinate identity: the force of the moving body is harnessed to disrupt the binary identity categories. In my own work on the fitness industry, I have embraced Deleuze's rhizomatic philosophy, first, to understand why, despite staunch criticism by feminist researchers, fitness practices have remained unchanged, and second, to explore how change might be initiated by creating different fitness practices (Markula 2006, Markula 2011).

Conclusion

In this chapter, I have highlighted several themes emerging from socio-cultural studies of the physically active body. While these 'body studies' now address diverse physical activities such as sport, action sports, exercise, and fitness, the body as a representation of identity remains the primary research topic. While gender politics is central, raced and sexed bodies, in addition to such 'new' identity categories as disabled and aged bodies, have become more visible. Relying strongly on media readings, this scholarship maintains that physically active bodies, particularly white male bodies, are normalized into dominant identities. In addition, there is an increasing acknowledgement of the matrix of domination by intersecting sexism, heterosexism, racism, ableism, and nationalism in sport.

In addition to media readings, identity formation is examined through individual sport and exercise experiences. Phenomenological researchers, particularly, have highlighted how the gendered body has been constructed through embodied physical activity experiences. Other scholars have further located individual body experiences within the structural constraints of power by drawing attention to what I have labelled 'embodied subjectivities.' Relying on insights from Bourdieu, Foucault, and Gramscian critical hegemony theory, they have demonstrated that individual athletes and exercisers, while aiming for normalcy, also resist it by questioning the 'normal' body or by participating in physical activities that challenge gender appropriateness. As their main conclusion, these investigations reveal the complex nature of physical activity experiences by evidencing the participants' persistent negotiation of compliance and resistance to normalcy. Despite exposing the contradictory process of embodied subjectivity formation, this research has not documented significant changes in the prevalence of dominant identities.

To find further ways to change the dominant definitions of the normal body, some researchers have turned to Foucault's disciplinary techniques in order to analyze the tight panoptic power relations that produce docile bodies. Although these investigations persuasively show the anatomo-political control that is exerted over physically active bodies, they have not yet provided suggestions as to how bodily discipline may be transcended. This research has, nevertheless, shifted the focus from the normalization of identity to the control of the body. As a result, these researchers argue that altering physical activity practices is one way to change the social construction of identity, subjectivity, and the self. To further advance the Foucauldian examinations, a Deleuzian perspective has offered some insight into how change in movement practice can facilitate social change. This approach aims, not only to provide socio-cultural research with new directions, but to instigate change beyond academia. As a related move, there has been increased interest in considering the impact of the 'material' body together with the discursively constructed body (identity) on the operations of physical activity in the current society.

Despite the dominance of the representational body, there is now a broader range of approaches to investigate the (moving) body. In addition, the material, physical, moving body and how it defines the landscape of physical activity and society at large has become a more visible feature of socio-cultural investigations of sport and exercise. Further research into the role of the physically active body as an agent of change, can offer potential insights into the discursive formation of sport and exercise. Although the emphasis on 'concrete' physicality is important, we might need deeper awareness of the body in the era of increasing virtualization of social life: How does the material, moving body operate in this terrain? As technology becomes a gradually more pervasive aspect of social 'reality', it also defines how we understand, know, and move our bodies. We nevertheless all have material bodies that continue to be subjected to multiple forces and thus, physically (in)active bodies, no doubt, will continue to be integral aspects of socio-cultural studies of sport, exercise, coaching, and physical activity.

Notes

1 See also the special issue on whiteness in the *Sociology of Sport Journal*, Volume 22, Issue 3.
2 See also *Journal of Sport and Social Issues* special issue, Volume 37, issue 1.

References

Barker-Ruchti, N. and Tinning, R. (2010) 'Foucault in Leotards', *Sociology of Sport Journal*, 27: 229–250.
Birrell, S. and McDonald, M.G. (2000) (eds) *Reading Sport: Critical Essays on Power and Representation*, Boston, MA: Northeastern University Press.
Bolin, A. (2003) 'Beauty or the Beast: The Subversive Soma', in A. Bolin and J. Granskog (eds) *Athletic Intruders*, Albany: SUNY Press.
Broad, K.L. (2001) 'The Gendered Unapologetic: Queer Resistance in Women's Sport', *Sociology of Sport Journal*, 2: 181–204.
Brown, D. (2006) 'Pierre Bourdieu's "Masculine Domination" Thesis and the Gendered Body in Sport and Physical Culture', *Sociology of Sport Journal*, 23: 162–188.
Capon, D. A. and Helstein, M. (2005) '"Knowing" the Hero: The Female Athlete and Myth at Work in Nike Advertising', in S.J. Jackson and D.L. Andrews (eds) *Identities, Commodities and the Politics of Representation*, London and New York: Routledge.

Carrington, B. (2010) *Race, Sport and Politics*, London: Sage.

Caudwell, J. (2006) *Sport, Sexualities and Queer Theory*, London: Routledge.

Chase, L.F. (2006) '(Un)disciplined Bodies: A Foucauldian Analysis of Women's Rugby', *Sociology of Sport Journal*, 23: 229–247.

Cole, C.L. (2000) 'Body Studies in Sociology of Sport', in J. Coakley and E. Dunning (eds) *Handbook of Sports Studies*, Thousand Oaks, CA: Sage.

Cooky, C., Wachs, F.L., Messner, M. and Dworkin, S.L. (2010) 'It's Not About the Game: Don Imus, Race, Class, Gender, and Sexuality in Contemporary Media', *Sociology of Sport Journal*, 27: 139–159.

Cox, B. and Thompson, S. (2000) 'Multiple Bodies: Sportswomen, Soccer and Sexuality', *International Review for the Sociology of Sport*, 35: 5–20.

Craig, M.L. and Liberty, R. (2007) '"Cause That's What Girls Do": The Making of a Feminized Gym', *Gender & Society*, 21: 676–699.

Dart, J. (2014) 'Sports Review: A Content Analysis of the *International Review for the Sociology of Sport*, the *Journal of Sport and Social Issues* and the *Sociology of Sport Journal* Across 25 Years', *International Review for the Sociology of Sport*, 49: 645–668.

Denison, J., Mills, J., and Jones, L. (2013) 'Effective Coaching as a Modernist Formation: A Foucauldian Critique', in P. Potrac, W. Gilbert and J. Denison (eds) *The Routledge Handbook of Sport Coaching*, London: Routledge.

Douglas, D.D. and Jamieson, K.M. (2006) 'A Farewell to Remember: Interrogating the Nancy Lopez Farewell Tour', *Sociology of Sport Journal*, 23: 117–141.

Duncan, M. and Aycock, A. (2005) 'Fitting Images: Advertising, Sport and Disability', in S.J. Jackson and D.L. Andrews (eds.) *Sport, Culture and Advertising*, London: Routledge.

Dworkin, S.L. and F.L. Wachs (2009) *Body Panic: Gender, Health, and the Selling of Fitness*, New York: New York University Press.

Elder, C., Pratt, A. and Ellis, C. (2006) 'Running Race: Reconciliation, Nationalism and the Sydney 2000 Olympic Games', *International Review for the Sociology of Sport*, 41: 181–200.

Elling, A. and Luijt, R. (2009) 'Different Shades of Orange?', in P. Markula (ed.) *Olympic Women and the Media*, Basingstoke, UK: Palgrave.

Francombe, J. (2010) '"I Cheer, You Cheer, We Cheer": Physical Technologies and the Normalised Body', *Television & the New Media*, 11: 350–366.

Giardina, M. and Metz, J. (2005) 'Women's Sports in Nike's America', in S.J. Jackson and D.L. Andrews (eds) *Sport, Culture and Advertising*, London: Routledge.

Groven Synne, K., Solbrække Nyheim, K. and Engersrud, G. (2011) 'Large Women's Experiences of Exercise', in E. Kennedy and P. Markula (eds) *Women and Exercise*, New York: Routledge.

Haravon Collins, L. (2002) 'Working Out Contradictions: Feminism and Aerobics', *Journal of Sport & Social Issues*, 26: 85–109.

Hargreaves, J. and Anderson, E. (2014) *The Routledge Handbook of Sport, Gender and Sexuality*, London: Routledge.

Hargreaves, J. and Vertinsky, P. (2007) 'Introduction', in J. Hargreaves and P. Vertinsky (eds) *Physical Culture, Power, and the Body*, London: Routledge.

Harris, J. and Clayton, B. (2002) 'Femininity, Masculinity, Physicality and the English Tabloid Press: The Case of Anna Kournikova', *International Review for the Sociology of Sport*, 37: 397–413.

Heywood, L. (2007) 'Producing Girls: Empire, Sport, and the Neoliberal Body', in J. Hargreaves and P. Vertinsky (eds) *Physical Culture, Power, and the Body*, London: Routledge.

Hills, L. and Kennedy, E. (2009) 'Double Trouble: Kelly Holmes, Intersectionality and Unstable Narratives of Olympic Heroism in the British Media', in P. Markula (ed.) *Olympic Women and the Media*, Basingstoke, UK: Palgrave.

Hockey, J. and Allen-Collinson, J. (2007) 'Grasping the Phenomenology of Sporting Bodies', *International Review for the Sociology of Sport*, 42: 115–131.

Howe, P.D. (2004) *Sport, Professionalism and Pain*, London: Routledge.

Jette, S. (2006) 'Fit for Two?: A Critical Discourse Analysis of *Oxygen* Fitness Magazine', *Sociology of Sport Journal*, 23: 331–351.

Jones, R.L., Glintmeyer, N. and McKenzie, A. (2005) 'Slim Bodies, Eating Disorders and the Coach–Athlete Relationship', *International Review for the Sociology of Sport*, 40(3): 377–391.

Kennedy, E. and Pappa, E. (2011) 'Love Your Body?: The Discursive Construction of Exercising Women's Lifestyle and Fitness Magazines', in E. Kennedy and P. Markula (eds) *Women and Exercise: The Body, Health and Consumerism*, New York: Palgrave.

King, S.J. (2003). 'Doing Good by Running Well', in J.Z. Bratich, J. Packer and C. McCarthy (eds) *Foucault, Cultural Studies, Governmentality*, New York: Simon & Schuster.

Koh, E. (2009) 'Heroes, Sisters and Beauties: Korean Printed Media Representation of Sport Women in the 2004 Olympics', in P. Markula (ed.) *Olympic Women and the Media*, Basingstoke, UK: Palgrave.

Kusz, K.W. (2007) *Revolt of the White Athlete: Race, Media and the Emergence of Extreme Athletes in America*, New York: Peter Lang.

Larsson, H. and Quennerstead, M. (2012) 'Understanding Movement: A Socio-Cultural Approach to Exploring Human Movement', *Quest*, 64: 283–298.

Lippe, G. van der (2002) 'Media Image: Sport, Gender, and National Identities in Five European Countries', *International Review for the Sociology of Sport*, 27: 371–395.

Lock, R.A. (2003) 'The Doping Ban: Compulsory Heterosexuality and Lesbophobia', *International Review for the Sociology of Sport*, 38: 397–411.

Loy, J., Andrews, D.A. and Rinehart, R. (1993) 'The Body in Culture and Sport: Toward an Embodied Sociology of Sport', *Sport Science Review*, 2: 69–91.

Lucas, S. (2000) 'Nike's Commercial Solution: Girls, Sneakers, and Salvation', *International Review for the Sociology of Sport*, 35: 149–164.

Malcolm, D. (2011) 'Sport Medicine, Injured Athletes and Norbert Elias's Sociology of Knowledge', *Sociology of Sport Journal*, 28: 284–302.

Markula, P. (2001) 'Beyond the Perfect Body: Women's Body Image Distortion in Fitness Magazine Discourse', *Journal of Sport & Social Issues* 25: 158–179.

—— (2006) 'Deleuze and the Body without Organs: Disreading the Fit Feminine Identity', *Journal of Sport & Social Issues*, 30: 29–44.

—— (2009) 'Introduction', in P. Markula (ed.) *Olympic Women and the Media*, Basingstoke, UK: Palgrave.

—— (2011) '"Folding": A Feminist Intervention in Mindful Fitness', in E. Kennedy and P. Markula (eds) *Women and Exercise*, New York: Routledge.

Markula, P. and Pringle, R. (2006) *Foucault, Sport and Exercise*, London: Routledge.

McDermott, L. (2011) '"Doing Something That's Good for Me": Exploring Intersections of Physical Activity and Health', in E. Kennedy and P. Markula (eds) *Women and Exercise*, New York: Routledge.

McDonald, M.G. (2005) 'Mapping Whiteness and Sport: An Introduction', *Sociology of Sport Journal*, 22: 245–255.

—— (2008) 'Rethinking Resistance: The Queer Play of the Women's National Basketball Association, Visibility Politics and Late Capitalism', *Leisure Studies*, 27(1): 77–93.

McGannon, K.R., Johnson, C.R. and Spence, J.C. (2011) 'I Am (Not) Big . . . It's the Pictures That Got Small: Examining Cultural and Personal Exercise Narratives and the Fear of Fat', in E. Kennedy and P. Markula (eds) *Women and Exercise*, New York: Routledge.

McGrath, S.A. and Chananie-Hill, R.A. (2009) '"Big Freaky-Looking Women": Normalizing Gender Transgression Through Bodybuilding', *Sociology of Sport Journal* 26: 235–254.

Mennesson, C. (2000) '"Hard" Women and "Soft" Women: The Social Construction of Identities among Female Boxers', *International Review for the Sociology of Sport*, 35: 21–33.

—— (2012) 'Gender Regimes and Habitus: An Avenue for Analyzing Gender Building in Sport Contexts', *Sociology of Sport Journal* 29: 4–21.

Messner, M.A. (2002) *Taking the Field: Women, Men and Sports*, Minneapolis: University of Minnesota Press.

Millington, B. (2014) 'Amusing Ourselves to Life: Fitness Consumerism and the Birth of Bio-Games', *Journal of Sport & Social Issues*, 38: 491–508.

Montez de Oca, J. (2013) 'Paradox of Privilege: Sport, Masculinities, and the Commodified Body', in B. Carrington and D.L. Andrews (eds). *A Companion to Sport*, Chichester, UK: Wiley Blackwell.

Pike, E. and Maguire J. (2003) 'Injury in Women's Sport: Classifying Elements of Risk Encounters', *Sociology of Sport Journal*, 20(3): 232–251.

Rail, G. (2012) 'The Birth of the Obesity Clinic', *Sociology of Sport Journal*, 29: 227–253.

Ravel, B. and Rail, G. (2006) '"The Lightness of Being Gaie": Discursive Constructions of Gender and Sexuality in Quebec Women's Sport', *International Review for the Sociology of Sport*, 41(3): 395–412.

Rinehart, R. and Sydnor, S. (2003) *To the Extreme: Alternative Sports, Inside and Out*, Albany: SUNY Press.

Roussel, P., Griffet, J. and Duret, P. (2003) 'The Decline of Female Bodybuilding in France', *Sociology of Sport Journal* 20: 40–59.

Safai, P. (2013) 'Sports Medicine, Health, and the Politics of Risk', in B. Carrington and D.L. Andrews (eds) *A Companion to Sport*, Chichester, UK: Wiley Blackwell.

Schultz, J. (2005) 'Serena Williams and the Production of Blackness at the 2002 US Open', *Journal of Sport & Social Issues*, 29(3): 338–357.

Scraton, S. and Flintoff, A. (2013) 'Gender, Feminist Theory, and Sport', in B. Carrington and D.L. Andrews (eds) *A Companion to Sport*, Chichester, UK: Wiley Blackwell.

Silva, C.F. and Howe, P.D. (2012). 'The (In)Validity of Supercrip Representation of Paralympic Athletes', *Journal of Sport & Social Issues*, 36: 174–194.

Smith, B. and Sparkes, A. (2009) 'Narrative Inquiry In Sport Psychology: What Can It Mean and Why We Might Do It?', *Psychology of Sport and Exercise*, 1–11.

Smith Maguire, J. (2007) *Fit for Consumption: Sociology and the Business of Fitness*, London: Routledge.

Spencer, N.E. (2004) 'Sister Act IV: Venus & Serena Williams at Indian Wells: "Sincere Fictions" and White Racism', *Journal of Sport & Social Issues*, 28: 115–135.

Stevenson, D. (2002) 'Women, Sport, and Globalization', *Journal of Sport & Social Issues*, 26: 209–225.

Theberge, N. (2002) *Higher Goals: Women's Ice-Hockey and the Politics of Gender*, Albany: SUNY Press.

—— (2007) '"It's Not About Health, It's About Performance": Sport Medicine, Health, and the Culture of Risk in Canadian Sport' in J. Hargreaves and P. Vertinsky (eds) *Physical Culture, Power, and the Body*, London: Routledge.

Thorpe, H. (2011) *Snowboarding Bodies in Theory and Practice*, Basingstoke, UK: Palgrave Macmillan.

—— (2014) 'Moving Bodies Beyond the Social/Biological Divide', *Sport, Education and Society*, 19: 666–686.

Thorpe, H. and Wheaton, B. (2013) 'Dissecting Action Sports Studies', in B. Carrington and D.L. Andrews (eds) *A Companion to Sport*, Chichester, UK: Wiley Blackwell.

Turner, B. (1984) *The Body and Society*, London: Sage.

Young, K. (2005) *Sporting Bodies, Damaged Selves*, Oxford: Elsevier.

—— (2012) *Sport Violence and Society*, London: Routledge.

Wenner, L.A. (2013) *Fallen Sports Heroes, Media, & Celebrity Culture*, New York: Peter Lang.

Wensing, E. and Bruce, T. (2003) 'Bending the Rules: Media Representations of Gender During the International Sporting Event', *International Review for the Sociology of Sport*, 38: 387–396.

Wesely, J. (2001) 'Negotiating Gender: Bodybuilding and the Natural/Unnatural Continuum', *Sociology of Sport Journal*, 18: 162–180.

Wu, P. (2009) 'From "Iron Girl" to "Sexy Goddess": An Analysis of the Chinese Media', in P. Markula (ed.) *Olympic Women and the Media*, Basingstoke, UK: Palgrave.

29

SPORT, PHYSICAL ACTIVITY, AND HEALTH

Jessica Lee

Introduction

Studies from around the world point to inadequate participation in physical activity and sport, with direct consequences on population health as evidenced by the 'growing obesity epidemic' and the advent of 'lifestyle diseases'. Governments are spending unprecedented amounts of money in an attempt to increase participation in physical activities. Therefore, no longer is public participation in physical activity and sports viewed as a matter of pleasurable, voluntary leisure time pursuit; rather, such activity has become an obligation with not only health but also moral implications. This shift and meaning of participation in physical activity and sports in our social milieu is worthy of examination.

Much of what we 'know' about participation in sports and physical activity is informed by large-scale epidemiological studies that tell us overall participation is low, and that women and girls, people with disabilities, ethnic minorities, and those of low socioeconomic status are less likely to be physically active (as I discuss later). Despite our best efforts and big budgets, there has been little success in changing physical activity behaviours through the use of policy models that emphasize positivist methods and individual responsibility. As such, there is a need for more extensive and theoretically rigorous research and analysis, in order to understand the meaning of physical activity in popular culture and indeed within people's own lives.

Studies of health that utilize social theory have proposed that individual health behaviours (such as sport and physical activity participation) are reflective of wider sociohistorical contexts within which people live their daily lives. As such, health practices such as diet and physical activity are learnt and embodied through the internalization of social surroundings (Warin *et al.* 2008; S. Williams 1995). From this perspective, popular public health discourses of individual responsibility and victim blaming, which suggest that lifestyles are simply a matter of personal choice, become particularly problematic (S. Williams 1995). A move beyond epidemiology is therefore required to investigate and to theorize the social and structural dimensions of *why* individuals and groups behave the way they do (G. Williams 2003). Current approaches to physical activity promotion often fail to consider the impact of social structures on meanings given to physical activity and health which affect actions and 'choices' concerning physical activity. This perhaps explains, in part, the limited success of interventions to increase physical activity at a population level. The use of qualitative understandings and social theory can help us further describe 'what is going on' in terms of reports of low participation rates and failing interventions.

The purpose of this chapter is to examine the appropriation of sport and physical activities from fun leisure time pursuits to obligated practices of good citizens for the sole purpose of increasing health. Specifically, I will examine, with the use of Bourdieu's social theory, how physical activity participation has been hijacked by the imperative for health and the associated pursuit of 'trim-ness'. In doing so I will highlight the growing links between elite sport and population physical activity participation, and how pervasive the notion of bodily movement for the purpose of health has become.

Sport and physical activity as health behaviours

From the second half of the twentieth century, physical activity became commonly linked with health benefits, following Jeremy Morris's seminal reports from investigations of London transport workers and British civil servants (Blair *et al.* 2004). Morris documented higher rates of coronary heart disease (CHD) in men who were sedentary at work (e.g. bus drivers) and in leisure compared to those who had more active jobs (e.g. bus conductors) or leisure pursuits (Heady *et al.* 1956). As such, in 1975 the first recommendations for health-related physical activity were published by the American College for Sports Medicine (ACSM) (Blair *et al.* 2004). This recommendation was updated in 1990 and 1995, and is credited by Blair (2004) with marking the shift away from performance-related fitness to one that accounts for health-related outcomes. The purpose of the recommendations was to provide a 'clear, concise, public health message' that would 'encourage increased participation in physical activity' (cited in Haskell *et al.* 2007: 1423). Current recommendations for health-enhancing physical activity were published in 2007 and suggest:

> To promote and maintain health, all healthy adults aged 18–65 years need moderate-intensity aerobic physical activity for a minimum of 30 minutes on five days each week or vigorous-intensity aerobic activity for a minimum of 20 minutes on three days each week.
>
> (Haskell *et al.* 2007: 1525)

This recommendation has been adopted by the World Health Organization (WHO), the U.S. Centers for Disease Control and Prevention (CDC), the British Heart Foundation and the UK's National Health Service (NHS), the Australian Health Department, and other national health and exercise organizations worldwide.

In more recent times lack of physical activity has been recognized in public health agendas as a major cause of death and chronic disease. Physical inactivity is currently considered overall as the third highest risk factor for global mortality, accounting for around 9% of premature deaths (WHO 2009). Furthermore, overweight and obesity are considered the next highest risk factors for global mortality (accounting for 5% of deaths) (WHO 2009), with physical inactivity being widely accepted as a 'cause' of overweight and obesity.

This potted history of physical activity promotion for health benefits outlines the beginnings and continuation of the now taken-for-granted link between physical activity and health. What we see today is a saturation in schools, the media, and popular culture of the imperative to be active to achieve or maintain health benefits and not least of all to achieve or maintain a 'healthy weight' (Evans *et al.* 2011). From a quick scan of national health and physical activity promotion campaigns (e.g. Change4Life UK, Measure Up Australia, Shape Up America) and popular culture artefacts, it is evident that the policy discourse suggests that all physical activity should be conducted with a view to gaining health. One prime example is the television series *The Biggest Loser*, where contestants challenge each other to lose the most weight (thereby personalizing the concern) by being subjected to vigorous physical activity training regimes (and restrictive diets) under the guidance of personal trainers who push, shout, and even ridicule their subjects to make them work harder to lose weight and seemingly gain health, although health markers are never measured as part of the show. Indeed, health and physical activity have become a commodity and an industry (Klein 2010), and the ideal of sport and play as an essential human right has been hijacked by a corporate health agenda. Metzl (2010) proposes that health has become 'the new morality'. I argue that, by association, physical activity and sport have themselves become acts of moral worth, a position which is discussed more thoroughly in the following section.

Berlant (2010: 26) suggests that the obese body 'serves as a billboard advert for impending sickness and death', while for Lebesco (2010: 72) fat people are urged to 'eat less and better, and to *move more*' (emphasis added). The link between physical activity and overweight and obesity is taken for granted in this exhortation to 'move more'. If one moves more, one will lose weight and become healthy, thereby implicating physical activity in the morality of health. A number of contemporary researchers (e.g. Lebesco 2010; Rich and Evans 2005) have labelled the so-called obesity epidemic a 'moral panic', and it is no coincidence that 'sloth' is considered a capital vice within Christian ethics. As a result, a great deal of hostility in the form of moral outrage is directed at individuals who are understood to be lazy, out of control, without will, and ignorant (Lebesco 2010). Those buying into the obesity epidemic are often proponents of the healthism discourse (Kirk and Colquhoun 1989), which states that health can be achieved 'unproblematically through individual effort and discipline, directed mainly at regulating the size and shape of the body' (Crawford, cited in Kirk and Colquhoun 1989: 149). The 'individual effort and discipline' referred to is in no small part directed at physical activity and, particularly for the overweight or obese person, is merely for the purpose of weight loss.

Despite dominant discourses and popular cultural understandings, the relationship between physical activity, overweight and obesity, and health is far from clear. Critical obesity researchers, having closely examined the plethora of epidemiological evidence, report a distinct lack of proportion between the hype surrounding obesity and the harm caused by fatness (e.g. Campos 2004; Gard 2011; Gard and Wright 2005). For example, Campos *et al.* (2006: 56) found that

> among the obese, little or no increase in relative risk for premature mortality is observed until one reaches BMIs in the upper 30s or higher. In other words, the vast majority of people labelled "overweight" and "obese" according to current definitions do not in fact face any meaningful increased risk for an early death.
>
> (2006: 56)

In addition, statistical linkages between body mass and mortality may be confounded by factors like fitness and exercise (Lebesco 2010). For example, over decades of research Steven Blair and colleagues have consistently found physical fitness to be a stronger mediator of health outcomes than body weight such that being thin is only beneficial to health if also physically fit and being fit reduces the hazards of obesity (e.g. Gibbons *et al.* 1983; Ortega *et al.* 2013).

The point here is that because of the moral panic around the obesity epidemic, despite scientific evidence to the contrary, physical activity and sport participation have become embroiled in a public health agenda. Due to the healthism discourse, participation in physical activity and sport has become an individual responsibility and is thus promoted as such. If one does not make the 'choice' to participate in physical activity or sport, one is choosing not to be healthy. There-fore, from a public health perspective, physical activity and sport have been reduced to simple choices with very little regard for the social structures that shape participation.

Elite sport, health promotion, and the obesity epidemic

Not only have the health and obesity agendas pervaded recreational or leisure time physical activity discourses. There are now several examples of how elite sport is used to increase mass participation under the guise of health promotion. Many elite sports clubs have jumped onto the obesity prevention bandwagon. Perhaps the most rigorously trialed and evaluated is the Scottish Premier League's (SPL) 'Football Fans in Training (FFiT)' program (Gray *et al.* 2013). The FFiT program recruited men aged 35–65 to take part in a 12-week group intervention at the SPL club they support. While the pilot programme yielded only moderate success in achieving its aim of reducing obesity (4.6% and 3.5% weight loss at 12-week and 12-month follow-up, respectively) it was rolled out to the entire SPL, and funded by the SPL Trust, the Football Pools, and the Scottish government (Gray *et al.* 2013). Similar campaigns have been initiated in England, offering obesity prevention programs aimed at children, for example, with Manchester City (Manchester City Football Club n.d.) and Aston Villa (Premier League 2012) in football and London Wasps and Saracens in Premiership Rugby (London Wasps n.d.; Sara-cens 2012).

In our recent cultural memories is also the London 2012 Olympic legacy to 'inspire a gen-eration'. London's mayor during the Olympic period, Boris Johnson, said, 'My perfect 2012 legacy would be a leaner, fitter London and I want us to work swiftly towards the elimination of childhood obesity' (Greater London Authority n.d.). As Rich (2012a) suggests, the 'inspire a generation' slogan as it relates to youth participation rates in sport and physical activity was particularly ambitious as there is scant evidence to support the claim that hosting the Olympic Games has created such a legacy elsewhere. Furthermore, the sport/physical activity and health link is once again highlighted with the mention of the elimination of childhood obesity, and as such, Rich suggests 'undertaking physical activity for other reasons such as the pleasure of movement, or experiencing connection with one's body or environment, can be quickly lost in the presence of the sort of elite performances celebrated during London 2012' (Rich 2012a: 65). While elite sport may have gained momentum in Great Britain following the 2012 Olympics, Rich (2012b) reminds us to be cautious of this legacy in school sport and physical education (and, I would suggest, in the public health arena). Using sport to tackle 'social ills' such as obesity and 'breed the next champion' can lead to school programmes which emphasize fitness testing and competitive sport which, as research consistently demonstrates, are often the very things that put young people off being active (Rich 2012b).

As evidenced in this section, elite sport has also become a vehicle in promoting physical activity for health rather than a fun leisure pursuit. If nothing else, these programmes serve to change the place of sport spectatorship and elite sport in our everyday lives. Furthermore, they perpetuate the discourse that health-enhancing physical activity should be meritocratic, pur-poseful exercise involving formal coaching, such as gym work and team sports, and add to the moral pursuit of health and physical fitness. In the following section, findings from an Australian ethnographic project are reported that explore the place and meaning of physical activity in young people's lives, demonstrating the pervasiveness of the healthism discourse and the idea of health-enhancing physical activity as formal sport and fitness training.

A sociological understanding of participation in sport and physical activity

If sport and physical activity are to be considered as such important markers of the health and well-being of individuals and communities, we must understand them sociologically. Humans, their lives and experiences, are not reducible to numbers. So what do we know about who is sufficiently physically active for health and who is not? And is that important? To answer these questions we need to examine the social structures and discourses that shape everyday people's experiences with sport and physical activity.

As with data on the relationship between obesity and health, the epidemiological evidence around participation in physical activities tells a partial and biased story. Based on participation statistics, it is often cited that girls and women (Bauman *et al.* 2012), those of low socioeconomic status (Trost *et al.* 2002), people of ethnic minority groups (Trost *et al.* 2002), people with disabilities (Rimmer *et al.* 2004), those in rural locations (Parks *et al.* 2003), and those with poor body image and/or overweight or obese (Metcalf *et al.* 2011) are less active than their counterparts in dominant social groups. However, there are certain cautions to taking these statistics at face value. First, research suggests that physical activity measurement surveys have tended to favour the types of activities engaged in by men, and as such, the types of activities that many girls and women participate in, such as less formal forms of physical activity and household chores are not measured. Similar points may be made regarding ethnic minority groups (Knez *et al.* 2012) and people living in rural areas (Lee and Macdonald 2009) where evidence shows that different forms of physical activity dominate and are not necessarily captured in traditional surveys. It is perhaps this poor understanding of the types and meanings of physical activity that contribute to our taken-for-granted knowledge about who is adequately physically active and who is not.

Furthermore, as mentioned in the previous section, given the social structures that mediate participation, it is superficial and erroneous to consider individual participation in sport and physical activity as a simple product of personal choice. There is a lot that the participation statistics cannot tell us, such as *why* all minority categories tend to be less active than members of dominant groups. Current approaches to physical activity fail to consider the impact of social structures on the meanings that people give to physical activity and health and which, in turn, affect actions and 'choices' concerning participation. A sociological perspective can help us examine the complex interplay of cultural forces, which shape people's engagements with sport and physical activity. A deeper sociological perspective (as opposed to the dominant positivist perspective that usually informs physical activity and health) shifts the focus from the individual to examine power and broader overarching structures (such as gender, class, race) that are out of the direct control of the individual but which have an inherent influence on shaping participation in sport and physical activity.

For this purpose, several researchers (this author included) have found the social theories of Pierre Bourdieu to be particularly useful (e.g. Dagkas and Quarmby 2012; Laberge and Kay 2002; Lee and Macdonald 2009, 2010). Others have drawn on Michel Foucault (e.g. McGannon and Spence 2010; Nelson *et al.* 2012), Basil Bernstein (Evans *et al.* 2010; Leow *et al.* 2012), and feminist theory (e.g. Rich *et al.* 2011) to examine how discourses and overarching institutions and structures shape participation in physical activities. As such, it is evident that physical activity and sport participation at a recreational level can be explained, understood, and critiqued using sociological tools from various perspectives.

By way of example, I will demonstrate how Bourdieu's notions of habitus, capital, and field can be used to understand rural young people's engagements with physical activity and sport.

Data in the following example are part of a large-scale, longitudinal, qualitative research project into the place and meaning of physical activity and physical culture in the lives of young people in Australia. The specific cohort referred to in this chapter were a sample of 11 rural young people (6 girls, 5 boys) ranging in age from 11 to 15 years old at the time of recruitment. Our full findings on this issue are published elsewhere (Lee and Macdonald 2009).

Over the three-year data collection period, strong gender differences appeared in the rural young people's participation in physical activities and their talk around health and fitness. In particular, variations were played out in the differentiation between the young women's and young men's participation in sport, and also in the ways in which they perceived physical labour. This is discussed in terms of how Bourdieu's notions of habitus and capital intersect with the particular rural social setting to shape certain actions. While gender differences in young people's participation in physical activities are often reported in quantitative studies, this analysis goes beyond participation statistics to explore the nature of the social worlds that produced gendered practices.

While most of the young women in the cohort did participate in recreational physical activities (tennis, swimming, trampoline), individual exercise (sit-ups, boxing bag), and/or physical labour, they did not perceive these forms of physical activity as legitimate because of the dominance of sport and exercise discourses. The young women involved in physical labour discussed these activities in terms of chores or responsibilities rather than physical activity, for example, 'It's not really a physical activity because I'm not doing it to get fit'. As these young women identified themselves as physically inactive despite participating in physical forms of labour and recreation, quantitative-based studies relying on self-report to measure physical activity participation would not capture these legitimate forms of physical activity.

Given the young women's talk about 'what counts' as physical activity and their somewhat restricted participation patterns, it is inferred that their conceptions of physical activity were not consistent with the rural feminine discourse perceiving a lack of legitimized feminine physical activity options. When asked about the physical activity options in their communities, the young women often mentioned activities and sports that they could not access like cricket and football (rugby league) clubs that did not have women's teams, and facilities like a skate park that were dominated by male 'skatey bums'. The only young woman in the cohort to be involved in a formal sport participated in equestrian events, particularly dressage, which, while it does include male participants, remains consistent with feminine discourses.

The young men in the cohort were involved in more sports, as there were more opportunities and facilities for what were perceived to be boys' sports. Of the young men who were not involved in organized sports, all were regularly involved in physical labour. In contrast to the young women, being involved in farming work constituted legitimate physical activity for the young men. The young men who were not involved in any sport were keen to demonstrate that they were nevertheless physically active in their farm chores such as wood chopping, sheep and cattle mustering, and shearing. Physical labour also appeared in these young men's descriptions of their leisure time.

Bourdieu's theoretical tools of 'habitus', 'capital', and 'field' are employed, which allow for an explanation of the interplay between social contexts and relationships in shaping rural young people's engagements with physical activity. Bourdieu described the embodiment of social rules, values, and dispositions as the habitus, which he defined as 'the durably installed generative principle of regulated improvisations . . . [which produces] practices' (Bourdieu 1977: 78). Therefore, one's apparently spontaneous choice of personal practices, including participation in sport and physical activity, are the product of embodiment of dispositions and norms that are derived from, and are indicative of, social conditions (Harvey and Sparks 1991). The habitus reflects a configuration of capital (economic, social, cultural, physical) comprising aspects of social currency that individuals possess in varying degrees and which are unequally distributed amongst social groups (Bourdieu 1986). A field (such as sport and physical activity) can be defined as a social arena characterized by struggles for dominant positions (Jarvie and Maguire 1994) to determine what constitutes the legitimate capital within that field and how that capital is to be distributed (Webb *et al.* 2002).

For this cohort of young people, gendered power appeared to be most dominant in the social order of the sport and physical activity field within the rural setting. Their habitus is shaped by the internalizing of this social setting. As the habitus is a set of dispositions that motivate action in the particular field, the rural young people's apparent choices about participation in physical activities reproduced the gendered order of the rural social setting. Bourdieu explains this relationship between the field and habitus as 'the relationship of immediate adherence that is established in practice between a habitus and the field to which it is attuned, the pre-verbal taking for granted of the world that flows from practical sense' (1990a: 68). Both the young men and the young women appeared to adhere to the gendered social order which placed the young women in a subordinate position in terms of legitimized activities and availability of facilities.

This model is not to be interpreted as overly deterministic. Evans's (2002) use of the concept *bounded agency* is particularly useful in this situation. In Bourdieu's terminology, bounded agency is demonstrated in the following quote: 'Agents shape their aspirations according to concrete indices of the accessible and inaccessible and, of what is and is not *for us*' (Bourdieu 1990a: 64, emphasis added). It is important to point out that this is not a conscious effort on behalf of the individual to 'adjust their aspirations to an exact evaluation of their chances of success' (1990a: 54); rather that the habitus, 'without violence, art or argument tends to exclude all "extravagances" ("not for the likes of us"), that is, all the behaviours that would be negatively sanctioned because they are *incompatible with the objective conditions*' (1990a: 56, emphasis added).

The case of the only woman to participate in a sport demonstrates her possession of the necessary social capital (access to equestrian clubs and coaches) and cultural and economic capital (knowledge of horse training and grooming methods, possession of land and equipment for horse riding), which afforded her the agency to participate in equestrian sport. As noted earlier, however, her access was available to an activity that is considered appropriate and legitimate for female participants. Rather than being structurally forced into certain actions, this young woman chose a sport that was consistent with her habitus. Bourdieu would term this occurrence as the 'logic of practice' (1990b).

The gendered nature of the rural young people's participation in physical activities arises from the habitus and the deeply instilled social order, and every performance both reproduces the gender norms of the field and reinscribes them upon the body. This performance of gender was not only evident in the young people's participation choices but also in the way they understood and spoke about sports and physical activities. For example, it was evident when one young man spoke of physical farm chores as 'sort of rough, it's a boy thing', and in one young women's comments about local facilities, '... based around all boys' stuff ... they should put more like female sports and stuff'.

This analysis provides insight into what may contribute to the reported discrepancy between boys and girls in rates of participation in physical activities, as noted earlier. The way that the young women conceptualized 'what counts' as physical activity brings into question the accuracy of self-report measures of participation rates. Physical activity as sport and exercise was the dominant discourse which rendered most of the rural young women to classify themselves as physically inactive, despite participating in varied forms of recreational physical activities and physical labour. In highlighting this issue with measurement, interpretation of participation statistics must also be assessed critically, particularly when they portray young women as problematic and 'at risk' due to their lower participation rates.

This study is significant and serves as a pertinent example of why sociological understandings of participation in, and meanings of, physical activity are vital. Warin *et al.* (2008) suggest that the universality of health promotion messages is problematic. As actions and indeed meanings of actions reflect local, social contexts, the 'gendered and classed *habitus* is at odds with current health-promotion policies or practices', as they 'do not take account of local and relational worlds' (Warin *et al.* 2008: 3). The lack of attention to gendered and classed meanings attached to health behaviours is highly problematic for the uptake of major health promotion initiatives. Moreover, as evidenced by the data in this section, it may limit the success of such programmes. The notion of gender performativity linked to bounded agency is important to consider, as it was demonstrated that the rural young women, in particular, were unlikely to participate in activities that contradicted what was acceptable according to their gendered habitus. Despite the growing body of evidence, it seems that governments and policy agencies do not access research of this type to inform campaigns and interventions, instead relying on the reproduction of popular discourses. Sociological understandings of participation in physical activities as demonstrated here can contribute to more holistic and successful approaches to policy development in the areas of health and participation in physical activity.

Conclusion and future directions

In this chapter I have offered an overview of cultural discourses around health and physical activity and evidence of how they are played out in the everyday lives of young people. I have argued that gone are the days of sport as an essential human right for the purpose of play and the joy of movement. Through public health campaigns and the pervasive popular media, physical activity and sport have been appropriated by the health agenda and we are encouraged to partake in physical movement for the sole purpose of weight loss and health gain (despite the tenuous link between these states). Thus, by its association with health, physical activity and sport participation has become the new 'moral' health behaviour. Indeed, elite sports clubs' association with promoting health and reducing obesity through their sport and the London 2012 'inspire a generation legacy' are further examples of the dominance of healthism and obesity discourse in our popular culture. Furthermore, evidence presented from an Australian longitudinal study suggests that indeed, the idea of playful engagement in bodily movement has been lost to the imperative of strict criteria relating to organized sports and fitness activities. Analysis utilizing Bourdieu's social theory demonstrates the importance of the social setting in shaping perceptions of, and participation in physical activity and how dominant discourses can open up and close off access to sport and physical activity for certain groups.

There are several implications stemming from this line of research. First, a sociological perspective brings into question the taken-for-granted truth in sport and physical activity participation statistics and measurement procedures. Second, it is questionable whether health promotion campaigns informed by positivist perspectives – which emphasize individual responsibility and choice and are popular in developed Western countries – are reaching their target audience, given the multitude of social structures such as gender and social class that shape engagements with sport and physical activities. It may be more damaging than beneficial to be focusing on health obligations, elite sports, and competition, as these elements often do not coincide with people's lived experiences. If governments intend to promote mass participation in physical activity for health benefits, perhaps their focus should return to legitimizing the creativity of play and the joy of movement rather than the morally charged obligation to be active for the purpose of health. This kind of policy shift would open up more opportunities to be active and enjoy movement, beyond the current exclusive arenas of sport and physical exercise. Finally, if we are to offer the wider population equitable and non-judgemental opportunities to be physically active, a consideration of sociological perspectives in understanding physical activity participation in people's everyday lives is essential.

References

Bauman, A.E., Reis, R. S., Sallis, J. F., Wells, J. C., Loos, R.J.F. and Martin, B.W. (2012) 'Correlates of Physical Activity: Why Are Some People Physically Active and Others Not?', *Lancet*, 380: 258.

Berlant, L. (2010) 'Risky Bigness: On Obesity, Eating, and the Ambiguity of "Health"', in J.M. Metzl and A. Kirkland (eds) *Against Health: How Health Became the New Morality*, New York: New York University Press.

Blair, S. N., LaMonte, M. J. and Nichaman, M. Z. (2004) 'The Evolution of Physical Activity Recommendations: How Much Is Enough?', *The American Journal of Clinical Nutrition*, 79: 913S.

Bourdieu, P. (1977) *Outline of a Theory of Practice*, Cambridge: Cambridge University Press.

Bourdieu, P. (1986) 'The Forms of Capital', in J.G. Richardson (ed.) *Handbook of Theory and Research for the Sociology of Education*, New York: Greenwood Press.

Bourdieu, P. (1990a) *In Other Words: Essays towards a Reflexive Sociology*, Stanford, CA: Stanford University Press.

Bourdieu, P. (1990b) *The Logic of Practice*, Stanford, CA: Stanford University Press.

Campos, P. (2004) *The Obesity Myth: Why America's Obsession with Health Is Hazardous to Your Health*, New York: Gotham Books.

Campos, P., Saguy, A., Ernsberger, P., Oliver, E. and Gaesser, G. (2006) 'The Epidemiology of Overweight and Obesity: Public Health Crisis or Moral Panic?', *International Journal of Epidemiology*, 35: 55.

Dagkas, S. and Quarmby, T. (2012) 'Young People's Embodiment of Physical Activity: The Role of the "Pedagogized" Family', *Sociology of Sport Journal*, 29: 210.

Evans, K. (2002) 'Taking Control of Their Lives? Agency in Young Adult Transitions in England and the New Germany', *Journal of Youth Studies*, 5: 245.

Evans, J., Davies, B. and Rich, E., (2010) 'Bernstein, Body Pedagogies and the Corporeal Device', in G. Ivinson, B. Davies and J. Fitz (eds) *Knowledge and Identity: Concepts and Applications in Bernstein's Sociology*, London: Routledge.

Evans, J., Rich, E., De Pian, L. and Davies, B. (2011) 'Health Imperatives, Policy and the Corporeal Device: Schools, Subjectivity and Children's Health', *Policy Futures in Education*, 9: 328.

Gard, M. (2011) 'Truth, Belief and the Cultural Politics of Obesity Scholarship and Public Health Policy', *Critical Public Health*, 21: 37.

Gard, M., and Wright, J. (2005) *The Obesity Epidemic: Science, Morality and Ideology*, Oxon, UK: Routledge.

Gibbons, L.W., *et al.* (1983) 'Association Between Coronary Heart Disease Risk Factors and Physical Fitness in Healthy Adult Women', *Circulation*, 67: 977.

Gray, C.M., Hunt, K., Mutrie, N., Anderson, A. S., Treweek, Shaun, S., and Wyke, S. (2013) 'Weight Management for Overweight and Obese Men Delivered Through Professional Football Clubs: A Pilot Randomized Trial', *International Journal of Behavioural Nutrition and Physical Activity*, 10: 121.

Greater London Authority (n.d.) *Committed to Tackling Obesity in London*. Available at: http://www.london.gov.uk/priorities/health/focus-issues/obesity (accessed 10 September 2013).

Harvey, J. and Sparks, R. (1991) 'The Politics of the Body in the Context of Modernity', *Quest*, 43: 164.

Haskell, W.L., Lee, I.M., Pate, R.R., Powell, K.E., Blair, S.N., Franklin, B.A., Macera, C.A., Heath, G.W., Thompson, P.D. and Bauman, A. (2007) 'Physical Activity and Public Health: Updated Recommendation for Adults from the American College of Sports Medicine and American Health Association', *Circulation*, 116: 1081.

Heady, J.A., Morris, J.N. and Raffle, P.A. (1956) 'Physique of London Busmen: Epidemiology of Uniforms', *Lancet*, 271: 569.

Jarvie, G. and Maguire, J. (1994) *Sport and Leisure in Social Thought*, New York: Routledge.

Kirk, D. and Colquhoun, D. (1989) 'Healthism and Physical Education', *British Journal of Education*, 10: 417.

Klein, R. (2010) 'What Is Health and How Do You Get It?', in J.M. Metzl and A. Kirkland (eds) *Against Health: How Health Became the New Morality*, New York: New York University Press.

Knez, K., Macdonald, D. and Abbott, R. (2012) 'Challenging Stereotypes: Muslim Girls Talk about Physical Activity, Physical Education and Sport', *Asia-Pacific Journal of Health, Sport and Physical Education*, 3: 109.

Leow, A.C.S., Macdonald, D., Hay, P. and McCuaig, L. (2012) 'Health Education Policy Interface: The Implementation of the *Eat Well Be Active* Policies in Schools', *Sport, Education and Society*, doi: 10.1080/13573322.2012.737777.

Lebesco, K. (2010) 'Fat Panic and the New Morality', in J.M. Metzl and A. Kirkland (eds) *Against Health: How Health Became the New Morality*, New York: New York University Press.

Laberge, S. and Kay, J. (2002) 'Pierre Bourdieu's Sociocultural Theory and Sport Practice', in J. Maguire and K. Young (eds) *Theory, Sport and Society*, Oxford: JAI.

Lee, J. and Macdonald, D. (2009) 'Rural Young People and Physical Activity: Understanding Participation through Social Theory', *Sociology of Health and Illness*, 31: 360.

Lee, J., and Macdonald, D. (2010) '"Are They Just Checking Our Obesity or What?": The Healthism Discourse and Rural Young Women', *Sport, Education and Society*, 15: 203.

London Wasps (n.d.) *Independent Schools Programme*. Available at: http://www.wasps.co.uk/education/independent-schools-programme (accessed 10 September 2013).

Manchester City Football Club (n.d.) *Strike a Balance*. Available at http://www.mcfc.com/community/manchester-programmes/health-and-activity/strike-a-balance (accessed 23 December 2013).

McGannon, K.R. and Spence, J.C. (2010) 'Speaking of the Self and Understanding Physical Activity Participation: What Discursive Psychology Can Tell Us About an Old Problem', *Qualitative Research in Sport and Exercise*, 2: 17.

Metcalf, B.S., *et al.* (2011) 'Fatness Leads to Inactivity, but Inactivity Does Not Lead to Fatness: A Longitudinal Study in Children', *Archives of Disability in Childhood*, 96: 942.

Metzl, J. M. (2010) 'Introduction: Why "Against Health"?', in J.M. Metzl and A. Kirkland (eds) *Against Health: How Health Became the New Morality*, New York: New York University Press.

Nelson, A., Macdonald, D. and Abbott, R. (2012) 'A Risky Business? Health and Physical Activity from the Perspectives of Urban Australian Indigenous Young People', *Health, Risk & Society*, 14: 325.

Ortega, F.B., *et al.* (2013) 'The Intriguing Metabolically Healthy but Obese Phenotype: Cardiovascular Prognosis and the Role of Fitness', *European Heart Journal*, 34: 389.

Parks, S.E., Housemann, R.A. and Brownson, R.C. (2003) 'Differential Correlates of Physical Activity in Urban and Rural Adults of Various Socioeconomic Backgrounds in the United States', *Journal of Epidemiology and Community Health*, 57: 29.

Premier League (2012) *N'Zogbia Backs Villa Vitality Programme*. Available at: http://www.premierleague.com/en-gb/news/news/2012-13/oct/charles-nzogbia-backs-villa-vitality-programme.html (accessed 23 December 2013).

Rich, E. (2012a) 'Beyond the Slogan: There Are Many Ways to *Inspire a Generation*', *Culture @ the Olympics*, 14: 64.

Rich, E. (2012b) *The End of the Affair? Why London 2012 'Inspiration' Could Be Short-Lived*. Available at: http://www.emmarich.me.uk/?p=352 (accessed 15 November 2013).

Rich, E., and Evans, J. (2005) '"Fat ethics" – The Obesity Discourse and Body Politics', *Social Theory & Health*, 3: 341.

Rich, E., Evans, J. and De Pian, L. (2011) 'Obesity, Body Pedagogies and Young Women's Engagement with Exercise', in P. Markula and E. Kennedy (eds) *Women and Exercise: The Body, Health and Consumerism*, Oxon, UK: Routledge.

Rimmer, J.H., Riley, B., Wang, E., Rauworth, A. and Jurkowski, J. (2004) 'Physical Activity Participation Among Persons with Disabilities: Barriers and Facilitators', *American Journal of Preventive Medicine*, 26: 419.

Saracens (2012) *Scrummy!* Available at: http://www.saracens.com/foundation/programmes/eat-well-live-well/scrummy/ (accessed 23 December 2013).

Trost, S.G., Owen, N., Bauman, A. E., Sallis, J. F. and Brown, W. (2002) 'Correlates of Adults' Participation in Physical Activity: Review and Update', *Medicine and Science in Sports Exercise*, 34: 1996.

Warin, M., Turner, K., Moore, V., and Davies, M. (2008) 'Bodies, Mothers and Identities: Rethinking Obesity and the BMI', *Sociology of Health and Illness*, 30: 97.

Webb, J., Schirato, T. and Danaher, G. (2002) *Understanding Bourdieu*, Thousand Oaks, CA: Sage.

Williams, G.H. (2003) 'The Determinants of Health: Structure, Context and Agency', *Sociology of Health and Illness*, 25: 131.

Williams, S.J. (1995) 'Theorising Class, Health and Lifestyles: Can Bourdieu Help Us?', *Sociology of Health and Illness*, 17: 577.

WHO (2009) *Global Health Risks: Mortality and Burden of Disease Attributable to Selected Major Risks*, New York: WHO.

30

RISK AND UNCERTAINTY IN SPORT

Stephen Lyng

The sociology of sport has been an expanding field of study in recent decades with increasing numbers of sociologists and scholars in other academic disciplines devoting attention to the growing significance of sports participation and spectatorship in contemporary social life. The specific topics studied by sports sociologists typically reflect the general disciplinary themes and issues of concern to sociology, including the influence of class, race, and gender on sport, the relevance of sport for processes of socialization and social change, the economic and political dimensions of sport activities, and related topics (see Frey and Eitzen 1991). However, one of the most distinctive features of sport has not been extensively researched by sport sociologists. I refer to the unique way in which uncertainty, and the closely related phenomenon of risk, figure into most sport activities.

There can be little doubt that one of the most highly valued aspects of sport, for participants and spectators alike, is the fact that the outcome of many sport endeavours is uncertain. On any given afternoon at the height of baseball or football season in the US, millions of sports fans can look forward to spending a few hours in front of their television sets or at particular sports venues watching their favourite teams take on opponents, with the reality-tested understanding that the outcome of these contests is never predictable, irrespective of the intensity of their hopes for victory. Similarly, sports participants usually develop a keen awareness of the limits of their capacity to predict the quality of their own or their teammates' performances on any particular outing, despite the significant time and effort they may devote to developing powers of control over such performances. Thus, in a social world where formulaic calculation and predictability are central imperatives in the operation of most institutions and organizations, including the entertainment media, many people find a refreshing escape from this rationalized reality in the unpredictability of sport.

Another way in which uncertainty appears as a defining characteristic of sport is in its connection to the corporeal nature of most sport activities. Since many (but not all) sports involve efforts to explore the limits of bodily capacities, the inherent vulnerabilities of the human body are often a central focus of concern for athletic performers, trainers, coaches, and spectators. Consequently, the uncertainties of bodily injury, usually expressed in terms of the technical-objectivistic definition of 'risk' (the *probability* of a measured degree of *damage* to the body – see Zinn 2008) is a distinctive feature of sport, at least with respect to the elevated risks of injury in many sports. It is not surprising then that in elite sport, where expectations of high-level athletic performance forces athletes to push the limits of the body to the maximum extent, the risks of injury to players are often what determines the long-term success or failure of individual athletes or teams. These considerations suggest that uncertainty and risk are essential features of sport – and yet, this dimension has not been extensively researched by sport sociologists.

In this chapter, I offer some reflections on the growing significance of uncertainty and risk in sport within the context of the late modern social order. As previously noted, uncertainty has always been endemic to sports, but I will suggest that recent social and cultural trends have altered the way that contemporary social actors respond to and make sense of the various uncertainties involved in sport activities. My view of these changes is informed by a longstanding scholarly interest in contemporary forms of voluntary risk taking, which I have conceptualized and analyzed in previous research as 'edgework' (Lyng 1990, 2005). Although this concept has been applied to a broad range of high-risk endeavours in the past two decades, the edgework perspective was initially developed to account for the rise of 'extreme' or 'adventure' sports in the late 1960s and 1970s, with a specific focus on the sport of skydiving (Lyng 1990; Lyng and Snow 1986). In the case of extreme sports, the central role of risk and risk taking seems obvious and is typically highlighted in attempts to draw a clear line between 'extreme' and 'traditional' sports (Rinehart and Sydnor 2003). The primary goal of this analysis is to challenge this way of distinguishing between adventure and traditional sports by asserting that risk and uncertainty have become more sociologically salient features of almost all sports today, a change that has been influenced more by the broader social and cultural context of sporting activities than technological or creative developments intrinsic to specific sports.

To explore the significance of uncertainty and risk in contemporary sports, I will begin by considering the conceptual clarity of the key terms of the analysis – the ideas of uncertainty and risk. Next, I review existing efforts to develop a sociological perspective on the relationship between risk and sport, demonstrating the evolution of this perspective over the past two decades and identifying the broader social forces and intellectual trends that may account for the rapid transformation of the perspective. After offering some suggestions for expanding the sociological perspective on risk and sport, I revisit the putative distinction between 'traditional' and 'extreme' sports and explore some of the contradictions in previous efforts to clearly differentiate these two areas of sports participation. Finally, I consider some implications of the present analysis for understanding the importance of risk and uncertainty in all forms of sport in the late modern era.

The nature of risk and uncertainty

As a preliminary step in the study of risk and risk taking in sport, it is important to consider matters relating to the conceptual clarity of the key terms of the analysis – risk and uncertainty. While one might expect a certain degree of imprecision in the use of these terms by common-sense actors, advancing the social scientific understanding of this topic requires that we strive for clearly drawn conceptual distinctions or, at least, approximate this ideal. The importance of this task for the present analysis can be better appreciated by considering the relevant literature on the study of risk and sport. An examination of this literature reveals several anomalies relating to the issue of risk. On the one hand, we find a sizable body of sociological research on the topic of sports-related injury (see Young 2004), and yet this topic is not usually framed in terms of risk (for exceptions, see Nixon 1993; Donnelly 2004). On the other hand, the notion of risk is often invoked by researchers who study 'extreme' sports (sometimes referred to as 'risk sports'), even though empirical evidence on injury and death rates indicates that these sports are often less dangerous than many traditional sports. Clarifying the meaning of risk and indicating how risk differs from the related concept of *uncertainty* may provide a way to make better sense of these anomalies.

While the need for a clearer definition of risk can be easily appreciated, generating such a definition is a more difficult task. As many commentators have noted, how risk is conceived and defined varies significantly between different academic disciplines and even *within* many of these disciplines. In an overview of the diverse conceptualizations of risk, Zinn (2008: 3–7) offers an organizing framework for distinguishing between the different 'risk epistemologies'. In this framework, different approaches to risk can be located along a continuum ranging from objective/realist orientations at one extreme to subject/constructionist orientations at the other. The purest expression of the objective/realist approach, adopted by disciplines focusing on technical risk assessment (insurance, epidemiology, toxicology), conceives of risk as the calculated probability of an objectively measured amount of damage that can accrue from a particular event. This approach to risk assumes that probabilities and harms can be objectively calculated through the application of appropriate scientific procedures and formulae and that the resulting measures reflect a reality independent of socially or psychologically based perceptual processes. In sport, epidemiological studies of injury and fatality rates across different varieties of sport typically employ this conception of risk, which makes it possible to identify and explore popular misperceptions about the dangers of various sports – for instance, the belief that extreme sports are characterized by high risk as compared to traditional sports (when the 'facts' may actually indicate otherwise).

At the other end of Zinn's (2008) continuum, risk is a product of social construction processes that are either inextricably intertwined with an objective reality of scientifically measurable dangers or align with socially and historically ascribed discourses or decision-making structures. The most radical versions of the constructionist perspective assert that risk exists only as a historical phenomenon and comes into existence through social processes. For instance, the 'governmentality' perspective, inspired by Michel Foucault's genealogical studies, focuses on the discourse structures emerging in the early Enlightenment that transformed uncertainty into risk – a conception of uncertainty as something that can be subjected to the calculative techniques involved in statistical-probabilistic analysis (Zinn 2008: 7). As Giulianotti (2009: 542–543) points out, governmentality theory identifies techniques of probabilistic risk calculation operating at two different levels – 'technologies of the state' and 'technologies of the self'. The former operate in the domain of sport when spectators with particular social characteristics or attendees of certain sporting events are identified through empirical analysis as being 'at risk' for hooliganism or other kinds of criminal activity, allowing police to employ pre-emptive strategies for controlling these possible outcomes. 'Technologies of the self' refer to self-governance through the use of knowledge systems that allow individuals to manage the uncertainties of their own personal lives. In both amateur and professional sports, these technologies produce self-governing subjects who take personal responsibility for managing injuries and maintaining health, perhaps through strict adherence to daily regimens advocated by sports medicine experts.

Between the two extremes of strict objectivism and strict constructionism, we find other epistemologies of risk that represent various mixes of objective, subjective, and social dimensions. These include the psychometric approach, which relies on statistical analysis of large-scale surveys to identify the psychological, emotional, and social factors that shape subjective perceptions of objective risks (Slovic 1999), and the cultural approach, which also accepts the objective reality of risks but incorporates an understanding of the role of culturally specific institutional factors in determining how certain objective risks are highlighted and socially constructed in public debate (Douglas and Wildavsky 1982). Just as the objective/realist and social constructionist conceptions of risk can be effectively applied in the realm of sport, it is also possible to envision useful applications of the psychometric and cultural approaches. Giulianotti (2009: 542) has suggested that psychometric analysis may be helpful in establishing correlations between social/demographic characteristics and participation in high-risk sports, although the resulting models cannot account for cultural variations in risk taking associated with national and regional identities. This limitation in psychometric analysis is specifically addressed by Douglas and Wildavsky's cultural approach. Focusing on cultural factors could help to explain one of the greatest ironies we currently face in sports-related risks – the fact that the rates of injury in many sports are very high and yet this problem has not received the sustained attention of policy makers or legal authorities. Sport injuries are not regarded as a public health problem in most Western societies, but comparable injury rates in other areas of social life (work, consumer products, etc.) would very likely attract the attention of public health officials (Donnelly 2004: 33).

What is apparent from this overview of risk epistemologies is that risk can be conceptualized in many different ways if we consider the broad range of thinking about risk extending from the abstract-theoretical formulations of positivist science to the practical constructions of common-sense perspectives. While technical concerns may dictate that risk be conceived as something that can be objectively measured in terms of clearly defined parameters, the sociological focus on the practical logics of common-sense actors encourages us to understand risk as what 'people' (understood as the products of psychological, historical, or cultural forces) think it is. And, as we have seen, the apparent polarity of these two views has been dispelled by risk perspectives that combine elements of both conceptions. Thus, we are confronted with one of the ironic consequences of the recent 'risk turn' in the social sciences. As new social scientific perspectives on risk have proliferated during the past two decades and the idea of risk has been applied to a wider range of human action and thinking, the meaning of risk has become less clear. Indeed, with the concept of risk encompassing an ever-increasing range of human experiences, one wonders if it has ceased to have any meaning at all![1] For sociologists interested in the connection between risk and sport, the expanding heterogeneity of risk conceptualization will present difficult challenges.

In light of these challenges, I suggest that the best way to advance the study of risk and sport at this time is to dispense with the debate over how best to conceptualize risk in favour of the more modest task of distinguishing between risk and uncertainty. Taking this step moves us in the opposite direction from the recent elaboration of multiple risk paradigms. To differentiate between risk and uncertainty, it is sufficient to return to one of the earliest efforts to define risk – Frank Knight's simple but elegant idea that risk is best understood as 'measurable uncertainties' (1921: 21). It is possible to conceive of risk in this concise way while still acknowledging some of the important insights of more recent efforts to define risk – recognizing, for instance, that beliefs about the possibility of 'measuring' uncertainty and the development of various technologies for doing so are historical and cultural artifacts, irrespective of any assessment of the objectivity of such measures. As Weber, Foucault, Giddens, Luhmann, and other social theorists have expressed in their own unique ways, the idea of risk as measurable uncertainty is one of the key indexes of the transition from pre-modern to early modern societies. The important point, though, is that even in the context of a modernity dominated by beliefs about calculated risks, uncertainties that *cannot* be measured and controlled still occupy a central place in human experience.

Thus, in the following reflections on the social dimensions of sport in the late modern era, I am guided by the related but distinct concepts of uncertainty and risk. Concisely and simply defined, uncertainty refers to future outcomes of present actions and circumstances that cannot be anticipated. And as a unique expression of uncertainty, risk arises when uncertainty is transformed into calculated probabilities of possible occurrences by rational procedures and technologies. Armed with the concepts of uncertainty and risk understood in this way, I will now explore the relevance of these ideas to the world of contemporary sport.

The emergence of the risk era in sports

As we have seen, the study of risk and sport has crystallized only recently as a distinct line of inquiry in the sociology of sport, although researchers from a variety of disciplines have maintained a longstanding interest in the study of sports-related injuries. Looking at early literature on risk and sport, the first formal reference to the topic appears in James H. Frey's Presidential Address to the North American Society for the Sociology of Sport in 1989, later published in the *Sociology of Sport Journal* (1991). Frey's address is especially noteworthy because it anticipated the rise of a new research stream in the sociology of sport fed by the expanding social scientific interest in risk beginning in the early 1990s. A close examination of Frey's address offers some interesting hints about the broader intellectual and social forces that contributed to this development.

Frey began his address by explaining why he had taken up the problem of risk and sport, and in doing so, provided a revealing account of how his scholarly interests were shaped by the intersection of his personal biography and the historical circumstances of the post-1960s era. First, he mentioned his involvement in an ongoing sociological study of a nuclear waste repository located near his home institution. Then he described how he had been inspired by another presidential address – this one delivered by James Short at the American Sociological Association Meetings of 1984 and later published under the title 'The Social Fabric at Risk' (1984). Finally, he indicated his interest in studying the sport of skydiving as part of a broader concern with the relationship between work and leisure. Most important, he sketched the historical backdrop of all three of these influences on his thinking by describing the emerging structure of what might be characterized today as a 'risk society.'[2]

> Interest in risk studies and the language of risk is expanding to a point where risk is a concern for scholars, policy makers, social agencies, and the general public. This is especially true when risk is associated with health and safety, technological change, environmental impact, and hazardous events. It is not uncommon to hear terms such as risk assessment, risk perception, risk communication, risk-taking, risk acceptance, comparative risk, risk management, and of course risk sport or risk recreation. Risk analysis is now a business ... that includes private and public entities who engage risk professionals in the assessment, regulation, and management of risk.
>
> (1991: 136–137)

Although Frey did not explicitly argue that the world of sports and social life in general were being transformed in some dramatic ways in the post-1960s era, it is clear that this was an implicit theme of his address. This is reflected in the way he connected emerging economic-technical problems (disposal of nuclear wastes), shifts in leisure practices (the growing popularity of the new sport of skydiving), and recent developments in intellectual thought (Short's presidential address) around the common theme of risk. The particular combination of these three influences on Frey's choice of a presentation topic may reflect in part the unique circumstances of his biography, but his exposure to these experiences was also a product of the specific social-historical conditions of this time period. Had he been a member of an earlier generation of sociologists, it is unlikely that the issue of nuclear waste disposal, the growing popularity of sports like sky-diving, or an agenda-defining essay on the topic of risk by a leader of his profession would have been a part of his personal experience.

The details of my own research program can be traced to a similar intersection of biography and history at this time, at least with respect to my sociological interest in risk and sport. Like Frey, my initial focus on the topic of risk resulted in part from an involvement with skydiving, although I suspect that my integration into the skydiving world was much more serendipitous than Frey's. For me, the connection to skydiving related to two practical problems I faced during my graduate school training – the need to supplement my meager salary as a graduate teaching assistant and the desire to maintain my currency as an airplane pilot while completing my graduate education in the late 1970s. Fortunately, I stumbled upon a common solution to both problems. I discovered that a local sport parachute center was looking for a 'jump pilot' for their weekend skydiving operations and, as a commercially rated pilot, I was qualified for the job. I knew very little about skydiving before taking this part-time job, so many months passed before I fully appreciated the potential that existed for conducting research on the local skydiving network and the sport of skydiving as a whole. However, my initial interest in studying the local skydiving scene eventually led to a more ambitious study of 'adventure' sports in general and a broader range of high-risk activities in other social domains that I eventually classified as forms of 'edgework' (Lyng 1990).

As a male growing up in the 1950s and 1960s who experienced traditional sports the way most males did in the US during these decades (participating in neighbourhood pick-up games and organized team sports in middle and high school), I was struck by how dissimilar skydiving was from any sport I had experienced in the past. In fact, the various activities surrounding the central event in skydiving – individuals jumping out of airplanes at high altitude and deploying their parachutes – seemed to belong more to the realm of subculture than sport, which was the way my coauthor and I conceptually framed these activities in the initial study of the local group (Lyng and Snow 1986). It is also noteworthy that many of the participants themselves rejected the classification of skydiving as a sport. Although a few skydivers embraced the sport label, these individuals were usually marginal to the main group of jumpers, who were generally insulted by the idea of viewing skydiving as merely a sport. For members of the latter group, being a skydiver was a core part of their identity and they viewed the shared (sub)cultural products, activities, and interactions with other 'hard-core' skydivers as a distinct style of life (see also Wheaton 2004).

Whether skydiving and similar pursuits are properly classified as sports or represent some other form of collective behaviour is an issue that has not been fully resolved today. However, for James Frey and myself, the accidents of personal biography that led us to conduct research on skydivers introduced us to a new phenomenon that reflected the unique historical circumstances of the late twentieth century. What we both found in skydiving was a collectively organized and culturally constructed form of embodied leisure activity that resembles traditional sports in some ways but also differs from these sports in several important respects. More importantly, skydiving is just one of many similar sports-like activities that came into existence in the post-1960s era that seemed to signify the birth of a new sporting movement. The range and complexity of characteristics exhibited by these new sporting activities partly account for the diversity of terms used to describe them: 'extreme,' 'alternative', 'lifestyle', 'whiz,' 'action-sports', 'panic sport', 'postmodern', 'postindustrial', and 'risk' sports (Wheaton 2004: 2). And if the plethora of labels applied to these activities indicates ambiguity about their defining qualities, further ambiguity is exhibited in the various attempts to describe the broader historical context in which this new phase of sporting activity developed. As suggested by the 'postmodern' and 'postindustrial' designations, many scholars have embraced different versions of the social/cultural discontinuity paradigm in an attempt to identify general structural imperatives that shape the distinctive qualities of new sports. In addition to postindustrialism and postmodernity, they are variously associated with historical transitions to late capitalism, consumer culture, or other discontinuous social or cultural formations.

While this body of work has produced many important insights about risk sports[3] and the socio-historical forces that may have shaped them, this style of analysis has had the less useful consequence of fuelling endless debates about the existence and nature of continuities or discontinuities between contemporary social life and the modern, industrial social order depicted by classical social theory. Although I see little to be gained by participating in such debates, I do share two basic assumptions with sports researchers who have adopted this style of analysis: first, the idea that the sporting activities that emerged in the post-1960s era do constitute a distinct form of sport, different from the varieties of sport that developed in earlier eras; and second, the belief that contextualizing post-60s risk sports within the socio-historical conditions of this period is crucial to understanding their unique character and significance. However, the way that I depart from previous analyses of this type is to refrain from drawing a bright line between traditional and risk sports and to treat both forms of sport as unique expressions of a more fundamental kind of human action – voluntary risk-taking behavior. As noted above, the thing that sets sport apart from most other human experiences and the quality that we seem to value most as sport participants and spectators is the opportunity it gives us for experiencing uncertainty and risk. We delight or despair in the unpredictability of competitive games and marvel at the way the objectivity of the body imposes itself on us with its vulnerabilities and performance uncertainties as well as its unrecognized potentials. Thus, the *voluntary* embrace of risk and uncertainty is an endemic feature of all sport,[4] although different forms of sport may reveal different attitudes and orientations towards the risks and uncertainties that participants confront. This variation in attitudes and orientations will be the reference point for my effort to differentiate traditional and risk sports.

Traditional versus risk sports: unique expressions of voluntary risk taking

With the emergence of the new sporting movement in the latter half of the twentieth century, there has been much discussion among participants, media professionals, and social scientists about how best to understand the nature of these leisure practices and the attraction they hold for participants. In the popular perception, these activities clearly belong to the realm of sport but they are distinguished from traditional sports by the level of danger involved in the activity – as suggested by the label 'extreme', post-1960s sports are often viewed as more dangerous than traditional sports. Thus, in regard to voluntary risk taking, perhaps extreme sports participants engage in riskier pursuits than participants in traditional sports. Although it is difficult to assess the actual danger of different sport activities because of the lack of relevant data, some researchers have pulled together scattered findings on patterns of sports-related injuries that challenge the popular perception.

Reviewing research from the US, Canada, New Zealand, and the UK, Phillip White (2004) found that the highest rates of serious injury and even death occur in sports that are regarded as traditional in the countries examined. In New Zealand and the UK, the most dangerous sport is rugby, followed by soccer, martial arts, field hockey, and cricket (2004: 316). In Canada, the highest rates of 'catastrophic' (fatal or permanently disabling) injury can be traced to four activities: snowmobiling, bicycling, boating, and swimming. Although risk sports such as hang-gliding and skydiving are included in the category of sports contributing to the highest number of fatalities in the UK, the other sports in this category include motor sports, horse riding, and water sports (2004: 317). Thus, these data demonstrate that the perception of risk sports as activities that involve much higher levels of risk taking than traditional sports is not supported by the available evidence (although this evidence is admittedly partial).

However, before we can accept the assertion that risk sports are not 'really' as dangerous as most observers may think, a caveat is in order. Interpreting the evidence on injuries and fatalities is complicated by the fact that these statistics cannot be regarded as direct measures of the inherent risks of the activities examined. This caution is based on the understanding that the likelihood of injury or death in skill-based activities like risk sports is determined by the *level* of skill one exercises in responding to the dangers at hand. As several subjects in my original study of skydivers informed me, 'Jumping out of airplanes is only dangerous to those who don't know what they are doing,' a general attitude shared by participants in other risk sports who devote significant time and energy to honing their skills for managing the specific dangers they confront (see Donnelly 1981). Although instances of insufficiently skilled individuals participating in risk sports do occur, self-selection and group-selection pressures typically ensure that this is a rare event, as reflected in the data on injuries and fatalities.

What is apparent from this examination of the empirical evidence on sports-related injuries is that traditional and risk sports cannot be distinguished from one another based on either the willingness to engage in risk taking or the degree of danger involved in the activity: both forms of sport can be subsumed under the general category of voluntary risk taking since participants in both categories of sport voluntarily assume risks and the likelihood of experiencing harm in these pursuits is actually greater for traditional athletes, despite popular beliefs to the contrary. Thus, if traditional and risk sports are more similar than different in these respects, what supports the claim by myself and others that these are different forms of sport? To answer this question, I will return to a conceptual contrast discussed above – the distinction between uncertainty and risk – and focus on how these two phenomena are incorporated into the goal orientation of both types of sport.

As we have seen, participants in traditional and risk sports must deal with a common task in the pursuit of their athletic endeavours – both groups of athletes must manage risks that are inherent to their sporting activities. For members of both groups, the probability of experiencing either minor or serious injury in sports pursuits is greater than the risks they face in any other daily activity. The same can be said about fatalities: the risk of dying while participating in the routines of social life in Western societies is generally low, but fatality rates for high intensity sports are higher than most other common activities (Paffenbarger *et al.* 1993). While the demand for managing the risks of injury or death is common to both traditional and risk sports, these risk management practices are linked to different ultimate goals. In both domains, risk management is a means to a higher end that structures most other aspects of the sporting experience.

For traditional sports, the ultimate goal of the sporting enterprise is defined by the value placed on competition and achievement (traditional sports are sometimes referred to as 'achievement sports'). Athletes compete with other athletes, as individuals or members of teams, in order to 'win' or demonstrate their athletic superiority. Thus, the ultimate goal of 'winning' influences the way athletes approach risks that inhere in their respective sports. To effectively manage risks in traditional sports, one must engage in proactive efforts to remain free of injuries that can interfere with training or performance, develop capacities and strategies for continuing to play when one is injured ('playing hurt'), and develop an awareness of when to take calculated risks to gain an advantage over one's opponents. In traditional sport, risk taking and risk management practices are subservient to the 'higher' goal of achieving distinction in demonstrating superior athletic ability or defeating opponents or both.[5]

While traditional sports participation involves voluntary risk taking, the primary focus is on controlling risks and reducing uncertainty. Participants in risk sports also engage in risk taking and risk management, not for the purpose of *reducing* uncertainty, but for the higher aim of *embracing* uncertainty. This difference in the ultimate goals of the sporting endeavour is what differentiates traditional and risk sports most fundamentally and is the basis for many of the other distinctive features of risk sports highlighted by previous analyses. Despite the popular stereotype of risk sport participants as fearless individuals willing to take any risk for the payoff of an 'adrenalin rush', these individuals actually have much more in common with traditional athletes in their commitment to the careful management of risks. Skydivers and other risk sport participants (rock climbers, BMXers, cavers, etc.) devote much time and effort to preparing for the central activities of their sport – checking equipment, developing action plans, practicing specific skills, and thinking about every possible contingency they may face. The purpose of these preparation efforts is to anticipate possible harms and develop strategies for controlling them. These efforts can be properly classified as a form of risk analysis that informs their later risk management practices, since they are based on a common-sense logic for measuring harms and the probability of experiencing them. However, the point of engaging in this kind of risk analysis and preparation is to minimize the possibility of harm from dangers that *can* be anticipated, in order to achieve a level of experience where one confronts and manages harms that *cannot* be anticipated. In other words, the ultimate goal of the endeavour is to transport oneself to a zone of uncertainty where embodied and largely unrecognized skills and capacities are summoned to ensure one's survival and well-being. Thus, in getting to this zone of uncertainty, one achieves a form of self-discovery and transcendence that is rarely attained in human experience. This is the primary attraction of risk sports.[6]

In short, what this analysis reveals is that voluntary risk taking is no less important to traditional sports as it is to risk sports. The modern conception of risk, and the derivative notions of risk calculation and management, are key knowledge components of both forms of sport. Where traditional and risk sports diverge, however, is in the way that risk-taking practices are structured by the higher goals of each form of sport. Traditional athletes take risks in the pursuit of athletic achievement (most often to defeat their opponents) and in the process, they seek to maximize their control over both risk and uncertainty – especially the uncertainty of competitive outcomes (winning or losing). In contrast, risk sport participants take risks in pursuit of self-knowledge and transcendence, which is achieved by moving past dangers that can be cognitively envisioned and rationally managed to confront those requiring 'instinctive' responses. At this level, risk sports are more accurately termed as 'voluntary uncertainty-seeking' rather than voluntary risk taking.

Notes

1 For example, Niklas Luhmann's (1993) system theory approach posits that risk is a dimension of all human decision-making.
2 This should not be read as an endorsement of Ulrich Beck's (1992) 'risk society' perspective. I use the term here to simply highlight the increasing importance of risk in contemporary social life.
3 Given the variation in the labels for these sports, I have chosen the term 'risk sports' in recognition of the widespread agreement among researchers that these sports generally involve positive attitudes towards risk taking.
4 Of course, this assertion must be qualified to take account of the coercive forces acting on professional athletes relating to the terms of their employment.

5 It should be acknowledged that traditional sports are often played in noncompetitive environments for the sheer enjoyment of participating in physical activity and developing athletic skills. However, non-competitive participation in traditional sports is still highly structured by the culture of competition in sports.

6 This part of the analysis draws on my earlier phenomenological studies of the 'edgework experience' (Lyng 1990; 2005), which cannot be reviewed here due to space limitations. Also, see Lyng (2014) for a theorization of self-discovery and transcendence in edgework practices in terms of the concept of 'hermeneutic reflexivity'.

References

Beck, U. (1992) *Risk Society: Towards a New Modernity*, London: Sage.

Donnelly, P. (1981) 'Four Fallacies, I: Climbing Is Not Really Dangerous', *Mountain*, 80: 38–40.

Donnelly, P. (2004) 'Sport and Risk Culture', in K. Young (ed.) *Sporting Bodies, Damaged Selves: Sociological Studies of Sports-Related Injuries*, Amsterdam: Elsevier.

Douglas, M. and Wildavsky, A.B. (1982) *Risk and Culture*, Berkeley: University of California Press.

Frey, J.H. (1991) 'Social Risk and the Meaning of Sport', *Sociology of Sport Journal*, 8: 136–145.

Frey, J.H. and Eitzen, D.S. (1991) 'Sport and Society', *Annual Review of Sociology*, 17: 503–22.

Giulianotti, R. (2009) 'Risk and Sport: An Analysis of Sociological Theories and Research Agendas', *Sociology of Sport Journal*, 26: 540–556.

Knight, F. (1921) *Risk, Uncertainty, and Profit*, New York: Houghton Mifflin.

Luhmann, N. (1993) *Risk: A Sociological Theory*, New York: Aldine de Gruyter.

Lyng, S. (1990) 'Edgework: A Social Psychological Analysis of Voluntary Risk Taking', *American Journal of Sociology*, 95: 851–886.

Lyng, S. (2005) 'Sociology at the Edge: Social Theory and Voluntary Risk Taking', in S. Lyng (ed.) *Edgework: The Sociology of Risk Taking*, New York: Routledge.

Lyng, S. (2014) 'Action and Edgework: Risk Taking and Reflexivity in Late Modernity', *European Journal of Social Theory*, 17: 443–460.

Lyng S. and Snow, D.A. (1986) 'Vocabularies of Motive and High Risk Behavior: The Case of Skydiving', in E. Lawler (ed.), *Advances in Group Processes*, vol. 3, Greenwich, CT: JAI.

Nixon, H. (1993) 'Accepting the Risks of Pain and Injury in Sport: Mediated Cultural Influences on Playing Hurt', *Sociology of Sport Journal*, 10: 183–196.

Paffenbarger, R., Hyde, R., Wing, A., and Jung, D. (1993) 'The Association of Changes in Physical Activity Level and Other Lifestyle Characteristics with Mortality among Men', *New England Journal of Medicine*, 328: 538–545.

Rinehart, R. and Sydnor, S. (eds) (2003) *To the Extreme: Alternative Sports, Inside and Out*, Albany: State University of New York Press.

Short, J. F. (1984) 'The Social Fabric at Risk: Toward a Social Transformation of Risk Analysis', *American Sociological Review* 49: 711–725.

Slovic, P. (1999) 'Trust, Emotion, Sex, Politics, and Science', *Risk Analysis*, 19(4): 689–701.

Wheaton, B. (2004) 'Introduction: Mapping the Lifestyle Sport-Scape', in B. Wheaton (ed.) *Understanding Lifestyle Sports: Consumption, Identity and Difference*, London: Routledge.

White, P. (2004) 'The Costs of Injury from Sport, Exercise and Physical Activity: A Review of the Evidence', in K. Young (ed.) *Sporting Bodies, Damaged Selves: Sociological Studies of Sports-Related Injuries*, Amsterdam: Elsevier.

Young, K. (2004) *Sporting Bodies, Damaged Selves: Sociological Studies of Sports-Related Injuries*, Amsterdam: Elsevier.

Zinn, J.O. (2008) *Social Theories of Risk and Uncertainty: An Introduction*, Malden, MA: Blackwell Publishing.

31

DOPING IN ELITE SPORT

Verner Møller

Doping in sport is a sensitive issue. It has been condemned by media, politicians, and sports organizations for more than fifty years. In the wake of Tommy Simpson's amphetamine-related fatal collapse at the Tour de France in 1967, the International Olympic Committee (IOC) introduced a list of prohibited substances. This list formed the basis of systematic drug testing at the Mexico Olympic Games in 1968.

The introduction of doping testing was a message to athletes that medical shortcuts in pursuit of sporting glory were unacceptable. But the message did not have its intended impact and there is much to suggest that doping continued to grow concurrently with advances in medical science and the commercialization of sport. A number of doping scandals – most notoriously the Team Festina affair at the 1998 Tour de France – made it clear that the use of performance-enhancing drugs was endemic in sport. If cycling was illustrative, the attempts by sports organizations to police the use of drugs within their respective realms had failed spectacularly.

This led to a unique collaboration between the IOC and governments worldwide resulting in the establishment of the World Anti-Doping Agency (WADA) in 1999. Through WADA a much more ambitious policy to combat doping has been enforced. The first World Anti-Doping Code (WADC) – the regulatory framework that every international sports organization must adopt to be eligible for participation in the Olympic Games – was published in 2003. The WADC has been revised twice: the first revision took effect on 1 January 2009; the second, finalized in 2013, took effect on 1 January 2015. Both revisions have further tightened the already demanding and far-reaching control system introduced in the 2003 WADC.

Despite all these efforts, recurrent positive tests show that performance-enhancing drugs are still used by athletes in search of a competitive edge. Unfortunately, the high-profile fight against doping has driven the practice further into the dark. Sports organizations' preferred strategy, to treat every positive test as exceptional and portray individual athletes who get caught in the control system as exceptional unsporting cheats, was to no avail when it was revealed that systematic doping was organized in entire cycling teams. At the same moment it became obvious that doping was as least as much a sociological as a psychological or educational problem and had to be understood as such, resulting in a steep increase in studies of the phenomenon. However, the fact that drug-using athletes have become much more careful means that the use of doping in sport has become harder to research.

This chapter focusses on the reliability problem in sociological research into doping in sport. The discussion begins with a brief examination of different work on the subject, followed by a critical assessment of the influence of literature on doping that was published prior to 1998. It will be shown how myth on doping promoted in books and interviews by anti–doping crusaders has uncritically been adopted by academic researchers and to some extent biased their work. Inspired by C. Wright Mills's *The Sociological Imagination*, the chapter then proposes a way to advance sociological doping research in an increasingly sensitive, secretive, and secluded milieu.

Doping research after Festina

If doping had been of little interest within the humanities and social sciences before 1998, the Festina affair was a watershed moment. In January 1999 Barrie Houlihan published *Dying to Win: Doping in Sport and the Development of Anti-Doping Policy*, which offered an analysis of the political challenges brought about by sport's doping culture. In 2000 Ivan Waddington published *Sport, Health and Drugs: A Critical Sociological Perspective* which examined the relationship between modern sports drug use and other public health issues. Whilst the first part of Waddington's book addresses a number of issues, including the ideology of health protection and conflicting commercial interests, abuse in child sport, and club doctors' dilemmas in professional football, the second part of the book is entirely devoted to sport and drugs. Here cycling and the 1998 Festina affair, unsurprisingly, are at the fore.

Tellingly, when Waddington decided to update this text, the end product, published in 2009 in collaboration with Andy Smith, was in effect a whole new book. It bears witness to the increasing significance of the doping issue that the new version, entitled *An Introduction to Drugs in Sport – Addicted to Winning?*, omitted the first part in order to close in on drugs in sport and still ended up being 60 pages longer than the original book.

Houlihan and Waddington focus on athletes' incentives to dope, as did earlier scholars such as the Norwegian Gunnar Breivik (1987, 1992), who used a game theory approach, and the Germans Karl-Heinrich Bette and Uwe Schimank (1995) who viewed doping as a result of the structural dynamics of elite sport. However, little concrete information was known about the extent of the problem. This resulted in an increased interest in quantitative doping research.

In the wake of the 1998 Tour de France, the Danish Ministry for Culture (which has sport under its jurisdiction) appointed a white-paper committee to explore the size of the problem. The committee initiated a survey targeting various sporting milieus that showed that no more than 1.3 per cent of Danish elite athletes had 'experience with performance–enhancing hormones, and of these 1.3 per cent very few indicated they had experiences with other doping means' (Kulturministeriet 1999: 50). The committee acknowledged that surveys of this kind have a 2 per cent uncertainty, thus implicitly admitting that the use of doping in Danish elite sport could be zero. However, in the same breath, the committee noted that when measuring areas associated with social taboos, prejudices, and crime, there is a tendency for respondents to underreport even if they are guaranteed anonymity.

Later, using a mathematical and statistical method developed in the 1970s to resolve the problem of underreporting, a group of German researchers investigated the use of doping among elite athletes in Germany and found a much higher level of doping than in the Danish survey. This method, 'the randomized response technique', was designed to demonstrate to respondents that their anonymity could not be breached, but this guarantee comes at a price. The method is restricted to measure intervals and thus is not very precise. Still, the result was remarkable. Between 25.8 and 48.1 per cent of athletes admitted to using or having used doping (Pitsch, Emrich and Klein 2005). The result appears to reveal a discrepancy between athletes' public statements on doping and their actual practice. A survey of Norwegian elite athletes' attitudes toward anti-doping suggests the same, as it revealed significant discontent with the control system despite athletes' generally positive public statements about these measures (Hanstad *et al.* 2009; Hanstad and Loland 2009).

In order to further understanding of athlete motivations to dope or to abstain, qualitative interview studies were applied either as a complementary tool or as a method in their own right.

In-depth interviewing made it possible to pursue athletes' knowledge and experience of drug use as well as their attitude to and personal consequences of the counteracting anti-doping system, it was thought. However, the findings of these studies are also mixed and uncertain, as the following examples should demonstrate.

A WADA-funded Swiss psycho-sociological study of young male elite cyclists' attitudes found that it was normal for the participants to consume dietary supplements and that they were attracted to doping and willing to use banned substances if necessary in order to pursue a professional career (Lentillon-Kaestner and Carstairs 2009). This finding is remarkable because even though it is common practice in qualitative interview research to guarantee interviewees anonymity, it is hard to come by athletes who in interviews are willing to talk openly about their use of or willingness to use banned substances. It cannot be ruled out that the data were influenced by the fact that the interviewer was of the opposite sex to the young male cyclists and that this subconsciously encouraged them to present themselves as more ambitious, bold, and courageous than they would have done had the interviewer been male.

Another interview-based project on doping in cycling, funded by the Australian government's anti-doping research programme, found, in contrast to the Swiss study, that the doping culture was a fading problem thanks to the influence of what the authors label 'the social peloton'. Based on interviews, the researchers concluded: 'Since doping was quite clearly seen as a threat to the sport's economic viability, and to the health and welfare of its workforce, there already seemed to be a degree to which the social peloton was working to reduce the impact of doping' (Hardie *et al.* 2010: 150). This study was led by a researcher who was also known by the interviewees for in-depth knowledge of cycling and for his coverage of cycling as a journalist. The informants recruited for this study were also guaranteed anonymity. Nevertheless, the quotes presented from the Australian interviews largely echoed what riders say about doping to public media, which could reflect the interviewees' perception of the interviewer and their (false) perception of his agenda.

The suspicion that qualitative data on controversial topics depends more on the interpersonal dynamics between interviewer and interviewee than is otherwise recognized by proponents of qualitative research was extended further by another Australian study on the use of complementary and alternative medicine in swimming. This study was carried out by a former elite swimmer, and it is clear from the lengthy quotes in the research findings that the data was generated in a trusting relationship with a shared understanding of the particular sport culture. In the interviews, the informants do not openly admit to doping (that is, illegal use of performance-enhancing substances or methods), but there is a subtext which makes it obvious that consumption of performance-enhancing substances was a natural part of being an elite swimmer. The athletes' main worry on doping is the risk of being caught without intending to 'dope', specifically when taking a supplement which they did not know contained banned substances. The athletes in the study were asked to explain how they would act in a particular thought-experiment on doping, when a coach informs them about a drug that he knew was used by athletes to great effect in sports that were non-signatories to the WADA code, and whether these athletes would take that substance. The response of one interviewee was striking: 'Once again, as an athlete, I would've gone, yup give it to me. As long as it is not banned and it's gonna help me get through the stuff . . . then yeah, give it to me' (Koh 2013: 253). Overall, there is no doubt that in the plethora of doping studies which have been conducted since 1998 there is plenty of valuable information. The difficulty lies in assessing the quality of the various contributions to form the bigger picture from the various, often contradictory studies.

Doping research before Festina

Prior to the 1998 Tour de France, scholarly books on doping were few and far between. In 1986 Tom Donohoe and Neil Johnson, experts in physiology and pharmacology, published *Foul Play: Drug Abuse in Sport*. As the title indicates, the authors were on an anti-doping mission on moral and medical grounds. The book explains the pharmacological effects and physiological dangers associated with the use of different performance-enhancing drugs, and the closing section of the book offers a worrying presentation of future challenges to sport, which the authors foresee will be pressing as medical science progresses. They fear that in the future scientists will aid the creation of 'artificial' athletes, with 'sperm banks and ova donated by gold medallists to produce "pre-programmed" athletes whose growth and development will be geared towards sporting achievement' (Donohoe and Johnson 1986: 126).

In 1991 Robert Voy, former chief medical officer for the US Olympic Committee, published *Drugs, Sport, and Politics*, in which he shared his experiences and concerns about the corruption of the Olympic spirit for the sake of winning at all cost, including through the use of drugs. The following year historian John Hoberman published his pioneering monograph *Mortal Engines: The Science of Performance and the Dehumanization of Sport* – explaining the mutual interest between scientists and athletes from the nineteenth century onwards in performance-enhancement substances, culminating in the politically motivated doping programmes in East Germany during the Cold War. The issue of doping was sometimes mentioned in passing in other critical books on sport to exemplify the perverse consequences of sporting obsession with records and winning. Together with journalist Les Woodland's *Dope: The Use of Drugs in Sport* (1980), the three books noted above became standard references in the expansive number of texts on doping produced in the wake of the Festina affair in order to analyze the dynamics of the problem.

The influence of pre-Festina doping research

The first in-depth social scientific analysis of doping in English was Barrie Houlihan's *Dying to Win*, published on the basis of research for the Council of Europe, and providing in particular a valuable contribution to understanding of political problems on the issue. In the opening chapter, Houlihan makes the precise observation that 'the pattern of sport that develops in a society is the product of that society in exactly the same way as the commercial and political systems are the product of deeper social values and attitudes' (Houlihan 1999: 13) This simple statement explains why doping and sport are inseparably connected. Doping is basically a result of the medicalization of society, wherein an ever-growing number of human conditions are transformed into treatable disorders (Conrad 2007). Fatigue and the age-related decline of functions are viewed as resulting from curable deficits rather than natural processes, whilst over-the-counter drugs are offered to remedy the slightest bodily discomfort.

In light of this it should be no surprise that athletes and their support personnel seek to exploit the profusion of drugs available to suppress pain, aid recovery, and enhance performance, whether in compliance with or in violation of the anti-doping regulations. And here we reach another important element of the doping conundrum identified in Houlihan's book: namely the uncertainty surrounding the problem.

Hitherto all attempts to produce an unequivocal definition of the problem have been unsuccessful. As a result, when WADA formulated the WADC in 2003, the agency opted for a definition devoid of content, to state instead: 'Doping is defined as the occurrence of one or more of the anti-doping rule violations set forth in Article 2.1 through Article 2.8 of the Code' (WADA, 2003: 8). Doping is thus 'defined' as infringement of WADA's regulations. The point of orientation is the annually negotiated prohibited list and prohibited methods. But those remain arbitrary. There is no reasonable explanation why some substances with proven performance-enhancing effects (such as caffeine and creatine) are accepted whilst other substances that have a performance-enabling but negligible performance-enhancing effect (such as ephedrine, which appears in over-the-counter cough syrup, and salbutamol, which is an efficient compound in asthma medication) are banned. There is no convincing argument why the performance-inhibiting stimulant cannabis is on the banned list whereas nicotine, which is associated with increased levels of haematocrit (the desired effect of those who use the hormone erythropoietin, or EPO, responsible for the production of the oxygen carrying red blood cells in the body) is not. By the same token, there is no convincing argument why it is legal for athletes to use an artificial environment like a hypoxic chamber (a room in which the level of oxygen can be reduced to simulate the effect of staying at high altitude in order to elevate the number of red blood cells) but illegal to use EPO injections to reach the same goal.

Houlihan deserves credit for having called attention to the unstable foundation of anti-doping policy and the fact that it is formed without a clear and distinct understanding of the problem it opposes. He observes correctly that 'each refinement in policy has been accompanied by a sharper insight into the issues and aspects of policy that remain unsolved' (Houlihan 1999: 171). The conclusion he draws from this is less convincing: 'There is an unfortunate number of examples of the identification of a problem which prompts a period of enthusiastic debate and policy-making, a period which slows considerably when the analysis of the problem leads to a greater awareness of the complexity of the issue or the cost of resources required for its resolution' (Houlihan 1999: 171). It could be argued that the cooling of the political interest in the doping issue when the immediate media furore abated was a positive sign that the 'moral panic' approach to the problem had been replaced by political after-thought and a sense of proportion. Houlihan's use of the term 'unfortunate' indicates that at this early stage in the global war on drugs in sport, he bought into the idea that doping was an alarming problem in need of sweeping political action. He does not include in his analysis the possibility that the enterprise had been pushed forward by anti-doping ideologists who, based on a blend of nostalgia, technophobia, purism, and health worshipping, exaggerated the problem; and that the 'doping' issue has thus been initiated on false premises in an attempt to protect the image and economic viability of sport, at a time when elite sport was portrayed as massively reliant on dangerous performance-enhancing drugs.

The likely explanation is that Houlihan was drawing on information provided by these anti-doping ideologists, at a time when literature on doping was sparse. Thus, Houlihan's description of doping in the early days of cycling provides a faithful reproduction of Voy's earlier account of different practices by Belgian, French, and British cyclists (Voy 1991: 6; Houlihan 1999: 33f).

Houlihan refers to Voy, but this reference is a dead end because Voy does not reveal where he picked up this information. His use of the terms 'allegedly' and 'supposedly' raise suspicion that he may have it from hearsay. Hoberman in his otherwise impressively well-researched and well-documented *Mortal Engines* also mentions the colourful description of cyclists' doping practice and offers a direct quote from Donohoe and Johnson:

> The French used a mixture known as "Caffeine Houdes" while the Belgians sucked on
> sugar cubes dipped in ether. The riders' black coffee was boosted with extra caffeine

and peppermint, and as the race progressed the mixture was spiked with increasing doses of cocaine and strychnine. Brandy was also frequently added to cups of tea. . . . Since drugs such as heroin or cocaine were widely taken in these tournaments without supervision, it was perhaps likely that fatalities would occur.

(Donohoe and Johnson 1986: 3; Hoberman 1992: 130)

When consulting Donohoe and Johnson to check where they got the information from, we once again find ourselves in a cul-de-sac. Given the similarity, it is tempting to think that Donohoe and Johnson have used Voy's account and spiced it up. Nevertheless, Voy's description has been reproduced numerous times in academic publications. The author of this chapter is as culpable as anyone, having referred to Voy's account in *The Doping Devil* (2008; first published in Danish in 1999). The image of uneducated nineteenth-century sportsmen's hazardous intake of strychnine, ether, and alcohol was so riveting I could not resist the temptation to pass it on to the reader. Voy's description was a useful illustration of how athletes were so obsessed by the will to win from the very beginning of modern sport that they would do anything short of killing themselves to achieve victory. It underpinned the argument that the Festina affair was not the result of a new generation of corrupt athletes' disrespect for the spirit of sport. For authors with an anti-doping agenda, the story was equally useful because it also demonstrated athletes' irresponsibility and thus supported the idea that doping should be banned in order to protect athletes against themselves. In other words, regardless of perspective, once published the story was simply too good *not* to be true.

The Arthur Linton myth

One of the most convincing arguments in the anti-doping crusaders' armoury centres on the danger of doping. Hence they cherish dramatic references to doping-related deaths even if the examples are anecdotal. Donohoe and Johnson's speculation that 'it was perhaps likely that fatalities would occur' is a modest example. Voy delivers a less vague example when he unreservedly claims: 'The first recorded drug-related death in the world of sport occurred in 1886, when an English cyclist died from an overdose of something called trimethyl, which was probably a form of ether' (Voy 1991: 6).

Voy does not mention the name of this cyclist. Instead we get the name in Houlihan's text as he mentions the consequences of the risky habits of heroin-strychnine-ether-brandy-dependant athletes: 'It was inevitable that the administration of these and other dangerous drugs would lead to fatality. The death of the cyclist Arthur Linton in 1886 may be the first recorded death of an athlete from an overdose of drugs' (Houlihan 1999: 34). One notes, in passing, that we have moved from fatalities being 'perhaps likely' to 'inevitable' in the intake of the these substances. There is little doubt that Houlihan has taken Voy's account at face value, but his honesty shows in a footnote when he alerts the reader to Donohoe and Johnson's differing account, in which Linton's death is stated to have occurred 'many years later from typhoid' (Houlihan 1999: 34).

In hindsight it is easy to suggest that Houlihan ought to have investigated whether Linton died in 1886 or in 1896 and thus which source was the more reliable of the two. One important explanation for why Houlihan opted for Voy's account in the body text is that it was the most fitting. If Linton did not die from an overdose of drugs in relation to a cycling event but from typhoid fever on 23 July 1896, two months after he had finished his last race, it would have been pointless to mention him at all. Once again, I admit to making the same sensationalist mistake, stating in *The Doping Devil* that Linton died in the wake of the first edition of the spring classic Paris-Roubaix race in 1896. Quoting a German source, I found the captivating claim,

'Linton died in mysterious circumstances after crossing the finish line in fourth place. It was later reported that his coach, the famous and notorious "Choppy" Warburton, had given him a "magic potion", so that, despite complete exhaustion, he could complete the race' (Møller 2008: 31). However, this myth was exposed as such by the historian Paul Dimeo, who made the effort to check all available material about Linton, which led him to the conclusion that 'we cannot say that his death was due to drug use because there is no evidence either way' (Dimeo 2007: 8).

The influence of other anti-doping myths

It is tempting to shrug off the old Linton myth as an unimportant curiosity. But it is not, as it is one among many myths that anti-doping idealists have produced in order to promote their cause. When the Danish cyclist Knud Enemark Jensen collapsed at the Rome Olympics in 1960 and subsequently died from sunstroke, it was rumoured that his death had been caused by the intake of amphetamines. Anti-doping idealists seized on Jensen's death as a promotional tool. If athletes die as a result of performance-enhancing stimulants, the sporting community will have to react. Consequently, in January 1963 European sports governing bodies held a convention where they tried to define doping as a prerequisite for the development of anti-doping policy. In 1965 doping controls were introduced in cycling, to the dissatisfaction of many professional cyclists. When in 1966 dissatisfied cyclists refused to take the doping test during the Road World Championships, their actions provoked the European Council to pass a resolution condemning athlete use of doping. In 1972 Ludwig Prokop, a member of the IOC's Medical Commission, who had pushed for an anti-doping policy since the 1950s, published a report in which he stated as a fact that Jensen's death was a consequence of amphetamine intake – notwithstanding the facts that his claim was unsubstantiated; that the medico-legal report sent from the Italian authorities to the Danish police in 1961 cleared Jensen of suspicion; and that Prokop himself admitted in an interview in 2001 that he had never seen documentation to prove that Jensen's death was caused by doping, thereby conceding that 'perhaps it was wrong of me to draw it out in the report' (Møller 2005: 467). This is another myth which has been established as a scientific truth on the basis of Voy's and Donohoe and Johnson's unscientific accounts, becoming a common reference in scholarly books and articles about doping in sports. It is mentioned as a fact in the books by Houlihan (1999) and Waddington (2000). In Waddington and Smith's updated 2009 version of Waddington (2000), the account has been rectified, but in the revised book we still find a third major myth, regarding the lethal danger of the aforementioned blood hormone EPO.

> EPO came onto the market in Europe in 1987 and it was followed almost immediately by a sudden spate of deaths of heart failure among professional cyclists. Between 1987 and 1990 fourteen Dutch riders and four from Belgium – all young and apparently healthy elite athletes – died suddenly . . . and the overwhelming probability is that some, if not all, of these unexpected and unexplained deaths were associated with the use of EPO; that all the deaths occurred amongst Dutch and Belgian riders also suggests the establishment of an early EPO 'grapevine' and distribution network in Holland and Belgium.
>
> (Waddington and Smith 2009: 223)

The rationale appears sound. The only problem is that the claim regarding a 'sudden spate of deaths' has little foothold in reality, as documented by Bernat López in his meticulous study of the case (López 2011). Checking the references in scientific articles, López found that there was no substantial evidence. The story stems instead from journalistic outlets which report dramatic descriptions by anti-doping crusaders, who need no evidence to profess that athletes who abuse EPO will see that their 'blood becomes mud', and who have no reservations in attributing the sudden death of young, healthy riders to abuse of EPO, even in cases where this interpretation makes little sense from a sporting or forensic point of view.

Once again I must confess to membership of the group of doping researchers who have reproduced this story, (Møller 2010) referring to Waddington and Smith (2009), who had referred to a UK newspaper, *The Independent on Sunday* (14 July 1991). Unfortunate as it may be, I succumbed to the tendency to lose critical sensibility when enthralled by information that is clearly not reserved for the typical reader of gossip columns.

A final example:

> Consider this. A number of elite-level athletes were asked if, hypothetically, they would be willing to take a pill that would guarantee them an Olympic gold medal even if they knew this pill would kill them, within a year. Over 50 percent of the athletes said yes.
>
> (Voy 1991: 115)

What Voy here presents as a fact about athletes' irresponsible obsession with winning is known as the Mirkin study. Although this study has never been published in a peer-reviewed journal, the understanding that Mirkin had asked over one hundred athletes and found to his own 'amazement, more than one-half of the athletes responding stated they would take the magic pill' (Mirkin 1982), this 'study' has been referred to in scholarly work as a proven truth about elite athletes' attitude. Waddington, for instance, uses it in his otherwise razor-sharp critique of the Peter Coni report on drug use in British sport; and this leads him to the optimistic conclusions that 'since perhaps 1983 the level of drug use in British athletics has reduced' and that 'British athletics is at present enjoying a noticeable recession in the level of drug use' (Waddington 2005: 481). The Coni report does not even mention 'Mirkin's study of over a hundred competitive runners, more than half of whom would take a magic pill that guaranteed them an Olympic gold medal, even if it would kill them within a year' (Waddington 2005: 481).

The Mirkin study inspired another anti-doping idealist, Bob Goldman, to do a follow-up study. 'The Goldman dilemma is one of the most cited results in the anti-doping literature becoming accepted "wisdom" regarding choices elite athletes make regarding drug use in sport' (Connor *et al.* 2013: 1). Goldman makes the same hypothetical offer to athletes, the only difference being that he let the athletes live up to five years after winning the gold medal. Goldman alleged that he has carried out this study repeatedly on a biannual basis from 1982 to 1995 and every time found that about half of the athletes would take up the offer. Connor *et al.* (2013) were sceptical, so they decided to conduct a control study that led to a completely different result. Out of 219 samples among elite track and field athletes, only two reported that they would make the deal. The rigorous study of Connor *et al.* seems to falsify Mirkin and Goldman and to have exposed yet another anti-doping myth.

The state of affairs and the lesson taught by C. Wright Mills

Connor *et al.* mention in their critique of Goldman's 'research' that 'the studies have not been peer reviewed' (Connor *et al.* 2013: 1). By doing so they imply that peer review is a safeguard of research quality. If this is true of natural sciences, it could not be farther from the truth for the human and social sciences. Peer review within these latter sciences is nothing but a delusional game promoted for bureaucratic purposes and accepted by human and social scientists as a way to improve the academic prestige of these research areas. Although there are many reasons to be sceptical about Goldman's dilemma (the difference between indicating a willingness to take a deadly pill and to actually take it appears to make it futile) the fact that the paper by Connor *et al.* has been peer reviewed does not warrant that the answers they received from the athletes is a true reflection of their inner thoughts. It may well be that the impact of the anti-doping campaign has taught elite athletes to present themselves in accordance with dominant public opinion. The surprisingly high number of athletes admitting to doping in Pitsch *et al.*'s survey, based on the randomized response technique, seems to suggest that conclusion.

So the conclusion that can be drawn from the observations above is that we do not really know what we have claimed to know about doping in sport except from the most obvious: that it is practiced by a number of athletes; that some of them test positive and receive quarantines; that there are doctors and scientists who assist athletes in their doping practices; and that political initiatives have been taken to oppose this practices. The things we know with certainty about the milieu of elite sports doping have come to light as a result of police investigations, or have been revealed by athletes or their support personnel in the interviews or biographies that are usually published in the wake of a major scandal or a positive doping test (e.g. Voet 2001; Hamilton 2012).

Peer review has proved unable to prevent sociological research into doping from being tainted by misinformation provided by athletes and anti-doping idealists. There is a web of reasons as to why sociology, like many other human science disciplines, has produced doping research that embraces unsubstantiated doping myths, trusts the public statements of athletes on doping, and puts faith in anonymized interview narratives and survey responses. But two of the most prominent threads in this web are the widening of the gaps between human science disciplines, and what C.W. Mills has identified as abstracted empiricism that 'often seems to consist of efforts to restate and adopt *philosophies* of *natural* science in such a way as to form a program and a canon for work in social science' (Mills 2000/1959: 57; italics in original). Human reality is too complex and diverse for any scholar to succeed in the ambition to present the truth about, in this case, elite sport's doping culture, and it is probably impossible to produce completely flawless research of any importance into the matter. One has to reconcile oneself with the fact that human and social science by nature is interpretive.

That said it is certainly possible to avoid severe pitfalls and to increase the credibility and validity of the research. Mills offers some good advice when he urges researchers to 'avoid the arbitrary specialization of prevailing academic apartments' (Mills 2000/1959: 225). To be a good sociologist one must also be a scrupulous historian, conscientious philosopher, and open-minded anthropologist as well as an empathetic psychologist. The challenge is 'to understand men and women as historical and social actors, and the ways in which the variety of men and women are intricately selected and intricately formed by the variety of human societies' (Mills 2000/1959: 225). Introspection and a continuous attempt to put oneself in the shoes of the individuals under study are fruitful strategies; however, they offer no guarantee that informants will not hide away crucial information, and indeed, the hotter the topic, the greater will be the likelihood of such evasion. Being aware of human beings' self-interest and taking possible personal agendas into account may help future researchers to listen and to read more carefully, and to avoid contributing to the adoption of unsubstantiated myths in sociological research.

References

Bette, K.H. and Schimank, U. (1995) *Doping im Hochleistungssport: Anpassung durch Abweichung*, Frankfurt am Main: Suhrkamp Verlag.

Breivik, G. (1987) 'The Doping Dilemma: Some Game Theoretical and Philosophical Considerations', *Sportwissenschaft*, 17: 83–94.

Breivik, G. (1992) 'Doping Games: A Game Theoretical Exploration of Doping', *International Review for the Sociology of Sport*, 27: 235–256.

Connor, J., Woolf, J., and Mazanov, J. (2013) 'Would They Dope? Revisiting the Goldman Dilemma', *British Journal of Sport Medicine*, doi:10.1136/bjsports-2012-091826.

Conrad, P. (2007) *The Medicalization of Society: On the Transformation of Human Conditions into Treatable Disorders*, Baltimore: Johns Hopkins University Press.

Dimeo, P. (2007) *A History of Drug Use in Sport 1876–1976: Beyond Good and Evil*, London: Routledge.

Donohoe, T. and Johnson N. (1986) *Foul Play: Drug Abuse in Sport*, Oxford: Basil Blackwell.

Hanstad. D.V. and Loland, S. (2009) 'Where on Earth Is Michael Rasmussen?' in V. Møller, M. McNamee and P. Dimeo (eds) *Elite Sport, Doping and Public Health*, Odense: University Press of Southern Denmark.

Hanstad, D.V., Skille, E.Å. and Thurston, M. (2009) 'Elite Athletes' Perspectives of Providing Whereabouts Information: A Survey of Athletes in the Norwegian Registered Testing Pool', *Sport und Gesellschaft*, Jahrgang 6: 30–46.

Hamilton, T. (2012) *The Secret Race – Inside the Hidden World of the Tour de France: Doping, Cover-ups, and Winning at All Costs*, New York: Bantam Books.

Hardie, M., Shilbury, D., Ware, I., and Bozzi, C. (2010) *I Wish I Was Twenty-One Now: Beyond Doping in the Australian Peloton*, Geelong: Deakin University.

Hoberman, J.M. (1992) *Mortal Engines: The Science of Performance and the Dehumanization of Sport*, New York: Free Press.

Houlihan, B. (1999) *Dying to Win: Doping in Sport and the Development of Anti-Doping Policy*, Strasbourg: Council of Europe Publishing.

Koh, B. (2013) *Athlete Motivation and the "Spirit of Sport": Understanding Doping and the Culture of Complementary and Alternative Therapy Use in Aquatic Sports*, Sydney: University of Technology Sydney.

Kulturministeriet (1999) *Doping i Danmark: En hvidbog* [Doping in Denmark: A White Paper], København: Kulturministeriet.

Lentillon-Kaestner, V. and Carstairs, C. (2009) 'Doping Use among Young Elite Cyclists: A Qualitative Psychosociological Approach' *Scandinavian Journal of Medicine and Science in Sport*, 20(2): 336–345.

López, B. (2011) 'The Invention of a Drug of Mass Destruction: Deconstructing the EPO Myth', *Sport in History*, 31(1): 84–109.

Mills, C.W. (2000/1959) *The Sociological Imagination*, Oxford: Oxford University Press.

Mirkin, G. (1982) 'High Risk Gamble to Obtain Winning Edge', *San Diego Union*, 13 July.

Møller, V. (2005) 'Knud Enemark Jensen's Death During the 1960 Rome Olympics: A Search for Truth?' *Sport in History*, 25 (3): 452–71.

Møller, V. (2008/1999) *The Doping Devil*, Norderstedt: Books on Demand.

Møller, V. (2010) *The Ethics of Doping and Anti-Doping: Redeeming the Soul of Sport?* London: Routledge.

Pitsch, W., Emrich, E., and Klein, M. (2005) 'Zur Häufigkeit des Dopings im Leistungssport: Ergebnisse eines www-survey', *Leipziger Sportwissenschaftlicher*, 46 (2): 63–77.

Voet, W. (2001) *Breaking the Chain: Drugs and Cycling. The True Story*, London: Yellow Jersey Press.

Voy, R. (1991) *Drugs, Sport, and Politics*, Champaign, IL: Leisure Press.

Waddington, I. (2000) *Sport, Health and Drugs: A Critical Sociological Perspective*, London and New York: Routledge.

Waddington, I. (2005) 'Changing Patterns of Drug Use in British Sport from the 1960s', *Sport in History*, 25(3): 472–496.

Waddington, I. and Smith, A. (2009) *An Introduction to Drugs in Sport: Addicted to Winning?* London and New York: Routledge.

Woodland, L. (1980) *Dope: Use of Drugs in Sport*, Newton Abbot, UK: David and Charles.

World Anti-Doping Agency (WADA) (2003) *World Anti-Doping Code*, Montreal: WADA.

32

SPORT FANS AND FANDOMS

William W. Kelly

It is a key feature of modernity that fans emerge out of mass culture audiences in search of intensified meanings and pleasure. They consume mass culture, but in their rapacious and determined consumption, they produce social communities, personal identities, and cultural artefacts. They create and inhabit fandoms, small worlds of persistent practice. This is certainly as true for sports as for any other modern arena of leisure and entertainment.

Sports are almost always watched as they are played, whether by anxious parents following a child's swim meet or by 100,000 ardent supporters at a FIFA World Cup final. Beyond the immediacy of spectating in situ, the amount of time and resources devoted by all of the world's media to the print, broadcast, and digital transmission of sporting events and news creates and feeds an insatiable global thirst for sport.

There are many ways, of course, that we watch, listen to, and read about sport events, from the most occasional, casual, and distracted spectators to those who follow sport in a sustained, knowledgeable, and passionate cast of mind, body, and emotion. It is the latter who are the fans, and they have overwhelmingly been the focus of social science research on those who follow sport. This chapter selectively surveys the long-standing and highly developed sociology of sport fandom, which itself is a core field of sport sociology.

To date, sport fan studies have focused overwhelmingly on the centre sports of Great Britain, Europe, and the United States, especially football (soccer) and baseball. They tend to analyze these fans in terms of identity or consumption, and the more incisive are set within theorizations of modern and postmodern culture and political economy. There are still residual judgmental debates about fans as authentic or as pathological (the exchange, for instance between Smith 1988, 1989; and Meier 1989). Studies of sport fandom are based on quantitative and qualitative methodologies and draw on a vast array of sources beyond academic research, including memoirs, fanzines (print and digital), interviews, and journalism. While sociologists have contributed centrally to the academic study of fans, they have been in continuous and constructive dialogue with colleagues in history, anthropology, psychology, geography, cultural studies, and media and communication studies, and we must consider some of this work as well.

Who are the fans?

How are fans to be defined among the broad spectrum of modern audiences, from the casual spectator to the committed supporter (Abercrombie and Longhurst 1998)? The distinctions are often taken as obvious – fans are those at the far end of vectors of frequency and intensity – but this in itself is not a nuanced basis of analysis. It may seem obviously productive to begin with the condition of sport fans framed more generally within fans across the many domains of mass culture, including music, television, film, fiction, fashion, gaming, and so forth. Surprisingly, however, there has been too little analysis that does this. Schimmel *et al.* (2007) are correct to bemoan this, although there are several notable exceptions (e.g. Gray *et al.* 2007, Redhead 1997).

In my own formulation, there are at least six features that sport fans share with other mass culture fans.

1   All fans are the most aggressive appropriators and the most brazen producers among mass culture consumers. Watching television, attending sport contests, listening to music, reading comics, and buying may always require some degree of active 'recoding'. But fans really are the guerrilla vanguard of such consumption, turning their 'reception' of commercial entertainment into a resourceful, often irreverent, 'production'.

2   Fans both know more and care more. It is not just the extent of what they know but the depth of how they feel that sets fans apart from the rest of the audience, yet this intersection of knowledge and passion is difficult to sustain. It is quite difficult, for instance, to follow a contest closely while participating fully in cheering at the same time. The chanting and clapping so necessary to sustain the mood can be quite a distraction to the concentration required of appreciating the finer points of the action. On the other hand, the pursuit and retention and display of ever more arcane knowledge can become a quite dispassionate objective. What and how much fans should know and what and how much fans should feel are nervous issues even for the fans themselves.

3   Fandom is serious play. Sports and music are consumed by a very large proportion of the national population, but usually for occasional entertainment. Professional baseball in the United States plays to tens of millions of stadium spectators each year, but very few of them come to an entire season of a team's 80 home games. The fans among them are those who seek much more than entertainment and invest this 'leisure' with much more drive and dedication. It is about one's personal identity, not entertainment desires.

4   Fans are also marked by seeking intimacy with the object of their attention – a personality, a programme, a genre, a team. Fans are not satisfied with the formal performances, with the mediated and staged glimpses of stars. They seek to get behind the curtain, to know more about the performers, to 'possess' them through tokens like autographs and bootleg tapes. Fandom is a gesture of intimacy toward commoditized culture, but such intimacy is not to be confused with identification. For several reasons, fans are often involved in an intense play between identifying and distancing. Keeping a certain social and physical distance can be an acknowledgement of propriety, it can be necessary for creative fantasy, and it can result from scepticism. By their very knowledge and passion, fans can be the most ardent of supporters but equally, the most arch of critics.

5   Being a fan can be a solitary, private pursuit and a richly collective sociality. Intimacy may be sought and gained as a fan with other fans as well as a solitary fan toward the object of adulation. In producing meanings and pleasures through acts of both social and aesthetic discriminations, fans often create and sustain communities of shared practices.

6 Finally, mass culture fans tread a fine line between the pleasure of fantasy and the pathology of fanaticism, between the excessive and the obsessive. It is never easy to determine when and how intimacy becomes idolatry and passion becomes pathological. The issue is rendered even more complex because society's official agents, the mainstream population, and the fans themselves may have incommensurable standards of normalcy and morality.

All of these conditions fit sport fans within a broader formulation of mass culture fandom, but our analyses also hinge on several distinctive features of sport as open-ended, physical contests. The outcomes are uncertain, the action is physical, and allegiance is partisan. Thus, in ways quite different than other mass culture fans, sport fans are shaped by suspense and by agonistic affiliation.

Fans in history and theory, from local identity to hyper-consumption

The debates in sport sociology and sport history about the utility of sharply demarcating modern sport from those sport-like physical contests in eras before (a line generally drawn somewhere in the nineteenth century) has generated similar debates about spectators and fans. Could there be such a category before strict rules governed play, delimited the players, and created special venues with stands and fences and admission charges? To be sure, in many of the cases of popular premodern proto-sport, it was impossible to draw a firm line between participants and observers, as with the in-and-out action of Native American lacrosse and the folk-ball games found in towns and villages across the British Isles. But as Allen Guttmann surveyed in his useful history *Sports Spectators* (1986) and as much research has demonstrated, premodern sporting events in many eras and societies drew large spectator audiences and even the passionate intensity that is resonant of modern fandoms. From the blood-thirsty crowds at the Mesoamerican ball games (Whittington 2001) and the Blue and Green 'circus factions' at the Roman Coliseum (Cameron 1976) to the 20,000 who gathered on Newmarket Heath in June of 1809 to watch Captain Barclay successfully walk 1,000 miles in 1,000 hours to win a 1,000-guinea bet (Radford 2001), fan passions seem to have a trans-historical genealogy (Quinn 2009).

By the mid- to late nineteenth century, fandoms of emerging modern sports were forming in two constellations – around urban working-class men, whose affiliations were generated by local, ethnic, and class loyalties for emerging professional teams or individual athletes (e.g. football, baseball), and around broader metropolitan followings of elite amateur team sports (e.g. inter-collegiate American football, athletics) or individual tournament sport athletes (e.g. in golf, horse racing, and boxing). Neither of these was an unmediated response to the sport contest. Oriard's early study (1993) was an incisive demonstration of how coverage and commentary in late nineteenth-century urban newspapers and weeklies educated a US metropolitan readership about the new sport of American football, creating a mass spectatorship and passionate followers of favourite teams.

By and throughout the twentieth century, major sport fandoms were shaped by highly structured leagues, territorially based clubs, stadium experience, print and later television mediated loyalties, a commoditized material culture (trading cards, kits, hats), and increasingly participatory venues (fan clubs, supporter associations, talk radio, fantasy leagues, etc.). Notable in twenty-first-century sports fandom are emergent formations of internet and/or digital media and an ever sharper tension between intimacy and distance. That is the explosive growth of fan numbers, the communicative powers of new media, and the competitive proliferation of sport media have brought ever more intimate probing of athletes as well as ever more distant possibilities of passionate and knowledgeable attachments to teams and athletes around the world. Along with the global flows of sport capital, media, and migratory athletes, we must add fan loyalties and fandom forms.

The transformations of sport spectators and fans produced by these historical changes in sport have been most often theorized at the intersection of identity and commodification. In the earlier stages of metropolitan modernity, fan identities were shaped by local team support, the immediacy and intimacy of the stadium experience, and lifelong interactions among family, workplace, and community. The expanding scale of professionalization, growing commercialization of sport, commodification of fan performance, economic dislocations, social mobility, and television technology all conspired to dilute and undermine fan formation (e.g. Marjoribanks and Farquharson 2012). They are 'debased' in the double sense of being deracinated and being less than real supporters. There has been determined resistance, from hooligan violence to independent supporter activism (Redhead 1997), but globalization and hyper-commodification insure that, with centre sports in the vanguard, the era of the 'post-fan' is upon us. For football, one of the most nuanced modelings of changing spectatorships and the nature of fans among them was that of Giulianotti (2002), who characterized four ideal types of spectator identity based on shifts from traditional identification with clubs to more fickle consumers and from hot to cool forms of support.

Crawford (2004) uses a very suggestive concept of fan career (in social and moral terms) to get beyond any simple notion that inauthentic consumers are replacing real fans. His study of a Manchester ice hockey team's supporters (2010) was an ethnographic demonstration that fandom may survive in an era of hyper-consumption. It is in this sense that fans remain the unstable core of commoditized culture (and its cultural commodities) because they are dangerously poised between the forces of production and the sites of reception, inclined both to disrupt with rude distortion and to comply with exemplary consumption. Fans represent the fondest hopes and worst fears of a sport capitalist.

Fan violence

The greatest attention in sport fan studies has been paid to organized fan violence, especially in football and most especially with English football. 'Football hooligan' studies have commanded some of the sharpest minds – and sharpest debates – for over four decades, since the provocative studies by Ian Taylor in the late 1960s. Over a decade ago, Dunning *et al.* (2002: 13) enumerated seven main academic approaches to the study of football fan violence, which have spanned the disciplines of history, sociology, anthropology, criminology, and social psychology (among the key contributions are Armstrong 1998, Dunning *et al.* 1988, Giulianotti *et al.* 1994, King 1997, Marsh *et al.* 1978, Taylor 1971, Williams 1991). Broadly, positions fall on one side or the other of the question of whether the logic of violence can be traced to more rational causes, particularly socioeconomic circumstances, or to more emotional motivations, especially the 'rush' of aggro. Among the many specific issues that have divided analysts are the degree of organization, the class background of hooligans, the extent to which hooligan violence takes place at the scene of the game and because of the sport or whether the sport and the game is a pretext for violence caused by other factors, distinctions between aggressive pose and violent actions, and the degree to which football hooliganism is trans-historical and transcultural.

Those outside this academic fray may tire of the scholarly battles, and non-British academics may be bewildered by the apparent squandering of intellectual resources on such a singular topic. Nonetheless, football is the 'world game', and violence, especially organized violence, has remained tenaciously present, simply changing in form and location. Hooliganism is often not just about class frustration, about shaping and displaying a particularly aggressive masculinity, and about a struggle to defend and invade territory, but also not infrequently about racism, homo-phobia, and misogyny. This is not the place to review in detail this literature (e.g. Giulianotti *et al.* 1994, Dunning *et al.* 2002) but the English studies and debates do offer a valuable foundation for historical and comparative research and for theorizing fandom in extremis.

Football hooliganism has also been debated particularly for the cases of Scotland, Italy, and Argentina in the past; important recent scholarship is the comparative football research by Ramón Spaaij across a number of European countries (e.g. Spaaij 2006) and new work on Italian UltraS (Guschwan 2007, Scalia 2009, Testa and Armstrong 2010). Unfortunately, little attention has been paid to fan violence across sports comparatively because there appears to be little correlation between fan violence and on-field violence. Michael Messner (1995) and others have richly documented the ways that a hyper-masculinity drives 'centre sports' in the United States, yet even the most physically violent – American football and ice hockey – have never experienced the organized fan aggression of football.

Fan psychology

Aggression and anger, excitement and the 'flow' of getting in the game may be central modal-ities of fan emotion, but there is a wider interest in the range of emotions that motivate and are stimulated by fan engagement. Much of the research into sport and emotion has focused properly on athletes and sport performance (see the very useful review by Duquin 2000). That which attends to spectators and fans is often found in the football hooligan debates (Maguire 1991 is a perspective from figurational sociology). But this is a small part of the story. Following a sport team commands loyalty and incites enmity, but it also produces intense states of joy and suffering, gratification and grief, pride and shame, intimacy and relief (Wenner 1994).

Fan emotions are generated by several circumstances. As Sugimoto (2007) shows, the charged atmosphere of a stadium or other venue during a contest – the continual suspense of uncertain outcomes, moment to moment, the collective effervescence of the crowd, and the vivid sensory world of sounds, sights, smells, and touch (Armstrong and Young 2000, Back 2001, Kytö 2011, Magazine 2007: 72–107, Schoonderwoerd 2011). For most fans, the intensity of the moment is deepened by their longstanding familiarity of the stadium experience – standing (and singing) in the same place in Liverpool's Anfield Kop (Williams *et al.* 2001), sitting in the same bleacher section of Chicago's Wrigley Field (Swyers 2010), or of Osaka's Kōshien Stadium (Kelly 2004), game after game. The sociality of continuing attendance is further enriched by the narrativity and nostalgia of games past and player memories recounted (Bairner 2014). Trujillo and Krizek found that 'true fans seem to have an emotional attachment to baseball that is resilient to ticket prices, labor disputes, and media spectacles. . . . Indeed, as they expressed their feelings and emotions, these fans revealed . . . powerful senses of identity, community, continuity, narrativity, therapy, spirituality, and self-discovery' (1994: 321).

And beyond those horizons, the fan experience is shaped by one's location in a local, regional, and even national context. As Robson (2000) describes for Millwall, the depth of passion on match day in the Lion's Den comes from the supporters' lived experience in that area of south-east London. Likewise, the emotions that underlie sport derbies around the world are generated by broader antagonisms between the two neighbourhoods, cities, or regions (Armstrong and Giulianotti 2001). Fan emotion is generated even by national ideology as well, as Archetti has argued for the Argentine 'cult of Maradona', who was celebrated as an exemplar of a particular form of class-based but nationalized masculinity: 'Maradona's performances were remembered in a kind of ritualised, commemorative bodily communion and as a genuine expression of joy' (1997: 34).

Issues of emotion in sport have brought sport sociology (and anthropology) to an uneasy relationship with psychology – uneasy because our social and cultural accounts are often sceptical of the claims of universal psychodynamics and/or neurobiological hardware that constitute much of sport psychology (Simons 2013 is a recent and somewhat popular synopsis of this work; see also Wann *et al.* 2000 and Wang 2006). And yet there is still potential collaboration here, especially on the issue of failure and loss. Only one player wins a Wimbledon championship; only one team wins the World Series. All others lose. The common lot of fans is that the sublime elation of success is so elusive and the sense of loss and failure is so perennial. How and why do fans remain loyal and tolerant and even hopeful in the face of continual disappointment? Klugman (2009) offered a Freudian account of the two loves that lie at the heart of fans' attachment to Australian Football League teams that is intriguing but which sounds almost masochistic. How might we address this question more comparatively and across the social and psychological disciplinary divides?

Stadium spectating and mediated spectating

Sports are played and watched in a vast range of spaces, artificial and natural, dedicated and borrowed – backyards, schoolyards, playgrounds, urban streets, and mountain slopes – but the enclosed stadium is our preeminent 'theatre of sport'. It is both the quintessentially modern monument to mass leisure and entertainment and an enduring echo of the spectacular sports of the ancient world – the stadium at Olympus, the Coliseum in Rome, the royal ball courts of Mesoamerica. A stadium at game time can attract tens of thousands of people, providing entertainment, food, shelter, clothing, law enforcement, and ongoing social relations. Deep and diverse emotions are invested not only in the experiences of watching a team but in the place itself where the spectating takes place. Romance, domestic quarrels, parent-child bonding, friendships, work, weddings, and fights – all take place in stadiums, thickening the sociality of fan identity.

This sociality of place, together with the potent immediacy of the event, has supported a general sense that watching sport in situ is the authentic experience, and those who come to watch and support are the 'true' local fans. John Bale, for instance, our premier geographer of sport, has written of sport venues as emotionally and symbolically imbued by fans as church, school, home, and heritage (1994), and he has also described the passionate love (topophilia) and fear (topophobia) that fans as well as players feel about their home venues and those of their most frequent rivals. This attachment is enacted through routinized rituals of attendance: assembling at the adjacent pub, holding tailgate parties in the stadium parking lot, wearing team clothing and kit, marching together into the stadium, collective cheering, the small rituals of particular seating sections, the after-game drinking, and so forth. All of this has been compellingly characterized by a number of ethnographic studies (e.g. Robson 2000 for Millwall; Kelly 2004 for Kōshien Stadium in Osaka; Magazine 2007 for Mexico City; Swyers 2010 for Wrigley Field in Chicago; and Keys 2013 for a rare historical exploration of sensory regimes in sport venues).

Other research, however, cautions us against presuming that sport-at-a-distance cannot also affirm fans and sustain fandoms. Many fans only experience the object of their commitment at home and in bars, via the television (Eastman and Riggs 1994; Gantz and Wenner 1995). The conviviality and excitement of media watching in sports bars is of a different order than, albeit of equal intensity to, being in the stadium. Eastman and Land (1997), Rowe (2004), and Boyle and Haynes (2009) have written persuasively of the very particular intimacy created by the visual technologies, verbal commentaries, and program strategies of sport television. As Weed (2007) argued about sports bars, perhaps it is less proximity to the event underway than proximity to others watching the same event that creates fan intimacy. And even television is unnecessary.

Grant Farred (2002), for instance, has written about his long-distance love of Liverpool FC from early childhood in South Africa, nurtured 'only' by occasional press reports and a fervent imagination; he never saw the team play, live or on television. This of course is now quite common; clubs in major sports around the world market themselves beyond even satellite broadcasting via internet pages and social media; there are Manchester United, Tiger Woods, and New York Yankees fan clubs on all continents, and Bale (1998) and King (2000) have theorized our need to 're-imagine locality' under these conditions, a theme I will take up below.

Fans and gender

Organized sports participation and spectatorship are still overwhelmingly male, at least in the aggregate. Sport has long been presumed to be 'naturally' about physical contests of aggressive physicality and masculine virtues and therefore largely played and watched by males. Sport has been defended as a 'male preserve', although the defensiveness of this phrase betrays an undertone of anxiety. Women's sports are deemed less interesting to watch, less profitable to broadcast, and less lucrative to sponsor because they are thought not to be on same level of skill and/or power as their male counterparts. LPGA pros noticeably lag in driving distance behind PGA pros; a majority of NBA players routinely dunk the ball while there is but a single current player in the WNBA (Brittney Griner) who will occasionally dunk; the litany is familiar, and the belief fuels the global sports economy. But this is such a transparently faulty logic of discrimination. If that principle really held, we men would all only watch and follow a sport at its most elite level. Why bother with Little League baseball or minor league baseball when we could be watching major league baseball? And even among MLB teams, why would anyone watch and support the hapless Chicago Cubs when one could be following perennial champions like the New York Yankees? But lost causes, lower leagues, and local school teams have never been deterrents to fan formation and often instill even more fan-aticism (Mainwaring and Clark 2012). There is a desperate and deep-rooted gender bias that still works against women's sport, female athletes, and female fans (Gosling 2007).

The central issues of gender and sport are treated elsewhere in this volume. Here it is worth noting that where scholars have looked, they have indeed found female fans, drawn by the same needs and desires as male fans, albeit facing greater obstacles to acceptance. (Women may be tolerated as fans on the pretext that they are 'really' watching as mothers, wives, and girlfriends, which is of course to dismiss them as not really fans at all!) But accounts such as those by Damousi and Cash (2009) and Mewett and Toffoletti (2011) on Australian rules football fans and Kelly Nelson (2000) on WNBA fans in the United States are testimony that the attractions and distractions of supporter passions can quickly cross gender divides.

Fans and fantasy

The digital frontier in sports is for some the cutting edge of fandom and for others the death knell of authentic sport followership. Whatever the future, it is important to appreciate that 'digital' and 'virtual' have multiple meanings in defining the fan experience. Early on, they referred to the long-distance fandoms encouraged by satellite, cable, and internet broadcasting of sport programming, including the sport television talk shows and 'sports talk radio' that were the forerunners of internet chat rooms, online blogs, and social media, which facilitate interactive communication and communal spaces for virtual fandoms (Bale 1998). This was carried forward through the medium of fantasy sport leagues (especially in the United States, using MLB baseball; Walker 2006), which allow fan-players to construct and manage 'teams' of players from many actual teams, the effect of which can be to cross-cut real team loyalties with one's fantasy team performance. The enormous popularity of 'Football Manager' marks the digitalization of this illusory blending of owner, manager, and fan. It also is an example of digital sport games more generally; in game-box and online formats and single-player and multi-player versions, sport games are among the best-selling and most played in the world (Witkowski 2012). In blurring the distinction between watching and doing, they not only attract and abet fans of 'live' sport, but they are now even used by coaches and athletes as part of their preparation and practice (Glanz and Schwartz 2010). No doubt the debates will sharpen about the effects of these multiple virtualizations of fan experience and their consequences for enhancing or displacing existing forms of sport fandom – and the sports and athletes that they follow. Plymire (2009) and Jonasson and Thiborg (2010) offer judicious speculations on the possible trajectories of e-sport, but it is still early in the technologies and in our capacities to appreciate their potentially transformative powers.

Future directions

Sport fan studies began with the centre sports of football in Britain and baseball in the United States and have taken up how these sports and their offspring have been followed elsewhere in the world (especially football fans in Europe and South America, Australian rules football fans, and baseball fans in Central America and Japan). Special attention has been paid to patterns of fan violence in football. Particular analytical weight has been given to assessing the effects of globalization and commodification on transformations – and, for some, erosion – of sport fans, their practices, and the dynamics of their identity construction.

These studies have produced rich insights, not only about the nature of fandom but more generally of sport. No doubt such lines of research will continue; for instance, just in 2013, FIFA has sanctioned clubs in Germany, Italy, France, the Netherlands, Scotland, Turkey, Cyprus, Russia, Poland, and Romania for the violent actions of their supporters, so clearly it remains a critical topic for sport sociologists. At the same time, though, sport fan sociology can fruitfully expand its horizons of inquiry in a number of directions. There are at least five that one might recommend:

1   Much more comparative work is required to appreciate the differences of fandom in centre sports, minor sports, and lifestyle sports. To what extent do our understandings from baseball, football, basketball, and other major sports apply to sports of limited exposure and alternative sports that avoid spectatorship and demand full-time commitment? Can there be fans of rock climbing and climbers?
2   What different forms of fandom are evoked by team sports versus individual sports? Features of boxing, tennis, golf, and other individual sports construct distinct experiences for fans, who may be drawn to the sport as a whole or who may follow a favourite boxer or golfer. However, the competitions are usually more occasional than team sports and the lack of league play also makes it difficult to generate the same oppositional fervour that is key to central sport fandoms.
3   We also yet have few comparative studies of gender, class, and world regional differences in fan identity and fandom practices.
4   We know that there are multiple sources and resources for fan self-fashioning – local identity, family allegiance, commercial appeal, spiritual quest, aesthetic pleasure, and so on.
5   Finally, much more is needed to understand the ways in which being a sport fan is embedded and enacted in everyday life. We need not only to locate fans within the broad spectrum

of sports but also to locate fans' sport practices within their everyday lives – apart from the overt moments of direct connection with the object of their attention, adoration, and affiliation – away from the stadium and the pub and the computer screen. How is one being a fan when one is not performing as a fan? The academic literature is not silent on this (Crawford 2004, Crawford 2010, and Stone 2007 are particularly suggestive), but it is much more developed in fan memoirs and fan fiction.

Sport fans and their worlds exhibit the common features of modern fandoms. They stand out from the audience for the depth of their knowledge and passion. They engage in serious play, not casual spectatorship. They test the limits of aggressive appropriation and the line between the pleasurable fantasy and pathological fanaticism. The suspense, the power, the expertise, and the partisanship at the heart of all sport forge the passionate and sustained commitments of their supporters. Fans are essential constituents of sport, not merely passive and peripheral receptors.

References

Abercrombie, N. and Longhurst, B. (1998) *Audiences: A Sociological Theory of Performance and Imagination*, Thousand Oaks, CA: Sage.

Archetti, E.P. (1997) '"And Give Joy to My Heart": Ideology and Emotions in the Argentinean Cult of Maradona', in G. Armstrong and R. Giulianotti (eds) *Entering the Field: New Perspectives on World Football*, Oxford: Berg.

Armstrong, G. (1998) *Football Hooligans: Knowing the Score*, New York: Berg.

Armstrong, G. and Giulianotti, R. (eds) (2001) *Fear and Loathing in World Football*, Oxford: Berg.

Armstrong, G. and Young, K. (2000) 'Fanatical Football Chants: Creating and Controlling the Carnival', in G. P.T. Finn and R. Giulianotti (eds) *Football Culture: Local Contests, Global Visions*, London and Portland, OR: Frank Cass.

Back, L. (2001) 'Sounds in the Crowd', in M. Bull and L. Back (eds) *The Auditory Culture Reader*, London: Berg.

Bairner, A. (2014) 'Emotional Grounds: Stories of Football, Memories, and Emotions', *Emotion, Space and Society*, 12: 18–23.

Bale, J. (1994) *Landscapes of Modern Sport*, Leicester: Leicester University Press.

Bale, J. (1998) 'Virtual Fandoms: Futurescapes of Football', in A. Brown (ed.) *Fanatics! Power, Identity and Fandom in Football*, London: Routledge.

Boyle, R. and Haynes, R. (2009) 'Consuming Sport: Fans, Fandom, and the Audience', in R. Boyle and R. Haynes (eds) *Power Play: Sport, the Media and Popular Culture*, Edinburgh: Edinburgh University Press.

Cameron, A. (1976) *Circus Factions: Blues and Greens at Rome and Byzantium*, Oxford: Clarendon Press.

Crawford, G. (2004) *Consuming Sport: Fans, Sport and Culture*, London: Routledge.

Crawford, G. (2010) *Theorising the Contemporary Sports Supporter: An Ethnography of the Supporter Base of the Manchester Storm*, Saarbrücken, Germany: Lambert Academic Publishing.

Damousi, J. and Cash, J. (2009) *Footy Passions*, Sydney: UNSW Press.

Dunning, E., Murphy, P., and Williams, J. (1988) *The Roots of Football Hooliganism: An Historical and Sociological Study*, London: Routledge & Kegan Paul.

Dunning, E., Murphy, P. Waddington, I., and Astrinakis, A.E. (eds) (2002) *Fighting Fans: Football Hooliganism as a World Phenomenon*, Dublin: University College Dublin Press.

Duquin, M. (2000) 'Sport and Emotions', in J. Coakley and E. Dunning (eds) *Handbook of Sports Studies*, Thousand Oaks, CA: Sage.

Eastman, S.T. and Land, A.M. (1997) 'The Best of Both Worlds: Sports Fans Find Good Seats at the Bar', *Journal of Sport and Social Issues*, 21: 156–178.

Eastman, S.T. and Riggs, K.E. (1994) 'Televised Sports and Ritual: Fan Experience', *Sociology of Sport Journal*, 11(3): 249–274.

Farred, G. (2002) 'Long Distance Love', *Journal of Sport and Social Issues*, 26(1): 6–24.

Gantz, W. and Wenner, L.A. (1995) 'Fanship and the Television Sports Viewing Experience', *Sociology of Sport Journal*, 12: 56–74.

Giulianotti, R. (2002) 'Supporters, Followers, Fans, and Flaneurs: A Taxonomy of Spectator Identities in Football', *Journal of Sport & Social Issues*, 26(1): 25–46.

William W. Kelly

Giulianotti, R., Bonney, N. and Hepworth, M. (eds) (1994) *Football Violence and Social Identity*, London: Routledge.

Glanz, J. and A. Schwartz (2010) 'From "Avatar" Playbook, Athletes Use 3-D Imaging', *New York Times*, 2 October 2010, available at: http://www.nytimes.com/2010/10/03/sports/03reality.html?_r=0.

Gosling, V.K. (2007) 'Girls Allowed? The Marginalization of Female Sports Fans', in J. Gray, C. Sandvoss and C.L. Harrington (eds) *Fandom: Identities and Communities in a Mediated World*, New York: New York University Press.

Gray, J., Sandvoss, C. and Harrington, C.L. (eds) (2007) *Fandom: Identities and Communities in a Mediated World*, New York: New York University Press.

Guschwan, M. (2007) 'Riot in the Curve: Soccer Fans in Twenty-First Century Italy', *Soccer & Society*, 8: 250–266.

Guttmann, A. (1986) *Sports Spectators*, New York: Columbia University Press.

Jonasson, K. and Thiborg, J. (2010) 'Electronic Sport and Its Impact on Future Sport', *Sport in Society*, 13: 287–299.

Kelly, W.W. (2004) 'Sense and Sensibility at the Ballpark: What Fans Make of Professional Baseball in Modern Japan', in W.W. Kelly (ed.) *Fanning the Flames: Fans and Consumer Culture in Contemporary Japan*, Albany: SUNY Press.

Keys, B.J. (2013) 'Senses and Emotions in the History of Sport', *Journal of Sport History*, 40: 21–38.

King, A. (1997) 'The Postmodernity of Football Hooliganism', *British Journal of Sociology*, 48: 576–593.

King, A. (2000) 'Football Fandom and Post-National Identity in the New Europe', *British Journal of Sociology*, 51: 419–442.

Klugman, M. (2009) 'Loves, Suffering and Identification: The Passions of Australian Football League Fans', *International Journal of the History of Sport*, 26: 21–44.

Kytö, M. (2011) '"We Are the Rebellious Voice of the Terraces, We are Çarşı": Constructing a Football Supporter Group through Sound', *Soccer & Society*, 12: 77–93.

Magazine, R. (2007) *Golden and Blue Like My Heart: Masculinity, Youth, and Power among Soccer Fans in Mexico City*, Tucson: University of Arizona Press.

Maguire, J.A. (1991) 'Towards a Sociological Theory of Sport and the Emotions: A Figurational Perspective', *International Review for the Sociology of Sport*, 26: 25–36.

Mainwaring, E. and Clark, T. (2012) '"We're Shit and We Know We Are": Identity, Place and Ontological Security in Lower League Football in England', *Soccer & Society*, 13: 107–123.

Marjoribanks, T. and Farquharson, K. (2012) *Sport and Society in the Global Age*, New York: Palgrave Macmillan.

Marsh, P., Rosser, E., and Harré, R. (1978) *The Rules of Disorder*, London: Routledge and Kegan Paul.

Meier, K.V. (1989) 'The Ignoble Sports Fan', *Journal of Sport & Social Issues*, 13: 111–119.

Messner, M.A. (1995) *Power at Play: Sports and the Problem of Masculinity*, Boston: Beacon Press.

Mewett, P.G. and Toffoletti, K. (2011) 'Finding Footy: Female Fan Socialization and Australian Rules Football', *Sport in Society*, 14: 670–684

Nelson, K. (2000) *Gender and Sexuality at Play: Women Professional Athletes and the People Who Watch Them*, Ph.D. thesis, Waltham, MA, Brandeis University.

Oriard, M. (1993) *Reading Football: How the Popular Press Created an American Spectacle*, Chapel Hill: University of North Carolina Press.

Plymire, D.C. (2009) 'Remediating Football for the Posthuman Future: Embodiment and Subjectivity in Sport Video Games', *Sociology of Sport Journal*, 26: 17–30.

Quinn, K.G. (2009) *Sports and Their Fans: The History, Economics and Culture of the Relationship between Spectator and Sport*, Jefferson, NC: McFarland & Company.

Radford, P. (2001) *The Celebrated Captain Barclay: Sport, Gambling and Adventure in Regency Times*, London: Headline.

Redhead, S. (1997) *Post-fandom and the Millennial Blues: The Transformation of Soccer Culture*, London: Routledge.

Robson, G. (2000) *No One Likes Us, We Don't Care: The Myth and Reality of Millwall Fandom*, Oxford: Berg.

Rowe, D. (2004) *Sport, Culture, and the Media: The Unruly Trinity*, Buckingham, UK: Open University Press.

Scalia, V. (2009) 'Just a Few Rogues? Football Ultras, Clubs and Politics in Contemporary Italy', *International Review for the Sociology of Sport*, 41: 41–54.

Schimmel, K.S., Harrington, C.L. and Bielby, D.D. (2007) 'Keep Your Fans to Yourself: The Disjuncture between Sport Studies' and Pop Culture Studies' Perspectives on Fandom', *Sport in Society*, 10: 580–600.

Schoonderwoerd, P. (2011) '"Shall We Sing a Song for You?": Mediation, Migration and Identity in Football Chants and Fandom', *Soccer & Society*, 12: 120–141.

Simons, E. (2013) *The Secret Lives of Sports Fans*, New York: Overlook Press.

Smith, G.J. (1988) 'The Noble Sports Fan', *Journal of Sport & Social Issues*, 12: 54–65.

Smith, G.J. (1989) 'The Noble Sports Fan Redux', *Journal of Sport & Social Issues*, 13: 121–130

Spaaij, R. (2006) *Understanding Football Hooliganism: A Comparison of Six Western European Football Clubs*, Amsterdam: Amsterdam University Press.

Stone, C. (2007) 'The Role of Football in Everyday Life', *Soccer & Society*, 8: 169–184.

Sugimoto Atsuo (2007) 'Agitation and Restraint: The Dialectic of Emotion in Sports Spectatorship', in W.W. Kelly (ed.) *This Sporting Life: Sports and Body Culture in Modern Japan*, New Haven, CT: Yale University.

Swyers, H. (2010) *Wrigley Regulars: Finding Community in the Bleachers*, Urbana: University of Illinois Press.

Taylor, I. (1971) 'Football Mad: A Speculative Sociology of Football Hooliganism', in E. Dunning (ed.) *The Sociology of Sport: A Collection of Readings*, London: Frank Cass.

Testa, A. and Armstrong. G. (2010) *Football, Fascism, and Fandom: The UltraS of Italian Football*, London: A & C Black.

Trujillo, N. and Krizek, B. (1994) 'Emotionality in the Stands and in the Field: Expressing Self through Baseball', *Journal of Sport & Social Issues*, 18: 303–325.

Walker, S. (2006) *Fantasyland: A Season on Baseball's Lunatic Fringe*, New York: Viking.

Wang, S. (2006) 'Sports Complex: The Science behind Fanatic Behavior', *APS Observer*, 19(5): 26–32.

Wann, D.L., Melnick, M.J., Russell, G.W. and Pease, D.G. (2000) *Sport Fans: The Psychology and Social Impact of Spectators*, London: Routledge.

Weed, M. (2007) 'The Pub as a Virtual Football Fandom Venue: An Alternative to "Being there"?', *Soccer & Society*, 8: 399–414.

Wenner, L.A. (1994) 'Loving the Game to Death: Heroes, Goats, and Spectator Emotion', *Journal of Sport & Social Issues*, 18: 299–302.

Whittington, E.M. (ed.) (2001) *The Sport of Life and Death: The Mesoamerican Ballgame*, New York: Thames and Hudson.

Williams, J. (1991) 'Having an Away Day: English Football Spectators and the Hooligan Debate', in J. Williams and S. Wagg (eds) *British Football and Social Change: Getting into Europe*, Leicester: Leicester University Press.

Williams, J., Long, C. and Hopkins, S. (eds) (2001) *Passing Rhythms: Liverpool FC and the Transformation of Football*, Oxford: Berg.

Witkowski, E. (2012) 'On the Digital Playing Field: How We "Do Sport" with Networked Computer Games', *Games & Culture*, 7: 349–374.

33

SPORT AND VIOLENCE

Ramón Spaaij

Introduction

Excessive violence has long been considered 'one of the major threats to the long-term future of sport as we know it' (Case and Boucher 1981: 9). Recent instances of sports violence suggest that this 'threat' has not waned. In the past few years, lethal violence has been reported in professional and amateur sports in different global regions. In September 2013, a baseball fan was stabbed to death at a Major League Baseball match between the San Francisco Giants and the Los Angeles Dodgers, sparked by an argument over the teams' rivalry (Ortiz 2013). A month later, in a particularly gruesome act of violence, an amateur football (soccer) game in Brazil turned into a double murder scene when a 19-year-old referee was decapitated by spectators after he had stabbed a player to death (Longman 2013). And in February 2012, in one of deadliest episodes of sports-related violence in modern history, 74 people were killed and hundreds injured when spectators invaded the playing field after a football match between Al-Masry and Al-Ahly in the Egyptian city of Port Said. Most of the deaths were caused by concussions, stab wounds and suffocation from the stampede.

However, other types of sports violence have also grabbed media headlines. In several countries, concerns persist over the long-term health impacts of sports-related head injuries to professional and high-school athletes (e.g. Associated Press 2013). In Australia, the longstanding public debate on the well-being of thoroughbred racehorses was reignited by the leg injury that prized racehorse Verema sustained during the running of the 2013 Melbourne Cup, which resulted in the mare being 'put down' (Thomas 2013). For critics of staged animal contests, this recent event showed once again that the horse-racing industry exploits and endangers animals.

These recent examples highlight the sheer diversity of sports-related violence. The term 'violence' is applied to numerous phenomena in or related to the realm of sport, and used to describe all sorts of events and behaviours that occur at all levels of sport from professional competitions to collegiate, high school and youth leagues. Scholars in the disciplines of sociology, psychology, criminology and law have investigated diverse forms of sports violence. However, they typically fail to recognize the full diversity of sports violence and limit their enquiries to the types of violence that are most commonly associated with organized sport, that is, violence among fans and violence among athletes (Young 2012). As a consequence, their perspectives and explanations are at best partial.

This chapter critically reviews and synthesizes the breadth of sociological theory and research on sport and violence. The chapter first discusses competing definitions and interpretations of what violence is and how it relates to sport in all its forms. It then examines how different sociological approaches understand and explain sports violence, and explores some of the similarities and differences between them. The main approaches discussed here are figurational sociology, collective behaviour, microsociological and masculinity theories. Following this discussion, the attention shifts to emerging issues in the sociology of sports violence, with a particular focus on animal violence in sport. Issues for future sociological investigation are also proposed.

What is sports violence?

Defining sports violence is an important task because it determines what behaviours and practices we render (in)visible, how we assess and respond to these, and where we look for explanations. For example, Young (2012: 13) laments the narrow customary parameters of definitions of sports violence and suggests that if these parameters are broadened to include a range of harmful or abusive behaviours within the context of sport, 'it becomes evident that the subject matter may be far more expansive and varied than commonly assumed.' This definitional concern similarly plagues the social sciences of violence more broadly, where the problems entailed in specifying violence in an unambiguous way are well established. Wieviorka (2009: 2), for instance, argues that what makes violence so difficult to define is the need to adopt a double perspective that recognizes both the 'objectivity' of violence and 'the way subjectivity influences how it is experienced, lived, observed, represented, desired or undergone by individuals, groups and societies'.

Definitions of sports violence can be seen to operate on a continuum that ranges from minimalist to extended definitions (Spaaij 2014). Figure 33.1 shows how four particular conceptions

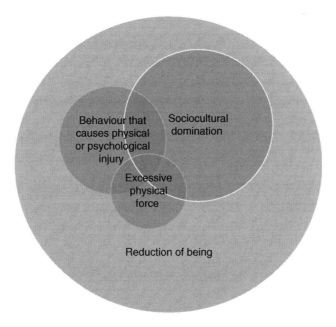

Figure 33.1 Defining sports violence: a continuum

of violence on this continuum relate to each other. A minimalist definition is that violence involves excessive physical force and physical harm to others. In this definition, violence is principally the coercive and destructive use of physical force. However, this does not imply that the exercise or suffering of violence is reduced to an exclusively bodily experience; on the contrary, violence entails a reduction of both the physical and the mental integrity of those against whom it is exercised (Zwaan 2007).

The adjective 'excessive' in this definition is of particular relevance to the study of sports violence because social norms concerning the use of violence in sport differ from those that govern most other societal domains. In many respects sports violence has never been viewed as 'real' violence (Smith 1983). Ritualized violence is built into the rules and structures of many competitive sports. Violent bodily contact is accepted as 'part of the game' in several contact sports and considered illegitimate only if it occurs outside the rules of the sport. More generally, competitive sport has impelled men and women to abuse and injure their bodies by over-training, playing when hurt, using performance-enhancing drugs and so on. This reveals the situationally specific nature of violence: the same behaviour that might be considered criminal in other contexts might be valued and celebrated by large segments of the sporting community. However, the opposite is also true, for example with regard to crowd behaviours that are criminalized and punished more heavily in the context of major sport events than in other societal spheres (e.g. Mastrogiannakis and Dorville 2012).

A somewhat broader definition is that sports violence is 'any behavior that causes either physical or psychological injury related to either a direct or indirect result of a sport experience' (Jamieson and Orr 2012: 4). Most scholars consider this behaviour in direct relation to the sport context, yet some include in their analysis the possibility of the diffusion of violent acts resulting from direct or indirect involvement in sport, where sports violence 'can occur in the home, school, workplace, recreational site, at events and many other venues due to the sport contest or involvement itself' (Jamieson and Orr 2012: 4). Whilst this definition has the advantage of being restrictive in its focus on 'physical or psychological injury', it can be criticized for not going far enough to deal with the complexity of sports violence, and for failing to consider the wider systems of power relations in which violence occurs.

Extended definitions of violence, on the other hand, draw attention to various modes of sociocultural domination that impede human realization and violate a person's rights or integrity. This definition stretches the notion of violence to include what Bourdieu calls 'symbolic violence', which refers to the largely unnoticed, partly unconscious domination that everyday discourses and practices maintain over a subject. This violence is 'exercised upon a social agent with his or her complicity' (Bourdieu and Wacquant 1992: 167). Bourdieu considers gender domination to be the paradigmatic form of symbolic violence, and it is this form of sociocultural domination that (alongside class domination) has attracted significant attention from sports sociologists. For example, several studies have identified how masculine hegemony is (re)produced in sport in ways that inferiorize women and their sports practices and achievements (e.g. Hargreaves 1986; Bryson 1987; Messner 2007). A distinctive advantage of this extended definition of sports violence is that it draws attention to a wider range of issues, social processes and practices that can be considered 'violent' even if they are not recognized as such in the common usage of the term. However, one could argue that this is precisely also its main disadvantage, namely, the meaning of 'violence' is stretched so far that it loses both its distinguishing character and its value as an analytical construct (Zwaan 2007).

Notwithstanding this critique, some conceptions of violence are broader still. Schinkel (2010), for example, defines violence ontologically as reduction of being (see Figure 33.1). For Schinkel

(2010: 50), violence is an aspect of every situation and (human) interaction since 'a reduction of being is necessary for such interaction to exist'. Violence can be seen as a sliding scale, where 'violence is relatively little present in interaction so long as the interacting actors are prepared to "change the aspect" of the other' (Schinkel 2010: 51). This ontological definition of violence is yet to be employed in the sociology of sport. However, its portrayal of violence as a sliding scale resonates in some respects with Smith's (1983) frequently cited typology that classifies sports violence into four types on a scale of legitimacy. *Brutal body contact* refers to violence performed within the official rules of the sport, hence legal in effect under the law and more or less socially accepted. Brutal body contact is inherent in heavy-contact sports such as boxing, ice hockey, rugby, Australian Rules football and American football. *Borderline violence* involves assaults that, although prohibited by the official rules of a given sport and the law, occur routinely and are more or less accepted by all concerned. The ice hockey fistfight, the late hit in American football and the high tackle in football are all examples of borderline violence. *Quasicriminal violence*, on the other hand, violates not only the official rules of the sport but also to a significant degree informal social norms that operate within the sporting environment. Quasicriminal violence, such as a forceful blow to the back of the head, can result in serious injury and is more likely to result in heavy punishment. Finally, *criminal violence* violates the official rules of the sport, the law and informal norms, and is not accepted. Such physical attacks usually take place prior to or after the sporting contest itself (Smith 1983).

While Smith's (1983) sociolegal typology is much narrower than the ontological definition of violence proposed by Schinkel (2010), it does enable a differentiated understanding of how the nature, severity and legitimacy of violence vary across different sports and change over time. More recently, Guilbert (2004) has sought to produce a typology that distinguishes three classes of sports practices: 'hard violence' sports that require bodily contact and where winning may require doing physical harm to the opponent (e.g. combat sports, mixed martial arts, basketball, soccer); 'soft violence' sports that allow other forms of violence, especially psychological and verbal violence (e.g. tennis, volleyball); and sports where violence is hidden or absent (e.g. swimming, shooting). Compared to Smith's (1983) typology, a major limitation of Guilbert's (2004) approach is that it suggests a singular, static image of each type of sport, thereby impeding a more dynamic understanding of sports violence and its multiple manifestations even within a single sport.

Recent sociological investigations into sports violence have sought to engage more fully with extended definitions of violence. One of the more sophisticated analyses is Young's (2012) conceptualization of a broad landscape of harmful or abusive behaviours under the notion of sports-related violence. Young's (2012) extended definition of sports-related violence incorporates both the process of violence and the damage or harm it causes, as well as questions of social justice. In so doing, it combines two dominant definitional positions – that of 'violence as force' and 'violence as violation' (Bufacchi 2005). For Young (2012: 15), sports-related violence refers to:

1   direct acts of physical violence contained within or outside the rules of the game that result in injury to persons, animals or property; and
2   harmful or potentially harmful acts conducted in the context of sport that threaten or produce injury or that violate human justices and civil liberties.

With this definition, Young (2012) aims to highlight the associations that underpin different forms of sports violence and explain these sociologically. It is to the main sociological approaches to sports violence that I now turn.

Sociological approaches to sports violence

Sociological approaches draw attention to the social conditions and social dynamics that enable, cause or impede sports violence. A focus on the broader social context within which sports violence occurs distinguishes these approaches from psychological perspectives that emphasize the personality characteristics, psychological states or particular situational dynamics that lead individuals or groups to act aggressively or violently. However, sociological approaches to sports violence are highly diverse. In this section, I examine four distinctive sociological approaches – figurational, collective behaviour, microsociological and masculinity theories – that have applicability to multiple modalities of sports violence, including player and crowd violence. The purpose of this discussion is not to provide an exhaustive account of all the different ways in which sports violence has been investigated and theorized; rather, the selective discussion of these four approaches seeks to illuminate how sports violence might be understood *sociologically* from a range of theoretical perspectives.

Figurational sociology

Violence and violence control are central themes in figurationalists' work on sport. Figurational sociologists have examined these themes in the context of a broader 'civilizing process' that entails the progressive tightening of externally and internally imposed controls over people's behaviour (Elias 1971; Elias and Dunning 1986). Modern sports, they argue, have undergone a civilizing process through the establishment of centralized rule-making and rule-enforcing bodies, a complex set of formally instituted rules which demand stricter control over the use of physical force, and clearly defined intra-game sanctions (e.g. penalties or sending-offs), as well as the institutionalization of specific roles whose task it is to control the game (e.g. the referee) (Elias and Dunning 1986). Yet at the same time, within the broader shift in the manner in which members of society relate to one another, sport enables people to experience a pleasurable upsurge of emotions, an enjoyable 'de-controlling of emotional controls' (Elias and Dunning 1986: 44), without many of its socially and personally dangerous implications. The quest for pleasurable excitement imposes heavy demands on the balance between pleasure and restraint in sporting contests. If there is too little tension, the contest becomes dull and risks losing its 'mimetic' function; yet, if there is too much tension, the ensuing excitement can pose a serious risk to contestants and spectators alike (Van Bottenburg and Heilbron 2006). A recurrent problem for organized sport in all its forms, then, is the need to strike an appropriate balance between pleasure and restraint.

Figurational sociology has had greater influence on the sociology of sports violence than any other sociological tradition, especially in the United Kingdom and continental Europe. While some of its most enduring appeal has been in the study of crowd violence and football hooliganism (e.g. Dunning *et al.* 1988, 2002; Bairner 2006; Reis 2006), its influence on scholarly debates about other types of sports violence and violence control is also evident (see also the chapter 6 by Dominic Malcolm in this volume).

Collective behaviour theory

While the figurational approach has been particularly influential in Europe and parts of Latin America, several North American sport sociologists have examined sports violence from a structural-functional perspective. The latter body of research is strongly influenced by the collective behaviour tradition and especially Smelser's (1962) 'value added' theory, which views collective violence as a hostile expression of underlying social strains and grievances. Smelser's (1962) theory posits that six conditions are necessary for a particular kind of collective behaviour to emerge: (1) structural conduciveness (social circumstances in which collective behaviour could result; e.g. spatial proximity, communication among the aggrieved); (2) structural strain (a social situation in which people feel dissatisfied with their social environment, e.g. perceived relative deprivation or injustice); (3) generalized belief (a shared belief in terms of who is responsible for the strain, whether they should be punished and whether participants will escape sanctions for their actions); (4) precipitating factors (a spark to ignite the flame, e.g. a dramatic event); (5) mobilization for action (participants who share a generalized belief become organized); and (6) breakdown or failure of social control (deterioration in the legitimacy of social control agents). Since the 1970s a number of North American studies have applied this theory to sports violence (for an overview of early studies, see Case and Boucher 1981).

The most systematic application of Smelser's theory in the sociology of sport is Lewis's (2007) work on celebrating riots, a major type of sports fan violence in North America. Lewis (2007: 87–90) posits that celebrating violence is likely to occur when certain conditions are present. First, a celebrating riot by fans of the winning team is more likely than a punishing riot by fans of the losing team. Second, a celebrating riot is more likely to occur after championship games due to the emphasis put on winning. Third, a celebrating riot is more likely to occur if the winning team has not won a championship for some time: 'the longer a team has gone without winning a championship, the more important the winning becomes and the more likely that there will be fan violence when the team does win an important victory' (Lewis 2007: 87). Fourth, a celebrating riot is enabled by sports fans' access to a natural urban gathering area where 'people want to be seen and to see others on the street' (Lewis 2007: 89). Finally, if a celebrating riot occurs, the typical rioters will likely be young white males. Although Lewis fails to provide a convincing explanation for this condition, it is corroborated by international research into sports crowd violence (e.g. Spaaij 2008).

Regretfully, Lewis does not situate the aforementioned conditions macrohistorically (as the figurational approach dictates), and relies almost exclusively on secondary data rather than the kind of rich observational data produced by microsociological studies of sports violence discussed below. Moreover, we do not know which (if any) of the conditions identified by Lewis (2007) apply to other forms of sports violence, such as player violence. However, his work posits some hypotheses that might be used to explore this issue. For example, Lewis's (2007: 136) hypothesis that 'the severity of fan violence varies directly with the importance in the status of the competition' is consistent with the premise of game-related perspectives regarding the meaning and significance of the match and the relationship between the contestants as a key determinant of fan violence (Jamieson and Orr 2012), and can possibly be extended to player violence. Lewis's recommendation that future research focus on relationships among rioters and the interaction between rioters and social control forces also opens the door for a more comprehensive understanding of possible links between different forms of sports violence, especially if we conceive of 'rioters' more broadly to include spectators, players and other actors. The microsociological approach developed by Collins (2008) is particularly well equipped to this task.

The microsociology of sports violence

Randall Collins's (2008) microsociological theory of violence differs radically from the aforementioned approaches. Rather than being concerned with a long-term social process (figurational sociology) or structural strain (collective behaviour theory), it focuses on the situation of human interaction in which violence is performed. According to Collins (2008), violence arises from a set of pathways around the confrontational tension that rises up whenever people come into antagonistic confrontation with each other. This tension stems from attempting to act against another person, and thus against one's own propensities to fall into solidarity and a common cognitive universe with that person. Any 'successful' violence, Collins argues, must overcome this tension.

The central argument to Collins's theory is that people are not wired for perpetrating violence and naturally abhor violence in many forms. Thus, techniques for carrying out violence must always be fitted to the task of overcoming confrontational tension. Collins identifies three dynamics that make sports violence possible. The first is the collective effervescence in build-ups of dramatic tension in the audience. The second is the degree of emotional resonance within a team: in team sports, players share collective emotions with their teammates, and successful performance depends on emotional resonance that keeps the team coordinated as well as energetic. The third kind of dynamics comprises 'emotional energy' (EE) contests between opponents: players are involved in an emotional interaction with their opponents, in which 'the player or team who gains EE wins at the point where the opponent loses EE. These are the emotional turning points of a game' (Collins 2008: 285). Collins (2008) contends that there are two features that predict player violence: the extent to which violent moves, efforts or threats are incorporated into the game action itself; and the extent to which players are protected, physically or socially, from being hurt. He further argues that spectators are subject to the same rhythms of dramatic tension – collective effervescence, emotional resonance and emotional energy. This explains why spectators may behave aggressively at roughly the same moments that players get into fights. However, the structure of involvement is different for players than for spectators, and hence their style of violence is different. Fights between players tend to have the form of symmetrical fair fights, while spectator violence is often a form of physical and numerical domination, or 'attacking the weak' (Collins 2008: 310), in a state of high confrontational arousal.

To date, Collins's theory is yet to be applied to manifestations of sports violence beyond those examined by Collins himself. There are interesting parallels to the figurational approach to sports violence, notably Collins's emphasis on self-control and the way sporting contests produce socially generated pleasurable excitement. However, Collins's approach strips these notions from the macrohistorical process within which figurational sociologists situate them. Herein lies a fundamental difference between microsociological and figurational approaches: while the former focuses on microsituations of violence, the latter is principally concerned with macrohistorical dimensions of violent situations.

Masculinity perspectives

Many forms of sports violence are highly gendered. Several sociologists argue that the association between violence and the production and performance of masculinity is key to understanding sports violence as it occurs within the competitive arena (between players, spectators, etc.) as well as in broader social relations (e.g. gender-based violence or domestic violence perpetrated by athletes). Masculine identity is vigorously pursued and negotiated by males, and competitive sports, especially heavy-contact team sports, offer an opportunity to construct hegemonic masculine identities both on and off the playing field (Weinstein *et al.* 1995; Messner 2007). Male-to-male physical violence and male-to-female physical, sexual and emotional aggression are often key elements in the performance of masculinity in competitive sporting environments (Pappas *et al.* 2004; Messner 2007).

One area of recent theory and research on gender, violence and sport focuses on the ways in which athletes negotiate dominant masculine discourses. Such discourses have been shown to be prominent in athletic cultures, and it is within these discourses that male athletes commit acts of violence to validate their masculinity among their peers and with themselves. Many male team sports at college, high school and professional levels emphasize and celebrate physical and psychological domination and aggression. Athletes who fail to meet these standards are often criticized or punished by fellow teammates and pushed to reach higher individual standards of performance by putting their bodies on the line (Messner 2007). Athletes learn to accept and normalize pain and injury as part of their participation in physically demanding sport (White *et al.* 1995; Coakley 2009). In this context, a recent report by the Institute of Medicine and National Research Council (2013) on sports-related concussions in high school and college athletes highlights the macho 'culture of resistance' that continues to dominate in contact sports, a culture where athletes are compelled to 'man up', not let their teammates or coach down and play with/through injury and pain. Sociological research shows that the association between athletic affiliation and sexual violence is mediated by peer contexts (e.g. Coakley 2009; Messner 2007). One of the more sophisticated analyses is Kreager's (2007) study of high school sport, peer networks and male adolescent violence. Combining masculinity and social learning per-spectives, Kreager shows that the positive association of heavy-contact sports (e.g. American football and wrestling) with serious male violence is mediated by peer relationships and that playing heavy-contact sports shapes subsequent violence in ways that participation in non- or light-contact sports (e.g. tennis and basketball) do not. His study verifies the argument that the contexts of heavy-contact sports produce conditions supportive of male violence, such that embeddedness in all contact-sport networks substantially increases the risk for serious violence.

The celebration of masculine prowess in sport further tends to involve the objectification and denigration of women. Sexual prowess and sexual conquest are greatly valued traits in mascu-line sporting cultures. Male athletes and spectators can bond through collective involvement in coercive forms of sexual practice or sexualized interaction (Flood 2008). In this process sexual violence can become normalized and accepted within athletic milieus and be exported outside the sporting arena, such as when athletes use sexual violence against women within a party scene (e.g. Crosset 1999; Pappas *et al.* 2004).

Crowd violence is equally associated with the production and performance of masculinities. Research consistently shows the assertion of aggressive masculinity among male spectators as a key source of crowd violence in general and football hooliganism in particular (e.g. Dunning *et al.* 1988, 2002; Armstrong 1998; Free and Hughson 2003). Football hooligans, for instance, celebrate an aggressive masculine identity that is constructed through (the threat of) violence, with the purpose of attaining an unambiguous sense of one's masculine status (Spaaij 2008). In a similar vein, research on *barras bravas*, the most active and violent Argentinian fan groups, high-lights the exclusively masculine morality in which crowd violence loses its negative connotation and acquires moral legitimacy among the fans and their broader communities (Garriga Zucal 2010; Alabarces *et al.* 2005).

Emerging issues in the sociology of sports violence

The approaches discussed here enable a sociological appreciation and understanding of dif-ferent forms of sports violence and their interrelationships. However, different types of sports violence have usually been treated as separate, independent spheres of social action. To rectify this, some scholars have attempted to link different types of sports violence in novel ways (Fields *et al.* 2007; Young 2012). In doing so, they draw attention to forms of sports violence that had previously been peripheral to sociological debates despite the ongoing public and media atten-tion they receive. This includes forms of violence that fit squarely within definitions that view sports violence as violation, most notably the extended definition proposed by Young (2012). Lack of space prevents me from examining these types of sports violence in full in this chapter. Instead, I will discuss one type of sports violence – violence against animals – that illustrates how emerging themes in the sociology of sport may be linked to more conventional types of sports violence.

Human-animal relations in sport are highly diverse but often involve animal contests or activities where animals potentially suffer harm and abuse, including so-called blood sports (Atkinson and Young 2008) (e.g. dogfighting, bullfighting, cockfighting, fox-hunting) and vari-ous types of racing competition (e.g. greyhounds, thoroughbred horses). Sociological studies of animal violence in sport are still relatively rare despite calls to probe this largely unexplored ter-rain (e.g. Franklin 1996). Figurational sociology is a notable exception, as it has long considered animal sports such as fox-hunting as central to debates on violence, civilization and sportization (Elias and Dunning 1986; Dunning 1999). Building on this tradition, Atkinson and Young (2005, 2008) highlight how racing greyhounds are enmeshed in wider formations of sports-related violence. They argue that racing greyhounds face four types of violence: breeding, training/ racing, housing/release and disposal violence. They explain this violence as a social process that is formed through the interwoven actions of social actors operating at different levels, including context players (e.g. owners, promotors, spectators, gamblers), conditions players (e.g. breed-ers, trainers) and regulation players (e.g. legislators, animal rights activists). These social chains of interdependence, they argue, are necessary to perpetuate tolerable deviance against racing greyhounds.

Other sociological studies highlight the cultural and historical specificity of social figurations that shape animal violence in sport. For example, Franklin's (1996) research combines social constructionist, ideational and figurational perspectives to examine the violent relationship that modern hunting and angling sports in Australia sustain with wildlife. Franklin contends that the cultural meanings of hunting and angling sports in Australia are inverted from those in the United States and the United Kingdom. Although in all three countries nature symbolism is invoked as part of nation-building processes, unique to the Australian context is an 'Austral-ianization' discourse that sought from Federation (1901) onwards to establish, maintain and privilege an indigenous nature and to banish introduced species that competed with indigenous species or blurred the 'Australianness' of Australian nature. As such, hunters and animal activists 'are brought into an ironic alliance in favouring and protecting indigenous species while seek-ing the destruction of most introduced species' (Franklin 1996: 54). Another important aspect of the inverted meaning of hunting and angling sports in Australia is that Australian hunters are not perceived as 'pleasure seekers' in the same way that hunters are perceived in the United States and United Kingdom. Instead, Australian hunting is seen more as work than pleasure (e.g. culling local population explosions, self-provisioning). Franklin (1996) also points to class differences in hunting and angling sports as a partial explanation. In both the United Kingdom and the United States, most people associated with hunting and angling have high social status or represent the new corporate sector hunter, whereas Australian hunters and anglers do not. As a consequence, the latter typically receive greater sympathy for hunting.

Conclusion

Sociological investigations have enhanced our understanding of sports violence in all its forms. However, there is no consensus among sociologists as to what sports violence is and how it is best explained. Sociological approaches to sports violence range from macrohistorical to micro-interactionist, each offering a particular analytical lens through which to view sports violence sociologically. The breadth of sociological theory and research on sport and violence provides a rich foundation upon which future studies can build. One pressing issue for further research is the need to examine and theorize more fully the associations between different types of sports violence, and in particular the connections of player and crowd violence with the broader landscape of sports-related violence (Young 2012). These different types of sports violence need to be examined as a whole as well as in pieces (Fields *et al.* 2007). A comprehensive sociological understanding of sports violence in all its forms will further necessitate greater dialogue between the different approaches discussed in this chapter. Such dialogue would help create a platform on which an integrated understanding of sports violence as a sociological phenomenon could be fostered.

References

Alabarces, P., *et al.* (eds) (2005) *Hinchadas*, Buenos Aires: Prometeo.

Armstrong, G. (1998) *Football Hooligans: Knowing the Score*, Oxford: Berg.

Associated Press (2013) 'Australians Assessing Injuries to the Head', *The New York Times*, 10 March.

Atkinson, M. and Young, K. (2005) 'Reservoir Dogs: Greyhound Racing, Mimesis and Sports-Related Violence', *International Review for the Sociology of Sport*, 40(3): 336–356.

Atkinson, M. and Young, K. (2008) *Deviance and Social Control in Sport*, Champaign, IL: Human Kinetics.

Bairner, A. (2006) 'The Leicester School and the Study of Football Hooliganism', *Sport in Society*, 9: 583–598.

Bourdieu, P. and Wacquant, L. (1992) *An Invitation to Reflexive Sociology*, Chicago, IL: University of Chicago Press.

Bryson, L. (1987) 'Sport and the Maintenance of Masculine Hegemony', *Women's Studies International Forum*, 10(4): 349–360.

Bufacchi, V. (2005) 'Two Concepts of Violence', *Political Studies Review*, 3: 193–204.

Case, R.W. and Boucher, R.L. (1981) 'Spectator Violence in Sport: A Selected Review', *Journal of Sport and Social Issues*, 5(1): 1–14.

Coakley, J. (2009) *Sports in Society: Issues and Controversies* (10th edition), Boston, MA: McGraw-Hill.

Collins, R. (2008) *Violence: A Micro-Sociological Theory*, Princeton, NJ: Princeton University Press.

Crosset, T. (1999) 'Male Athletes' Violence against Women: A Critical Assessment of the Athletic Affiliation, Violence against Women Debate', *Quest*, 51(3): 244–257.

Dunning, E. (1999) *Sport Matters: Sociological Studies of Sport, Violence and Civilization*, London: Routledge.

Dunning, E., Murphy, P., Waddington, I. and Astrinakis, A. (eds) (2002) *Fighting Fans: Football Hooliganism as a World Phenomenon*, Dublin: University College Dublin Press.

Dunning, E., Murphy, P. and Williams, J. (1988) *The Roots of Football Hooliganism: An Historical and Sociological Study*, London: Routledge.

Elias, N. (1971) 'The Genesis of Sport as a Sociological Problem', in E. Dunning (ed.) *The Sociology of Sport: A Selection of Readings*, London: Frank Cass.

Elias, N. and Dunning, E. (1986) *Quest for Excitement: Sport and Leisure in the Civilizing Process*, Oxford: Blackwell.

Fields, S.K., Collins, C.L. and Comstock, R.D. (2007) 'Conflict on the Courts: A Review of Sports-Related Violence Literature', *Trauma, Violence, & Abuse*, 8: 359–369.

Flood, M. (2008) 'Men, Sex, and Homosociality: How Bonds between Men Shape their Sexual Relations with Women', *Men and Masculinities*, 10(3): 339–359.

Franklin, A. (1996) 'Australian Hunting and Angling Sports and the Changing Nature of Human-Animal Relations in Australia', *Australian and New Zealand Journal of Sociology*, 32(1): 39–56.

Free, M. and Hughson, J. (2003) 'Settling Accounts with Hooligans: Gender Blindness in Football Supporter Subculture Research', *Men and Masculinities*, 6: 136–155.

Garriga Zucal, J. (2010) *Nosotros nos peleamos: Violencia e identidad de una hinchada de fútbol*, Buenos Aires: Prometeo.

Guilbert, S. (2004) 'Sport and Violence: A Typological Analysis', *International Review for the Sociology of Sport*, 39(1): 45–55.

Hargreaves, J.A. (1986) 'Where's the Virtue? Where's the Grace? A Discussion of the Social Production of Gender Relations in and through Sport', *Theory, Culture & Society*, 3: 109–121.

Institute of Medicine and National Research Council (2013) *Sports-Related Concussions in Youth: Improving the Science, Changing the Culture*, Washington, DC: Institute of Medicine.

Jamieson, L.M. and Orr, T.J. (2012) *Sport and Violence: A Critical Examination of Sport*, Oxford: Elsevier Butterworth-Heinemann.

Kreager, D. (2007) 'Unnecessary Roughness? School Sports, Peer Networks, and Male Adolescent Violence', *American Sociological Review*, 72: 705–724.

Lewis, J.M. (2007) *Sports Fan Violence in North America*, Lanham, MD: Rowman & Littlefield.

Longman, J. (2013) 'A Yellow Card, Then Unfathomable Violence, in Brazil', *The New York Times*, 31 October.

Mastrogiannakis, D. and Dorville, C. (eds) (2012) *Risk Management and Sport Events*, Paris: Le Manuscrit.

Messner, M.A. (2007) *Out of Play: Critical Essays on Gender and Sport*, Albany: State University of New York Press.

Ortiz, J.L. (2013) 'Taking Fanatic to the Extreme', *USA Today*, 27 September.

Pappas, N., McKenry, P. and Skilken Catlett, B. (2004) 'Athlete Aggression on the Rink and off the Ice: Athlete Violence and Aggression in Hockey and Interpersonal Relationships', *Men and Masculinities*, 6(3): 291–312.

Reis, H.H.B. (2006) *Futebol e violência*, Campinas, Brazil: Autores Associados/FAPESP.

Schinkel, W. (2010) *Aspects of Violence: A Critical Theory*, Houndmills, UK: Palgrave Macmillan.

Smelser, N.J. (1962) *Theory of Collective Behavior*, New York: Free Press.

Smith, M.D. (1983) 'What Is Sports Violence? A Sociolegal Perspective', in J.H. Goldstein (ed.) *Sports Violence*, New York: Springer-Verlag.

Spaaij, R. (2008) 'Men Like Us, Boys Like Them: Violence, Masculinity, and Collective Identity in Football Hooliganism', *Journal of Sport and Social Issues*, 32(4): 369–392.

Spaaij, R. (2014) 'Sports Crowd Violence: An Interdisciplinary Synthesis', *Aggression and Violent Behavior*, 19(2): 146–155.

Thomas, R. (2013) 'Why They Had to Kill Broken-Down Melbourne Cup Horse Verema', *The Daily Telegraph*, 6 November.

Van Bottenburg, M. and Heilbron, J. (2006) 'De-Sportization of Fighting Contests: The Origins and Dynamics of No Holds Barred Events and the Theory of Sportization', *International Review for the Sociology of Sport*, 41(3/4): 259–282.

Weinstein, M.D., Smith, M.D. and Wiesenthal, D.L. (1995) 'Masculinity and Hockey Violence', *Sex Roles*, 33: 831–847.

White, P., Young, K. and McTeer, W. (1995) 'Sport, Masculinity, and the Injured Body', in D. Sabo and D. Gordon (eds) *Men's Health and Illness: Gender, Power, and the Body*, Thousand Oaks, CA: Sage.

Wieviorka, M. (2009) *Violence: A New Approach*, London: Sage.

Young, K. (2012) *Sport, Violence and Society*, New York: Routledge.

Zwaan, T. (2007) `Theses on Violence and Violence Control', Unpublished manuscript, Amsterdam: University of Amsterdam.

34

SPORT AND SOCIAL INTERVENTION

Douglas Hartmann

The belief that sport is an important and almost uniformly positive arena of socialization, education, and opportunity for youth and young people has a long and much-touted history going back to the nineteenth century and the origins of modern sport itself. This concept or claim has been especially pronounced in countries (such as the United States) and institutional contexts (like schools) that lack a well-developed understanding of and/or commitment to sport for its own sake. American educational institutions, in fact, have long justified both interscholastic athletic competition and physical education as a means of building character, self-discipline, and pro-social attitudes among students. However, in schools and a host of other institutional domains, these ideals have often been understood and implemented in very different ways, approaches that seem to be connected with the populations and perceived characteristics of the populations being targeted.

For example, as historians have detailed, when competitive athletics took shape in modern industrial societies, the notion of development and life training through sports participation was largely the terrain of the middle and upper-middle classes who saw amateur athleticism as a training ground for socializing young men and preparing them for societal leadership. Sport here was both a male place and a masculinizing space. As these ideals about education and socialization through sport were popularized and expanded to the working, immigrant, and lower classes – especially ethnic and racial minorities (still mostly boys and young men) in the early twentieth century – they came to be oriented toward more rigid control and more dramatic personal level intervention. In other words, they were directed more toward the purposes of social containment, discipline, and individual transformation and change, what we might now call re-socialization or risk prevention. Eventually what emerged was a distinctive variation on the theme of sport-based education and development, a vision that focused less on cultivation and empowerment and more on intervention, re-socialization, and individual-level change. And what has become clear over the years is that this more interventionist, control-oriented vision of sport and youth development has tended to be understood and applied in ways that are racialized, gendered, and class-specific.

This chapter will provide an overview of scholarly research and thought on the latter and more specific of these two visions – namely, athletic involvement as a means for social intervention and individual-level change. It will begin by briefly elaborating on the historical origins and contemporary organizational manifestations of sport as intervention. The second section

will then highlight some of the limitations, misunderstandings, and pitfalls of sport-based intervention that have been identified by sport scholars. The third portion of the chapter will then
discuss recent theoretical innovations that lay out key principles underlying how sports-based
social interventions are best conceptualized so as to best make meaningful contributions to
intervention and change. The chapter will conclude by summarizing the implications for program design, policy implementation and assessment, and future research.

Historical origins and contemporary manifestations

In the United States, the ideology of sport as a positive, progressive force for social intervention
and individual transformation for youth and young people who were somehow marginalized or
disadvantaged took shape during the reforms of the turn-of-the-twentieth-century Progressive
Era. The most famous and well-researched example is the 'play movement' of the early 1900s,
which was promoted by progressive reformers who saw the development of parks and recreation programs as a way to socialize and 'Americanize' the waves of immigrant, ethnic, and racial
minority working classes moving into US cities (Cavallo 1981). But numerous Progressive Era
organizations such as the YMCA, YWCA, and the Boy Scouts all used sports and physical activities as key to their projects of adolescent socialization, transformation, and immigrant assimilation (Pope 1997). And it is also in this period that American schools, both public and private,
began to justify sporting activities as means of educating mass student populations as well as of
preventing delinquent and disorderly behaviours among their charges (Levey Friedman 2013).

As modern spectacle sport exploded into an industry and consumer phenomenon during
the twentieth century and came to be associated with mobility for minority communities and
progress for race relations more generally (Carrington 2010), these notions about the interventionist value of sport in marginalized (and often urban) communities continued to develop
and evolve, providing both rationale for youth sport funding as well as principles for program
design and implementation. One of the reasons for this continued emphasis on sport for poor
and disadvantaged youth is that young people in these communities have been more reliant
than others on public funding and facilities for their athletic opportunities (Wilson 1994). This
model has been driven less by the provision of goods to citizens and communities than by perceived public interests in organizing, stabilizing, and even controlling these communities and the
people therein. And as the old millennium gave way to the twenty-first century and neoliberal
transformations in social policy have taken hold, a whole new generation of such sport-based
social intervention programs, initiatives, and organizations has emerged.

This new wave of sport-based youth interventions has come in a variety of types and sizes.
Some are small, single-sport programs located in schools or operated at community centers or
other public facilities. Others are city-wide, multi-sport summertime projects, and still others
are run by sports experts at Olympic training centers or sports foundations. The initiatives
range from police athletic leagues to afterschool programs, and use sporting practices as diverse
as basketball, calisthenics, martial arts, and motocross to address an even broader array of social
problems and public concerns. Numerous well-regarded youth outreach and risk prevention
programs run by organizations such as the Boys and Girls Clubs, 4-H, and the YMCA that
include athletic activities are also involved, although these initiatives tend not to be sport-based
or even use physical recreation as a point of entry.

Several distinctive characteristics define and unify the diverse array of programs, organizations, and initiatives. One is that they still must be distinguished from other, less interventionist
(though no less structured) forms of youth sport and physical activity that are encouraged and
supported either for the sake of athletic development or for the sake of fun, fitness, recreation,

socialization, and health (or some combination thereof). Such programs would include youth athletic practices such as recreational sports, travel teams and leagues, interscholastic athletics as well as ordinary recreation, physical fitness, and child-centred play – all of which are sometimes lumped together under the heading of 'suburban sport,' with youth soccer providing a primary model (Andrews, Pitter, Zwick, and Ambrose 2003).

Second, this new generation of programs and initiatives does not tend to talk about intervention and social change in a general way but instead has been touted as an innovative, inexpensive, and remarkably effective approach to address a specific (if multifaceted) array of social problems and public concerns in urban and impoverished communities. This type of programming ranges from crime prevention and public health to day care, juvenile delinquency, and teenage pregnancy to gangs, drugs, and violence to education and economic revitalization. In fact, the most striking and original feature of contemporary interventionist initiatives may be their emphasis on risk reduction and crime prevention through sport. So pronounced is this orientation that some scholars have referred to this new movement as the 'social problems industry' in urban sport and recreation (Pitter and Andrews 1997). Midnight basketball programs – late-night, sport-based crime prevention programs that originated in the late 1980s and early 1990s during the first Bush administration – have been described as paradigmatic of this shift (see also Hartmann 2001). And once again: although the emphasis is not always explicit, these programs are almost uniformly targeted to poor, disadvantaged, and minority youth and young people, especially boys and young men of colour.

Both in the United States as well as in many other developed nations around the world, the recent emergence and re-orientation of sport-based social intervention programs, organizations, and initiatives under the racially charged banner of 'social problems' prevention has been driven by at least two primary structural forces characteristic of the neoliberal era. One factor involves the cutbacks and privatization of public parks and recreation facilities that began to emerge in the 1980s (Crompton 1998; Crompton and McGregor 1994; Schultz, Crompton, and Witt 1995). The other drivers are the even larger cutbacks, reorganization, and transformations of the welfare state under the conditions of neoliberalism of the same period (Harvey 2005).

The former dimension is a bit complicated. Part of the story has to do with the fact that, especially since the 1960s, youth sports provision has been defined by a market-driven 'two tiered' or 'two stream' system wherein 'people who have the access to the disposable income and free time necessary to consume these services' have their sport and recreation needs served, while 'the poor [and otherwise disadvantaged] are left with a shrinking pool of public . . . and private services, none of which they can afford' (Pitter and Andrews 1997: 86). Beginning with dramatic budget cuts to public parks and urban recreation departments in the 1970s and intensifying with rising liability costs and the elimination of 'extra-curriculars' in schools in the 1980s, funding and support for public parks, recreation, and sport provision – especially for program operation and staffing – stagnated in the late 1970s and early 1980s (Ingham 1985; Shivers and Halper 1981). By the mid-1990s, according to one report (Crompton 1998), parks and recreation budgets were slashed so dramatically at both state and local levels that reliance on external resources had almost doubled in the earliest years of this period (from 14 per cent in 1974–1975 to 24 per cent in 1987–1988), and the slide continued throughout the 1990s. These pressures and dynamics forced youth sport administrators and operators to turn to problems-based sports initiatives in order to provide sports and recreation opportunities to populations and communities with otherwise limited resources and facilities. In other words, sports-based social outreach and intervention programs have afforded funders and program providers a way to provide access to sports and physical recreation for otherwise underserved communities, focusing especially on poor youth and young people of colour living in urban, inner-city neighbourhoods.

However, a much broader and less sport-specific set of forces and interests has also been at play here. The Reagan-dominated 1980s were, after all, an era marked by the effort to privatize and scale back government services across a whole range of sectors and domains – 'retrenchment,' it is often called. And in many communities and for many funders, funding for sport-based social intervention was not so much about athletic participation per se as it was about trying to replace that whole range of social services and public programs that were being cut, curtailed, and significantly restructured.

This new, neoliberal policy niche helps explain the unique organizational structure of many of these initiatives: namely, how they are embedded in organizations and agencies outside the usual local and state governmental systems and operate according to a market-oriented logic based upon competition, effectiveness, and efficiency. In a more concrete, substantive sense, this broader policy context also helps account for the emphasis on containment, surveillance, and discipline that has taken hold in the neoliberal era (Simon 2007; Soss, Fording, and Schram 2011; Wacquant 2009). The idea, in short, is that as long as participants are involved in a controlled physical activity, their energies and risk-oriented proclivities are thus controlled and diverted toward other pursuits – pursuits that are physically contained and that have the additional benefit of being exciting, challenging, and physically demanding.

This context of risk reduction and crime prevention has made the economic, gendered, and especially racialized dimensions of sport-based social intervention pronounced. Evidence suggests that these ideals and funding structures have come to provide the structural and cultural context for the participation in all manner of sport and physical activity for disproportionate numbers of poor kids and children of colour in the United States (Hartmann and Manning, forthcoming).

Scholarly perspectives and critiques

Sport scholars have been fairly critical of the whole idea of social intervention through athletic participation, whether in its earliest, idealistic forms or the more explicit, problems-based focus of the recent neoliberal period. Some of these critiques stem from the usual criticisms that sport scholars have of all sport-based education and development visions and initiatives; others are more specific to intervention and change-based programming.

In the most general terms, the role of sport participation in contributing to educational attainment and social development has proven difficult for scholars to document systematically and conclusively, whether intervention oriented or more generally developmentally based (Hartmann 2008). Part of this difficulty stems from the fact that the pro-social, developmental effects of sports participation are deeply intertwined with all of the other activities and background variables associated with involvement in athletics that are well known to shape and determine educational attainment, childhood development, and the avoidance of delinquency. In other words, while sport participation is clearly associated with positive social characteristics, it is unclear if the association is causal or simply correlational. But a further challenge is that the empirical relationships between social development and educational attainment appear to be relatively uneven and mixed in the first place, perhaps stemming from the wide variation in sport-based initiatives and programming. Some use sport effectively and work well, others do not.

A second common criticism has to do with how sport-based education and development is understood – or not understood. Part of the problem here is that coaches and program operators may employ the *rhetoric* of education and youth development, but in actual practice their programs are often more oriented toward and interested in athletic performance and the development of sporting excellence for their own sake. For all of the talk of education and development, that is, many youth sports programs are still more about sport than they are about education or intervention.

Another variation on this theme is that even the most well-intentioned of these programs and initiatives often lacks a coherent conceptual foundation specifying both what they are trying to accomplish as well as how sport participation can be understood to contribute to that mission. The underlying assumption in many of the earliest sport-based social intervention initiatives was that the positive, pro-social impacts of sports participation happened almost automatically or inevitably without any special structure or planning. The emphasis on competition; the need for teamwork, sportsmanship, and self-discipline; the centrality of the body and physical control: these qualities and characteristics were embedded in and part of the unique structure of athletic activity. As such, sporting pursuits were expected to imbue otherwise undisciplined and disorderly young people with the principles of social order and self-control necessary to become good citizens and productive workers (Macleod 1983; see also Oriard 1991). (To a certain extent these principles and expectations applied to all youth, but they were typically viewed as even more important and in need of self-conscious application for young people from culturally distinct and socially disadvantaged backgrounds who were seen as in danger of being 'under-socialized'.) In contrast, sport scholars have insisted that the social and developmental benefits of sports participation are not as automatic, inevitable, and consistent as is often implied or assumed. Sport, according to this critique, actually produces *characters* as much as character, and the history books, sociological studies, and sports pages are all replete with stories and evidence that belie any easy or automatic or inevitable relationship between sport and positive social outcomes. In this view, the developmental impacts of any sport-based activity depend upon the communities that are targeted, how programs are understood, designed, and deployed, and the social and institutional contexts within which they are situated.

Other criticisms are more pointed and directed to sport-based social intervention specifically. One problem involves unrealistic promises and expectations. Many of the most interventionist, problems-oriented sports programs promise huge impacts in the neighbourhoods and communities in which they are enacted – expectations that are both inflated and based upon a misunderstanding of the potential community-level impacts of programs. Midnight basketball initiatives are a prime example: these programs came to national prominence and attention with claims of massive (30 percent and more) crime reduction in the neighbourhoods and communities in which they were originally located in the early 1990s. Yet more careful evaluation and assessment revealed that these trends were largely the result of a larger decrease in crime of the period and could not be attributed to programs that served at most a couple of hundred young men of colour only a few nights a week for several months a year. (This is not to suggest that the program was not successful; only that there was and is little evidence that the programs exerted the sizable community-level impact that was claimed at the time.)

The fact that ideas about intervention and prevention in and through sports are often based upon troubling racial, ethnic, economic, and gender stereotypes is another important line of scholarly critique. Such stereotypes stigmatize certain communities and populations even as they valorize and normalize mostly white, middle-class others. They also ignore the broader socio-economic conditions that account for the differences (and inequalities) that distinguish one from the other. Furthermore, sport researchers have found that sports-based programming implemented from the interventionist angle tends to be far more invasive and controlling than those targeted to more mainstream, suburban middle- and upper-class, and white populations. Children from poorer neighbourhoods and communities of colour often have their athletic involvement seen and organized as being about surveillance and control, and the need to cultivate discipline and re-socialization (Guest 2013; Hartmann 2001), often with a focus on reducing the threat to public order or safety that these individuals are perceived to present (Cole 1996).

And then there are even more basic questions of access, availability, and rates of activity and participation. In terms of race and class and gender, some of the bigger problems for youth and young people stem from limited access to sports facilities and opportunities, the low rates of activity and participation for recreation, fitness, and leisure among low-income and otherwise marginalized communities (Halpern 2006). Whatever their other benefits, the creation of opportunities for athletic involvement in these typically poor and marginalized communities is not one of the benefits of intervention-defined programming. Indeed, because of the controlling nature of these programs, this may even discourage participation and heighten inequalities in physical activity and athletic involvement.

A final line of scholarly critique of sport-based social intervention has to do with the role and function of sports-based initiatives in the larger landscape of public policy and social services aimed at variously disadvantaged minority populations. Although sport-based interventions are often supported and funded as replacements for neoliberal retrenchment and reorganization in other realms, these initiatives clearly can't replace all social services that have been eliminated or reconstituted as neo-liberalism has taken shape in American metropolitan areas. Yet, such programs are often justified in precisely that way, used as community relations ploys by public officials trying to make it look like they are taking steps to deal with the problems of urban crime, violence, and public safety without actually committing new resources, energy, or attention to the relevant communities. Such short-sighted and even cynical visions create unrealistic expectations about the immediate influence and effectiveness of the interventionist aspects of these sport-based initiatives. Far more disconcerting, such unrealistic expectations for sport-based interventions can actually serve to reinforce and exacerbate the problems faced by at-risk urban youth by deflecting public attention away from deeper social sources of their problems. 'If we are not cautious,' as Jay Coakley (2002: 23) put it, such programs 'may unwittingly reaffirm ideological positions that identify young people, especially young people of colour as "problems" and then forget that the real problems are deindustrialization, unemployment, underemployment, poverty, racism, and at least twenty years of defunding social programs that have traditionally been used to foster community development in ways that positively impact the lives of young people'.

Conceptualizing effective intervention

In the face of these criticisms and the continued growth of intervention-oriented youth sports programming, a new, more constructive, and forward-looking body of scholarship has begun to better theorize effective social intervention and risk prevention (Coakley 2002; Hartmann, 2012; Holt 2008; Kelly 2011, 2013; Martinek and Hellison 1997; Nichols 2007; Witt and Crompton 1997). Sport-based programming, according to these researchers, can be an important part of a whole package of community-based approaches to social intervention and risk prevention, but only when understood properly, targeted appropriately, and implemented under the correct conditions.

One of the first and most basic insights about effective, sport-based intervention is that there are many different visions of what intervention is and how sport is believed to contribute to it. For example, there are those who emphasize empowerment and skills building, others who focus on character building, re-socialization, and the constitution of self-discipline, and still others who see sport as a relatively simple means for containment and control of populations who are perceived to be disorderly and disruptive (Nichols 2004; Zarrett *et al.* 2008). These different approaches are not necessarily mutually exclusive; however, theorists insist that the most successful programs are those in which operators are strategic and self-conscious about what they are trying to accomplish and have a clear understanding of how sport contributes to those goals. Positive, pro-social outcomes through sport for any populations or communities are unlikely to happen, unless these outcomes are directly structured into program activities and goals. And here there is an irony: that the most successful sport-based interventions are usually *not* determined by their athletic but by their non-sport components.

This is a second major theoretical innovation. Time and again, case studies have revealed that the programs that are most promising and successful as for purposes of intervention and change are those that systematically incorporate non-sport, development-oriented elements (Hartmann 2003; Nichols 2007; Witt and Crompton 1996). This finding stems from the fact that sport is not automatically or inherently a positive, pro-social force but needs to be guided and directed in that fashion. That is, sport-based programming is best understood, like any other tool or technology, as an 'empty form' (MacAloon 1995) – a practice that can be positive, but can also be a problem if the energies involved in athletics are not channelled appropriately. The upshot is that the success of a sport-based social interventionist program is largely determined by the strength of its non-sport components, what it does with young people once they are brought into the program through sport. This is the 'plus sport' model which Coalter (2009) has described in the context of the literature on development discussed elsewhere in this volume (see also Hartmann and Kwauk 2011; Levermore and Beacom 2009).

A third theoretical point regarding effectiveness involves the opportunities that sport-based programs and organizations present to make connections to the programs, activities, and resources of other agencies, organizations, and initiatives working with marginalized, disadvantaged communities. Interventionist-minded sports policy makers and programmers have become well aware of the need to supplement, support, and extend their offerings and outreach by connecting with other like-minded and similarly engaged programs, agencies, organizations, and initiatives. These connections are crucial, not only in terms of generating non-sport programming in general, but in the context of limited resources and facilities and the importance of non-sport interventionist programming. Connecting with other organizations, institutions, agencies, and programming is a means of sharing knowledge, pooling resources, and intensifying and enriching programming.

For all of the emphasis on the non-sport aspects of sport-based social intervention, the sport-based components of such programs still cannot be ignored, taken for granted, or minimized. This is a fourth and final theoretical principle. Whatever else they may be, one of the most consistent characteristics of sport-based interventions is their ability to recruit and retain youth and young people in social programming. Not only are outreach and recruitment the first concern of any social policy initiative (you can't have a social program without participants), the unique ability to recruit and retain otherwise hard-to-reach populations has been true for virtually every program that has been studied. This cannot be taken for granted. There needs to be a balance between the sport-based and the non-sport-based aspects of a program, where sport is an important part of a whole package of resources and social supports requiring a level of investment and intensive, day-to-day involvement far beyond that of most sport-based intervention programs.

With all of these conceptual advances, documenting the effectiveness of sport-based intervention remains an ongoing challenge. More research is needed to see how to operationalize these principles and how programs achieve their effects – and for what populations and under what kinds of conditions and constraints programs are most likely to be successful. Fortunately, a more sophisticated framework for measurement and assessment is now in place as well (Baldwin 2000; Nichols and Crow 2004; Witt and Crompton 1997).

Conclusions and implications

This conceptualization of sport as a tool for social intervention whose influence depends upon the ends toward which it is directed, how it – and especially its non-sport elements – is implemented, and the ways it is connected (or not) with other social services and resources has a number of implications for program design, implementation, and operation. Perhaps the most basic and obvious point is that operators need to be clear and self-conscious about all of their goals and strategies. Just offering a sports program is unlikely to have any significant or systematic results. Many other factors are involved. Another key implication is that while sport has contributions to make to outreach, intervention, and risk prevention, these contributions are more complicated, intensive, and expensive than is usually believed.

The cost and complexity of sport-based intervention is important to realize because too often sport-based approaches are believed to provide a fairly simple relatively inexpensive solution to problems of socialization, development, and risk prevention. Nothing could be further from the truth. Sport-based program operators must be expert at and secure funding for both high-level, engaging sport programming as well as for extensive social interventionist activities and initiatives. They have to be both sport providers and social workers. Rather than having it easier than other youth workers, sport-based program organizers have a unique double burden requiring that they must be proficient at both sport and social intervention.

With these unique challenges and complexities in mind, it is important to stress and reiterate two final cautions about sport and intervention. One is about race. No matter what sport-based social intervention may have to contribute to improving the lives of urban, mostly minority youth in the United States and elsewhere, these initiatives do not tend to increase their access to sport and physical activity. Access to facilities and participation rates among young people from marginalized and disadvantaged backgrounds continue to slip, even as the number of problems-based sporting programs grows. Here it is also important to guard against the racial and economic stereotyping and stigmatizing that can happen in and through such programs, especially when young people are treated so differently in the sporting context. Too often, these initiatives can reinforce stereotypes – stereotypes about both minorities and the mainstream majority.

Second and finally, it is important not to expect too much from these sports-oriented initiatives, nor to treat them as a magic bullet or miracle elixir. Social intervention, risk prevention, and social change are complex and challenging enterprises under the best of circumstances – that is, even with abundant resources and using the most comprehensive and advanced programming. Given their typically limited resources and structure, sport-based programs by themselves, even when brilliantly conceived and properly implemented, will not always succeed. In fact, they may fail as often as they succeed. To believe anything else not only overestimates the social force of sport, it underestimates the difficulties of meaningful social intervention and change in the lives of youth and young people who have limited resources and face numerous social and cultural challenges. And as much as we strive for effective, sport-based social intervention, we must, as Coakley insisted, guard against allowing these programs to deflect public attention away from the deeper social sources of poverty, racism, and social marginalization faced by at-risk urban youth.

References

Andrews, D.L., Pitter, R., Zwick, D., and Ambrose, D. (2003) 'Soccer, Race, and Suburban Space', in R.C. Wilcox, D.L. Andrews, R. Pitter, and R.L. Irwin (eds) *Sporting Dystopias: The Making and Meanings of Urban Sport Cultures*, Albany: SUNY Press.

Baldwin, C.K. (2000) 'Theory, Program, and Outcomes: Assessing the Challenges of Evaluating At-Risk Youth Recreation Programs', *Journal of Park and Recreation Administration*, 18: 19–33.

Carrington, B. (2010) *Race, Sport and Politics: The Sporting Black Diaspora*, London/Thousand Oaks, CA: Sage.

Cavallo, D. (1981) *Muscles and Morals: Organized Playgrounds and Urban Reform, 1880–1920*, Philadelphia: University of Pennsylvania Press.

Coakley, J. (2002) 'Using Sports to Control Deviance and Violence among Youths: Let's Be Critical and Cautious', in M. Gatz, M.A. Messner, and S.J. Ball-Rokeach (eds) *Paradoxes of Youth and Sport*, Albany: SUNY Press.

Coalter, F. (2009) 'Sport-in-Development: Accountability or Development?', in R. Levermore, & A. Beacom (eds) *Sport and International Development*, Hampshire, UK: Palgrave Macmillan.

Cole, C.L. (1996) 'American Jordan: P.L.A.Y., Consensus and Punishment', *Sociology of Sport Journal*, 13: 366–97.

Crompton, J.L. (1998) 'Forces Underlying the Emergence of Privatization in Parks and Recreation', *Journal of Park and Recreation Administration*, 16(2): 88–101.

Crompton, J.L., and McGregor, B. (1994) 'Trends in the Financing and Staffing of Local Government Park and Recreation Services', *Journal of Park and Recreation Administration*, 12(3): 19–37.

Guest, A.M. (2013) 'Cultures of Play During Middle Childhood: Interpretive Perspectives from Two Distinct Marginalized Communities', *Sport, Education, and Society*, 18(2): 167–183.

Halpern, R. (2006) 'Physical (In)Activity among Low-Income Children and Youth: Problem, Prospect, Challenge', in Frances Scott (ed.) *Monographs of the Herr Research Center for Children and Social Policy*, Chicago: Erikson Institute.

Hartmann, D. (2001) 'Notes on Midnight Basketball and the Cultural Politics of Race and At-Risk Urban Youth', *Journal of Sport and Social Issues*, 25: 339–371.

Hartmann, D. (2003) 'Theorizing Sport as Social Intervention: A View from the Grassroots', *Quest*, 55: 118–140.

Hartmann, D. (2008) 'High School Sports Participation and Educational Attainment: Recognizing, Assessing, and Exploiting the Relationship', report prepared for the LA '84 Foundation, Los Angeles, CA.

Hartmann, D. (2012) 'Rethinking Community-Based Crime Prevention Through Sports', in R. Schinke and S.J. Hanrahan (eds) *Sport for Development, Peace, and Social Justice*, Morgantown: West Virginia University Press/Fitness Information Technologies.

Hartmann, D. and Manning, A. (forthcoming) 'Kids of Colour in the American Sporting Landscape: Limited, Concentrated, and Controlled', in M. Messner and M. Musto (eds) *Child's Play: Sport in Kids' Worlds*, New Brunswick, NJ: Rutgers University Press.

Hartmann, D. and Kwauk, C. (2011) 'Sport and Development: An Overview, Critique, and Reconstruction', *Journal of Sport and Social Issues*, 35(3): 284–305.

Harvey, D. (2005) *A Brief History of Neoliberalism*, New York: Oxford University Press.

Holt, N.L. (2008) *Positive Youth Development through Sport*, London: Routledge.

Ingham, A.G. (1985) 'From Public Issue to Personal Trouble: Well-Being and the Fiscal Crisis of the State', *Sociology of Sport Journal*, 2(1): 43–55.

Kelly, L. (2011) '"Social Inclusion" through Sport-Based Interventions', *Critical Social Policy*, 31(1): 126–150.

Kelly, L. (2013) 'Sports-Based Interventions and the Local Governance of Youth Crime and Antisocial Behavior', *Journal of Sport and Social Issues*, 37(3): 261–283.

Levermore, R. and Beacom, A. (2009) 'Sport and Development: Mapping the Field', in R. Levermore and A. Beacom (eds) *Sport and International Development*, Hampshire, UK: Palgrave Macmillan.

Levey Friedman, H. (2013) 'When Did Competitive Sports Take Over American Childhood?' *The Atlantic*, September 20.

MacAloon, J. (1995) 'Interval Training', in S.L. Foster (ed.) *Choreographing History*, Bloomington: Indiana University Press.

Macleod, D.I. (1983) *Building Character in the American Boy: The Boy Scouts, YMCA, and Their Forerunners, 1870–1920*, Madison: University of Wisconsin Press.

Martinek, T.J. and Hellison, D.R. (1997) 'Fostering Resilience in Underserved Youth through Physical Activity', *Quest*, 49: 34–49.

Nichols, G. (2004) 'Crime and Punishment and Sports Development', *Leisure Studies*, 23: 177–194.

Nichols, G. (2007) *Sport and Crime Reduction: The Role of Sports in Tackling Youth Crime*, London: Routledge.

Nichols, G. and Crow, I. (2004) 'Measuring the Impact of Crime Reduction Interventions Involving Sports Activities for Young People', *Howard Journal*, 43(3): 227–236.

Oriard, M. (1991) *Sporting with the Gods: The Rhetoric of Play and Game in American Culture*, Cambridge: Cambridge University Press.

Pitter, R. and Andrews, D.L. (1997) 'Serving America's Underserved Youth: Reflections on Sport and Recreation in an Emerging Social Problems Industry', *Quest*, 49: 85–99.

Pope, S.W. (1997) *Patriotic Games: Sporting Traditions in the American Imagination, 1876–1926*, New York: Oxford University Press.

Schultz, L.E. Crompton, J.L. and Witt, P.A. (1995) 'A National Profile of the Status of Public Recreation Services for At-Risk Children and Youth', *Journal of Park and Recreation Administration*, 13(3): 1–25.

Shivers, J.S. and Halper, J.W. (1981) *The Crisis in Urban Recreational Services*, East Brunswick, NJ: Associated University Presses.

Simon, J. (2007) *Governing through Crime: How the War on Crime Transformed American Democracy and Created a Culture of Fear*, New York: Oxford University Press.

Soss, J. Fording, R.C., and Schram, S.F. (2011) *Disciplining the Poor: Neoliberal Paternalism and the Persistent Power of Race*, Chicago: University of Chicago Press.

Wacquant, L. (2009) *Punishing the Poor: The Neoliberal Government of Social Inequality*, Durham, NC: Duke University Press.

Wilson, J. (1994) *Playing by the Rules: Sport, Society and the State.* Detroit, MI: Wayne State University Press.

Witt, P.A. and Crompton, J.L. (1996) *Recreation Programs That Work for At-Risk Youth*, Philadelphia, PA: Venture.

Witt, P.A. and Crompton, J.L. (1997) 'The Protective Factors Framework: A Key to Programming for Benefits and Evaluating Results', *Journal of Park and Recreation Administration*, 15(3): 1–18.

Zarrett, N. Lerner, R.M. Carrano, J. *et al.* (2008) 'Variations in Adolescent Engagement in Sports and Its Influence on Positive Youth Development', in N.L. Holt (ed.) *Positive Youth Development through Sport*, London: Routledge.

35

SPORT AND THE URBAN

Kimberly S. Schimmel

We live in an urban world. The 2010 report from the United Nations Population Division confirmed that for the first time in human history over half of the world's population lived in cities. And while many reading this Handbook probably take both cities and the presence of sport within them for granted, it is important to remember that in 1900, when England became the first country to urbanize, the world was still 86 percent rural and what we now recognize as sport largely existed as clubs and voluntary associations. It was not until 1920 in the US and 1931 in Canada that half of the population was located in urban settlements. The growth of cities was so rapid during the nineteenth and twentieth centuries that the time period is often referred to as the 'urban revolution'. So, seen within the context of several million years of human habitation on our planet, cities are a relatively new social invention, having only existed for the last 10,000 or so years. The social, cultural, and economic hegemony of cities, however, is even more recent (Palen 2005).

The record of scholarly concern with cities is nearly as long as the scholarly disciplines themselves. Some of sociology's original and most fundamental questions addressed the ways in which the city shapes social life, and the discipline's evolution was accelerated by a normative academic response to the many problems and challenges of modernism, including urbanization (Nevarez 2005). Concern about the urban spatial context within the sub-discipline of the sociology of sport, however, developed much more slowly. Actually, historians of sport were the first to document, through case studies of specific cities, that sport development and urban development were intertwined, and also that early sport was promoted both as a means to escape urban problems and as a method for building urban communities (see, for example, Reiss 1981). Reflecting on this important historical research, sociology of sport scholars, informed by classical theories of social development, began to formulate broader conceptual lenses through which to analyze sport-city connections, taking into account the urbanizing landscapes and expanding capitalist economic system that transformed the societies of Europe and North America.

A rich literature now exists within the sociology of sport that addresses the urban context. My goal in this chapter is to represent some of the conceptual diversity in this area and reflect the broad trends in the sociology of sport scholarship that, much like the field of urban studies (see Bowen, Dunn, and Kasdan 2010) and sociology more generally, defy neat compartmentalization. I have constructed three themes around which to organize the material, each representing a current focus of *sport and the urban* scholarship. I explain how each theme has developed over time, identify key sociologically oriented theorists associated with each, and show the ways in which the sociology of sport both draws from and contributes to their insights. In the last section of the chapter, I identify possible future themes that are likely to emerge as our field responds to what we now recognize as the first urban century. Before beginning, however, I must offer several caveats to the reader. First, though the literature below is grouped thematically for organizational clarity, it is important to recognize that the themes are overlapping and intertwined, as are many of the issues that thread through the scholarship I review here. Second, given space limitations, my discussion is necessarily simplified and I therefore overlook important nuances within each of the scholarly works I include. Finally, my review does not cover the corpus of knowledge in the sociology of sport related to the urban context; rather, I am selecting some illustrative pieces published in sociology of sport venues to show thematic development and theoretical connections. In the first section I group together sociology of sport scholarship that analyzes how sport has been used by urban elites in pursuit of non-sporting goals such as place promotion and real estate development. These works can be viewed as contributing to a broader political-economic-theoretical perspective for examining the effects of political decision-making upon the interconnected processes of sport and urban development.

City-building: politics and profits

The term *political economy* refers to a broad scholarly paradigm in which scholars from a wide range of disciplines and sub-disciplines generate questions related to the interactions of economic, political, and cultural affairs. This work continues the tradition of Karl Marx (1818–1883), the influential European social theorist who was born in agrarian Germany but who spent most of his adult life in industrializing London. There, Marx witnessed as a daily part of urban life the exploitation and hardships of the new class of wage labourers alongside the accumulating wealth and comfort of the industrialists (Palen 2005). Marx surmised that the structural dynamics of capitalism, that is the market economy, determine social relations. *Urban* political economy did not flourish until the late 1970s and early 1980s when a number of scholars – influenced by the Marxist-inspired insights of French sociologist-philosopher Henri Lefebvre, British geographer David Harvey, and Spanish-born, French-trained Manuel Castells – began to flesh out a paradigm that emphasized the importance of analyzing particular features of capitalism in any assessment of urban life.

As Nevarez (2005) explains, although urban political economy traces its concern for the structural dynamics of capitalism to Marx, it is his fellow German social theorist Max Weber (1864–1920) who provides a way to understand how human action both supports and reproduces it. Weber's work on individual social action emphasized how humans creatively and intentionally organize their social relations to accomplish a wide variety of objectives, thus making it possible to analyze motives within dominant authority structures. This work opened up the theoretical possibility that urban power and political contingency could be analytically combined with historical conjunctures of the economy. Thus, urban political economists adapted 'neo-Weberian premises to the neo-Marxist problematic and identified the social production of urban space – that is, city building – as the institution that organizes the material interests and galvanizes the political dominance of urban elites' (Nevarez 2005: 5123). Urban governance therefore includes both the decisions made by politicians and those made by place-based entrepreneurs in search of profits.

Sociologists of sport have contributed to this perspective by analyzing the inextricable connection between the development of sport and the development of cities through the extension of capitalism's production-consumption relations into the realm of sport culture. Earlier, historians of sport had documented how urbanization created both the demands and the means for the development and growth of sports (see Hardy 1997). However, in their influential essay, sociologists of sport Alan Ingham and Robert Beamish (1993) argued that historians had merely identified the conditions necessary for the creation of commercial sport, but these conditions were not sufficient for the integration of sport into the market. Thus, Ingham and Beamish employed the concepts of 'valorization' from Marx and 'instrumentally rational action' from Weber to establish a general framework to explain the development of sport 'in different places and at different times' (1993: 169). Their analysis focused on the creation of the consumer market for commodified sport in the United States, but the overarching political economic framework, they argued, explains the same changes throughout Western capitalist societies. The urban environment created an expanding cash nexus between people and gave entrepreneurs the potential opportunity to stimulate consumer needs, one of which was for sport, in order to accumulate profits.

Just as sport entrepreneurs' roles in the development of sport have attracted the attention of our sub-discipline, so too have their roles in the development of cities. Sociologists of sport have shown that sport-related actors have both the power and the resources necessary to influence urban development. One of the first to document this was George Lipsitz (1984) who analyzed the ways in which stadium construction in the 1960s was used in three US cities as a tool for promoting public and private spending for urban development. Lipsitz showed how public and private actors used stadium construction to reclaim the built environment in ways that biased financial capital, service sector capital, and affluent populations. Schimmel, Ingham, and Howell (1993) extended this argument in vignettes concerning US professional sport team franchise relocation in the 1980s. Their research focused more attention than Lipsitz's on the mobility of private capital and the competition within and between cities for capital investment. This work paved the way for Schimmel's case study (1995, and updated in 2009) of sport and urban growth politics, published in Bale and Moen's edited collection titled *The Stadium and the City* (1995), the first book of its kind to expose the stadium as global icon of the modern city.

Subsequently, sociologists of sport have contextualized the sport-capital-urban development relationship in a number of ways. Picking up in the 1990s, Whitson and Macintosh (1996), Lenskyj (1996), and Heitzman (1999) for example, focus on the construction of sport facilities to attract sport mega-events, such as the Olympic Games. Kidd (1995) investigated how postmodern design elements were incorporated into sports stadiums to encourage consumption activities. More recently, the analysis of sport infrastructure has broadened to include policies and practices of neoliberal regulation. For example, Friedman, Andrews, and Silk (2004) view sports facilities as a part of a larger themed landscape that provides false images of urban revitalization without changing the underlying conditions of urban poverty. Silk and Andrews (2008) further explore efforts to regulate, manage, and market 'sterile' urban landscapes and spaces of play and sport. Their case study of Memphis, Tennessee, offers a multi-dimensional account of the complex ways in which urban bodies, power, mobility, and forms intersect within the contemporary city. Spirou (2010) examines the intersection of race, class, and political representation in Chicago and traces that city's history of urban renewal projects along with the influence of professional sport. He suggests that through public-private partnerships, business interests are so entrenched that their influence in future stadium developments is assured, despite local residents' opposition. Sam and Scherer (2010) focus attention on the proposal to build a world-class rugby stadium in Dunedin, New Zealand. Their important work introduces a new element of power in controlling the nature of stadium debates: internet technologies. Sam and Scherer expose the manner in which stadium proponents used highly orchestrated public relations strategies to bypass traditional media and disseminate unfiltered messages that supported their cause. As a final example, an edited collection by Andrews and Silk (2012) examines sport, politics, and cultural consumption within the context of neoliberalism.

The sociology of sport has made an important contribution to our overall understanding of the integrated economic and political complexities of city-building. This scholarship demonstrates the contested nature of urban space and reveals connections between sport actors, economic actors, and political actors. In short, this work establishes that politics matters in urban economies and that sport matters in urban politics. In the next section I turn to the sociocultural consequences of living in these urban places.

City life: culture and community

It is not surprising that so many of the classical social theorists who witnessed the rapid development of cities at the end of the nineteenth century would have pondered the cities' social effects upon increasingly concentrated residents. Of note, in addition to Marx and Weber, Ferdinand Tönnies (1855–1936), Emile Durkheim (1858–1917), and Georg Simmel (1858–1918) all critiqued the urban-industrial context for causing a heightened sense of individualism, loss of emotional attachment, and loss of community. As people moved from rural areas into urban residences and transitioned from agrarian to industrial occupations, traditional forms of social bonding were disrupted. Altered, too, were the patterns of everyday life and tempos associated with nature's rhythms, replaced by consciously directed human action, calculated, hurried, and measured. Forming and sustaining attachment to others and to a larger sense of community became much more difficult in this fast-paced, competitive context. Social theorists frequently analyzed these changes through the use of logical constructs or 'ideal-types', presenting a 'then versus now' perspective in which the social ties of the rural past were compared to the urban present (and speculative future). For example, Tönnies' best-known work, *Gemeinschaft und Gesellschaft (Community and Society)*, published in 1887, contrasted features of what he believed to be past small, intimate communities with the large-scale, impersonal activities of modernity. Simmel, likewise, was deeply concerned by what he feared would be the future's eroding sense of community and the social-psychological consequences of an urban lifestyle where calculated sophistication would replace meaningful relationships. The frameworks of these classical theorists helped establish the discipline of sociology and influenced the work of subsequent generations of social scientists, which ultimately provided those interested in studying sport as a cultural phenomenon with numerous analytical tools with which to begin.

It is fair to say that one of the most significant contributions the sociology of sport has made to a deeper understanding of urban life has been in conceptualizing the ways in which sport as a *dominant cultural form* is connected to the construct of community. Sociologists of sport are perhaps uniquely positioned to provide such insights, given that the core focus of the field (sport) is a socially created activity associated with both individual and collective identities. An important part of our field's contribution in this regard is related to elite sports teams and events, and exposes how dominant urban actors use sport to assert new forms of civic identity, connect a desire for collective bonding to urban development agendas, and promote a sense of 'we' that does not structurally exist. These things are achieved, in part, by including sport in a larger discourse about community. Sociologists of sport have developed a sophisticated analysis of the sport-community relationship contributing to a broader social scientific understanding of capitalism. They show us that relations in capitalism are not simply ones of production-consumption; they are also cultural relations.

Gregory Stone (1981) was the first sociologist of sport to focus on community. His essay inspired others to think more deeply about sport's connection to the concept of community in the urban context, leading to Ingham, Howell, and Schilerproort's (1987) influential publication, which is still being cited by scholars today. It draws upon Marxian notions about the connection between community and the development of social classes, classical sociological theories of community, and the (then) newly emerging 'urban growth machine' perspective in urban studies. Professional sport can, they suggest, contribute to our imagination of the community-as-a-whole, but the discourse of community is constructed in ways to naturalize the private interests of capital to appear in the public good. One of the major contributions of this essay is that it sets the groundwork for conceptualizing the sport–urban–community relationship from the perspective of hegemony, linking capitalism and culture, and linking sport to the cultural expression of power. Hegemony, Italian Marxist philosopher Antonio Gramsci's most influential concept, emphasizes that power relations are not sustained by brute force, but rather by securing 'common consent' from subordinate groups. This insight – that consent for urban development schemes can be more easily manufactured when connected to sport and appeals to community – began to figure prominently in subsequent sociology of sport research.

In addition to more deeply conceptualizing the relationship between sport and community, a number of case studies published in the sociology of sport literature provide empirical evidence that sport is used to construct a hegemonic discourse about urban culture that is both powerful and problematic. This work critically analyzes the ways in which public resources such as land and tax revenues are directed toward privately owned sports clubs and franchises. For example, an early publication by Sage (1993) shows how groups in Denver leveraged public funds in pursuit of private profit by legitimating stadium construction as a community-as-a-whole benefit. Scherer (2001) investigated the narratives surrounding the National Hockey League's Winnipeg Jets and found that local politicians and media promoted the team as a symbol of local and global identity. Local Jets fans actively embraced this narrative, helping to secure public funding for the team's stadium. Smith and Ingham (2003) focus on the city of Cincinnati, uncovering the efforts by local sports team owners and politicians to evoke community support (both financial and emotional) for their professional team. They conclude that rather than generating a sense of solidarity, the team served to further divide local residents along class, urban/suburban, and fan/non-fan lines.

In 2010, Sam and Hughson edited a special issue of the journal *Sport in Society* (volume 13, number 10) focusing on sport in the city; a dominant theme in those case studies is the multiple and complex ways in which identities and communities are created, changed, and exploited. For example, in that issue Gee and Jackson (2010) investigate localized representations of hegemonic masculinity through the mediated construction of 'Speight's Space' in New Zealand, sponsored by the beer brewery of the same name. They conclude that the 'holy trinity' of sport, masculinity, and alcohol effectively defines the inhabitants of this space and of the city itself. When civic elites argue that more public money is needed to build a new stadium and prevent a team from moving out of the city, they also tap into deep-seated anxieties about the potential loss of identity constructed through the 'holy trinity'.

And finally, I include here the work of Scherer and Davidson (2011), who draw upon Ingham and MacDonald's (2003) further elaboration of community/communitas and explore how a neoliberal urban identity was produced in the Canadian city of Edmonton. Scherer and Davidson demonstrate how the city's print media coverage of the National Hockey League's Edmonton Oilers incorporated a variety of social identity–based groups as civic elites attempted to showcase the city as a diverse and welcoming cosmopolitan centre. They conclude that in the name of 'building an image of a global cosmopolitan "community"', business and civic leaders forwarded Edmonton's arriviste status, securing the "need" for a professional men's hockey franchise and the public support it requires' (2011: 174).

While much of the sociology of sport literature on urban culture and community is related to elite/professional sport, it is not our sub-discipline's only focus. For a broader analysis of this theme, readers should start with the book edited by Wilcox, Andrews, Pitter, and Irwin (2003), titled *Sporting Dystopias: The Making and Meanings of Urban Sport Cultures*. This rich collection of case studies and essays includes topics such as youth cultures in an urban drop-in centre, racial identity and suburban soccer clubs, and an intriguing entrée into the culture of urban ticket scalpers. This, combined with recent work such as Giardina and Cole's (2012) exploration of race, class, and inner-city life in New Orleans and Kidder's (2013) study of parkour, masculinity, and the city demonstrate the manner in which different groups have appropriated sport as a symbol of group affiliation in urban contexts. The insightful analyses of sociology of sport scholars help us more fully understand how sport is a significant and meaningful ingredient in city life, both to the elites who manipulate it and to the people for whom it represents a lifestyle, tradition, vocation, or identity. In the next section I turn to a theme that in many ways can be seen as a synthesis of the first two. It includes a spatial analysis of the city set against broader contemporary trends and geopolitical transformations whereby distinctive strategies are used to represent cites as exciting, clean, and safe places to work and play.

City space: spectacle and security

Today's cities bear little resemblance to those experienced by classical social theorists during the 'urban revolution'. In the late twentieth century a major shift from industrial to post-industrial capitalism, along with attendant changes in how the economy is regulated, transformed urban built environments. A shorter cycle of investment, more flexible forms of production, and changes in the production and circulation of commodities aided the mobility of capital. City governments, moving away from managerial functions and into entrepreneurial roles (Harvey 1989), now provide a wide array of public subsidies, including tax abatements, low-interest loans, direct grants, revenue bonds, and land allocation in the attempt to attract capital investment and stimulate development. New corporate towers and luxury apartments alongside bars, restaurants, festival marketplaces, and shopping malls aim to develop urban cores into sites that serve business professionals and middle-class residents and attract visitors. Fuelled by a culture of consumption, the post-industrial city is symbolically projected as 'spectacular urban space' (Harvey 2001: 92), competing for tourism revenues and fixed capital investment from corporate, government, and retail sectors.

Within the past two decades, sociology of sport scholars have focused on different aspects of this late capitalist moment. Much of this work draws from and contributes to the conceptual frameworks advanced by neo-Marxist scholars David Harvey, Manuel Castells, and Henri Lefebvre (mentioned above). In addition, sociology of sport scholarship related to urban space has made important connections to French situationist Guy Debord, whose theory of spectacle is often viewed as a reworking of Marxian notions of alienation. Taken together, these intellectual traditions demonstrate deep concern for the exploitation of subordinate groups in society, a concern that has echoed in the sociology of sport literature since the 1970s (Ingham and Donnelly 1997). In a fruitful line of research that began with a focus on Montreal, Belanger (2000) for example finds Debord's theory of spectacle useful to examine the privatization of urban space for the purposes of capital accumulation associated with the city's two sport venues. Belanger found that nostalgia for the old arena was manipulated in ways that transferred authenticity and the history of authority to private capital promoting spectacular urban consumption. Silk (2004), influenced in part by the work of Manuel Castells, critically investigates the spatial expressions of capitalism in Memphis, where public policy was aimed at creating a tourist-oriented downtown, ultimately creating new lines of social inequality within the city. In 2011 (volume 46, number 2) the *International Review for the Sociology of Sport* dedicated a special issue to the theme of 'sporting spectacles in the city'. In that publication, Friedman and Andrews (2011) draw together insights from David Harvey regarding contemporary urban governance with Debord's notion of spectacle and Lefebvre's concept of spatial representation, to explore power relations through the construction of Major League Baseball's Nationals Park in Washington, DC. Even more recently, Silk and Andrews (2012) present a thorough exploration of urban spaces of sporting consumption through Harvey's 'capital space' concept. In these and other works, sociologists of sport show us that within the larger context of neoliberal finance-led, state-sponsored urban (re)development, urban sporting spaces often exist in close proximity to citizens who cannot afford the price of admission and upon whom the burden of increased taxation is disproportionately placed. Moreover, breakdowns in barriers to free trade and the free flow of capital are now accompanied by an increasing fortification of barriers between urban spaces and disruption of the flow of people throughout the city.

Part safe space, part spectacle (Perry 2003), this new urban landscape had to be carved out of the remnants of the industrial past and tourists cordoned off from the harsh realities of existence for 'mobility frozen' (Ingham and McDonald 2003) urban residents. 'Islands of affluence' (Judd 1999) hide the overall decline of the post-industrial city, reducing it to a distorted representation of the real thing. Revitalized spaces with newly developed cultural attractions, walled off from the presumed dangerous places (and people), are created to solve urban image and social control problems. These spaces are defended by measures that solidify the relationships with capital, making them 'secure' for capital investment. Railroads, highways, and bridges are used to establish rigid zones of demarcation between the 'good' and the 'bad' parts of a city. Buildings and other barricading structures can serve the same purpose. But space can also be reclaimed through intensive policing and surveillance. As these reclaimed spaces and tourist zones became larger, policing tactics extended into ever further reaches of cities (Graham 2004; Schimmel 2006).

At the present historical moment, new relationships are emerging – and established ones intensifying – between sport culture and transforming urban environments. A number of sociologists of sport are focusing attention on the ways in which new urban spaces of the post-9/11 era are increasingly viewed as terrain on which military tactics and weaponry are necessary to protect capital investments, control crowds, and prevent and respond to terrorist attacks. This means that in addition to the various transformations wrought by post-industrial capitalism, the urban landscape is being shaped by domestic/'homeland' security doctrines. Altered too, are the experiences of people who live in, work, and visit urban areas. Sociologists of sport argue that both the escalating economic expenditures devoted to sport spaces and the intensifying militarization justified by the need for security have led to measures that downgrade the quality of life for urban residents who are routinely surveilled, digitally scanned, corralled, barricaded, and patted down (Schimmel 2012).

Readers interested in this area of sociology of sport scholarship should start with a special issue of the *International Review for the Sociology of Sport* published in 2012 (volume 47, number 3) that focuses on 'terrorism'. The essays and case studies in this issue, originating from Europe, Australia, Africa, and North America, make a strong argument that sport is connected to the militarization of urban civil society and that status-differentiated cultural power is reinforced and defended by the state. Toohey and Taylor (2012), for example, show that many of the security measures implemented before and during the Sydney 2000 Summer Olympics remained as a legacy after the games. Sugden (2012) focuses on the nature of terrorist threats and the scale of security operations mobilized for the London 2012 Summer Games, critically analyzing the civil liberty consequences for its citizenry. Schimmel documents how US military doctrine and US Supreme Court jurisprudence legally equates the National Football League with a government defense contractor and transforms residents of Super Bowl host cities into citizen soldiers. These and other issues associated with urban security represent an emerging trend in sociology of sport research and embody some of the challenges and opportunities our sub-discipline faces. It is to those points that I now turn.

Future directions for the sociology of sport

I began this chapter with reference to the rapid nineteenth-century change in human settlement that resulted in our current urban world. The prognosis resulting from such intensified urbanization is that nearly all of the globe's population growth will occur in urban areas, causing an escalation of the world's slum inhabitants to about 2 billion by the year 2030. Also by that same year, the Global South will contain almost 80% of the world's populace (Gaffikin and Perry 2012). Cities in the Global South and those in other nations with rapidly growing economies are entering their own periods of change, not the least of which are issues associated with hosting sports mega-events in a new era of global significance. As of this writing, we know the developing regions of the world that will host the globe's largest events stretching to the year 2022 when the FIFA Men's World Cup Finals will be in Qatar. However, despite the population growth, emerging economic influence, and shift in global spotlight to cities of the Global South, urban theory suffers from an overshadowing Global North focus. Most urban theory derives from cities with industrial heritage, which itself is 'overreliant on a US-centric lens' (Gaffikin and Perry 2012: 703).

These interrelated realities present the sociology of sport sub-discipline with the opportunity to lead the active construction of theory and engaged practices that make clear and consistent distinctions between people and places and appreciates how urban diversity is experienced and understood differently in all parts of the world. Giulianotti and Klauser (2010) make a similar point with specific reference to researching security-related issues and processes at sports mega-events in the Global South. They call for a research agenda that investigates critically the 'specific properties and diverse effects of sports mega-event securitization' (58) in both the Global North and the Global South.

I suggest that in order for this and other research trajectories to be fully informed, we must engage in reciprocal bridge-building with our colleagues located in all parts of the world. This requires us to find more ways to overcome language differences that separate us and isolate our bodies of knowledge. Sociologists of sport across the globe view with informed scepticism any notion that sports can act as a solution to general urban problems. Although sport may create a sense of attachment that is important at an interpersonal level, sport does not significantly improve the economic, social, and political realities of everyday urban life. While acknowledging that sport is meaningful at personal levels and can contribute to civic initiatives, it is important to keep in mind that the city is not a unitary entity that benefits uniformly from sport-related policy. The Brazilian street protests, amidst preparations for that nation's hosting of FIFA's 2014 Men's World Cup Finals and the 2016 Olympic Summer Games, are a testament to this fact. The sociology of sport has much about which it can be proud; our field has tackled some of the most important and vexing problems associated with cities from industrialization up to our current historical moment. Our field has documented that since the rise of sport in the urban-industrial context, ethnic assimilation, class conflict, control of urban space, and ethnic and gender relations are inseparable from the promotion of sport. Forging links between scholars located in different socio-political and economic contexts will position our field to address the issues related to *sport and the urban* in whatever happens next.

References

Andrews, D.L. and Silk, M.L. (eds) (2012) *Sport and Neoliberalism: Politics, Consumption and Culture*, Philadelphia, PA: Temple University Press.

Bale, J. and Moen, O. (eds) (1995) *The Stadium and the City*, Keele, UK: Keele University Press.

Belanger, A. (2000) 'Sport Venues and the Spectacularization of Urban Spaces in North America,' *International Review for the Sociology of Sport*, 35(3): 379–398.

Bowen, W.M., Dunn, R.A. and Kasdan, D.O. (2010) 'What Is "Urban Studies"?: Context, Internal Structure, and Content', *Journal of Urban Affairs*, 32(2): 199–227.

Friedman, M.T. and Andrews, D.L. (2011) 'The Built Sport Spectacle and the Opacity of Democracy', *International Review for the Sociology of Sport*, 46(2): 181–204.

Friedman, M.T., Andrews, D.L. and Silk, M.L. (2004) 'Sport and the Façade of Redevelopment in the Postindustrial City', *Sociology of Sport Journal*, 21: 119–139.

Gaffikin, F. and Perry, D.C. (2012) 'The Contemporary Urban Condition: Understanding the Globalizing City as Informal, Contested, and Anchored', *Urban Affairs Review*, 48(5): 701–730.

Gee, S. and Jackson, S.J. (2010) 'The Southern Man City as Cultural Place and Speight's Space: Locating the Masculinity-Sport-Beer "Holy Trinity" in New Zealand', *Sport in Society*, 13(10): 1516–1531.

Giardina, M.D. and Cole, C.L. (2012) 'Race, Class, and Politics in Post-Katrina New Orleans', in D.L. Andrews and M.L. Silk (eds) *Sport and Neoliberalism: Politics, Consumption, and Culture*, Philadelphia, PA: Temple University Press.

Giulianotti, R. and Klauser, F. (2010) 'Security Governance and Sport Mega-Events: Toward an Interdisciplinary Research Agenda,' *Journal of Sport and Social Issues*, 34(1): 49–61.

Graham, S. (ed.) (2004) *Cities, War, and Terrorism: Towards an Urban Geopolitics*, Oxford: Blackwell.

Hardy, S. (1997) 'Sport in Urbanizing America: A Historical Review', *Journal of Urban History*, 23(6): 675–708.

Harvey, D. (1989) *The Condition of Postmodernity*. Oxford: Blackwell.

Harvey, D. (2001) *Spaces of Capital: Towards a Critical Geography*, London: Routledge.

Heitzman, J. (1999) 'Sports and Conflict in Urban Planning: The Indian National Games in Bangalore', *Journal of Sport and Social Issues*, 23: 5–23.

Ingham, A.G. and Beamish, R. (1993) 'The Industrialization of the United States and the "Bourgeoisfication" of American Sport', in J. Maguire, E. Dunning and R. Pearton (eds) *The Sporting Process*, Champaign, IL: Human Kinetics.

Ingham, A, G. and Donnelly, P. (1997) 'A Sociology of North American Sociology of Sport: Disunity in Unity, 1965–1996,' *Sociology of Sport Journal*, 14: 362–418.

Ingham, A.G., Howell, J.W. and Schilerproort, T.S. (1987) 'Professional Sports and Community: A Review and Exegesis', *Exercise and Sport Science Reviews*, 15: 427–465.

Ingham, A.G. and McDonald, M. (2003) 'Sport and Community/Communitas', in R. Wilcox, D.L. Andrews, R. Pitter and R.L. Irwin (eds) *Sporting Dystopias: The Making and Meanings of Urban Sport Cultures*, Albany: State University of New York Press.

Ingham, A. & McDonald, M. (2003). Sport and community/communitas. In R. Wilcox, D. Andrews, R. Pitter & R. Irwin (Eds.), Sporting dystopias: The making and meaning of urban sport cultures (pp. 17–33). New York: SUNY Press.

Judd, D. (1999) 'Constructing the Tourist Bubble', in S. Fainstein and D. Judd (eds) *The Tourist City*, New Haven, CT: Yale University Press.

Kidd, B. (1995) 'Toronto's SkyDome: The World's Greatest Entertainment Centre', in J. Bale and O. Moen (eds) *The Stadium and the City*, Keele, UK: Keele University Press.

Kidder, J.L. (2013) 'Parkour, Masculinity, and the City', *Sociology of Sport Journal*, 30: 1–23.

Lenskyj, H. (1996) 'When Winners Are Losers: Toronto and Sydney Bids for the Summer Olympics', *Journal of Sport and Social Issues*, 20, 392–410.

Lipsitz, G. (1984) 'Sports Stadia and Urban Development: A Tale of Three Cities', *Sport and Social Issues*, 8, 1–18.

Nevarez, L. (2005) 'Urban Political Economy', in G. Ritzer (ed.) *Encyclopedia of Sociology*, Cambridge, MA: Blackwell.

Palen, J.J. (2005) *The Urban World*, New York: McGraw-Hill.

Perry, D. (2003) 'Urban Tourism and the Privatizing Discourses of Public Infrastructure', in D. Judd (ed.) *The Infrastructure of Play: Building the Tourist City*, Armonk, NY: M.E. Sharpe.

Reiss, S.A. (1981) 'Power without Authority: Los Angeles' Elites and the Construction of the Coliseum', *Journal of Sport History*, 8(1): 50–65.

Sage, G. (1993) '"Stealing Home": Political, Economic, and Media Power and a Publicly Funded Baseball Stadium in Denver', *Journal of Sport and Social Issues*, 17: 110–124.

Sam, M.P. and Scherer, J. (2010) 'Fitting a Square Stadium into a Round Hole: A Case of Deliberation and Procrastination Politics', *Sport in Society*, 13(10): 1458–1468.

Scherer, J. (2001). 'Globalization and the Construction of Local Particularities: A Case Study of the Winnipeg Jets', *Sociology of Sport Journal*, 18: 205–230.

Scherer, J. and Davidson, J. (2011) 'Promoting the "Arriviste" City: Producing Neoliberal Urban Identity and Communities of Consumption During the Edmonton Oilers' 2006 Playoff Campaign', *International Review for the Sociology of Sport*, 46(2): 157–180.

Schimmel, K.S. (1995) 'Growth Politics, Urban Development, and Sports Stadium Construction in the United States: A Case Study', in J. Bale and O. Moen (eds) *The Stadium and the City*, Keele, UK: Keele University Press.

Schimmel, K.S. (2006) 'Deep Play: Sport Mega-Events and Urban Social Conditions in the USA', *Sociological Review*, 54(s2): 160–174.

Schimmel, K.S. (2009) 'Political Economy: Sport and Urban Development', in E. Smith (ed.) *Sociology of Sport and Social Theory*, Champaign, IL: Human Kinetics.

Schimmel, K.S. (2012) 'Protecting the NFL/Militarizing the Homeland: Citizen Soldiers and Urban Resilience in Post-9/11 America', *International Review for the Sociology of Sport*, 47(3): 338–347.

Schimmel, K.S. Ingham, A.G. and Howell, J.W. (1993) 'Professional Team Sport and the American City: Urban Politics and Franchise Relocation', in A.G. Ingham and J.W. Loy (eds) *Sport in Social Development: Traditions, Transitions and Transformations*, Champaign, IL: Human Kinetics.

Silk, M.L. (2004) 'A Tale of Two Cities: The Social Production of Sterile Sporting Space', *Journal of Sport and Social Issues*, 28(4): 349–378.

Silk, M.L. and Andrews, D.L. (2008) 'Managing Memphis: Governance and Regulation in Sterile Spaces of Play', *Social Identities*, 14(3): 395–414.

Silk, M.L. and Andrews, D.L. (2012) 'The Governance of the Neoliberal Sporting City', in D.L. Andrews and M.L. Silk (eds) *Sport and Neoliberalism: Politics, Consumption and Culture*, Philadelphia, PA: Temple University Press.

Smith, J. and Ingham, A.G. (2003) 'On the Waterfront: Retrospectives on the Relations Between Sport and Community', *Sociology of Sport Journal*, 29(4): 252–275.

Spirou, C. (2010) 'Cultural Policy and the Dynamics of Stadium Development', *Sport in Society*, 13(10): 1423–1437.

Stone, G. (1981) 'Sport as Community Representation', in G. Lüschen and G. Sage (eds) *Handbook of Social Science and Sport*, Champaign, IL: Stipes.

Sugden, J. (2012) 'Watched by the Games: Surveillance and Security at the Olympics', *International Review for the Sociology of Sport*, 47(3): 414–429.

Toohey, K. and Taylor, T. (2012) 'Surveillance and Securitization: A Forgotten Sydney Olympic Legacy', *International Review for the Sociology of Sport*, 47(3): 324–337.

Whitson, D. and Macintosh, D. (1996) 'The Global Circus: International Sport, Tourism, and the Marketing of Cities', *Journal of Sport and Social Issues*, 20: 278–295.

Wilcox, R.C., Andrews, D.L., Pitter, R. and Irwin, R.L. (2003) *Sporting Dystopias: The Making and Meanings of Urban Sport Cultures*, Albany: State University of New York Press.

36

SPORT MEGA-EVENTS

Wolfram Manzenreiter

Introduction

Sport mega-events are high-profile and large-scale sport competitions of international, or more to the point, global significance that attract large audiences of both onsite spectators and media coverage followers (Horne and Manzenreiter 2006: 1; Tomlinson and Young 2006: 3). They are not just about sport, having assumed a key role in urban or regional place promotion and development strategies. Satisfying entrepreneurial interests as well as public developmental goals, they generate social collaterals extending far beyond the tournament itself (Cornelissen and Swart 2006: 108). They are multi-dimensional and multi-functional cultural performances, which include play, dramatic acting, ritual and ceremonial behavior (MacAloon 2006). Probably of most importance from a sociological perspective, however, is their significance for the collective imagination: they provide a stage for the display of collective achievements and the experiences of sharing and belonging.

So far scholars have failed to come to an unambiguous and commonly accepted definition. Yet many studies identify a number of common characteristics, like their fixed and short-term duration (Hiller 1998), their regular reoccurrence within an international event calendar (Roche 2003; Kelly 2011), their 'out of the ordinary' status (Roche 2000; MacAloon 2006), their economic impact (Preuss 2004; Gratton, Shibli and Coleman 2006) and their susceptibility to political use and abuse (Tomlinson and Young 2006; Schimmel 2001). In concrete terms, the Summer Olympic Games and the men's football World Cup feature most prominently in academic debate as well as in popular conceptions of true sport mega-events. While these two supernovas of global sports are clearly unrivalled in terms of size, spectatorship, market value and media reach, they share most commonalities with a number of slightly or significantly smaller 'second-order sport mega-events', such as the European football championships (Manzenreiter and Spitaler 2012), the Pan American Games (Curi 2011) or the Commonwealth Games (Black 2007). If market size, TV spectatorship and public attention are taken as benchmarks, there is good reason to restrict the applicability of the term 'sport mega-event' to the former two. At the same time, the distinction between first- and second-order mega-events is useful in acknowledging their impact on the conceptualization, perception and management of sport competitions that are more or less minor in size but which attract attention only among certain international populations or in limited regions of the world.

Even though sport mega-events epitomize the centrality of sport within global consumer culture more than any other sport-related phenomenon, the study of these events only recently took centre stage among social scientists. Horne and Manzenreiter (2006) state that the sociology of sport mega-events took off during the final decade of the twentieth century after innovations in media technologies, the consolidation of transnational media networks and ever-expanding corporate marketing strategies had backed up the expansionary drive of the Olympic Games, the FIFA World Cup and some of the second-order sport mega-events in their wake. Next to this seminal introduction to the sociological study of sport mega-events and Roche's groundbreaking investigation of the linkages between mega-events and modernity (Roche 2000), noteworthy volumes on selected aspects of sport mega-events include the collection on *National Identity and Global Sports Events* (Tomlinson and Young 2006), the *Palgrave Handbook on Olympic Studies* (Lenskyj and Wagg 2012), the edited volume on *Leveraging Legacies from Sports Mega-Events* (Grix 2014) and a number of journal special issues published for the *Third World Quarterly* (25/7: The Allure of Global Games, 2004), *British Journal of Sociology* (63/2: Olympic and World Sport: Making Transnational Society?, 2012), *Urban Studies* (48/5: Security and Surveillance at Sport Mega-Events, 2011), *Sport in Society* (16/2: Security and Sport Mega-Events, 2013), *Sustainability* (5: Sustainable Mega-Events, 2013) and some issues of *The International Journal of the History of Sport* that deal with specific sport mega-events from comparative historical perspectives.

In this chapter, I reflect on what the available social scientific scholarship on sport mega-events has brought to light on their significance for community building, urban development and the formation of collective identities and global civil society. Key thematic areas that we identify in the literature include their representational and presentational functionalities; the local and global political economies of hosting; the articulation of dissent and protest by social movements; and the micro-politics of sport mega-events infiltrating the everyday lives of people. Hence this chapter elaborates on the sociological understanding of sport mega-events as collecting points for a variety of aspirations by differing stakeholders. We understand sport mega-events as powerful social sources that serve as catchment sites for the projection of messages to others, whether in the form of public authorities conveying ideas of (international) stature, patriotism, development and growth or social groups voicing diverging viewpoints, dissent or specific demands. A sociologically informed study of sport mega-events tries to make sense of all these aspects, answering the question of what sport mega-events transmit about societies and their economic and political structures, but beyond that, what these events suggest about the nature and pathways of modernity.

Sport mega-events, identity and nationalism

What makes sport mega-events sociologically distinctive from expositions, art fairs, film festivals and other cultural hallmark events is first of all their global reach and unrivalled popularity in drawing more attention than any other event. This appeal is partly expressed by the ever-growing numbers of participating teams and athletes, national delegations, sport officials, and media accreditations. But the nature of true globality becomes most visible by the equally increasing head counts of onsite live spectators and the mediated mass participation of global TV audiences crossing all borders of nationality, ethnicity, age cohorts and social class. Particularly in times when the success or failure of mega-events is counted in millions of TV spectators, the distributional channels of the international media play a leading role in the spectacularization of sport mega-events. Spectacles in general aspire after grandeur and acknowledgement as unique, exclusive and extraordinary, and they use ritual symbolism, awe-inspiring performances and breath-taking staging techniques in order to achieve these goals, which actually are often just means for quite different ends. As the whole spectacle adapts itself around its own sensual, audiovisual potentials, it is the sensually stimulating, dynamic and exciting form that diverts mass attention away from cleavages and fissures behind the surface of the spectacle.

In recent years, media spectatorship has increasingly spread out from private living rooms into the public, searching for the shared experience of cheering in sport bars and communal bonding in makeshift public theatres providing live broadcast on giant screens. These forms of long-distance involvement are clear indicators that sport mega-events capture people's imaginations in ways that other types of hallmark events seldom do. They provide narratives about how the world is and ought to be, and as a result sport mega-events become focal points for a wide range of group dynamics and social processes relating to the construction and confirmation of senses of self, community, difference and otherness.

Sport has contributed to processes of nation-building as well as the expansionary politics of colonization; in response to the cultural imperialism of European powers, sport also assumed a prominent role for the assertion of national identity in postcolonial processes of state-building. Sport is crucial for the reaffirmation of national civil societies, as its symbolism is useful in the formulation of narratives and discourses about the character, culture and historical trajectory of a people. Such constructions can take the form of ethnic or civic nationality and may refer to a highly selective, mythical or even invented sense of history (Jarvie 2003: 540–541). By their very nature, the constructions of national communities feature forces of social inclusion and exclusion, thereby categorizing subjects into different status groups and drawing the lines of effective membership. Hogan (2003) argued that in diverse national contexts, discourses of national identity and sport are gendered and ethnicized, and these selecting forces also come to the fore at sport mega-events.

In all such instances sport nationalism has been identified as a particular expression of collective identity. It is a particular form of cultural nationalism, substituting for more outright forms of political nationalism. Sport media studies have pointed at the crucial role of the media for the discursive construction of collective identities within the framework of the modern nation. Particularly with reference to the naturalizing impact of institutions and the centrality of the media in modern society for the shaping of discourse and consciousness, scholars have made use of the concept of banal nationalism (Billig 1995) to mark sport as a primary site for the reinforcement of national imagery and the crystallization of national orientation. Past achievements in sport have often forged close symbolic linkages between specific sports and specific nations. The idea that sport and sporting achievements contribute to a nation's greatness and at times help to transcend internal strife or propel national reconciliation is widely echoed in the language of mainstream sport media reporting, not exclusively but also prominently on sport mega-events.

A large body of scholarship discusses the ways in which sporting activities and tournaments project a sense of community to those watching or discussing these events. Sport mega-events magnify the collective forces of unification and identification since they do not just constitute another platform for the symbolic display of a grand history or the revival of past glories or sporting rivalries that are of high significance for traditional supporters in sport and usually fuel the standard narratives of media sport reporting. Whereas spectators at regular league games or lower-scale sport conventions usually hold a stake in a team or otherwise a deeper personal relationship to the kind of sport they are watching, crowds at sport mega-events are best characterized as ephemeral, otherwise dissociated, makeshift communities of the event culture. In that regard, and paradoxically, they may be more real than Anderson's 'imagined communities' of the nation – which is usually at stake at sport mega-events.

Nationalist or patriotic sentiments are not just linked to the success of one's team but also spurred by the role of being actively involved as a member of the host community or among the many thousands of volunteers recruited for the effective and smooth staging of the event. Being host to the world, and in direct exposure to the foreign gaze enacted by the sport event tourists and the massive media coverage, locals often are prone to submit to the rhetoric of national solidarity in order to deliver in time and fashion.

The global and local political economies of mega-events

Sport mega-events have always provided a stage for the symbolic contestation of modernity between elites and masses, as well as among different models of development. As the Cold War rivalry between the communist bloc and the 'Free World' has shown, both in sporting competitions and in hosting them, sport spectacles acquired not only high importance as points of reference for the collective orientation of national societies toward international audiences, but also for the dissemination of ideologically loaded messages, despite the self-declared political neutrality of world sport. Studies on countries from the periphery, which have hosted the flagship events of contemporary global sporting culture, demonstrate the significance that sports mega-events have acquired for promoting 'official' versions of public culture in these regions as well. With the end of the binary world order, neoliberalism has come to replace the political ideologies of democracy and socialism as hegemonic discourses informing the rationale and objectives behind the hosting of sport mega-events.

The growth curve of sport mega-events has been spectacular and continuous ever since the Los Angeles 'Hollywood Games' in 1984 had shown for the first time that sourcing out the hosting of mega-events to a consortium of private and semi-public actors could establish new business opportunities and purportedly produce economic surpluses. A substantial amount of the new literature on sport mega-events thereafter has been drawn to the critical analysis of financial flows, investments, expenses and revenue distribution. Although most of these studies have demonstrated that public authorities usually must shoulder the largest part of the financial burden while profits are privately pocketed, often by foreign and multinational corporations, the myth of the event as an economic growth machine appears to be self-sustaining. Bidding wars and beauty contests in which potential host cities and nations compete against each other have intensified, defying the overwhelming evidence on the underestimation of costs and overestimation of gains. This apparent paradox has opened up another branch of critical investigation into power asymmetries, the often murky processes of political decision-making, and corruption and collusion of interests in the context of the bidding for and hosting of sport mega-events (Jennings and Sambrook 2000; Grix 2014).

Inspired by globalization theory, critical political geography has argued that the shifting landscape of global capitalism has given rise to the 'entrepreneurial city' in response to a general tendency of central states to withdraw from regional policy (Hall and Hubbard 1996). Local governments reacted to the challenge of an increasingly global competition by crafting new kinds of development strategy, based on new entertainment products from cultural industries, pooled financing, and public-private partnerships (Andranovich, Burbank and Heying 2001). Sport mega-events in this regard are seen as crucial for global competition not only because of their short-term economic impact and mid-to-long-term contribution to the labour market, business vitality and fiscal income, but also because of the message they deliver about a place and its people on their ability to attract mega-events and deliver in appropriate fashion to global audiences. What is truly remarkable in relation to the underlying dynamics of globalization is that in recent years, cities and governments from developing countries have joined the hosting circuit, often with the support and encouragement of the proprietary rights-holders of sport mega-events which are located in the Global North. Subscribing to the sociopolitical construction and marketing of hosting as a legitimate and fundamental aspect of development policy (Cornelissen 2009), hosts in the Global South adopted event hosting as an opportunity to overturn international stereotypes of backwardness, unreliability or waywardness. Instead they aimed at gaining currency from the symbolic display of national accomplishment and cultural authority on the international stage where their showcase events were meant to give proof of the level of socioeconomic development and the advance toward modernity. At the same time, they should demonstrate the political reliability and managerial capabilities of the host societies to international partners and potential investors (Manzenreiter 2010).

While hallmark events of all kinds have long been able to forge alliances between corporate and governmental interests by drawing on the shared interest of capitalizing on the positive image of a place, technological developments in transport and communication, the globalization of the media and the unparalleled growth of demand for leisure and amenity-oriented services are all of central significance for understanding the attraction and centrality of event-based development strategies within contemporary urban policies (Hall 1992; Roche 2000). National and city governments are also using sport mega-events to leverage more urban reconstruction projects in relatively short spaces of time and against lower levels of resistance by local groups that are directly affected by the construction craze, for example by the enforced relocation of people which has become a familiar consequence of hosting. While cities all over the world are tempted to use sport mega-events to push through unpopular or controversial projects, hosts from newly industrializing countries – where demand for urban reconstruction is high and funding abundant, where corruption and collusion are widespread and authorities wield the power to muscle through anti-social policies despite opposition – have been most aggressive in extensive refurbishment of the city landscape.

The list of actors and stakeholders would be incomplete if we forget that entire industries have come into being around the organizing, mediatizing (Miller *et al.* 2001; Kellner 2003), securing (Houlihan and Giulianotti 2012), regulating and governing of mega-events (Allison 2005; Manzenreiter and Spitaler 2012). New players are not only delivering these services to the host organization but also pursuing their own specific agendas. Hence, at the forefront of stakeholders, alongside the host authorities, are sponsoring partners, usually multinational corporations seeking to explore global marketing opportunities, the media networks that are selling time and visibility to corporate enterprises, and international sport federations. For example, the IOC (International Olympic Committee), FIFA (world football's governing body) or UEFA (European football's governing body) negotiate the marketing rights between host organizations, local or national governments, and corporations. These sport federations, like other international non-governmental organizations (or NGOs), are key in the constitution of global cultural order, while their leading officials are often virtually unaccountable.

Hosting sport mega-events nowadays demands an extensive engagement with global civil society. Given the highly mediated exposure of host cities and nations across the world, the demand for strategic image management has particularly been heightened by the highly idealist rhetoric of universal peace and international friendship underpinning the philosophies of the Olympic movement and other sport federations. The potential to realize shared, global modes of identity and interdependence, making real the sense of a global civil society (Tomlinson and Young 2006: 1), has often been used to legitimize the expenses or emergency politics of hosting, and even the investment in bidding to stage the sport mega-event. However, the appeal to universal values (or, better, to Eurocentric norms in the disguise of universality) is in marked contrast to the *Realpolitik* of hosting: various studies have shown how sport federations have come to influence financial policies, law-making and domestic security in host territories. In many instances special measures have been enacted to place IOC, FIFA or UEFA policies over national law, while setting the conditions for security and commercial activity at the mega-event (Hage-mann 2012; Cornelissen 2012). However, there is some doubt whether mega-events such as the Olympics really function as a 'Trojan Horse transporting the state's control assets into the local realm' (Fussey *et al.* 2012: 274), because the configuration of local, national and international actors and stakeholders ultimately prevents any single actor from imposing its overarching goals.

Nonetheless the unequal distribution of economic and social burdens, the paradoxes of universalism in a particular sport ideology, and the growing awareness of the flawed rhetoric of event-based urban development policies appear to be behind the sport federations' recent concern with legacy. Shifting the debate from economic gains to the managed delivery of benefits for the hosting society, including the well-being of the local population, eco-friendly staging practices and increased sport participation rates must be understood as strategic moves in response to a growing uneasiness with corruption scandals within the sport federations them-selves, the rapidly growing costs of hosting events, and the inherent contradictions behind local aspirations for making the city fit for global consumption. In that regard, legacy is a thoroughly political notion. It appears to be common-sense and appealing, but camouflages the uneven distribution pattern of legacies. It is well known that sport mega-events generate tangible leg-acies that are carved into the urban infrastructure and intangible legacies that are written into the popular memory. Whereas the latter kind of legacies tend to be universal and accessible to all, the former are rather selective and particular in nature, benefiting the interests of elites from commerce and politics (Horne 2014); this in turn encourages resistance.

Protest, conflict and social movements

Cornelissen (2012) argued that global sport – particularly its highly commercialized and corpo-ratized forms – has become one key field for advocacy networks that resist neoliberal forms of globalization. Sport sociologists have turned to examine global social movements which reflect rising awareness of the devastating effects of global capitalism, in neocolonial relationships with regions from the Global South, the exploitation of Third World labour in sporting goods manu-facturing and environmental damages caused by the sport industries (Harvey and Houle 1994). The sociological literature focuses on advocacy against working conditions in the global com-modity chain in the production of sporting goods (Sage 1999); the employment of new social media to rally border-crossing support for a common cause (Wilson 2007); the take on sport as a facilitator for the international peace movement (Wilson 2012); and, the work of NGOs in the field of developmental aid and international cooperation (Darnell 2013).

In the context of sport mega-events, resistance to the 'hegemonic Olympic industry' among activists and residents living in host cities (Lenskyj 2000, 2008) led to the formation of early social movements. When preparing for sport mega-events, hosting authorities have often been prompted to employ neoliberal social policies that impact on the local population in mark-edly different ways. In order to guarantee returns from private and public investments into the renewed inner city, authorities have come to intensify security and encompassing surveillance activities within the highly commercialized and functionally compartmentalized cityscape. The gentrification of the city and similar forms of urban redevelopment one-sidedly benefit tourists and the better-off groups of society, whereas marginal communities are often bypassed, sidelined or simply expelled. In the context of hosting the Olympic Games, resistance against forced housing evictions or the privatization of public space has been particularly virulent because these policies directly conflict with the official Olympist ideology of peace and harmony.

Public protests and campaigns by NGOs against the negative impacts of hosting have become regular accompaniments to the games. In its incipient form, the protest movement has been exclusively concerned with a local agenda, speaking on behalf of the socially underprivileged, protesting against environmental pollution, demanding more accountability and transparency from their elected politicians and the abolition of policies that produce negative impacts for local communities. However, there is considerable ambiguity over the ownership of the mega-event platform and the master tropes of its narrative. Is the event owned by the sport governing body, the organizing committee, the host city or nation or the sponsors? With more and more voices joining the choir, sport mega-events are 'an exploited resource within a political economy of collective attention' (Dayan 2008: 397).

In recent years, the Olympic Games and other major sport-events have become targeted by global social movements with quite a different and more far-reaching agenda. Employing Dayan's theory of the hijacking or piggybacking of media events by means of transmitting complementary, contradictory or challenging counter-narratives, Price (2008) demonstrated how global civil society organizations have seized the Olympic platform to reach out to audiences worldwide and define the games to their advantage. Exploring the efforts by international human rights NGOs to leverage public opinion on China's human rights record, Brownell (2012) argued that it is precisely because the Olympic Games strengthen a sense of membership in an 'imagined global community' that they mobilize civil society toward transnational debates. The formation of global civil society actors that are using the sport mega-event for the transmission of their own messages has been discussed as an unintended intangible legacy of mega-events (Manzenreiter 2014).

More recently, Harvey *et al.* (2014) provided a salient account of the most influential global social movements challenging the global sport order. They argue that these movements, like the international women's rights movement, human rights movements or global environmentalist movements, actually have the power to challenge the social forces impacting through the sport order on civil society at local, regional and global levels. Alterglobalization is the name for a large spectrum of such global social movements that do not reject globalization but support alternative forms while urging that purely economic concerns may not be put before values of democracy, justice, environmental protection, and human rights. These global movements are characterized by a shift in scale from the state level to multiple other levels; their flat organizational structures, devoid of hierarchical structure, that encourage new forms of interaction; and their specific aim of developing new, more humane forms of globalization. The discussion of 'transnational civil society' or 'global civil society' in sport centers on the social, 'bottom-up' or grassroots aspects of globalization, notably on issues of human development, peace-building and social justice (Giulianotti 2011). However, as Cornelissen (2012: 331) observed, sport mega-event contestation has a dual nature – with a set of domestic dynamics that are enabled by an international context. Sport mega-events thus provide a political space in which the transnationalization of local issues and the localization of transnational dynamics occur simultaneously.

The 'everyday' of mega-events

The sport mega-event itself extends over a short time span that encompasses four extended, overlapping and interpenetrating cycles (Kelly 2011). The gap between original bid planning, nomination, preparation and eventual hosting is a decade at minimum, and these cycles overlap with other bid cycles in an unending rhythm of sport mega-event development (Rowe 2012). Local residents are exposed to the dynamics of all of these cycles. They become involved right at the start of the event cycle which begins with feasibility studies, extensive lobbying and the creation of a rationale and its narrative. During this period, event lobbyists pursue widespread support or consent. In the second phase, after the bid has been secured and host communities are mobilized for frantic infrastructure construction and the complete preparation of the event, the local public is carefully schooled in the spirit of the master theme in ways that connect to the official mega-event history. The event period itself is followed by the legacy period in which the books are closed, reports are published and a retrospective theme is fashioned to engage broadly in the culminating project of legacy-making. Now that legacy concerns have become part of the entire event temporality, the orientation to future outcomes, post-event usage and public memory are colouring every step of managerial decision-making between planning, design, implementation and recording (Manzenreiter 2014). The mnemonic technologies of memorizing, recording and projection generate a generation's collective memories of the past and, for future generations, the imagination of the past. Mega-events thus resemble public investments in the future. They are mid-term projects of a short-term occurrence that sometimes in the future may serve as a particular long-term reading of the past.

It is important to keep in mind that there are multiple ways of watching the mega-event, which unfolds for many as a live event. Sport mega-events in general provide space for encounters between people who are otherwise disconnected for reasons of age, status and interest. A characteristic feature of the event is multigenerational or multi–age group inclusivity encompassing hosting communities, visitors from outside and to some degree distant media spectators as well. For these spontaneous and ephemeral event communities, sport mega-events are late modernity's version of rituals that celebrate community and the charismatic. There is always the promise of sharing truly heroic moments and the aura emanating from global sport heroes which arguably is at the core of the universal appeal of sport mega-events (Roche 2000: 7). Within the time-space of the sport mega-event, appearances of charisma and aura (as well as the bureaucratic control of it) are fairly predictable, thereby standing in marked contrast to a world which is often experienced as excessively rationalistic and as lacking any dimensions beyond the mundane in everyday life.

As 'experiential commodities,' sport mega-events can offer their participants the resources to construct subjectivity, personhood and identity. They provide a rare opportunity for witnessing history in progress, where those who have been 'there' can connect their own biography with the immortal moments of the special and the spectacular. However, the magical moment – which was once a special, extraordinary occurrence with strong religious and mythical undertones – has nowadays turned into a normative principle of consumer culture and late-modern lifestyles. Savvy event designers carefully outline and craft the contemporary mega-event to provide aesthetically and emotionally highly condensed experiences. Within a clearly demarcated place and for an exactly defined period of time, mega-events thus suspend everyday life (Gebhardt 2001: 20). Providing a rationale for merry-making, masquerade and temporary escape, they premise agency and subjectivity for the individual in the crowd. As the action shifts back and forward between the arena and the tribunes, the functional distinction between performer and spectator is blurred. The crowds in the stadium – and at public places where live screening is available – become part of the party and turn into active performers. Camera crews scrutinize the seated rows for particularly eye-catching shots and immediately channel these images of the happy crowd into the feed for stadium screens or live broadcast. This demonstrates how fans and observers are transgressing the traditional constraints of their passive side-role, to become active performers of their own script under the gaze of fellow spectators and TV cameras. The pronounced global 'mediatization', including the spread of digital social media, has enhanced the possibilities for vigorous transnational civil disputes across the whole event cycle (Rowe 2012: 291). Locals are more likely to be involved in these struggles, since they are more prone to carry the burden of the event. They are confronted with the financial costs of hosting and infrastructure investment. Residents also have to come to terms with multiple interferences in daily life when the event visitors take over the city, traffic is rerouted, town quarters are closed, consumer prices go up, and national laws are suspended. Yet it must be noted that the solidarity generated by the feeling that 'the world is watching' often causes potential critics to engage in self-censorship, and may actually lessen support for advocacy groups.

Conclusion: future directions

From a mid- to long-term perspective, it may be argued that despite the imminent impact which sport mega-events have on local communities throughout the cycle, in the end these events turn out to be only passing and ephemeral occurrences that leave little tangible impact on daily existence. In order to come to terms with this paradoxical observation, more research is needed on the micro-and meso-sociological dimensions of sport mega-events, probing the 'everyday' level and how these events shape the life experience of locals, visitors and other parties involved. Our understanding of these events would be advanced by more 'thick descriptions' of everyday discourses and the social channels in which they arise and are circulated.

In addition, there is a clear need for more critical analyses of sport mega-events as 'Trojan horses' of consumerist ideologies and neoliberal policies, and the impact that they have upon new forms of social division and stratification. The widening of social inequalities, the marginalization of the poor and the exclusion of the 'precariat' are all acute transformations of societies in the Global North and South. Since the principal agents, such as the sport federations, corporate partners and the professional class of event organizers, are identical, I would argue here that these diverse observations represent an urgent call for studies of the relations between sport mega-events and the neocolonial structures of transnational capitalism.

References

Allison, L., ed. (2005) *The Global Politics of Sport: The Role of Global Institutions in Sport*, London: Routledge.

Andranovich, G., Burbank, M. and Heying, C. (2001) 'Olympic Cities: Lessons Learnt from Mega-Event Politics', *Journal of Urban Affairs* 23(2): 113–131.

Billig, M. (1995) *Banal Nationalism*, London: Sage.

Black, D. (2007) 'The Symbolic Politics of Sport Mega-Events: 2010 in Comparative Perspective', *Politikon: South African Journal of Political Studies* 34(3): 261–276.

Brownell, S. (2012) 'Human Rights and the Beijing Olympics: Imagined Global Community and the Transnational Public Sphere', *British Journal of Sociology*, 63(2): 306–327.

Cornelissen, S. (2009) 'A Delicate Balance: Major Sports Events and Development', in R. Levermore and A. Beacom (eds) *Sport and International Development*, New York: Palgrave Macmillan.

Cornelissen, S. (2012) '"Our Struggles Are Bigger Than the World Cup": Civic Activism, State-Society Relations and the Socio-political Legacies of the 2010 FIFA World Cup', *British Journal of Sociology*, 63(2): 328–348.

Cornelissen, S. and Swart, K. (2006) 'The 2010 Football World Cup as a Political Construct: The Challenge of Making Good on the African Promise', in J. Horne and W. Manzenreiter (eds) *Sports Mega-Events: Social Scientific Analyses of a Global Phenomenon*, Oxford: Blackwell.

Curi, M. (2011) 'The Pan American Games in Rio de Janeiro 2007: Consequences of a Sport Mega-Event on a BRIC Country', *International Review for the Sociology of Sport* 46(2): 140–156.

Darnell, S. (2013) *Sport for International Development and Peace*, London: Bloomsbury.

Dayan, D. (2008) 'Beyond Media Events: Disenchantment, Derailment, Disruption', in M. Price and D. Dayan (eds) *Owning the Olympics: Narratives of the New China*, Ann Arbor: University of Michigan Press.

Fussey, P., Coaffee, J., Armstrong, G., and Hobbs, D. (2012) 'The Regeneration Games: Purity and Security in the Olympic City', *British Journal of Sociology*, 63(2): 260–284.

Gebhardt, W. (2001) 'Feste, Feiern und Events: Zur Soziologie des Außergewöhnlichen', in W. Gebhardt, R. Hitzler and M. Pfadenhauer (eds) *Events. Soziologie des Außergewöhnlichen*, Opladen: Leske und Budrich.

Giulianotti, R. (2011) 'The Sport, Development and Peace Sector: A Model of Four Social Policy Domains', *Journal of Social Policy* 40(4): 757–776.

Gratton, C., Shibli, S. and Coleman, R. (2006) 'The Economic Impact of Major Sports Events: A Review of Ten Events in the UK', in J. Horne and W. Manzenreiter (eds) *Sports Mega-Events: Social Scientific Analyses of a Global Phenomenon*, Oxford: Blackwell.

Grix, J. (ed.) (2014) *Leveraging Legacies from Sports Mega-Events: Concepts and Cases*, London: Palgrave Pivot.

Hagemann, A. (2012) 'From the Stadium to the Fan Zone: Host Cities in a State of Emergency', in W. Manzenreiter and G. Spitaler (eds.) *Governance, Citizenship and the New European Football Championships: The European Spectacle*, London/New York: Routledge.

Hall, M. (1992) *Hallmark Tourist Events: Impacts, Management, and Planning*, London: Belhaven Press.

Hall, T. and Hubbard, P. (1996) 'The Entrepreneurial City: New Urban Politics, New Urban Geographies?', *Progress in Human Geography* 20(2): 153–174.

Harvey, J. and Houle, F. (1994) 'Sport, World Economy, Global Culture, and New Social Movements', *Sociology of Sport Journal* 11(4): 337–355.

Harvey, J. *et al.* (2014) *Sport and Social Movements. From the Local to the Global*, London: Bloomsbury.

Hiller, H. (1998) 'Mega-Events and Urban Social Transformation', in C. Persson, T. Andersen and B. Sahlberg (eds) *The Impact of Mega Events*, Östersund: Midsweden University.

Hogan, J. (2003) 'Staging the Nation: Gendered and Ethnicized Discourses of National Identity in Olympic Opening Ceremonies', *Journal of Sport & Social Issues* 27(2): 100–123.

Horne, J. (2014) 'Managing World Cup Legacy', in S. Frawley and D. Adair (eds) *Managing the Football World Cup*, London: Palgrave Macmillan.

Horne, J. and Manzenreiter, W. (2006) 'An Introduction to the Sociology of Sports Mega-Events', in J. Horne and W. Manzenreiter (eds) *Sports Mega-Events: Social Scientific Analyses of a Global Phenomenon*, Oxford: Blackwell.

Houlihan, B. and Giulianotti, R. (2012) 'Politics and the London 2012 Olympics: The (In)security Games', *International Affairs* 88(4): 701–717.

Jarvie, G. (2003) 'Internationalism and Sport in the Making of Nations', *Identities: Global Studies in Culture and Power* 10(4): 537–551.

Jennings, A. and Sambrook, C. (2000) *The Great Olympic Swindle*, London: Simon and Schuster.

Kellner, D. (2003) *Media Spectacle*, London: Routledge.

Kelly, W. (2011) 'Beijing 2008 and the Limits of Exceptionalism', in W. Kelly and S. Brownell (eds) *The Olympics in East Asia. Nationalism, Regionalism, and Globalism at the Center Stage of World Sports*, New Haven: Yale CEAS.

Lenskyj, H. (2000) *Inside the Olympic Industry*. New York: SUNY Press.

Lenskyj, H. (2008) *Olympic Industry Resistance*. New York: SUNY Press.

Lenskyj, H. and Wagg, S. (eds) (2012) *The Palgrave Handbook of Olympic Studies*, Basingstoke, UK: Palgrave Macmillan.

MacAloon, J. (2006) 'The Theory of Spectacle: Olympic Ethnography Revisited', in A. Tomlinson and C. Young (eds) *National Identity and Global Sports Events: Culture, Politics, and Spectacle in the Olympics and the Football World Cup*, New York: SUNY Press.

Manzenreiter, W. (2010) 'Global Movements, Sports Spectacles and the Transformation of Representational Power', *Asia Pacific World* 1(1): 37–55.

Manzenreiter, W. (2014) 'Magical Thought and the Legacy Discourse of the 2008 Beijing Games', in J. Grix (ed.) *Leveraging Legacies from Sports Mega-Events: Concepts and Cases*, London: Palgrave Pivot.

Manzenreiter, W. and Spitaler, G. (eds) (2012) *Governance, Citizenship and the New European Football Championships: The European Spectacle*, London/New York: Routledge.

Miller, T. *et al.* (2001) *Globalization and Sport. Playing the World*. London: Sage.

Preuss, H. (2004) *The Economics of Staging the Olympics: A Comparison of the Games 1972–2000*, Cheltenham, UK: Edward Elgar.

Price, M. (2008) 'On Seizing the Olympic Platform', in M. Price and D. Dayan (eds) *Owning the Olympics, Narratives of the New China*, Ann Arbor: University of Michigan Press, 86–114.

Roche, M. (2000) *Mega-Events and Modernity: Olympics and Expos in the Growth of Global Culture*, London: Routledge.

Roche, M. (2003) 'Mega-events, Time and Modernity: On Time Structures in Global Society', *Time & Society* 12(1): 99–126.

Rowe, D. (2012) 'The Bid, the Lead-Up, the Event and the Legacy: Global Cultural Politics and Hosting the Olympics', *British Journal of Sociology* 63(2): 285–305.

Sage, G. (1999) 'Justice Do It! The Nike Transnational Advocacy Network Organization, Collective Actions, and Outcomes', *Sociology of Sport Journal* 16(3): 206–235.

Schimmel, K. (2001) 'Sport Matters: Urban Regime Theory and Urban Regeneration in the Late-Capitalist Era', in C. Gratton and I. Henry (eds) *Sport in the City: The Role of Economic and Social Regeneration*, London: Routledge.

Tomlinson, A. and Young, C. (2006) 'Culture, Politics, and Spectacle in the Global Sports Event: An Introduction', in A. Tomlinson and C. Young (eds) *National Identity and Global Sports Events: Culture, Politics, and Spectacle in the Olympics and the Football World Cup*, Albany: State University of New York Press.

Wilson, B. (2007) 'New Media, Social Movements and Global Sport: A Revolutionary Moment and the Sociology of Sport', *Sociology of Sport Journal* 24(4): 457–477.

Wilson, B. (2012) *Sport and Peace: A Sociological Perspective*, Oxford University Press.

37

SPORT AND ENVIRONMENTALISM

Brian Wilson and Brad Millington

In this chapter we critically examine the perspectives and activities of a relatively new and extremely influential 'breed' of environmentalist: what we call the sport management environmentalist, or 'SME'. The SME is a corporate or corporate-linked environmentalist – a manager, organizer, promoter or other that is often (though not always) affiliated with a sport mega-event. SMEs can also be major sport organizations (i.e. those hosting sport mega-events), corporations (e.g. Mizuno or General Electric), environmental NGOs (e.g. Greenpeace) or members of governments lobbying to host a sport mega-event. In this regard, our definition of SMEs parallels the view that sport management in general involves the practices 'of *all* people, activities, businesses, or organizations involved in producing, facilitating, promoting, or organizing any sport-related business or product' (Pitts and Stotlar 2007: 4; cf. Petersen *et al.* 2011: 7; emphasis added).

Every two years some of the highest profile SMEs meet at the biennial World Conference on Sport and the Environment to discuss, highlight and celebrate their work. That an organizing partner for and major presence at this conference is the United Nations Environment Programme (UNEP), and that celebrity SME-supporters like Prince Albert of Monaco have been featured presenters at the conference, speaks to the SME's recognized role as a leader in the environmental movement. Perhaps the best example of the leadership and impact of SMEs can be seen in the work of the most powerful SME, the International Olympic Committee (IOC) – an organization that has immense influence over the environment-related activities of those who govern some of the world's major (Olympic) cities, and that relies heavily on its major corporate sponsors. Put simply, the SME has emerged as an important force in contemporary society.

Our examination and critique of the perspectives and activities of SMEs comprises three interrelated arguments. The first of these is that SMEs' preferred approach to dealing with environmental problems is based on a set of seldom questioned and in some ways dubious assumptions. These pertain most of all to the closely related concepts of sustainability and ecological modernization. The second argument is that SMEs' approach to promoting their activities and leadership on environmental issues is an excellent example of what theorist-activist Slavoj Žižek (1999) and others refer to as a 'post-political' approach. That is to say, SMEs generally promote an 'un-contentious' form of politics, and a belief that 'we all agree' on both the problems at hand when it comes to the environment and the most desirable pathways forward. This anticipates our third argument: that the post-political responses proffered by SMEs are undemocratic to the extent that they quell (or tacitly aim to quell) alternative and more 'radical' solutions to environmental problems whilst at the same time privileging the interests of those who benefit economically from (for example) sport mega-events. Indeed, the nature of post-politics is such that 'agreeable' environmental solutions are necessarily profitable ones as well (Swyngedouw 2010).

We elaborate on these three arguments in the following sections. First, we offer a broad overview of existing research on sport and environmental issues as background and context for our analysis. Following this, we provide a brief history of the SME and its emergence, identify characteristics of the archetypical SME and describe the set of assumptions that underlie SMEs' sustainability-driven approach. We then discuss some of the environmental strategies privileged and practiced by SMEs and discuss the seldom mentioned but very real problems with these practices. Finally, we define the term 'post-politics' and explain why this term is helpful for describing how SMEs have responded to critiques of sport mega-events and their environmental impacts. We conclude with recommendations for reimagining SME-led, post-political approaches to dealing with environmental problems.

Background and context: sport and the environment

Although this chapter focuses on the corporate-influenced environmentalist activities of what we term SMEs, it is important to recognize that research in this specific area fits within a growing, but still relatively small, tradition of sociological research on sport and the environment.

The early days of this research tradition included David Chernushenko's 1994 text *Greening Our Games* and his detailed assessment therein of how and why some organizations disingenuously promote an eco-friendly image (i.e. 'greenwash'). Despite this critique, Chernushenko's key message was effectively that 'environmentally friendly sport can be good for business' – a view that was subsequently critiqued by Helen Lenskyj (1998) for positioning the natural environment as a resource to be managed by humans who are equally concerned with economic and social issues, rather than as something with intrinsic worth. Brian Stoddart's (1990) analysis of the internationalization of golf in the 1980s and 1990s is another important early contribution. Stoddart identified environment-related problems associated with the construction and maintenance of golf courses, and thus, like Lenskyj, shed light on contemporary problems inherent to consumer culture and sport (cf. Wheeler and Nauright 2006). John Bale's (2001) work was similarly illuminating in that he identified and described how 'predictable' consumption experiences for tourists and sport fans led to the manipulation and destruction of many natural environments.

Since these early writings, sociologists of sport have begun to examine a variety of environment-related topics and issues (for overviews, see Mincyte *et al.* 2009 and Wilson and Millington 2013). Included here are studies on sport-related environmental activism and resistance (Atkinson 2009; Lenskyj 2002; Stolle-McAllister 2004; Wheaton 2007), perceptions of participants in sports known to have especially negative environmental impacts (Stoddart 2012), stakeholder negotiations pertaining to sport-related developments and environmental issues (Hayes and Horne 2011; Kearins and Pavlovich 2002; Pitter 2009), and the particular forms of environment-related 'ethical consumption' that have been featured by those working in the fitness industry (Mansfield 2009).

Of particular pertinence to this chapter are studies that identify and describe how sport-related organizations and industry members have in recent years become aware of the need to appear environmentally friendly, and have thus promoted themselves as leaders of a sport-related environmental movement. For example, with the IOC having proclaimed in 1994 that the 'environment' would be the third pillar of the Olympic movement (alongside 'sport' and 'culture' – Cantelon and Letters 2000), local organizing committees have sought in recent years to brand their events as the 'greenest Games ever' (Hayes and Horne 2011; Karamichas 2013; Lenskyj 1998, 2002). In doing so, organizing committees have devised both pro-environment activities and robust promotional strategies en route to countering (or, at least, to promote the view that they are countering) the heavy environmental impacts of 'welcoming the world' to one's city.

Along with SMEs promoting mega-events like the Olympics are the various sport managers and promoters involved in less prominent, though still significant, sport-related environmental-ist work. In this context, many in the golf industry have emerged as leading SMEs as well. As we found in a recent study (Millington and Wilson 2013), members of the golf industry have developed slick pro-environmental campaigns as a way of changing golf's reputation from one associated with negative environmental impacts to one that involves leading the way towards environmentally friendly sport. Indeed, in the face of concerns from environmentalists over pesticide-induced harms, golf industry members in the 1960s commonly denied that pesticides could unduly affect humans, animals and natural environments. Yet within a span of two decades, industry members had adopted a *proactive* strategy to take leadership on environment-related issues as a way of both satisfying environmentally concerned golfers and staving off stringent government regulations (see also Millington and Wilson 2014b). In other words, and to borrow a phrase from Hoffman (2001), environmentalism moved from heresy to dogma in the golf industry over time.

In recent years, the IOC and golf industry members have been joined by an assortment of other SMEs who now claim to be taking leadership on environment-related issues. These individuals and organizations work together to varying degrees to promote the idea that sport managers who run, organize and/or promote events and activities are working together with a shared vision of 'greener sports'. In many cases, SMEs' vision for 'greening sport' is supple-mented by claims that sport-related environmental work will have direct and positive impacts that go *beyond* sport as well. The most common and powerful claim is that the benefits of hosting sport mega-events can be used to leverage pro-social and pro-environment changes of all kinds within cities hoping to host an event. As one example, promotion of Formula One racing has included the view that reducing the emissions of race cars will aid those attempting to reduce *all* road emissions; innovation will effectively have a 'trickle down' effect (Wilson and Millington 2013).

Ecological modernization, post-politics and the sport management environmentalist

Having established that SMEs have taken leadership on environment-related issues in recent years, it is crucial to consider the implications of this development. To do this, we explore a series of questions intended to promote thinking about the benefits of and problems with SME-led environmentalism. These include: (a) what are the characteristics of the SME?; (b) what assump-tions and incentives underpin SME-led forms of environmentalism – and are there reasons to be concerned about SME leadership on public and environmental health-related issues?; and (c) how is consent generated for SME leadership and SME-driven decision-making on these issues?

Characteristics of the SME

There are several features of SMEs that distinguish them from sport mega-event organizers and sport managers of years past. First, the SME is known to openly acknowledge that sport-related activities can negatively impact the natural environment. This is a noteworthy admission if we consider that historically many industries denied that there was strong evidence that their practices may negatively impact the environment (Hoffman 2001). As noted earlier, our prior research outlined a transition from a moment when members of the golf industry denied that golf course management practices could be harmful for the environment (in the 1960s) to a moment when industry proclaimed leadership on environmental issues (from the 1980s onwards – Millington and Wilson 2013, 2014a).

Second, SMEs are known to respond to environment-related concerns using a 'sustainability' approach. That is to say, SMEs see progress on environment-related issues to be inseparable from progress on economic and social issues. SMEs are usually quite clear about this point. For example, the Vancouver Olympic Games Organizing Committee (VANOC) stated on the opening page of their publicly released 2009–2010 sustainability report that 'sustainability means managing the social, economic and environmental impacts and opportunities of our Games to produce lasting benefits, locally and globally' (VANOC 2010: 2). Thus, by adopting a sustainability approach, VANOC and other SMEs work within an incentive system driven by 'the triple bottom line' – which refers to the interrelated economic, social and environmental drivers that underlie sustainability.

Third, SMEs claim to prioritize collaboration with other stakeholders in their work on environment-related issues. For example, the World Conferences on Sport and the Environment promote collaborations between environmental NGOs (e.g. Greenpeace), governments, corporations and sport mega-event organizers/managers. As the homepage for the most recent conference in Sochi indicates, the 'biennial World Conference on Sport and the Environment is one of the IOC's key advocacy initiatives in the field of the environment, and gathers together representatives from the Olympic family, governments, the UN system, academic institutions and NGOs' (UNEP 2013).

Such claims of effective collaboration are based on the idea that discussions between people from different sectors who share a vision of sustainable sport and society can lead to mutually agreed upon solutions to questions about how sport can be more sustainable and how it can contribute to the promotion of sustainability in the wider society. It is worth emphasizing here that the environmental NGOs involved in these conferences and in stakeholder relationships with event organizers are, according to the definition we offer at the beginning of this chapter, a form of SME. That is to say, such NGOs actively support environmentalist work related to sport mega-events and promote the vision of sustainable sport that is at the core of SME-related work. For example, Greenpeace Australia was a partner in Sydney's successful bid for the 2000 games. This distinguishes them from activist organizations like Earth First! that challenge the hegemony of organizations like the IOC and the legitimacy of the sustainability approach that they advocate for.

Fourth, the SME is a promoter of technology-oriented solutions to environmental problems – solutions believed to emerge from the sort of innovative thinking that corporations are motivated to do in a marketplace where more efficient 'green' technologies are highly valued. There are numerous (well-advertised) instances where such technology-driven changes led to 'greener' facilities and sport-related practices. Leading up to the Vancouver 2010 games, for example, the 'latest technologies' were used in the construction of venues like the Vancouver Olympic Centre (curling) and the Richmond Oval (speed skating) with the goal of capturing 'the heat generated by refrigeration units to heat other parts of the building[s]' and the re-circulation of waste heat to heat spectator areas and water (Canadian Olympic School Program, n.d.). New technologies are also central to many of the carbon offsetting initiatives that are supported by SMEs who encourage sponsors and those who attend mega-events to contribute to various kinds of carbon-saving projects as a way of neutralizing the games' overall impacts.

Fifth and finally, SMEs tend to be strong supporters of voluntary and gradual forms of environment-related regulation. This position on regulation should be unsurprising in the sense that SMEs – as supporters of sustainability as a 'triple bottom line' approach to dealing with environment-related issues – would see forms of regulation from those outside industry to be insensitive to the economic realities faced by those interested in promoting sustained economic growth. Being open to harsher forms of regulation from government would also fly in the face of the idea that consumers should be the ones who 'regulate' the conduct of SMEs through the choices they make as paying spectators at events. This stance is directly related to SMEs' position that sport mega-events, when run by responsible and environmentally sensitive sport managers/ promoters (i.e. SMEs!), can be leveraged for the good of the environment more generally.

Ecological modernization and SME-driven environmentalism: assumptions and problems

Although sustainability is the term most often used to describe the approach that guides the environment-related work of SMEs, sociologists of the environment commonly suggest that sustainability-related practices are, in fact, underscored by principles associated with what is known as 'ecological modernization' (EM). Gibbs (2000: 11, drawing on Hajer 1995) has succinctly argued that sustainability is the 'central story line' of the policy discourse of ecological modernization. Put simply, aspects of the more nuanced ecological modernization concept commonly make their way into the more accessible and marketable language associated with sustainability (Wilson 2012a, 2012b).

So, what is ecological modernization, and how does it relate to the work of SMEs? In short, EM involves the view that industrialization can be altered using innovation/technology so that production and consumption become 'cleaner' and 'greener' (Mol 2002; Spaargaren and Mol 1992). The idea is that processes of industrialization progress through three different stages, from 'industrial breakthrough', to the construction of an 'industrial society', to finally the development of a 'super-industrial society' stage. In the last of these, technologies are developed that can deal with (and ultimately overcome) the environmental impacts of capitalism (Hannigan 2006: 27). Advocates of 'strong versions' of EM[1] see this move towards a super-industrial society as taking place through strategic (but limited) government interventions, and especially through negotiations and collaborations between industry, non-governmental organizations and consumers. The idea is that industry will respond to demands for improvements on environmental performance by developing new and 'greener' technologies. A classic example of this is Coca-Cola's development of energy-efficient coolers that used 'hydrocarbon' cooling systems (instead of hydrofluorocarbons, or HFCs) for use during and after the Sydney 2000 Olympics – a development that took place in response to criticisms from Greenpeace (and related concerns about consumer backlash) leading up to the Sydney Games (Chernushenko *et al.* 2001).

There are a number of assumptions that underpin an EM approach to dealing with environment-related problems. There are also some compelling concerns that have been raised by critics of EM. For example, an EM approach is based on the idea that economic development and progress on environmental issues are compatible (Wilson 2012a, 2012b). The problem here, however, is that businesses that are by mandate driven to pursue profit can ultimately be concerned with *appearing* 'green' – acknowledging that some pro-environmental technologies may in themselves lead to money savings. The point here is that some businesses are known to make minimal changes to their environmental practices whilst investing in the promotion of a pro-environment image (a process known as 'greenwashing' – Lubbers 2002). It is also well known that many businesses take leadership on environment-related issues in an attempt to stave off governments that could choose to implement harsher and potentially costly (but, presumably, more environmentally friendly) regulations. All this is to say that EM claims about the compatibility of economic and environment-related goals are not as unproblematic as they seem at first pass (Millington and Wilson 2013; Wilson 2012a, 2012b; Wilson and Millington 2013).

Another assumption at the foundation of EM thinking is that humans will be able to develop technologies needed to deal with the ever-evolving activities of industry and their environmental impacts. Holding such an assumption requires immense faith in human ingenuity and the power of new technologies to deal with often unforeseeable environmental issues. Thomas Homer-Dixon (2000) suggested in his book *The Ingenuity Gap* that such faith is unfounded, a position that gained some credibility during the Deepwater Horizon oil spill in the Gulf of Mexico, where there were several failed attempts to plug the oil leak.[2] We have raised questions elsewhere about how such uncertainties might be relevant to sport as well, noting that the unintended consequences of holding environment-impacting mega-events are perhaps still unknown (Wilson and Millington 2013; Wilson 2012a, 2012b).

We made a similar point in our recent research on the golf industry, where we showed how the industry's faith in the 'latest science' meant that some pesticides that were ultimately shown to be quite dangerous for humans and non-humans were used on golf courses until sufficient evidence of risk was identified (Millington and Wilson 2013). Such problems have inspired many who do work on environmental issues to recommend that industry and others adopt a 'precautionary approach' – a more cautious strategy for dealing with the uncertainties of environment-impacting activities. In a not unrelated way, one of us has also offered a detailed critique of the assumptions that underlie the use of carbon offsetting practices by sport mega-event organizers. The main assumption made by these SMEs is that one can reasonably calculate how much money needs to be invested in a particular carbon offset project to effectively 'offset' the carbon emissions that result from a carbon-emitting activity like building a sport stadium or travelling to a sport event. The point made by critics is that being 'carbon neutral' says little about how local ecosystems were potentially disrupted in the preparations for and holding of sport mega-events. For example, building a highway through an environmentally sensitive green space to an event venue still impacts that particular green space, even if the carbon emissions associated with that construction project are offset. Moreover, the criteria used for assessing what 'counts' as an emission associated with holding a sport event and what counts as an appropriate offset project are not straightforward either (see Wilson 2012a, 2012b for an extended discussion of these issues).

Additionally, and as we have also discussed elsewhere (Millington and Wilson 2013; Wilson 2012a), there is evidence that increases in efficiency do not necessarily lead to decreases in environmental impacts – noting that a more efficient technology may allow for or inspire more overall consumption (e.g. if the development of a less expensive and more eco-friendly vehicle led to an increase in the number of people buying and driving vehicles – cf. Foster *et al.* 2010).

Post-politics, environmental managerialism and the SME

The questions we will raise and engage at this point, in light of these concerns about SMEs' environmentalist work, are: how is it that SMEs have been able to take a relatively unchallenged leadership role on sport-related environmental issues? How are the factions of environmental activists that would conventionally be critical of, or at least suspicious of, SME-related activities responding to these SME-led developments? What role is government playing in the monitoring of SMEs' environment-impacting activities?

Our responses to these questions are heavily influenced by the work of authors like Žižek (1999) and Swyngedouw (2010) who have argued that political decision-making in the current historical moment commonly takes places through consensus-building among stakeholders, instead of through contentious *confrontations* between stakeholders with markedly different viewpoints and agendas. This current arrangement has been called 'post-political'.

While such forms of decision-making may seem innocuous, even desirable, critics have pointed to ways that the processes underlying post-political decision-making contribute to a situation whereby consent is generated for particular approaches to dealing with environmental issues – and for the exclusion of others. Specifically, and as Swyngedouw (2007) notes, consensus is commonly 'built around the inevitability of neoliberal capitalism' (p. 24). What this means in practical terms is that those who are negotiating solutions to environment-related issues must do so with the shared assumption that regulating industry is detrimental. This is because heavy-handed government intervention (that is antithetical to a neoliberal ideology – cf. Harvey 2005) is thought to undermine market-driven mechanisms for attaining the 'triple bottom line' goal of sustainability. Put simply, the question of *not* using a sustainability-driven approach to dealing with environmental problems is not up for debate if a consensus-building exercise that includes corporate-affiliated stakeholders is to take place.

It becomes increasingly obvious here why those who are cynical about neoliberal capitalist approaches to environmental problems would also be cynical about post-political decision-making. For example, a main frustration for those who have fought for years to promote major social and cultural shifts in environment-related behavior is that sport mega-event organizers and promoters – whose environmental activities remain controversial for reasons outlined throughout this chapter – have seemingly inoculated themselves against critiques by *agreeing with the critiques*. Ben Pitcher (2011) put this well in an essay discussing post-politics and activism more generally:

> [I]t's entirely possible for us [i.e. radical activists] to take these key social actors to task, but it is a strategy that fails to work . . . because our critique is met not with rejection, but a form of agreement: yes, sexism, racism, unsustainability and homophobia are all terrible things, and we are all working to get rid of them. There is no antagonism here, and no real possibility of conflict.

More than this, though, those who were previously targets of such critiques now proclaim to have identified the best approach (i.e. sustainability) to dealing with the environment-related problems they were at least partly responsible for in the first place – and further claim to be legitimate leaders in the response to these problems! The underlying idea is that the work of the radical environmental activists of years past is no longer needed, because 'new' environmentalists (e.g. SMEs) are now leading the charge. And whilst a variety of stakeholders – even 'traditional' activists – might be enlisted in arriving at environmental solutions, the concepts of sustainability and ecological modernization are effectively unassailable. As one might expect, environmental NGOs like Greenpeace Australia that partnered with Olympic Games organizers leading up to the Sydney 2000 Olympics came under attack for what many saw as a compromised position on environmental issues (see Beder 2002).

The underlying issue here is that while SMEs are concerned with environmental issues, the social and cultural transformations that many more radical environmentalists advocate – which might include fewer sport mega-events, and/or the re-use of designated locations for events – are not adopted. The input of more radical environmentalists may be sought when it comes to tweaking an already decided sustainability strategy. Harvey Neo's study of such consultations around golf course development in Singapore is an excellent example of this. Neo's (2010) study revealed that government acted as a facilitator of discussions between environmentalists and developers about how to construct environmentally friendly golf courses. The problem with this post-political configuration was, according to Neo, that the development of golf courses in the first place was never questioned nor rendered debatable. Put simply, the decision to develop had already been made before consultations took place. This is an excellent example of Swyngedouw's (2007) argument that negotiations between stakeholders take place in an environment where particular forms of and approaches to development and sustainability are 'inevitable'.

Findings of this kind also raise questions about why government representatives would support a post-political arrangement that appears to implicitly support the interests of business. Environmental sociologists like John Hannigan (2006) offer a form of response to such questions when they describe how many governments are in the difficult situation of fulfilling a 'dual mandate'. The mandate requires, on one hand, the facilitation of economic growth, and, on the other hand, the development and implementation of strategies intended to protect the environment. To satisfy this dual mandate, Hannigan (2006) suggests that governments adopt an 'environmental managerialist' approach. As he describes:

> [G]overnments often engage in a process of 'environmental managerialism' in which they attempt to legislate a limited degree of protection sufficient to deflect criticism [e.g. about environmental concerns] but not significant enough to derail the engine of economic growth. By enacting environmental policies that are complex, ambiguous and open to exploitation by the forces of production and accumulations the state reaffirms its commitments to strategies for promoting economic development.
>
> (Hannigan 2006: 21)

It is no stretch to suggest that by endorsing the work of SMEs – as governments do through their presence at and encouragement of the pro-environment work that is showcased at World Conferences of Sport and the Environment, and by allowing SMEs to influence decisions around urban development leading up to sport mega-events – governments are engaging in the 'managerialist' processes described by Hannigan. In our research on environmental regulation and golf in Ontario, Canada, we suggested that the Ontario provincial government was acting in accordance with environmental managerialist principles in its decision to exempt golf courses from an otherwise comprehensive ban on the use of pesticides for cosmetic purposes in the province (Millington and Wilson 2014b). The government justified the decision by suggesting that there were already stringent guidelines used to regulate how pesticides are deployed on golf courses. What we found was that the regulatory bodies that decide on acceptable and unacceptable uses of pesticides include members of lobby groups for the pesticide industry. Although we acknowledged that the government legislation was quite progressive and pro-environment in other respects, we found the contradictions pertaining to the golf exception striking, and only explainable by referring to the environmental managerialism concept. Such an arrangement is post-political in the sense that government is, in this instance, leaving negotiations around how to use pesticides to a mix of stakeholders who are influenced in some cases by an incentive system (i.e. profit for the pesticide industry) that is not inherently inclined towards the health of the natural environment and/or humans. Žižek's (2002: 303) suggestion that the 'ultimate sign of post-politics in all Western countries . . . [is when] government is reconceived as a managerial function, deprived of its proper political dimension' is especially germane here.

Conclusion: from practice to theory

As the closing speaker at the World Conference on Sport and the Environment in Vancouver in 2009, David Chernushenko noted that there has been 'significant progress from theory to action at all levels' when it comes to sport and the environment, and that relevant stakeholders 'are now discussing sustainable development in its full sense, and not just environmental protection' (as reported in Du Bois 2009).

There are two interesting and, we think, problematic assumptions underlying Chernushenko's comments. The first assumption is that moving from theory to action is 'progress'. In this chapter we have attempted to problematize the idea that 'moving ahead' with 'sustainable sport' is not *necessarily* an environmentally friendly move. The second and related assumption made by Chernushenko is that tying economic progress with progress on environmental issues is what is best for the environment. Chernushenko, who is well aware of this problem – he outlines some of these problems in his own writing about sport and environmental issues – still seems unwaveringly committed to a sustainability approach for SMEs based on this assumption.

In light of the problems with sustainability and the related ecological modernization concept that underpin SME-driven environmentalist work, we would argue, contrary to Chernushenko, that what is needed in the current moment is a *return to theory* – a return to thinking about alternate ways of seeing relationships between sport managers, sport mega-event organizers and the environment. By returning to theory, we would be in a better position to see not only why a SME-driven approach to environmental problems unjustifiably narrows the range of options that could be adopted for dealing with sport-related environmental concerns – but we would also be in a better position to consider how we might develop more democratic decision-making processes on sport-related environmental issues. Thus, what we are advocating for are critical, theoretically informed, context-sensitive analyses that help us see the assumptions that underpin any strategy for dealing with environmental problems (the approach we adopted in this chapter). We also see a need for theories of social change intended to inspire thinking about 'what is possible', and for devising 'minor utopian' visions of a future where decisions about how to deal with sport and environment-related issues are made by those who are mandated to prioritize environmental and related public health concerns, not by those who are ultimately working towards profit goals. Said another way, future work might ask and seek to answer questions commonly overlooked in the 'age of the SME' – for example, whether the most environmentally responsible decision might involve *not* holding a sport mega-event at all, or whether the environmental benefits that sport mega-events are 'leveraged' to achieve can be arrived at *without actually holding* a sport mega-event in the first place.

To be clear, and in conclusion, our suggestions and arguments are not intended to undermine the accomplishments of those who work in an ecological modernist model or those who have successfully supported the development of many innovative and important 'green' technologies. What we have attempted to do is demonstrate that there is a need to re-politicize the taken-for-granted responses to environmental problems that are privileged and promoted by SMEs and others. The ultimate goal here is to open up more spaces for dialogue about the range of possibilities for dealing with sport-related environmental issues.

Notes

1 Following Christoff (1996), we distinguish stronger versions of EM from weaker versions of EM that are more directly aligned with the deregulation and open markets approaches to environmental issues that characterize neoliberal responses to environmental concerns.

2 The oil spill began in April 2010 after a series of explosions on BP's Deepwater Horizon oil rig in the Gulf of Mexico. Bryant (2011) reports that 10 different techniques were employed in trying to halt the oil flow. It wasn't until July 15, 2010, that the well was capped; it was sealed permanently on September 19, 2010. Eleven people died as part of the disaster. As of this writing, it is the biggest offshore oil spill in American history.

References

Atkinson, M. (2009) 'Parkour, Anarcho-Environmentalism, and Poiesis', *Journal of Sport & Social Issues*, 33(2): 169–194.

Bale, J. (2001) *Sport, Space, and the City*, West Caldwell, NJ: Blackburn.

Beder, S. (2002) *Global Spin: The Corporate Assault on Environmentalism*, White River Junction, VT: Chelsea Green Publishing Company.

Bryant, B. (2011) 'Deepwater Horizon and the Gulf Oil Spill – The Key Questions Answered'. Available at: http://www.theguardian.com/environment/2011/apr/20/deepwater-horizon-key-questions-answered (accessed 1 March 2014).

Canadian Olympic School Program (n.d.) *Environmental Sustainability and the Vancouver 2010 Olympic Winter Games*. Available at: http://cdnolympic.files.wordpress.com/2013/09/sustainability_en.pdf (accessed 3 December 2013).

Cantelon, H. and Letters, M. (2000) 'The Making of the IOC Environmental Policy as the Third Dimension of the Olympic Movement', *International Review for the Sociology of Sport*, 35(3): 249–308.

Chernushenko, D. (1994) *Greening Our Games: Running Sports Events and Facilities That Won't Cost the Earth*, Ottawa: Centurion.

Chernushenko, D., Van der Kamp, A. and Stubbs, D. (2001) *Sustainable Sport Management: Running an Environmentally, Socially, and Economically Responsible Organization*, Nairobi: United Nations Environment Programme.

Christoff, P. (1996) 'Ecological Modernisation, Ecological Modernities', *Environmental Politics* 5(3): 476–500.

Du Bois, D. (2009) '"Living Lightly" Visionary Shares Insights on Olympic Sustainability Conference'. Available at: http://energypriorities.com/entries/2009/04/wcse_chernushenko.php (accessed 4 December 2013).

Foster, J.B., Clark, B. and York, R. (2010) *The Ecological Rift: Capitalism's War on the Earth*, New York: Monthly Review Press.

Gibbs, D. (2000) 'Ecological Modernisation, Regional Economic Development and Regional Development Agencies', *Geoforum*, 31(1): 9–19.

Hajer, M. (1995) *The Politics of Environmental Discourse: Ecological Modernisation and the Policy Process*, Oxford: Oxford University Press.

Hannigan, J. (2006) *Environmental Sociology*, 2nd edition. New York: Routledge.

Harvey, D. (2005) *A Brief History of Neoliberalism*, New York: Oxford University Press.

Hayes, G. and Horne, J. (2011) 'Sustainable Development, Shock and Awe? London 2012 and Civil Society', *Sociology*, 45(5): 749–764.

Hoffman, A. (2001) *From Heresy to Dogma: An Institutional History of Corporate Environmentalism*, Stanford, CA: Stanford University Press.

Homer-Dixon, T. (2000) *The Ingenuity Gap: Can We Solve the Problems of the Future?* New York: Knopf.

Karamichas, J. (2013) *The Olympic Games and the Environment*, New York: Palgrave Macmillan.

Kearins, K. and Pavlovich, K. (2002) 'The Role of Stakeholders in Sydney's Green Games', *Corporate Social Responsibility and Environmental Management*, 9(3): 157–169.

Lenskyj, H. (1998) 'Sport and Corporate Environmentalism: The Case of the Sydney 2000 Olympics', *International Review for the Sociology of Sport*, 33(4): 341–354.

Lenskyj, H. (2002) *The Best Olympics Ever: Social Impacts of Sydney 2000*, Albany: SUNY Press.

Lubbers, E. (ed.) (2002) *Battling Big Business: Countering Greenwash, Infiltration and Other Forms of Corporate Bullying*, Monroe, ME: Common Courage.

Mansfield, L. (2009) 'Fitness Cultures and Environmental (in)Justice?', *International Review for the Sociology of Sport*, 44(4): 345–362.

Millington, B. and Wilson, B. (2013) 'Super Intentions: Golf Course Management and the Evolution of Environmental Responsibility', *The Sociological Quarterly*, 54(3): 450–475.

Millington, B. and Wilson, B. (2014a) 'The Masters of Nature: Golf, Non-Humans, and Consumer Culture', in J. Gillett and M. Gilbert (eds) *Sport, Animals & Society*, New York: Routledge.

Millington, B. and Wilson, B. (2014b). 'An unexceptional exception: Pesticides, golf and environmental regulation in Canada'. *International Review for the Sociology of Sport*. Advance online publication. doi: 10.1177/1012690214526878.

Mincyte, D., Casper, M.J. and Cole, C. L. (2009) 'Sports, Environmentalism, Land Use, and Urban Development', *Journal of Sport & Social Issues*, 33(2): 103–110.

Mol, A.P.J. (2002) 'Ecological Modernization and the Global Economy', *Global Environmental Politics*, 2(2): 92–115.

Neo, H. (2010) 'Unravelling the Post-Politics of Golf Course Provision in Singapore', *Sport and Social Issues*, 34(3): 272–287.

Petersen, P.M., Parks, J.B., Quarterman, J. and Thibault, L. (2011) *Contemporary Sport Management*, 4th edition, Champaign, IL: Human Kinetics.

Pitcher, B. (2011) 'Radical Subjects after Hegemony', *Subjectivity*, 4: 87–102.

Pitter, R. (2009) 'Finding the Kieran Way: Recreational Sport, Health, and Environmental Policy in Nova Scotia', *Journal of Sport & Social Issues*, 33(3): 331–351.

Pitts, B.G. and Stotlar, D.K. (2007) *Fundamentals of Sport Marketing*, 3rd edition. Morgantown, WV: Fitness Information Technology.

Spaargaren, G. and Mol, A.P.G. (1992) 'Sociology, Environment, and Modernity: Ecological Modernization as a Theory of Social Change', *Society and Natural Resources*, 5(4): 323–344.

Stoddart, B. (1990) 'Wide World of Golf: A Research Note on the Interdependence of Sport, Culture, and Economy', *Sociology of Sport Journal*, 7(4): 378–388.

Stoddart, M. (2012) *Making Meaning Out of Mountains*, Vancouver: UBC Press.

Stolle-McAllister, J. (2004) 'Contingent Hybridity: The Cultural Politics of Tepoztlán's Anti-Golf Movement', *Identities: Global Studies in Culture and Power*, 11(2): 195–213.

Swyngedouw, E. (2007) 'Impossible/Undesirable Sustainability and the Post-political Condition', in J.R. Krueger and D. Gibbs (eds) *The Sustainable Development Paradox*. New York: Guilford Press.

Swyngedouw, E. (2010) 'Apocalypse Forever? Post-political Populism and the Spectre of Climate Change', *Theory, Culture & Society*, 27: 213–232.

UNEP (United Nations Environment Programme) (2013) *10th IOC World Conference on Sport and the Environment Kicks Off in Sochi*. Available at: http://www.unep.org/newscentre/default.aspx?DocumentID=2752&ArticleID=9671 (accessed 3 December 2013).

VANOC (Vancouver Organizing Committee) (2010) *Vancouver 2010 Sustainability Report 2009–2010*. Available at: http://www.olympic.org/Documents/Games_Vancouver_2010/VANOC_Sustainability_Report-EN.pdf (accessed 4 December 2013).

Wheaton, B. (2007) 'Identity, Politics, and the Beach: Environmental Activism in Surfers Against Sewage', *Leisure Studies* 26(3): 279–302.

Wheeler, K. and Nauright, J. (2006) 'A Global Perspective on the Environmental Impact of Golf', *Sport in Society*, 9(3): 427–443.

Wilson, B. (2012a) *Sport & Peace: A Sociological Perspective*, Don Mills, ON: Oxford University Press.

Wilson, B. (2012b) 'Growth and Nature: Reflections on Sport, Carbon Neutrality, and Ecological Modernization', in D. Andrews and M. Silk (eds) *Sport and Neo-Liberalism: Politics, Consumption, and Culture*, Philadelphia, PA: Temple University Press.

Wilson, B. and Millington, B. (2013) 'Sport, Ecological Modernization, and the Environment', in D. Andrews and B. Carrington (eds) *A Companion to Sport*, Malden, MA: Blackwell Publishing.

Žižek, S. (1999) *The Ticklish Subject*, London: Verso.

Žižek, S. (2002) *Revolution at the Gates*, London: Verso.

38

SPORT AND MEDIA

Lawrence A. Wenner

This chapter considers the development of the socio-cultural study of sport and media within the sociology of sport disciplinary tradition. Now vibrant, important, and substantial, media inquiry did not always play a featured role in the sociology of sport. Today, it is difficult to imagine how there could be big-time sport without big-time media.

The relatively late arrival of the socio-cultural study of sport and media was influenced by the *terroir* of two disciplines – sport studies (including the sociology of sport) and media studies – both of which were emerging and, being a bit insecure in the academy, were seeking legitimacy. Early media studies built academic legitimacy through a reliance on hard social science models and focusing on the 'serious' social effects (e.g. propaganda, violence) of mass media on different audiences. Physical education and sports studies increasingly became scientized as kinesiology and exercise science. In both settings, studying something popular, like mediated sports, worked against scientific legitimacy efforts.

With the rise of British cultural studies, sport and media studies gained 'permission' to engage each other without apology. Making inroads in the 1980s, media became essential to the sociology of sport, with the door also opened to sport in media studies. As the study of sport and media advanced, recognition of their intermix became so fundamental that neologisms such as 'mediasport' were created (Wenner 1998). In this fusion, many saw a cultural power greater than the sum of its parts. This conclusion is warranted as mediasport merges two of Althusser's (1971/2000) ideological state apparatuses (or ISAs) in a way that gathers unique powers through masking its force in the twin pleasures of sport and media consumption. Following Althusser, essential reasons for studying the dynamics of the mediasport mix are that 1) 'in its contemporary hypercommodified form, the ideological contours and ethical sensibilities of mediasport dominate the cultural meanings that are associated with sport,' and 2) 'as it fulfills its market roles, mediasport strategically reaches out to us to narrate understandings of sport in the context of broader social relations' (Wenner 2013b: 83–84).

Whether motivated by critical concerns over power or inequality or social process, the study of mediasport entails understanding the intersection of core components in the communication process:

1   senders/institutions/production/encoding,
2   messages/content/texts/representation/signification, and
3   receivers/audiences/fandom/consumption/decoding.

Most scholars agree that communication is a fluid process entailing all these matters, with reference to the political-economic climate, everyday lived experiences, and active struggles over material and symbolic resources.

What follows is a brief phylogenetic characterization of four stages in the development of sport and media research. The treatment traces the area's evolutionary path and considers overarching concerns with: 1) 'money and power' (i.e. commercialization, advertising, mega-events/spectacle, globalization, celebrity) and 2) 'framing and identities' (i.e. gender/sex, race/ethnicity, ability/disability, national/local).

Mediasport 1.0: childhood (1975 to 1989)

Adumbrated by Johnson's *Sports Illustrated* reports (1969) about how the money and demands of television had changed sport, Buscombe (1975) and Real (1975) offered critical analyses of televised football on opposing sides of the Atlantic. Published in premier outlets, by BFI and the *Journal of Communication*, their work meshed overarching concerns with political economy and nationalism with semiological analysis of televisual logics in producing commodified spectacle. While there were debates over television's harm to sport and historical accounts characterizing television's merger with sport, Buscombe and Real's critical sensibilities sparked mediasport inquiry.

Much 1970s research featured discrete studies. Here, work began to assess how televisual codes restructure the experience of sport, the culture of sport journalism, and racial bias in media coverage. Only one coherent research program emerged during this period. Set in media psychology, the Bryant-centered research group showed how strategies and characterizations of announcers, particularly those emphasizing drama, conflict, and violence, most influenced spectator enjoyment. This research frames a long line of disposition theory inquiry and parallels research in sport psychology on spectator engagement that continues to inform studies of mediated fandom (see Raney 2006).

A complementary media gratifications study (Gantz 1981) helped frame television sports viewing as an active and resourceful enterprise. Foreshadowing a substantial line of research, motives were identified for televised sports viewing (thrilling in victory, rooting for favorites, curiosity about outcome, etc.) that were linked to affective 'feelings' and behaviors prior to, during, and after sports viewing (Wenner and Gantz 1998).

The 1980s brought more theoretically savvy efforts to explain how media language shaped understandings of sport and continued cultural studies concerns over the ideological workings of mediated sport. Research established mediated sport as contested terrain with coverage systematically disadvantaging women and encouraging hegemonic masculinity and heteronormativity.

No work was more influential in framing mediated sport as contested terrain than Whannel's (1983) *Blowing the Whistle*. By placing media centrally in a Marxist critique of the cultural politics of sport, Whannel focused on power in institutional arrangements, pointing to important new intersections for the mediasport agenda: commodification, globalization, nationalism, and struggles over gender, race, ethnicity, and class.

In Australia, similar work anchored by Rowe foreshadowed his ongoing importance to mediasport inquiry. Here, key arguments made about mediasport's role in legitimating 'masculine hegemony', 'capitalist rationality', and 'militaristic nationalism' (McKay and Rowe 1987: 261–264) were amplified in *Power Play* (Lawrence and Rowe 1986), perhaps the first scholarly collection to feature a media-centric view of sport. Works such as this, and Jackson and McPhail's (1989) volume featuring leading critical scholars assessing Olympics coverage, showed how essential media analysis was for understanding the sport spectacle and sport mega-events.

Consensus grew during Mediasport 1.0 that the research agenda required interlocked under-standings of media and sport institutions, textual tendencies and preferred meanings, and audi-ence reception. *Media, Sports, and Society* (Wenner 1989), organized by those components in showcasing research strategies for an overarching agenda, served as a 'handbook' to advance legitimacy for mediasport inquiry. Meshing with Whannel and Rowe's roles in framing inquiry in the UK and Australia, studies in this work stimulated research in North America.

Mediasport 2.0: adolescence (1990 to 1998)

While Mediasport 1.0's childhood progressed slowly, research agendas matured quickly during Mediasport 2.0's adolescence. Here, emergent scholars (e.g. Andrews, Bruce, Jackson, Boyle, Haynes) with lasting impact joined foundational scholars (e.g. Whannel, Rowe, Real, Duncan, Kane, Gantz, Bryant, Wenner) in continuing important research lines. With leading sociology of sport jour-nals – *International Review for the Sociology of Sport, Sociology of Sport Journal*, and *Journal of Sport and Social Issues* – regularly publishing media-centric research, the 'arrival' of media to sport sociology during Mediasport 2.0 was more evident than the entry of sport into media studies, especially in the United States, where cultural studies drove interest in the mediasport nexus. Outside the US, the founding of a sport and media working group within the International Association for Media and Communication Research in the early 1990s signaled sport's rising legitimacy in media studies.

Two UK-centered books on television and sport frame Mediasport 2.0. One, Barnett's *Games and Sets* (1990), presents a pessimistic cultural history of the evolutionary relationship of sport and television. The second, Whannel's *Fields in Vision* (1992), was the first sole-authored work to consider the range of mediasport inquiry. Blending a critical cultural studies backbone with overarching concern over ideology and power, Whannel showcased how production, content, and reception elements *should* and *could* be studied as a cohesive whole. Many areas Whannel touched on became key themes during Mediasport 2.0. Here came focused research on institu-tions and production, the globalization-spectacle-nation nexus, representation of identities and celebrity, and the dynamics of reception.

Research on institutions examined how sport and media organizations conspire in mutual benefice to grow markets and profits. Wernick's (1991) concerns over hypercommodification driven by 'circuits of promotion' were evident in political-economic critique and figurational analysis. Research 'followed the money' and an integrated global web of relationships to decon-struct synergies, cross-ownership, and how sports spectacle prioritized the needs of advertisers and sponsors in building allegiances among viewers.

Research on production and professional practice blended Ellul's (1964) concerns over 'la technique', evident in a focus on media conventions, with those of occupational sociology, evident in a focus on work cultures, norms, and routines. Studies show how television cre-atives shape sport as media events and use televisual language to stimulate themes of drama and conflict amidst conservative values emphasizing competitive success, naturalizing capitalism, and reinforcing dominant ideologies of masculinity, femininity, and race. Studies of reporters characterized sports journalism as not only a 'toy department' but a 'boy department'. Women journalists often embrace the values of male sport and see women's sport as second tier, but face challenges to their covering men's sports.

Research on globalization, spectacle, commodification, and nation deconstructed the tricks of the 'glocalization' trade that use media to make the global local. Focus was given to how institutional priorities within the mediasport complex conspire to shape mega-event spectacles through symbolic imaginaries of athletes and nations to build allegiances and audiences in ways that mutually benefit capitalism and nationalism.

Collectively, much Mediasport 2.0 research suggests that, driven by goals to maximize pleasure, grow audiences, and 'situate the sell', sport media reliance on technique and assertions that will not disrupt present power relations or cultural sensibilities is endemic. No evidence confirms this assessment more than research showing how media helps sustain gender as the great divide of sport. From absence to trivialization to ambivalence in covering female athletes, to celebrative constructions of violence and instrumentality that perpetuate hegemonic masculinity, to tendencies towards naturalizing heteronormativity and homophobia, the evidence has been overwhelming and daunting (Duncan 2006). Substantial work on gender made this area of inquiry the first to produce book-length treatments (Creedon 1994; Daddario 1998; Davis 1997; Trujillo 1994) and an enduring line of longitudinal research (Cooky *et al.* 2013).

When compared to gender-centered research, Mediasport 2.0 inquiry on racial and ethnic castings was nascent. Still, bottom line assessments concerning race meshed with those about gender. Reliant on stereotypes, media narratives were found to essentialize and naturalize difference, as 'black' and 'white' are constructed as distinct categories that emphasize black athleticism and the leadership and work ethos of white athletes (Davis and Harris 1998).

In intriguing ways, Mediasport 2.0 research on racial representations transacted with emergent interest in media constructions of sporting celebrity. Studies of 'good blacks' and 'bad blacks' (Wenner 1995) shed light on the complexities, tensions, and contradictions in media coverage of the rise and fall of sporting heroes. Fusing core elements in mediasport inquiry (e.g. globalization, commodification, gender, and race), the rise of celebrity studies at this time also served to amplify interest in morals, the body, and pleasures.

Exploration of audience pleasure in consuming mediated sport was a key feature of Mediasport 2.0 reception research. Research here explored the position of audience subjects, and tactics for spectators for empowerment and resistance, and was influenced by key work in cultural studies as well as Foucault, Lacan, and other post-structuralists, audience ethnographies, and reader-oriented analyses of discourse. Work examining the rituals and meaning of fanship complemented maturing research on audience gratifications and dispositions to fan enjoyment. Important myths about 'football widows', spousal battles over sports viewing, and the powerlessness of female viewers began to be debunked (cf. Bryant *et al.* 1998; Wenner and Gantz 1998). Empirical evidence showed that female agency in response to male preoccupation with sport was active; women who were not sports fans followed their own interests during game broadcasts and imbalances in sports interests were typically accommodated in relationships with little friction.

With key research lines developing, Mediasport 2.0's passage was marked by a second *de facto* handbook. The volume, *Mediasport* (Wenner 1998), as a more inclusive 'community organizing' effort, recognized mediasport as an artefact of the postmodern condition, with papers that interrogated institutions, texts, and audiences that were increasingly sensitive to commodification, globalization, and technology.

Mediasport 3.0: early adulthood (1999 to 2006)

By the close of Mediasport 2.0, research agendas had matured and studies featured diverse theoretical lenses and methodological tactics. Positivist, phenomenological, figurational, and postmodern vantage points had standing. Yet, foundational concerns with power and ideology drove the agenda. The influences of post-structural critical theory, cultural studies, semiotics, and variously disposed feminisms were clear. Persuasive evidence from studies of 'money and power' and 'framing and identities' showed how the big sport–big media fusion often served as a conservative, even retrograde, socio-cultural force.

Two trends flavored Mediasport 3.0: 1) the publication of noteworthy books focusing on diverse aspects of the sport-media nexus, and 2) further institutional mainstreaming of sport and media research, notably within communication studies in the US. Three authored books ushering in Mediasport 3.0 signaled the area's coming of age; by offering overarching syntheses, these publications were also employed as textbooks, which furthered the mainstreaming of mediasport perspectives. Brookes (2002) centered on representations of national, gender, and racial identities, and while considering globalization and production, paid relatively little attention to audiences. More far-ranging successful treatments by Rowe (1999) and Boyle and Haynes (2000) brought useful histories, political–economic analysis, and assessment of professional norms and textual tendencies within sport media.

Diverse edited collections extended these authored efforts. Studies in Birrell and McDonald's *Reading Sport* (2000) interrogated sporting power and used the intersectional analysis of race to deconstruct media representations of gender and sexualities. Policy concerns anchored Roche's (1998) collection, which centered on how media symbols of identities transact with mega-events and football. Bernstein and Blain's (2003) *Sport, Media, Culture* 'announces' mediasport's emergence as a 'major research field' with studies of global/local tensions and gender and racial identities. Similarly, Brown and O'Rourke's (2003) *Case Studies in Sport Communication* 'announces' sporting rhetoric and narrative as legitimate fields of inquiry for communication studies. In contrast, Rowe's (2004) compilation of previously published *Critical Readings* showcases mediasport research as established rather than emergent. Collectively, these works share text-centric critical tactics, overarching concerns with identities and mega-events, and little study of media audiences.

Directly addressing this ongoing deficiency, Wann, Melnick, Russell, and Pease's (2001) *Sports Fans* takes stock of social-psychological inquiries into sports spectatorship in and out of mediated settings. This work represents a companion to ethnographic and qualitative studies of audience resourcefulness in exploring the polysemic possibilities of mediated texts in order to produce pleasure and resistance. Wann *et al.* (2001) also provide an important counter to critical work that is reliant on texts and the assumption that audiences simply consent to the reception and internalization of dominant ideologies.

The complexities of increasing commodification within sport were considered in key works. Anchored in Bauman's (2007) notions of 'consumer sociality' and 'liquid modernity', Crawford's (2004) *Consuming Sport* shows that agency in sport consumption and fanship, while active and resourceful, necessarily references naturalized commodity logics. The omnipresence of consumer culture's transaction with sports media is a key feature of both Horne's (2006) *Sport in Consumer Culture* and Andrews's (2006) *Sport-Commerce-Culture* — works that consolidate influences from two key scholars. Horne's treatment brings political–economic analysis of the forces at play, anchoring globalization in media–centered consumerization and how promotional logics interact with identities. Andrews's fluid postmodern analysis deconstructs media excess and corporatized strategies. Diverse cross-national comparisons of how the media drive commodification and undergird the globalization of sport through televisualization are synthesized in Miller, Lawrence, McKay, and Rowe's (2001) *Globalization and Sport* and featured in Silk, Andrews, and Cole's (2005) *Sport and Corporate Nationalisms*. An important first work on advertising (Jackson and Andrews 2005) provides critical assessments of promotional narratives and the strategic employment of identities of nation, gender, race, and bodily health by multi-national corporations (notably Nike) in the sport marketplace.

The manufacture of celebrity has been important to both the commodification of mediated sport and the pleasures of its consumption. Providing critiques of gender, racial, and national identities, Andrews and Jackson's (2001) collection showcases tactics for deconstructing power relations that are embedded in corporatized discourses of sporting celebrity. Focusing on gender and the complexities of masculinities, Miller's *Sportsex* (2001) and Whannel's *Media Sport Stars* (2002) show the flexibility of corporate discourse to be 'strategically ambiguous' in recognition of changing sexual sensibilities that serve to reorganize hegemonic masculinity.

At this time, complementary research progressed on media making. Through fieldwork and interviews, Lowes's (1999) *Inside the Sports Pages* shows how newsroom structures, beats, and source relations serve to make sport reporting complicit with goals to sell sport as spectacle. Boyle's (2006) *Sports Journalism* critically engages key literature and the occupational enterprise. Boyle's meta-analysis focuses on three themes – globalization, digitization, and marketization – that drive increasingly promotional sport media. Related work by emerging scholars (Billings 2004; Bruce 2001; Hardin 2005) illuminates the fragmented professional identities of women sportswriters and the 'normalizing' of gender, racial, and national bias in coverage.

Important institutional developments accompanied these hallmark works. The International Sociology of Sport Association and North American Society for the Sociology of Sport now featured steady calls for mediasport papers. Marking legitimacy in communication and media studies, the first Summit on Communication and Sport in 2002 foreshadowed an ongoing series of conferences. Here, communication scholars plotted disciplinary legitimation strategies, including authoring a seminal statement about the contours for studying communication and sport beyond its media interface. Focusing on 'how members in the community of sport communicatively enact, (re)produce, consume, and organize sport' (Kassing *et al.* 2004, p. 373), their efforts illumined studying sport in interpersonal, organizational, family, coaching, and other communicative contexts.

Other developments firmed sport's place in communication and media studies. In 2002 a Media and Sport Section of the International Association for Media and Communication Research grew from a working group. In 2003 Pennsylvania State University's Curley Center for Sports Journalism became the first communication research institute focused on sport in the US. The year 2004 brought 'named' legitimacy as the journal *Culture, Sport, Society* was retitled *Sport in Society: Culture, Commerce, Media, Politics*.

The area's first officially named handbook signaled critical mass for mediasport research. The heft and range of Raney and Bryant's (2006) *Handbook of Sports Media* went far beyond earlier such publications. By examining not only established (gender, race) and emerging (disability, bodies) research concerning 'framing and identities' and established lines of inquiry about 'money and power' (globalization, mega-events), the collection provided much-needed focus on sport media consumption (enjoyment, fanship, violence) and the discrete aspects of sport media industries in print, television, radio, cable, and online. Most importantly, the volume pointed to roads ahead in understanding the new media environment for sports, such as in gaming, blogging, and fantasy sports.

Mediasport 4.0: middle age (2007 to present)

Major works and institutional initiatives advanced in Mediasport 4.0. The area's first scholarly journal, the *Journal of Sports Media*, was launched with a professional culture focus (reporting, announcing, public relations) complementing socio-cultural research. In 2008 publication of the *International Journal of Sport Communication* brought the area's first research quarterly.

In 2008 the Broadcast Education Association became the first US scholarly organization to feature a sports division. The 2010 launch of the Sports Communication Interest Group made the Association for Education in Journalism and Mass Communication the largest organization to sanctify mediasport inquiry. In 2013 the launch of *Communication and Sport*, the first journal broadly embracing media and communication studies, in tandem with the International Association for Communication and Sport as the area's first scholarly society, marked a critical juncture. Further escalating this trend, in 2014 the Communication and Sport Interest Group was formed within the International Communication Association.

Revealing the maturity of mediasport inquiry, major works during this period included second-generation textbooks (cf. Billings *et al.* 2012; Kennedy and Hills 2009). In tandem, new contributions from foundational scholars marked the field's center at the nexus of studies in globalization and commodification. Whannel's (2008) *Culture, Politics, and Sport* reprised earlier work and argued afresh that the field's concerns with identities and pleasures were necessarily subservient to forces of globalization and commodification. Rowe's (2011) *Global Media Sport* updates how processes of globalization, mediatization, and sportification interact in the digital age. He explores the prospects for resourceful 'executive fandom' and digital connectedness to temper the glocalization strategies that advance imperialistic goals by organizations, corporations, and nations.

Other projects by foundational scholars focused on hypercommodification and the marketization of sport through advertising and celebrity. A long research line (see Wenner 2013c) showed how media narratives reappropriate cultural logics about sport to bring 'dirtied' meaning to 'pollute' other quarters of culture where sporting logics may be 'matter out of place' (Douglas 1966: 43). These studies advanced a mediasport-specific 'dirt theory' of narrative ethics studies that meshed reader-oriented and ethical criticism to reveal how advertising narratives rely on constructions of 'imagined communities' (Anderson 1983) which were 'dirtied' in this way to model and channel the pleasures of mediated sport into consumption. Studies in *Sport, Beer, and Gender* (Wenner and Jackson 2009) focused on a 'dirty' holy trinity, documenting the promotional strategies that brewers use to naturalize alcohol and its reception in sporting contexts. Commodification and the globalization of sporting celebrity were featured in two volumes: Sandvoss, Real, and Bernstein (2012) considered media discourses celebrating global sport stars, whilst Wenner (2013a) examined how media characterize fallen sports heroes in ways that do not taint the value of sporting celebrity as a media product.

Mediatization of the Olympic Games received much attention. Distinct in considering production, texts, and audience, Billings's (2008) *Olympic Media*, examining the tactics of television producers and announcers in companion to viewers' perceptions, showed the nuanced ways in which nation, gender, and race are negotiated and presented in this spectacularized mega-event. Similar nuance was featured in two collections (Bruce *et al.* 2010; Markula 2009) examining media coverage of female Olympic athletes. Featuring global comparisons, critical analyses moved beyond the tendencies for liberal feminisms and ideological constructions of male hegemony to oversimplify media symbolic annihilation, trivialization, and ambivalence in covering female athletes. By engaging intersectionality (gender, race, nationality) and post-structuralist readings, these collections, as well as Hundley and Billings (2010), broadened critical analysis of media, sport, and identities.

Two collections on fandom (Earnheardt *et al.* 2012; Hugenberg *et al.* 2008) assessed motives, identities, and engagement associated with traditional sports broadcasts and new media articulations (blogs, social media, gaming, fantasy sports). Still, studies in *Sport and Its Female Fans* (Toffoletti and Mewett 2012) showed how media constructions continue to 'other' female fans and reinforce female fanship of male sport as 'authentic'. Mirroring media presumptions, most women sports bloggers continued to see 'the privilege afforded men's sports as natural' (Hardin and Whiteside 2013: 164).

Interest in how digital and social media were changing the sport media equation quickened in Mediasport 4.0. Although television's 'second screens', Facebook, Twitter, fantasy sports engagement, and ubiquitous blogging clearly changed the *terroir* of sport media, the nature of that change and its meaningfulness in terms of media democratization are less clear. The potential for digital media to disrupt overarching tendencies for sport media to reinforce dominant cultural ideologies and maintain current power relations remains the subject of much debate (Hutchins and Rowe 2012, 2013).

New ways of communicating and experiencing sport became possible as fans and athletes became media-makers not under the control of legacy mediasport entities. For many, such as Sanderson (2011), the interactive communication dynamic of social media necessarily changed sport. Others are less sure and highlight the adaptability of old media and sport organizations in becoming co-developers (and co-owners) of the new digital mediaplex. Dart (2012) argued that such new media, anchored to old, will feature different articulations of 'old issues' that reproduce dominant cultural arrangements.

That three handbooks close Mediasport 4.0 is significant. Their appearance both marked the study of media and sport as central to socio-cultural understandings about sport across the academy and pointed to the rising importance of digital media in sporting cultures. Billings's (2011) *Sports Media*, the first volume in the Broadcast Education Association's electronic research series, marked the growing legitimacy among foundational and emerging scholars of new media research. Pedersen's (2013) *Handbook of Sport Communication*, the field's heftiest compilation to date, had twenty percent of its chapters focused on new media. Nearly as substantial, Billings and Hardin's (2014) *Handbook of Sport and New Media* focused entirely on the new digital mediasport environment. Framed by familiar issues of globalization, political economy, fandom, and the like, the volume's organizing triad of production, content, and reception, suggests that much new mediasport study will grow from established foundations.

Looking ahead

This chapter has presented a phylogenetic survey of research on sport and media. Mediasport 1.0 was marked by exploration as the field found its footing in key areas. Mediasport 2.0, marked by growing legitimacy within sport and media studies, featured a second generation of key scholars, diverse engagement with cultural studies and critical theory, and growing research programs on institutions and production, globalization and commodification, framing and identities, and reception. Mediasport 3.0 signaled the area's coming of age with key works by seasoned scholars bringing synthesis as the institutionalization of sport and media in the research community broadened. Mediasport 4.0 brought further evidence of the area's maturity as journals were launched, places were found in longstanding scholarly organizations, universities started academic programs and centers, and a scholarly society was established.

Much evidence confirms that mediated sport consumption is the source of abundant pleasure and significance for audiences which have the capacity to ignite resourcefulness and to reappropriate meaning, often in resistance to institutional narratives. But if one steps back and looks at what has driven mediasport research, it is clear that concerns over the tenor of agency in the face of the mediasport cultural complex are considerable. To many, the weight of findings about the sport-media nexus symbolize much about what is wrong with sport today: its globalization, corporatization, and commodification; its reliance on spectacle, mega-events, and celebrity; its tendencies to reinforce dominant cultural ideologies; and, its tendencies to essentialize and naturalize difference through characterizations of nation, race, gender, and other identities.

Given the firmness of such findings, it is difficult to see meaningful change ahead, even in the face of new and social media. McLuhan's (1964) basic lessons provide reminders that 'new', when it comes to media, is a relative term and that new media often draft old. Further, given arguments such as Bauman's (2007) about the limits of human agency in 'liquid modernity' and how understandings of power have been naturalized within the confines of the consumerist model, it seems more likely that the 'democratization' offered by new sports media may be enveloped by a larger 'consumerist syndrome' that has altered sensibilities about agency through a 'masturbatory sociality' focused on individual pleasure and instant gratifications.

Following Bauman (2007), the collective evidence concerning the sport-media nexus points to much 'collateral damage'. Mediasport is a powerful, influential, and ultimately conservative socio-cultural force. The plentiful pleasures that it brings in engagement often mask that this is the case. In today's corporatized and hypercommodified environment, the prospects for meaningful change are challenging. Yet, as Bauman notes concerning our increasing containment within naturalized consumerist logics, we have no choice but to try.

Thus, rather than stay the course and merely continue to pile on the rather consistent evidence that has been amassed about mediasport research's meta-concerns of 'money and power' and 'framing and identities', prioritizing other tactics seems essential. As Whannel (2013: 15) notes, like other specialist fields, mediasport risks 'developing an enclosed and inward mentality'. While there is much nuance to understanding the dynamics at play, the bottom line socio-cultural understandings concerning mediasport seem both stable and distressing. Thus, Whannel's (2013: 16) suggestion – to engage the 'wider purpose' of research 'to be heard and read' by 'working harder at becoming public intellectuals' – seems particularly apropos. Similarly, Rowe's (2014) bottom line assessment of why media studies and sport matters invokes Silverstone's (1999: 152) assessment that 'it's all about power', and thus reminds us that socio-cultural research on mediasport is inexorably embedded in politics and needs to be linked to policy. Moving forward in Mediasport 5.0, we will need more work such as Scherer and Rowe's (2013) recent project that connects understandings about sport media to policies that enable cultural citizenship.

References

Althusser, L. (1971/2001) *Lenin and Philosophy and Other Essays*, New York: Monthly Review Press; trans. Ben Brewster.

Anderson, B. (1983) *Imagined Communities*, London: Verso.

Andrews, D. L. (2006) *Sport-Commerce-Culture: Essays on Sport in Late Capitalist America*, New York: Peter Lang.

Andrews, D.L., and Jackson, S. (eds) (2001) *Sport Stars: The Politics of Sporting Celebrity*, London: Routledge.

Barnett, S. (1990) *Games and Sets: The Changing Face of Sport on Television*, London: BFI.

Bauman, Z. (2007) *Consuming Life*, Cambridge: Polity.

Bernstein, A., and Blain, N. (eds) (2003) *Sport, Media, Culture: Global and Local Dimensions*, London: Frank Cass.

Billings, A.C. (2004) 'Depicting the Quarterback in Black and White: A Content Analysis of College and Professional Football Broadcast Commentary', *The Howard Journal of Communications*, 15(4): 201–210.

—— (2008) *Olympic Media: Inside the Biggest Show on Television*, London: Routledge.

—— (ed) (2011) *Sports Media: Transformation, Integration, Consumption*, New York: Routledge.

Billings, A.C., Butterworth, M.L., and Turman, P.D. (2012) *Communication and Sport: Surveying the Field*, Thousand Oaks, CA: Sage.

Billings, A.C., and Hardin, M. (eds) (2014) *Routledge Handbook of Sport and New Media*, London: Routledge.

Birrell, S., and McDonald, M.G. (eds) (2000). *Reading Sport: Critical Essays on Power and Representation*, Boston, MA: Northeastern University Press.

Boyle, R. (2006) *Sports Journalism: Context and Issues*, London: Sage.

Boyle, R., and Haynes, R. (2000) *Power Play: Sport, the Media and Popular Culture*, London: Pearson.

Brookes, R. (2002) *Representing Sport*, London: Arnold.

Brown, R.S., and O'Rourke, D.J. (eds) (2003) *Case Studies in Sport Communication*, Westport, CT: Praeger.

Bruce, T. (2001) 'Second Sight: Experiencing Life through the Eyes of Women Sports Writers', in J. Hughson and C. Hallinan (eds) *Sporting Tales: Ethnographic Fieldwork Experiences*, Sydney: Australian Society for Sports History.

Bruce, T., Hovden, J., and Markula, P. (eds) (2010) *Sportswomen at the Olympics: A Global Comparison of Newspaper Coverage*, Rotterdam: Sense.

Bryant, J., Zillmann, D., and Raney, A. A. (1998) 'Violence and the Enjoyment of Media Sports', in L. A. Wenner (ed.) *Mediasport*, London: Routledge.

Buscombe, E. (ed.) (1975) *Football on Television*, London: BFI.

Cooky, C., Messner, M.A., and Hextrum, R.H. (2013) 'Women Play Sport, but Not on TV: A Longitudinal Study of Televised News Media', *Communication and Sport*, 1: 203–230.

Crawford, G. (2004) *Consuming Sport: Fans, Sport, and Culture*, London: Routledge.

Creedon, P.J. (ed.) (1994) *Women, Media and Sport: Challenging Gender Values*, Thousand Oaks, CA: Sage.

Daddario, G. (1998) *Women's Sport and Spectacle: Gendered Television Coverage and the Olympic Games*, Westport, CT: Praeger.

Dart, J. (2012) 'New Media, Professional Sport and Political Economy', *Journal of Sport and Social Issues*. doi: 10.1177/0193723512467356.

Davis, L.R. (1997) *The Swimsuit Issue: Hegemonic Masculinity and* Sports Illustrated, Albany: SUNY Press.

Davis, L.R., and Harris, O. (1998) 'Race and Ethnicity in U.S. Sports Media', in L.A. Wenner (ed.) *Mediasport*, London: Routledge.

Douglas, M. (1966) *Purity and Danger: An Analysis of the Concepts of Pollution and Taboo*. London: Routledge & Kegan Paul.

Duncan, M.C. (2006) 'Gender Warriors in Sport: Women and the Media', in A.A. Raney and J. Bryant (eds) *Handbook of Sports and Media*, Mahwah, NJ: Erlbaum.

Earnheardt, A.C., Haridakis P.M., and Hugenberg, B.S. (eds) (2012) *Sports Fans, Identity, and Socialization: Exploring the Fandemonium*, Lanham, MD: Lexington.

Ellul, J. (1964) *The Technological Society*, New York: Vintage.

Gantz, W. (1981) 'An Exploration of Viewing Motives and Behaviors Associated with Television Sports', *Journal of Broadcasting*, 25: 263–275.

Hardin, M. (2005) 'Stopped at the Gate: Women's Sports, "Reader Interest", and Decision-Making by Editors', *Journalism and Mass Communication Quarterly*, 82: 62–77.

Hardin, M. and Whiteside, E. (2013) 'How Do Women Talk Sports? Women Sports Fans in a Blog Community', in K. Toffoletti and P. Mewett (eds) *Sport and Its Female Fans*, New York: Routledge.

Horne, J. (2006) *Sport in Consumer Culture*, Houndsmills, UK: Palgrave Macmillan.

Hugenberg, L.W., Haridakis, P.M., and Earnheardt, A.C. (eds) (2008) *Sports Mania: Essays on Fandom and the Media in the 21st Century*, Jefferson, NC: McFarland.

Hundley, H.L., and Billings, A.C. (eds) (2010) *Examining Identity in Sports Media*, Thousand Oaks, CA: Sage.

Hutchins, B., and Rowe, D. (2012) *Sport Beyond Television: The Internet, Digital Media and the Rise of Networked Media Sport*, London: Routledge.

—— (eds) (2013) *Digital Media Sport: Technology, Power and Culture in the Network Society*, London: Routledge.

Jackson, R., and McPhail, T. (eds) (1989) *The Olympic Movement and the Mass Media: Past, Present and Future Issues*, Calgary: Hurford.

Jackson, S.J., and Andrews, D.L. (eds) (2005) *Sport, Culture and Advertising: Identities, Commodities and the Politics of Representation*, London: Routledge.

Johnson, W. (1969) 'TV Made It All a New Game', *Sports Illustrated*, 22 December, 86–102.

Kassing, J.W., Billings, A. C., Brwon, R. S., Halone, K. K., Harrison, K., and Krizek, B. (2004) 'Communication in the Community of Sport: The Process of Enacting, (Re)Producing, Consuming, and Organizing Sport', *Communication Yearbook*, 28: 373–410.

Kennedy, E., and Hills, L. (2009) *Sport, Media, and Society*, Oxford: Berg.

Lawrence, G., and Rowe, D. (1986) *Power Play: The Commercialization of Australian Sport*, Sydney: Hale and Iremonger.

Lowes, M.D. (1999) *Inside the Sports Pages: Work Routines, Professional Ideologies, and the Manufacture of Sports News*, Toronto: University of Toronto Press.

McKay, J., and Rowe, D. (1987) 'Ideology, the Media and Australian Sport', *Sociology of Sport Journal*, 4: 258–273.

McLuhan, M. (1964) *Understanding Media: The Extensions of Man*, New York: McGraw-Hill.

Markula, P. (ed) (2009) *Olympic Women and the Media*, Houndsmills, UK: Palgrave Macmillan.

Miller, T. (2001) *Sportsex*, Philadelphia, PA: Temple University Press.

Miller, T., Lawrence, G., McKay, J., and Rowe, D. (2001) *Globalization and Sport: Playing the World*, London: Sage.

Pedersen, P. (ed.) (2013) *Routledge Handbook of Sport Communication*, London: Routledge.

Raney, A.A. (2006) 'Why We Watch and Enjoy Mediated Sports', in A.A. Raney and J. Bryant (eds) *Handbook of Sports and Media*, Mahwah, NJ: Erlbaum.

Raney, A.A., and Bryant, J. (eds) (2006) *Handbook of Sports Media*, Mahwah, NJ: Erlbaum.

Real, M.R. (1975) 'The Superbowl: Mythic Spectacle', *Journal of Communication*, 25(1): 31–43.

Roche, M. (ed.) (1998) *Sport, Popular Culture, and Identity*, Aachen: Meyer and Meyer.

Rowe, D. (1999) *Sport, Culture, and the Media: The Unruly Trinity*, Buckingham, UK: Open University Press.

—— (ed.) (2004) *Critical Readings: Sport, Culture and the Media*, Maidenhead, UK: Open University Press.

—— (2011) *Global Media Sport: Flows, Forms and Futures*, London: Bloomsbury.

—— (2014) 'Media Studies and Sport', in J. Maguire (ed.) *Social Sciences in Sport*, Champaign, IL: Human Kinetics.

Sanderson, J. (2011) *It's a Whole New Ballgame: How Social Media Is Changing Sports*, New York: Hampton.

Sandvoss, C., Real, M., and Bernstein, A. (eds) (2012) *Bodies of Discourse: Sports Stars, Media, and the Global Public*, New York: Peter Lang.

Scherer, J., and Rowe, D. (eds) (2013) *Sport, Public Broadcasting, and Cultural Citizenship: Signal Lost?* London: Routledge.

Silk, M., Andrews, D.L., and Cole, C.L. (eds) (2005) *Sport and Corporate Nationalisms*, New York: Berg.

Silverstone, R. (1999) *Why Study the Media?* London: Sage.

Toffoletti, K., and Mewett, P. (eds) (2012) *Sport and Its Female Fans*, New York: Routledge.

Trujillo, N. (1994) *The Meaning of Nolan Ryan*, College Station: Texas A&M University Press.

Wann, D.L., Melnick, M.J., Russell, G.W., and Pease, D.G. (2001) *Sports Fans: The Psychology and Social Impact of Spectators*, New York: Routledge.

Wenner, L.A. (ed.) (1989) *Media, Sports, and Society*, Newbury Park, CA: Sage.

—— (1995) 'The Good, Bad, and the Ugly: Race, Sport and the Public Eye', *Journal of Sport and Social Issues*, 19: 227–231.

—— (ed.) (1998) *Mediasport*, London: Routledge.

—— (ed.) (2013a) *Fallen Sports Heroes, Media, and Celebrity Culture*, New York: Peter Lang.

—— (2013b) 'The Mediasport Interpellation: Gender, Fanship, and Consumer Culture', *Sociology of Sport Journal*, 30: 83–103.

—— (2013c) 'Reflections on Communication and Sport: On Reading Sport and Narrative Ethics', *Communication and Sport*, 1: 188–199.

Wenner, L.A., and Gantz, W. (1998) 'Watching Sports on Television: Audience Experience, Gender, Fanship, and Marriage', in L.A. Wenner (ed.) *Mediasport*, London: Routledge.

Wenner, L.A., and Jackson, S.J. (eds) (2009) *Sport, Beer, and Gender: Promotional Culture and Contemporary Social Life*, New York: Peter Lang.

Wernick, A. (1991) *Promotional Culture: Advertising, Ideology and Symbolic Expression*, London: Sage.

Whannel, G. (1983) *Blowing the Whistle: The Politics of Sport*, London: Pluto.

—— (1992) *Fields in Vision: Television Sport and Cultural Transformation*, London: Routledge.

—— (2002) *Media Sport Stars: Masculinities and Moralities*, London: Routledge.

—— (2008) *Culture, Politics, and Sport: Blowing the Whistle, Revisited*, London: Routledge.

—— (2013) 'Reflections on Communication and Sport: On Mediatization and Cultural Analysis', *Communication and Sport*, 1: 7–17.

39

SPORT AND NEW MEDIA

Matthew David and Peter Millward

The conception of 'new media' as digitally distributed communications belies a distinction between the 'new' digital media that arose through cable and satellite sports television, and the even newer 'new' media of Internet-based live-streaming. The former is associated with the intensified commercialization of sports 'fandom'; the latter has become associated with 'de-commodification', or at least a significant challenge to dominant forms of 'hyper-commodification'. Whilst Castells (2009) has attended to the rise of global network corporations tied to the first 'digital revolution', only recently has more attention been paid to the second 'digital revolution'.

This chapter synthesizes the small but growing body of research on new media and sport in four parts. First, we outline Castells's 'network society' theory, noting tensions between early non-network digital distribution and later network forms. Second, we detail the 'first digital revolution', which saw sports broadcasting via dedicated cable and satellite media give rise to a new global hyper-commercial industry. Third, we outline the 'second digital revolution', where fully distributed media networks create radical new affordances that challenge existing broadcast models of distribution that arose during the first digital revolution. Fourth, we show how these two digital revolutions now coexist: established digital broadcasters remain profitable, even whilst new commercial players struggle and non-commercial actors, such as those able to freely share live streams of events, proliferate. The network revolution builds upon, rather than simply abolishes, the products and processes of the 'industrial revolution': we should not be surprised that the two digital sports new media revolutions might coexist. Our analysis is significant because it illustrates how new media has contributed to the globalization of formerly domestic sporting competitions, and yet it affords the contradictory possibilities of hyper-commercial and de-commodified mediations.

The rise of the network society

The development of the Internet has proved central to advances in information and communication technologies (Castells 2001). The use and scope of 'new' media technologies grew as a result of the emergence of the Internet, and have afforded it further capabilities. Manuel Castells (1996/2000) argued that the 'network society' developed as global economic restructiving of society – such as the fall of Soviet 'state socialism' – allowed people and organizations across the world to connect, and these connections were mediated by technological innovations in communication. Rapid accelerations of such innovations and, specifically, the growing use of the Internet gave rise to an intensification of globally connected practices. Subsequently, the capitalist 'mode of production' fundamentally changed from the primacy of industrial innovation (around energy and physical force/manipulation) towards the primacy (in business innovation) of information storage, manipulation and distribution.

Castells saw the emerging society as consisting of networks of people and organizations (which he refers to as 'nodes') connected by digital links. In this network, 'capital' can flow between globally dispersed 'nodes' in what he called 'a space of flows', and in instantaneous 'timeless time' (2000). Castells (1996/2000) argued that digital networks are now the primary form of social organization across the globe and that this made previously established and unquestioned national boundaries – and state regulations – increasingly porous or 'lighter'. At this stage of his analysis, these key actors were primarily seen as firms, states and other 'corporate' actors. 'Mass self-communication' – the rise of billions of individual citizen 'broadcasters' who are networked to each other across the world, such as through social media (Castells 2009: 63–71) – was discussed in his later work.

For Castells, in the 'network society', actors bound by national cultures and state laws are out-performed by those who are able to exploit advantages and evade inhibitions – wherever encountered. Castells (1996/2000) referred to this change as 'capitalist perestroika', arguing that the efficiency of network organizations is dependent upon their abilities to integrate useful nodes into their 'space of flows' and bypass any 'places' that obstruct transnational organizational goals. Thus, networks and nodal actors in the space of flows are stronger than those that are territorially bound. 'Capital' is key to his discussion, and is largely synonymous with power. Following Bourdieu (1986), he saw 'capital' as material and symbolic, encompassing the economic (i.e. money, property), cultural (education, 'taste') and social (i.e. trust, personal connections), but added to this discussion by defining 'informational' forms (Castells 1996/2000). Knowledge and information are power and likely to be able to be quickly transported across the space of flows. The mobility of informational capital in the network society marks it as dynamic, and this might drive transformations of material capital and 'traditional' symbolic forms of status and valuation.

Castells's (1996/2000) suggestion that the new technologies empowering the space of flows in the network society have generated 'timeless time', or the globally simultaneous 'now', has a particular significance for the emergence of globally networked sports media. Where the first digital revolution afforded the rise of a new global and hyper-commercial sport media industry through the availability of live sport through digital television, the second creates the possibility of global free-sharing of mediated sports coverage such as through online peer-to-peer sharing of live sport through Internet platforms. Hutchins and Rowe (2012) point out that the new commercial applications of Internet and mobile media have not replaced television as the primary screen through which mediated sport is viewed. However, the second digital revolution does offer a threat to the commercial foundations that currently govern global corporate pay-per-view and subscription digital television. The fact that people continue to watch sport on television screens raises interesting questions about how elite – and globalized – sports leagues – such as the (English) F.A. Premier League (or EPL; see Millward 2011) – might be positioned in a 'networked' new media-supported transnational society.

To explore these issues, we outline two digital revolutions: first, the digital revolution that saw the rise of global hyper-commercial digitally mediated sports leagues; and second, global sport in the age of a networked revolution that affords global sharing of digital products (see David 2010). We take the EPL, 'the global football league', as the key illustration in each case, but show how it highlights general, but not universal, tendencies.

The first digital revolution: the global hyper-commercialization and new mediatization of elite sport

The EPL has been described as 'transnational' on account of its increasing number of overseas players, managers and coaches in the post-Bosman era (Millward 2013). For Castells (1996/2000), key agents in the network society will occupy the most lucrative space, which is increasingly global. The EPL sells broadcast rights in 211 countries, generating rapidly rising revenues, with £178m for the three years from 2001, £325m for 2004/5–2006/7 seasons, 2007/8–2009/10 seasons at £625m (Wilson 2007) and 2010/11–2013 seasons at £1.437bn (Harris 2013). The 2013/14 to 2015/16 seasons renewal saw a 55 per cent increase in value to £2.23bn (Harris 2013). Domestically, this revolution in digital broadcasting also changed the landscape for elite English clubs. In 1988 the British Satellite Broadcasting company (BSB) challenged the then-analogue broadcasters BBC and ITV's rights to screen games, and although they did not succeed in securing matches, the fee rose from £3.1m to £11m per season, of which 75 per cent was retained by clubs in the top division. With English football's restructuring into the F.A. Premiership in 1992, later rebranded as the F.A. Premier League, the first five-year broadcast contract was won by BSkyB (a merger of Sky TV and BSB) for a reported £304m, rising to £670m for the three years from 1997, whilst 2009's three-year domestic broadcast renewal was worth £1.782bn. The 2013/14–2015/16 deal was worth £3.018bn (*The Guardian* 2012).

BSkyB is both principal broadcaster of EPL games and its 'marketing partner'. Broadcasting contracts have encouraged football fans to take up subscription offers (Boyle and Haynes 2004) but, in return, BSkyB's advertising of the EPL has opened up new markets for the league to attract new supporters. The co-development of global broadcasters and global leagues in an era of digitization is also found in other sports (Hutchins and Rowe 2012: 13, 177). The National Football League (NFL in American football) generates over US$4bn each year from its global digital broadcasting rights sales, with the Super Bowl XLVI (2012) drawing in a global television audience of 166.8 million people through NBC's coverage of the game (Florio 2012). Meanwhile, the Indian Premier League (IPL in cricket) broadcast to audiences of 145 million in its country of domicile (Majumdar 2011, cited in Hutchins and Rowe 2012: 23), but drew in digital viewers from across the world – specifically in Europe, Australia, North America and the Middle East (*Sport on the Box* 2012).

Evens and Lefever (2013) outline the contradiction at the heart of the digitally afforded revolution in Belgian football coverage, a migration from free terrestrial broadcasting to pay-per-view/subscription-based digital coverage. There is now more 'choice' in terms of channels and events being broadcast, but for those who cannot afford to pay, there is less choice. Whilst prices vary, one transnational commonality has been that when sports rights migrate from free-to-air terrestrial providers to global commercial digital providers, the audience is required to pay more. Higher 'subscription' prices for consumers are the outcome of the first digital revolution. Just as there are tensions over how revenues are distributed amongst sporting actors (sports, leagues, clubs, players, etc.), there is now competition emerging between new media platforms. The Internet might be a commercial challenger to digital (satellite or cable) television. However, Goldsmith (2013) points out that whilst Internet rights to distribute Australian Football League coverage raised AU$153m for the 2012–2016 period, the television rights were sold for over AU$1bn, a ratio of over six to one. Goldsmith observes that television remains the dominant medium, but that it is evolving within an increasingly integrated digital environment. The Internet is not replacing television; rather, it offers to reinvent the relationship between fans and television. As television becomes exclusively digitized, its distinctiveness from other digital media declines: it becomes the digital hub around which circulate other digital media such as computers, tablets, games consoles and even mobile telephones. This confluence of hardware and the integration of computing functions within devices (the fusion of telephone, email, web, apps, services, etc.), is key to the logic of the network society, what Castells (1996/2000: 62) calls the most powerful dimension of the informational mode of development: 'the growing convergence of specific technologies into a highly integrated system'. Digital broadcasters have responded to the advent of second-stage new media by launching Internet platforms. For instance, Sky Go is a subscription-based online television service offered by BSkyB that allows users to watch live and on-demand content on computers, smart phones and computer game consoles through an Internet connection. The first digital revolution continues to transform the practice of 'watching' sport (from the stadium to the television, and now synchronized with screens), but what defines this revolution remains the extent to which the viewer's access remains doubly mediated, both digitally and financially. The integration of digital television broadcasting with the Internet may forward or challenge this dynamic of global hyper-commercialization.

The second digital revolution: global sharing and streaming

Widespread free-sharing of music over the Internet predates online sharing of live sport. Yet, music (and later film) file-sharing was based on technical developments that emerged from research into the more efficient distribution of digital television images. During the 1980s, Moving Picture Expert Group (MPEG) research into compressing visual data aimed to enable digital distribution of live television (Musmann 2006; David 2010). Still, even when compressed, such data was so large as to require dedicated cable or satellite channels, and could not be sent via ordinary Internet cables. The initial driver for compression was relatively cheap (hence profitable) digital television, for which sports broadcasting was the spearhead. These compression formats enabled the launch of Sky Sports in 1992. The MP3 (audio layer III) version of the MPEG compression format came later. MP3 was first released in 1993. It was used for global distribution of recording, producing, mastering and manufacturing functions within record companies and underwent various revisions until 1998. As such, MP3 was initially developed as part of the first (commercial) digital revolution. However, in 1999, Sean Fanning's Napster software combined MP3 compression with an Internet file search programme to initiate the second digital revolution – free online sharing (David 2010).

The second digital revolution in music saw each new form of free sharing become the target of legal sanction (David and Kirkhope 2006). Ongoing developments in technical capacity and legal evasion laid the foundations for what became the second digital revolution in sport a decade after Napster. When Napster's central server was successfully targeted for 'contributory infringement', new 'peer to peer' (P2P) software emerged that did not require a central server to facilitate exchanges between peers. Unmediated peer sharing enabled free circulation by removing intermediaries that could be easily targeted and closed down. Uploaders (those whose files are copied by downloaders) were then targeted. This encouraged torrent-based 'peers to peer' (Ps2P) software that allows downloaders to make copies from a torrent of uploads. A downloader cobbles one copy from a multitude (the torrent) of uploader files. Torrents make individual uploader identification impossible. Prosecutors turned to torrent trackers such as the Pirate Bay. Trackers do not host content but enable downloaders to locate torrents. Targeting trackers saw the physical relocation and virtual distribution of their servers. It also encouraged 'live-streaming'. Live-streaming is where digital content (such as a sporting event) broadcast commercially by one provider is re-routed via a streaming channel. Any number of viewers may watch the stream without going to the original (commercial) broadcaster. Viewers watching but not making a copy cannot be prosecuted. Those re-routing content are hard to target as they are rarely in the same country as the broadcaster. Streaming channels evade liability if they agree to investigate and act upon reported IP infringements. This takes time, and with new streams popping up all the time, such 'takedowns' are relatively ineffectual. The movement towards streaming has had monumental consequences for the distribution of television, and in particular live sport.

MP3 compression relies on the 'filling in' done by the brain when listening to sound. MP3 audio files can therefore be radically shrunk. This enabled fast uploading and downloading, even with the kinds of bandwidth most domestic Internet users had at the turn of the millennium. Live visual content required far more bandwidth than domestic Internet users had until very recently. Higher bandwidths were available from commercial broadcasters (via cable and satellite). Such compression of visual content that could be achieved made this initial technical monopoly (providing what could not be provided via the Internet) both possible and profitable. Live broadcasting of digital content required that such content could be downloaded at the same speed as it was being performed. Whilst downloaders could wait for a large film file to download before watching it, live-sports broadcasters relied upon the faster bandwidth available via satellite and cable television channels to ensure they could offer higher-quality live images than could be viewed over the Internet. The claim that 'you cannot see the ball' (something said of the first live television sports broadcasts in the 1930s – see Barnett 1990) was true in the early days of live sports Internet streaming, but this is no longer the case. For these reasons the second ('free') digital revolution in sport began to be felt only in 2009 (see Birmingham and David 2011), ten years after it had begun in music with Napster in 1999 (see David 2010).

A decade of legal-technical challenges by music companies against music sharing led music sharers to arrive at technology that allowed torrents and streaming. These new technical systems, and improvements in Internet bandwidth (allowing for faster connections), mean that Internet users can now stream free live sport broadcasting at a high level of quality, which is comparable in quality to the images that are provided by commercial digital service providers. Sports leagues and commercial broadcasters making live coverage digitally available across the world enable the possibility that such content can be rerouted back across a networked world via streaming channels. Such streams may be free of charge to view. The easy and free availability of its matches became apparent to the English Premier League in 2009, and its chief executive, Richard Scudamore (2009), came to view live-streaming as 'a very real threat' to the commercial attractiveness of the huge broadcasting rights deals that had become central to EPL finances. Indeed, the EPL came to view live-streaming as 'theft', even if legal systems across the world do not always support this position. Indeed, in the UK, as long as services that provide streaming channels agree to look into and take down channels found to be streaming copyright-infringing content, the channel itself cannot be held liable for the content its users choose to stream (Birmingham and David 2011). The speed with which rights holders can scan and contact streaming-channel providers has increased, so that some streams are now taken down during the sports event. However, jurisdictional differences, the speed of legal action relative to event duration, and the vast numbers of alternative streams that are available (especially for the most popular sport events), all mean that it is impossible to prevent fans from accessing high-quality streams free of charge.

Live streaming requires high bandwidth and greater data compression but this has become less of a technical problem over time, posing commercial problems for those seeking to prevent this practice. In the very years when file-sharing was rising and sales of recorded music were in sharp decline, the commercial value of digital sports broadcasting was growing in all significant markets (Hutchins and Rowe 2012). Yet, the suggestion that sports fans (whose loyalty to a 'club' might be seen as binding) will continue to pay for digital access is not as clear as it once appeared to be (Birmingham and David 2011; David and Millward 2012; Kirton and David 2013).

We have previously explored the ways in which established broadcasters have sought to portray live streaming in negative ways, with reference to 'bad quality' and 'sad consumers' (David and Millward 2012). First, EPL chief spokesman Dan Johnson told BBC News (2011) viewers that 'what they [the fans] care about is the quality; and they care about the quality of the broadcast so a broadcast you know, where the broadcasters invest very heavily in production – like the BBC, like [B]Sky[B] – they produce a quality product and people will choose it on that basis'. Johnson's comment followed a European Court of Justice recommendation that the 'parallel importing' of broadcasts within Europe should be allowed – in effect, permitting the live-streaming of football. While some live streams are lower in quality than televised broadcasts, time and technological advancements have seen exponential improvements with NetResult conceding that there are now 'good quality streams' available (Christopher Stokes, quoted in Smith 2009). Second, on the 'sad consumers' of live streaming, as part of its 'Internet football piracy' alert, BBC News framed the typical live-stream viewer as someone watching matches alone in their bedroom. Whilst 'going to the match' is the pinnacle of both commitment and sociability for many (Millward 2011), most non-attending fans also understand the appeal of watching football to be its social nature. BBC News' portrayal of live-stream viewers stands in clear contrast to this: whilst many fans watch matches at home, the isolated individual frame stands in stark contrast to the broadcasters' own presentation of television football viewing as a communal activity (whether at home with family/friends or in public places). Watching matches on a relatively small computer screen limits scope for watching with others, and hence the 'sad' frame may hold some continued resonance with audiences. However, as digital television and PC/computer converge, the 'private small screen/public big screen' distinction will fall away, thus it will be interesting to monitor the continuing relevance of the 'sad consumer' frame in future.

Widening the net beyond the confines of association football, Hutchins and Rowe (2012: 17) argue that whilst sports with more limited global geographical appeal will have less scope to generate large revenues from globalized commercial digital rights deals, such sports will also suffer less threat to such revenues from unauthorized 'piracy'. Rather, they argue that those sports and leagues that have gained a global reach in the age of digital broadcasting will also be those that suffer the greatest risk of loss from unlicensed streaming and file sharing. However, as Hutchins and Rowe also suggest, this situation also challenges commercial stakeholders which have invested in other increasingly global sports distribution deals, such as Formula One motor racing, Italian and South American association football and Indian and Australian cricket. It is ironic, then, that one of the earliest cases of legal action against a live-streaming channel was the failed attempt by the Australian FoxSport to pre-emptively bar the US site Channelsurfing.net from streaming the 2007 A-League Australian Football Cup Final, an event FoxSport had bought the exclusive rights to broadcast (Hutchins and Rowe 2012: 37). Despite the free streaming of the event being advertised five days in advance of the broadcast, FoxSport could not get a 'cease and desist' order enforced on a foreign-based company in time. Hutchins and Rowe highlight similar actions against streaming channels for infringement in relation to Ultimate Fighting Championship coverage, elite level American football, basketball and baseball leagues, as well as the Australian Tennis Association. As is the case in the EPL's attempts to close down streaming channels, success in closing channels and even blocking hosting sites have all been circumvented by various factors, notably the time delays involved in issuing, checking and enacting 'cease and desist' orders, jurisdictional differences and the many diverse sites that are streaming these events (Birmingham and David 2011, David 2011, David and Millward 2012). The International Olympic Committee claimed a degree of 'success' in identifying (and closing) over four thousand unauthorized streaming channels across the world during the course of the

2008 Beijing Olympiad (Hutchins and Rowe 2012: 38). However, we cannot easily measure the 'success' of these interventions relative to how long it took for such channels to be blocked in each case, and just how many alternatives were available at any particular time. For London 2012, the organizing committee set out restrictions for athletes and spectators on what they could and could not do with their mobile phones (Goggin 2013: 31–32), attempting to protect highly valuable and complex digital rights that had been negotiated and paid for by various broadcasters and advertisers across the world. The prohibitions issued were both an indication of the significance of digital rights to the modern Olympics, and evidence of the threat posed by unauthorized digital coverage. Whilst five days was not enough to enact a 'cease and desist' order in 2007, time scales have shrunk radically since then, with many streaming channel providers now taking only hours or less to close down channels found to be streaming copyrighted content. However, in the 'space of flows', all blocked nodes are bypassed, and in the age of 'timeless time', new streams emerge faster than it takes for older ones to be closed down (cf. Castells 2000, 2009).

The current state of affairs

In music, the commercial release of the compact disc in 1982 saw a golden age in recorded sales, but this came to an abrupt end in 1999, after which recorded music sales started to crumble (Sandell 2007). A decade after the CD, 1992 saw the birth of the EPL and its 'marketing relationship' with BSkyB's Sky Sports, a first digital revolution in sports broadcasting that saw a parallel golden age in revenue generation. In a similar fashion, one decade after Napster, 2009 witnessed a 'signal' event in relation to this golden age of commercial digitalization that may come to be seen as sport's 'Napster Moment' as Setanta UK – one of the UK's broadcasters of a multitude of elite sports, including the EPL – applied for bankruptcy, having failed to generate the subscription revenues it had anticipated, and on which it had based its bidding rights. Setanta UK's failure to generate sufficient subscription revenues flowed from a combination of only having a limited number of EPL matches in the bundle of rights it had secured (fewer than its rival BSkyB), and a general failure to realize the levels of digital television subscription that analysts had been predicting, and which bids reflected. Giulianotti and Robertson (2009) note that 'expert' analysis had predicted that 80 per cent of UK households would have taken up a satellite television subscription by the early years of the millennium, but in reality the figure was just under half that. Whilst digital television subscription rates have risen, such increases were not as great as had been expected, leaving Setanta UK insufficient funds to pay for the rights. Setanta UK was very quickly replaced by ESPN, which soon found it could not prosper and withdrew from the next round of rights bidding, being replaced by British Telecom (hereon BT). Setanta UK's collapse and the subsequent withdrawal of ESPN was not a death blow to global commercial digital sports broadcasting. The availability of free alternatives simply meant that new commercial providers have been unable to gain a sufficient foothold to establish themselves relative to the one dominant and formerly fully monopolistic provider (BSkyB). At the time, many saw new media free streaming as an alternative to subscription payment as a direct and significant threat to digital sport's fundamental business model (David 2011; Birmingham and David 2011). This has, to date, not proved to be the case. The EPL's £3.018bn domestic rights deal for 2013/14–2015/16 seasons with BSkyB and BT certainly suggests that even if a second (free) digital revolution is underway, the first (hyper-commercial) digital revolution remains active in its attempt to fend off new media rivals.

In July 2013 the EPL won a court order that forced UK Internet providers to block the popular live-stream hosting website FirstRow1.eu – operating from Sweden – on the grounds that the site systematically encourages copyright-infringing streaming (Lee 2013). This move follows multiple site blocks that mimic earlier and failed attempts to quash file-sharing by the music industry (see David 2010). This may not have resulted in a reduction of live streaming, as streams still exist on other channels. Whilst unable to block alternatives, legal rights holders are also seeking their own alternative channels – BT, for example, have set up a new channel called BT Sport to broadcast matches. Indeed, it followed up its purchase of EPL rights with those to screen rugby union's Premiership for four seasons from 2013/14 season, paying £152m (Rees 2012). Just as the EPL and BSkyB had acted as marketing partners from the 1992/93 season (see Millward 2011), so BT hope that sport can help to build its market share in the provision of Internet broadband. BT Sport is given free to view on televisions and/or computers for customers who subscribe to the mother company's broadband. As such, those who have paid BT for the Internet access that would allow them to live stream can now legally watch those matches whose broadcast rights are owned by the company.

However, a little over two months after BT Sport launched, Martin (2013) claimed that there were concerns amongst investors that the company had overestimated the size of the market for its sports television channels and had seen its share price fall: less than 30 per cent of BT customers were using the channel and it had failed to make serious further inroads into the broadband market. BT responded by purchasing exclusive rights to UEFA Champions League matches in the UK for three seasons beginning in 2015/16 and paying £897m. BT invested heavily seeking to gain enough content to make their new channels attractive enough to grow their audience share. However, unlike BSkyB, which grew its market share with a monopoly over both rights and the delivery infrastructure, BT, like Setanta UK and ESPN before, have to contend with both a dominant existing commercial rival, and an array of free new-media-facilitated alternatives. BT is caught between free alternatives that limit its scope to grow the market and subscription-based digital channels like Sky Sports. In this case, we might argue that Castells's (1996/2000: 18–22) informational 'capitalist perestroika' – which points to a transition to network capitalism – is partially demonstrated. Commercial success in sports media remains bound to non-networked digital distribution (dedicated cable and satellite) and legal monopolies. The networked 'mode of development' has not been subordinated to the prevailing (capitalist) 'mode of production', even whilst new technical affordances have not 'overthrown' the dominant (non-network-based) economic regime. Castells's non-reductive account of relations between modes of technical development and modes of production is essential to grasp contemporary (new) media dynamics. However, his attention to how far capitalism has reinvented itself in recent years (relative to the failure of the Soviet Union to adapt to network affordances – Castells 1998: 55–58), perhaps underestimates the extent to which capitalism remains dependent upon forms of 'control' that the network mode of development does not support and may in fact challenge.

Conclusions

The term 'new media' has been used to refer to the rise of global digital satellite and cable-enabled broadcasting of sport (Boyle and Haynes 2004). The term 'new media' has also been used to refer to the rise of global digital networked alternatives to 'traditional' television broadcasts of sport (Hutchins and Rowe 2012). This chapter has highlighted and sought to move beyond this conceptual slippage. The global digital transformation of elite sports and sports media since the 1990s coincides with what Castells describes as the transition to the network society. However, while his work in the 1990s focused upon networked computing, his recent work (2009) explores 'global multimedia networks', such as businesses that fuse broadcast media and Internet services. It needs to be recalled, however, that the rise of global digital media companies in the 1990s – those that hyper-commercialized sport's broadcasting and who used sports rights ownership to drive their recruitment of paying customers – did not use 'networked' (Internet) distribution, but rather direct and one-directional digital vehicles (in other words, non-Internet cables, aerials and satellites). Until very recently, domestic Internet channels could not support the transmission of live visual data of any quality and scale. The first digital sports media revolution, whilst it was digital, was not fully networked. The combination of legal broadcast rights and full control over the distribution infrastructure (the cables and satellites) created a market and technical monopoly for early digital players like BSkyB. What Castells called 'capitalist perestroika' was not as 'networked' as the blanket term 'digital revolution' might imply. Vertical control remained in both ownership and architecture. The first digital revolution remained something beamed from above. The advent of greater compression and faster Internet broadband speed has afforded streaming channels that have opened up a second digital revolution in sports media, one that is both digital and fully networked in the sense of its horizontal and distributed infrastructure. Nonetheless, this revolution from below has not led to the 'sky' falling in for the hyper-commercialized model of sports broadcasting, even as the less entrenched commercial players in the digital sports broadcasting market have struggled (and often failed) to adapt, control and/or engage with the more open affordances of digital networks.

If the term 'new media revolution' implies one order replacing another, then the term may be misleading. The rise of networked digital sharing may have created an alternative space within the network society, but it does not appear to actually threaten to remove the 'dominant' commercial order. Those at the margins have found alternatives to paying. However, this may not bring down the 'centre' but entrench those that have already come to occupy the most profitable positions. Caught between dominant players with large subscription bases (and hence pockets with which to bid for rights renewals) and non-dominant actors who increasingly choose free alternatives, the scope for new commercial players to enter and prosper is very limited. 'New media' afford multiple possibilities in both the strengthening and weakening of commercial forces in sports broadcasting.

References

Barnett, S. (1990) *Games and Sets: The Changing Face of Sport on Television*, London: British Film Institute.

BBC News (2011) 'Premier League TV Football Choice "Upheld" by EU Advice', 3 February. Available at: www.bbc.co.uk/news/business-12355022 (accessed on 5 June 2011).

Birmingham, J. and David, M. (2011) 'Live-Streaming: Will Football Fans Continue to Be More Law Abiding Than Music Fans?' *Sport in Society*, 14(1): 69–81.

Bourdieu, P. (1986) 'The Forms of Capital', in J.E. Richardson (ed.) *Handbook of Theory of Research for the Sociology of Education*, London: Greenwood.

Boyle, R. and Haynes, R. (2004) *Football in the New Media Age*, London: Routledge.

Castells, M. (1996/2000) *The Rise of the Network Society*, Oxford: Blackwell.

Castells, M. (1998) *End of Millennium*, Oxford: Blackwell.

Castells, M. (2000) 'Materials for an Exploratory Theory of the Network Society', *British Journal of Sociology*, 51(1): 5–24.

Castells, M. (2001) *The Internet Galaxy*, Oxford: Oxford University Press.

Castells, M. (2009) *Communication Power*, Oxford: Oxford University Press.

David, M. (2010) *Peer to Peer and the Music Industry: The Criminalisation of Sharing*, London: Sage.

David, M. (2011) 'Music Lessons: Football Finance and Live Streaming', *Journal of Policy Research in Tourism, Leisure and Events*, 3(1): 95–98.

David, M. and Kirkhope, J. (2006) 'The Impossibility of Technical Security: Intellectual Property and the Paradox of Informational Capitalism', in M. Lacy and P. Wilkin (eds), *Global Politics in an Information Age*, Manchester: Manchester University Press.

David, M. and Millward, P. (2012) 'Football's Coming Home? Digital Reterritorialization, Contradictions in the Transnational Coverage of Sport and the Sociology of Alternative Football Broadcasts', *British Journal of Sociology*, 63(2): 349–369.

Evens, T. and Lefever, K. (2013) 'The Struggle for Platform Leadership in the European Sports Broadcasting Market', in B. Hutchins and D. Rowe (eds) (2013) *Digital Media Sport: Technology, Power and Culture in the Network Society*, New York: Routledge.

Florio, M. (2012) 'Super Bowl Draws Record Total Audience of 166.8 Million', *NBC Sports*, 6 February. Available at: http://profootballtalk.nbcsports.com/2012/02/06/super-bowl-draws-record-total-audience-of-1668-million/ (accessed on 7 November 2013).

Giulianotti, R. and Robertson, R. (2009) *Globalization and Football*, London: Sage.

Goggin, G. (2013) 'Sport and the Rise of Mobile Media', in B. Hutchins and D. Rowe (eds) (2013) *Digital Media Sport: Technology, Power and Culture in the Network Society*, New York: Routledge.

Goldsmith, B. (2013) '"SporTV": The Legacies and Power of Television', in B. Hutchins and D. Rowe (eds) (2013) *Digital Media Sport: Technology, Power and Culture in the Network Society*, New York: Routledge.

The Guardian (2012) 'Premier League Sells Domestic TV Rights to Sky and BT for £3.018bn', 13 June. Available at: www.theguardian.com/football/2012/jun/13/premier-league-tv-sky-bt (accessed on 10 November 2013).

Harris, N. (2013) 'REVEALED: Asia Driving Boom as Premier League Foreign TV Cash Hits £2.23bn', *Sporting Intelligence*, 9 September. Available at: www.sportingintelligence.com/2013/09/16/revealed-asia-driving-boom-as-premier-league-foreign-tv-cash-hits-2-23bn-160901/ (accessed 7 November 2013).

Hutchins, B. and Rowe, D. (2012) *Sport Beyond Television: The Internet, Digital Media and the Rise of Networked Media Sport*. New York: Routledge.

Kirton, A. and David, M. (2013) 'The Challenge of Unauthorised Online Streaming to the English Premier League and Television Broadcasters', in B. Hutchins and D. Rowe (eds) (2013) *Digital Media Sport: Technology, Power and Culture in the Network Society*, New York: Routledge.

Lee, D. (2013) 'Premier League Wins Piracy Block of First Row Sports', *BBC Online*. Available at: http://www.bbc.co.uk/news/technology-23342349 (accessed on 7 November 2013).

Majumdar, B. (2011) 'The Indian Premier League and World Cricket', in A. Bateman and J. Hill (eds) (2013) *The Cambridge Companion to Cricket*, Cambridge: Cambridge University Press.

Martin, B. (2013) 'BT Slips on Sports Channel Worries', *The Telegraph*, 23 October. Available at: http://www.telegraph.co.uk/finance/markets/marketreport/10400527/BT-slips-on-sports-channel-worries.html (accessed on 7 November 2013).

Millward, P. (2011) *The Global Football League*, Basingstoke, UK: Palgrave.

Millward, P. (2013) 'Spatial Mobilities, Football Players and the World Cup: Evidence from the English Premier League', *Soccer and Society* 14(1): 20–34.

Musmann, H.G. (2006) 'Genesis of the MP3 Audio Coding Standard', *Consumer Electronics, IEEE Transactions*, 52(3):1043–1049.

Rees, P. (2012) 'BT Signs Exclusive Deal to Broadcast Premiership Rugby from 2013', *The Guardian*, 12 September. Available at: http://www.theguardian.com/sport/2012/sep/12/premiership-rugby-bt-deal-broadcast, (accessed on 7 November 2013).

Sandall, R. (2007) 'Off the Record', *Prospect Magazine*, 137 August. Available at: http://www.prospect-magazine.co.uk/pdfarticle.php?id=9735 (accessed 26 March 2015).

Scudamore, R. (2009) 'Call It by Its Name – This Is Theft', *The Guardian*, 23 November.

Smith, P. (2009) 'Interview: NetResult CEO Christopher Stokes on Tackling Football TV Pirates'. Available at: http://paidcontent.co.uk/article/419-interview-netresult-ceo-christopher-stokes-on-tackling-football-tv-pira/ (accessed on 10 June 2011).

Sport on the Box (2012) 'CRICKET: ITV Secures New Four-Year IPL Deal', 30 March. Available at: http://sport-onthebox.com/2011/03/30/itv-secures-new-four-year-ipl-deal/ (accessed on 7 November 2013).

Wilson, J. (2007) 'Premier League Is World's Favourite League', *The Telegraph*, 6 November.

40

SPORT AND THE NATION IN THE GLOBAL AGE[1]

Frank J. Lechner

The opening ceremony of the 2012 Olympic Summer Games in London offered a global television audience an unusual sight. It reminded viewers of British contributions to world culture, like iconic children's literature and the invention of the World Wide Web, and showed James Bond escorting Queen Elizabeth to a helicopter for a jump into the stadium. More surprising to foreign eyes, the spectacle also featured dancing doctors and nurses who represented the National Health Service, apparently a major point of pride for modern Britain in producer Danny Boyle's vision. The gesture may have been unique – and therefore worked as a proper postmodern claim to national distinction – but in using the global media stage to make their national point, the London organizers followed a venerable tradition. That tradition goes back at least to the controversial 1936 Berlin Olympiad, used by the Nazi regime to bolster its reputation in spite of its own reservations about universal sport and the star turn by Jesse Owens that called myths of Aryan superiority into question (Guttmann 2006). At the 2000 games in Sydney, to take a more recent example, Australian organizers offered the world a version of harmony and peace, telling an uplifting story of national reconciliation in the form of an enacted dream sequence that combined aboriginal, white settler, and new immigrant symbolism (D'Agati 2011: 156–57). In 2008 China presented itself with characteristic communist understatement at the Beijing Games, using 'traditional' drummers, characters, and fireworks in a large-scale, tightly scripted ceremony, produced by filmmaker Zhang Yimou, to display both its traditional 'Brilliant Civilisation' and the new 'Glorious Era' (Chen *et al.* 2012). Staging the Olympics enabled those and other nations to 'inflect these standard rituals with nationally specific meanings' (Hogan 2003: 106), positioning 'the nation as a player on the global stage' by turning tradition and history into a 'local, arrogated version of the [universal] ideal' (Tomlinson 1996: 600). Of course, step one in such national self-assertion before a global audience is getting the right to host. The International Olympic Committee has effectively exploited such national needs to its financial advantage.

International sport competition provides other national benefits as well. If few countries go to the expensive trouble of hosting the Olympic Games or the men's football (soccer) World Cup, the experience of participation pays off for many more. In a very modest way, small country teams earn a moment of global recognition as a handful of athletes marches into an Olympic stadium along with delegations from major powers, the parade itself obviously marking the importance of national attachments even at a site where 'Olympism' is supposed to reign. For purposes of national identification, sporting success matters more – for example, great swimmers and track champion Cathy Freeman for Australia in 2000, great divers, gymnasts, and table tennis players for China in 2008, and tennis player Andy Murray first at the 2012 London Olympiad and then at Wimbledon the following year. National team victories in major sport typically generate even more excitement, creating shared public memories that become part of a national conversation. Canadian hockey fans, that is most Canadians alive at the time, remember the day in September 1972 when Paul Henderson scored the winning goal at the end of the decisive game in the Challenge (or Summit) Series between Canada and the Soviet Union (Hayes 2001). Americans, more fickle hockey fans, enjoyed a similar moment of collective ecstasy when a rag-tag team of young players defeated the Soviets' Red Machine in the 1980 Winter Games, soon memorialized as the 'Miracle on Ice'. England's victory over Germany in the 1966 World Cup final, televised live for the first time, commanded an audience of about half the UK population and set off national celebrations, perhaps more impressive in nostalgic hindsight (Mason 2006). Those festivities were still low-key by comparison with the unprecedented national joy and 'love of Orange' in the Netherlands after the unexpected Dutch victory over Germany in the 1988 European football championships semi-final (Kok 2008). In sport, if not in politics, Germany has helped to boost other countries' national identities. Endlessly discussed, now constantly available via the Internet, such defining moments in national sport histories connect generations of fans. Real images of real performance give content to nations as imagined communities.

Not all international competition bolsters national identities. For example, by contrast with the opening ceremony at the 1984 Los Angeles games, which had been drenched in Americana and Hollywood glitz, the centennial Olympiad in Atlanta in 1996 focused more on region than nation, celebrating the 'new South' in music and a story sequence – complete with thirty chrome trucks, supposed icon of the area – followed two weeks later by a closing event conducted partly in New Orleans funeral style (D'Agati 2011: 166–67). The regional focus had been even more striking at Barcelona four years earlier, where organizers staged a Catalan, rather than Spanish, creation myth, King Juan Carlos I entered the stadium accompanied by the Catalan anthem, and the monarch spoke in Catalan to declare the games open – all part of the successful 'Catalanisation' of the games that caused tension with the national government (D'Agati 167–69; Kennett and de Moragas 2006). Viewed from a different angle, the Olympics also make nations more similar, for example through the standard rules the IOC imposes on sport and sport federations that want to qualify for inclusion in the games. Much of the actual staging of the event, including the opening ceremony, is subject to an elaborate IOC script that organizers must follow. Both the Olympics and the men's World Cup, to mention just the peak events in the global sporting system, also depend on commercial sponsorship and media coverage, which require that they be made fit for global consumption by an audience not divided along national lines. Precisely what is 'national' about national teams or top performances becomes questionable at a time when many professionals pursue opportunities outside their country of origin, with many swimmers training in the US, basketball players joining the National Basketball Association, star football players gravitating toward select European leagues, and so on. Athletic performance by nationally identified actors intersects with a professional market system that pays far less attention to traditional symbolic boundaries.

As these examples show, international competition enables nations to flex their symbolic muscle, yet the globalization of sport also puts them at risk. On the one hand, global games give ample play to national sentiment. In the global age, nations remain actors on courts and fields. Shared sport experience shapes national identities. If by those identities we refer to a primary way peoples answer the 'who are we?' question, sport certainly plays a key role. For such reasons, sociologists of sport have noted strong links between sport and nation, arguing that sport demonstrates the continued resilience and vitality of nations, even in, and partly due to, globalization (Bairner 2001; Hargreaves 2002; Maguire 1999: 83). That same sport experience undermines national distinction in other ways, as people in different countries play by the same rules, sport allows for the expression of multiple identities, and corporations turn events and teams into media commodities. For such reasons, some left-leaning sociologists of sport think 'playing the world' is just as likely to lead to the 'unmaking' of nations, which they tend to treat as outdated fictions that may still serve some state or business purposes (Miller *et al.* 2001). Reflecting on the real-world tensions captured by these contrasting views, recent studies of sport have moved away from an either/or approach to nations in globalization and toward a subtler understanding of how national identities are redefined and globalization includes 'glocal' variety (Giulianotti and Robertson 2004).

In that way, the sociology of sport has productively addressed bigger issues in contemporary social science, most notably the fortunes of the nation. On one side, scholars have long argued that most nations have deep ethnic roots, culturally complement the modern state, and therefore will continue to shape collective aspirations in the global age. Critics of this view contend that such recently invented, somewhat arbitrary identities are historical constructs that emerged only in a particular context and are now bound to fade as new ties and identities globally rise to the fore, supplanting the old, contentious form of cultural and political division. At least some work in this field paints a more complex picture, suggesting that the strength and salience of things national depend on issues and contexts, and that the redefinition of national identities in response to common global challenges is likely to take different forms in different settings (Lechner 2008). The serious business of immigration or international conflict may matter most in assessing these scenarios, but sport, as an object of popular attention and passion, perhaps more transparently shapes and displays national transformations. Supplying evidence of both 'national' and 'post-national' games, the sociology of sport aids opposing sides in the old debate but, by adding further nuance, ultimately makes the complex, 'glocalized' picture more plausible, suggesting that the evolution of nations in the global age follows no single scenario.

National games

Since the nineteenth century, modern nations have played modern games. As states engaged in nation-building, devising institutions to integrate people and polity in new ways, they also organized leisure activities to suit the community their leaders envisioned. Starting in England in the nineteenth century, and continuing through post–World War II decolonization, most aspiring nation-states adopted a 'national game'. English cricket set an example. Always perceived as an English invention, it became more popular after 1800 as rules were codified, violence on and off the pitch diminished, Parliament legalized the game, and a growing literature touted its spiritual, essentially English qualities, making it a model of order and civilization in times of change, one that flourished due to 'an interconnected physical attraction and moral code which tied players, spectators and administrators in a joint enthusiasm' (Sandiford 1998: 11; Malcolm 2013: 33–38). Public schools did much to promote it, and in the classic novel *Tom Brown's Schooldays*, the main character famously declares that it 'is more than a game. It's an institution'. Newspapers kindled interest, reporting on games and helping to create the image of the first true national cricket star, W.G. Grace, at the end of the century. Though never the most widely played game, and in spite of tension over issues like professionalism, for Victorians it nonetheless became the embodiment of Englishness. With prominent cricket figures also influential in the political arena – perhaps slightly overstated by a scholar who calls the cricketing and political empire 'one and the same' (Sandiford 1998: 13) – the national game diffused through the colonies to become the 'imperial game' as well. That diffusion confirmed England's sporting prowess, not to mention its dominance in other spheres, but later made it a victim of its early success. The spread of football, a rival to English national allegiance, tells a similar story, though it achieved greater success outside British dominions.

By different paths, other people and countries turned British sporting exports into their own national games. It started early in Australia, where settlers first brought pastimes like cricket with them to prove their Englishness and bask in imperial nostalgia, before the game served to express a love-hate relationship with the motherland and create the 'first stirrings of nationalism', aided by victory in an 1877 Test match over a visiting English team (Cashman 1998a: 39). In India, cricket became part of Britain's civilizing process, focused first on the elite, in the second half of the nineteenth century. Not until much later did it gain wider support, making the game look 'more Indian than English' to most Indians, as a prominent commentator put it – and again, of course, Test victories over the old colonial power, from 1952 onward, helped nationalize cricket (Cashman 1998b). Long popular as the established imperial game in the West Indies, cricket took on new meanings in the islands' twentieth-century struggle for independence, becoming 'a vehicle of the nascent democratizing nationalist order' as homegrown stars, most of them black, turned the West Indies team into an innovative powerhouse – a process marked, once again, by key victories over England, including the first dramatic and liberating Test victory in England's 'own backyard' at Lord's cricket ground in 1950 (Beckles 1998a: xv–xviii). In spite of competition from even more deliberately nationalist games, rugby union came to express a similar oppositional identity in Ireland, linking all 32 counties on the 'Gaelic' fringe in a 'we-ideal' against the 'Anglo-Saxon' English, expressed as always in the qualities of star players and a supposedly distinct playing style (Maguire and Tuck 2005). For the Argentinian state, trying to find ways to assimilate immigrants around 1900, an authentically Argentinian form of football served as a popular national discourse that appealed to working and middle class alike; prominent publications advocating the crafty, individualistic 'criollo' style over English precedent and second-place finishes in the 1928 Olympics and the first World Cup in 1930 confirmed to a large, mostly male public the country's special football virtues (Archetti 1999; Alabarces and Graciela Rodríguez 2000). Respected and self-respecting countries, these examples suggest, had to have their own national game(s).

Nationalizing games did not just happen from within. As in the development of other identities, linking sport and national identity typically involved dialogue of sorts. Again, an early example comes from Australia, where cricket tours did not just help Australians 'invent' themselves as such in contrast to the English but also shaped English views of Australians as a new kind of people, initiating a changing relationship that changed self-understandings on both sides (Bradley 1995). In a slightly different way, Greek commentators used the international recognition the country earned for its remarkable victory in the 2004 European football championship, only the second time the Greeks even participated, in a kind of virtual dialogue with foreign fans to accentuate its Christian and Hellenic identity as a distinctive contribution to European culture (Tzanelli 2006). Asserting a national identity in a sporting arena does not stop at claims that 'we' differ from 'them' in a particular way but also incorporates (if sometimes to reject) what 'they' think of 'us'. How much real 'dialogue' takes place in the stands or the sport pages is debatable, of course, but imagining community typically involves imagining what others make of it.

Using sport for national self-definition became the global thing to do. International competitions, as noted, helped to reinforce that norm. In many countries, elites acted on it by selecting one or a few legitimate sports that carried their approval, leaving popular dissemination to enthusiastic entrepreneurs (and, of course, successful athletes) – a process at work in India's embrace of cricket but applicable elsewhere (Kaufman and Patterson 2005). Such elites and popularizers used media to create a national mystique around the national game, typically projecting a national essence onto it. Beyond those similarities, however, national games also showed cross-national differences (Guttmann 1994). Most obviously, the choice of primary sport, insofar as it was a choice, varied – for example, cricket more commonly within the (former) British Empire, football more often outside of it. The extent of direction from above varied as well – turning a form of gymnastics into 'the' German national sport at the outset took concerted effort (Hofmann 2004), and forceful guidance from communist bosses helped (and for a time hurt) the cause of table tennis in China (Guttmann 2004: 209–10). The precise meaning attached to the national game also differed – it was typically greater in places where newly formed symbols had special 'work' to do, as in Argentina's response to immigration and in the West Indies' struggle for cultural independence. However globalized they may appear, games like football or cricket therefore also display distinct local adaptations, a range of cricket or football cultures, plural (Finn and Giulianotti 2000). Apart from 'the' national game, of course, players and fans may enjoy others as well, complicating the overall domestic 'sport space' and creating distinctive national composites. Recent scholarship has provided a good picture of the range of variation but still no single theory to explain it. For example, it remains puzzling that neither football nor cricket took hold in Canada, which developed a sport space and culture quite different from that of Great Britain.

Post-national games

Early-modern nation-building did more than give cultural backing to emerging states: it also made the nation the norm. Living up to it proved problematic, of course, where nation and state did not align. From its European outset, the national project also ran into other difficulties, each a way of questioning the normality of the nation, as the sport record illustrates. Ostensibly 'national' games have long had 'post-national' qualities as well, for example due to always more-than-national or transnational sport organizing, or to the inconstancy of national significance attributed to games, or to rivals supplanting distinctly national sports or teams.

Even as nation-states cultivated distinction, they also acted alike. Elites learned and borrowed. Upgrading institutions involved standardization. In international society, codes of national conduct emerged. So it happened in sport: sport leaders copied and adapted, leisure activities were increasingly organized in regular competitions, and rules of games were adjusted to international codes. For all their national baggage, modern sport took similar forms in different places. Modernization focused athletic contests on common rules and records (Guttmann 1978). Using new technologies, sport reporting and sport talk that drew in large groups of spectators increasingly surrounded major games everywhere (Werron 2010). For most games, national borders limited the relevant audience and the sport conversation took place in national languages, yet many sports followed a similar path in becoming modern. National games have always been more-than-national.

The status of 'national' games is not fixed in any case, showing that the nation is not a uniform, and uniformly important, container of identities. In the West Indies, for example, cricket traditionalists lament the 'collapse of the nationalist sensibility within which West Indies cricket came to an ideological maturity', which they attribute in part to the cultural impact of globalization, detect in declining quality of play and the rise of competing options, and blame for the weakening of national identity beyond sport (Beckles 1998b: 1, 93). In Uruguay, once a small but unusually successful football power, which the game had pulled 'out of the shadows of universal anonymity', the decline of domestic play and the migration of top players contributed to a 'football bankruptcy' that affected the longstanding close identification of game and nation (Giulianotti 2000). By contrast, when France, not previously known as a great football power,

won the 1998 World Cup on home territory, that victory had an unexpected national, even unifying impact, partly due to the undeniably great contributions of ethnic minority players – 'les
Bleus' mattered to the country in a way they had not before (Dauncey and Hare 1999).

The meaning or content of national games varies as well, further challenging the nation-as-
norm. Occasional success in international settings, as France enjoyed in 1998 and Greece in
2004, can revive certain national associations. In other cases, that national meaning is more
contested. For example, many commentators attributed the international success of great Dutch
teams in the early 1970s to their 'distinctively Dutch' brand of 'total football', in turn treated
as a reflection of some deep Dutch essence, but others questioned whether the Dutch shared a
distinct tradition and played in a way that displayed any particular values – in the Netherlands
and elsewhere, self-critical, at times ironic, debate is part of the national sport conversation
(Lechner 2007). Beyond fans and aficionados, public perception may not in fact link sport and
national identity as tightly as conventional sport talk suggests. For example, some limited empirical research in England, based on interviews in the early 2000s, suggests that conservatively
inclined fans might leap from football support to national pride but many others resist the urge,
because they care little about the English team or 'bracket' football interest from politically suspect patriotism (Abell *et al.* 2007). Even in relation to national teams, therefore, spectator identities need not align neatly with a single, national identity; as in relation to club teams, traditional,
'hot' supporters may increasingly be replaced by 'cool,' cosmopolitan consumers (Giulianotti
2002). And even the seemingly 'hot' support may have more to do with an opportunity to party,
as Greek, English, or Dutch football fans abroad have been known to do, than with any deeper
national traditions. Activated mainly by major sporting events, imagining community only in
discrete episodes, such ludic nationalism comes and goes.

Besides the similarities, change, and variation just noted, other evidence suggests that the
national meaning of sport involvement, or the role of sport in framing such identities, may
be at risk of declining. In football, for example, major professional clubs have lost some of
their national aura. When Manchester United defeated Real Madrid in the European Cup
semi-final in 1968, a prominent commentator noted that the team stood as 'heroes of England'
whose 'English temperament, fibre and morale' had won through (conveniently ignoring the
presence of Irish players), which reflected a taken-for-granted 'nationalistic interpretation' of
European competition that also chided the dubious character of foreigners (King 2003: 4–7).
When United faced Bayern Munich in 1999, that nationalist view had not disappeared, but a
far more diverse team (with seven foreigners) also drew more guarded, even critical comments,
illustrating how 'major European football clubs are becoming differentiated from the nation
and different forms of solidarity are emerging around and against them when they play other
European competition' (King 2003: 11). In United's case, that included a more blasé domestic
audience partly unified in rooting against a club perceived as overbearing and a transnational fan
base that made it one of the most lucrative sport franchises in the world. In football, as in many
other sports, we-ideals need not center on the nation. Other trends point in a similar direction.
As in developed countries more sports become available to more people as amateur participants
or relatively passive consumers, in the form of a menu of options, local variety increases but
contrasts across localities decline (Maguire 1999). Insofar as national identities of old depended
on such contrasts, that trend spells potential atrophy.

American exceptions

Like any other proper sport power, the United States has its national game – two in fact. Baseball,
of course, came first. In some ways, the game evolved much like football and cricket (Seymour

1960; Werron 2010). Starting in New York in the 1840s, fuzzy rules turned into definite laws of the game, standardizing it across large regions and making performance measurable. Railroads enabled teams to travel, creating increasingly regular league play. Professionals soon dominated, their exploits avidly followed by newspapers and later radio for an ever-expanding audience. As in other polyglot countries, the game appealed, and was used to appeal, to different classes and ethnic groups. And of course its advocates promoted it from an early stage as the 'national pastime': it was 'our game,' said the poet Walt Whitman, reflecting 'American Dash, Discipline, Determination' and many other alliterative virtues in the words of Albert Spalding, star pitcher and baseball executive (Spalding 1911/1992: 4). The 'national game' took on 'mythic qualities' (Rossi 2000). Among those qualities, according to Spalding and many others, was its eminently democratic thrust – made more real at the highest professional level when, in another pattern familiar elsewhere, the identities of game and nation were reinterpreted after World War II, in the American case to include African Americans.

Though a normal national game, baseball also had and has comparative quirks that have made it exceptional in the eyes of its American aficionados (Cogliano 2004). At the outset, Americans were unusually insistent to make it so, disclaiming any connection between the American game and British precedents. Efforts to export the game, for example in Spalding's famous 1888–1889 world tour, did not bear fruit as they did for British football and cricket, helping to turn American baseball's focus toward national competition on a sport 'island' quite separate from others. With Major League Baseball at the center of the professional baseball world, international competition has never played a national role in baseball of the sort described above, and the initial versions of Major League Baseball's World Baseball Classic stirred little national passion, suggesting that 'dialogue' and cross-national comparison did not fuel American sport nationalism. Perhaps even more than fans of other games (though cricket writers might disagree), Americans have invested baseball with national meaning, making 'The Star-Spangled Banner' part of pregame ritual and singing the game's praises in an extensive nationalizing literature.

American football became a national game much later (MacCambridge 2005). Like baseball, it is in some ways a normal national game. Elite fans like Theodore Roosevelt had long thought of it as uniquely American in its fair play and martial, masculine vigor, stressing how much it differed from British precedent. After a rowdy start, the rules of football standardized to contain violence and facilitate both amateur and later professional cross-regional competition. When the professional game took off after World War II, coaches put their stamp on it, systematizing preparation and strategy perhaps more than in any other sport. Exploiting fan interest in a game well suited to television, the National Football League became a model commercial sport league, cutting-edge in the way it turned games and players into consumable commodities. Even more than American football at other levels, the NFL's marketing strategy has portrayed the game as an exercise in patriotism and crafted its championship game, the Super Bowl, as the most-watched American ritual usually laden with patriotic symbolism. Though less venerated in a romantic national literature, by the late twentieth century football had become 'America's game'. Like baseball, however, it also had its special features. Even more than baseball, American football has appeared to Americans as exceptionally American, a different species of sport than forms of rugby elsewhere. For lack of serious diffusion, international competition means even less than in baseball. Thanks to a distinct organizational base, notably in colleges and universities but including high schools as well, American football has formed a world unto its own, accentuating the island-like quality of the US in the global sporting system. Combined with baseball, which it has come to overshadow in popularity, it marks an exceptional sport culture, which by its engrained routines creates a kind of 'banal', everyday nationalism (Billig 1995) that ties American fans, and at times a larger public, into a more-than-imagined community.

Some innovations on the 'island', like basketball and volleyball, have had a great impact abroad. Though Americans did not invent professionalism, American commercial sport marketing and media packaging have also influenced the business of sport elsewhere. In turn, foreign talent has altered domestic games in both baseball and basketball. Yet America's involvement in global sport, for example in major international competitions, still matters much less to fans and a larger public than regular domestic competition, with the exception of individual sports like golf and tennis. Similarly, the country's soccer teams have not attracted the kind of passionate interest that is common in many other countries, traced by some authors to the un-American game's early crowding-out from an already occupied sport space (Markovits and Hellerman 2001). Though American soccer is belatedly growing in popularity and quality, the lack of such passion has itself become a trope in media commentary framing 'their' odd interest in the game to contrast with 'our' sensible indifference (Buffington 2012), another instance of a sport serving to define American distinction in a distinctive way. But, in the US as elsewhere, the status and content of even such longstanding collective self-interpretations are subject to reinterpretation, which future soccer success may yet accomplish. The interplay of self-reinforcing national and more recent post-national tendencies affects even the largest nationally bounded sport spaces.

Conclusion

A generation's work in the history and sociology of sport has shown the varied resilience of nations and national identities, new pressures exerted on them by globalization, and the complex ways national identities are being redefined in sporting arenas. That work has shed much light on issues that matter to all of social science and to thoughtful sport observers, supporting a more subtle picture of nations and national identities than was once commonly accepted.

As some examples above have shown, many sporting nations develop a we-sense through participation in the global sporting system, importing a particular mix of sports to form their own sport space, adapting foreign examples to devise national styles, demonstrating special qualities in competition against others, using tournaments for national self-display, and feeding national sentiment on the thrill of winning or losing. In world society, nations identify themselves through sport. Identities thus created may be imagined or invented, terms often applied to national communities, but many sport records are now long enough to make old roots feel quite real.

In the 'global age', nations also face constraints and challenges in using sport to form distinct identities, since international competition allows for the expression of many identities, common rules standardize sport across borders, labor markets in major sports dilute athletes' national attachment, and corporate media, owners, and sponsors treat sports as commodities. The imagination at work in sporting venues need not be national.

The sport record also shows that, more than a century after the first links between sport and nation crystallized, those links are being transformed, as the status and significance of national identification vary, the meaning and content of common traditions are redefined, and national identities are contested and disputed. Few postmodern nations provide the fixed cultural anchor nineteenth-century sport enthusiasts envisioned. For that reason, students of sport recommend thinking of nations and national identities as always in process.

Though exposed to the same trends as any other country, the United States also stands out in its distinctively home-grown sports, the continued use of sport in the routine affirmation of national sentiment, its relative disregard for normal national use of international competition, and its outsized, some would say imperial, impact abroad. In sport, at least, Americans have had good reason to think of themselves as exceptional. Yet the many bridges to their sport island may force even them to rethink their national distinction.

Note

1 I would like to thank Richard Giulianotti for his comments on an earlier version of this chapter.

References

Abell, J., Condor, S., Lowe, R.D., Gibson, S. and Stevenson, C. (2007) 'Who Ate All the Pride? Patriotic Sentiment and English National Football Support', *Nations and Nationalism*, 13(1): 97–116.

Alabarces, P. and Graciela Rodríguez, M. (2000) 'Football and Fatherland: The Crisis of National Representation in Argentinian Soccer', in G.P.T. Finn and R. Giulianotti (eds.) *Football Culture: Local Contests, Global Visions*, London: Frank Cass.

Archetti, E.P. (1999) *Masculinities: Football, Polo, and the Tango in Argentina*, Oxford: Berg.

Bairner, A. (2001) *Sport, Nationalism, and Globalization: European and North American Perspectives*, Albany: State University of New York Press.

Beckles, H. McD. (1998a) *The Development of West Indies Cricket. Volume 1: The Age of Nationalism*, Kingston: The Press University of the West Indies.

Beckles, H. McD. (1998b) *The Development of West Indies Cricket. Volume 2: The Age of Globalization*, Kingston: The Press University of the West Indies.

Billig, M. (1995) *Banal Nationalism*, London: Sage.

Bradley, J. (1995) 'Inventing Australians and Constructing Englishness: Cricket and the Creation of a National Consciousness, 1860–1914', *Sporting Traditions* 11(1): 35–60.

Buffington, D.T. (2012) 'Us and Them: U.S. Ambivalence Toward the World Cup and American Nationalism', *Journal of Sport & Social Issues* 36(2): 135–54.

Cashman, R. (1998a) 'Australia', in B. Stoddart and K.A.P Sandiford (eds) *The Imperial Game: Cricket, Culture and Society*, Manchester: Manchester University Press.

Cashman, R. (1998b) 'The Subcontinent', in B. Stoddart and K.A.P Sandiford (eds) *The Imperial Game: Cricket, Culture and Society*, Manchester: Manchester University Press.

Chen, C.C., Colapinto, C. and Luo, Q. (2012) 'The 2008 Beijing Olympics Opening Ceremony: Visual Insights into China's Soft Power', *Visual Studies* 27(2): 188–95.

Cogliano, F.D. (2004) 'Baseball and American Exceptionalism', in A. Smith and D. Porter (eds) *Sport and National Identity in the Post-War World*, New York: Taylor and Francis.

D'Agati, P.A. (2011) *Nationalism on the World Stage: Cultural Performance at the Olympic Games*, Lanham, MD: University Press of America.

Dauncey, H. and Hare, G. (eds) (1999). *France and the 1998 World Cup: The National Impact of a World Sporting Event*, London: Frank Cass.

Finn, G.P.T. and Giulianotti, R. (eds) (2000). *Football Culture: Local Contests, Global Visions*, London: Frank Cass.

Giulianotti, R. (2000) 'Built by the Two Varelas: The Rise and Fall of Football Culture and National Identity in Uruguay', in G.P.T. Finn and R. Giulianotti (eds.) *Football Culture: Local Contests, Global Visions*, London: Frank Cass.

Giulianotti, R. (2002) 'Supporters, Followers, Fans, and *Flaneurs*: A Taxonomy of Spectator Identities in Football', *Journal of Sport & Social Issues* 26(1): 25–46.

Giulianotti, R. and Robertson, R. (2004) 'The Globalization of Football: A Study in the Glocalization of the "Serious Life"', *British Journal of Sociology* 55(4): 545–68.

Guttmann, A. (1978) *From Ritual to Record: The Nature of Modern Sports*, New York: Columbia University Press.

Guttmann, A. (1994) *Games and Empires: Modern Sports and Cultural Imperialism*, New York: Columbia University Press.

Guttmann, A. (2004) *Sports: The First Five Millennia*, Amherst: University of Massachusetts Press.

Guttmann, A. (2006) 'Berlin 1936: The Most Controversial Olympics', in A. Tomlinson and C. Young (eds), *National Identity and Global Sports Events*, Albany: State University of New York Press.

Hargreaves, J. (2002) 'Globalisation Theory, Global Sport, and Nations and Nationalism', in J. Sugden and A. Tomlinson (eds.), *Power Games: A Critical Sociology of Sport*, London: Routledge.

Hayes, S. (2001) 'America's National Pastime and Canadian Nationalism', in S.G. Wieting (ed.), *Sport and Memory in North America*, London: Frank Cass.

Hofmann, A. (ed.) (2004) *Turnen and Sport: Transatlantic Transfers*, New York: Waxmann.

Hogan, J. (2003) 'Staging the Nation: Gendered and Ethnicized Discourses of National Identity in Olympic Opening Ceremonies', *Journal of Sport & Social Issues* 27(2): 100–23.

Kaufman, J. and Patterson, O. (2005) 'Cross-National Cultural Diffusion: The Global Spread of Cricket', *American Sociological Review* 70: 82–110.

Kennett, C. and Moragas, M. de (2006) 'Barcelona 1992: Evaluating the Olympic Legacy', in A. Tomlinson and C. Young (eds) *National Identity and Global Sports Events*, Albany: State University of New York Press.

King, A. (2003) *The European Ritual: Football and the New Europe*, Aldershot, UK: Ashgate.

Kok, A. (2008) *1988: Wij Hielden van Oranje*, Amsterdam: Thomas Rap.

Lechner, F.J. (2007) 'Imagined Communities in the Global Game: Soccer and the Development of Dutch National Identity', *Global Networks* 7(2): 215–29.

Lechner, F.J. (2008) *The Netherlands: Globalization and National Identity*, London: Routledge.

MacCambridge, M. (2005) *America's Game: The Epic Story of How Pro Football Captured a Nation*, New York: Anchor Books.

Maguire, J. (1999) *Global Sport: Identities, Societies, Civilizations*, Cambridge: Polity Press.

Maguire, J. and Tuck, J. (2005) '"A World in Union"? Rugby, Globalisation and Irish Identity', in J. Maguire (ed.), *Power and Global Sport*, New York: Routledge.

Malcolm, D. (2013) *Globalizing Cricket: Englishness, Empire and Identity*, London: Bloomsbury.

Markovits, A. and Hellerman, S.L. (2001) *Offside: Soccer and American Exceptionalism*, Princeton: Princeton University Press.

Mason, T. (2006) 'England 1966: Traditional and Modern?' in A. Tomlinson and C. Yung (eds), *National Identity and Global Sports Events*, Albany: State University of New York Press.

Miller, T., Lawrence, G., McKay, J. and Rowe, D. (2001) *Globalization and Sport: Playing the World*, London: Sage.

Rossi, J.P. (2000) *The National Game: Baseball and American Culture*, Chicago: Ivan R. Dee.

Sandiford, K.A.P. (1998) 'England', in B. Stoddard and K.A.P. Sandiford, *The Imperial Game: Cricket, Culture and Society*, Manchester: Manchester University Press.

Seymour, H. (1960) *Baseball: The People's Game. Volume 1: The Early Years*, New York: Oxford University Press.

Spalding, A.G. (1911/1992) *America's National Game*, Lincoln: University of Nebraska Press.

Tomlinson, A. (1996) 'Olympic Spectacle: Opening Ceremonies and Some Paradoxes of Globalization', *Media, Culture & Society* 18: 583–602.

Tzanelli, R. (2006) '"Impossible Is a Fact": Greek Nationalism and International Recognition in Euro 2004', *Media, Culture & Society* 28(4): 483–503.

Werron, T. (2010) *Der Weltsport und Sein Publikum: Zur Autonomie und Entstehung des Modernen Sports*, Weilerswist: Velbrück.

41

THE MIGRATION OF ELITE ATHLETES

Raffaele Poli and Loïc Ravenel

Introduction

Football is often considered as an activity which has developed hand in hand with the process of globalization. As the late historian Eric Hobsbawm wrote, 'There is nothing that illustrates globalization better than the evolution of football in recent years. This sport has become truly international, and teams are no longer tied to a particular country, and even less to a city. There is a nucleus of world class players who are recruited and run around the world, as happened before for the divas of the opera or the great conductors'[1] (2000: 132). In his book on the cosmopolitan vision, German sociologist Ulrich Beck also proposes a parallel between football and globalization. He underlines that players under contract with Bayern Munich, the club in his hometown, 'are neither from Bavaria, nor from Munich; they are of many different nationalities, speak many different languages and have many different passports'. For him, 'Bayern Munich stands for a profane cosmopolitan "We" in which the boundaries between internal and external, the national and the international have long since been transcended' (2006: 11).

In different ways, Eric Hobsbawm and Ulrich Beck refer to football as a showcase for globalization and cosmopolitanism. To bolster their reasoning, both of them refer to the international migration of professional football players. Approaching this theme from the opposite direction, many authors advocate considering the mobility of athletes rather than an expression of the globalization process. For example, in the introduction to their seminal book on sport as a global arena, John Bale and Joseph Maguire state that 'the connection of locating sports migration with the issue of globalization is seen as crucial' (1994: 5). On one hand, the migration of top-level athletes is considered as a perfect example to illustrate globalization.[2] On the other hand, authors like referring to the latter phenomenon to explain the rise in the international mobility of athletes, and more generally to highlight the ever-increasing transnational dimension of sport (Giulianotti and Robertson 2007). In all cases, the migration of professional athletes is highlighted. As a consequence, this issue has become a fashionable one in the study of sport from a social science perspective. Indeed, the increase in the volume of publications dealing with this theme recently led to the publication of the first consolidated books in this area of study (Gillon, Grosjean and Ravenel 2010; Maguire and Falcous 2011).

From a sociological point of view, such analysis of player migration in elite football raises two main issues which can be summarized using two key concepts. The first one is identity, which helps us to question the effects of migration, especially at a local and national level. The second is globalization. Generally, this can be analyzed using economic theories, but such frameworks are not normally sufficient as globalization has not led to the disappearance of cultural, historical or geographical patterns. In addition, a more relational approach on the circulation of players and the creation of networks brings a deeper understanding. These networks rely on existing relationships within societies and constantly adapt to new opportunities. Leading to a more functional integration of territories beyond national borders, these processes exemplify the way in which migration contributes to the formation of a global economy in the sports industry.

In this paper, we focus our attention specifically on football (soccer). First of all, this choice is guided by its worldwide diffusion (Gillon *et al.* 2010) as much for the number of registered players as for the game's nature as a global sporting spectacle. Football's globalization has allowed for the rise of a global market within the game, and thus all the resulting migration of elite athletes. In addition, our reflection relies on the academic work produced by the CIES Football Observatory, a research group of the Swiss International Centre for Sports Studies. Since its creation in 2005, the observatory has analyzed the evolution of the professional football player market with reference to international migrations, and provides the original issues and findings which we draw together and discuss in the following pages.[3]

Player migration and identities

Identity at a local level

Identity issues deriving from the migration of athletes in team sports can firstly be related to the perception that the presence of players imported from abroad threatens the process of identification for supporters of clubs located in that specific living area. This perception derives from the assumption that fans have a preference for local footballers, with whom they can more easily identify. While this assumption may be true, it is hard to state to what extent it corresponds to reality. While empirical evidence has been provided to show the link between sporting success and match attendances (Simmons 1996; Scelles *et al.* 2013), the same does not hold true for the fielding of local players and numbers frequenting stadia. The relationship even seems to be inverse: attendances in the big-5 European leagues,[4] since 1995, have increased in line with the increase in the number of expatriate players.[5] For example, in France, Paris-Saint-Germain played the first part of the 2013–2014 season with more than 8.4 expatriate players per game (Poli, Ravenel and Besson, 2013) and attendances at the Parc des Princes broke records. One might thus consider that the driving force for identification is actually success rather than squad make-up. This is clearly confirmed by the much greater popularity of the most successful teams compared to lesser performing clubs. It is hard to find evidence of the importance of player origin for supporter identity, even when looking at very popular but mainly unsuccessful teams. In this case, too, club tradition and familial heritage probably play a more crucial role than squad composition. Success with imported players seems to be preferred to failure with local representatives. While the achievement of success with a majority of local footballers may be reasonably considered as the ideal configuration, this may be called into question when applied to a club that has developed into a global brand with a worldwide fan base (Richelieu and Desbordes 2009). The process of deterritorialization (Poli 2005) and the development of 'remote supporters' (Hognestad 2003; Lestrelin 2010) go hand in hand with a redefinition of the 'local', a notion that becomes pretty much dependent on the origin of supporters. For a Japanese fan supporting Manchester United, for example, the 'local' player is probably more likely to be Shinji Kagawa of Japan rather than Paul Scholes of England. This process is also exemplified by the ever-increasing tendency to choose imported players as captains, despite a lack of deep quantitative analysis on this issue.

Identity at a national level

The recruitment of foreign players by professional clubs also raises issues related to identity at a national level. This has to do with the historical role of football, and, broadly speaking, sport, in nation building, stimulating national pride and also a sense of belonging. Indeed, the structural configuration of sport as a competitive activity favours the process of drawing borders between the 'We' and the 'Others' (Bromberger 1995; Barth 1998; Jaska 2011). For over a century, international competitions have been developed to oppose teams or athletes symbolically representing a nation within a carefully designed scenario which is structured around national anthems and flags. Sporting events and performances have become so important for the national narrative that the highest state authorities all over the world can no longer afford to ignore them, and further proactively use them for political purposes. Within this context, in team sports the importation of players by professional clubs has rapidly become an important issue. Since the 1920s, football associations and state authorities have considered foreign footballers as a threat to national identity. Indeed, foreigners are prevented from playing for the national team in international competitions and their presence in national clubs is often considered as an obstacle for the development of local talent. While debatable insofar as it could also be argued that skilled imported players can to a certain extent help local players to raise their own technical levels, this assumption has led to the introduction of quotas limiting international player migration. Until the end of the 1980s, European clubs in most team sports were prohibited from including more than three foreign players. In some nations and for specific periods, quotas were even stricter. This situation drastically changed in the mid-1990s, when a ruling from the European Court of Justice obliged sporting institutions to guarantee the freedom of movement of all players holding an EU passport, as well as for citizens of non-EU states having concluded free circulation agreements with the European Union. Again, sporting authorities claimed that this would put into danger the power of sport, and more particularly football, to promote the identification of a nation, despite being unable to provide clear evidence. Conversely, many scholars suggest that the role of sport to stimulate national identity has never been as important as today within the context of globalization (Tomlinson 1996; Roche 2006; Gillon *et al.* 2010). Indeed, due to their extreme media exposure, international sporting mega events are more than ever the ideal occasion to project ideas of nation and identity in a world where borders are constantly challenged. From this perspective, sport has become a very important refuge for identity.

Player migration and globalization

Following a definition provided by the economic geographer Peter Dicken (2003), globalization can be divided into two main concepts: internationalization and trans-nationalization. Internationalization is considered as an increase in the general volume of international flows, and we can see that this trend has influenced all sports during the last decade (Gillon *et al.* 2010). Transnationalization is understood as a diversification of migratory routes and their spatial fragmentation between multiple states. This concept will help us to understand the mechanisms underlying the player labour market.

Internationalization: the increase of player migrations

Table 41.1 clearly illustrates the impact of the Bosman ruling[6] on club recruitment policies. In just five seasons, between 1995 and 2000, the percentage of expatriate players taking part in the five major European leagues increased from 18.6% to 35.6%, and the number per club has more than doubled (from 4.6 to 10.2). Although the rise in the number and proportion of expatriate footballers has slowed down since then, an overall increase has continued without interruption to the present day.[7] On a larger scale, as of 1 October 2013, 36.8% of the footballers under contract with 500 clubs in the 31 top division clubs in Europe were expatriates – a new record (Besson, Poli and Ravenel 2014). The latter represented the majority of squad members in five national associations: Cyprus (63.8%), England (60.4%), Italy (54.1%), Turkey (53.1%) and Belgium (51.4%). This general increase in the number of expatriates goes hand in hand with the increase in their diversity. In 2013, 82 nationalities were represented in the big-5 leagues, compared to only 31 in the 1960/61 season.

More and more leagues worldwide have reached a level of professionalization which allows them to sign players from abroad. The development of professional football is particularly remarkable in Asia, both in the south-eastern part of the continent (South Korea, Japan, China, Thailand, etc.) and in the Middle East (Qatar, United Arab Emirates, Bahrain, etc.). Professional leagues have also flourished in other countries were football has traditionally not been the leading sport: the United States, Australia and India, for example. The professionalization of the game on a global scale demonstrates an increase in the international mobility and diversity of players.

In this context of internationalization, certain countries have become progressively more specialized in the training of footballers and their exportation (Table 41.2). They have comparative advantages that are accentuated by global competition. This specialization can be explained by several factors: the number of trained players is connected to the population size of the country (Brazil, France, Argentina) and this is amplified by the successes and profile of the relevant national team (Brazil, Argentina, Spain, Uruguay). The quality of the training system available has a role as seen in France, Serbia, Croatia and the Netherlands. The economic weakness of the local championship also promotes interest in producing players.

Such figures indicate that the labour and transfer market of footballers now has a truly global reach. However, a more detailed study of international transfer flows shows that the latter do not

Table 41.1 Evolution of the number of expatriate players ('big-5' leagues)

Season	%	Number per club
1960/61	8.5	2.0
1965/66	5.9	1.4
1970/71	6.0	1.3
1975/76	8.1	1.8
1980/81	8.5	1.8
1985/86	9.1	1.9
1990/91	14.7	3.3
1995/96	18.6	4.6
2000/01	35.6	10.2
2005/06	37.3	10.3
2010/11	43.5	11.4

Source: CIES Football Observatory

Table 41.2 Top exporting countries, national players only (2010)

Rank	Country	Exported players
1.	Brazil	283
2.	Argentina	215
3.	Serbia	150
4.	Uruguay	96
5.	France	77
6.	Spain	77
7.	Colombia	71
8.	Portugal	57
9.	Croatia	57
10.	Netherlands	51
11.	Slovakia	51

Source: (Besson, Poli and Ravenel 2011)

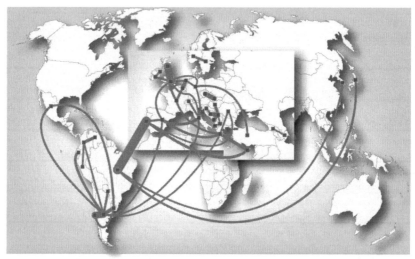

Number of flows between two associations

116   50   20

Figure 41.1 Most common migratory pathways in 2010 (at least 20 flows)
Source: (Besson, Poli and Ravenel 2011)

equally relate to all national markets. On the contrary, there are still privileged migratory routes. For example, Portugal remains by far the main country of destination for Brazilian players. Africans from former French colonies are over-represented in France, and South Americans are still over-represented in Spain and Italy. Such stable preferences reflect the historical and cultural links between the countries. Of course, geographic proximity can also reinforce such migration patterns, as shown on Figure 41.1, which reveals the most common migratory pathways in 2010.

Transnationalization of careers: a relationalist approach

At the same time, the fragmentation of a career between different countries shows a trend towards transnationalization: four expatriate footballers out of ten in the big-5 leagues have played for clubs located in more than two countries during their professional career and such figures have been increasing since the middle of the 2000s. The main beneficiaries of this are players originating from financially underprivileged continents who tend to cross more borders than their counterparts from richer areas of the world. This demonstrates the economic nature of the transnationalization process. Indeed, the transfer costs for young South American players and, even more so, their African counterparts are more affordable than those for footballers trained in richer economies. As a consequence, the former are particularly sought after by professional clubs and intermediaries following a speculative strategy consisting of increasing the market value of players 'on the move', through their circulation. The over-representation of Africans and Latin Americans among forwards also partially explains their greater international mobility. Offensive players are generally the best paid and those for which clubs are the most keen to spend money in transfer fees. This also enhances the transfer speculation which surrounds them. The over-representation of players from less developed countries in these positions may thus reflect a sociological adaptation to economic opportunities.

Less ideological than rational choice or Marxist perspectives,[8] the relational approach could be developed using network theories. In relationalism the unit of analysis is neither individuals, as in rational choice theories, nor macro structures, as in Marxist approaches, but social networks through which players migrate. The analytical frameworks of global commodity chains (Gereffi and Korzeniewicz 1994), global value chains (Klein 2010) and global production networks (Dicken 2003) are particularly useful in understanding what is at stake in this transnationalization process. Clubs can be considered as industrial units that gradually develop football skills and players as commodities whose transfer rights are bought and sold in order to generate added value. Since 1994 the number of football player transfers has multiplied by 3.2 and the total value of transfers fees by 7 (KEA and CDES 2013). Despite the financial crisis in the European economy, the transfer market has emerged as a growing economic sector and the total amount of transfers generated during the 2013 transfer window by the big-5 leagues exceeded for the first time the sum of €2 billion. Such financial opportunities imply that more and more clubs and agents are active at a transnational level in the search for young and promising footballers whose skills still need to be developed in order for them to be further transferred to wealthier teams and leagues. In reality, the upward transnational career paths of leading players at the very best clubs in the world only concern a tiny minority of footballers. However, this does not prevent a full range of actors from club officials to player agents working on a daily basis to set up potentially lucrative channels and opportunities that form the basis of the whole migration system for professional football players.

This new economic sector attracts new investors who expect high profitability, generated by growing transfer fees. The Third Party Ownership (TPO) system is an example of such an emerging market which uses existing migration networks. TPO refers to the practice of a third party (society, investment fund, agent, etc.) to acquire rights in the future transfer fees of a player. In this situation, the individual player should maximize the number of transfers during a career to ensure the highest possible profits. Existing relations between clubs and countries are reinforced as they can facilitate movements which are disconnected from sporting issues. Clearly, in this type of transaction agreement, one must not only consider the migration of a player from the sociological perspective of identity but also as a phenomenon that questions the 'values of sport' and far wider ethical issues. First of all, we must question the integrity of players in this situation: have they lost their human status in becoming commodities? They are under pressure from investors who decide career choices and opportunities on their behalf. Both physical and moral integrity are also in danger. How can sport continue to transmit values of friendship, respect and effort in this situation? The integrity of sporting events is in question too, as it can be argued that the interests of the investors are disconnected from sport results, specifically when their players are distributed amongst several teams. The owner of various players' economic rights can have financial stakes in different clubs and thus the power to manipulate match results and the sporting destiny of teams.

As for rational choice theories, relationalism considers that economic stakes play a crucial role in driving the action of individuals within networks. From this perspective, economic divisions between countries tend to favour the emergence of transnational networks, which will consequently increase the volume of international transfer flows. As for Marxist approaches, relationalism applied to player migration considers that it is very important to analyze power relationships between actors involved in transfer networks. On the one hand, this allows us to understand the impact of economic and political macro structures at an individual level. On the other hand, the study of the empirical functioning of transfer networks permits us to understand the strategic actions deployed by the different parties involved to better their position within such networks and to broaden their sphere of influence.

But, in relationalism, the consequences of player migration cannot be determined in advance. The international flows of footballers are not considered as intrinsically positive or negative, but must be analyzed on a case-by-case basis. However, the detailed analysis of transfer networks and player career paths allows generalizations on possible outcomes. For example, statistical evidence can be provided to stress the importance of top league experience in a home country – before migration – in achieving a more successful career abroad. From this perspective, migration is generally positive both at an individual and collective level when the player in question has already proven himself in a national league. A move can be less successful without such prior national league development.

While individuals involved within transfer networks know the risks for a player to migrate at a very young age, competition for talent and financial considerations drive the general lowering of the age of international migration. The latter went down from 26 years of age in the 1980s to currently around 22 years of age (Poli, Ravenel and Besson 2011). Competition between intermediaries also promotes the scouting of ever younger players. A survey carried out in 2011 on licensed agents and contracted players domiciled in the five biggest European markets has shown that only 42% were already professional players (Poli and Rossi 2012). This confirms that agents are above all interested in young talent that has the potential of an upward career path and which can further enhance their own careers. As a consequence, the social situations surrounding talented young players can easily lead them to make ill-informed career choices. In such a competitive sector as professional football, where the supply of labour constantly overtakes demand, these problems can heavily undermine the potential benefits of international migration both at an individual and collective level.

Conclusion

The migration of elite athletes is a key feature of contemporary sport. Such migration configures the identity of many elite athletes, such as in the cases of US basketball players all over the world (FIBA 2013), rugby players drawn from the south hemisphere (Gillon *et al.* 2010: 49), Cuban and Dominican baseball players in the United States or Kenyan runners winning races worldwide (Bale and Sang 1996). But football, with its advanced forms of globalization, provides an outstanding case study. Its development as a truly global industry has further driven the increase in international player movement and more individuals than ever before are now involved in the transfer process. Networks also have a crucial role to play. However, they are composed of multiple actors who are often competing against each other as they try to manage the transfer and take advantage of their prized asset. Licensed and unlicensed agents – to whom it is possible to refer using the broader notion of intermediaries – are also key figures. Their connections with players and club representatives, on behalf of whom they also often work, are essential to understanding career pathways and, more specifically, migration patterns.

In such a competitive and hierarchical sector as professional football, it is inevitable that a significant number of players will not achieve an upward career path. While migration is often a prerequisite for access to the wealthiest leagues, international migration can prove to be detrimental to long-term career success. Financial speculation linked to young footballers – especially from underprivileged countries – and within the context of the creation of transnational value chains only serves to aggravate the situation.

In a business sector which involves the movement of players as both workers and human beings, it is essential that football governing bodies and state authorities collaborate to ensure the enforcement of existing rules on transfer and labour rights. To preserve the potentially positive impact of international mobility both on an individual and collective level, it is also crucial that football governing bodies at the national and international level continue to proactively investigate and implement new ways to regulate the market in accordance with state laws.

Notes

1 Translated into English from the French version.
2 See also Poli (2010a) for more examples.
3 More information is to be found on the CIES Football Observatory's website at http://www.football-observatory.com.
4 The five major European football championships ('big-5') are the English Premier League, the Spanish Primera Liga, the Italian Serie A, the German Erste Bundesliga and the French Ligue 1. These leagues comprise the wealthiest clubs in the world, which have the financial means to attract the best-performing players regardless of their origin.
5 The notion of expatriate refers to footballers who are employed by a club that is outside of the national association where they began playing and from where they departed following recruitment by a 'foreign' club.
6 The 'Bosman ruling', decreed in 1995 by the European Court of Justice, has obliged the national football associations and national football leagues of all European Union countries to review their regulations and to allow for the free circulation of players holding an EU passport. This ruling has allowed clubs to take advantage of new recruitment possibilities and accelerated the globalization of European football.
7 More information is to be found on the CIES Football Observatory's website at www.football-observatory.com.
8 For more details, see Poli (2010a)

References

Bale, J. and Maguire, J. (eds) (1994) *The Global Sports Arena: Athletic Talent Migration in an Interdependent World*, London: Frank Cass.
Bale, J. and Sang, J. (1996) *Kenyan Running: Movement Culture, Geography and Global Change*, London: Frank Cass.
Barth, F. (1998) *Ethnic Groups and Boundaries: The Social Organization of Culture Difference* (5th edition), Prospect Heights, IL: Waveland.

Beck, U. (2006) *The Cosmopolitan Vision*, Cambridge: Polity Press.

Besson, R., Poli, R., and Ravenel, L. (2011) *Global Player Migration Report 2011*, Neuchâtel: CIES.

Besson, R., Poli R., and Ravenel L. (2014) *CIES Football Observatory's Demographic Study*. Neuchâtel: CIES.

Bromberger, C. (1995) *Le Match de football: ethnologie d'une passion partisane à Marseille, Naples et Turin*, Paris: Éditions de la Maison des Sciences de l'Homme.

Dicken, P. (2003) *Global Shift: Reshaping the Global Economy Map in the 21st Century* (4th edition), London: Sage.

FIBA (2013) *International Basketball Migration Report*, Mies: FIBA. Available at: http://www.fiba.com/asp_scripts/downMana.asp?fileID=4240 (accessed 5 March 2014).

Gereffi, G., and Korzeniewicz M. (eds) (1994) *Commodity Chains and Global Capitalism*, Westport, CT: Praeger.

Gillon, P., Grosjean, F., and Ravenel, L. (2010) *Atlas du sport mondial*, Paris: Autrement.

Giulianotti, R., and Robertson, R. (2007) 'Sport and Globalization: Transnational Dimensions', *Global Networks*, 7(2): 107–112.

Hobsbawm, E. (2000) *Les enjeux du XXIe siècle: entretien avec Antonio Polito*, Bruxelles: Complexe.

Hognestad, H. (2003) 'Long-Distance Football Support and Liminal Identities Among Norwegian Fans', in N. Dyck and E. Archetti (ed.) *Sport, Dance and Embodied Identities*, Oxford: Berg.

Jaksa, K.L. (2011) 'Sports and Collective Identity: The Effects of Athletics on National Unity', *SAIS Review of International Affairs*, 31(1): 39–41.

KEA and CDES (2013) 'Study on the Economic and Legal Aspects of Transfers of Players'. Available at: http://ec.europa.eu/sport/news/20130207-study-on-transfers_en.htm (accessed 15 December 2013).

Klein, A. (2010) 'Sport Labour Migration as a Global Value Chain', in J. Maguire and M. Falcous (eds) *Sport and Migration: Borders, Boundaries and Crossings*, London: Routledge.

Lestrelin, L. (2010) *L'autre public des matchs de football. Sociologie des « supporters à distance » de l'Olympique de Marseille*, Paris: Éditions de l'EHESS.

Maguire, J., and Falcous, M. (eds) (2011) *Sport and Migration: Borders, Boundaries and Crossings*, London: Routledge.

Poli, R. (ed.) (2005). *Football et identités: les sentiments d'appartenance en question*, Neuchâtel: CIES.

Poli, R. (2010a) 'Understanding Globalisation through Football: The New International Division of Labour, Migratory Channels and Transnational Trade Circuits', *International Review for the Sociology of Sport*, 45(4): 491–506.

Poli, R. (2010b) *Le marché des footballeurs. Réseaux et circuits dans l'économie globale*, Bern: Peter Lang.

Poli, R., Ravenel, L. and Besson, R. (2011) *Annual Review of the European Football Players' Labour Market*, Neuchâtel: CIES.

Poli, R., Ravenel, L., and Besson, R. (2013) *Big-5 Weekly Post*, 55, Neuchâtel: CIES. Available at: http://www.football-observatory.com/IMG/pdf/wp55_eng.pdf (accessed 5 March 2014).

Poli, R., and Rossi, G. (2012) *Football Agents in the Biggest Five European Football Markets: An Empirical Research Report*, Neuchâtel: CIES. Available at: http://www.football-observatory.com/IMG/pdf/report_agents_2012-2.pdf (accessed 15 December 2013).

Richelieu, A., and Desbordes, M. (2009) 'Football Teams Going International: The Strategic Leverage of Branding', *Journal of Sponsorship*, 3(1): 10–22.

Roche, M. (2006) 'Mega-events and Modernity Revisited: Globalization and the Case of the Olympics', *Sociological Review*, 54: 25–40.

Scelles, N., Durand, C., Bonnal, L., Goyeau, D., and Andreff, W. (2013) 'Competitive Balance versus Competitive Intensity Before a Match: Is One of These Two Concepts More Relevant in Explaining Attendance? The Case of the French Football Ligue 1 over the Period 2008–2011', *Applied Economics*, 45(29): 4184–4192.

Simmons, R. (1996) 'The Demand for English League Football: A Club-Level Analysis', *Applied Economics*, 28(2): 139–155.

Tomlinson, A. (1996) 'Olympic Spectacle: Opening Ceremonies and Some Paradoxes of Globalization', *Media Culture and Society*, 18(4): 583–602.

42

SPORT AND THE CORPORATE WORLD

Barry Smart

Introduction: the corporate world of sport

Sport has become increasingly immersed in the corporate world and ever more dependent on the lucrative financial returns that flow from commercial sponsorship, endorsement contracts, and media broadcasting rights. Sport events, teams, and athletes are now known not only for the competitive tournaments and performances with which their identities have become synonymous, but also, by virtue of an increasingly pervasive corporate logic that structures the sporting world, as commercial brands (Gratton *et al.* 2012; Perelman 2012; Smart 2005, 2007). Sport teams and athletes are ranked not only in terms of their competitive sporting performances and tournament successes but also, as is the case with sport events, according to commercial brand value. The three events considered in the corporate world to be the most valuable sporting properties are the Super Bowl, the Summer Olympic Games, and the FIFA World Cup, with estimated brand values of $470 million, $348 million, and $147 million respectively (Forbes 2012).

The Summer Olympic Games and the FIFA World Cup are the two most popular and prestigious truly global sporting events. Their economic significance and cultural appeal transcend national and ideological boundaries, override differences of religion, class, and ethnicity, and provide the corporate world with unrivalled commercial opportunities to increase global brand awareness and extend market penetration of their products and services.[1] Although the Super Bowl is televised around the world, it nevertheless remains fundamentally an American sporting cultural ritual and does not have the global reach or appeal of the Olympic Games, the FIFA World Cup, or other sporting events with a more credible claim to global status, including cricket and rugby union World Cups (Martin and Reeves 2001). The NFL's Super Bowl XLVII of 2013 was broadcast from the Mercedes-Benz Superdome in New Orleans to 185 countries in 30 different languages, but in comparison to other genuinely more global sports, the Super Bowl has continued to leave the great sporting public around the world relatively unmoved; 'for the United States to consider the Super Bowl as the most popular *international* sporting event requires both an excessive amount of hype . . . and an equal amount of solipsism' (Martin and Reeves 2001: 223, 228).

The Super Bowl is now as much of a corporate advertising extravaganza as a sporting event, with some observers arguing that the real competition is no longer between the teams playing but between advertising agencies and corporate brands pitching their wares in the commercial breaks (Martin and Reeves 2001: 221). As Lab42, a Chicago-based market research company that conducted a survey on the Super Bowl, discovered, 'American adults prefer watching Super Bowl commercials to the game itself' (Beltrone 2013).

Sport, industry, and economy

Whether the focus is on the competitive sporting contests of classical antiquity, traditional folk games, or modern, formally constituted, rule-governed sports, an economic dimension has been consistently present, but from the late nineteenth century following professionalization, commercialization, and increasing media coverage of sport it has grown in significance (Rader 1984; Smart 2005, 2007; Gratton *et al.* 2012).

Victorious competitors in the ancient games held in Olympia achieved fame and glory and had statues erected in their honour. When they returned home to their communities, they frequently received compensation in the form of material rewards, which might include money, exemption from taxation, free accommodation and food, as well as other payments in kind (Crowther 1996: 34; Andreff 2008:13). Indeed, a form of professionalism, in the sense of athletic guilds bargaining for the rights of athletes, participating in the organization of events, and operating to protect the material interests of athletes, was a significant feature of the ancient Olympics, and early forms of sponsorship have been traced back to the fifth century BC (Kissoudi 2005; Toohey and Veal 2007). Gambling on outcomes was a prominent feature of traditional folk games as well as most pre-modern sporting activities, and by the seventeenth century money transactions were an increasingly frequent feature of prize fighting, horse racing, bowls, tennis, and cricket, as the commercial potential of sports began to be recognized and exploited (Birley 2003). But it was in the course of the late nineteenth century, with growing international capitalist economic development and spectacular industrial fairs and exhibitions, that signs truly began to accumulate of sport's increasing incorporation into the rapidly expanding world of commerce.

One of the earliest prestigious international events where the growing affinity between industry, business, and sport became increasingly evident in the course of the second half of the nineteenth century was the 'Universal Exhibition' or 'World's Fair', an economic and cultural spectacle which began in London with the Great Exhibition in May of 1851 and subsequently has been held at regular intervals around the world. The imminent prospect of the Great Exhibition was described in November 1850 by Marx and Engels (1850/1978: 499–500) as a 'great world congress of products and producers . . . [and as] striking proof of the concentrated power with which modern large-scale industry is everywhere demolishing national barriers and increasingly blurring local peculiarities of production, society and national character among all peoples', a powerful economic and cultural capacity subsequently emulated by modern sports.

In a report following the inaugural modern Olympic Games in Athens Pierre de Courbetin (1896/1897: 1) remarked that just as Universal Exhibitions had collected together 'the powers and achievements of art, industry and science', so too sportsmen from around the world had begun to meet on 'common ground' and that the growth of international sport reflected the 'great cosmopolitan tendencies' of the time. The introduction of world's fairs and exhibitions in the nineteenth century has been recognized as a significant influence on the development of international sport in general and the modern Olympic Games in particular:

> Competitions in sports have been part of the programmes and by-programmes since 1851. . . . Sport and games including gymnastics had been systematically represented in world's fairs since 1867. . . . The combination of an international gymnastic festival

and athletic competitions with the Paris Fair of 1889 may be seen as prototype for the linking of Olympic Games with the world's fairs of the years 1900, 1904, and 1908.

(Borgers 2003: 7–8)

The early Olympic Games were heavily dependent upon the organizational and financial infrastructure provided by the world's fairs. The 1900 Paris Olympics and 1904 St Louis Olympics lacked a designated organizing committee and relied on the exhibitions with which they were closely associated. In both cases the sports programmes were 'dispersed over the whole period of the exhibition'; indeed, athletes returning from the Paris Olympics complained that sports events were effectively marginalized (Borgers 2003: 18–19). De Coubertin was particularly concerned about the impact that the exhibition's emphasis on commerce and entertainment might have upon the Olympic ideal he was attempting to cultivate and lamented the fact that they had been 'taken over by a big fair where their philosophical value vanished into the thin air' (cited in Borgers 2003: 18). The fear was that commercial interest in the Olympics would corrupt the amateur ethos deemed integral to a resurrection of the ancient games. But de Coubertin simultaneously recognized that for the early-modern Olympics there was no option: the 'alliance' with exhibitions was essential for 'budgetary reasons' (cited in Borgers 2003: 19). Comparable financial 'alliances' with the corporate world, albeit far greater in scale, have proven to be no less essential for late-modern Olympic Games.

An economic and cultural affinity between sport and the corporate capitalist world was identified by the German social and economic analyst Max Weber early in the twentieth century. Reflecting on the competitive nature of modern capitalism, Weber commented that 'in the United States, the pursuit of wealth . . . tends to become associated with purely mundane passions, which often actually gives it the character of sport' (1904–05/1976: 182). In 1904 Weber spent six months in the USA and experienced at first hand the rapidly growing enthusiasm for sport on university campuses, the extent of press interest in and coverage of sport, and the disciplined and 'businesslike earnestness' with which sports events were being conducted (Scaff 2011: 49, 141, 143, 146–47). While in the USA, Weber presented a lecture at the Congress of Arts and Science at the World's Fair in St Louis, in conjunction with which the 1904 Games of the III Olympiad were held (Kent 2008). At this time the modern Olympic movement was struggling to gain control over the organizing and planning of the games.

At the II Olympiad in Paris in 1900, staged in the shadow of a World's Fair (Exposition Universelle), some sports events had been confusingly listed as part of the trade fair, and in a comparable fashion the 1908 Games of the IV Olympiad in London took place in the midst of, and required the invaluable assistance of, another international fair, the Franco-British Exhibition of Science, Arts and Industries. The cost of the stadium used for the games, which became known as 'White City after its ugly concrete structures', was met by the Franco-British Exhibition (Kent 2008). As the Official Report of the London Games records,

> agreement was finally concluded on January 14, 1907 . . . that the Exhibition Committee should construct at their own cost all the racing tracks and buildings necessary for carrying out the Olympic Games, and should provide all necessary equipment, attendants, advertisements . . . and should advance to the British Olympic Association the sum of £2,000 for current working expenses. The proceeds of the admission of the public were to be divided between the Franco-British Exhibition and the British Olympic Association in the proportion of three to one
>
> (British Olympic Council 1909: 26)

The modern Olympics and the corporate world: London 1908, 1948, and 2012

At the beginning of the twentieth century, the Olympic Games was beginning to distinguish itself from the universal exhibitions of modern industry and was acquiring a measure of independence. As the twentieth century developed, the quadrennial games would have an increasingly significant impact on 'the environmental and architectural transformation of their host cities' and, by virtue of advances in television and communication technology, the Summer Olympics would become *the* global sports event (Borgers 2003: 8).

By the end of the twentieth century, the Olympic movement had come to terms with professionalism. In 1971 the International Olympic Committee (IOC) removed the term 'amateur' from the Olympic Charter and subsequently amended eligibility regulations to allow athletes to receive compensation for time spent away from work while training and competing. In addition, athletes were allowed to accept sponsorship from National Olympic Committees, sporting organizations, and business. Following a further IOC initiative in 1986, international sports federations governing each Olympic sport were given the authority to determine whether professional athletes could participate in Olympic events (Barney *et al.* 2004; Toohey and Veal 2007).

Analysis of the three London Summer Olympic Games illustrates the growing impact of a commercial ethos on sport and the increasing involvement of the corporate world.

London 1908

With limited resources at their disposal, and very limited government support, the IV Olympiad held in London in 1908 was heavily dependent on finance provided by the Chamber of Commerce with additional funds raised through a *Daily Mail* newspaper public appeal. There was no Olympic Village, so athletes were placed in boarding houses and hotels, mainly in and around the London area. The lack of financial backing and support for the majority of the 2,008 athletes (1,971 men, 37 women) representing the 22 National Olympic Committees was a matter of great concern, as was the broader issue of professionalism and fake-amateurism which was having an impact on many sports (Kent 2008; IOC 2013).

Although the early Olympic Games did not attract a great deal of interest from business, there were nevertheless emerging signs of the corporate world's awakening to the possible benefits of association with sport. From the late nineteenth century, sports goods companies began to emerge in Europe and America, including Spalding, Slazenger, Dunlop, J.W. Foster & Sons (later to become Reebok), Converse, Wilson, and Gebruder Dassler (from which Adidas and Puma subsequently developed) (Smart 2007: 11–14). In addition, corporations began to recognize the positive commercial value to be derived from association with prestigious sporting events. For example, in 1898 in England, Bovril welcomed endorsement by the league champions Nottingham Forest football club, and in the USA, Spalding worked to ensure that their equipment was visible at all Amateur Athletic Union (AAU) track meets (Kent 2008; Marshall and Cook 1992).

In respect of the early Olympic Games, there were several signs of developing corporate interest. The 1904 games held in St Louis were criticized in Europe for having been over-commercialized. Spalding, the sports goods company, provided a significant proportion of the facilities and was a major sponsor of the III Olympiad. Coubertin subsequently expressed the view that holding the games in 'utilitarian America' had been a 'misfortune' (cited in Brownell 2008: 48). At the London 1908 Olympics, Oxo gained the catering rights for the marathon event and provided booths along the route offering 'an Oxo Athletes' Flask containing Oxo for immediate use; Oxo, hot and cold; [and] Oxo Soda', and in the same event free samples of WAWKPHAR Antiseptic Military Foot Powder were provided to competitors (Jenkins 2008: 192–93; Kent 2008: 159). Organizers of Olympic events sought to attract advertising from commercial sponsors and 'in the booklet describing the race procedures and listing entrants for the marathon, readers were exposed to full-page advertisements for Schweppes Soda Water and Dry Ginger Ale, Vaughton's Medal and Badge Makers and Wawkphar's Antiseptic Military Foot Powder' (Barney *et al.* 2004: 23). At the Fifth Olympiad in Stockholm, there was a further incremental increase in commercialism with companies purchasing 'sole rights' to promote and sell products in and around the Olympic venue (Barney *et al.* 2004).

London 1948

The years between the IV and XIV Olympiads held in London in 1908 and 1948 were marked by a number of significant developments which constituted portents of the future commercial value of the games. Towards the end of 1913, Pierre de Courbetin adopted what would ultimately become the iconic commercially invaluable symbol of the Olympic Games, its brand, the five interlocking rings representing the five continents and the 'universality of Olympism' (The Olympic Museum 2007: 3). The prominence of business and commercial enterprise at the VII Olympiad in 1930 in Antwerp led Courbetin to warn of the growing risks to which the games were becoming exposed, and the VIII Olympiad in Paris demonstrated how vulnerable the games were as product advertising appeared in the stadium for the first (and only) time and 'the 320-page guide to the games published by the Organizing Committee . . . featured ads on 256 different pages' (Barney *et al.* 2004: 27). For the next games, held in Amsterdam, the IOC ruled that Olympic stadiums and buildings should be free of advertising, but 'rights packages' were sold by the organizers (Barney *et al.* 2004: 28). Another very notable development was that Coca-Cola began its enduring relationship with the Olympic Movement:

> Our relationship with the Olympic Games started at Amsterdam 1928, when a freight ship arrived in the Dutch capital delivering both the US Olympic Team and 1,000 cases of *Coca-Cola* to the Olympic Games. Bottles of our classic sparkling drink were sold at kiosks around the Olympic Stadium and rowing course.
> (Coca-Cola and the Olympic Games: Our History n.d.)

As in 1908, the 1948 London Olympics, the 'austerity Olympics', had to proceed with little government support. Following the end of the Second World War, emphasis was placed upon 'make do and mend', allowing commercial and business interests to make further inroads into the Olympic Movement (Hampton 2008: 3; 2012: 19). Making do was unavoidable because the UK was still recovering from the war. London had been badly bombed, rationing of food, clothing, and petrol was in force, and few resources could be directed to the XIV Olympiad (Hampton 2012). This was the context in which a corporate interest in the Olympics stealthily continued to develop, with a variety of companies providing sponsorship, including Nescafé, International Combustion Ltd, Gillette, Martel Brandy, Ovaltine, Quaker Oats, Sloane's Liniment, Guinness, Brylcreem, and Coca-Cola. As Hampton (2008: 33) observes,

> The official souvenir magazine was filled with so many advertisements – for items like Gilbey's gin, Craven 'A' cigarettes, Stein's garters and Aertex underwear – that it is difficult to find the articles. Any company that paid £250 was permitted to use the five ring Olympic emblem.

Increasingly appreciative of the marketing value the Olympics provided, corporations took every opportunity to draw attention to their close association with the games. Notwithstanding the ban on advertising in stadiums, Dunlop went so far as to declare its involvement 'in huge letters on the track' at the Herne Hill Velodrome in London (Hampton 2008: 262; see also 61, 63, 75).

In media terms both the 1908 and 1948 London Olympics were notable. The 1908 games were the first to be filmed by moving cine camera and the 1948 games were the first to receive national television coverage (Hampton 2012, 2008). The BBC paid £1,000 for radio and television transmission rights for the 1948 London Olympic Games, a figure dwarfed by the £60 million reportedly paid to transmit the 2012 London Olympics (Magnay 2012). The sale of broadcasting rights has become a major source of income for the sport industry in general and for global sport events in particular. The total global value of the broadcasting rights for the 2010 Winter Olympic Games (Vancouver) and the 2012 Summer Olympic Games has been estimated to be US$3.83 billion, an increase of 'US$1,258 million ... [on] the cumulative broadcast revenue earned from the 2006 and 2008 Olympics' (Gratton *et al.* 2012: 78).

The growing corporatization of the Olympics

From the 1928 Amsterdam Games, the issue of corporate interest and intrusion became an increasing matter of concern for the IOC. Acute ambivalence is perhaps the most appropriate way to describe the IOC's early reaction, because whilst commercialization was regarded as anathema to Olympic values, the rising costs of staging the games made sources of finance an increasingly vital matter. The development of the Olympic Games from the X Olympiad in Los Angeles in 1932 to the XXIII Olympiad held in the same city in 1984, through to the present, is marked by increasing commercialism. A number of significant developments reveal the complex ways in which the Olympics have responded to increasing business interest and corporate encroachment, but a key moment is the unanticipated business acumen and commercial exploitation of the Los Angeles Games in 1932 by Helms Bakeries, which had a 'bakery goods supply contract for the Olympic Village' (Barney *et al.* 2004: 33). Following the games, Helms continued to capitalize on the Olympic association by manufacturing products such as 'Helms Olympic Bread' and employing Olympic rings and words in marketing. This prompted the IOC to move to legal registry to protect 'Olympic words and insignia' from commercial 'exploitation *without authority*', a development which prepared the ground for the establishment in 1985 of a lucrative marketing rights initiative, The Olympic Partner (TOP) Programme and subsequent forms of bespoke legislation to protect sponsors (Barney *et al.* 2004: 31, 33, 49, emphasis added; Smart 2007: 22; Addley 2012).

If the 1932 Olympic Games were notable for prompting the Olympic Movement to recognize the need to protect its sign values from unauthorized commercial exploitation, the 1984 games 'rewrote the rules for the staging of the international sporting event [and] introduced a new economic order'; and demonstrated that the corporate world was more than capable of delivering a successful sports event at a profit (Tomlinson 2008: 67). In 1982 the IOC had established a commission to explore new sources of financing to fund the Olympic Movement, and the following year research began on the development of an international Olympic marketing programme. As a consequence of the city of Los Angeles preventing the use of public money, the games in 1984 were the first Olympics to be funded entirely from corporate sponsorship and marketing revenue and the first to be profitable since 1932 (Close *et al.* 2007: 11). The following year, the IOC explicitly embraced the corporate world and endorsed commercialism by approving 'the launch of the TOP Programme', a prestigious and lucrative commercial sponsorship programme designed to create 'an orderly marketplace with the creation of specific programs targeted to meet the interests of all the Modern Olympic Movements partners' (IOC 2001; Barney *et al*. 2004: 231).

The increasing corporatization of the Olympic Games is illustrated by a number of additional developments, including commercial and corporate involvements of IOC members, many of whom are developers and financiers, the growing role corporations have played in the organizing and funding of the games, and the increasing emphasis placed upon 'the business opportunity for growth' exemplified by the Olympics and illustrated by the Beijing Organizing Committee for the games as it sought to encourage further corporate involvement in 2008 (Close *et al*. 2007: 21). In the period prior to the 2008 games, the Beijing Organizing Committee placed great emphasis on the marketing opportunities awaiting corporate partners and emphasized that a partnership with the 2008 Olympic Games would 'provide a unique Olympic marketing platform for both Chinese and foreign enterprises [and would] encourage ... Chinese business entities to enhance their corporate image and brand awareness through their Olympic association, [as well as] provide quality services to sponsors and maximize the return on their investments' (Chinese Olympic Committee 2004).

The period between the XXIII Olympiad in Los Angeles in 1984, which firmly established the 'consumerist union of commerce, sport and television' (Rowe 1996: 556), and the XXX Olympiad in London in 2012 is marked by rapidly rising broadcasting rights revenue and growing commercial sponsorship income as the Olympic Movement increasingly embraced corporatization (IOC 2012).

As Jacques Rogge, IOC president, acknowledged in a reference to the vital contribution of the corporate world to the Olympic Movement:

> Without the support of the business community, without its technology, expertise, people, services, products, telecommunications, [and] its financing . . . the Olympic Games could not and cannot happen.
>
> (International Olympic Committee, n.d.)

London 2012

When in 2005 London won the bid to host the 2012 Summer Games, the global economy was continuing to grow and the United Nations (2005: iii) reported that it had 'considerable momentum' and that prospects remained 'positive'. But the economic crisis that commenced in 2007 meant that preparation for and indeed the staging of the XXX Olympiad itself took place in very different circumstances, in the midst of an economic and cultural climate of austerity. However, notwithstanding the constraints arising from a global banking and sovereign debt crisis, UK government support for the games increased substantially, rising from an estimated budget of £2.4 billion in 2005 to a budget of £9.3 billion by the end of 2011, the expectation being that a global sporting event could provide a 'boost to the economy' (Batty 2011). In turn, in the period up to 2012, Olympic broadcasting rights and TOP sponsorship programme revenue generation had continued to increase (see Table 42.1), confirming the growing commercial value of the games to the corporate world (Murray 2012).[2]

In 2012 there were eleven commercial worldwide partners in the TOP programme: Coca-Cola, Acer, Atos, Dow, General Electric, McDonald's, Omega, Panasonic, P&G (Procter & Gamble), Samsung. and Visa. In addition, all National Olympic Committees continued to manage their own locally based sponsorship programmes to support their sport development activities and Olympic teams, albeit in non-competing categories to the TOP sponsors (IOC 2012:

Barry Smart

Table 42.1 Olympic Marketing Revenue: The Past Five Quadrennia

Source	1993–1996	1997–2000	2001–2004	2005–2008	2009–2012
Broadcast	1,251	1,845	2,232	2,570	3,914
TOP Programme	279	579	663	866	957

Source: IOC (2012: 6). All figures in USD millions.

17–40). The London 2012 Organising Committee (LOCOG) put in place a local sponsorship programme which granted 'exclusive marketing rights' within the UK to seven additional commercial partners including Adidas, BMW, BP, British Airways, BT, EDF, and Lloyds TSB, as well as to a further seven 'Olympic Partners', including Adecco, Arcelor Mittal, Cadbury, Cisco, Deloitte, Thomas Cook, and UPS (IOC 2012: 41–45).

The exercise of increasingly unbridled corporate power over the Olympics can be traced back to the corporate takeover of the games in Los Angeles in 1984, which inaugurated an increased commodification of all the iconic Olympic properties, including rings, flag, motto (*citius, altius, fortius*) and flame (Barney *et al.* 2004; Tomlinson 2005). The scale and extent of the corporate presence in the London 2012 Games led to a variety of criticisms that private corporations were 'calling the shots'(*The Guardian* 2012; Milne 2012). Three of the companies in the TOP programme, Dow Chemical (producers of the wrap for the Olympic Stadium), Rio Tinto (manufacturer of the Olympic medals), and BP ('official sustainability partner') attracted particular criticism, as did the IOC for including them as sponsors. Association with such an iconic sporting event allowed these corporations to appear as good corporate citizens and to distract attention from ongoing protests about their responsibility for forms of environmental destruction and community devastation (Greenwash Gold 2012; O'Connor 2012).

In preparation for the 2012 Olympics in London, the UK parliament passed specific legislation to protect the commercial interests of the games and the corporate sponsors involved. The London Olympic Games and Paralympic Games Act of 2006 added further to the protections inscribed in law through the 'Olympic Symbol etc (Protection) Act' of 1995, which had already made legislative provision for 'the use for commercial purposes of the Olympic symbol and certain words associated with the Olympic games' (Legislation.gov.uk 1995: chapter 32). The 2006 act amended the previous legislation and provided a higher level of protection to the games and corporate sponsors in addition to that already available through contract law and copyright. The act created the Olympic Delivery Authority for the games and granted it 'exclusive control of the advertising space and street trading licences around Olympic venues and the power to investigate and prosecute breaches of the Olympic Association Right and the London Olympics Association Right' (James and Osborn 2011: 416). The commercial protections inscribed in the legislation have been described as 'unparalleled in English Law' and as exemplifying 'the creep of commercialism' transforming the culture and spirit of the Olympics (James and Osborn 2011: 416). The act went much further than prohibition of unauthorized use of Olympic symbols and associated words and terms by designating the London Olympics Association Right as encompassing '*any* representation of *any kind* that is likely to suggest to the public that there is an association between the London Olympics and any goods or services, or any person who provides goods or services' (James and Osborn 2011: 421).

The aim of such legislation is to uphold the commercial value of Olympic properties, the symbols and iconography, by protecting the rights of corporate partners, the sponsors who have paid for authorized use of Olympic signs and words. Notwithstanding the wide-reaching character of the legislation, corporations that were not official partners of the IOC or LOCOG found ways of avoiding legal prohibitions, ways of creatively associating themselves with the games, and the company with the most successful track record in this respect has been Nike.

Nike Games

Early in 2012 Nike introduced a campaign called 'Make It Count' featuring sportsmen and sportswomen across a number of fields. A survey of Tweeters subsequently revealed that the Nike brand was the most associated with the Olympic Games even though it had no official sponsoring relationship, unlike its close commercial rival Adidas (Addley 2012).

Nike has a longstanding reputation for ambush marketing. At the Barcelona Olympics in 1992, Nike sponsored press conferences with the all-conquering USA Basketball 'Dream Team', led by Michael Jordan, half of whose members had lucrative endorsement contracts with Nike, despite Reebok being the games' official sponsor. There was also a stand-off between Nike-contracted players and the US Olympic Committee, which had received $4 million from Reebok. The contract stipulated that American medal winners would wear jackets bearing the Reebok emblem in award ceremonies, but the Nike contingent in the basketball team initially refused to do so and only complied when advised that they could wear the jackets in a manner that did not identify the offending brand (Smart 2005: 110–112). In Atlanta in 1996, Nike built its Nike Village adjacent to the Olympic athletes' village, bought up a large quantity of advertising billboard space around Olympic venues, and gave Nike flags to spectators. In 2012, as well as the 'Make It Count' campaign, Nike ran a 'Find Your Greatness' advertising campaign featuring unknown athletes engaging in various sports in places with the name London in the frame – London, Ohio; London Plaza; Little London, Jamaica; London Hotel; London Gym; London Field; London, Nigeria; London, Canada; London Fire Dept; London Primary; and London Avenue – with the following 'attitude' narrative:

> There are no grand celebrations here, no speeches, no bright lights, but there are great athletes, somehow we've come to believe that greatness is reserved for the chosen few, for the superstars, the truth is greatness is for all of us, this is not about lowering expectations, it's about raising them for every last one of us, because greatness is not in one special place, it is not in one special person, greatness is wherever somebody is trying to find it.
>
> (Sweney 2012)

The Nike 2012 television ambush marketing campaign was launched to coincide with the opening ceremony of the games and was supplemented by a poster campaign with straplines such as 'Greatness doesn't only exist in SW19' (referring to Wimbledon, which hosted the Olympic tennis tournament), 'Greatness doesn't need its own anthem', and 'Greatness doesn't need a stadium' (Sweney 2012). Just as Nike had ambushed earlier games by sponsoring teams – for example, in Beijing they sponsored Chinese teams in 22 of 28 Olympic sports – in 2012 they were the official sponsors of the US basketball team and provided the uniforms and medal stand apparel, even though Adidas was once again an official games sponsor (Badenhausen 2012). Furthermore, adding to their Olympic ambush marketing reputation and corporate profile at the games, Nike provided the Volt Collection footwear for the US team and other athletes who chose to wear the very distinctive neon-yellow shoes (Briggs 2012).

Barry Smart

Concluding remarks: the corporatized sporting world

Modern sport is now thoroughly corporatized. Sports events, sports teams, individual athletes, the stadiums and venues where competition takes place, as well as the array of media which now relay matches and tournaments to fans and viewers around the world, are imbued with the interests, values, and signs of the corporate world. Sponsorship and media coverage are the lifeblood of modern sport and their articulation constitutes a cultural-commercial force field. Global sports events such as the IOC Olympic Games and the FIFA World Cup also present opportunities for processes of 'creative destruction' as host cities and countries are radically transformed in the course of providing appropriate stadiums, venues, and associated transport and other forms of infrastructure, developments which have proven highly lucrative for corporate interests, simultaneously financially costly for host cities, and also destructive of the traditional fabric of the host environments made subject to forms of architectural and urban renewal which 'in the context of the current globalization process [produce] the homogenization and unification of all cities' (Perelman 2012: 12).

Late modern sport is thoroughly corporatized and global in scope. A sport-media-corporate constellation, a close articulation between sports events, teams, and athletes, broadcasting organizations, and corporate sponsors, a corollary of the increasing globalization of the sport market, has transformed the ethos of sport, transformed its economic value, social meaning, and cultural significance. Sport travels effortlessly across national borders and is the ideal vehicle for capitalism's cosmopolitan pursuit of global markets (Aris 1990: 169). While sport retains a vestige of genuine aesthetic value and continues to serve as a medium for expressions of community belonging, it is thoroughly imbued with the commodity form and is now a 'vast capitalist enterprise within the entertainments industry' (Perelman 2012: 123), a major global business, and an integral part of the corporate world.

Notes

1 The Summer Olympic Games and the FIFA World Cup are truly global sporting events. At the London Olympic Games in the summer of 2012, over 10,000 athletes from 204 countries competed in 300 events, and 204 national teams participated in the qualification process for the 2010 FIFA World Cup, held in South Africa.
2 For data on the highest media broadcasting rights deals for the 2010/12 Olympic Games cycle, see Murray (2012: 7).

References

Addley, E. (2012) 'Olympics 2012 Branding "Police" to Protect Sponsors' Exclusive Rights', *The Guardian*, 13 April. Available at: http://www.theguardian.com/sport/2012/apr/13/olympics-2012-branding-police-sponsors (accessed 25 March 2015).
Andreff, W. (2008) 'The Globalization of the Sports Economy', *Rivista di diritto ed Economia dello Sport*, IV(3):13–32.
Aris, S. (1990) *Sportsbiz: Inside the Sports Business*, London: Hutchinson.
Badenhausen, K. (2012) 'Why Nike Owns US Olympic Basketball', *Forbes*, 20 July 2012. Available at: http://www.forbes.com/sites/kurtbadenhausen/2012/07/20/why-nike-owns-us-olympic-basketball/ (accessed 15 August 2013).
Barney, R.K., Wenn, S.R. and Martyn, S.G. (2004) *Selling the Five Rings: The International Olympic Committee and the Rise of Olympic Commercialism*, Salt Lake City: University of Utah Press.
Batty, D. (2011) 'Jeremy Hunt Rejects Calls for "Austerity" Olympics', *The Guardian*, 31 December 2011.
Beltrone, G. (2013) 'Ads Trump Football in Super Bowl Survey: More Consumers Cite Spots than Sport as Favorite Part of the Big Game', *Adweek*, 24 January 2013. Available at: http://www.adweek.com/news/advertising-branding/ads-trump-football-super-bowl-survey-146776 (accessed 4 June 2013).

Birley, D. (2003) *A Social History of English Cricket*, London: Aurum Press.

Borgers, W. (2003) 'From the Temple of Industry to Olympic Arena: The Exhibition Tradition of the Olympic Games', *Journal of Olympic History*, 11(1): 7–21.

Briggs, B. (2012) 'Nike Takes Marketing Gold with Neon-Yellow Shoes', NBC News. Available at: http://www.nbcnews.com/business/nike-takes-marketing-gold-neon-yellow-shoes-934825 (accessed 10 December 2013).

British Olympic Council (1909) *The Fourth Olympiad London 1908 Official Report*, London: British Olympic Association.

Brownell, S. (2008) *The 1904 Anthropology Days and Olympic Games: Sport, Race and American Imperialism*, London: University of Nebraska Press.

Chinese Olympic Committee (2004) 'Beijing 2008 Olympic Games Sponsorship Programme', 27 March. Available at: http://en.olympic.cn/coc/marketing/2004-03-27/121869.html. (accessed 20 August 2013).

Close P., Askew D., and Xin, X. (2007) *The Beijing Olympiad: The Political Economy of a Mega-Sporting Event*, Abingdon, UK: Routledge.

Coca-Cola and the Olympic Games: Our History (no date). Available at: http://www.coca-cola.co.uk/olympic-games/coca-cola-and-olympic-games-history.html (accessed 25 June 2013).

Coubertin, P. de (1896/1897) Preface to *The Olympic Games BC 776–AD 1896*, London: H. Grevel & Co.

Crowther, N.B. (1996) 'Athlete and State: Qualifying for the Olympic Games in Ancient Greece', *Journal of Sport History*, 23(1): 34–43.

Forbes (2012) 'The Forbes Fab 40: The World's Most Valuable Sports Brands'. Available at: http://www.forbes.com/sites/mikeozanian/2012/10/17/the-forbes-fab-40-the-worlds-most-valuable-sports-brands-4/ (accessed 10 December 2013).

Gratton, C., Liu, D., Ramchandani, G., and Wilson, D. (2012) *The Global Economics of Sport*, London: Routledge.

Greenwash Gold (2012) 'Greenwash Gold 2012 Medals Awarded'. Available at: http://www.greenwashgold.org/ (accessed 13 August 2013).

The Guardian (2012) 'London 2012: Olympic Protests Planned against "corporate dominance"', 25 July. Available at: http://www.theguardian.com/world/2012/jul/25/olympics-protests-planned (accessed 25 March 2015).

Hampton, J. (2008) *The Austerity Olympics: When the Games Came to London in 1948*, London: Aurum Press.

Hampton, J. (2012) *London Olympics 1908 and 1948*, Oxford: Shire Publications.

International Olympic Committee (no date) 'Commercial Partnerships'. Available at: http://www.olympic.org/commercial-sponsorships (accessed 25 July 2013).

International Olympic Committee (IOC) (2001) *Marketing Matters: The Olympic Marketing Newsletter*, Issue 19. Available at: http://www.olympic.org/Documents/Reports/EN/en_report_273.pdf (accessed 25 July 2013).

International Olympic Committee (IOC) (2012) *IOC Marketing: Media Guide*. Available at: http://www.olympic.org/Documents/IOC_Marketing/London_2012/IOC_Marketing_Media_Guide_2012.pdf (accessed 13 August 2013).

International Olympic Committee (IOC) (2013) 'Factsheet: the Games of the Olympiad'. Available at: http://www.olympic.org/Documents/Reference_documents_Factsheets/The_Olympic_Summer_Games.pdf (accessed 26 April 2013).

James, M. and Osborn, G. (2011) 'London 2012 and the Impact of the UK's Olympic and Paralympic Legislation: Protecting Commerce or Preserving Culture?', *The Modern Law Review*, 74(3): 410–429.

Jenkins, R. (2008) *The First London Olympics*, London: Piatkus Books.

Kent, G. (2008) *Olympic Follies: The Madness and Mayhem of the 1908 London Games*, London: JR Books.

Kissoudi, P. (2005) 'Closing the Circle: Sponsorship and the Greek Olympic Games from Ancient Times to the Present Day', *International Journal of the History of Sport*, 22(4): 618–638.

Legislation.gov.uk (1995) *Olympic Symbol etc (Protection) Act 1995*. Available at: http://www.legislation.gov.uk/ukpga/1995/32/introduction (accessed 15 August 2013).

Magnay, J. (2012) 'London 2012 Olympics: BBC Wins Broadcasting Rights for All Games for the Next Eight Years', *The Telegraph*. Available at: http://www.telegraph.co.uk/sport/olympics/9408315/London-2012-Olympics-BBC-win-broadcasting-rights-for-all-Games-for-the-next-eight-years.html (accessed 10 July 2013).

Marshall, D.W. and Cook, G. (1992), "The corporate (sports) sponsor", *International Journal of Advertising*, Vol. 11, Spring, pp. 307–24.

Martin, C.R. and Reeves, J. L. (2001) 'The Whole World Isn't Watching (but We Thought They Were): The Super Bowl and US Solipsism', *Culture, Sport, Society*, 4(2): 213–236.

Marx, K. and Engels, F. (1850/1978) 'Neue Rheinische Zeitung Revue May–October 1850', *Collected Works* Vol 10 1849–51, London: Lawrence and Wishart.

Milne, S. (2012) 'This Is a Corporate Lockdown, Why Not an Olympics for All?', *The Guardian*, 11 July.

Murray, C. (2012) 'Olympic Games Set to Break $8bn Revenues Barrier in Four-Year Cycle Ending with London 2012', *Sportcal*, 26 July. Available at: http://www.sportcal.com/pdf/gsi/Sportcal_Issue26_6-9.pdf (accessed 8 December 2013).

O'Connor, A. (2012) 'Olympic Protest Groups Join Forces to Shame Sponsors', *The Times*, 16 April 2012.

The Olympic Museum (2007) 'The Olympic Symbols'. Available at: http://www.olympic.org/documents/reports/en/en_report_1303.pdf (accessed 25 June 2013).

Perelman, M. (2012) *Barbaric Sport: A Global Plague*, London: Verso.

Rader, B.G. (1984) *In Its Own Image: How Television Has Transformed Sports*, London: Free Press.

Rowe, D. (1996) 'The Global Love-Match: Sport and Television' *Media Culture & Society*, 18(4): 565–582.

Scaff, L.A. (2011) *Max Weber in America*, Oxford: Princeton University Press.

Smart, B. (2005) *Modern Sport and the Cultural Economy of Sporting Celebrity*, London: Sage.

Smart, B. (2007) 'Not Playing Around: Global Capitalism, Modern Sport and Consumer Culture', *Global Networks*, 7(2): 113–134.

Sweney, M. (2012) 'Olympics 2012: Nike Plots Ambush Ad Campaign', *The Guardian*, 25 July. Available at: http://www.theguardian.com/media/2012/jul/25/olympics-2012-nike-ambush-ad?guni=Article: in%20body%20link (accessed 15 August 2013).

Tomlinson, A. (2005) 'The Commercialisation of the Olympics: Cities, Corporations and the Olympic Commodity', in K. Young and K.B. Walmsley (eds) *Global Olympics: Historical and Sociological Studies of the Modern Games*, Bingley, UK: Emerald Group Publishing.

Tomlinson, A. (2008) 'Olympic Values, Beijing's Olympic Games, and the Universal Market', in M.E. Price and D. Ayan (eds) *Owning the Olympics: Narratives of the New China*, Ann Arbor: University of Michigan Press.

Toohey, K. and Veal, A.J. (2007) *The Olympic Games: A Social Science Perspective*, Wallingford, UK: CAB International.

United Nations (2005) *World Economic Situation and Prospects 2005*. Available at: http://www.un.org/esa/policy/wess/wesp2005files/wesp2005.pdf (accessed 2 August 2013).

Weber, M. (1904–05/1976) *The Protestant Ethic and the Spirit of Capitalism*, London: George Allen & Unwin.

43

SPORT, INTERNATIONAL DEVELOPMENT AND PEACE

Simon C. Darnell

Introduction

Sport connects to international development and peace in multiple ways. For example, the International Olympic Committee (IOC) and the United Nations General Assembly (UNGA) now recognize April 6 – the date of the beginning of the first modern Olympics in 1896 – as the International Day of Sport for Development and Peace (United Nations 2013). There are a host of non-governmental organizations (NGOs) that now use sport to meet international development goals, such as those within the streetfootballworld network that reaches more than 60 countries and 700,000 children (streetfootballworld 2013). And sport, international development and peace have become matters of public policy, illustrated by government support for UK Sport's International Inspiration program (UK Sport 2013) or the Instituto Nacional de Deportes, Educación Física y Recreación in Cuba that offers fully subsidized scholarships to foreign students in sport and physical education (Huish and Darnell 2011). Overall, the increased number of organizations and stakeholders mobilizing sport towards the goals of development and peace – such as gender empowerment, health promotion, education, poverty reduction and conflict resolution – and the nascent Sport for Development and Peace sector (Giulianotti 2011a), suggest a more concerted effort by policy makers, sports stakeholders and civil society to organize sport in socially and politically beneficial ways.

At the same time, sport connects to more overt political struggles for equitable and sustainable development as well. For example, social activists have centred attention on the massive public spending for the 2014 World Cup and 2016 Summer Olympics in Rio de Janeiro, Brazil, a city and country with significant inequality and under-capacity in health and education (BBC 2013). Such examples serve as a reminder that sport is not an essential force for, or tool of, international development but rather a social, cultural and political phenomenon and institution with significant implications for development and peace (Darnell and Black 2011). Therefore, the questions that frame this chapter are: what does sociological literature to date suggest about the likelihood of achieving sustainable and/or transformative development through SDP activities? In turn, what future research is needed, and what questions should be asked, to support a critical sociological analysis of sport, international development and peace?

The chapter proceeds in three main parts. In the next section, a brief overview of the history and emergence of the SDP sector is offered. Recent research is then discussed that illustrates some of the positive aspects of SDP activity, and also some of the cautions and limitations that deserve consideration. The final section discusses future directions in the sociological analysis of Sport for Development and Peace.

History and politics of international development

The history of sport in the service of development and the social good has been analyzed elsewhere in some detail (Giles and Lynch 2012; Kidd 2008; Levermore and Beacom 2009), as have the political shifts and decisions that have contributed to the institutionalization of the SDP sector (Coalter 2013; Darnell 2012; Okada and Young, 2012). The intention here is not to repeat this literature but to draw out some of its sociological implications. At least three points are germane.

First, current initiatives of sport-for-development should be considered against the history of sport itself, within which struggles for social development have taken place. Kidd (2008: 371) offers a useful summary of this history:

> To be sure, social development through sport has a long history. Its aspirations can be traced back to the "rational recreation" interventions of the improving middle and working class in the late nineteenth century, the "playground movement" of the early twentieth century and the confessional and workers' sports movements of the interwar period, among other antecedents. A more recent incarnation has been the "midnight basketball" interventions in the United States and Canada. International social development through sport dates back to nineteenth-century colonising.

This history suggests that the logic of sport for social development is not new, but also that the 'power of sport'[1] for achieving development stems less from sport's inherent social positivity and more from its intractability from broader relations of power and political processes.

Second, there is a particular history of international development – from the colonial aspirations of the eighteenth and nineteenth century through to new forms of twentieth-century internationalism – that should be considered when contextualizing the current mobilization of sport-for-development. In the years immediately following World War II, relatively powerful nations began to assume new responsibility for the development of the so-called Third World, and this era of international development served to establish a relationship of northern stewardship that has been roundly criticized for maintaining traditional vectors of colonial rule and demonizing the poor as 'under-developed' (Escobar 1995). While it is overly simplistic to claim that current programmes and policies of sport-for-development and sport-for-peace merely repeat this history of northern stewardship, SDP programmes are at the least implicated in the current structures and politics of international inequality, and subject to critiques of development as modernization. As Giles and Lynch (2012: 91) state:

> Indeed, sport for development is not called sport for cultural self-determination or sport for political representation. Instead, the use of the word development identifies such initiatives as being part of the broader political processes associated with development.

In the new millennium, these broader politics remain largely dominated by neo-liberal philosophy, often with a focus on resource extraction, infrastructure and private ownership as the preferred approach to development, particularly in Africa and Asia (Kapoor 2011). From this perspective, government ownership and regulation are eschewed, and non-governmental organizations become key development stakeholders (Choudry and Kapoor 2013), a fact evident in the SDP sector as well (Giles and Lynch 2012; Giulianotti 2011a).

Third, though, the current institutionalization of the SDP sector also owes much to relatively new approaches to international development and aid that have emerged in the past two decades. A shift away from strict economic policy (though not necessarily away from neo-liberal philosophy) and towards 'softer' development based on the pursuit of social and cultural capital was both a response to the inequalities exacerbated by market fundamentalism and a means for attracting and leveraging new development aid and funding (Coalter 2013: 31). This new context set the stage for an increased interest in sport amongst traditional development stakeholders; by the time the UN General Assembly passed Resolution 58/5, entitled 'Sport as a means to promote education, health, development and peace'[2] in November 2003, the institutional momentum of the SDP sector was apparent.

A critical sociology of SDP is thus confronted with the argument that sport appears 'tailor made' for the dominant neo-liberal development philosophy (Levermore 2009), particularly given that the current organization of global, commercial sport is often less than amenable to the humanist values that underpin SDP activity (Maguire 2011). The histories of sport and development, respectively, also draw attention to issues of power and agency within the structures and operations of the SDP sector. As both a critical scholar and a self-described indigenous practitioner of sport-for-development, Mwaanga explains:

> The SDP movement of the last decade constitutes a progressive social movement of revolutionary proportions when it is perceived that, as part of the African Renaissance, African people are leading the way in overcoming the challenges confronting them as a continent.
>
> (2010: 61)

While a critical analysis of SDP is not simply a matter of assessing who is (or is not) in charge of SDP activities, relations of power – historical, structural and discursive – are likely solidified and/or challenged when sport is mobilized for development and peace on an international scale. Such issues are discussed further below.

Research

With the preceding overview in mind, this section reviews current research findings. The review is necessarily selective and aims to demonstrate the ambivalence regarding the extent to which SDP activities are successful in facilitating sustainable development and social change. The studies discussed focus on low and middle income countries (LMICs),[3] the global South, and/or the Two-Thirds World. Whilst all of these labels are imperfect in capturing and describing unequal development on a global scale, they also tend to obscure the fact that sport-for-development programmes have taken place within the ostensibly 'developed world' of North America (for example, through Midnight Basketball) and Europe (for example, Positive Futures).[4] The focus on the global South below is not meant to essentialize SDP as a 'southern' issue, but to recognize that specific parts of the world (i.e. Africa, Asia) constitute the preferred sites of development within post-colonial societies, structures and imaginations (McEwan 2009).

According to the United Nations Inter-Agency Task Force (2003), sport-for-development programmes fall into three categories depending on their development focus: social issues, health and education, and economic development, a categorization to which peace and reconciliation should be added. In each of these categories, recent research shows some important and positive contributions of SDP activities.

In relation to social issues, there is evidence that SDP programmes or interventions can make a positive contribution to social cohesion and integration, or even anti-oppression. For example, Okada and Young's (2011) analysis of the Siem Reap Hotel Football League (SHFL) in north-ern Cambodia, a region faced with extreme poverty and the legacy of genocide, found that community football served as a site for improved social integration and understanding. As they state (2011: 22), the SHFL "operates as a context in which social problems may be acknowl-edged, considered and addressed, as well as bringing otherwise diverse and differentiated groups together in potentially respectful and healthy ways." In this way, sport can provide a relatively safe site for social actors to discuss structures of exclusion and dominance that are often exacerbated amidst development inequalities.

More pointedly, research by feminist scholars like Kay (2009) and Saavedra (2009) has argued that the success of SDP programmes in championing and supporting gender empowerment stems from the fact that sport participation often offers girls and young women an opportunity to assert their agency and challenge patriarchy. This is the case precisely because the participation of girls and women in sport is still often considered to be a transgressive activity (Saavedra 2009). For example, Kay's (2009) study of the GOAL project in Delhi, India, found that amidst deeply patriarchal social structures, sport-based programming provided an opportunity for girls and young women to acquire important knowledge related to reproductive health and to improve their confidence, social standing and relationships.

In turn, economic development is also relevant to SDP research. A good example is Hay-hurst's (2013) recent analysis of global funding chains in sport-for-development that link funders like northern governments or transnational corporations to southern NGOs. Based on inter-views with members of a Ugandan sport-focused NGO, Hayhurst demonstrated that the per-sonal and social benefits of sport participation were part of a process of seeking to secure some measure of economic sustainability for local women; to this end, the organization managed its own for-profit business in nut processing with financial yields returned to local female farmers and re-invested in the NGO's programmes. Such efforts afford local people a measure of eco-nomic independence whilst also allowing the organization to attempt to distance itself from financial dependence upon foreign donors. As Hayhurst (2013: 14) concludes: "NGOs based in the Two-Thirds World may increase their independence, creativity and innovation through social entrepreneurial strategies that are intertwined with/tacked on to SGD (sport, gender, development) interventions." In addition, sport can play a positive role in the development and conversion of different forms of social capital into economic security as underserved or mar-ginalized individuals and communities use the participatory and community features of sport to seek and secure employment (Spaaij 2011).

In terms of health and education, a primary focus of SDP activity has been the organization of sport to combat and reduce the spread of HIV/AIDS, particularly in sub-Saharan Africa. Organi-zations like Grassroots Soccer have used the popularity and convening features of soccer/football to offer life skills training to children (Grassroots Soccer 2013) while the Kicking AIDS Out! (KAO) network, an initiative begun in 2001 by the Zambian-based EduSport Foundation and the Norwegian Development Agency, connects partners from Africa, North and South America, Europe and Asia and shares curricula, best practices and expertise (Kicking AIDS Out! 2013).

Some recent research suggests positive results of such initiatives. Roberts *et al.*'s (2012) assess-ment of KAO programming within the community based sport programme EMIMA in Dar es Salaam, Tanzania, found that children who participated in HIV/AIDS education programming through sport-focused peer coaching demonstrated better knowledge of, and more positive intentions towards, engaging in safe behaviour such as condom use when compared to children who had taken part only in the school-based national curriculum. The researchers conclude: "the sport-based approach is an effective means of communicating desirable information about safe sex behaviors to a population of at-risk adolescents" (Roberts *et al.* 2012: 156). Particularly in the context of reduced public infrastructure and a lack of national policies or curricula regarding HIV/AIDS in some African countries (Njelesani 2011), sport-based programming can make a positive contribution to fighting the pandemic.

Further, recent research also demonstrates that sport holds some potential for making a positive contribution to peace and post-conflict reconciliation. Wilson *et al.'s* (2013) assessment of post-election violence in Kenya in 2007 and 2008 found that elite runners from that country were able to utilize their profiles, reputations and connections in order to mobilize support for peace and reconciliation efforts. Particularly in a country like Kenya that enjoys an international reputation in the sport of running, there is:

> immense potential for celebrity athletes . . . to make a positive impact in contexts where these athletes have local connections and the local knowledge that allows them to facilitate event organization and make context-sensitive strategic decisions.
>
> (Wilson *et al.* 2013: 22)

Other recent research studies have also demonstrated the possibility of peace and reconciliation through sport. Cross- or inter-community sports programmes in divided societies have been shown to facilitate some physical engagement and social understanding between youth and adults (Gasser and Levinsen 2004; Lyras and Welty Peachy 2011; Sugden 2010). As well, the hosting of sports events designed specifically and strategically to integrate members of different communities within post-conflict situations has been found to create interactive experiences that may go some way towards bridging deeply engrained ethnic or cultural divisions (Schulenkorf 2010). When taken en masse, this research leads scholars like Keim (2012: 16) to conclude, "Peace through sport can be a reality if certain factors are taken into consideration," namely the recognition of different cultures and languages, the integration of various stakeholders, the promotion of positive role models and attention paid to choices of time and venue when hosting and organizing sport.

These findings all suggest positive development and peace benefits of sport; however, current research has also identified some of the limitations, and even negative effects, of sport-for-development and sport-for-peace.

In relation to social issues, critical scholars have cautioned that SDP activity may serve to secure processes of social reproduction more so than self-determination for marginalized people (Donnelly *et al.* 2011; Hartmann and Kwauk 2011). It is here that the context of neo-liberalism is particularly important; the neo-liberal focus on individuals as agents of their own development often requires those individuals to conform to, rather than resist, the dominant structures and logic of social and economic life. When viewed through this lens, sport-for-development may offer a way to 'teach' social actors how to survive in a competitive world. This 'reproductive vision' of sport-for-development

> is not really about structural transformation and change. Rather, it is primarily about sport's ability to resocialize and recalibrate individual youth and young people that, in turn, serves to maintain power and hierarchy, cultural hegemony, and the institutionalization of poverty and privilege. It is, in other words, a fundamentally reproductive vision of development.
>
> (Hartmann and Kwauk 2011: 291)

433

This is not to say that creativity or even resistance is absent within such processes. Rather, the options available to many SDP programmes in pursuing social change are often produced and constrained by the logic of neo-liberalism itself. For example, in Hayhurst's (2013: 14) study, SDP NGO staff looked to social entrepreneurship as a means of economic independence, but this was not a free choice as much as "a viable strategy for survival in an increasingly competitive and unstable economy." Any autonomy enjoyed by girls and young women as a result of such initiatives cannot, therefore, be attributed to the making of positive individual choices (Hayhurst 2013).

When it comes to health and education in SDP, critical scholars have also questioned the impact and logic of the SDP approach. From a structural perspective, the mobilization of sport for addressing HIV/AIDS, particularly in sub-Saharan Africa, has been criticized for a lack of sustainable funding, poor planning and coordination, and, perhaps most importantly, for its isolation from the wider HIV/AIDS community (Mwaanga 2010). Indeed, from a policy perspective, the sport-for-development field has been criticized for making elevated claims as to its efficacy while often lacking both a theoretical understanding of development or a framework for isolating or accounting for the role of sport therein (Coalter 2013). Further, the absence of a relationship with the wider health NGO community or HIV/AIDS policy circles (Lindsey and Banda 2011) limits comparative learning and the sharing of best practices.

With that said, there is also a critique that such programmes tend to focus on life skills, individual choices and responsibility at the expense of broader – and more challenging – analyses of how and why HIV/AIDS has disproportionately affected people in LMICs or the global South. Forde's (2014) critical reading of SDP educational curricula argues that knowledge of HIV/AIDS in SDP tends to be constructed through discourses of risk, individualism and deficiency that serve to place the onus on individuals to change their behaviour. When considered against the legacy of the World Bank's Structural Adjustment Programs (SAPs) in Africa in the 1980s, which reduced public capacity to combat HIV/AIDS (Njelesani 2011), initiatives like George W. Bush's President's Emergency Plan for AIDS Relief (PEPFAR) that promoted abstinence-only solutions (Giles and Lynch 2012), or policies forbidding the teaching of condom use (Maro *et al.* 2009), it is disingenuous to reduce the struggle of preventing HIV/AIDS in Africa to individual choice. Mwaanga's (2010: 64) critique of the individualization of HIV/AIDS is worth quoting here:

> Sports empowerment should never be promoted only as a matter of feelings (or perceptions) of inner strength at the expense of addressing how groups can increase access to resources that in turn increase control of aspects that matter in their lives, such as addressing poverty.

Further, if school-based HIV/AIDS education has not proved effective in places like Tanzania (Roberts *et al.* 2012), and sport-for-development programming is being positioned to fill this void or as an alternative to public policy (Maro *et al.* 2009: 32), this may say less about the efficacy of SDP programming and more about the need to question the reasons that HIV/AIDS preventative education has failed in the first place.

In relation to peace and reconciliation, while the case can be made that even the incremental or micro effects of reconciliation through sport and physical activity are significant, recent assessments of sport-for-peace programmes suggest that their impact may be limited by the local politics, understandings and demands regarding sport itself. Schulenkorf *et al.*'s (2013) assessment of the Football for Peace (F4P) programme in Israel found a wide range of community perspectives in relation to SDP programming that belied the straightforward and intended implementation of the programme. For example, the interest in, and demand for, competitive football and opportunities for elite success meant that attempts by programme officials to attach 'softer' development and peace messages to the sport were not necessarily accepted by participants.

Several implications emerge from such findings. One, the competitive ethos of global, commercial sport may infiltrate even grassroots SDP initiatives in ways that make it difficult to presume softer benefits of peace and reconciliation. Two, despite attempts to organize SDP initiatives in a non-political manner and in neutral spaces, Schulenkorf *et al.*'s (2013) research suggests that SDP programmes or interventions may actually be sites of community negotiation unto themselves, where social actors define and/or resist the terms and politics of membership. This points to the need to view SDP activities as spaces where sport, development and peace are interpreted, defined and contested rather than simply achieved (or not). Finally, the assessment of F4P illustrates human agency within SDP. If sport-for-peace programmes only succeed if and when 'appropriate structures and processes are in place' (Schulenkorf *et al.* 2013: 14), then the focus of SDP programming and research should be the people, politics and social structures of local contexts, more so than the organization and implementation of sport itself. In the final section, I explore this theme further in discussing future research.

Future directions

Given the research cited above, there is a need for future studies of sport, international development and peace that are sociologically informed. In this final section, I suggest several vectors of analysis that this work might follow.

First is the question of monitoring and evaluation (M&E) of SDP activities. As Okada and Young (2012: 22) state:

> Generally speaking, it is difficult to evaluate the outcomes of sport in development sectors, especially when the targets are based on abstract characteristics, since these outcomes are often intangible and take a long time to become evident and measure robustly and with accuracy.

According to Levermore (2011a and 2011b), M&E does take place in SDP but tends to be based on positivist methodologies, with participatory methods sometimes deployed. Positivist approaches have been criticized for being top-down, overly quantitative, conducted through a 'tick-box approach' or on a one-off basis, or imbued with notions of scientific rationality that are presumed to be universal but tend to secure colonizing knowledge flows (Levermore 2011a). A challenging implication of this is the question of why, and indeed whether, M&E of SDP needs to take place at all. As Levermore (2011a: 352) suggests, "One of the critical perspectives arguments surrounds whether programmes really need evaluation."

It is likely the case that the hegemonic climate of global funding chains (Hayhurst 2013), rational sport science (Maguire 2011) and neo-liberal development policy combine to construct and maintain the necessity of M&E in SDP, particularly through positivist methods. Yet, options remain available for sociologists to support novel approaches to data collection and analysis. In light of critiques that structures and relations of knowledge/power in SDP subjugate local knowledge relative to that derived by academics and funders (Nicholls *et al.*'s 2011), Participatory Action Research, which strives to include participants in the design of research studies, holds potential for producing new forms of data (Darnell and Hayhurst 2011). In turn, theoretically informed approaches to SDP in the tradition of critical pedagogy may encourage researchers and practitioners to imagine and integrate new approaches to social change through sport (Darnell 2012).

This is not an uncontroversial approach, to be sure. Coalter (2013) has argued that positivist, independent and quantitative assessments of sport-based development programmes are needed in order to maintain a critical, detached and scientific view on the sector that resists the evangelism plaguing the SDP sector. At the same time, Coalter (2009) has also identified and discussed the difficulties of M&E research, namely that it is susceptible to simple assessments of outcomes that lack theoretical grounding or a process orientation. In sum, there is no panacea, nor is there likely to be a consensus, regarding the correct way to evaluate SDP; therefore critical sociologists are likely to face decisions regarding the methodology and data that is most useful for making sense of the complexities and ambivalence within SDP.

This leads to the second issue, which might be termed the processes of reception, interpretation and even resistance within SDP activity. Research by Schulenkorf *et al.* (2013) and Guest (2009) illustrate that SDP programmes may be interpreted by participants or targets differently than intended by programme officials, governments and funders. This suggests the need for theoretical flexibility in research that keeps relations of power in mind but does not presume their effects on people nor their strict interpretation by social agents. In the specific field of SDP, there have been calls "for an appreciation of the intricacies, complexities, and nuances in the way that F4P (and SDP work more generally) is received" (Schulenkorf *et al.* 2013), with Mwaanga (2010: 62) highlighting the "deafening silence of alternative and non-western voices in the general SDP discourse." Indeed, and with notable exceptions, much SDP activity still follows traditional flows of resources and knowledge from the north to the south that may serve to perpetuate colonial discourses, which draws attention to the need for new approaches to research that may interrupt such conventional structures.

Finally, it will continue to be important for sociologists to study not only the participants and presumed beneficiaries of SDP activities, but also the international organizations, stakeholders and individuals that tend to enjoy leadership within the sector. This is important given the social and political diversity within and between SDP NGOs; research suggests that officials within SDP NGOs critically reflect on their own practices and do not neatly adhere to stable or particular development ideologies (Giulianotti 2011b; Hayhurst 2013). It is also important given that not all stakeholders within SDP approach the relationships between sport, development or peace in the same way. As the introduction of this chapter suggests, it is likely that SDP organizations with educational mandates (such as Grassroots Soccer) view the social development implications of soccer/football very differently than do Brazilian social movement activists protesting the World Cup, even though both could be considered part of a sport-focused NGO community or broader civil society.

In turn, there remains a need to interrogate, in the tradition of reflexive theory/method, the ways in which people are drawn to SDP service and work. In their recent text on sport-for-development, Schinke and Hanrahan (2012: 4) state: "At the heart of each of us is a desire to contribute to a community and be part of its advancement." Such statements raise important questions regarding the processes by and through which the "desire to contribute" is constructed and learned, a line of inquiry I have explored previously (Darnell 2007, 2013). While these writings have sometimes been interpreted as an analysis of the socially constructed and racialized Other, they were primarily intended to analyze the subject positions of SDP stakeholders. This kind of critical inquiry is necessary in order to support future leaders of SDP who possess not only technical skills but also the critical and historical grounding necessary to recognize and challenge colonial residue and oppressive knowledge production within SDP. As Coalter (2013) has shown, the recent policy rhetoric surrounding SDP has tended to amplify the benefits of sport; important questions remain to be asked about how this amplification – and even evangelism – influences the identities of SDP stakeholders amidst the contemporary politics of global inequality. When stakeholders imagine changing the world through sport, what does the process of this change look like? And what does this imagination say about Others, however they may be constructed?

These questions, like others to be asked of SDP, need to be contextually grounded. It is reasonable to conclude that when bringing a sociological perspective to bear on the relationships between sport, international development and peace, any analysis will need to consider its specific features, from the types of institutions and organizations involved to the historical, geographical and political settings. While beholden to these specificities, if grounded in solid theory and method, future studies can shed new light on the complex and ambivalent relationships between sport, international development and peace.

Notes

1 Former UN Secretary-General Kofi Annan has made several references to the 'power of sport' in recent years. For example, see http://kofiannanfoundation.org/newsroom/press/2010/04/kofi-annan-we-must-use-power-sport-agent-social-change.
2 See http://daccess-dds-ny.un.org/doc/UNDOC/GEN/N03/453/21/PDF/N0345321.pdf?Open Element.
3 The World Bank classifies countries according to gross national income (GNI). Based on 2012 numbers, countries with a per capita GNI of $1,035 or less are considered low income, while per capita GNI of $1,036–$4,085 constitutes a lower middle income country (World Bank 2014).
4 Midnight Basketball refers to a series of programmes in the United States in the 1980s and 1990s that were organized around the concept that providing constructive sporting activities for inner-city youth would occupy their time and, in turn, contribute to reducing crime (Hartmann and Depro 2006). Positive Futures was a similar prevention and diversionary programme based in the UK and funded by the Home Office. It deployed sport, among other activities, to support youth deemed to be at risk of substance abuse and committing crimes (Crabbe 2008).

References

BBC (2013) 'Protests Disrupt FIFA Visit to Brazil World Cup Venue'. Available at: http://www.bbc.co.uk/news/world-latin-america-24453842 (accessed December 31, 2013).
Choudry, A., and Kapoor, D. (2013) *NGOization: Complicity, Contradictions and Prospects*, London: Zed Books.
Coalter, F. (2009) 'Sport-in-Development: Accountability or Development', in R. Levermore and A. Beacom (eds) *Sport and International Development*, London: Palgrave Macmillan.
Coalter, F. (2013) *Sport-for-Development: What Game Are We Playing?* London: Routledge.
Crabbe, T. (2008) 'Avoiding the Numbers Game: Social Theory, Policy and Sport's Role in the Art', in M. Nicholson and R. Hoye (eds) *Sport and Social Capital*, Oxford: Butterworth-Heinemann.
Darnell, S.C. (2007) 'Playing with Race: Right to Play and the Production of Whiteness in "Development through Sport"', *Sport in Society*, 10: 560–579.
Darnell, S.C. (2012) *Sport for Development and Peace: A Critical Sociology*, London: Bloomsbury Academic.
Darnell, S.C. (2013) 'Orientalism through Sport: Towards a Said-ian Analysis of Imperialism and "Sport for Development and Peace"', *Sport in Society*, 1–15.
Darnell, S.C., and Black D.R. (2011) 'Mainstreaming Sport into International Development Studies', *Third World Quarterly*, 32: 367–378.
Darnell, S.C., and Hayhurst L.M.C. (2011) 'Sport for Decolonization: Exploring a New Praxis of Sport for Development', *Progress in Development Studies*, 11: 183–196.
Donnelly, P., Atkinson, M., Boyle, S., and Szto, C. (2011) 'Sport for Development and Peace: A Public Sociology Perspective', *Third World Quarterly*, 32: 589–601.
Escobar, A. (1995) *Encountering Development: The Making and Unmaking of the Third World*, Princeton: Princeton University Press.
Forde, S. (2014) 'Look After Yourself, or Look After One Another? An Analysis of Life Skills in Sport for Development and Peace HIV Prevention Curriculum', *Sociology of Sport Journal*, 31: 287–303.
Gasser, P.K., and Levinsen, A. (2004) 'Breaking Post-War Ice: Open Fun Football Schools in Bosnia and Herzegovina', *Sport in Society*, 7: 457–472.

Giles, A.R., and Lynch, M. (2012) 'Postcolonial and Feminist Critiques of Sport for Development', in R.J. Schinke and S.J. Hanrahan (eds) *Sport for Development, Peace and Social Justice*, Morgantown, WV: Fitness Information Technology..

Giulianotti, R. (2011a) 'The Sport, Development and Peace Sector: A Model of Four Social Policy Domains', *Journal of Social Policy*, 40: 757–776.

Giulianotti, R. (2011b) 'Sport, Transnational Peacemaking, and Global Civil Society: Exploring the Reflective Discourses of "Sport, Development, and Peace" Project Officials', *Journal of Sport & Social Issues*, 35: 50–71.

Grassroots Soccer (2013) 'What We Do'. Available at: http://www.grassrootsoccer.org/what-we-do/ (accessed 31 December 2013).

Guest, A.M. (2009) 'The Diffusion of Development-Through-Sport: Analysing the History and Practice of the Olympic Movement's Grassroots Outreach to Africa', *Sport in Society*, 12: 1336–1352.

Hartmann, D., and Depro, B. (2006) 'Rethinking Sports-Based Community Crime Prevention: A Preliminary Analysis of the Relationship Between Midnight Basketball and Urban Crime Rates', *Journal of Sport & Social Issues*, 30: 180–196.

Hartmann, D., and Kwauk, C. (2011) 'Sport and Development: An Overview, Critique and Reconstruction', *Journal of Sport and Social Issues*, 35: 284–305.

Hayhurst, L.M. (2013) 'The "Girl Effect" and Martial Arts: Social Entrepreneurship and Sport, Gender and Development in Uganda', *Gender, Place & Culture*, 1–19.

Huish, R., and Darnell, S.C. (2011) 'Solidarity, Counter-hegemony and Development: Exploring New Dimensions of Cuba's Sport-based Internationalism', *Canadian Journal of Latin American and Caribbean Studies*, 36: 139–164.

Kapoor, D. (2011) *Critical Perspectives on Neoliberal Globalization, Development and Education in Africa and Asia*, Rotterdam: Sense Publishers.

Kay, T. (2009) 'Developing through Sport: Evidencing Sport Impacts on Young People', *Sport in Society*, 12: 1177–1191.

Keim, M. (2012) 'Developing Peace through Community Sport in Multi-ethnic South African Contexts', in R.J. Schinke and S.J. Hanrahan (eds) *Sport for Development, Peace and Social Justice*, Morgantown, WV: Fitness Information Technology.

Kicking AIDS Out! (2013) 'Our International Network: Where Are We?'. Available at: http://www.kickingaidsout.net/WhatisKickingAIDSOut/Pages/NetworkMembers.aspx (accessed 31 December 2013).

Kidd, B. (2008) 'A New Social Movement: Sport for Development and Peace', *Sport in Society*, 11: 370–380.

Levermore, R. (2009) 'Sport-in-International Development: Theoretical Frameworks', in R. Levermore and A. Beacom (eds) *Sport and International Development*, Basingstoke, UK: Palgrave Macmillan.

Levermore, R. (2011a) 'Evaluating Sport-for-Development: Approaches and Critical Issues', *Progress in Development Studies*, 11: 339–353.

Levermore, R. (2011b) 'The Paucity of, and Dilemma in, Evaluating Corporate Social Responsibility for Development through Sport', *Third World Quarterly*, 32: 551–569.

Levermore, R., and Beacom, A. (eds) (2009) *Sport and International Development*, Basingstoke, UK: Palgrave Macmillan.

Lindsey, I., and Banda, D. (2011) 'Sport and the Fight against HIV/AIDS in Zambia: A "Partnership Approach"?', *International Review for the Sociology of Sport*, 46: 90–107.

Lyras, A., and Welty Peachey, J. (2011) 'Integrating Sport-for-Development Theory and Praxis', *Sport Management Review*, 14: 311–326.

Maguire, J.A. (2011) 'Development through Sport and the Sports–Industrial Complex: The Case for Human Development in Sports and Exercise Sciences', *Sport in Society*, 14: 937–949.

Maro, C.N., Roberts, G.C., and Sørensen, M. (2009) 'HIV/AIDS Education in Tanzania: The Experience of At-Risk Children in Poorer Communities', *Vulnerable Children and Youth Studies*, 4: 23–36.

McEwan, C. (2009) *Postcolonialism and Development*, London: Routledge.

Mwaanga, O. (2010) 'Sport for Addressing HIV/AIDS: Explaining Our Convictions', *Leisure Studies Association Newsletter*, 85: 61–67.

Nicholls, S., Giles, A.R., and Sethna, C. (2011) 'Perpetuating the "Lack of Evidence" Discourse in Sport for Development: Privileged Voices, Unheard Stories and Subjugated Knowledge', *International Review for the Sociology of Sport*, 46: 249–264.

Njelesani, D. (2011) 'Preventive HIV/AIDS Education through Physical Education: Reflections from Zambia', *Third World Quarterly*, 32: 435–452.

Okada, C., and Young, K. (2011) 'Sport and Social Development: Promise and Caution from an Incipient Cambodian Football League', *International Review for the Sociology of Sport*, 47: 5–26.

Roberts, G.C., Maro, C., and Sorensen, M. (2012) 'Using Sport to Promote HIV/AIDS Education among At-Risk Youths in Sub-Saharan Africa', in R.J. Schinke and S.J. Hanrahan (eds) *Sport for Development, Peace and Social Justice*, Morgantown, WV: Fitness Information Technology.

Saavedra, M. (2009) 'Dilemmas and Opportunities in Gender and Sport-in-Development,' in R. Levermore and A. Beacom (eds), *Sport and International Development*, Basingstoke, UK: Palgrave Macmillan.

Schinke, R.J., and Hanrahan, S.J. (eds) (2012) *Sport for Development, Peace and Social Justice*, Morgantown, WV: Fitness Information Technology.

Schulenkorf, N. (2010) 'Sport Events and Ethnic Reconciliation: Attempting to Create Social Change between Sinhalese, Tamil and Muslim Sportspeople in War-Torn Sri Lanka', *International Review for the Sociology of Sport*, 45: 273–294.

Schulenkorf, N., Sugden, J., and Burdsey, D. (2013) 'Sport for Development and Peace as Contested Terrain: Place, Community, Ownership', *International Journal of Sport Policy and Politics*, 1–17.

Spaaij, R. (2011) *Sport and Social Mobility: Crossing Boundaries*, London: Taylor & Francis.

Streetfootballworld (2013) Available at: http://www.streetfootballworld.org/ (accessed 31 December 2013).

Sugden, J. (2010) 'Critical Left-Realism and Sport Interventions in Divided Societies', *International Review for the Sociology of Sport*, 45: 258–272.

UK Sport (2013) 'Working in Partnership to Inspire, Empower and Transform Lives through Sport: International Development through Sport'. Available at: http://www.uksport.gov.uk/pages/international-inspiration/ (accessed 31 December 2013).

United Nations (2003) 'Sport for Development and Peace: Towards Achieving the Millennium Development Goals, Report from the United Nations Inter-Agency Task Force on Sport for Development and Peace'. Available at: http://www.un.org/wcm/webdav/site/sport/shared/sport/pdfs/Reports/2003_interagency_report_ENGLISH.pdf (accessed 31 December 2013).

United Nations (2013) 'UN Assembly Proclaims 6 April International Day of Sport for Development, Peace'. Available online at: http://www.un.org/apps/news/story.asp?NewsID=45689 (accessed 31 December 2013).

Wilson, B., Van Luijk, N., and Boit, M.K. (2013) 'When Celebrity Athletes Are "Social Movement Entrepreneurs": A Study of the Role of Elite Runners in Run-for-Peace Events in Post-Conflict Kenya in 2008', *International Review for the Sociology of Sport*, published online October 9, 2013. doi 10.1177/1012690213506005.

World Bank (2014) 'How We Classify Countries'. Available at: http://data.worldbank.org/about/country-classifications (accessed 20 February 2014).

44

SPORT AND GLOBALIZATION

Richard Giulianotti

Introduction

Since the early 1990s, globalization has been arguably the most substantial and significant subject for research and debate across the social sciences. This 'global turn' in academe has mirrored the ubiquity of globalization as a subject of comment and discussion across the public sphere, whether in politics, business, the media, sport, and other social realms.

The sociologist Roland Robertson (1992) played a critical role in initiating analysis of globalization processes. For Robertson (1992: 8), globalization should be defined in a dual sense, as referring 'both to the compression of the world and the intensification of consciousness of the world as a whole'. In other words, globalization involves, first, greater levels of transnational *connectivity* or interconnectedness, for example in financial markets, production of commodities, telecommunications (including social media), migration, and tourism; and second, we have greater levels of social *reflexivity* regarding the world *per se*, as illustrated by constant references in sport, education, politics, and business to 'global' issues, problems, or strategies.

Globalization is also a multi-faceted and long-term historical phenomenon, extending back to at least the fifteenth century and European exploration of the world. Globalization is not, therefore, a recent and one-dimensional process, associated with, for example, neo-liberal economic policies or Western modernization. Moreover, in interpreting globalization, we should ensure that we avoid slipping into the usage of simplistic binary oppositions, such as 'the local versus the global', and instead focus on the complex interdependencies that lie behind such terms. For example, the concept of *glocalization*, advanced by Robertson (1992, 1995), helps us to explain the fluidity of local-global interrelations. One aspect of glocalization, for instance, refers to how some transnational cultures (such as world-popular sports or musical genres) are adapted and transformed by different social groups at everyday level.

In the following discussion, I draw on these broad standpoints to explore the interrelationships between sport and globalization processes.[1] The chapter is divided into three main parts. First, I outline briefly sport's main historical features with reference to globalization processes since the nineteenth century. Second, I consider the main political and economic aspects of globalization and sport, with reference to the diversity of political actors and the global sport economy. Third, I examine the socio-cultural dimensions of global sport with regard to debates on cultural imperialism and cultural creativity and hybridity.

Global sport history: 'take-off' and beyond

Robertson (1992, 2007) traces globalization back to at least the fifteenth century, and identifies six key phases within this global history. Arguably the most notable of these was the 'take-off' phase, which ran from the 1870s to the mid-1920s, and was marked by very rapid forms of globalization, such as in the fast development of communications, the construction and spread of different national 'traditions', the growth of international organizations, the staging of international exhibitions, and the first global war.

Sport was a highly important constituent of this take-off phase in two obvious ways. First, most important, many modern sports underwent very rapid forms of global spread, development, and institutionalization during this time. For example, the British sports of football, cricket, rugby union and rugby league, and boxing were variously spread into Europe, Africa, Asia, South America, and Australasia through a mix of colonial, trade, and educational connections and influences. British sport culture inspired the establishment and 'take off' of many global sport events, such as the Olympic Games. Meanwhile, reflecting both stronger international connections and powerful forms of global consciousness, world sport governing bodies such as the IOC (1894) and FIFA (1904) were founded and attracted growing memberships. The transnational institutionalization of sport was also advanced by the standardization of rules for different sporting disciplines, which allowed diverse social groups to learn and to play the same games; by the establishment of many sports clubs and competitions across the world; and by the international movement of sport coaches and athletes, who brought the technical skills of sporting disciplines to new audiences.

Second, sport fed significantly into wider globalization processes that were central to the 'take-off' phase. Athletes, teams, and sport competitions came to reflect and intensify the making of local or national identities and 'traditions', for example through the display of national flags, the singing of anthems, and the hosting of VIPs at international events. Some nations and regions developed their own specific sport traditions, which projected distinctive forms of cultural and national identity, often in conscious resistance to British influence in sport and society. In Ireland, for example, the Gaelic Athletics Association formally codified and institutionalized Irish sports such as hurling and Gaelic football, in opposition to 'colonial' British games. The *Turnverein* (German gymnastic movement) challenged British sporting influence in Central Europe. American independence and 'exceptionalism' were reflected in the separate development of distinctively 'national' sports like baseball and American football. For many nations, early sporting successes served to forge much stronger forms of national solidarity; examples here include Australians in cricket, New Zealanders in rugby union, and Uruguayans in football. These 'take-off' developments within sport also highlight how global processes may serve to sharpen (rather than to threaten) forms of local and national identity.

Overall, in historical terms, the sport-globalization relationship during the 'take-off' phase was two-way and interdependent: just as the diffusion of sport was largely underpinned by growing transnational connectivity and consciousness, so sport also contributed to the making of this critical 'take-off' phase of globalization.

Robertson indicates that, after the 'take-off' phase, globalization has gone through three other key phases. Briefly explained with reference to sport, these are the:

• 'struggle for hegemony' (mid-1920s to late 1960s) phase, which was marked by struggles and conflicts over the 'dominant globalization process', such as capitalism, communism, fascism, and colonialism. These struggles included the world wars, the Cold War, and wars of national liberation; this phase also witnessed early attempts to establish global governance through the League of Nations and the United Nations. In sport, this phase saw the growth of international sport governance and sport tournaments; and more extensive national ideologies and rivalries in major sport events.

- 'uncertainty' phase (late-1960s to 2000s), which was marked by the end of the Cold War, spread of nuclear weapons, greater global consciousness, rise of global civil society, emergence of global media systems, stronger ethnic, gender, and sexual identities, more multicultural nations, and the rise of Islam as a global force. In sport, this phase was marked by, for example, the growth of sport mega-events as 'global' events; civil rights struggles in sport along 'race' and gender lines; stronger transnational media coverage of sport; and the presentation of sport as a force for global unity.

- 'millennial' phase (from 2000 onwards), which has been marked broadly by the rise of climates of fear, instability, and insecurity, in particular following the 9/11 attacks on the United States, the subsequent 'War on Terror', the rise of militant Islamism, and conflicts in Afghanistan, Iraq, and Syria; transnational economic instability, through the world economic downturn from 2007 onwards; conflicts over systematic governmental regulation and surveillance of individuals and social groups (such as through accessing 'private' electronic messages); cultures of self-openness, such as through social media; and the growth of global civil society, particularly in response to global poverty. In sport, these millennial features are reflected in many ways, including the extensive focus and vast expenditure on security at major sport events; the instant transmission of sport-related opinions and identities through social media; and the emergence of the 'sport for development and peace' sector, which uses sport to promote non-sport social goals.

These phases establish the historical and contemporary contexts in which different aspects of the sport-globalization nexus are played out. I turn now to explore the political and economic aspects of global sport before examining socio-cultural issues.

Global sport politics and economics

In this section, I explore in turn two major issues regarding the political and economic aspects of globalization that are relevant to sport. These issues relate to the growing range and complexity of political actors, and the structure of the global economy.

Global sport politics

The global politics of sport have acquired greater significance since the 1990s, and highlight the growing number, diversity, and interplay of political stakeholders within different sports. These stakeholders may be clustered into four general categories which tend also to be associated with specific political policies and ideologies.[2]

First, we have market-based *individual* political actors who favour and benefit particularly from highly commercial practices and from neo-liberal or free-market policies in global sport. These policies are reflected, for example, in those sports clubs which prioritize the maximizing of commercial revenues, such as through high ticket prices for seats or the aggressive pursuit of new consumers of team merchandise at global level. The biggest beneficiaries of individualistic free-market policies are the world's wealthiest elites, the largest and richest sport clubs (such as Manchester United, Real Madrid, New York Yankees, Dallas Cowboys, and so on), private media corporations, and top international athletes and their agents.[3]

Second, we have *national* or nation-centred political actors who pursue 'neo-mercantile' policies that are intended to maintain national-level governance and interests in sport. In the broader political context, nation-states provide the strongest illustrations of these policies; in sport, these political actors include national sport governing bodies and associations, public-sector national media organizations, and national governmental departments that engage with sport.

Third, we have *international* political actors who act to maintain or strengthen the frameworks of *international governance*. International sport federations and international governmental organizations (such as the European Union and the United Nations) are illustrative.

Fourth, we have a broader and diverse set of political actors who are part of *global civil society* with a very varied focus on world social issues such as development, peace, tolerance, humanitarian aid, and social justice. In sport, these actors include non-governmental organizations, social movements, and critical journalists, who tend to be variously engaged in activities that include sport-related development projects or campaigns against racism, sexism, and homophobia.

Taken as a whole, the interplay of these different kinds of political actors serves to produce the contemporary politics of global sport. Three further points follow from this model.

First, the model reflects the continuing significance of national political actors in sport, and also the wider observation that national entities and the nation-state *per se* still have substantial influence within the global context (Calhoun 2008). For example, the world's most prominent and richest sport leagues operate primarily at national levels, for example in England, Spain, Italy, and Germany in European football, or in India in cricket, or (almost entirely) in the United States in American football, basketball, and baseball. In addition, it is nations and their cities which host sport mega-events, in part to boost their 'brand' identities and 'soft power' on the global stage (Nye 2008).

Second, in globalization theory, there has been recurring discussion of how global governance may be established according to democratic and socially just principles (Archibugi *et al.* 1998; Held 1995). In effect, these arguments interconnect the two themes of international governance and global civil society. In sport, such possibilities have been explored by critical NGOs and social movements (such as Transparency International, or 'Play the Game'),[4] and by some prominent international sport officials. For example, Jérôme Champagne, who stood for election as FIFA president in 2015, drew on the arguments of the French intellectual Jacques Attali (2009) to argue that world football's governing body should seek to become a model of 'planetary democratic government.'[5]

Third, and often cross-cutting these political stakeholders within sport, we find complex issues of political identification and belonging. Some pessimistic political analysts have argued that globalization will inevitably feature a greater array of conflicts, such as a 'clash of civilizations' between Western, Muslim, Orthodox, Eastern, and other peoples (Huntington 1993). In sport, illustrations here might include the conflicts and tensions surrounding nations in the Balkan region, or the phenomenal growth of the sport security industry, which is focused in particular on protecting major events from attacks by radical Islamist groups. Yet, much more commonly, the major rivalries in sport tend to be far more localized, and involve opposing clubs and their supporters who live relatively near to each other and who share many similar cultural traits. Again, in the global context, these sport-derived oppositions highlight the continuing significance of locality and nationality as important anchors for collective identification and belonging.

Overall, these complex political structures and processes within global sport are substantially shaped by the global sport economy, to which I now turn.

Global sport economy

The global sport economy may be understood as reflecting the broader world economy, in being principally structured to promote the interests of wealthy individuals, nation-states, and corporations that are based in the 'global North' (largely western Europe, North America, and Australasia). Through his 'world system theory', Wallerstein (1974, 2003) indicated that the global economy featured three types of nation-state:

- *Core* nations such as the United States, western European nations, and Japan, which are highly developed, well-established, rich, and strongly governed;
- *Peripheral* nations, such as in sub-Saharan Africa, which have little development, weak governments, and are open to continuous conflicts;
- *Semi-peripheral* nations, which in recent times have included post-communist transition societies or the so-called BRICS (Brazil, Russia, India, China, South Africa), have experienced rapid economic growth, have governments with modest powers, and harbour limited commodity diversity or technological development.

This three-fold structuring of the global sport economy helps us to explain labour markets in leading sports. For example, in baseball or football, the best young athletes in peripheral nations are developed in training camps in order to be hired or sold into the major leagues in core nations in North America or western Europe. Semi-peripheral nations experience similar flows of their top athletes into these core nations, while at the same time also exploiting peripheral nations in the same way.

We may add to Wallerstein's perspective by exploring issues of social class and ideology within the global sport economy. Several scholars have examined how, for example, the world economy is dominated by elite groups of the transnational rich. Some scholars refer to these groups as 'globals', to reflect their high levels of wealth and freedom to travel (Bauman 1998; Elliott and Urry 2010). For Sklair (2001), these groups represent a highly privileged 'transnational capitalist class' (TCC), which is largely made up of corporate executives and key officials, pro-capitalist politicians and professionals, consumerist groups in key sectors such as business and media, and 'globalizing state bureaucrats'. They possess a global outlook and identity, diverse national origins, and high consumption levels, notably in luxury goods and services. The TCC also promote a powerful 'culture-ideology of consumerism' which has taken root across their own nations and transnationally.

Globals and members of the TCC may be identified as key figures in the ownership and control of leading sports. They are to be found among the leaders and officials of national and, in particular, international sport federations such as FIFA, UEFA, the IOC, the NFL, NBA, and MLB; the legions of 'corporate partners' at sport clubs and sport events at national and international levels; the professional groups and entrepreneurs that 'service' the commercial side of the sport, for example as lawyers, financial advisers, and player agents; and the wealthier audiences that are targeted by sport tournaments and clubs to purchase higher-priced seats, merchandise, and products advertised by corporate partners.

These elite groups tend to advocate, and to benefit particularly from, neo-liberal economic and social policies. Associated particularly with the New Right policies of the Reagan and Thatcher regimes in the United States and UK during the 1980s, and largely sustained thereafter, neoliberal policies feature economic deregulation, national and transnational free markets, low and reduced levels of income tax and welfare spending, and the privatization of state assets (Harvey 2005). Neo-liberalism's wider impacts have included the growing size and influence of major transnational corporations, greater levels of economic volatility (through more extreme booms and slumps), increasing levels of social inequality, mass opposition (such as in the election of left-wing governments in much of South America), and social conflicts (notably in industrial disputes).

Neoliberal policies have underpinned the political-economic transformation of global sport since the late 1980s. Neoliberalism served to deregulate the wider media environment, enabling major sport leagues such as basketball's NBA (in North America), American football's NFL, and football's English Premier League to sell broadcasting rights to transnational media corporations for ever-higher sums. In European football in particular, rapidly growing competitive inequalities took hold, assisting elite clubs to dominate by recruiting the best athletes, so that, for example, the wealthiest teams from the richest leagues (England, Spain, Italy, and Germany) have monopolized the premier competition, the European Champions League, since the mid-1990s.

Transnational corporations (TNCs) have become more prominent in the neoliberal global sport economy, notably in television rights and advertising. Media corporations, such as the former News Corporation group controlled by Rupert Murdoch, have built up vast global businesses through sale of live televised sport to world markets. Major corporations also wrap sport events in the 'culture-ideology of consumerism' to advertise products to global viewers. Moreover, elite sport clubs such as the New York Yankees and Real Madrid come to resemble TNCs in their own right, in terms of their global branding strategies, pursuit of new consumers in the richest markets, and recruitment of players across global labour markets.

We should note, however, that neoliberalism in global sport is not an uncontested process and does undergo forms of 'glocalization': that is, it is manifested in varied and selective ways in different locations and sports.[6] For example, unlike European football nations where there is largely a 'free market' in player recruitment and movement, North American sports continue to operate a 'draft system', which allows poorly performing teams to have first pick of young college athletes in order to improve the competitive balance within their leagues. In European football, there are marked differences between the English Premier League and the German Bundesliga over the social impact and influence of neoliberal policies: compared to England, for example, German stadiums tend to be larger and to offer relatively low admission prices for many ground sections. In several nations (notably England, Germany, and France), the football leagues operate a collective selling of television rights in their negotiations with media corporations; collective selling enables the leagues to share out television money in a more even (if far from egalitarian) way across their member clubs than would be the case if individual clubs were free to sign their own contracts with pay-TV networks. In effect, neoliberalism in sport has been challenged on specific issues by some supporter movements, for example through criticism of the high cost of stadium admission prices, television subscription charges, or 'official' merchandise that is produced at very low cost by production plants in South-East Asia. Moreover, on this latter point, critical campaign groups such as War on Want have organized campaigns against specific aspects of neo-liberalism in sport, such as the exploitation of workers in these sport merchandise production plants.[7]

Overall, the global politics and global economy of sport point broadly to the hegemonic position of higher social classes and TNCs. At the same time, this influence is challenged by weaker stakeholders within sport's political landscape. These power interrelationships are also evidenced with respect to the socio-cultural dimensions of global sport, to which I now turn.

Global sport: socio-cultural dimensions

In this section, I explore two key socio-cultural aspects of global sport, relating to debates on cultural imperialism and on cultural creativity and hybridity.

Richard Giulianotti

Cultural imperialism

According to some scholars, globalization is driven by different forms of cultural imperialism (see Tomlinson 1991 for a review of arguments). Cultural imperialism refers to the process by which the dominant political and economic position of some societies enables them to dominate global culture, including sport. These arguments often harness a neo-Marxist perspective, which attributes a particular determinant power to political economy with respect to all other spheres or structures in society. Most scholars who advance theories of cultural imperialism are also critical of this process, notably in how it serves to disempower weaker societies.

Different theories of cultural imperialism point to how Western nations and corporations have dominated non-Western societies (Hamelink 1995; Latouche 1996; Ritzer 2004; Said 1994). The initial evidence indicates that these theories may be strongly applicable within sport. For example, the world's most popular sports – such as football, cricket, baseball, basketball, and rugby – are all British or American in origin, and relied on these associations with such powers to spread globally, particularly through the entangled routes of empire, trade, education, and politics. In turn, as Western sports have dominated, so the established 'body cultures' within non-Western regions, notably sub-Saharan Africa, were largely marginalized or erased. More recently, to borrow from Wallerstein's position, we find that many peripheral and semi-peripheral nations – across Africa, Asia, South America, and eastern Europe – have come to receive a constant televised drip-feed of 'spectacular' elite sport from 'core' nations, such as American basketball and western European football. In turn, when faced with these powerful, glamorous, global competitors, many local sport clubs and leagues in these poorer locations fail to develop effectively or fall into decline. Finally, cultural imperialism arguments contend further that the dominant meanings and identities within sport are largely defined and shaped by powerful nations and regions. Thus, in international sport organizations, sport media, and other public spheres, we find that athletes from different nations and regions are discussed in ways that reflect pro-Western perspectives: white, North American, and North European athletes are portrayed as cool, rational, scientific, and methodical, whereas athletes of African or Latin American extraction tend to be described as expressive, unpredictable, and even irrational.

One particularly important version of the cultural imperialism thesis views globalization as basically a story of *Americanization*.[8] This perspective contends that American cultural institutions dominate the beliefs, tastes, identities, and lifestyles of different societies across the world. American corporations – such as Amazon, Apple, Coca-Cola, CNN, Disney, Facebook, HBO, McDonald's, Microsoft, MTV, and Nike – play a critical role in promoting their products and, more broadly, the highly individualistic, consumerist, American way of life across global markets (Crothers 2007). Ritzer (2004), for example, has contended that contemporary globalization is driven by three inter-related forces: Americanization, capitalism, and McDonaldization (or forms of rationalization along the lines of the McDonald's fast-food corporation).

In sport, Americanization is evidenced in the transnational influence of corporations such as Nike, the assiduous marketing of American sport leagues (such as the NFL and NBA) and sport stars (such as Michael Jordan and Tiger Woods), and the prevalence of Americanisms in sport (such as the use of cheerleaders or the staging of 'Monday night' games to suit television audiences). However, sport also highlights some crucial limitations and flaws in the Americanization thesis. For example, in terms of global participation and popularity, American sports have been outperformed by the non-American sports of football (the world's truly global sport) and, to a lesser extent, cricket (hugely popular in South Asia, and with a highly successful World Cup in place since 1975). A further problem relates to the false assumption within the Americanization

446

thesis that the United States itself is a culturally uniform nation; rather, the United States is a highly diverse nation, particularly due to its wide range of migrant communities.

As these observations indicate, theories of cultural imperialism, including the Americaniza-tion thesis, tend to have some significant flaws. These approaches tend to be rather 'economistic' and deterministic, in terms of assuming that economic power equates to cultural domination. According to this logic, the citizens of diverse societies across the world passively consume the products (including the sport) of North America or Europe. Conversely, as I discuss below, a plethora of rich studies in non-Western locations highlights how different societies engage critically with global sport, to create distinctive meanings, techniques, and styles of play. The successes of Latin American football players, South Asian or Caribbean cricketers, and Central American baseball players testify to how adept these regions have been in adapting sports.

Finally, a further issue in the early twenty-first century concerns the extent to which the 'global North', particularly the United States, continues to be a hegemonic force in politics, eco-nomics, and sport (Wallerstein 2003). American military power and foreign policy were badly exposed by the disastrous invasions and occupations of Afghanistan and Iraq. Chronic failures in the American financial system led to a lengthy world economic downturn from 2007 onwards – highlighting how the American economy was highly influential at the global level, yet was itself built on very unstable foundations. Moreover, other, non-Western nations have emerged to pursue transnational influence and to exercise their economic and political power, often in marked differentiation to the 'global North'. Substantial attention has been directed towards the highly populous 'BRICS', led in particular by China. Additionally, oil-rich Gulf states such as Qatar and Dubai have among the world's highest levels of GDP per capita, and thus, along with China, have amassed substantial investment portfolios across the world. The global aspirations of these nations are reflected through sport, particularly in bidding successfully to host mega-events such as the Beijing 2008, Sochi 2014, and Rio 2016 Olympics, and the Brazil 2014, Russia 2018, and Qatar 2022 World Cup finals in football. These nations also exercise greater influence in the governance of sport, particularly in the case of India and cricket (Rumford 2007); and in the 'culture-ideology of consumerism', we see sponsors such as the Russian oil giant Gazprom and Emirates airlines (based in Dubai) wrapping themselves around the sport products/events that are beamed out to global audiences. Thus, while we do find significant aspects of Americani-zation at play, there have been many more transnational influences in evidence in the cultural politics of sport, particularly over the past decade or so.

Cultural creativity and hybridity

An alternative set of arguments to those on cultural imperialism highlights the cultural creativity of social actors in making, adapting, and transforming transnational culture. Globalization theo-rists have advanced various keywords, such as 'hybridization', 'creolization', 'vernacularization', and 'indigenization', in order to capture these processes (Appadurai 1995; Burke 2009; Friedman 1999; Hannerz 1992; Pieterse 2007).

Sport may be used to illustrate the key points within these theories. For example, since at least the late nineteenth century, North and South American nations have been largely hybrid soci-eties, featuring complex mixes of migrant communities. Sport provides one vital cultural space in which these hybrid identities come together, often to explore and to generate new forms of national identity. Archetti (1998), for example, has examined how, in Argentina, hybrid forms of national masculine identity have been constructed and explored in football and polo. Distinctive ways of interpreting and discussing particular sports take root in different societies. For exam-ple, in football, Latin American spectators tend to be far more critical of 'robust' challenges by players than is the case in Northern Europe. 'Creolization' might be reflected in how weaker, peripheral societies have developed, in part, their own particular skills and techniques in order to beat more powerful opponents: for example, in cricket, South Asian players are particularly adept at slow spin bowling, while in the Caribbean there was a particular emphasis on aggressive stroke-play and ultra-fast bowling. Forms of creolization are also evident in the particular types of fan subculture that are engendered: thus, we find that American, Cuban, and Japanese baseball spectators have different ways of showing their support for their favoured teams; the same point might be made about English, German, Italian, and Argentinian football supporters, or Australian, English, Indian, and West Indian cricket fans. And, of course, the cultural histories and identities of sport teams are wrapped up in distinctive civic and national solidarities, and their specific rivalries and oppositions.

Social and cultural globalization is characterized by intensified levels of transnational connectivity, which serve in turn to underpin the exchange and blending of cultural practices across different societies, and also the greater fluidity of social identities. Heightened transnational social connectivity is associated particularly with the media (including social media such as Facebook and Twitter), and with travel and migration. These processes may 'disembed' or 'deterritorialize' people from specific geographical locales, so that identities may, for example, become relocated or repositioned (such as with ethnic enclaves) or shaped by shared transnational interests (such as with global fan groups).

In sport, globalization is marked by some shifting in social identification with clubs, national teams, and individual sport stars. Here, I suggest two ways in which such transitions tend to occur. First, *migration-based* fandoms feature substantial numbers of fans with cross-national team or sport identification. Examples here might include the large Irish diaspora in North America which follows Gaelic games such as Gaelic football and hurling; or Mexican, Turkish, North African, and other migrant 'nationalities' who follow their hometown teams at a long geographical distance, most commonly through transnational media or, on occasion, when these clubs visit the migrants' host cities.

Second, *media-based* fandoms are associated with those who have little initial biographical or social connection to the team in question. Conversely, many of these fans rely on transnational mass media to establish and to maintain their identification. For example, tens of thousands of Norwegian football fans identify strongly with different English football clubs; this identification has been largely inspired by live Norwegian television coverage of English fixtures since the 1960s (Hognestad 2009).

At the everyday level, the interface between sport and globalization is marked also by substantial levels of selective borrowing, adaptation, and transformation of spectator practices at the transnational level. Football provides some particularly vibrant illustrations of such a 'subcultural switchboard' at the transnational level, notably as supporters borrow and adapt practices from their counterparts across northern and southern Europe and South America, with North American and Japanese fans also getting in on the act. As these social and cultural exchanges take hold, it becomes increasingly difficult to identify the 'original' source of specific spectator practices. A similar point on 'origins' may be made on other aspects of sport that have been subject to substantial transnational exchange; for example, in elite-level sport, we find that 'hybrid' coaching techniques, tactical systems, and playing styles have been created as a result of long-term transnational social links and exchanges.

Finally, we should consider the issue of cosmopolitanism, which has been important to some social scientific discussions on the social aspects of globalization (Rumford 2011). By 'cosmopolitan' (as in a 'cosmopolitan society' or 'cosmopolitan sport'), I am referring to social circumstances that involve relatively high levels of interaction with other cultures (whether in terms of peoples, goods, images, or ideas). For some analysts, everyday life is marked by 'banal' cosmopolitanism, as other cultures are encountered in increasingly routine ways, such as through cuisine, literature, mass media, music, or social interaction with migrant communities (Beck 2006). In sport, this banal cosmopolitanism is evidenced in a host of ways: as ever more foreign players join sport leagues at different levels; as television provides more and more coverage of international sport leagues; as coaches bring new methods and ideas in from different nations to shape how their athletes train or how their teams play; and as towns and cities regularly host sport teams and supporters from different nations.

The social impacts of, and responses to, banal cosmopolitanism may take many varied forms. In some instances, we have seen generalized backlashes against migrant groups and cultures through the rise of right-wing anti-immigration movements, and, in sport, forms of crowd racism and xenophobia towards foreign athletes (cf. Barber 1995). More broadly, however, routine interaction with other social groups and with different cultural identities, practices, and beliefs will also contribute to greater levels of cultural hybridity. We see this process occurring in many sports, perhaps most obviously in how the skills and techniques of international athletes are adapted, mimicked, or emulated by those in the host society. In turn, banal cosmopolitanism has also helped to inspire the promotion of cosmopolitan ethics within sport. Some examples of these cosmopolitan ethics may be found in how different stakeholders within sport – notably sport federations, non-governmental organizations, and campaign groups – have initiated campaigns against racism and xenophobia, to promote the citizen rights of ethnic minorities and other marginalized groups. The issue of cosmopolitan ethics in sport connects strongly to the wider political theme of 'global civil society', discussed earlier in this chapter.

Overall, to sum up this discussion of global sport's socio-cultural features, we should certainly recognize that significant aspects of cultural imperialism continue to be 'in play'. However, we also find that globalization is characterized very strongly by the creativity and critical agency of social actors within sport, which gives rise in turn to significant and complex forms of cultural hybridity and cosmopolitanism.

Conclusion

Sport provides social scientists with a vibrant and insightful field for studying wider globalization processes, particularly in highlighting the complex interplays between structural forces and critical and creative forms of human agency. Historically, the making of global sport underwent a crucial 'take-off' phase in the late nineteenth and early twentieth centuries. Subsequent phases of sporting globalization were rooted in increasingly extensive levels of transnational connectivity and global consciousness, and were characterized in particular by more complex global conflicts and insecurities. Against that broad background, the political economy of global sport has been marked by a growing range of stakeholders, and by the dominance of neo-liberal economic influences that are both supported and managed by governing bodies in sport, to the particular advantage of core sporting nations, TNCs, and wealthy elites. In turn, and in line with substantial parts of the cultural imperialism thesis, these particular social interests have significantly influenced the socio-cultural contours of global sport. However, at the everyday level, sport allows us to identify many compelling expressions of critical cultural creativity by social actors, which in turn give rise to fluid and vibrant forms of cultural hybridity and cosmopolitanism.

As a field of research inquiry that encompasses a vast terrain, the globalization and sport interface may take a multitude of different turns. Understandably, there has been substantial research interest in recent years in the areas of sport for development and peace, mega-events, identities (particularly for spectators), and media and communication. From the discussion forwarded in this chapter, I would suggest four future research areas for exploration. First, research may explore in more detail how the 'millennial' phase of globalization is both underpinned and shaped by global sport in regard to such themes as conflict, security and insecurity, identity, and transparency. Second, research may examine more closely the workings and impacts of political and economic structures and forces within global sport, such as in relation to athlete labour markets, the transnational production of sport merchandise, and the development of sport 'consumer' markets. Third, on the socio-cultural dimensions of global sport, we may investigate more fully how individuals, groups, and organizations at the everyday level experience and engage with transnational sport in diverse ways. Fourth, in line with my comments on global civil society and cosmopolitan ethics, future research should adopt a more critical, normative approach towards the study of sport. Such an approach should examine in particular how relatively weak stakeholders, especially at civil society level, may be empowered more fully in terms of governance and their participation within global sport.

Notes

1 The analysis presented here draws substantially on Giulianotti and Robertson (2004, 2009, 2012, 2013).
2 For an earlier application of this broad four-fold model to football, see Giulianotti and Robertson (2012).
3 For a survey of the financially largest sport clubs, see http://www.forbes.com/sites/kurtbadenhausen/2012/07/16/manchester-united-tops-the-worlds-50-most-valuable-sports-teams/ (accessed on 25 August 2014).
4 See http://www.transparency.org/news/feature/sport_and_corruption_game_on and http://www.playthegame.org/ (accessed on 25 August 2014).
5 http://www.jeromechampagne2015.com/documents/fifa.which-fifa-for-21st-century.pdf.
6 On glocalization in football, see Giulianotti and Robertson (2004, 2009).
7 See, for example, http://www.waronwant.org/olympics-home (accessed on 25 August 2014).
8 See Beck *et al.* (2003) for critical discussions of these arguments.

References

Appadurai, A. (1995) 'Playing with Modernity: the Decolonization of Indian Cricket, in C.A. Breckenridge (ed.) *Consuming Modernity*, Minneapolis: University of Minnesota Press.
Archetti, E. (1998) *Masculinities*, Oxford: Berg.
Archibugi, D., D. Held and M. Kohler (1998) *Re-Imagining Political Community*, Cambridge: Polity.
Attali, J. (2009) *A Brief History of the Future*, New York: Arcade.
Barber, B. (1995) *Jihad vs McWorld*, New York: Ballantine.
Bauman, Z. (1998) *Globalization: The Human Consequences*, Cambridge: Polity.
Beck, U. (2006) *Cosmopolitan Vision*, Cambridge: Polity.
Beck, U., N. Sznaider and R. Winter (eds) (2003) *Global America?*, Liverpool: Liverpool University Press.
Burke, P. (2009) *Cultural Hybridity*, Cambridge: Polity.
Calhoun, C. (2008) *Nations Matter*, London: Routledge.
Crothers, L. (2007) *Globalization and American Popular Culture*, Lanham, MD: Rowman & Littlefield.
Elliott, A. and J. Urry (2010) *Mobile Lives*, London: Routledge.
Friedman, J. (1999) 'Indigenous Struggles and the Discreet Charm of the Bourgeoisie', *Journal of World-Systems Research*, 5(2): 391–411.
Giulianotti, R. and R. Robertson (2004) 'The Globalization of Football: A Study in the Glocalization of the "Serious Life"', *British Journal of Sociology*, 55(4): 545–568.
Giulianotti, R. and R. Robertson (2009) *Globalization and Football*, London: Sage.
Giulianotti, R. and R. Robertson (2012) 'Mapping the Global Football Field: A Sociological Model of Transnational Forces within the World Game', *British Journal of Sociology*, 63(2): 216–240.
Giulianotti, R. and R. Robertson (2013) 'Sport and Globalization', in D. L. Andrews and B. Carrington (eds) *A Companion to Sport*, Oxford: Wiley-Blackwell.
Hamelink, C.J. (1995) *World Communication: Disempowerment and Self-Empowerment*, London: Zed Books.
Hannerz, U. (1992) *Cultural Complexity*, New York: Columbia University Press.

Harvey, D. (2005) *A Brief History of Neoliberalism*, Oxford: Oxford University Press.

Held, D. (1995) *Democracy and the Global Order*, Cambridge: Polity.

Hognestad, H.K. (2009) 'Transglobal Scandinavian? Globalization and the Contestation of Identities in Football', *Soccer & Society*, 10(3/4): 358–373.

Huntington, S.P. (1993) 'The Clash of Civilizations', 72(3): 22–48.

Latouche, S. (1996) *The Westernization of the World*, Cambridge: Polity.

Nye, J. (2008) 'Soft Power and the Beijing Olympics'. Available at: http://belfercenter.hks.harvard.edu/publication/18502/soft_power_and_beijing_olympics.html (accessed 25 August 2014).

Pieterse, J.N. (2007) *Ethnicities and Global Multiculture*, Lanham, MD: Rowman & Littlefield.

Ritzer, G. (2004) *The Globalization of Nothing*, Thousand Oaks, CA: Pine Forge.

Robertson, R. (1992) *Globalization*, London: Sage.

Robertson, R. (1995) 'Glocalization', in M. Featherstone, S. Lash and R. Robertson (eds) *Global Modernities*, London: Sage.

Robertson, R. (2007) 'Open Societies, Closed Minds: Exploring the Ubiquity of Suspicion and Voyeurism', *Globalizations*, 4(3): 399–416.

Rumford, C. (2007) 'More Than a Game: Globalization and the Post-Westernization of World Cricket', *Global Networks*, 7(2): 202–214.

Rumford, C. (2011) *Cosmopolitan Spaces: Europe, Globalization, Theory*, London: Routledge.

Said, E. (1994) *Culture and Imperialism*, London: Chatto and Windus.

Sklair, L. (2001) *The Transnational Capitalist Class*, Oxford: Blackwell.

Tomlinson, J. (1991) *Cultural Imperialism*, London: Continuum.

Wallerstein, I. (1974) 'The Rise and Future Demise of the World Capitalist System: Concepts for Comparative Analysis', *Comparative Studies in Society and History*, 16(4): 387–415.

Wallerstein, I. (2003) *The Decline of American Power*, New York: New Press.

INDEX